Neither Right
nor Left

Neither Right nor Left

Fascist Ideology in France

Zeev Sternhell

Translated by
David Maisel

PRINCETON UNIVERSITY PRESS
PRINCETON, NEW JERSEY

To my aunts, Clara and Clementyna, in memory of the difficult years

Published by Princeton University Press, 41 William Street, Princeton, New Jersey 08540
In the United Kingdom by Princeton University Press, Chichester, West Sussex

Originally published as *Ni droite, ni gauche: L'Idéologie fasciste en France* © Éditions du Seuil 1983

Library of Congress Cataloging-in-Publication Data
Sternhell, Zeev.
   [Ni droite, ni gauche. English]
   Neither right nor left : fascist ideology in France / Zeev Sternhell ; translated by David Maisel.
     p.   cm.
   Includes bibliographical references and index.
   ISBN 0-691-00629-6 (alk. paper)
   1. Fascism—France—History. I. Title.
JA84.F8S7313 1995
320.5'33'0944—dc20   95-11286

First Princeton Paperback printing, 1996

Printed in the United States of America by Princeton Academic Press

10   9   8   7   6   5   4   3   2   1

Contents

Acknowledgments

I should like to thank several institutions whose assistance has been invaluable. Most of this book was written in 1980, when, freed from my usual teaching duties, I was able to devote all my time to research at the Institute of Advanced Studies of the Hebrew University, Jerusalem. Apart from the material conditions necessary to my purposes, I found there an ideal atmosphere for reflection and writing, and I should like to take this opportunity to express my gratitude to the director of the institute, Professor Aryeh Dvoretzky, the assistant director, Dr. Shabtai Gairon, and all the administrative staff, whose tireless efforts make the researcher's work in the institute so pleasant and profitable.

In 1979 I had the privilege of teaching in the Departments of History and Political Science at the University of California, Los Angeles, where I began work on this book. This great university not only places at the disposal of the researcher a remarkable library, which includes, notably, the Gaston-Mennevée Archives, whose importance is obvious to every expert on French history and politics in the twentieth century, but also provides him with a first-class intellectual environment. I was particularly fortunate in having the opportunity to enjoy a warm relationship with my colleagues Andrzej Korbonsky, David Fisher, Hans Rogger, Susan Rubin Suleiman, Ezra N. Suleiman, Eugen Weber, and Robert Wohl. At the neighboring campus at Berkeley, I had a friendly and profitable relationship with A. James Gregor.

The Leonard-Davis Institute of International Relations and the Research Commission of the Faculty of Social Sciences at the Hebrew University in Jerusalem kindly placed at my disposal over a period of several years the financial assistance I required to amass the necessary documentation. However, the photocopying machine cannot meet every requirement: in addition to this service, the researcher must also avail himself of interlibrary loans. The program between the National and University Library in Jerusalem and the French libraries works wonderfully and cannot be praised too highly.

I should like, finally, to express my gratitude to Mrs. Evelyne Cohen and Mr. Georges Bensimhon, who took on the task of correcting the original French manuscript. Their concern, their critical sense, and above all their friendship have been of inestimable value to me. Dr. Yohanan Manor, my colleague at the Hebrew University, has been a perspicacious reader of the manuscript and a faithful friend, and I wish to acknowledge my debt to him here. In Mario Sznajder and Itzhak Brudny I found intelligent and conscientious assistants with pride in their work, and I wish to thank them heartily. Last but not least, my thanks are due to my irreplaceable collaborator, Mrs. Marcelle Adjej, who was always able to understand and decipher a difficult manuscript and transform it into a text of perfect lucidity. Her admirable conscientiousness has never failed.

Mount Scopus, Jerusalem
April 1982

Most of the reading and writing for the English edition of this book has been done during the 1983–84 academic year, which I was fortunate to spend at the Institute for Advanced Study in Princeton. I am grateful to the institute's director and the fellows of the School of Social Science for allowing me to spend there one of the best years of my academic career.

The long discussions with Albert H. Hirschman, Lionel Gossman, Wolf Lepenies, Anson Rabinbach, Dominique Schnapper, Jerry Siegel, and Michael Walzer have been a wonderful experience.

My final thanks go to Mr. David Maisel for a faithful and intelligent English translation of my work.

Princeton and Jerusalem
October 1984

Preface to the
Paperback Edition

"Few books on European history in recent memory have caused such controversy and commotion," wrote Robert Wohl in a major review article of *Neither Right nor Left* published in 1991 in the *Journal of Modern History*.[1] Indeed, most of the questions analyzed in this book still rouse passions in Europe and provoke reactions that may seem strange to the American reader. In continental Europe, unlike the English-speaking world, the debate on fascism, the interwar period, and World War II is never restricted to the relatively limited circle of the academic community. This debate easily becomes a public issue and very often generates violent confrontations. For many people, to think of fascism as a phenomenon inseparable from the mainstream of European history and to consider the fascist ideology as a European ideology that took root and developed not only in Italy and, in a violent and extreme form, Germany but also in France can lead to parallels and comparisons that are still difficult to accept. Some consider this view an insult to their country and do not fail to say so. It is certainly much more convenient to restrict fascism to its Italian version, to treat it as merely a local accident if not an aberration; it is even more reassuring to see it as something involving only a few opportunists particularly clever at seizing an exceptional opportunity.

On the other hand, to allow fascism a theoretical dimension, to see it as possessing a body of doctrine no less solid or logically defensible than that of any other political movement, to conceive of it as a system of thought and a political option comparable to any other movement or ideology, involves a painful revision of a whole series of assumptions.

Such a step raises the question not only of the "fascist minimum" but also of the historical importance of the fascist ideology in France. What happens when one applies the tool forged through the comparative study of fascism to a particular case, that of France? Does fascism prove to be a marginal phenomenon without any real influence on the intellectual climate of the country? Or is one dealing, on the contrary, with a system of thought and a political outlook whose full importance would really be manifest only after the great defeat of 1940? Is it reasonable to suggest that democratic and liberal France, Jacobin France, nurtured not only the ideology of the French Revolution but also its antithesis?

A detached and clearheaded analysis of French history and politics shows that France is not only a country where the prevailing tradition is universalistic and individualistic, strongly rooted in the French Revolution, rationalist, democratic, and either liberal or Jacobin in coloring. It is also a country that, like Germany, gave birth at the end of the nineteenth century to a particularistic and organicistic tradition, often dominated by a local variant of cultural nationalism that was sometimes, but not always, of a biological and racial character, very close to the *volkisch* tradition in Germany. From the end of the nineteenth century, this other political tradition launched an all-out attack on liberal democracy, its philosophical foundations, its principles, and their application. It was not only the institutional structures of the Republic that were questioned, but the whole heritage of the Enlightenment.

This other tradition, contrary to a certain misconception that is soothing for national susceptibilities, is by no means a marginal ideology in twentieth-century France. On the contrary, its influence on intellectual and political life has been considerable, and it has impregnated society to a far greater degree than is generally admitted. From the end of the nineteenth century, these two traditions fought each other but also coexisted, often in the same work, in the thinking of the same person, independently of the celebrated left-right dichotomy. The traditional concept of a left-right conflict takes into account the realities of the period only very partially, and it often fails to take them into account at all.

In this respect, the most interesting and significant case from the end of the nineteenth century is that of Ernest Renan. The standard textbook on the history of ideas, the *Nouvelle Histoire des Idées politiques,* states in connection with the famous *Réforme intellectuelle et morale* that "nowhere was the violence of the shock of the events of 1871 better to be seen than in the case of the 'sceptic' Ernest Renan."[2] This explanation, which is supposed to represent the accepted opinion on this question, is characteristic of a certain tendency prevalent in current French history-writing: to give excessive importance to circumstances. Thus, the evolution of ideas, like human behavior in general, is far too readily described as merely a reaction to political events.

In fact, it was not the shock of the defeat of 1870 that created the antimaterialist reaction of the end of the nineteenth century any more than the collapse of 1940 gave rise to the revolt against "materialism" represented by the ideology of the national revolution. The rejection of the Enlightenment, of individualism, utilitarianism, and bourgeois values, of democracy and majority rule, of the idea that society is no more than a collection of individuals and that its ultimate aim is to serve individual interests—or, in other words, the principle of the absolute primacy of the individual in relation to society—was not the outcome of any conjuncture of events, and it existed independently of them. The rejection of these principles, to which a rejection of Marxism was very soon added, and which can be summed up precisely as a revolt against materialism, constitutes the basis of an alternative political tradition. Essentially, it is a phenomenon connected with the nature of civilization, and this other political tradition appears first of all as a cultural question, in the broadest sense of the term. To be sure, it is not solely nor, still less, exclusively a cultural question, but it is a cultural question first of all.

From this point of view, Renan constitutes the natural line of departure. *La Réforme intellectuelle et morale* is undoubtedly a result of the defeat of 1870. Most of its contents, however—all that is really of importance—is already to be found in a long article published in *La Revue des Deux Mondes* in November 1869, nearly a year before the battle of Sedan. In this essay, Renan expressed what was before the *année terrible* and what was to remain after the *année terrible,* his essential political thinking. He condemned above all "the idea of the equal rights of all men, the way of conceiving government as a mere public service which one pays for, and to which one owes neither respect nor gratitude, a kind of American impertinence," the claim "that politics can be reduced to a mere consultation of the will of the majority."[3]

After having poured scorn on the United States, Renan urged Napoleon III to adopt "the truly coservative programme," which was the only one that could hold back "that materialist conception" that is inherent in democracy and that finally could only give rise to "a sort of universal mediocrity." Whatever the case, he concluded, and whatever the future held in store—and here Renan ventured onto particularly slippery ground and predicted in 1869 that France "appears . . . still for a long period to be likely to avoid a Republic"—it was "probable," he said, "that the nineteenth century will be . . . regarded in the history of France as the expiation of the Revolution."[4]

This analysis was repeated, often word for word, in *La Réforme:*

Enervated by democracy, demoralized by its very prosperity, France has expiated in the most cruel manner its years of aberration. . . . France as formed by universal suffrage has become profoundly materialist; the noble concerns of yesteryear—patriotism, an enthusiasm for beauty, the love of glory—have vanished with the noble classes which represented the soul of France. The judgment and government of things have been transferred to the masses, and the masses are heavy and coarse, dominated by the most superficial ideas of interest.[5]

Sedan was thus conceived as the defeat of a political culture that was "the negation of discipline" and that tended "to diminish the state to the advantage of individual liberty." Faced with a Prussia that had preserved all the virtues of a "quasi-feudal regime, a military and national spirit carried to the point of uncouthness," France was now paying the penalty for the "philosophical and egalitarian conception of society," together with "the false politics of Rousseau." Renan taught his own generation and his innumerable disciples in the following generation that "a democratic country cannot be well-governed, well-administered, well-ordered." That, in his opinion, was the reason why the defeat of 1870 could not be regarded as the consequence of a rash policy or of military incompetence but represented the breakdown of an entire political culture. It was a certain form of relationship between people, a certain way of life, and an ideology dominated by the pernicious Jacobin values that had led the country to decadence. The defeat, he said, simply had the effect of "tearing away all the veils" so that "defects of temperament which one had merely suspected" suddenly "appeared in a sinister manner."[6]

The foremost of these defects was "materialism." A key idea if there ever was one, antimaterialism constituted the backbone and the common denominator of all the tendencies that, from Sedan to Vichy, were in revolt against the heritage of the eighteenth century, against liberal and socialist utilitarianism. "Materialism" was the summation of what Renan called "the sickness of France":[7] "While we were going care-

lessly down the slope of an unintelligent materialism or an over-
generous philosophy," he said, "nearly losing all memory of a national
spirit, . . . [it was] Prussia, which had remained a country of the *ancien
régime* and thus preserved from industrial, economic, socialist, and revolutionary materialism, which vanquished the virility of all the other
peoples."[8]

According to Renan, democracy and socialism were forms of materialism, but there was also a "bourgeois materialism,"[9] yet another aspect of the same mediocrity that since the end of the eighteenth century
had carried all before it. It was materialism that was the cause of the
French decadence; it was liberal and bourgeois materialism that were
defeated at Sedan. This basic idea recurred in an almost identical manner at the time of the defeat of 1940: once again, it was materialism that
was accused of having eaten away the body of the nation. The difference was, however, that since the turn of the century, liberal and bourgeois materialism had been supplemented with Marxist and proletarian
materialism. Renan, to be sure, was already aware of the dangers of
socialist materialism, but it was not until the 1890s that Marxism, with
its various political parties, its tendencies and ideological groupings,
became a force of the first importance. In the summer of 1940, materialism was once again made responsible for all the disasters that had be-
fallen the country.

Despite the shock that followed the two defeats, it must be admitted
that these at the most only helped in creating an atmosphere or conditions favorable to a revision of the materialist values. Defeats accelerate
a movement that already exists; they do not create one. The Republic
was set up in September 1871, and France progressively developed the
most advanced system of liberal democracy on the European continent.
At the same time, however, it also gave rise to its antithesis and stage by
stage produced a second political tradition. The evolution of this tradition did not cease after the Battle of the Marne in summer of 1914, and
it continued throughout the interwar period. In July 1940, the long
antimaterialist impregnation rose to the surface and the great antimaterialist revolution was set in motion.

It is interesting to note that the dissidents of the generation of 1890,
like those of the generation of 1930, did not always have many new
elements to add to Renan's criticism of the revolution, democracy, and
individualism. By what sleight of hand did the writer of *La Réforme
intellectuelle et morale* become one of the great names of French democracy? Is it that the scholar entirely eclipsed the political thinker? Or

is it that his anticlericalism was enough to find him favor with the republicans?

There is, of course, his famous lecture "Qu'est-ce qu'une nation?" given at the Sorbonne in 1882. In reading this manifesto of natural rights, this proclamation of the rights of people to self-determination, in scrutinizing this text which is in fact the application to a specific case of the principles of the French Revolution and which is in flagrant contradiction to the spirit of *La Réforme,* one wonders what Renan's evolution would have been if he were not under the obligation of justifying the demand for the return of the annexed territories. If he had been in the place of Mommsen, Ranke, or Treitschke, would Renan in 1882 have defined the life of a nation in terms of a "daily plebiscite"?[10] In 1871, Renan had thought that the Prussian victories represented a "victory of the *ancien régime,* of the principle which denies the sovereignty of the people" over the French Revolution: like Drumont, Déroulède, and, later, Maurras, Renan came to the conclusion that it was urgently necessary to reject the old nationalism of 1848 and even the whole revolutionary tradition. But how, in that case, in the name of what universal principle, could one demand the return to France of Metz and Strasbourg?

Renan's was a specimen case. For Barrès, Sorel, and Maurras, as well as for the minor figures—a Lemaître, a Bourget—he was a revered intellectual master, and in the 1930s Mussolini spoke of Renan's "pre-Fascist illuminations."[11] At the same time, the innumerable streets and *lycées* named after Ernest Renan and the place given to the writer of the *Vie de Jésus* in school textbooks bear witness to his status in the republican liturgy and mythology. As a figure, Renan exemplified a problematic phenomenon that changed very little between 1870 and 1940: the coexistence—in this case, in the work of one and the same person—of a fundamental duality.

Seventy years later, one found the same analysis, the same general approach, in Emmanuel Mounier.[12] Mounier is also regarded as a kind of republican saint and had considerable influence, quite incommensurate with the intrinsic value of his work. Like Renan before him, Mounier pondered the reasons for the defeat. Once again, the collapse was blamed not on the conduct of operations, a lack of preparedness and leadership, or questionable policies, but on the liberal-democratic political culture. Like Renan, Mounier looked at the recent past to determine the nature of the trouble, what remedies ought to have been applied, and what direction should be taken from that point on. Once

again it was the ideological modernity, the heritage of the Enlightenment, that was responsible for the fall of France.

Indeed, the founder of *Esprit* provides a most revealing and characteristic example of the profound ambiguities of this school of thought,
which proclaimed a will to revolution based on a rejection of Marxism
and of capitalism and liberal democracy. Indeed, Mounier's rejection of
the liberal order, as well as his analysis of the sickness of French society,
had affinities with the ideas professed by other nonconformist groups,
including those that were protofascist or already fascist. At the same
time, a nonselective examination of his writings reveals that Mounier's
involvement in the national revolution in 1940–41 and his decision to
revive publication of the journal *Esprit* did not derive from a single
error of judgment but rather resulted from the positions he had adopted
during the decade preceding the war.

From its foundation until its prohibition by the Vichy government in
August 1941, *Esprit* made a veritable onslaught on liberal democracy.
Its rejection of the "established disorder" was nothing other than the
rejection of a certain political culture normally associated with the heritage of the French Revolution, universal suffrage, and the essential principles of liberalism. Mounier thus had certain ideas and certain political
reflexes that were common to fascists and those who, like himself, were
not fascists but contemplated with various degrees of sympathy the
fascist struggle against the established order.

I feel one must insist on this point. This merciless criticism of liberal
democracy was directed not only against the workings of the regime—
its weaknesses and institutional faults—but also against the very principles of a certain political culture. This rejection of the basic principles of
political liberalism, on the one hand, brought the ideology of "personalist democracy" close to that of the *Ordre nouveau* group and, on the
other, caused both trends, after they had developed a theory of an organic or communitarian society, to join the true fascists in a single revolt against individualism and materialism. Moreover, this rejection of
individualism and materialism in their liberal and Marxist forms accounts for the acceptance by dissidents like Mounier or L'Ordre nouveau and the "Jeune Droite" groups of the defeat of France: in their
view, the overthrow of the liberal Republic would open the way for the
revolution whose coming they had continually proclaimed throughout
the decade preceding the war.[13] This continuous denunciation of the
principles of liberal democracy, this obsessive condemnation of the decadence of France (made inevitable by the individualism and materialism

inherent in the system that had grown out of the French Revolution), made Mounier's thought and the ideology of *Esprit* adjacent on certain points to the ideology of fascism.

The obsession with decadence and rejection of the principles of democracy and liberalism manifested by dissidents and rebels like Mounier went together with the belief that elections and party politics, pressure groups, and coalition governments could only mean compromise and therefore corruption. They all refused to have anything to do with such a republic, and, through the very logic of their political positions, the rebels and revolutionaries who hated the practices of the totalitarian regimes nevertheless drew close to those other rebels and revolutionaries who also detested the bourgeois and liberal Republic but had already formulated a fascist ideology. For these people who all shared the same antiliberal and antidemocratic mentality, there was no doubt that the system was doomed. This antiliberal and antidemocratic bias went together with a violent rejection of Marxism: anti-Marxism, anticapitalism, and antiliberalism were the common denominator of all these different variants of the revolt and were a fitting expression of their essence, namely, the rejection of "materialism."

Thus, different schools of thought all shared the same rejection of the liberal order, constituting a kind of outer circle around the hard core of fascist thought. This was the real importance of the fascist ideology. Its widespread dissemination and influence were possible only because of the channels of transmission provided by the nonconformist milieu. In these groups, one may have hated the totalitarian state, but one could not avoid identifying oneself with the fascist criticism of bourgeois society, liberalism, and democracy. It was because it was not only the bourgeois world that was attacked, but also a number of universal principles readily associated with the bourgeoisie, that the harsh criticisms of the regime brought their full weight to bear. These criticisms, in fact, were directed less against a system of government that, in a divided society, considerably weakened the executive authority than against democracy itself. The obsession with decadence and the sense of participating in the collapse of an individualistic and basely materialistic civilization were the common elements in this way of thinking.

The most striking and doubtlessly most significant case, the one that illustrates in the most concrete manner the extraordinary ambivalence of these ideas, is that of the National School of Youth Cadres at Uriage, a small spa near Grenoble in nonoccupied France. The school was founded in September 1940 by Captain of Cavalry Pierre Dunoyer de Segonzac and recognized as an official institution by a law of the Vichy regime in December of that year.[14] The community of Uriage represented the realization of the ideas of *Esprit* and was one of the vehicles of the national revolution. It is historically important because of its character as a highly influential laboratory of ideas, its status as an official organ of the regime, and the fact that it reflected the reaction to the defeat of France of a major sector of the Catholic intelligentsia. But what is even more important is that the *Esprit*-Uriage intellectual complex throws a great deal of light on the intellectual dissidence of the interwar period and on the Vichy national revolution.

Uriage is also the most impressive example of a collective attempt to obscure the realities of that period. For nearly half a century, the former members of Uriage succeeded in propagating the myth that this institution was conceived from the beginning as a center of resistance to the occupying power. The fact that among the former members, their sympathizers, and their ideological friends there were many who made a great career for themselves in the postwar period (the most famous being the celebrated journalist Hubert Beuve-Méry, founder of the newspaper *Le Monde* and its editor for twenty-five years) does much to explain the respectful silence that, until recent years, has surrounded the Uriage experiment.

The reality was far more complex than the myth suggests. The school of Youth Cadres at Uriage, as its name indicates, was established not to wage the struggle against the Germans but to train the elites of the new regime and to prepare the activists of the national revolution for their tasks. The frame of reference of this revolution was fixed by the Vichy legislation promulgated by Pétain between July and December 1940. Steeped in Catholic antiliberalism, the school adopted the *Esprit* ideology as the conceptual framework of its educational program: anti-individualism, antiliberalism, anti-Marxism, and a rejection of democracy, on the one hand, and, on the other, a cult of order, hierarchy and elitism, and reserved admiration for the German, Italian and Portuguese youth movements.[15]

The members of Uriage threw themselves into the national revolution with great enthusiasm. In the old château where the school was set up, they instilled a cult of Marshal Pétain and absolute obedience to the head of the French state, and they devoted themselves eagerly to the task of re-creating a France that would be "communitarian," profoundly Catholic, violently antimaterialistic, and "spiritualistic" in the sense given to these terms in the initial period of the 1930s by Mounier or Robert Aron, who in November 1933 wrote, together with Arnaud Dandieu, an extraordinary "Letter to Adolf Hitler, Chancellor of the Reich."[16] At Uriage, they sought to lay the foundations of a new civilization: virile, heroic, chivalrous. They were scornful of the bourgeoisie and their values; they attacked the "established disorder." This expression, coined by Mounier in the 1930s, from that time onward became the code word used by all elements in the personalist camp to assault the principles and institutions of democracy. With regard to democracy, they opposed the following formula: "authority, hierarchy, organization, interdependence, restriction of liberty."[17] There was an absolute fidelity to Pétain and his policies: "The school teaches the future leaders, in accordance with the guidelines laid down by the Marshal, the profound natural laws, the present-day organization, and the necessary or desirable reforms relative to the family, work, and society."[18] It was only to be expected that the measures of repression undertaken by Vichy, the handing over of anti-Nazi refugees to the Germans, the racial laws and the roundups of Jews by the French police in the occupied zone failed to arouse any reaction among the "knights" of Uriage.

This point should be emphasized. The members of Uriage took part eagerly and with conviction in the cultural and political revolution of Vichy, which was rightly called a national revolution. It was a "conservative revolution," in the sense the term possessed in Germany, where it meant the local variant of a revolt against modernity, liberalism, and democracy. They felt that to serve Vichy was the best, in fact the only, way of saving the country from decadence. Segonzac understood perfectly well the nature of the difference between himself and General de Gaulle: he reproached the latter for being "a conservative."[19] Indeed, de Gaulle was simply a classical conservative, while Segonzac was a revolutionary conservative. That is why the members of Uriage refused the option of Gaullism. De Gaulle, who merely called on people to fight the enemy, seemed to have no other aim than the liberation of French territory and the restoration of national sovereignty. The leader of the Free French sought to restore France, just as it was, to its rightful place in the world, not to create a new civilization.

That was the reason why the members of Uriage felt that this classical form of conservatism failed to satisfy the requirements of the period. But there was more to it than that. De Gaulle probably aroused their suspicions, doubts, and anxieties even more by allying himself with the feeble and materialistic bourgeois democracies. At the same time, Vichy was launching a revolution that, eradicating the principles of 1789, aimed at transforming society from top to bottom, instilling new values and destroying the liberal, democratic, and secular heritage of the Enlightenment and the French Revolution. We should remember that the personalists had always felt the attraction of the great antimaterialist revolt taking place on the other side of the French border, both to the east and to the south. When the time came that they had to choose between what seemed to them to be an ordinary, conservative nationalism and the great leap forward made possible by the new regime, they resolutely opted for the revolution.

For them, as for Renan in 1870, true patriotism meant first of all carrying out an intellectual and moral reform. That is why they condoned the most sordid aspects of Vichy—the Vichy of racial persecution, the Vichy of dictatorship. Protected by Pétain and his government, they only began to break away from the regime when its subjection to Germany became intolerable. The members of Uriage finally abandoned Vichy not because of a rejection of the principles represented by the revolution of 1940, but out of anti-German patriotism. One should remember that the real difference between the Vichy of Pétain and that of Laval was not the dictatorial and totalitarian nature of the latter but its degree of dependence on Germany.

The return to power of Pierre Laval on 18 April 1942 signaled the beginning of a reversal of policy, marked by the famous collaborationist speech of 22 June in which the new head of government declared his hopes for a German victory. On 8 November the Anglo-American armies landed in North Africa, and three days later the Wehrmacht invaded the free zone. Official policy hardened toward the Uriage school, and on 27 December Laval signed a decree ordering its closure. The cadres of the school went over to the opposition and then, increasingly, entered the armed Resistance. It is nevertheless worth noting that de Gaulle was under no illusions concerning the nature of this tardy change of direction: at the beginning of 1944 he refused to receive Segonzac, who had come to Algiers. When, finally, he yielded unwillingly to the entreaties of Henri Frenay, a friend of Segonzac and one of the founders of the "Combat" resistance movement, who made great efforts to retrieve the Vichyist Catholics before it was too late, he treated Segonzac, whom he regarded as just another "Vichyist," "with a hostile coldness." It was only through personal friendships that "Segonzac obtained *in extremis* an FFI [Forces Françaises de l'Intérieur] military command."[20]

The last phase of the organized activities of the Uriage group was not the least interesting. When the school closed, the hard core of its members decided to create an Order to perpetuate the Uriage community.[21] Beuve-Méry was one of the three members of the Council of the Order and was second in command to Segonzac, the undisputed leader who expected and was given absolute obedience. The Order of Uriage was less concerned with liberating French territory than with providing a solution to the "crisis of civilization."[22] The members of Uriage were preparing, in fact, for the revolutionary situation that inevitable came about with the defeat of Germany. They wished to provide the country with its new revolutionary cadres.

The ideology that the Order offered the communities of the Uriage network, which on the eve of Liberation extended throughout the length and breadth of the country—from Marseilles and Toulouse via Lyons, Grenoble, and Saint-Etienne to Paris, Roubaix, and Rennes—was always the same: anti-Communist, anti-individualist, anti-Masonic, elitist, and somewhat sexist. The Order did not pursue an overtly anti-Semitic policy, but Jews were firmly excluded from it.[23] A document entitled "The Policies of the Order" condemns those Frenchmen for whom "the interests of an International—whether capitalist, Jewish, Freemason or Communist"—have priority over "the national interests."[24]

When they entered the Resistance, the national revolutionaries of Uriage never abandoned their ideas. The means had changed, but the objective remained the same. As Liberation took a direction quite different from the one the personalists had hoped for, however, their ideological baggage, like their commitment to the national revolution, soon proved extremely embarrassing, and the former members of Uriage, like many people of their generation, endeavored to throw a modest veil over this troublesome past.

The work of repression and banalization began from the first days of Liberation. Essentially, it meant isolating Vichy from the period previous to the national revolution and reducing its place in twentieth-century history to a minimum. This complex process took three forms, which, although independent and different from one another, very often crossed and overlapped. The first—the most banal—originated in the necessity for many men, who either professed fascist ideas in the 1930s or collaborated with the Vichy regime, to cover up this embarrassing past. Since the 1940s, after having done much to facilitate the moral collapse of France in the spring of 1940, these people often have had brilliant careers, which they have used to vindicate their former ideas and political activities. Whether we are dealing with Thierry Maulnier, the brilliant writer and journalist who was elected to the Academie française, or the well-known political thinker Bertrand de Jouvenel, both of whom became liberals, their new "conversions" strongly affected how they viewed the past and the role they played between the wars. What, after all, is simpler than to interpret one period in the light of the next? What is easier than to conceive of people as being made all of one piece and never varying?

To reason in this way is to make what is after testify in favor of what is before: the postwar in favor of the prewar. One can thereby avoid questioning the ideas professed by a major section of the interwar generation. Yet a close examination of these ideas reveals the profound attraction fascism held for important and often unexpected sections of the public and the intellectual world. The broad dissemination of these ideas does not, as some claim, attest to their unimpeachably nonfascist character, but, on the contrary, demonstrates that a fascist type of thought was at that time very prevalent, that its roots went deep, and that its influence was considerable. That eminently respectable people professed such ideas means not that they were ideas entirely foreign to fascism, but simply that fascism was then part of the intellectual baggage of eminently respectable people. That after the war many of these people became convinced democrats, passionate liberals, and declared philo-Semites unfortunately changes neither the significance of fascism nor that of their former ideas. People can change and have the right to do so, but they do not have the right to distort their own history or that of their time.

These surviving figures from the past are not, however, the only ones to have "rewritten" their history. Contemporary members of the intelligentsia, who were not themselves involved, have also contributed to the distortion. In 1981, the well-known publishing house Plon published a new edition of Robert Brasillach's *Notre avant-guerre*. This, as we know, was one of the closest works to the Nazi ideology ever published in France. The notice on the cover informs us that Brasillach "was condemned to death for his political opinions." Brasillach distinguished himself under the Nazi occupation by his denunciatory articles filled with violent hatred. In October 1941, as chief editor of *Je suis partout*, he demanded an exemplary punishment for the perpetrators of anti-German actions, as well as for all those guilty "of an at least passive complicity. These people who are sometimes arrested for distribution of tracts and illegal action in the most bourgeois milieux are, in effect, moral accomplices. What are we waiting for in order to strike at them? What are we waiting for in order to shoot the communist deputies already imprisoned?" Brasillach even succeeded in horrifying the German officer Gerhard Heller, the literary censor attached to the propaganda services of the German "embassy" in occupied Paris, by saying of the Jews, "One must kill them all, even the young children."[25]

Forty years later, Plon—with no mention of Brasillach's virulent nazism—would have us believe he was sentenced to death for his political opinions rather than for demanding the execution of members of the Resistance, for visiting the eastern front, or for a relationship with Germans that made him one of the great symbols of high treason.

"The Problem of Memory" was the title given by Jeannie Malige to her preface to the memoirs of Bertrand de Jouvenel. Such a problem does indeed exist, but in a sense quite different from that intended by Malige, and in order to perceive its acuteness one need only read Jouvenel's famous report on his interview with Hitler in *Paris-Midi* of 28 February 1936 and compare its tone with that of his recollections published in 1979.[26]

In his 1936 article, Jouvenel was eager to stress the German chancellor's desire for peace, and he expressed his admiration for this man who extended his hand in friendship to France. He unabashedly portrayed Hitler as strongly attached to a "foreign policy entirely directed toward friendship with France." As a result of this meeting, Jouvenel wrote, "I have to revise all my ideas about the dictator," and he added, "What, this simple man who speaks quietly, reasonably, pleasantly, with humor—is this the fearful mob orator who has roused the whole German people to frenzy, and in whom the whole world has seen an eventual threat of war? . . . He laughs candidly; his face comes close to mine. I no longer feel at all intimidated. I also laugh. I see the features at close quarters, the lips that form a gay, droll smile."

But Jouvenel was not content to praise only the man: he eulogized the entire system. Near Hitler's residence—small, simple, modern— Jouvenel noticed that the "shrubs at the corner nearest the balcony had been trampled down, the sign of a recent outburst of popular enthusiasm" for a regime that, he thought, was truly of the people. Jouvenel contrasted "Nazi good-naturedness" with "Prussian formality." He expressed an admiration for Nazi egalitarianism: party dignitaries and typists fraternized in the House of the Party, and it was the doorkeeper at the law courts who led "the corporation of the magistrature" at the "national ceremonies on the first of May."[27]

Nothing of this is found in the six pages (including two pages of quotations) of the chapter entitled "That Famous Interview" in *Un Voyageur dans le siécle*. The stir caused by this article is put down to a "machination of Ribbentrop," who "made a fool of" Pierre Lazareff's senior reporter. As for the interview itself, it is described either as a faux pas or as a professional obligation: "The reporter only reported what the interviewee said."[28]

One can hardly believe one's eyes, for when one considers the spirit of this interview, the atmosphere in which it takes place, the total message it seeks to convey, and the "local color" it describes and bears in mind the particular sensibilities of the French public and its receptivity to certain types of argument, Bertrand de Jouvenel's reporting was no less pro-Nazi than Robert Brasillach's reports from Nuremberg a year later.[29] Moreover, this celebrated interview, with its panegyric of nazism, which Jouvenel today claims was required by his profession, had been sought by him in a way that leaves no doubt about either his sentiments or his purpose. Jouvenel was closely associated with Otto Abetz, the famous Nazi agent and specialist in German propaganda in France, adviser to Joachim von Ribbentrop on French affairs, and future German "ambassador" to occupied Paris. Jouvenel asked him to obtain for him a meeting with Hitler. In a letter of 22 January 1936, Jouvenel wrote:

Dear Otto, I am here for three weeks. During this time, do you think we can carry out our Berchtesgaden project? You know that *Paris-Soir* now has a circulation of 2,200,000. I don't need to tell you how anti-German the newspaper is. Let's give it something, for heaven's sake, and it will change its tone!

Give my best regards to the Baron Ribbentrop and be assured of my very affectionate friendship. Bertrand.[30]

Hitler himself was well aware of the intentions of the French journalist, who was at the time very active in the campaign for a rapprochement with Nazi Germany, and he spoke about them in his speech at the Reichstag on 7 March 1936.[31]

Another instructive example of the reconstruction of the period can be seen in the way Jouvenel now emphasizes his Jewish origins. This former Doriotist who in the 1930s was not afraid, as a member of the political bureau, to endorse the campaigns of the Parti Populaire Français against "Judeo-Marxism," today claims to be particularly proud of his status as "half Jew."[32] Fifty years ago, however, the brilliant journalist bitterly reproached the left (which saw him as a German propagandist)[33] for risking a "new War of Rights" in order to defend "the socialist widow and the Jewish orphan."[34] With Pierre Drieu La Rochelle, he traveled to Berlin to be present at a racist lecture given by his friend before the leaders of the Hitler Youth and the Association of National-Socialist Students.[35]

At the end of 1938, Jouvenel once more went to Germany, this time to Nuremberg to cover, on behalf of the anti-Semitic journal *Gringoire,* the National-Socialist Party Congress. He wrote about it in the issue of 9 September 1938, in an article whose complaisance toward the Nazi regime was surpassed only by that of his pro-Hitler reporting, again in *Gringoire,* on 10 November 1938, the day after the famous Kristallnacht (Crystal Night). Jouvenel must have written his article, "Il y a 15 ans, Hitler échouait," commemorating the failed putsch of 1923, a short time before the night of the pogrom in which dozens of Jews were massacred, but neither on the day after nor at any time in the following months did Jouvenel express any reservations concerning nazism. On the contrary, his best-known work of the period, *Après la défaite,* published in 1941 in praise of the Nazi spirit, was immediately translated into German and became a widely advertised instrument of Nazi propaganda.[36]

No less interesting is the case of Thierry Maulnier. Maulnier is coauthor of a work called *L'Honneur d'être juif,* written in praise of the Jews—"these people who prevent the world from sleeping."[37] The writer, who wished to "gather up in one basket all the fabulous fruits of the tree of Judea," came to the conclusion that "all the upheavals, metamorphoses and mutations that have changed the face of our planet—until we have reached the other planets—had Jews as their creators and promoters."[38] This work made a "rough inventory" of the Jewish origins of everyone and everything of importance in the twentieth century (one could multiply references and examples), from Picasso and Proust, whose mothers were Jewish, to Bergson, Husserl, and Joseph Kessel, to Eisenstein, Marcuse, and Léon Blum.

Léon Blum! What was not said about Blum in *Combat,* the journal edited by Thierry Maulnier, at the time of the Popular Front? What injury, what insult, what base insinuation, what vulgar accusation was he spared by Maulnier's friends and collaborators, by the journals and reviews to which Maulnier contributed? Did not Maulnier himself, in an article written in the purest tradition of Drumont anti-Semitism, advocate the practice of a "reasonable anti-Semitism" toward the Jews, who had "become our masters"? Maulnier was willing to exonerate the

Jews of only one accusation against them: their domination of Western society was to be attributed not to any "premeditated designs" but to "their cleverness in taking advantage of circumstances" and exploiting "historical situations." Having said this, he then proceeded to analyze in an impartial, academic tone the various aspects of anti-Semitism:

Anti-Semitism can be approached either from the humanistic point of view—the point of view of historical and moral justification—or from the point of view of political effectiveness or "revolutionary" effectiveness, if you will. These two approaches are not necessarily connected. Anti-Semitism can have a philosophical validity (if the Jews are really a force of corruption and enslavement of the people) and yet have no practical application in France (if it is impossible or very difficult to mobilize the French people against the Jews). Or, on the other hand, anti-Semitism can be devoid of philosophical validity (if the Jews are innocent of all the crimes of which they are accused) and yet have a usable practical effectiveness (if anti-Semitism is a good means of crystallizing revolutionary tendencies).

The brilliant young editor of *Combat* concluded, "We have no wish to point a moral."[39]

The historian, coming half a century later, has no wish to point a moral either. His task is to explain, not to moralize or make value judgments. However, he cannot help wondering if Thierry Maulnier's refusal to point a moral was not symptomatic, on the eve of the war, of a certain state of mind and a certain outlook, and if it did not have something to do with the events that overtook France such a short time afterward.

The second reason for this process of repression, the one that has been most often invoked and not only by political leaders like presidents Pompidou, Giscard d'Estaing, and Mitterrand, was the necessity to achieve national reconciliation.

In this regard, 1947 was the crucial year: it was then that the first taboos were broken. In April of that year, Jean Paulhan, cofounder of *Les Lettres françaises*, the organ of the literary resistance, undertook the de facto rehabilitation of his friend Marcel Jouhandeau by publishing him in his *Cahiers de la Pléiade*. A notorious and vicious anti-Semite, Jouhandeau had belonged to the hard core of collaborationists, and in September–October 1941 he had participated in the famous Weimar meeting at which the French supercollaborationists came together to promote the Nazi war effort. The spokesperson for the group was Jacques Chardonne, an early collaborator who in 1940 published vitrioic articles in *La Nouvelle Revue française*.[40] The publication of

Jouhandeau by Paulhan—who wanted France to be given back "all its voices"[41]—began the legitimization of the most notorious collaborators. Soon the writers among them, together with their publishers,[42] regained their place in the world of letters. Jouhandeau was propelled to the forefront of the Paris literary scene, and Henri de Montherlant and Paul Morand became members of the Académie Française. Lucien Rebatet, condemned to death in 1946, was republished by Gallimard in 1951. One could easily multiply such examples.

It was always through the great gateway of antibolshevism and in the name of *désengagement* that the former collaborators who had been weeded out, and those who had fled to other countries to wait for better days, returned to respectability. Such was the case for a whole bevy of intellectuals who, without playing a role comparable to that of Chardonne or Montherlant, had been much promoted by the German propaganda services in France. These services had judged the writings of Alfred Fabre-Luce, Jouvenel, and several dozen other writers extremely useful to the Nazi cause.][43] Thanks to the cold war, these people came back cleared, rehabilitated, and sometimes triumphant, after having greatly contributed to lowering the "threshold of acceptability" of the intellectual collaboration.[44]

The following text of Raymond Aron, published in 1983, is characteristic of this state of affairs. One of the Free French from the outset, Aron, writing in London, had condemned Montherlant, Chardonne, and Fabre-Luce. Forty years later, however, his perspective changed completely, and political exigencies modified his view of the past.

Today I would not write any of these articles just as they stand. They are to be found in the collection *L'Homme contre les tyrans,* published first in New York in a series edited by Jacques Maritain, and then in Paris after the Liberation. Since then, Alfred Fabre-Luce has several times analyzed the positions he adopted between 1940 and 1944; the third volume of the *Journal de France* was unknown to me when I discussed the first two. Nor had I read the introduction to the *Anthologie de la nouvelle Europe,* which dates from the end of 1941, and which in London would have angered me. Since then, we have so often found ourselves in the same camp that I would feel it to be tiresome to revive old polemics. Renan placed forgetfulness in the first rank of the virtues necessary for politics. I can only hope that Fabre-Luce finds forgetfulness as easy as I do.[45]

Undoubtedly, this is a rather extraordinary example of relativism in historical judgment, a relativism that supports a vision of the 1940s as an exceptional period to which the usual norms do not apply. The best argument that is offered for this point of view (even Aron shares this predisposition) is precisely the "reconversion" to liberalism of all these people who, through the 1930s and the Vichy period, never ceased fighting democracy, liberalism, capitalism, and socialism, which they regarded as aspects of the "materialist" sickness constantly eating away at French society.

The third form taken by Vichyist apologetics is more complex and basically relates to problems concerning the interpretation of fascism in general and French fascism in particular. The controversy resurfaced violently in autumn 1994: the debate that took place at that time was not the first on the subject, but it was suddenly invested with concreteness and drama, being placed in a new context.

A few months earlier, in April 1994, Paul Touvier, having for more than forty years enjoyed the generous support of a section of the French church, and having benefited from an attitude of good will on the part of President Pompidou, had become the first French citizen to be condemned for crimes against humanity. This condemnation implicitly signified a revision of the concept of the Vichy regime prevailing for half a century. In September the polemic was suddenly reactivated by the appearance—attended with a fuss of which only the Latin Quarter is capable—of the work of journalist Pierre Péan, *Une Jeunesse Française, François Mitterrand 1934–1947.*[46] This new biography, written with the assistance of the president of the republic, investigated the past of the chief personage of the state. There were few authentic revelations for professional historians, who knew that Mitterrand, a genuine "national revolutionalry" and a high official of the Vichy government, joined the Resistance rather late. To discover that at the beginning of 1943 the future president, who had just been awarded the Francisque, the Pétainist equivalent of the Legion of Honor, was still writing in the Vichy press is hardly a surprise.[47] Readers favorable to Mitterrand might say that the Francisque might well have been a suitable cover for someone who was already beginning to be active in the Resistance. The less well disposed could say that the future president's choice of the Resistance came late in the day, that it was well after Stalingrad and long after the Anglo-American landing in North Africa, and that in any case, those who had been in the Resistance from the beginning were not decorated with the Francisque.

There are several reasons why the book caused such a stir. First of all, the public was struck by the fact that the career of the president of the Republic not only was not at all extraordinary, but was representative of the intellectual and political development of a major part of the elite of the period. Consequently, the "banality of evil" represented by Vichy became apparent to many French people with a new clarity. Second, in a long televised interview the president, taking up the traditional apologetic, explanatory themes, refused to assume responsibility on behalf of the French nation for the misdeeds of the Vichy regime. This was tantamount to saying that Vichy did not really belong to French national history, but at the same time Mitterrand's biography demonstrated how natural a phenomenon the Vichy regime had been for many people of his generation. Mitterrand also claimed to have been unaware of the nature of the anti-Semitic policies of the Vichy regime.[48] Finally, the readers of this best-seller learned that their president, having for more than half a century maintained very close relations with the man who had been the key figure in the deportation of Jews to Auschwitz, still expressed his admiration for the personality of René Bousquet and refused to pass moral judgment on the conduct of his friend, indicted on 3 April 1991 for crimes against humanity.[49]

For an explosion of this kind to take place one had to await the arrival of a new generation—one more demanding, more pugnacious, and more sensitive, because it was free of the burden of the "dark years." It was a generation that wanted to know and not to cover things up. It was undoubtedly this new generation that was responsible for the holding, on 16 July 1993, fifty-one years after the great roundup of July 1942, of the first official commemoration, presided over by the premier, of Vichy's "racist and anti-Semitic persecutions." It was public opinion, again, that caused the practice of placing presidential wreaths on Pétain's tomb to be discontinued in November 1993. But above all, this new mentality was strikingly expressed in the indictment of Paul Touvier and René Bousquet for crimes against humanity. These two personalities were representative, each in his way, not only of the national revolution, but also of the way in which the political and judicial establishment refused for half a century to face the reality of those difficult years.

Secretary-general of the police in 1942–43 and directly dependent on head of government Pierre Laval, Bousquet had in recent years become the living symbol of the concrete results of the national revolution and of the willingness of the Vichy regime to collaborate with Nazi Germany. As head of the French police, he bore direct responsibility for the deportation of 59,000 Jews. More than four-fifths of all the deportees were handed over to the Nazis by his force: the German police in occupied France were few in number and consisted of less than three thousand men. The huge roundups were carried out on Bousquet's orders and executed by French police. In the roundup of 16 and 17 July 1942, thirteen thousand people were arrested in Paris, of whom four thousand were children. The youngest was two years old.[50]

Nowadays, Bousquet's name is associated primarily with the fate of the children, for it was on the express demand of the French authorities that children under six, separated from their parents and exempted by the German legislation, were also deported. The French administration did not wish to be burdened with these orphans. Two thousand children of less than six years of age were thus sent to Auschwitz, contrary to the wishes of the Germans themselves.[51] The charge of crimes against humanity made against Bousquet on 1 March 1991 accused him of "having knowingly been an accomplice to the violent abduction of children in the occupied zone and the free zone, having sent telegrams on the eighteenth, twentieth and twenty-second of August 1942 asking for the planned measures of arrest, internment and handing-over to be extended to groups in the free zone, and especially the children, who had previously been exempted."[52]

Assassinated on 8 June 1993, Bousquet could not finally be judged, but these facts had been well-known in 1949 when the secretary-general of police—the right-hand man of Laval and one of the top civil servants of the regime—was brought, like the other secretary-generals of the Vichy government, before the High Court of Justice. Acquitted of "harming national defense interests," Bousquet was declared "guilty of infamous actions" and given the penalty, systematically applied at that period, of five years' loss of civil rights. Then, at the same time, this penalty was waived because he was declared to have "participated actively and consistently in the resistance against the occupier."[53] Thus, seven years after the Vel d'Hiv' (Winter Velodrome) roundup of July 1942, René Bousquet was consecrated a "Resistance fighter" in the same way as Jean Legay, his representative in the occupied zone, and as such directly responsible for the ruthless manner in which the rounding up of Jews was carried out. Dismissed from his police function in 1945 (an administrative, not a penal measure), Legay was rehabilitated in 1955 "for acts of resistance."[54] Twenty-four years later, in March 1979, he was charged with crimes against humanity, but he died in 1989 without having been judged.

François Mitterrand was opposed to putting Bousquet on trial again, just as he had probably intervened indirectly on his behalf in 1949.[55] But it would be wrong to think that this was simply a matter of friendship. Mitterrand considers Vichy to have been an exceptional period, a period in parenthesis, as it were, where even men of high intellectual and moral caliber could tilt as easily to one side as to the other. One could have been a Vichyist, a collaborator, or a member of the Resistance at different times or simultaneously and still have deserved well from one's country. One could even have remained a Vichyist to the end, participated in the "final solution," and served one's country well. As the president tells us: "It is unjust to judge people for errors which are explicable in the atmosphere of the period."[56] If the moral validity of this statement is more than questionable, its historical significance is very clear. Mitterrand is right: a considerable part of the war generation was impregnated with ideas that were taken up by the national revolution, and they entered into the service of the regime believing it was working for a national revival.

We should note what François Dalle, the president's friend in youth, speaking of their student years in the Latin Quarter on the eve of the war, said: "We were close to *Combat* [Thierry Maulnier's fascist review], which guided our political opinions." He continued, "At that period, we speculated a great deal about fascism. We found that of Mussolini and Salazar to be attractive. We thought Mussolini would not follow Hitler. We were bourgeois, Catholic students, distant from money-matters. . . . We already knew that the war was lost, because our armaments were as useless as our leadership. . . . We were cannon-fodder. . . . We were influenced by *Gringoire* and *Je suis partout,* and, without being anti-Semitic, one could speak in our case of ostracism through contamination."[57]

Mitterrand wanted to avoid the Bousquet trial, for the indictment of this great state official—later a respected businessman and a celebrated figure in the Parisian social scene—would rapidly have assumed the proportions of the trial of a whole elite, a whole state apparatus, the whole enormous administrative, cultural, judicial, military, and educational machine, which, like the young Mitterrand himself, voluntarily placed itself at the service of the dictatorship.

The case of Paul Touvier illustrates another aspect of this same problematic. Touvier was the head of intelligence and operations of the militia in Savoy and later in the Rhone area—regions where the armed Resistance was particularly active. Having succeeded in avoiding capture, he enjoyed from the start the protection of the church. Thanks to this systematic and continuous assistance, he found refuge in many different monasteries, and when he was finally arrested in 1989, it was in a monastery of *intégristes* (supporters of pre-Vatican-II-style Catholicism). While Touvier was a fugitive and should have been sought by the police, a highly placed ecclesiastical figure, Canon Duclair, petitioned General de Gaulle to pardon him in 1963. The request was refused, but it was granted by President Pompidou, and the pardon was issued on 23 November 1971. Meanwhile, in 1967 a statute of limitations for crimes committed more than twenty years earlier had come into effect, and Touvier was no longer in danger of going to prison. Why, in that case, one may ask, was he granted a presidential pardon, which no longer had any practical significance? Was it really—as was claimed in one of the arguments used on behalf of Touvier and his family—to permit Paul Touvier's children to benefit from an inheritance from their grandfather?[58]

From Pompidou's point of view, the pardon was more than a humanitarian gesture. The act of pardoning had symbolic value and possessed historical significance: "Has not the moment come to cast a veil over the past, to forget those times when the French did not like each other, tore each other apart and even killed each other?" asked the president of the republic in September 1972.[59] Pompidou, who readily admitted to having displayed a very cautious attitude during the Occupation, was—like Mitterrand and Raymond Aron—of the opinion that forgetfulness was a political virtue and that national reconciliation had its price. It was no doubt in order to promote forgetfulness and reconciliation that French state television suppressed Marcel Ophuls's celebrated film *The Sorrow and the Pity,* which appeared a few months before Touvier's pardon, in April 1971. The film was able to appear on the screens of French television only ten years later. In October 1990, when Bousquet's indictment was being prepared, did not Georges Kiejman, President Mitterrand's minister of justice, continue to speak of the necessity of maintaining the "civil peace"?[60]

The second important aspect of the official view of fascism and Vichy revealed by the Touvier affair came to light in 1992. The law of 1964 on the imprescriptibility of crimes against humanity permitted the associations of members of the Resistance to lodge two charges against Touvier, in 1973 and 1974. After a long legal battle, these charges led in 1989 to the arrest of the former militiaman, but, on 13 April 1992, the Chambre d'accusation of the Parisian Court of Appeal, the equivalent of a grand jury, declared that Touvier would not be put on trial for two reasons: on six counts there were insufficient grounds for prosecution, and on the seventh count, the assassination of seven Jewish hostages, for which there was enough ground for prosecution, Touvier could not be judged because his crime could not be defined as a crime against humanity. The tribunal said that the former militiaman had not participated in the execution of a scheme carried out in the name of "a state that was practicing a policy of ideological hegemony." Vichy, it claimed, "was not a totalitarian state," which means that the officials who served it could not be classed with the officials of the Nazi state and consequently could not be judged guilty of crimes against humanity.[61] The court's historical analysis and its consequences caused a great stir both in the public at large and in the ranks of professional lawyers. The dismissal was rejected, and Touvier was finally judged and given a life sentence on 20 April 1994.

This interpretation of the nature and significance of the National Revolution was not invented by the Parisian Court of Appeal. It forms an integral part of the ideas prevailing in the majority of French historiography and was accepted by the French public for nearly half a century. In a work of great intellectual probity published in 1987, the historian Pierre Milza summed up the situation by demonstrating that, in contrast to the ideas put forward in *Neither Right nor Left*, one finds "a near-consensus in the history-writing of the French universities, especially among the representatives of the 'new political history' school grouped around René Rémond . . . for whom French fascism was no more than marginal, and who rightly believe that the Vichy regime did not belong to the same category as those which sprang up between the wars in Italy and Germany."[62]

Indeed, for many years the interpretation whose foundations were laid by René Rémond in the 1950s was dominant both among the public and in French historiography. This was that France had never produced an autonomous fascist tradition, and that fascism never had any importance or significance there. It was only an importation from abroad, a vague imitation and consequently extremely limited, without any real hold on society. It was claimed that the Vichy regime belonged to the counterrevolutionary tradition that began with Joseph de Maistre and continued with Charles Maurras and Action française: "The so-called national revolution was far more of a counterrevolution than the revolution which the fascist movements wished to promote," wrote Rémond in October 1994.[63] In replying in this way in *Le Monde* to my analysis of Vichy, which had appeared in the journal two weeks earlier,[64] the president of the Fondation Nationale des Sciences Politiques reiterated the ideas contained in his work published forty years before and regularly reprinted since that time. That work has served as a manual and, some say, a Bible for several generations of French students.[65]

Here, however, we must modify this picture somewhat. Just as the indictment of Bousquet and the Touvier trial, impossible to imagine not so long ago, was the product of a change of mentality and the appearance of a new generation of French people, so a new school of historiography has arisen in the last few years that is open to a questioning of Rémond's general thesis. This new approach implicitly recognizes the fact that Rémond's interpretation has had the effect of paralyzing historical investigation in France for the space of an entire generation. It has recently found expression in two major works: *La République,* by Maurice Agulhon, and l'*Histoire des Droites en France,* edited by Jean-François Sirinelli and Eric Vigne, representatives of the new generation.[66] But, as Pierre Milza has shown, it is always the René Rémond school of "political history" that claims to speak on behalf of French historiography. It is thus necessary for us to have a clear understanding of its ideas.

Because he starts with the axiom that France never produced a fascist ideology or a revolutionary right, Rémond conceives of Vichy as an anachronistic phenomenon without any hold on society and thus without any real importance. That is why, in the last edition of *Les Droites En France* (1982), a work of five hundred pages, chapter six—"1940–1944: Vichy, the National Revolution and the Right"—takes up a little less than eight pages. That is also the reason why anti-Semitism is almost absent from the book and hardly touched on in Rémond's most recent work, *Notre Siècle,* published in 1991.[67] The racial laws of October 1940 and June 1941 are not even mentioned, any more than the roundups, the collaboration, and other forms of repression, all of which had the same purpose: to replace, once and for all, the idea of a society made up of free citizens endowed with equal rights with the theory of the organic unity of the nation.

Anti-Semitism, however, was not merely an aberration but a political tool of great importance. Anti-Semitism permits us to give a concrete reply to the only question that really matters: what is the true nature of the French nation? Is it a collection of citizens, as the French Revolution would have it, or is it a large extended family huddled around its church, bound together by the cult of its dead and connected by ties of blood? It was undoubtedly this total form of nationalism, the nationalism of "blood and soil," that triumphed in the summer of 1940. *Volkisch* nationalism was never a monopoly of the Germans. This type of nationalism, which regarded itself as an ethic, a total conception of the politically desirable, and which sought to create a new form of relationship between the individual and the collectivity, did not date only from the defeat of 1940. This nationalism, which denied the existence of any universal norms, which had a vision of society shut in upon itself, came into being in France at the end of the nineteenth century and exploded in the Dreyfus Affair. But Rémond never treated the Dreyfus Affair as constituting a whole; on the contrary, he marginalized the political and ideological totality formed by Boulangism and anti-Dreyfusism and included it in that category without consistency or true identity, known as Bonapartism. Thus, Rémond remains captive to an explanatory schematization that forces him to minimize the intellectual significance of the revolutionary Right. He can only conceive of Vichy as reactionary, dust-covered, and irrevocably turned toward the past, and not as it was: the concretization of the French version of fascism.

Of course, if the totalitarian character of the system were to be made absolutely indisputable, the Vichy regime would have to have been provided with a single party. The nonexistence of such a single party was the pillar of the court's argument in favor of the nontotalitarian character of the Vichy regime. But in Italy and Germany a single-party system was always merely a means, never an end. The Fascist and Nazi parties were the only ones to survive, but the real power was soon concentrated in the hands of the leader, in his capacity of head of state (e.g., Hitler) or head of government (e.g., Mussolini). Moreover, it is an interesting fact that Pétain enjoyed a status that was both nominal and real, closer to that of Hitler than of Mussolini. The Duce in Italy had less absolute power than the Marshal in France: Mussolini was deposed in July 1943 by the king and put in prison with the assent of the dignitaries of the National Fascist party. This was something that could never have happened to Pétain, who was answerable to nobody. In April 1944, nine months after the fall of Mussolini, he was still being cheered in the streets of Paris. Even if this manifestation could not be compared with the scenes of enthusiasm that in August greeted de Gaulle, it nevertheless demonstrates the popularity of the Marshal on the very eve of Liberation. Pétain remained untouchable to the end.

Pétain, who never had to struggle to gain power, had no need of a party. He only needed to prohibit all parties. On the other hand, how can one gain a true picture of the nature of the Vichy regime without mentioning that the police repression in the nonoccupied zone was often harsher than in Italy, that in many respects the Mussolini regime was more lenient than Pétain's and that it was fifteen years after the fascists came to power that the racial laws were promulgated in Rome? Need one add that these laws were never applied on the Italian peninsula with the rigor with which they were carried out in France?

Finally, one must insist on the depth and quality of the roots of the national revolution. A serious ideological analysis of the national revolution leads necessarily to the conclusion that the Vichy regime undoubtedly carried out the ideological and political program found not only in Boulangism and anti-Dreyfusism, in the work of Barrès and Maurras, but also in that of Renan and Taine. Anyone who attempts an analysis of the legislation of the Vichy regime, anyone who seeks to study the rationale of the national revolution, will quickly discover that this was only a case of applying the principles contained in Renan's *La Réforme Intellectuelle et Morale de la France,* Taine's *Origines de la France Contemporaine* and *Histoire de la Littérature Anglaise* (one of the earliest examples of social Darwinism), and Barrès' theory of the Soil and the Dead.[68]

Like all the other European national revolutions, the national revolution in France did not appear out of a void. The Vichy regime was heir to a long tradition that was both indigenous and European: it represented the revolt of an intellectual and political France that had never accepted the philosophy of ideological modernity. In concrete terms, this revolt, as expressed at the turn of the century, in Boulangism and anti-Dreyfusism, took the form of a rebellion against liberal democracy. As in Italy and Germany, this rebellion against the "materialism" of the Enlightenment, whether in its bourgeois or proletarian form, had an undoubted attractiveness for a large section of the educated classes. It was the seductiveness of this antimaterialism, very often amounting to a real fascist temptation, that explains the sympathy of the majority of Italian intellectuals for the young movement led by Mussolini, and of a great part, of the German academic world first for the "Conservative Revolution" School and later for nazism. A large number of French intellectuals did not behave very differently in 1940. The new regime immediately gained the support of the elites: those elites who, throughout the 1930s, had been favorably disposed to the great "antimaterialist" revolt and proclaimed their rejection of what in certain nonconformist circles was called "the established disorder," which was nothing other than democracy.

Introduction

The purpose of this book is to attempt an analysis of fascism as it is reflected in French society. It aims to grasp the nature of a particular political phenomenon, to reconstruct an ideology, to apprehend the characteristics of a certain spirit and outlook, as they were manifested in the proving ground of France. France, as it happens, offers especially suitable conditions for such an endeavor, since the fascist period in France was marked by movements and ideologies but not by a fascist regime. For it is before coming to power, before pressures and compromises have transformed them into governmental groups like all the others, that ideologies and movements may be discovered in their purest form. The nature of a political ideology always emerges more clearly in its aspirations than in its application.

It was in France that the radical right soonest acquired the essential characteristics of fascism, and it was in France, also, that this process was most rapidly completed—on the eve of the outbreak of the Great War. The term did not exist yet, but the phenomenon existed, complete with a solid conceptual framework. To become a political force, it required only the proper social and economic conditions: widespread unemployment, an impoverished middle class, a terrorized petite bourgeoisie. The rise of the fascist ideology in France cannot be ascribed to the war alone, and even less to the triumph of Mussolini in Italy or of nazism in Germany. To be sure, in France also the war played an infinitely important role in producing the psychological, economic, and social conditions in which fascist ideas could be transformed into a political force, but neither with regard to the people involved nor with regard to movements and ideologies was the war the complete break it is generally thought to have been.

If the rise of fascism cannot be ascribed to the war, it can be said that, all things considered, fascism was the product both of a crisis in liberal democracy and of a crisis in socialism. It was a rebellion against bourgeois society, its moral values, its political and social structures, its way of life. Fascism thus seems an expression of a rupture signaling a crisis of civilization, and for that reason fascism, although it drew sustenance from the crisis of Marxism, was no mere reflection of or reaction to Marxism, but on the contrary a phenomenon with considerable intellectual independence.

Fascism and Marxism have one point in common: both want the destruction of the old order of things that gave rise to them and its replacement with new political and social structures. In this respect the fascist ideology is a revolutionary ideology, even if it does not wish to impair all the traditional economic structures, and even if it intends to strike at capitalism and not at private property or the idea of profit. In a bourgeois society practicing liberal democracy, an ideology that glorifies the state to such a degree as to identify it with the nation and regards politics as so important as to make the state the sole arbiter of social life and spiritual values, an ideology that considers itself, when all is said and done, the very antithesis of liberalism and individualism, is a revolutionary ideology. An ideology that propounds an organic society is bound to be unsympathetic to political pluralism, just as it can only reject the more blatant forms of social injustice.

The very term *fascism* has to be examined. Indeed, few terms in the political vocabulary have been more employed than this one, and yet few contemporary political concepts are so fluid and so ill defined. In its most limited sense the term refers simply to the Italian political regime of the interwar period, but it can also be employed as a banal term of political invective—being regarded, in that case, as the supreme insult, to be used against any political adversary whatsoever.

Thus, very few major political figures of the twentieth century have not been somebody's fascists at one time or another, and even fewer have been the political movements to which this epithet has not at some time been applied. What, then, is fascism and who is a fascist when the socialists are "social fascists" to the communists, and when Italian conservatives, Prussian Junkers, and French Croix de Feu are in turn considered "fascists" by the very people who are regarded as fascists by the orthodox Marxists?

Even today, when some excellent works enable us to understand the fascist phenomenon with a clarity that was scarcely possible previously, there is still no definition that is generally acceptable or regarded as universally valid.[1] In comparison with socialism or communism, fascism remains a relatively unexplored subject, and its very heterogeneity only serves to obscure still further a political idea that is already ambiguous enough. In the interwar period, fascism—which, among other things, was a form of extreme nationalism and hence of particularism—was as widespread in the great industrial centers of western Europe as in the undeveloped countries of eastern Europe and was as attractive to the leading intellectuals of the time as to illiterate peasants. Thus, without any clearly defined social foundation, fascism seems to lack consistency, texture, or even any real existence, and, moreover, its intellectual origins are vague and confusing. As a result, some authorities reasonably enough doubt the possibility of ever arriving at a conception of fascism that can satisfy the requirements of scientific precision,[2] while others, unwilling to face the problem, less reasonably deny the very existence of fascism.[3]

But are the problems any less serious where democracy or socialism is concerned? Are they not, on the contrary, inherent in any effort of conceptualization necessary for a real knowledge of history? And are not the concepts themselves too broad for the words that are intended to convey them? There is obviously no single example in history that corresponds to a "model" or "ideal type" (in the Weberian sense of the term) of democracy, socialism, or communism. Much the same applies to fascism: Italy in the twenties or thirties could not claim to be an "ideal" fascist state any more than the Parti Populaire Français (PPF), the British Union of Fascists, or the Legion of the Archangel Michael was an ideal fascist party.

Compared to communism or socialism, however, fascism has one fundamental weakness: it lacks a single source comparable to Marxism. If communism and socialism have very diverse and often opposing and antagonistic regional variations, these variations are always contained within the framework of Marxism. In the case of fascism, such a framework does not exist, and the historian has to try to discern the common denominator or "fascist minimum"[4] shared not only by the various political movements and ideologies that claimed to be fascist but also by those that disclaimed the title but nevertheless belonged to the family.

With regard to fascist ideology as such, the difficulties are even greater. For a very long period, it was usual to regard fascism either as

entirely lacking a system of ideas or as having rigged itself out, for partisan purposes, in the semblance of a doctrine that could not be taken
seriously and that did not deserve even the minimum of consideration
given to the ideas of any other political movement. This attitude was
perhaps not always unconnected with a basic refusal to see fascism as
anything else than a mere accident of European history: to admit that it
had intellectual substance would have meant granting it an importance
in the history of our time that people on both the left and the right, for
similar or contrary reasons, were unwilling to allow it. To admit that
fascism was anything other than a simple aberration, an accident, an
outburst of collective folly, or a phenomenon that could be explained
simply by the economic crisis, to observe that in nearly all the European
countries there existed homespun fascist movements that were not
simple imitations or caricatures of the Italian movement, to concede
that the armed bands of Rome and Bucharest, Paris and London, Berlin
and Vienna were backed by a body of doctrine no less logically defensible than that of the democratic or liberal parties, and to recognize, finally, that the ideas put forward did not belong only to the rejects of
society—the dregs of the great European capitals—manipulated by
international high finance would have required the revision of a whole
scale of values, of a whole chain of reasonings. This they were not willing to do.[5]

In this connection, it must be said that the official Marxist interpretation of the history of the interwar period, whereby fascism is alleged to
have been merely the tool of monopolistic capitalism and its ideology a
mere rationalization of imperialist interests, was a major obstacle to a
comprehensive understanding of the phenomenon. For a long time, the
idea that fascism could have been a mass movement possessing an ideology that reflected the realities and contradictions of modern society
was inconceivable and hence indefensible for anyone who did not wish
to be regarded as an "objective" ally of fascism. For many years, historians could only reflect an attitude that, however reassuring to a large
section of public opinion, could only hinder any attempt at a deeper examination of a major phenomenon of our time.

The present analysis of fascism in France covers the period from the
end of the nineteenth century to just after the fall of the Third Republic.
It begins at a time when the term *fascism* did not yet exist, about thirty
years before the appearance on the political scene, first in Italy and then
in France, of the first movements to describe themselves as fascist; it

ends with the collapse of liberal democracy in France, at the very moment when these movements appeared to be victorious, although in fact this period was far more the beginning of the end of fascism than its culmination. It was during this period that the French fascist movements lost their autonomy, and thereafter they were condemned to evolve in an inauthentic environment; for even if the ideological collaboration of Jacques Doriot, Déat, and Bucard with the Germans was a logical and natural conclusion of their development, it took place in special conditions, under the shadow of the Nazi victory, amid all the betrayals and acts of treachery that the defeat of 1940 entailed.

With regard to the origins of fascism the late 1880s are the necessary point of departure. It is then that one can first clearly discern the signs of an intellectual evolution without which fascism could never have come into being. It is then that one first finds a synthesis of a new kind of nationalism and a certain type of socialism, a synthesis that Georges Valois as well as Pierre Drieu La Rochelle, Paul Marion, Mussolini, Giovanni Gentile, and Oswald Mosley recognized as the very essence of fascism. These, indeed, were the years of incubation of the fascist phenomenon. An examination of this period reveals the national roots of French fascism, its intellectual independence with regard to other fascist movements, and the intrinsic quality of fascism as a universal phenomenon that found expression in various national movements. This period also bears witness to the rapidity with which fascist ideology matured, and to the continuity of this school of thought in France and in twentieth-century Europe.

To be sure, fascism never succeeded in coming to power in France: the traditional right was sufficiently powerful there to be able to look after its own interests. That was the case everywhere in Europe: the fascists never really succeeded in shaking the foundations of the bourgeois order. In Paris, Vichy, Rome, and Vienna, in Bucharest, London, Oslo, and Madrid, the conservatives were perfectly conscious of the difference between the fascists and themselves and were not deceived by a propaganda that sought to place them in the same category. Admiral Horthy, generals Antonescu and Franco, King Victor Emmanuel, and Belgian and British conservatives like Colonel-Count François de La Rocque, Marshal Pétain, and Pierre-Étienne Flandin were well aware that Ferencz Szalasi, Corneliu Zelea Codreanu, and José Antonio, Mussolini, Léon Degrelle, and Mosley, like Doriot, Déat, Bucard, Drieu, and Brasillach, represented a movement and a mentality that they accepted only owing to the force of circumstances. In fact, neither of these two groups permitted the confusion to continue: each side rid itself of the other as soon as the opportunity arose.

In France, the traditional right was so firmly entrenched that no revolutionaries could upset it, and it never found itself in the extreme situation, which overtook conservatives elsewhere, of having to place itself in the hands of the fascists. But the French traditional right did not have to call in the fascists for the excellent reason that when the time came, it revealed itself to be much more vigorous and readier for revolutionary changes than most of its counterparts in other countries. The French traditionalists were not fascists in the strict sense of the term, but they were not conservatives either. In many respects, the traditionalists who reached power in the summer of 1940 were also genuine revolutionaries, no less so than the famous German school of "conservative revolution." Nevertheless, the long struggle between the right and fascism—between all the right-wing factions and all the fascists—remains one of the most fascinating and least-known chapters in French politics in the period between the creation of Georges Valois's Faisceau in the middle of the twenties and Marcel Déat's campaign for the founding of a totalitarian, single-party system during the first months of the Vichy regime.

That conflict did not go back only to the interwar period; it came into being with the appearance, at the end of the nineteenth century, of a radical, popular, and socialistically inclined right, which heralded and prepared the way for the fascism of the twenties and thirties. This prefascism (which ideologically was already a mature form of fascism) immediately clashed with the conservative right; their collaboration on specific issues for particular purposes cannot conceal their essential opposition. Indeed, this latent antagonism only needed a suitable opportunity in order to break out violently into the open. The traditional, liberal, and conventional right played the same role toward prefascism and then toward fascism itself that social democracy plays toward communism in times of extreme crisis.

The study of fascism in France is particularly interesting for other reasons as well. First, one should mention the remarkably high intellectual standard of French fascist literature and thought. Apart from the work of Gentile, nowhere else in Europe was there a body of fascist ideological writings of comparable quality. Next, it should be pointed out that, in addition to the mystical, irrational, romantic, and emotional side of fascism, French fascism had a "planist," technocratic, one might say almost "managerial" aspect. This important but often ne-

glected aspect of fascism grew out of the crisis of socialism of that period, itself the result of the incapacity of Marxist thought to respond to
the challenge presented by the crisis of capitalism. More than anywhere
else, every conceivable kind of fascist sect, clique, and group flourished
in France. This multiplication of schools and tendencies no doubt contributed a great deal to the political ineffectiveness of French fascism,
but it also attests to its ideological richness and its potential. Fascist influence in France was much deeper and far more groups were affected
than is generally believed or recognized.

Speaking of that time of preparation, the period before the First
World War, Bertrand de Jouvenel was right enough when he said, a
quarter of a century later, "Historians of the future will ask if France,
were it not for the explosion of August 1914, would not have been the
first country to have a national revolution."[6]

This celebrated intellectual of the PPF, and great admirer of Mussolini
and Hitler, was not the only observer of the French political scene during that period to ask questions of this kind. His colleague, Drieu La
Rochelle, even made a preliminary contribution to an answer:

Undoubtedly, when one looks back on that period, one sees that certain elements of a fascist atmosphere came together in France around 1913, before they
did elsewhere. There were young people from various classes of society who
were filled with a love of heroism and violence, and who dreamed of fighting
what they called the evil on two fronts—capitalism and parliamentary socialism—and who were similarly disposed toward both. There were, I think,
people in Lyons who called themselves socialist-royalists or something of that
nature. A marriage of nationalism and socialism was already being envisaged.
Yes, in France, in the groups surrounding the Action Française and Péguy, there
was already a nebulous form of fascism.[7]

A similar opinion was expressed by Pierre Andreu, a Sorelian who
joined the PPF. In 1936 he published in *Combat*, a journal for fascistically inclined intellectuals, an article with a self-explanatory title:
"Fascism 1913." In this article he described the coming together, just
before 1914, of the outer wing of the Action Française and Sorelian syndicalism, united in their detestation of liberal democracy, intellectual-
ism, and bourgeois culture. After giving an account of this meeting, he
advocated a return to the sources of national socialism and a renewal of
the former alliance between the antiliberal and antibourgeois right and
the antidemocratic left. Andreu went to the trouble of unearthing the
old leftist writings of Charles Maurras,[8] and he compared the killings
ordered by Clemenceau at Draveil in 1908 to the events of February

1934. It is always the same bourgeois, democratic, liberal Republic, he said, that fires on the people: on 6 February it killed the veterans, and on the ninth it sent the police against the workers.[9]

Likewise, the writers of *Combat* who, throughout the year that saw the rise and victory of the Popular Front, had praised Georges Sorel and the Cercle Proudhon for having sought an alliance of the "revolutionary force" with the "force of national restoration"[10] reaffirmed that tradition, advocating the same kind of synthesis. They undoubtedly represented a similar school of thought with the same ideals, the same loyalties, the same mentality. The figures they admired were not only Sorel, Maurice Barrès, and Maurras but also Charles Péguy, the Marquis de La Tour du Pin, and Pierre-Joseph Proudhon. This form of fascism, already fully developed, was infinitely more subtle, more cultured, more sophisticated than the simplistic approach of Gustave Hervé in *La Victoire* or the brutality of *Je suis partout*. It was a fascism of people who do not die the violent death of agitators and rabble-rousers but end their days as members of the Académie Française. It is precisely this ordered, elegant, intellectual quality that has caused some authorities to doubt if this particular school of thought was authentically fascist. At any rate, there is no doubt that by the time it reached its full development this "salon fascism" was already well established in the French political tradition, and on the eve of Munich and the great collapse of 1940 its hour seemed to have arrived.

Long before the time of Drieu and Andreu, however, in the days when he founded the Faisceau, Georges Valois had already declared, "We find all we need here at home."[11] Philippe Barrès likewise replied to the opponents of the Faisceau who tried to "make out that the doctrines of fascism are essentially Italian" that "they are French."[12] Valois was quite correct in claiming that it was Barrès, the author of *Les Déracinés* and *L'Appel au soldat*, the Boulangist deputy for Nancy, the militant nationalist of the turn of the century, who had "had a premonition of fascism and first given expression to it" and "who had been the first to envisage the possibility and the necessity of fusing socialism with nationalism," and he called Barrès's *La Cocarde* "the first fascist journal."[13] Valois repeated this idea at every opportunity, and the careful reader of Barrès will not fail to acknowledge the correctness of this claim of kinship on the part of the founder of the Faisceau. He had gone over *Scènes et doctrines du nationalisme* with a fine-tooth comb and come to the conclusion that Barrès had foreseen and foretold the vast operation begun in Europe after the First World War.[14] Fifteen years later, in the months preceding the second war that that generation was to experience, René Vincent, writing in *Combat*, the most sophisticated and the most Barrèsian of the fascist reviews of the thirties, insisted on the unquestionable timeliness of Barrès. Praising his work *Leurs figures* in his article, "Retour à Barrès," Vincent spoke of the tremendous influence of this great writer on the youth of the period before the First World War.[15] Jean de Fabrègues also spoke of this,[16] and two years previously Drieu had invoked the authority of Barrès as one who, "like us, wished to fuse all the French traditions."[17] Even Doriot looked back to Barrès,[18] and dozens of texts written by the intellectuals of the PPF seem to have flowed directly from the pen of the national-socialist militant of the turn of the century.

Together with Barrès, the other great influential writer was Sorel, "the intellectual father of fascism."[19] "In assimilating and transcending democracy and socialism,"[20] wrote Valois, Sorel achieved something that, in his opinion, provided the basis and formed the originality of fascism and distinguished it from Leninism: the capacity to mobilize not only the proletariat but also the bourgeoisie and to call forth the combined vitality and energies of these two generally hostile classes. In Valois's opinion, the peculiarity of fascism was precisely this capacity to transcend contradictions, to mobilize energies, and to inspire the bourgeoisie to use its social and economic activities for the greatness of the country and the benefit of the community as a whole. He thought it one of the glories of fascism that it had adopted Sorel's idea that an active, demanding proletariat gave back the bourgeoisie its creative energy. A fully expanding modern economy could not, without risk of a total collapse such as the Soviet Union had recently experienced, forgo one of its main supporting elements. Therefore, one ought not to suppress the bourgeoisie but to utilize it, not to empty it of its substance but to place it under the direction of a syndicalist and corporatist state, a national state founded on "a close alliance with the working people"[21] and capable of imposing the national will on economic forces.

Like Valois, who wanted to revive the experiments of the Cercle Proudhon on a much larger scale, the rebels of the thirties, such as Drieu and Maulnier, faced with the Popular Front, dreamed of "the renewal of French society and the birth of a new world." They asked whether what had been possible before the war and its carnage had destroyed the hope of bringing together "the least corrupt element of the revolutionary force" and "the force of national restoration" was still possible in their own time, and their answer was positive. Such an al-

liance, they believed, was always possible and feasible, and it was necessary for the future of the nation and of civilization, for it represented a
"desire to assure a better future for oppressed and depredated classes,
and a desire to restore grandeur and order to the nation. There can be a
valid French order only if no Frenchman is excluded from it, and there
can be a strong society only if all partake of its benefits." [22]

This idea was repeated by the radical, revolutionary fascist right
throughout the half century between Boulangism and the Vichy revolution. Not only did the ideas not change, but even the style and vocabulary remained the same.

For the rebels against the established order of the interwar period, the
alliance of the Sorelians and Maurrassians was the prototype of an
ideal synthesis, the only one that could break the republican consensus
and counteract the collusion "between the revolutionary leaders, the
politicians and the financiers." [23] From the Blanquists in the days of Boulangism to the former Maurrassians, socialists, and communists who
opposed the Popular Front, this was how all of them defined the republican consensus. Because he had condemned social democracy more violently than anyone else, seeing it as the cornerstone of a system based on
the acceptance by the proletariat of the rules of liberal democracy, the
"old proletarian fighter" Sorel seemed, when social democracy triumphed in the summer of 1936, to be the prophet of any future attempt
to destroy this unnatural alliance, to gain the adherence of "the forces
today led astray by wordy, political and corrupt socialism." [24]

It was in order to attempt to put the national-socialist synthesis into
practice that the Maurrassians and revolutionary syndicalists founded
the Cercle Proudhon in December 1911. This circle was undoubtedly
one of the most significant developments bequeathed by the prewar generation to the generation that came out of the trenches. Led by Georges
Valois, a Maurrassian who was formerly an anarchist and later a fascist,
and the revolutionary syndicalist Édouard Berth, who after the war
drew near to communism, the Cercle Proudhon brought together those
nationalists and syndicalists who believed that "democracy was the
greatest error of the last century," because it allowed the most abomi-
nable exploitation of the workers and the setting up of the capitalist regime, and thus a substitution of the "laws of gold for the laws of blood,"
and that, accordingly, "if one wishes to preserve and to augment the
moral, intellectual and material capital of civilization, it is absolutely
necessary to destroy the democratic institutions." [25]

The Cercle Proudhon was the culmination of several years of tentative efforts, the concrete expression of a type of political thought that had already reached maturity by 1909. It was in August of that year that Sorel published his *La Déroute des mufles* in Italy—a work in which he presented the Action Française as the movement that was to put an end to the reign of stupidity in France. Four months later, when *Terre libre*, a national-syndicalist and anti-Semitic journal, began to appear, Sorel published *La Révolution dreyfusienne*, one of the most powerful indictments that had been written of the coalition that had emerged from the famous affair. On 14 April 1910, in an impressive article in *L'Action française* entitled "Le Réveil de l'âme française," Sorel praised the work of Péguy, another former Dreyfusard, who had just published *Le Mystère de la charité de Jeanne d'Arc*.

The aim of the Cercle Proudhon, wrote Valois, was to provide "a common platform for nationalists and leftist antidemocrats." [26] Placing itself under the authority of Proudhon, it also took inspiration from Sorel—two great thinkers who had "prepared the meeting of the two French traditions that had opposed each other throughout the nineteenth century: nationalism and authentic socialism uncorrupted by democracy, represented by syndicalism." [27]

The founders of the Cercle saw Sorel as the truest disciple of Proudhon. They admired his anti-intellectualism, his antiromanticism, his dislike of Kant, his Bergsonism, and his contempt for bourgeois and liberal values, democracy, and parliamentarianism. Thus, Gilbert Maire stressed the great difference between a syndicalism based on an authentic Marxism, "a philosophy of arms and not of heads" that "saw the social revolution in a mystical light," and a democratic Dreyfusard socialism, a socialism of unnatural alliances. [28] The Maurrassians welcomed Sorel so gladly because he enabled them to invoke Marx against Jean Jaurès, the interests of the proletariat against the solidarity of the "republican defense," syndicalism against socialism, and the new social sciences against Rousseau, the eighteenth century, democracy, and liberalism.

In place of the bourgeois ideology and as an alternative to democratic socialism, the Cercle Proudhon propounded a new ethic suited to the alliance of nationalism and syndicalism, those "two synthesizing and convergent movements, one at the extreme right and the other at the extreme left, that have begun the siege and the assault on democracy." [29] Their solution was thus intended as a complete replacement of the liberal order. They wished to create a new world—virile, heroic, pessimistic, and puritanical—based on the sense of duty and sacrifice: a world where a morality of warriors and monks would prevail. They wanted a society dominated by a powerful avant-garde, a proletarian elite, an aristocracy of producers, joined in an alliance against the decadent bourgeoisie with an intellectual youth avid for action. When the time came, it would not be difficult for a synthesis of this kind to take on the name of fascism.

For the generation of the thirties, the values of this synthesis arrived at before the war lay precisely in its total negation of democracy, of the French Revolutionary principles of the law of numbers, in its championship of youth, of activitistic minorities, of heroic values, in its constant campaigns against both large-scale capitalism and bourgeois culture, and in its merciless attacks on conservatives. "Conservative, now there's a word that is bad from the start," said Thierry Maulnier, addressing the object of his indictment. "We are not the splendid young people that have been hoped for," he continued, "the *milice sacrée* that the traditional right hopes will arise so that it will be able to prolong the age of horses and carriages, to defend Tradition, Property, Family, Morality, and, with a bit of luck, to revive the happy period of our conservatives' boyhood, the period when one still had servants." [30]

Far from it: this new, vigorous, revolutionary young party rose up with all its strength against both the socialist and democratic left and the bourgeois right, that "party of blindness, timidity, passivity, fear and egoism." This "new militia," for the first time since, at the turn of the century, it confronted the left "with ambitions, not regrets, not with the past but with the future," now saw its time arrive: "It had fought . . . and in certain foreign countries, after the war, it triumphed." That was the clearest lesson that the generations of 1890 and 1914 had to offer the French youth of the 1930s. Maulnier now summed up this experience and launched an appeal:

It is once more time to begin, like the prewar syndicalists, to combat both the political and the social forms of the regime, for they are inseparable. Today unscrupulous politicians mobilize crowds of workers in defense of the political regime that permits and necessitates their enslavement. It is not inappropriate to remind these imposters that the birth of the First Republic coincided with the Le Chapelier law that delivered up the workers defenselessly to capitalist exploitation; it is not inappropriate to remind them that the Second Republic came to birth in the blood of the June insurgents, and the Third Republic in the blood of the Commune. The Blums and the Jouhaux have forgotten this rather too easily.

The democratic Republic, whether the first, second, or third of that name, can only be for us the great enemy of the people, the symbol of its centuries-old oppression and the massacres that ensured it. It is against this blood-filled idol, it is against *capitalist democracy* itself and against all the parties, down to the communists, that, depending on it, become its defenders, that one must direct the battle.

Democracy and capitalism are one and the same evil: they can only be overthrown together. A regenerated nation, a better future, a flourishing peace can only spring up on their ruins. The people do not have to defend the real liberties: they still have to win them.[31]

One finds these ideas, developed by the rebels of the turn of the century, advocated by all the members of the interwar generation of fascists: as much by Valois, Hervé, Jouvenel, Jean-Pierre Maxence, Drieu, Brasillach, and the hundreds of intellectuals around them as by the agitators and killers, Bucard's followers, Joseph Darnand's militiamen, the anti-Semites of Henry Coston and Louis Darquier de Pellepoix, and the little journalists of *La Solidarité française* or *Le Franciste*.

One finds this same continuity of ideas in Bergery's *La Flèche* and Déat's *La Vie socialiste*. Indeed, the latter, a theoretical monthly journal published by the right wing of the Section Française de l'Internationale Ouvrière (SFIO), the French socialist party, seemed to revive the "pure French socialism" of the former *Revue socialiste* directed by Benoît Malon, which Édouard Drumont had approved of and which was very much in the Proudhon tradition, violently anti-Marxist and often anti-Semitic. Immediately after the split in the SFIO in July 1933—a split that led to the official emergence of neosocialism—the "néos" expounded the same kind of voluntarist, anti-Marxist socialism, rooted in an old "truly French" tradition, associated with the names of Proudhon, Sorel, Malon, Georges Renard, and Gustave Rouanet.[32] They had much in common with the leader of frontism, Bergery, whose departure (at the same time as Jouvenel's) from the Radical party and development toward a very "left-wing" form of fascism seems like a repetition of the revolt of the old Boulangists who had come out of radicalism. Indeed, like Alfred Naquet, Charles-Ange Laisant, and Henri Michelin—former parliamentary radicals, all situated on the extreme left of the political spectrum, who became Boulangists—Bergery and Jouvenel asked only one thing of the party: the fulfillment of its promises, the carrying out of the old radical program.

To a considerable degree, the generation of 1930 returned to the preoccupations of the generation of 1890, somewhat increasing their scope. It is true that, in the intervening years, the fundamental problems had hardly changed: the victory in the First World War had obscured them for a moment, but the worldwide crises of the twenties and thirties only made them worse. Moreover, the European or even global character of these crises—the revolutionary crisis of the early twenties, the economic and financial crisis at the end of that decade, the international crisis and drift toward war throughout the thirties—created a state of unrelieved tension that made some say that "crisis is endemic to society" and others that this was a crisis of the old and obsolete, a structural crisis, a "total" crisis: a crisis of capitalism, of bourgeois society, of liberal democracy. Both trends, in their own way, took up the same battle that had been fought by the generation of 1890: from the first stirrings of Boulangism to the death throes of the Third Republic, it was the essential nature of a society, of a way of life, of a civilization that had been called into question.

Thus, at the beginning of the twentieth century, France was a kind of laboratory in which the original political syntheses of our time were created. It was in France also that the first battles took place between the liberal system and its opponents. Similarly, it was in France that one saw, in Boulangism, the first attempt at a fusion of nationalism and social radicalism. It was in France, again, that one saw both the first right-wing mass movements, such as the Ligue des Patriotes, the Ligue Anti-sémitique, and the Jaune movement, and the first of those left-wing trends, such as Hervé's and Hubert Lagardelle's, that ended by leading their adherents to the threshold of fascism. Products of a crisis of liberalism—one of the gravest Europe had known—these currents of thought finally met on the eve of the First World War. The fascist spirit had now reached maturity. It was in France, finally, that one saw, on a scale comparable only to that seen in Italy before 1918, a phenomenon that one must take into account if one wishes to understand fascism: the shift to the right of elements that were socially advanced but fundamentally opposed to liberal democracy.

Regarding these, it should be pointed out that in France the sources of the fascist movement, as well as its leaders, were to be found as much on the left as on the right of the political spectrum, and often more to the left than to the right. To be sure, this was also the case elsewhere in Europe. Thus, the fascist positions of the labor minister Oswald Mosley in Great Britain and the group of Italian revolutionary syndicalists surrounding Mussolini and the warm welcome given nazism by Henri De Man, president of the Parti Ouvrier Belge (POB), parallel the reactions of the Doriotist militants, of Déat's followers, and of certain of Bergery's collaborators. The tradition was an old one, extending from the extreme left-wing radicals of the time of Boulangism, to Sorel, Lagardelle, and Hervé, to Déat, Doriot, and the thousands of ex-socialists and ex-communists who surrounded them. No other communist party lost as many members of its political bureau to a fascist party as the French one did. From the period of Boulangism right up to the time of the Collaboration, the French left never ceased to augment the ranks of the right-wing and even extreme right-wing parties, of the prefascist and already fully fascist movements. This was one of the recurring factors in French political life, and one of the main constituent elements of French fascism.

The wish to break with the liberal order was the connecting link between the Boulangist rebellion of the Blanquists, the former Communards, and the extreme left-wing radicals and the fascistically inclined or already fully fascist revolt of the neosocialists, the frontists, and the PPF. For both of these groups what really mattered was not the nature of the revolution but the very fact of a revolution. For both of these groups the nature of the regime that succeeded liberal democracy mattered much less than ending liberal democracy. This total rejection of the established order motivated one of the most important factors in the rise of fascist ideology: the transition from left to right. For if, throughout Europe, the extreme left was the traditionally revolutionary element, it soon became clear that the supposedly subversive character of socialism was largely theoretical. Each in turn and in its own manner, the various socialist movements all took the social-democratic path of compromise with the established order. In France, the Dreyfus affair only confirmed this tendency by consecrating an alliance between socialism and the bourgeois center for the defense of democracy. In deciding to join forces with the liberal bourgeoisie, French socialism initiated a policy that it was to pursue continuously throughout the twentieth century.

This shift from left to right occurred in three successive generations. At the end of the 1880s some Blanquists, a number of Communards, and some radicals of the extreme left turned to Boulangism, principally because they saw it as a means of overthrowing the liberal, bourgeois Republic. The regime, for which this was the first great confrontation, then included the possibilists among its supporters. For the first time in the history of European politics, the right wing of the socialist movement entered into an alliance with the liberal center. The system of alliances between moderates, like the process of integrating social democracy into the liberal system, came into being at that time and lasted for more than half a century,[33] just as a synthesis between social radicalism and national radicalism came into being during the Boulangist and nationalist revolt of the last years of the century. The "leftists" of the time—Henri de Rochefort, Ernest Granger, Ernest Roche, Laisant, Naquet—attacked the failings of bourgeois society, while the nationalists of Paul Déroulède's circle and the Ligue des Patriotes assailed the weaknesses of parliamentary democracy. All the members of these groups, whatever their differences, agreed that liberalism was the main enemy.

The second generation in which this shift to the right took place embarked on this process on the eve of the Great War. For some of its members the war had little effect on the process; for others it merely speeded it up. Four names represent the second group: Sorel, Berth, Lagardelle, and Hervé—participants in the theoretical activity of *Le Mouvement socialiste*. This review, run by Lagardelle, was one of the best that had ever existed in Europe, and the influence of its contributors on the development of the syndicalist extreme left was considerable. The theory of ethical socialism developed by the revolutionary-syndicalist school now spearheaded this revolt against both liberal democracy and social democracy.

The Sorelian synthesis of the two forces opposed to liberal democracy—socialism and nationalism—had already existed before the war, and took place regardless of it. Sorelian socialism itself can be seen as a form of revisionism that testified to the failure of Marxist determinism: industrial society had not developed as expected, a polarization had not taken place, and the proletariat had lost its fighting spirit. For Sorel, nothing was more despicable than the form of Marxist orthodoxy exemplified by Karl Kautsky, than the immobilism of that left wing that used a petrified Marxism, frozen into hackneyed formulas, to excuse its own impotence. Confronted with Kautsky, Sorel already preferred the point of view of Eduard Bernstein; in fact, it was with Sorel that the process began of "transcending Marxism," which reached its culmination with Henri De Man's *Au-delà du marxisme* and Marcel Déat's *Perspectives socialistes*. Going "beyond" Marxism in practice generally led to positions outside Marxism and very far away from it.

However, the socialism conceived in ethical terms of Sorel, Roberto Michels, and Arturo Labriola was an important contribution to political thought, for it played a tremendous role in the development of the national-socialist synthesis, both before 1914 and between the wars. It soon became clear that a conception of socialism in terms of universal values, independent of concrete historical circumstances, a conception of socialism in vitalist, intuitive, Nietzschean, and Bergsonian terms, was to have a definite influence on the development of Marxist ideology. Indeed, Sorelian socialism insisted from the beginning on the importance of the ethical dimension of Marxism, and Sorel stressed the moral content of Marx's thought as a tool of historical analysis and a means of transforming society. Sorel launched into a comprehensive criticism of the deterministic aspect of Marxism, whose materialistic and mechanistic element he deplored. The further he went in his criticism of the vulgarization of Marxism, of that orthodoxy that he regarded as unintelligent and unfaithful to Marx's real intentions, the more he inveighed with an ever-increasing violence against the social-democratic derivative as represented by Jaurès.

Sorel's form of socialism was in fact undergoing a metamorphosis. Despite its formal connection with labor syndicalism, it aimed increasingly at the moral regeneration of society as a whole, and the rescue of civilization rather than the liberation of the working class. Sorelian revisionism is in fact an idealistic form of revisionism, and its labor terminology cannot alter that fact. The ease with which Sorel turned to nationalism and anti-Semitism only a few years after publishing his *Reflections on Violence* shows how superficial this anti-intellectual laborism was.

Indeed, Sorel's ethical socialism owed as much to Nietzsche and Bergson as to Gustave Le Bon, Benedetto Croce, and Vilfredo Pareto. A close examination of Sorel's theory of myths reveals that Sorel regarded socialism as far more than the labor movement. Socialism to him was not only the creation of a particular class in modern society but also an ideological aspiration toward a different human order.

Thus, the spiritual and ethical renewal that was integral to the Marxism of the beginning of the century, just as it was in the 1930s, constituted a crucial turning point. In enabling socialism to be regarded as independent of the working class, it made possible a socialism without a proletariat. To Sorelian revolutionary syndicalists, to the nonconformists of the interwar period, socialism was more pedagogic than economic, and relatively indifferent to the class conflict. In the final analysis, therefore, no essential relationship appeared to exist between socialism and the proletariat. Just as all labor movements were not socialist, so all socialists were not proletarians, and socialism was not necessarily associated with any particular social structure. The interwar generation claimed that there was an "eternal socialism," a socialism valid for all men, for all times. From the moment when they, like the revolutionary syndicalists before them, lost faith in the revolutionary virtues of the proletariat, they turned toward the only historical force that could still serve as an agent of moral regeneration and social transformation. When the time came, the nation replaced the proletariat, and the transition from revolutionary syndicalism to national socialism took place quite naturally. As soon as it became obvious that the proletariat had neither the means nor the energy nor the desire to be the savior of heroic values, it was replaced by what appeared to be the great rising force: the nation.

Hervé and Lagardelle made this transition under the impact of the war. The war, they claimed, had demonstrated that the motive force of history was not the class but the nation. The idea of classes had lost its value for them, and Hervé's journal, *La Guerre sociale*, was renamed *La Victoire*—a name that this former left-wing weekly retained a quarter of a century later when it became the first journal to reappear in occupied Paris. Lagardelle, the editor of *Le Mouvement socialiste*, joined Valois's Faisceau and Bergery's frontists, and finally became Marshal Pétain's minister of labor.

Immediately after the First World War, Gustave Hervé founded a national-socialist party. His second in command was Alexandre Zévaès, a former deputy for Isère, a former Guesdist, and an orthodox Marxist, who in the interim had become the defender of Jaurès's murderer. This party—the second national-socialist party founded in France, which soon after its founding declared its enthusiasm for Mussolini and Italian fascism—in August 1919 won the support of the old socialist leader Jean Allemane, who wrote, "We have the duty of enlightening the working class concerning its real interests and showing it that they are identical with those of the nation."[34]

Yet, if the outbreak of the First World War created favorable conditions for the spectacular change of direction of Lagardelle, Hervé, and Allemane, this about-face really had a long preparation and was not a simple outcome of the war. Its origins went back to the Dreyfus affair at the beginning of the century.

Indeed, if the vast majority of French socialists followed Jaurès in taking the path of democracy without meeting any effective resistance from Jules Guesde, an active minority opted for an out-and-out opposition. Sorel, Lagardelle and the contributors to *Le Mouvement socialiste*, and syndicalist leaders like Émile Pouget and Victor Griffuelhes regarded the affair as an enormous hoax. Once again, they said, as in 1789, 1830, and 1848, the bourgeoisie had utilized the revolutionary capacities of the proletariat to protect its own interests. Once again, the proletariat had become the bourgeoisie's watchdog. Once again, in the name of liberty and the Republic, democracy and secularism, it had been cheated by its political leaders, who had persuaded it to save its own exploiters, its own oppressors.

The conclusion, then, was simple: since democracy and the bourgeoisie are inseparable and since democracy is the most effective offensive weapon the bourgeoisie has invented, democracy has to be overthrown in order to destroy bourgeois society. Lagardelle, Sorel, Berth, and Hervé all agreed that not only did democracy not serve the interests of socialism, as Jaurès believed, but it was its mortal enemy. In a parallel manner, Maurras and Valois believed that democracy brought the nation to the verge of extinction. Socialism and nationalism thus discovered their common enemy, whose elimination was necessary to their own existence.

Together with the revolt against the established order and a growing awareness of the national entity, a third cause of the switching of sides (as exemplified by Sorel) was a certain form of non-Marxism, anti-Marxism, and, finally, post-Marxist revisionism. "National" socialism, without which fascism could never have come into being, first appeared at the end of the 1880s, and the tradition continued without interruption until the Second World War. It has generally been overlooked that, until that time, the currents of thought opposed to Marxist orthodoxy were very strong in French socialism. The legitimacy of "national" socialism was questioned only very late, around 1930, when Marcel Déat's ideas in *Perspectives socialistes* were described by the left-wingers of the SFIO as "neosocialist." It was not until 1933 that the *Vie socialiste* group—under the nominal leadership of Pierre Renaudel, a close associate of Jaurès's, but in reality led by Déat—was excluded from the socialist party. Only after it had been tainted by collaboration with the Germans was a "national" socialism definitely discredited.

The socialist left was not the only group to provide members for fascist or quasi-fascist formations: the liberal center also played its part, contributing both Bertrand de Jouvenel and Gaston Bergery. These two "Young Turks" of the Radical party (the first was to become Doriot's economic expert and the second Marshal Pétain's ambassador) played a far from negligible role in the formation of a certain fascist outlook. One need only recall Jouvenel's contribution to the "planist" and technocratic aspect of fascism and Bergery's to the idea that one should fight liberal democracy and communism at home instead of engaging in ideological warfare against the fascist and Nazi dictators.

However, it was the revision of Marxism that constituted the most significant ideological aspect of fascism. In many respects, the history of fascism can be described as a continuous attempt to revise Marxism and create a national form of socialism. From Sorel to Déat and Henri De Man, who had much influence on French socialism, one factor remained constant—the desire to "go beyond" Marxism. But if, in the words of the title of De Man's most famous book, one goes "beyond" Marxism without reaching social democracy, one finally finds oneself outside Marxism. The work of Georges Sorel, like that of Arturo Labriola and the Italian revolutionary syndicalists, was a "leftist" transcendence of Marxism, while that of Déat and De Man was originally a revision of Marxism coming from the right. Their solutions differed, but the questions they raised were fundamentally the same, just as their different forms of revisionism led to the same political consequences.

From the beginning of the century, the great question on which the orthodox Marxists and the dissidents—from both the right and the left—were divided was, Is classical Marxism still capable of acting as a means of changing society? Does it remain the key to the interpretation of history? Can it be used to foresee the future? For both the leftist revisionists and those who had come from the right, the reply was, to various degrees, negative. Thus, in 1906, Sorel, in the midst of an already very productive career, wrote his *Reflections on Violence*, which remains to this day a classic of revisionism, but of a leftist, voluntarist, and vitalist form of revisionism. Five years later, Sorel inspired the creation of the Cercle Proudhon, and his writings of that period were already quasi-fascist. The shift toward fascism had therefore already taken place before the Great War, and was unconnected with it. It was completed as soon as Sorel and the revolutionary syndicalists of France and Italy became convinced that Marxism provided no real answer to the crisis of capitalism and that the proletariat would never bring about the revolution.

Increasingly, the idea gained ground—not only among theoreticians like Sorel and Berth but also among genuine activists like Émile Janvion—that the true revolutionary force, the one that would finally overthrow liberal democracy, was the nation and not the proletariat. At the same time as Sorel, the revolutionary syndicalists in Italy came to this conclusion: they threw themselves enthusiastically into the war not out of patriotism, as is often thought, but because they saw it as an instrument of revolution. Since war is a conflict between nations rather than between classes, the nation was seen as the foremost agent of revolution, and Italian revolutionary syndicalism became the backbone of fascist ideology.

The "leftist" form of revisionism did not survive the war. In the years following the war, a very different form of revisionism flourished, at first sight closer to the Bernstein tradition but in reality quite different in spirit. This was a "planist," technocratic, "managerial" form of revisionism, which maintained that between traditional capitalism and the proletarian revolution was a third option—the celebrated "intermediate regimes" referred to by Marcel Déat. At the same time, all these variants of revisionism were contained within the same conceptual framework, which was their common denominator and their factor of continuity, namely, the rejection of materialism. Liberal and bourgeois materialism was as abhorrent to them as Marxist proletarian materialism. On that point all the rebels, from the turn of the century onward, were agreed.

The true ideologist of this new form of revisionism—to which not only some of the leading figures in the ideological collaboration with Nazi Germany, such as Déat and Jean Luchaire, but also simple Vichyists like Lagardelle and Belin and supporters of Doriot who stopped en route, such as Jouvenel, contributed—was undoubtedly Henri De Man.

In 1926 De Man published *Zur Psychologie des Sozialismus*. Four years later, when an Italian translation of the book appeared, Mussolini expressed his interest in the work in a letter to the author: "Your criticism of Marxism is much more pertinent than that of the German or Italian reformists: it is also definitive, since it comes after the events of 1914–1919 that destroyed whatever 'scientific' element still remained in Marxism." [35] Mussolini was particularly appreciative of the idea that a corporative organization and a new relationship between labor and capital would eliminate "the psychological distance in which—more than in the clash of economic interests—one sees, precisely, the germ of class warfare." [36]

Mussolini had perfectly understood the nature of De Man's revisionism, and he recognized its true significance. He realized that the work of the Belgian socialist provided fascism, whether one liked it or not, with a kind of legitimacy. De Man, moreover, never disavowed this fact. Quite the contrary: while not concealing his objections to fascism, he was willing to acknowledge that there were aspects that he found positive. "Having said this," he wrote, "I beg you [Mussolini] to believe that no prejudice prevents me from following daily, insofar as one can from reading, with an ardent concern for objective information, the doctrinal and political work that you are undertaking." De Man continued:

It is precisely because, belonging, like you, to the "generation of the front," and influenced, like you, by the ideas of Georges Sorel, I do not close my mind to any manifestations of creative force, it is precisely because I am not afraid to do justice to certain organizational aspects of the fascist enterprise, that I follow its progress with a passionate interest. This passion stems both from my anxieties and from my hopes. My anxieties, because I believe that history will credit the leaders of our period only with those actions that they have done in order to accomplish the two great tasks of our civilization: to provide people with greater concrete liberty and to provide mankind with greater political unity. My hopes, because I have to believe that a man of your intellectual dynamism is too much possessed by the eternally revolutionary forces of the spirit not to seek the perfecting and perpetuation of his work—and its acceptability to the ideals of one's youth—in the revolutionary task par excellence: the organization of liberty and peace.[37]

It was no accident that De Man mentioned Sorel and stressed the long-term influence of the author of *Reflections on Violence*, or that he wrote to the Italian leader in a tone of historical complicity. Henri De Man's "planist" reformism, like Marcel Déat's, was a response both to the crisis of capitalism and to the incapacity of orthodox socialism to rise to the challenge. The basic problem preoccupying this new revisionism was the same one that concerned Sorel and the prewar revolutionary syndicalists. This no doubt explains the similarity of their intellectual developments.

Seen in this context, the events of the summer of 1940 are less surprising and the dissolution of the Parti Ouvrier Belge by its president is less inexplicable. On 28 June 1940, De Man, succeeding Émile Vandervelde, who had died in 1938, published a manifesto addressed to the socialist activists asking them to accept the Nazi victory as the starting point for the construction of a new world. This work is a classic of fascist literature.

The war has brought about the overthrow of the parliamentary regimes and the capitalist plutocracy in the so-called democracies.

For the laboring classes and for socialism, this collapse of a decrepit world, far from being a disaster, has been a deliverance.

Despite all the setbacks, sufferings and disillusionments we have experienced, the way is clear for the two causes that embody the aspirations of the people: European peace and social justice.

Peace did not arise through the voluntary agreement of sovereign states and rival imperialisms, but it could arise out of a Europe united by arms, in which economic frontiers have been leveled.

Social justice did not arise from a regime claiming to be democratic but that in reality was dominated by the power of money and the professional politicians, a regime grown increasingly incapable of any bold initiative, of any serious reform. It could arise out of a regime in which the authority of the state is strong enough to undermine the privileges of the propertied classes and replace unemployment by the obligation for all to work. . . .

You should therefore continue to pursue our economic activities, but regard the political role of the Parti Ouvrier Belge as terminated. This role was a fruitful and glorious one, but a different mission now awaits you.

Prepare yourselves to enter the cadres of a movement of national resurrection that will embrace all the living forces of the nation, of its youth, of its veterans, within a single party—that of the Belgian people, united by its fidelity to its King and by its desire to realize the Sovereignty of Labor.[38]

This text represents neither a rupture nor an aberration in the ideological development of a whole school of socialism in the French-speaking countries. For years, De Man had developed a political ideology that in all respects was already fascist. During these years, however, De Man was not just one thinker among others, or an isolated socialist revisionist: he was a leader of a great socialist party, and his conduct as president of that party and his writings during the German occupation were merely the logical outcome of a process that had been in operation for nearly twenty years.

In the case of the younger and less known Marcel Déat, this ideological development took place during the same period, but his writings only began to appear in 1930, when the Librairie Valois published his *Perspectives socialistes*, which paralleled the Belgian writer's *Au-delà du marxisme*. Three years later, Déat founded a new socialist party, the Parti Socialiste de France (PSF), which already had a fully fascist ideology, and which aimed at transforming the world but without passing through Marxism. Thus, Déat's speech as the leader of the collaborationist and pro-Nazi Rassemblement National Populaire (RNP) at the first congress of the movement, which took place at the Palais de la Mutualité in Paris on 14 and 15 June 1941, hardly differed from the one he had made in the Palais de la Mutualité eight years earlier as the SFIO deputy for the twentieth *arrondissement* in Paris. Returning to the famous "néo" slogan "Ordre, autorité, nation," and invoking the authority of Henri De Man as he had always done at the beginning of the thirties, Déat concentrated on the theme of the state and the nation:

"The state that socialism requires," he said, "should be not only a national state but an authoritarian state." [39]

Déat then proceeded to give a brief explanation of national socialism that could have been given in very similar terms at any time from the end of the nineteenth century onward:

Those who at first were deceived by the false mystiques of a bad nationalism serving the greater interests of international capitalism have gradually come to realize that there exists a body of workers, and that these will stand aloof from the nation as long as the state has not become, instead of the instrument of the domination of a class or of particular interests, the tool for the liberation of the proletariat. They have realized, I say, that nothing will be possible as long as the state and the nation are not the state and the nation of everyone, and as long as the nation has not become a national community in which everyone has, in addition to the possibility of living decently and normally, the possibility of developing the expectations and potentialities within him until he realizes his being and his personality. Having understood this, they arrived at the same revolution as ourselves via the nation, whereas we discovered the nation via the incomplete idea of a revolution of the classes.[40]

In the period of ideological collaboration with Germany, Déat once more recalled the heritage of Proudhon, Barrès, and Sorel. He thus brought to a close half a century of national-socialist thinking.

History and sociology have restored to us a sense of the unalterable originality of national surroundings. . . . But one must go farther and rediscover the biological notion of the race. . . . A race, too, is not just something to be preserved, it is the point of departure for the conquest of a future. It requires purification and defense, improvement and selection, or, as Nietzsche said, self-transcendence. France is thus invited to tighten its "ethnic identity," to practice eugenics, to have a demographic policy, and to ensure its ideological survival in order to preserve its spirit and maintain its historical role. What can be so outrageous about this state of affairs, in which the body regains its position next to the soul? Is this not a return to Greece via Sparta, that fine breeder of men, which Barrès praised in a book of particular lucidity?[41]

He ended:

This new idea of a living community in which an abstract fraternity is replaced by a kinship of blood, in which everyone has the same rights to the protection of the community, and is given the same opportunities at the beginning, but receives duties whose importance is determined by one's capacities, and in which the existence of a hierarchy does not exclude equality of sacrifice at critical moments—all these are new concepts. There is no break with the past, however: French liberty, like German liberty, is part of an order, and the same is true of equality. It forms a totality in which each person can develop, a total man in a total society, without clashing with others or crushing them, without anarchy.

This, in short, is the definition of socialism, which is not a mere adjustment of interests between rival classes more or less arbitrated by the state, but the subordination of all to the whole.

It is no longer a matter of Marxism, of the universalization of the proletariat, or of internationalism. It is a question of a national socialism that has lost or forgotten nothing of its true spirit.[42]

From Barrès in the days of Boulangism to Déat after the 1940 defeat, national socialism always pursued a particular aim: "the integration of the proletariat into the nation."[43] It was in order to be consistent with this idea that Marcel Déat insisted that the revolution should be directed against both the "old left" and the "old right," "the diehards of the left and right," the "ill-weaned nurslings of Maurrassism."[44] Similarly, he maintained that one ought to destroy "economic liberalism, which is a bourgeois materialism, which is paralleled by the labor materialism of Marxism, both indubitably children of rationalism"—which is "inverted fanaticism."[45] In attacking materialism and rationalism, Déat doubtless wished to discredit the old traditions of the Enlightenment before beginning to lay the foundations of the new order.

The wheel had come full circle. In Déat's writings one does not find a single basic idea that had not, in one way or another, been expressed by Barrès fifty years before.

In the forties, as at the turn of the century, there were two main right-wing trends: on the one hand, the conservatives and the liberals, who accepted the basic rules and principles of liberal democracy, and thus the established social order, and, on the other hand, the dissidents and the revolutionaries, whose rejection of those very principles throughout the half century before the summer of 1940 had prepared the downfall of democracy in France.

My analysis differs fundamentally from that of René Rémond who in the fifties divided the right into three streams—traditionalist (or legitimatist), liberal (Orléanist), and populist and authoritarian (Bonapartist)[46]—which could cross and intermingle but have nevertheless, from the restoration of the French monarchy in 1815 to the present, preserved their separate identities. Rémond's brilliant exposition portrays accurately the realities of the nineteenth century up to the first years of the Third Republic, but its pattern no longer fits from Boulangism onward. With Boulangism began the era of mass politics: the modernization of the European continent, the technological revolution, and the democratization of political life created a new social and ideological reality. These new conditions produced the new right—a right that was popular and even proletarian, but violently anti-Marxist, a right that pre-scribed an organic, tribal form of nationalism, a nationalism of Blood and Soil, of the Land and of the Dead. This new right represented a re-sponse to the problems of modern society; Bonapartism reflected the very different concerns of preindustrial society. Thus, the revolutionary right, the prefascist right, and later the fascist right all corresponded to needs that Bonapartism could not even conceive of.

Ideologically, the new right reflected the great intellectual revolution of the turn of the century, combining social Darwinism, racism, the so-cial psychology of Le Bon, and Nietzsche's philosophical revolt. Politi-cally, whereas Bonapartism thought in terms of a coup d'état supported by the great mass of peasants eager for stability, for whom dictatorship was above all a means of assuring public order and the protection of private property, the new right wished to create a new morality, a new type of society, and new rules of political behavior. The cultural integra-tion of the lower classes, the increasing nationalism of the masses, uni-versal suffrage, the general rise in literacy, and the dissemination of daily newspapers politicized society to a degree hitherto unknown. A struggle for public opinion began, a struggle for or against the existing system, for or against the accepted order.

Also with Boulangism there came into being within the right two opposing blocs that confronted one another up until the defeat of France in 1940: on the one hand the conservatives, who took their place next to the liberals and accepted the value system of liberal democracy, and on the other hand the revolutionaries, who wanted to destroy the political structures and to sweep away those same liberal-democratic values. This new revolutionary right had little in common with Bo-napartism, which, despite its populist and authoritarian character, be-longed to a society where the participation of the people in the political process was limited. Furthermore, Bonapartism lacked two essential modern ingredients of the revolutionary right: anti-Marxist radicalism and organic nationalism. As a result, it did not have an ideology of its own, elaborated—like that of the revolutionaries—by leading intellec-tuals of the period, and consequently it lacked the intellectual force that, throughout the half century preceding the defeat of 1940, assured the revolutionary right of its influence.

It was this revolutionary right of the turn of the century that laid the groundwork for fascism. Thus, not only did French fascism, despite its political weakness, come closest to the ideal, the "idea" of fascism in the

Weberian sense of the term, but France was also the country in which the fascist ideology in its main aspects came into being a good twenty years before similar ideologies appeared elsewhere in Europe, particularly in Italy. French fascism was thus in every respect an indigenous school of thought: in no way can it be regarded as a foreign importation, or—from the 1920s onward—as a vague imitation of Italian fascism.

The fascist movements—all the fascist movements—had the same lineage: a revolt against liberal democracy and bourgeois society, and an absolute refusal to accept the conclusions inherent in the general outlook, in the explanation of social phenomena and human relations, of all the so-called "materialist" schools of thought. The rise of fascism appears to have been one of the by-products of the crisis of Marxism and the crisis of liberalism, one of the consequences of the enormous difficulties encountered by both Marxism and liberal democracy before the realities of the twentieth century.

Thus, the historical circumstances of the half century preceding the Second World War gave rise to the essence of fascism: a synthesis of organic nationalism and anti-Marxist socialism, a revolutionary ideology based on a simultaneous rejection of liberalism, Marxism, and democracy. In its essential character, the fascist ideology was a rejection of "materialism" (liberalism, Marxism, and democracy being regarded as merely the three faces of one and the same materialist evil), and it aimed at bringing about a total spiritual revolution. Fascist activism, with its marked tendency to elitism, favored a strong political authority freed from the trammels of democracy and emanating from the nation, a state that represented the whole of society with all its different classes. Planism, economic dirigism, and corporatism were important elements in fascist thought, in that they expressed in concrete terms the victory of politics over economics and placed all the key positions in the economy and society in the hands of the state.

A classic ideology of rejection, fascism implied the repudiation of a certain political culture associated with the eighteenth century and the French Revolution, and sought to lay the foundation of a new civilization, a communal, anti-individualist civilization that alone would be capable of perpetuating the existence of a human collectivity in which all layers and classes of society are perfectly integrated. The natural framework of such a harmonious, organic collectivity was the nation: a nation that boasted a moral unity that liberalism and Marxism—both productive of factionalism and discord—could never provide. These, then, are the main features of a "minimal" characterization of fascism: fascism derived its power from its universality, from its being the product of a crisis of civilization.

The history of fascism is also in many respects the history of a desire for modernization, for renewal, and for the adaptation of political systems and theories inherited from the preceding century to the demands and necessities of the modern world. Resulting from a general crisis whose symptoms had been clearly apparent from the end of the last century, fascism manifested itself throughout the whole of Europe. The fascists were all completely convinced of the universal character of the wave that bore them, and their confidence in the future was consequently unshakable.

People from many different backgrounds and with eventful intellectual histories contributed to the formulation of the fascist ideology. Each one brought his own share, each one stressed a particular aspect of their common rejection of the existing systems, but all were united in rejecting what they felt to be the essence of those systems—"materialism," whether liberal and bourgeois materialism or Marxist and proletarian materialism. This opposition to "materialism" was the common denominator uniting Sorel, Arturo Labriola, Michels, De Man, Berth, Gabriele D'Annunzio, Angelo O. Olivetti, Barrès, Enrico Corradini, Mussolini, Gentile, Mosley, Degrelle, José Antonio, Codreanu, Drieu, Déat, Brasillach, Rebatet, Jouvenel, Maulnier, and so many others.

These people, to be sure, differed on many subjects, and at various periods professed different ideas. None of them formulated the whole of fascism, and the writings of none represent an ideal model of the fascist ideology, but the same applies, after all, to all the socialists after Marx and all the liberals after Hobbes and Locke. The differences between the fascists were no greater—in fact they were less—than those between J. S. Mill and Spencer, Tocqueville and T. H. Green, Bernard Bosanquet and Leonard T. Hobhouse, Proudhon and Ferdinand Lassalle, Kautsky and Jaurès and Bernstein, and Beatrice and Sidney Webb and Léon Blum, and yet, despite their differences, some of them appear to belong to the liberal school and others to the socialist school. The affinity between them is sufficiently great that their names are found in any work dealing with liberalism or socialism.

Fascism, like liberalism, socialism, and communism, was a universal category with regional and cultural variants. This was especially the case since the "age of fascism" was a period associated with a certain ideology and movements connected with that ideology rather than a period characterized by a certain type of regime. Fascism attained power only in Italy and, for a very short period, in Romania. That fascism never came to power in France does not mean that there was no French fascism. Does the failure of the French communists demonstrate the nonexistence of communism in France? Was there no French socialism before 1936 or 1981?

As a historical phenomenon, fascism can be perceived on three levels: it is an ideology, it is a movement, and it is a regime. Undeniably, where the history of ideas is concerned, the First World War was not the major break it was in so many other spheres. Fascism belonged not just to the interwar period but to the whole period of history that began with the modernization of the European continent at the end of the nineteenth century. It was the intellectual revolution of the turn of the century, the entry of the masses into politics, that produced fascism as a system of thought, as a sensibility, and as an attitude toward the essential problems of civilization. The Great War and the economic crisis produced the necessary sociological and psychological conditions for the setting up of fascist movements, but they did not give rise to the fascist ideology. As a system of thought, fascism was not "invented" on the Piazza di San Sepolcro, any more than communism came into being in the train that carried Lenin toward the Finnish frontier; it originated in the great ideological laboratory of the Belle Époque.

However, if fascism was to be found throughout Europe, its effect was not the same everywhere. One should retain one's sense of proportion and remember that though the revolutionary right won a resounding victory in Germany and Italy, it did not do so in France. The rebels and the revolutionaries played a major role in the formation of a certain sensibility, of a certain widespread mentality, but they nevertheless had to wait until the summer of 1940 to win the last of a long series of battles, beginning with Boulangism and the Dreyfus affair. Thus, while the influence of the radical right on French politics was considerable, French society resisted the rise of this revolutionary movement in a way not found beyond the Rhine or the Alps. This, at any rate, was the case until the final days of the Third Republic, but one must remember that the revolution embarked on by the Vichy government—the most important since 1789—can really be understood only in relation to the long process of "antimaterialist" impregnation—antiliberal, antidemocratic, and anti-Marxist—of the half century before the defeat of 1940.

The history of that period presents innumerable ambiguities. It is perhaps not inappropriate to illustrate this point with two examples. The

Dreyfus affair has undoubtedly become the symbol of the great wave of anti-Semitism that arose in Europe at the end of the nineteenth century. It provoked an explosion of strong passions and clearly revealed the precariousness of the Jewish condition. At that time, France was the center of anti-Semitic agitation in Europe. However, this celebrated affair also had another aspect: it gave rise to a controversy that not only resulted in clashes in the streets but also provoked reflections on the fundamental principles of political philosophy. For a number of years the entire country was intensely involved in a debate of universal significance. Few indeed are the nations that can claim for themselves the credit of having transformed, regardless of political considerations, a miscarriage of justice into a national trial of conscience, and fewer still are those that can boast of having overruled reasons of State for the sake of certain universal principles.

A generation later, when French society had been deeply affected by fascist influence, Léon Blum took office as prime minister of France. To be sure, Xavier Vallat, Maurras, Maulnier, and Brasillach were all extremely active at that time and their influence was increasing, but the fact remains that it was a Jew who presided over the triumph of the Popular Front. Thus the situation during that period was much more complex than is often alleged.[47]

It is perhaps precisely this fact that makes the study of the radical right in France so interesting. Here the revolt took place within a society that, unlike the Italian and German societies, had produced the most important liberal revolution in history and the only one to take place on the European continent. The French Revolution had molded the character of the nation and deeply affected it. In France, liberal democracy was not something imported from abroad but an inseparable part of the collective consciousness, and its overthrow would have required a mobilization of forces far greater than the comparatively modest effort required of the revolutionary right in Italy and Germany.

The same can be said of the economic and social conditions that existed in France. The process of industrialization, which proceeded at a much slower rate in France than in Germany and northern Italy, did not have the destabilizing effect in France that it had in the neighboring countries. French society was never as deeply affected by its economic growth and consequently never reacted with the same violence. France was able to modernize stage by stage, and its relatively slow rate of development enabled it to preserve a very great stability.

This stability, in turn, favored the creation and perpetuation of an alliance between democratic socialism and liberalism. The fact that the socialist movement as well as the liberal bourgeoisie functioned within the republican system and had a vested interest in preserving the existing order served to increase the resistance of that system to the onslaughts of the radical right throughout the half century before the Second World War. It is these fundamental considerations and not particular circumstances such as the war and the economic crisis that explain the great difference between the fate of liberal democracy in Germany and Italy and France.

However, the historical picture has still another aspect. Isolated from the Vichy period, the thirties in France appear to be tremendously dissimilar from the identical period in Germany or Italy, but, taken together with the forties, these difficult years take on a somewhat different aspect. In the space of a few months, the France of 1940 drew considerably closer to its two neighboring countries. Undoubtedly, the summer and autumn of 1940 were a truly revolutionary period that changed the face of the land. Very little now remained of the France of 1789: the old democratic tradition failed to resist the shock of a great national crisis—the defeat and the occupation of part of the national territory.

In the autumn of 1940, Vichy France, of its own volition, fell into line with Italy and Germany, and that is yet another reason why the study of the fascist and revolutionary right in France is of far greater interest even than the study—itself fascinating—of the history of the country in the first half of the twentieth century.

CHAPTER ONE

From One Prewar Period to Another

The Crisis of "Old Things":
Democracy, Liberalism, Socialism

The thirty years that preceded the First World War and the decade that followed it formed a truly revolutionary period in the history of Europe. In the space of less than half a century the condition of society, the form of life, the rate of technological progress, and in many respects people's way of looking at themselves underwent a greater change than at any other time in modern history. The growth of industry and technology transformed manners and morals, radically altered the pace of life, brought into being great metropolitan cities, and had a profound effect on life in the provinces.

In the second and third decades of our century, there was a strong and widespread awareness of living in a world that was changing with unprecedented rapidity. As Henri De Man wrote, "In reality, there are not many qualitative changes in the history of mankind that can be compared, as regards their revolutionary significance for society and culture, with the change from mechanical movement to electrical movement, from the technique of the lever to the technique of waves, from the cogwheel to the electric wire and wireless transmission, from material to energetic work processes, from mechanistic thought to functional thought."[1] De Man felt that the world of that period was a world in gestation, "which differed as much from the world of our grandparents as that differed from the world of their ancestors six thousand years ago."[2] And he concluded, in a manner very characteristic of his generation, "We are living in the midst of the greatest social revolution that history has ever known. There is an old world that is passing away and a new world that is being born."[3]

However, if it was only in the interwar period that this consciousness of the new situation became practically universal, a presentiment of the upheavals that were to overtake an entire civilization already existed at the end of the nineteenth century. Indeed, in the sphere of ideas, that period was already deeply affected by a resurgence of irrational values, by a cult of instinct and sentiment, and by an affirmation of the supremacy of the forces of life and the affections. The rationalist and "mechanistic" explanation of the world that had been dominant in European thought from the sixteenth century onward now gave way to an "organic" explanation, and the new importance given to historical values and various idealistic factors amounted to a condemnation of rationalism and individualism. The role of the individual was made subordinate to that of society and of history. To state the matter differently, for the generation of 1890—Le Bon, Barrès, Sorel, Georges Vacher de Lapouge, and others—the individual had no value in himself, and therefore society could not be regarded simply as the sum of the individuals who composed it.[4] This new generation of intellectuals was violently opposed to the rationalistic individualism of the liberal order, to the dissolution of social bonds that existed in bourgeois society, and to the "utilitarianism and materialism" that prevailed there.[5] It was precisely in this desire to overturn the prevailing order of values that the most clear-sighted fascist intellectuals of the interwar period perceived the origins of fascism. Gentile defined fascism as a revolt against positivism.[6]

That revolt, which was also an attack on the way of life produced by liberalism, an opposition to the "atomized" society, led to a glorification of the institution that was felt to represent the element of unity—the nation. This glorification of the nation, the emergence of a nationalism involving a whole system of defenses and safeguards intended to assure the integrity of the national body, was a natural outcome of the new conception of the world. The new school of thought, rejecting the system of values bequeathed by the eighteenth century and the French Revolution and assailing the foundations of liberalism and democracy, had a very different image of things: "The selectionist morality gives one's duty toward the species the position of supremacy that Christianity gives one's duty toward God," wrote Vacher de Lapouge.[7]

Here we must insist on something of great importance for an understanding of subsequent developments. The antirationalist reaction that questioned the underlying principles of both Marxism and democracy was not the mere product of a literary neoromanticism that affected only the world of arts and letters. These principles were challenged in the name of science, and this was the real significance of the intellectual revolution of the first quarter of the twentieth century. When one sees them in this context, one can understand the nature and scope of the new directions taken in many fields in this period: the new humanistic and social sciences, Darwinian biology, Bergsonian philosophy, Ernest Renan and Hippolyte Taine's interpretation of history, Le Bon's social psychology, and the so-called Italian school of political sociology—Pareto, Gaetano Mosca, and Michels—all opposed the basic premises of liberalism and democracy. The new social sciences, which inherited many aspects of social Darwinism (this was especially true of anthropology and social psychology), created a new theory of political conduct. They thus contributed to an intellectual climate that helped to undermine the foundations of democracy and to enable fascism to come to power.

The positivist character of their scientific method cannot alter the fact that the objective criticisms of given realities of Mosca, Pareto, and Michels amount, in actuality, to sweeping attacks on democracy. The rational explanation of the irrational provided by the theory of elites constitutes a bridge between social research and fascist practice. This explanation by the Italian school of political sociology contributed to the development of revolutionary syndicalism and nationalism, and in many respects represented the meeting point of these two schools of thought. A conception of man as being essentially motivated by the forces of the unconscious, a pessimistic idea that human nature is unchangeable, led to a static view of history: human conduct cannot change, since psychological motivations always remain the same. According to this view, in all periods of history, whatever the current ideology, under whatever regime, human behavior is unchanging, and therefore the character of a regime is finally of little importance in itself. Moreover, these three authors, like Max Weber at a later date, were agreed that the social sciences could not provide a basis for value judgments either of political structures or of ideologies. This scientific objectivism, based on a vision of man as an essentially irrational being, thus played an important role in undermining the foundations of democracy, and the theory of elites associated with Mosca, Pareto, and Michels remained until the forties one of the most formidable offensive weapons against both Marxism and democracy.[8] Their writings influenced every form of rebellion against democracy, liberalism, and Marxism; nationalists, syndicalists, and nonconformists of every kind referred to them, but in fact, from the end of the nineteenth century, all the social sciences contributed to the erosion of the spirit of optimism, of faith in the individual and in progress, without which it is difficult to conceive of the survival of democracy.

Here we must mention another important factor. From Mosca and Pareto at the turn of the century and Michels on the eve of the First World War up to De Man and Déat, the social sciences—sociology, anthropology, political science, psychology, and Bergsonian philosophy— were working toward what seems, at least in retrospect, to have been an attempt to create an alternative system to Marxism—a system that could give a total explanation of things comparable to the one given by Marx's. But this long-drawn-out competition with Marx involved not only people like Pareto, Michels, and Mosca but also Weber and even, by implication, Émile Durkheim and Freud. De Man's revision of Marxism was based on psychology, and it was by no means fortuitous that his major work was called, in the best tradition of Gustave Le Bon, *Zur Psychologie des Sozialismus.*[9]

Throughout the interwar period, the influence of these modern disciplines was enormous. They were the only ones with enough authority to be able to speak, along with Marxism, in the name of science, and they were the only ones to provide revisionism with its conceptual foundations.

Thus, at the beginning of the century, these new social sciences, particularly psychology and anthropology, which in turn influenced sociology, political science, and historical research, provided both the antiliberal and the anti-Marxist reactions with their conceptual framework. They also helped to fuse the ideas of the generation of 1850 (Darwin, Arthur de Gobineau, Wagner) and those of the generation of 1890 into a complete and coherent system. The old romantic outlook, the old historicist tendencies, the old theory of the unconscious origins of the nation, the idea of living forces that make up the soul of the people thus received scientific legitimation. One sees the reappearance, modernized and adapted to the requirements of mass society, of the old principles of the subordination of the individual to the collectivity and the integrity of the national body. These new theories completely rejected the traditional mechanistic conception of man that made human behavior dependent on rational choices. The idea became prevalent that feelings and the unconscious played a far greater role in politics than did reason, and this, by a logical process, engendered a contempt for democracy, its institutions, and its machinery.

The biological and psychological determinism of Le Bon, Vacher de Lapouge, Barrès, Drumont, and even Taine, and of innumerable publications in every field of intellectual endeavor led finally to racism.

According to Le Bon, a people's life, its institutions, its destiny are "simply the reflection of its soul,"[10] or, that is to say, the "moral and intellectual characteristics" that "represent a synthesis of its whole past, the heritage of all its ancestors, the motivation of its conduct."[11] "Human conduct," he said, "is inexorably predetermined" because "each people is endowed with a mental constitution that is as fixed as its anatomical characteristics," and these "fundamental, unchanging characteristics" derive from a "special structure of the brain."[12] Here Le Bon introduced the idea of race that, he said, "is becoming increasingly prevalent and tends to dominate all our historical, political and social conceptions."[13] He often returned to this theme, claiming that race "dominates the special characteristics of the soul of crowds,"[14] and represents the influence of past generations on the living.

The critical attitude to individualism, democracy and its institutions, parliamentarianism, and universal suffrage owed a great deal to this new view of man as an essentially irrational being, confined by historical and biological limitations and motivated by sentiments, associations, and images, never by ideas.

The belief in the dominance of the unconscious over reason, the stress on deep, mysterious forces led, as a natural and necessary consequence, to an extreme anti-intellectualism. To rationalism, to the critical spirit and its manifestations, the rebels of the end of the nineteenth century opposed intuitive feelings, emotions, enthusiasms, an unthinking spontaneity welling from the depths of the popular subconscious. Thus, for the generation of 1890, as for the generation that emerged from the trenches, the motive force of political conduct was the unconscious will of the people. This anti-intellectualism was paralleled, moreover, by a demagogic populism that decried intelligence and the use of words and glorified action, energy, and force. Barrès, for instance, no longer asked which doctrine was true, but which force would enable one to act and be victorious.[15] This was the basis of the new nationalism that came into being at the end of the last century and hardly altered until the time of Munich.

The new nationalists sang the praises of every source of power, and all its forms: vitality, discipline, social and national cohesion. Convinced that nothing can be accomplished unless one joins the majority, the crowd, Barrès, the committed intellectual par excellence, was able to "savor deeply the instinctive pleasure of being part of a flock."[16] He deliberately sacrificed the values of the individual to collective values: "What gives an individual or a nation its values is that its energies are tensed to a greater or lesser degree," he maintained.[17] Thus, the new nationalism of the turn of the century was a mass ideology par excellence, designed to embrace and to mobilize the new urban strata.

Based on a physiological determinism, a moral relativism, and an extreme irrationalism, nationalism, in the definitive form it assumed at the beginning of this century, well expressed this new intellectual direction. The new ethics that Barrès developed in the last years of the nineteenth century and that he opposed to the Jacobin mystique at the time of the Dreyfus affair was perhaps the most striking expression of the transformation of French nationalism. To be sure, it was Péguy's achievement to have stamped an important fringe of that nationalism with the mark of his universalistic genius, but his voice was scarcely audible among the chorus of such journalists, writers, and agitators as Rochefort, Drumont, Gustave Tridon, Barrès, and Maurras and such scientists as Jules Soury, Le Bon, and Vacher de Lapouge, for it was this form of determinism that provided the conceptual framework for the nationalism of the end of the century, and its underlying racial argument was precisely the main legacy of the generation of 1890 to the generation of 1930.

These two generations had another point of resemblance: like the neonationalists of the 1890s, the fascists of the interwar period rejected the political and social consequences of the industrial revolution and of liberal and bourgeois values. Moreover, just as the turn-of-the-century nationalists could not imagine their revolt without the support of the masses, so the fascist ideology was a mass ideology par excellence. One could multiply these parallels. Was not fascism also an anti-intellectual reaction, a reaction of the feelings against the rationality of democracy? Was it not a kind of reflex of the instincts? Did it not also have a cult of physical force, of violence, of brutality? All this explains the importance attached to the setting, the attention paid to decor, great ceremonies, parades—a new liturgy that substituted songs, torches, and processions for deliberation and discussion. In this respect, fascism seems a direct continuation of the neoromanticism of 1880–90, but the scale of that revolt was determined by the mass society that the generation of 1890 was only beginning to glimpse.

However, the intellectual malaise, the political tensions, the social conflicts that characterize the end of the nineteenth century and the beginning of the twentieth were already manifestations of the enormous difficulties experienced by liberalism in adapting itself to the age of the masses. It was toward the end of the century that one began to feel the full impact of the intellectual revolution effected by Darwinism, of the industrialization and urbanization of the European continent, and, finally, of the long-drawn-out process of the growth of a popular nationalism.

Contemporaries had no doubt that they were entering a new period. "The age we are entering will be truly the ERA OF THE MASSES," wrote Le Bon. "It is no longer in the councils of princes but in the heart of the masses that the destiny of nations is being prepared."[18] The entry of the new urban masses into the political arena posed problems for the liberal regime that had not previously existed. Liberalism is an ideology based on rationalism and individualism; it is the product of a society that was supposed to have stopped undergoing structural changes, and in which political participation was necessarily very limited. At the end of the century, an increasing number of people questioned the usefulness of an ideology in which the new social strata, the millions of workers and wage earners of all categories crowded together in the great industrial centers, could find no place. The crisis of liberalism had its roots in the enormous contradictions that existed between the idea of individualism and the way of life of the urban masses, between the traditional concept of the natural rights of man and the new laws of existence that the generation of 1890 discovered in social Darwinism. The great changes that took place after the First World War are really comprehensible only if one examines them against the background of this first prewar period.

The crisis of the liberal order, which persisted throughout the half century before 1940, found its first expression as a mass political movement in Boulangism.[19] The struggle of the radical and Blanquist extreme left against liberal democracy can be explained, first and foremost, by the politicization of the new urban masses. This revolt of the extreme left, with which a number of Guesdists sympathized, aimed at destroying the centrist consensus, but in the face of this radical, nationalist, and Blanquist activism there arose a great coalition of moderates that already included the socialist right wing.

The great importance of Boulangism lies in the fact that it was the first meeting point in France of nationalism and a certain non-Marxist, anti-Marxist, and already post-Marxist socialism. It is in the achievement of this synthesis, which had a long future before it, that the significance of the National party resides: it attracted emergent socialism wherever it appeared. The Guesdist and Blanquist extreme left was perfectly aware that Boulangism represented a revolt against bourgeois society and liberal democracy. Paul Lafargue and Émile Eudes, the spiritual heir of Louis Auguste Blanqui and his chief disciple, were convinced that it was their duty to support Boulangism in its attack on the established order. Antiparliamentarianism was in any case one of the most characteristic features of the struggle of the extreme left against liberalism.[20]

Antiparliamentarianism, heir to a Jacobin tradition that reappeared in the extreme-left radicals, combined with two other elements: Blanquism and nationalism. Blanquism was directed against the bourgeois order and nationalism against the political order that expressed it. These three elements united in a common opposition to liberal democracy. Their fusion toward the end of the 1880s found its first expression in Boulangism, and ten years later it reappeared in anti-Dreyfus nationalism. At the beginning of the twentieth century, this rebellion was represented by the Jaune movement, then by a certain form of nonconformist syndicalism, and finally by the Cercle Proudhon. After the war, this synthesis bore the name of fascism.

Boulangism exemplified this particular phenomenon to an exceptional degree. It represented an alliance of all the political forces that wished to destroy the immobilism of the parliamentarian regime at any cost; it was the first of the waves of assault that were to assail liberal democracy. In Boulangism one observes, for the first time, a phenomenon that would henceforth characterize prefascist movements and later fascism: the shift toward the right of elements with advanced but fundamentally antiliberal social conceptions, which professed either a dubious Marxism or a frankly anti-Marxist form of socialism, or, as on the eve of the war, abandoned Marxism for that other form of solidarity, nationalism.

Here we must indicate the importance, during that period, of those independent socialists who advocated a French, national socialism and who, when confronted with a foreign socialism, elaborated theories supposedly more in conformity with the national temperament and milieu. The ideas expressed by the writers of *La Revue socialiste* were very much in agreement with those of the Boulangists and made a serious contribution to the propagation of a socialistically inclined nationalism or a nationalistically inclined socialism. This form of French socialism, which constantly criticized Marxism, actually consecrated the legitimacy both of Boulangism and of social anti-Semitism. The closely related ideas of these two schools of thought provided a framework for the great post-Boulangist alliance that laid the foundations of anti-Dreyfusism, and demonstrate the ease with which one moved from left to right during that period and throughout the history of the Third Republic.

Gustave Rouanet, who was not a Boulangist but who *was* a Dreyfusard (which makes his criticism of Marxism all the more significant), provides a perfect example of this way of thinking. Just before the rise of Boulangism, he wrote, "Purely materialist, the ultimate stage in the evolution of the German historico-fatalist school that was a reaction against eighteenth-century philosophy, *Marx's thought was essentially anti-French.* Hence the complete rupture with our traditions, with our old socialist parties, effected by his translators, the religious depositaries of his thought both in its form and in its content. But a people does not, any more than a period, break easily with its past. We believe that this fruitless rupture has been disastrous for socialism in general."[21]

Unlike "German socialism," which is full of a "hatred of French thought," "French socialism . . . came out of the Revolution." The great difference between them, said Rouanet, is that "while the present socialism wishes to undo the work of the Revolution, French socialism considers itself its natural, indispensable complement."[22]

Rouanet was an adept of the great Jacobin tradition: he could only conceive of socialism as an extension of "the most glorious event not only in the history of France but in the history of the world."[23] He was horrified by Marx's comparison of the French Revolution, the English revolution, and the German Reformation, regarding it as an absolute sacrilege. A future collaborator of Jaurès's, he opposed Marxism because he believed it incompatible with the old revolutionary tradition. Its victory, he thought, would mean the end of French socialism.

This notion of a German socialism as against a French socialism, of a historical concept that is based on the principle of "class antagonism" and ignores the "antagonism of ideas,"[24] was very characteristic of the end of the nineteenth century. It was prevalent in many different left-wing circles and provided a common ground for left-wing Boulangists of Blanquist, Guesdist, and radical origins, for the independent socialists around Benoît Malon (who, like Rouanet, sought to demonstrate the existence of a purely French brand of socialism), and for social anti-Semites such as Auguste Chirac of *La Revue socialiste* and Drumont, whom Malon spoke of with enthusiasm. It was this community of ideas that enabled Barrès to bring out *La Cocarde* in 1894 and permitted the formation of the great post-Boulangist coalition, and it was the same anti-Marxist ideology that made possible the synthesis between Maurrassian nationalism and revolutionary syndicalism. After the war, it was again the rebellion against Marxism that gave rise to the revisionism of Henri De Man and of Marcel Déat, and enabled the various "planist," dirigist, and neosocialist schools of thought to come into being. These movements all aimed, within the framework of a nationally oriented spiritual revolution, at offering an alternative to Marxism.

To be sure, a revision of Marxism does not in itself necessarily entail a shift to the radical right. When this retreat from the ideological positions of the revolutionary left was accompanied by an acceptance of the basic principles and rules of liberal democracy, a form of democratic socialism resulted that, with Bernstein, Jaurès, and Filippo Turati, took root in western Europe. However, when this revision of Marxism was accompanied by a deep "antimaterialism," an appeal to irrational values, an antiliberalism, a rejection of parliamentarianism and the party system, an authoritarianism, and an appeal, beyond class interests, to national unity, the fascist equation was always possible. In times of crisis this synthesis became almost inevitable.

From the very beginning, national socialism was a mass movement. It had its party apparatus and its shock troops: it was more than just a popular ideology. It also had its popular power base. The Boulangist revisionist-socialist *comités*, the powerful and well-structured Ligue des Patriotes, the Marquis de Morès's *bandes*, and finally the Ligue Antisémitique and Jaune movement prefigured the fascism of the interwar period not only ideologically but also in their methods of recruitment and action. Issuing mainly from the poorer quarters, these action groups, often feared by the police, had real power in the streets, and the authorities always regarded them as a serious threat to the regime. Like the fascist and quasi-fascist *ligues* of the 1930s that were disbanded by the government of the Popular Front, these action groups of the end of the century could be crushed only when the entire machinery of repression at the disposal of the Republic was brought to bear against them. The Ligue des Patriotes was disbanded at the beginning of 1889; ten years later the most important nationalist and anti-Semitic leaders were either sentenced, like Jules Guérin, to long terms of imprisonment or, like Déroulède, sentenced to banishment.

The Ligue des Patriotes was the first mass party in France to have a nationalist and authoritarian ideology—at once militaristic, populist, anti-Marxist, and socialistic. It was also the first to have modern methods of organization, propaganda, and action in the streets.[25] Like Léon Blum in 1936, Ernest Constans in 1889 and René Waldeck-Rousseau in 1898–99 knew that, to ward off successive attacks against the democratic consensus, these action groups had to be smashed.

The rebels of the end of the nineteenth century, like the fascists of the twenties and thirties, regarded socialism and nationalism as two different aspects of antiliberalism, two aspects of one and the same rejection of democratic individualism, two ideologies that conceived of the individual only as an element in an organic whole. "The socialist idea is an organizational idea if it is purged of the liberal poison that is not necessary to it," wrote Barrès.[26]

In place of parliamentarianism, the Boulangists had a cult of the leader; instead of the current, allegedly meaningless institutions, they believed in authority; and they replaced capitalism with a form of populism accompanied by a frenzied antibourgeois rhetoric calculated to stir the lower classes to action. Short-lived as it was, Boulangism demonstrated that the left was not always impervious to the cult of the strongman, that it could easily accept the overthrow of a republic that did not correspond to its ideals, and that it was susceptible to a demagoguery that would deliver up the great financiers to the vindictiveness of the mob. It was the very success of this combination of ideological concepts and political and social forces generally regarded as antithetical that demonstrated its seriousness, revealed the vulnerability of liberal democracy, and proclaimed the arrival of a new age.

The crises of the turn of the century and those of the interwar period stemmed from the same problem: how does one overcome the difficulties of adapting liberal democracy to a mass society? The participation of these masses in the political life of modern society and their political mobilization (which in these periods went together) always resulted in a form of mass nationalism, and this in turn led to a long series of assaults on democracy. That was certainly the case in France between 1885 and 1940, but that country always knew how to respond to this phenomenon. Indeed, as soon as the first major crisis—the Boulangist rebellion—appeared, the celebrated republican defensive reflex asserted itself. This took the form of a great coalition that included all the moderate elements of the left—all those who, successively and to an increasing extent, accepted the legitimacy of the liberal order. The same process was to be repeated with Dreyfusism and the Bloc Républicain, and later with the Popular Front.

Thus, the alliance of the Guesdists, Blanquists, and extreme left-wing radicals in the days of Boulangism was opposed by a coalition of radicals and opportunists already supported by the right-wing socialists known as the possibilists. Ten years later, when the radical right once more seemed to hold the popular quarters of the big cities in its grip, the liberal center was able to confront it only because of the support of all the factions of socialism. At the time of the Dreyfus affair, French socialism abandoned its revolutionary pretensions and helped to found the Bloc: outside the liberal and democratic consensus there now remained only the revolutionary syndicalism of Sorel and Berth, Hervé and the *Guerre sociale* group, Lagardelle and the *Mouvement socialiste* group, and Janvion and the *Terre libre* group.

All these nonconformist groups of the pre-First World War period in one way or another developed toward fascism or ideological collaboration with Germany. The same was true of the generation of 1930: the rebels could not resist the attraction of fascism, or, at any rate, of an ideological abdication to the dictatorships. The only left-wing elements that did not yield were, on the one hand, the orthodox Marxists, loyal to their party, with its organization and discipline and fidelity to the Soviet Union, and, on the other hand, those whose socialism was inseparable from their commitment to democracy and who regarded the cause of the proletariat as intimately connected with the protection of liberty. And yet, for all that, even Léon Blum's democratic socialism had to summon up all its Marxist faith to resist the ideological pressures of neosocialism, and the leaders of the SFIO decided that a policy of doctrinal rigidity was not too high a price to pay for that resistance.

The Cartel of left-wing parties and especially the Popular Front were expressions of the same defensive reflex that had enabled the liberal Republic to overcome the two great crises of the end of the nineteenth century. The common front of the liberal bourgeoisie and the proletariat, of the Marxist or Marxist-leaning left and the liberal center, was always directed against one and the same danger: the power wielded in the streets by the radical right and the creation of a quasi-revolutionary political climate. This was the case both in 1888–99 and in 1934–36: the radicalization of the right had the immediate effect of causing a shift of the vast majority of the left toward the center and its integration into the liberal and bourgeois consensus. In 1936, this process embraced the

Communist party, just as a generation earlier it had brought the Guesdist and Allemanist parties into the republican alliance.

But this continuous process of shifting toward the center was always paralleled by the emergence, on the right, of a new force, younger and more aggressive, with a more radical ideology, which in turn renewed the attacks on liberalism and democracy. From the collapse of anti-Dreyfusism was born the Action Française. Then, ten years later, the Maurrassians helped to found the Cercle Proudhon, which gave rise, after the war, to the Faisceau of Georges Valois.

The Right as a Mass Movement

At the turn of the century, the ideological trend that expressed the new intellectual climate in the most tangible way and in a manner accessible to the greatest number was anti-Semitism. In France, anti-Semitism made its appearance on the political scene with Boulangism. It was then that the first national socialists discovered its revolutionary power and its capacity to mobilize the masses. Rochefort, Granger, Roche, Barrès, Francis Laur, the successors of Proudhon and Alphonse Toussenel, certain Blanquists, and some Communards all helped to implant the idea that anti-Semitism was a progressive and nonconformist tendency, part of a revolt against the established order—in short, an element of socialism. Thus, in 1898, when the old Ligue Antisémitique was refounded, Drumont was able to state that "anti-Semitism has never been a religious question: it has always been an economic and social question." [27] In the same way, the Ligue Antisémitique claimed to be fighting "Jewry, the enemy of French interests, and the Judaizing accomplices of cosmopolitan financiers," [28] and, finally, defined anti-Semitism as "a politically neutral terrain" [29]—the only one on which French unity could be recreated.

Everywhere in the anti-Semitic literature of the period one finds the same theme: the necessity of uniting all social classes, all good Frenchmen, who, said Drumont, "would be ready to embrace one another if the Jews, paid by Germany, were not always there to promote discord." [30] It was because he believed that this unity could generate a revolutionary energy that Barrès considered anti-Semitism the "popular formula" par excellence. [31]

This aspect of anti-Semitism—its ability to mobilize and integrate the masses—was well appreciated by all the movements opposed to liberal democracy. Morès, the organizer of the first shock troops of national socialism, said that "the next revolution,"[32] that "necessary social revolution,"[33] a purification of the national body, would be aimed against the Jews, whose "hour would come" as soon as the masses became aware of the tremendous power represented by a union of the "workers' syndicalist organization" and the "anti-Semitic movement."[34]

The whole of the radical right shared this conviction. Barrès, Rochefort, and Drumont, the Action Française, the Jaunes, and the syndicalists of *Terre libre* all believed that anti-Semitism was an ideology that could provide the revolt against the established order with a popular character, a sociological content, and, finally, a concrete example of what an antiliberal society could mean. In this vein, Henri Vaugeois wrote in 1900, "The two passions (plebiscitary and anti-Semitic) that are appearing in this country are undoubtedly the only revolutionary forces that nationalism can at present set against the parliamentarianism that delivers us up to the foreigners."[35] Two years later he wrote, "Nationalism will have to be anti-Semitic, and thus antirevolutionary, or it will not be whole, integral."[36]

In Vaugeois's opinion, revolutions and counterrevolutions are identical in that they have the same object: the overthrow of the existing order. One looked forward to a revolution—a national, social, anti-Semitic revolution that would bring in a new order, but one in the great French republican tradition. There could be no question of a return to the situation before 1789 or before 4 September. This revolution or counterrevolution would necessarily be a reaction against the principles of the open society that at the end of the nineteenth century governed the lives of the French people.

As an instrument of unification of the people, anti-Semitism was a political concept and not simply hatred of the Jews. Because they believed in its capacity to integrate all the social classes, the nationalists saw anti-Semitism as a common denominator that could serve as a platform for a mass movement against liberal democracy and bourgeois society. The further step of concluding that anti-Semitism permitted nationalism to appear as the doctrine of national consensus was easy to take, and taken soon enough. Anticipating a definition that had a future before it, Morès called this doctrine the doctrine of the *faisceau*.[37]

Morès, however, was aware that the necessary precondition for the realization of the *faisceau* was the integration of the proletariat into the body of the nation, and he expressed this idea in a number of propositions that anticipated the program of the Jaunes and constitute a classic example of national-socialist thinking: "One must suppress the proletariat; one must give these people something to defend, something to conquer." [38] And the precondition for this suppression of the proletariat and its integration into the nation was the great anti-Jewish revolution.

Thus began the political activation of all the social groups affected by technical progress and capitalist exploitation that found it particularly difficult to adapt to the conditions of an industrial society. By concealing the reality and inventing a mythical evil, the anti-Semites were able to transcend social divisions, conflicts of interest, and ideological contradictions.

The new right was quick to recognize the advantages to be gained from anti-Semitism. It felt that anti-Semitism filled a certain gap, supplied a need, and that without it nationalism could not survive. The Maurrassians made anti-Semitism one of the cornerstones of integral nationalism: they had a far more definite conception of it than many other right-wing groups. After the failure of Boulangism, Maurras wrote, "Everything seems impossible or terribly difficult without the providential appearance of anti-Semitism. It enables everything to be arranged, smoothed over, and simplified. If one were not an anti-Semite through patriotism, one would become one through a simple sense of opportunity." [39]

Unable to define itself in any other way than in terms of opposition, the nationalism of the turn of the century used racism and anti-Semitism as a means of stigmatizing everything it was against. The Jew symbolized the anti-nation: he was all that was negative—the cosmopolitan in opposition to whom, and yet at the same time in consequence of whom, national sentiment could finally emerge. For the new right, anti-Semitism was not only a useful political strategy but also a ferment that could help in that search for an identity of which nationalism is an expression.

Anti-Semitism, however, was not only to be found on the nationalist extreme right. At the beginning of the century, it was a basic element of the ideology of the Jaunes, of Sorel and Berth's revolutionary syndicalism, and of a certain extreme left-wing nonconformism (that of Hervé's *Guerre sociale* and Lagardelle's *Mouvement socialiste*, for instance). Anti-semitism was an essential part of the revolt against the liberal and social-democratic consensus, and for that reason the anti-Semitic movement of the interwar period added nothing essential to the ideas of its predecessor at the end of the last century. During the half century that had elapsed since then, the basic problems had remained the same.

Anti-Semitism was by no means an ideology without supporters.

During 1898–99 it was a genuine mass movement, and the anti-Semitic disturbances of that period were extremely serious. In Algiers, notably, where four of the six deputies were anti-Semites and where the anti-Semitic leader Max Régis became mayor, the settlers were in open revolt against the metropolis. In the Chamber of Deputies, proposals for anti-Jewish legislation received as many as 158 votes, which, although not a majority, was an appreciable number. Anti-Semitism was indeed an important aspect of the national-socialist revolution, and the anti-Semites wished to destroy both the concepts and the political structures of democracy. Beginning in the 1890s and throughout the twentieth century, this was to be the classic function of anti-Semitism.

For the second time in a decade, the socialists, like the communists throughout Europe in the 1930s, were confronted with a dilemma: should they choose the lesser of two evils and join the republicans, or should they refuse to take part in a struggle that, from the point of view of Marxist orthodoxy, did not concern the proletariat? Thus, one was faced, from the last quarter of the nineteenth century, with one of the key problems of European history. In the France of 1900, the socialists did not easily resign themselves to joining the republican consensus. Indeed, the socialist activists committed themselves only when, after a long period of hesitation, doubt, and wavering, anti-Semitic groups seemed in danger of progressively taking over the streets. As late as 20 January 1898, the socialist leaders published a celebrated manifesto in which they refused to take part in "a struggle between two rival factions of the bourgeois class"—a struggle that they claimed was financed by Jewish capitalists who were attempting, by means of the rehabilitation of Dreyfus, to gain the support of the nation for their reprehensible activities. The old anti-Semitic element in French socialism was at that point very much in evidence, as was the necessity of explaining Dreyfusism in a way that would tally with basic Marxist doctrine. The party activists followed Jaurès, who himself had hesitated a great deal, only when it became clear that, as Rouanet said, "not only the bourgeois Republic but also the social Republic was in danger."[40] In other words, it was only after a year and a half of agitation and disturbances and an attempted coup d'état that the various socialist factions came to the conclusion that the interests of the proletariat and the bourgeoisie agreed on one essential point: they both required the democratic system. The socialists did not bring their full weight to bear until the anti-Semitic *ligues* demonstrated their control of the streets and they had begun to lose their sway over the urban masses.

The appearance on the political scene of the radical right as a mass movement created a new and unprecedented situation: an interdependence between the bourgeoisie and the proletariat. This community of interests laid the foundations of the Bloc and the various forms of tacit collaboration between the bourgeois center and the left. At the same time, however, these new relationships between political parties representing opposing social classes and ideologies, this mutual acceptance of the democratic consensus, soon aroused the violent criticism of democracy of the revolutionary syndicalists.

From 1902 to 1906, the dates of the two great electoral campaigns that consecrated the victory of this alliance of the center and the left, there occurred a second series of attacks against the democratic, liberal consensus. Now that anti-Dreyfusism had been defeated, the revolt against democracy was represented by three different tendencies: the Jaune movement, the Action Française, and the nonconformist extreme left. Pierre Biétry and the Jaunes lost their impetus fairly soon, but the Maurrassians, the revolutionary syndicalists, and the associates of Hervé and Lagardelle came together at various times during the long periods of gestation previous to the two world wars. All things considered, this new generation of national socialists followed much the same path as that taken a quarter of a century earlier by the Boulangist and anti-Dreyfus left. Like the Blanquists and radicals who provided the first wave of national socialism with the nucleus of its activists, the "leftists" of the period before the First World War prepared the way for the third wave of national socialism—that which bore the name of fascism.

A Proletarian Anti-Marxism

Despite its relatively short period of existence, the Jaune movement is a phenomenon of great interest. It was really with the emergence of the Jaunes that one saw the popular, socialistically inclined movement of the right acquire for the first time a truly proletarian dimension. Founded by revolutionary syndicalists, the Jaune movement, which was created in accordance with an ideology developed in the last decade of the nineteenth century, constituted an authentic workers' movement. Around Biétry and his supporters gathered the remnants of the *ligues*, Rochefort and the remaining Blanquists, and the old stalwarts of anti-Semitism, Drumont and the *Libre Parole* group. In 1906, the Maurrassians attempted to win the support of the Jaunes. They already saw that the Jaunes could bring to their own movement a social dimension desperately needed.

In 1906, after four years of intensive work, Biétry was elected deputy for Brest, and the movement began to aspire to political action on a large scale. Like the *ligues* of the 1890s and the fascist movements of the 1930s, the Jaune movement could not resist the temptation to engage in active politics and exploit the opportunities provided by liberal democracy. In France, no political movement has ever existed that, after having poured scorn on the parliamentary regime, refused, when the opportunity arose, to try its luck at the polls. However, until 1940, at any rate, the parliamentary democracy in that country was strong enough to withstand the successive attacks of the forces arrayed against it, to neutralize them, and finally to assimilate them. What in fact took place was that, in agreeing to play the game according to the democratic rules, the radical right implicitly accepted the legitimacy of democracy and consequently found itself operating in an area unsuited to its specific character and unfavorable to its development, with the result that every such right-wing movement disintegrated, giving way to a direct or indirect successor that, in turn, experienced the same rapid development and the same disintegration.

One could say that in many respects the Jaune movement was like an earlier version of the Parti Populaire Français. Biétry himself was the ideal prototype of a fascist leader. A great trainer of men, indomitably courageous, a true man of the people, this former syndicalist was widely hailed as a "leader," "valiant and sublime," and was the object of a veritable cult in the movement's press of Paris and the provinces.[41]

Based on the principle of the absolute authority of the party leader over his followers, the Jaune movement was Biétry's special preserve, as the PPF was later Doriot's. Arousing an extraordinary enthusiasm and devotion among those who regarded themselves as his "soldiers," Biétry excited a ferocious hatred in his enemies. It was not only the socialist workers who detested him: at the turn of the century he was the most hated man in France. Not until Doriot appeared on the scene did one see the emergence of a similar phenomenon. Indeed, Biétry appears today to be the real precursor of the communist leader who founded the PPF. With him, national socialism ceased to be the preoccupation of aristocratic adventurers like Morès, journalists like Drumont and Rochefort, and intellectuals like Barrès, and became proletarian.

For the first time, it became evident that there could be a violently anti-Marxist proletarian mass movement with a clear ideology that could seriously rival the Marxist left-wing forces.

The Jaune ideology on the one hand echoed the main national-

socialist doctrines of the end of the last century, and on the other heralded those of the 1930s. The many political programs put out by *Le
Franciste* or *La Solidarité nationale* or by François Coty's *L'Ami du
peuple* had little to add to the ideas contained in the many Jaune publications. These advocated a "French socialism"[42] and a "national syndicalism"[43] that would prepare the way for "a national unity of workers
and employers."[44] To facilitate "a reconciliation of the classes through a
program of social justice,"[45] the Jaune movement promoted two concepts that had been much favored in left-wing Boulangist circles in the
1890s: the joint ownership of property and the sharing of profits. Readopting these ideas, which had been advanced by Barrès and Naquet
(this Boulangist leader, who became an anarchist at the turn of the century, wished that a share of "mechanical power" be given to the workers
just as land had formerly been distributed to the peasants), the Jaunes
advocated the sharing of industrial property by the workers. A necessary corollary of this collaboration of the classes would be the collaboration of capital and labor, for according to a doctrine of national socialism found in almost identical form in fascism there are two kinds of
capital: "speculative capital and working capital."[46] The latter was a key
factor in the promotion of productivity, collective wealth, and prosperity, and it was essentially different from the capital of the stock exchange, which was often Jewish or foreign and brought about the enslavement of the people.

   The Jaune movement was an authentic, spontaneous working-class
phenomenon. In the first years of the twentieth century, it had an undoubted working-class power base. Like the left-wing Boulangism that
had succeeded in taking root in recently developed industries, in the republican milieu of provincial towns, and in the popular quarters of
Paris, the Jaunes had a considerable following among the workers.[47]
They also tried to bring into being a genuine corporatism, but the employers, who could conceive of workers' organizations only in the context of class warfare, failed to seize their opportunity. It had been demonstrated that the industrial proletariat was not necessarily unreceptive
to a certain form of national socialism or plebeian anti-Marxism, and
was not totally unsympathetic to an ideology at once anticapitalist, anti-
Semitic, and authoritarian. This receptivity to an anti-Marxist yet popular and socialistically inclined viewpoint was the consequence of a
socio-economic and political situation that prevailed at a given moment
in a particular society, and not of relationships of production.

   This was well understood by the Action Française, and it was precisely for this reason that it detached itself from the Jaune movement and transferred its interest to the extreme left-wing dissidents. The Maurrassian right had come to the conclusion that the working class, represented by the Confédération Générale du Travail (CGT) and the extreme left wing of the socialist party, was ready for an insurrection against the bourgeois Republic and democracy. Particular attention was therefore paid to the "red" workers, and everything possible was done to encourage the new antirepublican and antidemocratic tendencies, to win over the revolutionary potential of the CGT, and to gain the support of its members. At that time, the opposition of the extreme left appeared to be sufficiently strong to allow the Maurrassians to hope that they could find there the popular forces that could undermine the regime.

Nationalism and Syndicalism

The mood of the years preceding the First World War strangely recalled the atmosphere of discouragement, disaffection, and disenchantment with the established order that prevailed just before the rise of Boulangism. The parallels with the situation in the late 1880s are striking. Two decades after the Boulangist phenomenon, there was a similar malaise among the same social classes and a similar clash between the moderate left and the extreme left—a clash that led to similar alliances. To certain syndicalists and their allies, the Radical Republic was as discreditable as the Opportunist Republic had been to their predecessors the left-wing radicals, the Blanquists, and the former Communards. The radicals' hatred for Jules Ferry was paralleled by the horror with which the labor activists regarded Clemenceau. The Radical Party of 1908 appeared to have reached the same low point as the Opportunists of twenty years before, and liberal democracy was subject to the same accusations and the same suspicions.

The nationalist awakening before the war,[48] the emergence of what has sometimes been called "the generation of Agathon,"[49] can be explained at least partly by this disenchantment with liberal democracy of a large section of the proletariat, of the rank and file of the great urban centers, and of intellectual youth. The breakaway of certain popular groups was basically caused, as it had been twenty years earlier, by the Republic's inability to satisfy the legitimate aspirations of those who had been its most ardent defenders. The members of the proletariat who in the 1880s had hailed the Republic as the beginning of a new era, and amid the troubles of the Dreyfus affair had championed what they believed to be a new revolution, now suddenly realized that they had once again been deceived, for the bourgeoisie had once more turned the victory to its sole advantage.

In many respects the Dreyfus affair appeared to the labor activists to be an enormous hoax. For all those who, to halt the wave of nationalism, had consented to a common front of the workers and the liberal bourgeoisie, despite the dangers presented by such an alliance for the newly aroused class consciousness of the proletariat, the affair had ended in a failure. For the labor leaders who had defended the regime and, to ensure the survival of liberal democracy, placed the physical might of the organized proletariat—albeit belatedly—at its disposal, the only tangible result of their victory had been the rise of radicalism and the transformation of the socialist party into a parliamentary party like the others. This socialism very soon took on the coloring of its "renegades"—Alexandre Millerand, Aristide Briand, René Viviani— and this radicalism no less quickly assumed the complexion of the Clemencist repression.[50]

All the attacks on liberal democracy—whether Hervé's insults or Sorel and Berth's theories about proletarian violence and the necessity of reviving a Marxism bogged down in reformism and Dreyfusism or the rebellion of Griffuelhes, Lagardelle, and Pouget—shared one overriding concern: stemming the tide of Dreyfusism that threatened to swamp the working class.

Immediately after 1 May 1906, *Le Mouvement socialiste, La Guerre sociale*, and the CGT, supported by the extreme left wing of the socialist party and nonconformists like Sorel, launched a violent campaign not only against Clemenceau and his methods but also against the political and social system that brought them into being and against the Dreyfusard alliance that perpetuated them. Lagardelle, Alphonse Merrheim, Pouget, Griffuelhes, André Morizet, Robert Louzon (who wrote a violent anti-Dreyfusard attack, "The Failure of Dreyfusism or The Triumph of the Jewish Party"),[51] Hervé, and Berth all took part in a huge campaign to ensure that nothing like the affair would ever take place again and that the working masses would never again rise up in protection of democracy.

In April 1907 an international conference was held in Paris that well expressed the spirit of that rebellion. It was a gathering of all the "leftists" of European socialism, the guardians of doctrinal purity, such as Arturo Labriola, Roberto Michels, and Hubert Lagardelle, who never ceased to upbraid the official socialist movement for having accepted the rules of democracy and substituted class collaboration for class struggle.[52] In that prewar period, Lagardelle never wearied of singing the praises of the general strike and of condemning "pseudosocialist theories of class collaboration and democratic and social peace."[53] Lagardelle saw the "parliamentary activities" of the socialist parties and the gulf between these parties and the groups of labor revolutionaries who had gained an awareness of their revolutionary role through struggle as the main cause of "the depth of the socialist crisis," and he said that a struggle was in progress between "a purely parliamentary socialism and revolutionary labor socialism."[54]

In much the same way, Roberto Michels regarded the exodus of the revolutionary syndicalists, overruled at every party congress, as a loss that would change the character of Italian socialism. That exodus began in 1907:[55] the Sorelians left in order to fashion an ideology that ultimately would become the conceptual framework of Italian fascism. Before this happened, they had toyed with the idea of creating a political syndicalist party—a party of bourgeois intellectuals with socialistic ideas, a vigorous opposition party that would have been a far more formidable opponent for the bourgeoisie than the isolated syndicalists. But in any case, said Michels, the project would have been stillborn, since modern democracy, "which is a regime and a struggle of the *masses*, leaves no room for parties of an *elite* who do not know what to do with large numbers."[56]

It was not until the First World War, however, that the situation was ripe for the creation of such a party and the transmutation of such ideas into a political force. Thus, just before the war, Labriola embraced a militant nationalism, and later retreated into an "eternal" socialism of the kind envisaged by De Man; Michels became a fascist; and Lagardelle, after joining Valois's Faisceau and Bergery's frontists, became a minister under Marshal Pétain. A certain concern for the preservation of doctrinal purity and a certain fidelity to the prewar revolutionary spirit fired these people with an overwhelming desire to destroy the liberal order. The same was true of Hervé and Zévaès, admirers of Mussolini and founders of a new national-socialist party.[57] Later, in the case of Déat, of Doriot and the intellectuals of his circle, and of De Man, one sees the same phenomenon: whatever revolutionary ardor remained when the Marxist faith of the opponents of democratic socialism disappeared became a desire to destroy both Marxism and liberal democracy.

The leftists of the pre-First World War period, like the nonconformists of the thirties, felt that there was an inherent incompatibility be-

tween socialism and democracy, socialism and parliamentarianism, socialism and bourgeois liberties. On the other hand, the new elitist
theories met with a deep response in the wing of socialism that advocated direct action as against social democracy and, among the labor
avant-garde, the conscious and activist minority that was to lead the
proletariat to revolution. To the socialism that advocated the conquest
of power by means of universal suffrage, to the tame bourgeois socialism
that accepted the passwords and rules of liberal democracy, syndicalism
opposed the revolutionary violence of a proletarian elite. Michels, accordingly, was able to claim that the elitist theory, which regarded the
masses as a source of energy but denied them the capacity to determine
the direction of social evolution, in no way contradicted the materialist
concept of history and the idea of class warfare.[58] And Émile Pouget
claimed that direct action by the proletariat could "express itself in a
benevolent and peaceful way or in a very forceful and violent manner,"
and that the great difference between syndicalism and "democratism"
was precisely that "the latter, through universal suffrage, permits the unaware, the unintelligent to assume control . . . and stifles the minorities
that contain the seed of the future."[59] Thus we see that the socialist extreme left preached a contempt for democracy and parliamentarianism
together with a cult of violent revolution by conscious activist minorities.

Finally, since, as Sorel stated, experience had taught the working class
that "democracy can work effectively to prevent the progress of socialism," the syndicates would have the task of initiating the reaction
against the established order.[60] It is therefore not particularly surprising
that, speaking about the future of universal suffrage, Victor Griffuelhes
should say, "It is clear to me that it should be relegated to the lumber
room."[61] And Lagardelle was therefore correct in maintaining that
"French syndicalism was born out of the reaction of the proletariat
against democracy"—which, he claimed, was never anything but a
"popular form of bourgeois domination."[62] Sorel, Pouget, and Lagardelle were all careful to point out, each in his own way, that socialism
could be based only "on an absolute separation of classes and on the
renunciation of any hope of a political renewal."[63] This meant, in fact,
the abandonment of electoral and parliamentary politics and the inval-
idation of the socialist party. If the incompatibility between class and
party, between "class and opinion,"[64] was the very basis of syndicalism,
and if, in trying to combine the two, the socialists were attempting to do
the impossible, the syndicalists of necessity had to take up a position of
noninvolvement that, in effect, eliminated the proletariat as a left-wing

political force. The Action Française was the first to recognize both the significance of the antidemocratic tendency that had grown up in revolutionary syndicalism and the implications of the position of neutrality adopted by the CGT.

The Action Française, always sensitive to the development of ideas in labor circles, was quick to stress its points of resemblance with revolutionary syndicalism, especially as at that time the essence of revolutionary syndicalism was the rejection of anything that even remotely resembled bourgeois values or collaboration with the bourgeoisie.

Like Berth, who condemned "anarchism as the negative, lazy and abstract protest of the individual," favoring instead a "labor Napoleonism,"[65] Pouget declared that the methods of action of a confederal organization could not be based on the "vulgar democratic idea; they do not express the consent of the majority arrived at through universal suffrage."[66] Pouget believed that if democratic procedures were adopted in labor circles, "the lack of will of the unconscious and nonsyndicalist majority would paralyze all action. But the minority is not willing to abandon its demands and aspirations before the inertia of a mass that the spirit of revolt has not yet animated and enlightened. Consequently, the conscious minority has an obligation to act, without reckoning with the refractory mass."[67] No one, he claimed, has the right "to recriminate against the disinterested initiative of the minority," least of all "the unconscious" who, compared to the militants, are no more than "human zeros."[68] This out-and-out elitism linked up with that of Pareto and Michels, and after the First World War finally turned against socialism. These elitist characteristics reappeared in the thinking of Henri De Man, Bertrand de Jouvenel, and Marcel Déat, and were among the main features of their transition to fascism.

The Sorelians, as well as some of its own adherents, could only regard revolutionary syndicalism as representing the very antithesis of a democratic society. There can be little doubt that a society based on the principles advocated by Sorel, Berth, Pouget, Lagardelle, and Griffuelhes would have possessed most of the major characteristics of a fascist society. Led by "the conscious, the rebellious,"[69] who have a boundless contempt for democracy, universal suffrage, parliamentarianism, and the bourgeois way of life, this syndicalist society would forge a new type of man, characterized by "the boldness, the marvelous discipline" demonstrated by an army of striking workers.[70]

To illustrate the essential qualities of this man of the new society, Berth—who liked to draw parallels between work and war, between the virtues of labor and the military virtues—quoted a passage from Proudhon that spoke of "companies of workers, *true armies of the Revolution*, in which *the worker, like the soldier in his batallion*, maneuvers with the precision of his machines."[71] Berth had learned from Sorel that the direction that would be taken by this society of producers, raised on "social myths," is impossible to foresee; its character is unforeseeable by its very nature. But because it rebels against the scientific outlook and individualistic anarchy of the bourgeoisie, it would totally replace the condition of bourgeois life with a new dynamic and activist reality. The role of the producer in this new proletarian society would be to lay the foundations of a new, virile, and mighty civilization that would be the antithesis of the one created by the bourgeois, that eternally "rootless person," that "cosmopolitan, for whom there are no fatherlands or classes," that merchant who "understands nothing of honor, . . . a value not quoted on the stock market."[72]

Undoubtedly, certain revolutionary syndicalists regarded themselves as a new aristocracy leading the huge army of proletarians to war—social war. Like Sorel and Berth, the other theoreticians of syndicalism were subject to the influence of Nietzsche. They fully sympathized with his contempt for the bourgeois mentality and had no trouble turning his "superman" into a revolutionary. His concept of an elite and his glorification of violence, heroism, dynamism, and faith—in short, his stress on activism—radically altered the Marxism that the syndicalists had professed until then. From that time onward, they emphasized the creative powers of the individual and his capacity to change the course of history.

The revolutionary idea thus came to be associated with faith and willpower and no longer only with a consciousness of historical evolution, and for that reason the encounter with the Action Française was not an accident but the result of a very similar conception of political ideals and historical forces. This encounter centered on the *Cahiers du Cercle Proudhon*.

Why was this new group named after Proudhon? From its very inception, the Action Française considered the author of *La Philosophie de la misère* one of its "masters." This philosopher had a place of honor in the weekly section of the journal of the movement entitled, precisely, Our Masters. Proudhon, of course, owed this privileged place in *L'Action française* to what the Maurrassians saw as his antirepublicanism, his anti-Semitism, his loathing of Rousseau, his disdain for the French Revolution, democracy, and parliamentarianism, and his championship of the nation, the family, tradition, and the monarchy.[73]

The *Cahiers du Cercle Proudhon* took up these same themes, but laid greater stress on Proudhon's socialism. Moreover, like Maurras, who admired him because, "quite apart from his ideas, Proudhon had a feeling for French politics,"[74] the *Cahiers* were at pains to point out how worthy of respect was a man who, in addition to his passion for order, attempted to prove the supremacy of France and demanded for the French nation, "which has produced the finest flower of human civilization," the right to command the rest of Europe.[75] Valois, in turn, insisted on the "revolutionary passion of Proudhon," which, instead of causing him to launch attacks against French society and property, made him turn against the true culprits: Jewish capitalism and the social order imposed by foreigners.[76] Berth, next, presented Proudhon as the representative of a "Gallic" socialism—a peasant, warrior socialism with a strong feeling for unity and order, a socialism drawn "from a pure French source."[77] Finally, Gilbert Maire wrote, "He dared to express more openly than anyone else the utility of direct action, the beauty of violence in the service of reason."[78]

The Sorelians and Maurrassians shared this intellectual revolt against the heritage of the Enlightenment and the French Revolution. They regarded Sorel as a disciple of Bergson and "an enthusiastic adherent of the intuitive philosophy,"[79] since Sorel had never failed to come to the defense of Bergson,[80] just as he had always expressed his appreciation of Le Bon and Pareto.[81] The same was true of Berth and Valois, who were well acquainted with the Italian school of sociology and referred to it in their writings.[82] All this helps to explain the "fundamental convergence" of "the ideas of the Action Française and syndicalist aspirations," which was based on the conviction that "nationalism, like syndicalism, can triumph only through the complete eviction of democracy and the democratic ideology."[83]

Valois declared that the "junction" between syndicalism and nationalism had already been made,[84] whereas Berth believed that this "dual revolt" could take place only with "the complete eviction of the regime of gold and the triumph of heroic values over the ignoble bourgeois materialism that is stifling present-day Europe. In other words, this awakening of Force and Blood against Gold . . . must end with the downfall of the plutocracy."[85] And this war waged by "these two great currents of national energy . . . , both of them antiliberal and antidemocratic," against "big capital" and "high finance" was at the same time a struggle against French decline and decadence.[86]

Indeed, the Sorelians, like Barrès around 1890 and Drieu and Maulnier around 1930, had an acute sense of decadence: their work was dominated by a perception of the decay of a whole civilization. "Bourgeois decadence, labor decadence, national decadence—it is all one," said Berth.[87] Berth took up Sorel's idea that socialism cannot be implemented in a country in a state of economic decay, where heavy industry is undeveloped and where a timid and retrogressive petite bourgeoisie continues to vegetate. A revolutionary proletariat can thrive only where there is a powerful and equally bold and revolutionary bourgeoisie.[88] But decadence is not only economic and social; it embraces the whole of political and cultural life and impregnates customs and manners and morals.

Sorel thought that the Dreyfus affair could never have happened if France had not already been declining for many years. The Russian novel, neo-Catholicism, anarchism, the aesthetics of the Jews of *La Revue blanche*, cosmopolitan salons, and the paintings of the impressionists and the fauvists all demonstrated how deep the sickness went.[89] This feeling of living in the twilight of a civilization was very strong with the rebels of the turn of the century, as it had been with their immediate predecessors, and would be with their successors in the interwar period. Toussenel had already lamented "the general shipwreck of public morals," in a period "in which the blood seemed to be frozen in the heart";[90] Morès constantly repeated that "the crisis is near,"[91] and Drumont warned continually of "the final catastrophe."[92]

To arrest this decadence, one had to wipe out the spiritual inheritance of the eighteenth century and reject bourgeois values, liberalism, and individualism, together with faith in progress and in the natural rights of man. The moral outlook of the generation of 1914, like that of the generation of 1930, was violently opposed to the "humanitarian mysticism"[93] of democracy; it was sympathetic to Marxism because "the Marxist philosophy, steeped in the idea of warfare . . . , made class struggle the main motive force of history,"[94] and it glorified conflict not only because violence, in its view, engendered greatness but also because violence "could, in certain cases, constitute a revolutionary event of the first order."[95] For the same reasons that the representatives of this moral outlook considered themselves close to Marxism, they were also patriotic, for "patriotism can also have a revolutionary significance," and "the man of the people is much more a part of his country than the man of the wealthy classes," that cosmopolitan vagabond "uprooted by an encyclopedic culture and an idle existence." [96] A national and class solidarity can exist only in a society that rejects the "atomistic and purely mechanical conception whereby man is no more than simply a carrier of merchandise," [97] and for that reason socialism and patriotism alike require the destruction of democracy. And, as for democracy, that corrupter of morals, not only does it "postulate an easy life, comforts, the commodities of existence, an anarchic liberty, a reduction in working hours, an indefinite increase in leisure," [98] but it is "by nature hostile to the organization of labor" [99] and consequently "the worst possible terrain for a genuine class struggle." [100] Thus, the revolutionary syndicalists, like the socialists, accused democracy of obscuring social realities and differences and of encouraging ideological debate to the detriment of real relationships of production. All this, finally, could have no other effect than to assure the survival of a system of capitalist exploitation sustained and strengthened by the mediocrity of a decadent civilization, by the baseness of a vulgar optimism, and by the obfuscation of a coarse, empty ideological debate.

All these themes recurred almost word for word in the fascist and quasi-fascist literature and journalism of the thirties. That rebellion against the liberal and bourgeois order revealed the same propensities, the same loyalties, the same mentality as the earlier one, and when Valois in the twenties and Drieu in the thirties claimed that fascism was simply a variant of socialism, they were only reviving, in a somewhat modernized form, an idea that already in 1912 was not particularly new. The writers of *Combat*, for instance—Pierre Andreu, Thierry Maulnier (the writer of the interwar period closest to Barrès), and Jean Saillenfest— were perfectly aware of this and readily acknowledged their ideological lineage. As Saillenfest wrote, "In crossing the frontier of the Alps, fascism passed through the gateway of a national experience: under a foreign name, ideas that had originated in France came back to us, illustrated and put into practice. Did not the main features of fascism already potentially exist in prewar French social nationalism and syndicalism?" [101]

Maulnier gave a very clear answer to this question in "The State of Force versus the Liberal Society," an important article of historical and political analysis written at the beginning of 1938. In order to overthrow the liberal society, he advocated the creation of a very broad front embracing "all the nonproletarian social categories" affected by "the economic tyranny of a caste" and based on the liberation of "syndicalism from its antinational proletarian ideology." Thus, "a syndicalism purged of its materialist and proletarian deviations, a nationalism purged of its sentimental and idealized tendencies, which make it a weapon in the hands of the present masters of the state, could one day pass beyond their present stage of sterility in the positive creation of a new form of community." [102]

This synthesis could henceforth find expression in "mighty popular movements" whose supreme aim was not "the domination of a class but the affirmation of the national unity beyond class divisions and the restitution of the state beyond competition for economic power." Such popular movements were "the 'nationalist' and 'fascist' movements of these last years," which represented "a colossal effort to impose a communal unity on the warring classes." Maulnier concluded, "Whatever the future of these movements may be, it is clear that they have brought the historical and biological infrastructure of human communities back to the forestage of history, abandoned for a moment to class competition, and thus given rise to the only kind of synthesis strong enough to resolve the enormous antagonism created by industrial development between the tools of economic power and the old world of human relationships." [103]

The First Corporatism

Having arisen out of an opposition to the conservative, conformist nationalism of the respectable Ligue de la Patrie Française, and ill disposed toward moderates of any kind, the Action Française at the turn of the century was a real laboratory of new ideas and aimed to be a fighting movement with a popular membership. The Maurrassian movement at that time was a radical, combative young movement, sufficiently close to a certain form of national socialism to attempt a genuinely fascist synthesis. First of all, the left-wing Maurrassians deliberately laid stress on the element they had in common with the extreme left-wing socialists: a hatred of democracy and liberalism. To the integral nationalists, democracy was antinational; to the revolutionary syndicalists, it was antisocial. To both, it had no legitimacy, it was contrary to nature—it symbolized evil. Consequently, from 1900 onward, one finds in Action Française circles a "socialist-monarchist" or "monarchist-socialist" ideology. Maurras himself used this expression to describe the Marquis de La Tour du Pin,[104] or when speaking of an "eternal socialism" that he claimed La Tour du Pin represented.[105] During that period Maurras also toyed with the idea of a journal that would be "nationalist in direction with a few socialist propensities." But he knew well enough how to temper his left-wing tendencies, and when it came to naming a program he preferred the term *social equilibrium* to *social justice*.[106]

The Maurrassian movement at that time, still faithful to its origins, waged a long campaign against conservatism, liberalism, and capitalism—against the social atomization that existed in bourgeois society. This campaign reached its height in 1908, in the violent confrontations between the CGT and the Clemenceau government. In the eyes of the labor activists, the day of bloodshed at Draveil represented the supreme failure of democracy. One day, at the *Bourse du Travail*, a center of mutual aid, workers' education, and labor exchange, a huge black flag appeared at a third-floor window with a bust of the Republic attached by the neck to its folds. Maurras was quick to react: "The hanging of Marianne in front of the *Bourse du Travail* is the most significant act of our history since 14 July 1789. Do you understand that, you conservative bourgeois?" he wrote.[107]

It was this common struggle against liberalism and bourgeois society, this vision of a world given up to "economic anarchy, generator of the labor crisis," which raged in the name of liberty, that served as the basis of the attempts of the Action Française to erect a common platform with the proletariat.[108] Until just before the war, the movement tried to cultivate relations with syndicalism, not only because it appeared to be an obvious ally in the fight against the Republic but also because it was regarded as an element of stability that could easily become a factor of conservatism. The Action Française saw the corporative character of syndicalism as a virtue: based on tangible affinities and concrete interests, the labor movement reflected social and economic realities and for that reason constituted an element of organization and stratification. Through its anti-individualism, syndicalism helped to ward off the forces that threatened to destroy the nation. "A *pure* socialist system would be free of any democratic element," wrote Maurras already in 1900. "It would submit to the rules of the hierarchy inscribed in the constitution of nature and the spirit."[109]

At the annual national congresses of the Action Française, the question of relationships with labor circles was particularly important. It was Georges Valois who generally dealt with these matters. His conclusions always followed the same pattern. A new ideological situation had come into being, he said, and it had to be brought to its fulfillment by seeking an alliance of all the political and social forces opposed to democracy. It should be pointed out in this connection that the Maurrassians never believed that this hypothetical alliance of nationalism with syndicalism would imply a renunciation of labor identity. On the contrary: "In all respects, we regard the spirit of class as an excellent phenomenon, which completely destroys the democratic spirit," said Valois addressing the congress.[110]

In syndicalism, the Action Française found a strong force of anti-individualism. While "democracy wants a nation composed of individuals . . . , syndicalism builds up the body of the nation," said Valois,[111] and in *La Monarchie et la classe ouvrière* he stated the matter even more explicitly: "The syndicalist movement replaces the masses of individuals that the Republican state wishes to have under it with the professional groupings by which the traditional French monarchy was supported."[112]

Jean Rivain reached the same conclusion in a careful analysis of Sorel's essay "The Socialist Future of the Syndicates." "The socialists understand very well the necessity of corporative autonomy," he wrote,[113] and he was surely not mistaken. Did not Sorel regard the syndicate as "a body that would have the monopoly of labor" in the factory "in the same way as formerly the guild had the monopoly of production in our cities?"[114]

The attempts of the Maurrassians to influence syndicalism or to encourage the emergence of a current of syndicalism that would be close to them were not always unsuccessful. Émile Janvion, who had waged a violent anti-Masonic and antirepublican campaign in the spring and summer of 1908, the following year founded a bimonthly review, *Terre libre*, in which antirepublican syndicalists and anti-Semites joined forces. In fact, this union of the left-wing Maurrassians and certain elements of revolutionary syndicalism took place on two levels: on the intellectual and ideological level in the Cercle Proudhon and on the level of syndicalist activism through their collaboration in *Terre libre*. Together with Paolo Orano's *La lupa* in Italy, these two points of encounter were among the most serious and ideologically most advanced initiatives of European national socialism. Indeed, where theory is concerned, these meeting points, despite their small scale and ephemeral character, remain an essential yardstick for any understanding of the fascist synthesis.

However, the left wing of the Action Française that joined forces with Berth under the patronage of Maurras and Sorel and gave its blessing to Janvion was not the only political group that continually sought the support of labor. By its very significance, this move prompted the royalist movement—which was also much more varied in its makeup than appears at first sight—to set off in search of a social dimension suited to it. The person who took on this task was Firmin Bacconnier, a self-educated printer who had become a royalist.

In April 1907, Bacconnier founded a bimonthly journal, *L'Accord social*, which in October 1908 became a weekly. The first issue of *La Guerre sociale* had come out in December 1906, and *Terre libre* appeared in November 1909. The times were decidedly propitious for new nonconformist publications in opposition to the existing order. *L'Accord social* attacked Clemenceau and his policy of confrontation with labor, and invoked the authority of Sorel and Lagardelle against the republican consensus, political socialism, individualism, and pacifism. The particular preoccupation of this journal, however, was the restructuring of social relationships. Most of the ideas expressed in it were taken up again by the various fascist movements twenty years later. Indeed, corporatism as expounded by "socialist monarchism" has a very modern ring to it. The antithesis of liberalism and individualism, it was to be the instrument par excellence of the integration of the proletariat into the body of the nation.

The corporation, however—and this was an important aspect of the system—was not regarded simply as a private association unconnected with the national community as a whole. On the contrary, it was to "provide the basis for our political reconstitution" and was "invested with a social and political function." [115] Not only did it eliminate "the wild, disloyal competition of liberalism," but it created social organisms that should function under "state control," [116] for "a concern for the general interest is undoubtedly a matter for its authorized guardian, the state. . . . The state has the right to intervene, which it does by means of its agents." [117]

For the "social traditionalists," the corporation was an important element in the state—both a channel of transmission and a framework for organizing the masses. It has an "educative function," said Léon Thoyot, who stressed the many-sidedness of the activities and duties of a corporation. [118] Bacconnier elaborated further. He said, "The term 'corporative regime' has a much wider connotation: it embraces any human collectivity united by a common social task or professional interest. There not only exist corporations of commerce and industry and arts and crafts, but there are also religious and intellectual corporations." [119] He concluded, "A monarchy can be said to be corporative when the state is master and sovereign in general matters and the corporations of all kinds are supreme, under state control, in purely local, corporative matters." [120]

The difference, indeed, is fundamental. In this area, the corporatism of *L'Accord social* was much closer to the fascist model than one might at first think. Here, it was a matter not of counterbalancing the influence of the state but of placing the corporations at the service of the state, as later in Italy. It is also a common error to regard the corporatism advocated by the French extreme right as a prolongation of the system of the ancien régime. While *L'Accord social* was by no means loath to sing the praises of those long-gone days, neither was it so naive as to want to revive a bygone era. Quite the contrary.

In fact, *L'Accord social* contributed more than any other contemporary source to the development of a preliminary version of a genuine theory of the corporative state. Its writers regarded corporative institutions as model examples of organizations that subordinated economic to noneconomic interests. Bacconnier and his colleagues never questioned the principle of the supremacy of the political, which was the cornerstone not only of the thinking of the Maurrassians but also of most prefascist and fascist ideology. The word *corporation* was understood in its etymological sense of "constituting a body"—which was also held to be the chief attribute of the state, that which guaranteed its life and unity.

It was for this reason that, despite all the differences between corporatism and Marxism, the nationalists felt so close to the revolutionary syndicalists. Did they not both abhor "liberals and conservatives,"[121] those "satiated democrats" of the "social defense"?[122] Did they not both reject "the enormous trickery of anticlericalism," the "hypocrisy of social laws," the "tyranny of parliaments"—in short, the "republican imposture"?[123] Above all, did they not both advocate the same methods, the same "savage principles"?[124] As Jacques Hélo, a close associate of Bacconnier's, said in his lucid account of the relations between the new corporatist right and the revolutionary syndicalists, "If one looks closely, is the syndicalist 'Direct action' anything other than the 'Politics first' of the royalists? Both of these formulas express revolutionary doctrines: doctrines of violence, unheeding of constitutional legality. Both, moreover, justify themselves by practical success."[125]

The war was to disorganize these attempts at a rapprochement. For a few years it looked as if the Union Sacrée might make some changes in political life, but it soon enough became quite clear that the war had made no difference. The four years of hostilities had changed neither the social situation nor the main ideological tendencies nor the facts of politics. It quickly became obvious that everything had to be taken up again just where the prewar generation had left it on the day of mobilization. Thus, the middle of the next decade saw the emergence of the Faisceau of Georges Valois, immediately followed by the rise of the *jeunes équipes* (young groups), the great wave of revision and "modernization" of socialism, and the different syntheses and various attempts to go "beyond" Marxism, nationalism, and liberalism that constituted the fascism of the thirties. The idea of "transcending" oppositions, of acting outside the framework of the traditional political parties and conventional ideologies, then reached its climax: the desire to break away at all costs from "the old and outworn," from democracy and liberalism and also from Marxism, which already appeared to be part of the established order, weighed heavily on a large part of public opinion in France and was a major element in the fascist penetration of the country.

In those crisis years, there were undoubtedly many French who sensed in this revolt against liberal democracy and bourgeois society a certain rebellious freshness, a certain flavor of youth. During that period of uncertainty and atomization, when individualistic liberalism seemed to be headed for disaster and capitalism had to grapple with endless crises, an even greater number of people, in order to avert catastrophe, began to respond enthusiastically to appeals for unity, responsibility, and solidarity between the classes.

CHAPTER TWO

The Revolution
of the Moralists

Revolutionary Syndicalism, or the
Antimaterialist Critique of Marxism

The critique of Marxism that had been engaged in from the beginning of
the century by socialists of various kinds led to two different consequences, sharing the same point of departure but ultimately very far
apart. The liberal form of revisionism, as exemplified by Bernstein and
Jaurès, was based on the idea of compromise with the established order.
Neither Bernstein nor Jaurès regarded liberal values as "metaphysical
harlots," as Lafargue called them.[1]

Unlike this liberal revisionism, that of the pre-1914 "leftists" represented not only a total rejection of the established order and its social and political structures but also a revolt against its moral values,
against the type of civilization that found expression in bourgeois society. This current of thought was characterized above all by a violent
antimaterialism, which led to both an ethical and a spiritual revision of
Marxism. The revolutionary syndicalists were the first, at the turn of the
century, to rebel against materialism in every form—not only its liberal
and bourgeois manifestations but also the Marxist and proletarian.
Consequently, even when very little of Marxism remained with these
men who had come from the left or the extreme left, a horror of bourgeois life and a hatred of a basely materialistic society persisted. Thus,
the path followed by Sorel, Lagardelle, Hervé, Michels, and the Italian
revolutionary syndicalists was by no means an illogical one.

The generation of the interwar period underwent a similar development. An implacable logic linked the ideas expressed by Henri De Man

at the Conference of Heppenheim in 1928 to his manifesto of the Parti Ouvrier Belge of 3 July 1940. In his exposition of ethical socialism at Heppenheim, De Man forcefully stated that "vital values are superior to moral values" and that "the aims of socialism cannot be deduced from any given causes in the capitalist milieu, and particularly not from the struggle of a class for interests and power."[2] Similarly, shortly after the Nazi conquest, he said in an appeal to Belgian socialists:

In linking their fate to the victory of arms, the democratic governments have accepted in advance the verdict of the war. This verdict is clear. It is a condemnation of regimes where speeches replace acts, where responsibilities are lost in the verbosity of assemblies, where the slogan of liberty serves to support an egotistic conservatism. It calls into being a period in which an elite prefers a short, dangerous life to a long, easy one, and, seeking out responsibility instead of evading it, constructs a new world. In that world the spirit of community would prevail over class egoism, and work would be the only source of dignity and power. The socialist order will be realized not as the manifestation of a class or party but as the binding force of a national solidarity that will soon be continental if not worldwide.[3]

Here one touches the heart of the matter. De Man, Déat and the neo-socialists, and Paul Marion and the other communists who went over to the Parti Populaire Français may have abandoned their Marxism, but not their taste for revolution and their desire to regenerate society. Their revolution, however, now became an ethical revolution, a spiritual revolution, a political and national revolution. This was the classic conceptual framework of a fascist revolution, the ideal meeting point where former socialists, nationalists, and former Maurrassians could come together once more. Sorel and Berth's association with Barrès and Valois in the offices of *L'Indépendance* and the *Cahiers du Cercle Proudhon* was paralleled in the 1930s by the revisionists' association with Drieu La Rochelle, Brasillach, and Maulnier in fighting the same opponent.

Anti-Marxism led ethical socialists, out-and-out modernists, "planists"—the advocates of a planned economy—to join forces with the neonationalists in their fight against materialism. Whether this materialism took the form of liberal democracy or Marxism was finally of little importance: in both cases it was regarded as the same bourgeois evil. This evil could take an economic, political, or social form, but above all it was moral, for the rebels and revolutionary syndicalists, like the ethical socialists of the thirties, were above all moralists. Sorel and Michels before 1914 and De Man and Déat between the wars primarily attacked materialism, whether bourgeois, liberal materialism, the mechanistic or-

thodox Marxist variety, or the opportunism practiced by the social
democrats. In that respect, the evolution of Sorel, Lagardelle, Berth,
Labriola, and Michels is extraordinarily interesting, for it anticipated
that of the generation of 1930 and gave a new dimension to all the currents of political nonconformity of that time.

Sorel became a Marxist in 1893,[4] when he began contributing to
the Marxist journal *L'Ère nouvelle*. Noteworthy among his contributions to the journal were two long articles, "L'Ancienne et la nouvelle
métaphysique"[5] (The Old and the New Metaphysics) and "La fin du
paganisme"[6] (The End of Paganism), both classical Marxist essays. In
the latter article, Sorel even spoke of the "idealist bric-a-brac" that the
Marxists were accused of neglecting (something he never did again).[7]
During this period, he was concerned—a preoccupation that was evident in his first book,[8] and was to be present in all his subsequent
books—with the problem of decadence. Sorel took to task the Christian
ideology that had overcome the martial spirit, the extreme individualism that had undermined and finally destroyed the fabric of the ancient world. "The Christian ideology," he wrote, "severed the links that
existed between the spirit and social life; everywhere it sowed seeds of
quietism, despair and death,"[9] and since he examined the past only to
discover if it was possible "to make a few useful reflections about the
present," he added, "Utopian socialism would have had equally disastrous results if it had had a lasting influence instead of being swept away
by the wave of capitalism."[10] Marxism, on the other hand, is "a doctrine
of life that is good for strong peoples. It reduces ideology to the role of
an artifice for the summary exposition of reality; it holds that economic
development is the necessary condition for the creation of a new society; it teaches men to want to acquire the rights that they are able to
bear responsibility for."[11]

Sorel claimed that Christianity had destroyed the Roman world by
emancipating property. The "clear consciousness of the absolute individualism of property" in turn brought about the "emancipation of the
individual." Man was henceforth regarded as "no longer owing anything to the collectivity, each person being exclusively preoccupied with
his spiritual interests without concerning himself with the interests
of the country."[12] In the period when he was an enthusiastic Marxist,
Sorel saw individualism as the root of all evil, and on this point he
never changed his opinion. In fact, he continued to be violently anti-
individualistic even when he had long since ceased to be a Marxist in
the orthodox sense of the word. Revolutionary syndicalism was a form

of anti-individualism, and the left-wing Maurrassians understood this immediately. On the eve of the First World War, it was once again the hatred of bourgeois, individualistic, liberal, and decadent civilization that led Sorel to allow the Cercle Proudhon to use his name in the most developed attempt of that period at a national-socialist synthesis.

"Christian egoism," claimed Sorel, gives rise to the bourgeois spirit;[13] "bourgeois wisdom" takes over society and proves fatal to the martial spirit.[14] Sorel said that even if one cannot maintain that Christianity destroyed the martial spirit of the Romans, it "drew conclusions from the peaceful, bourgeois evolution of the Empire."[15] The bourgeois spirit was inimical "to the ancient concept of the heroic society," and not until Saint Augustine was it realized that "this *metaphysical shopkeeper's* fanaticism was idiotic."[16] The same, he claimed, was true "in all the modern countries": If "the martial spirit grew weaker and the bourgeois spirit became predominant, the social idea grew weaker also."[17] This was a process that was bound to take place "unless the people were strongly affected by a collectivist propaganda."[18] In the case of France, a propaganda of this kind had been favored by "the warlike early development of French democracy" in the time of the Revolution and the Empire.[19] This "new *revolutionary paganism*" had produced "an amazing revival of a spirit quite close to the spirit of antiquity,"[20] and had given rise to a period of grandeur that will find its equivalent in the future only in "the scientific transformation of society by socialism."[21] Finally, only when "the worker in heavy industry will replace the warrior of the heroic society and machines will replace weapons"[22] will the moral dissolution of the modern world, the product of Christian and bourgeois individualism, be arrested.[23]

Sorel's preoccupation, in his first period of activity, with the moral character of a given age and society remained characteristic of him in the period of the Cercle Proudhon and *L'Indépendance*. One can say that this obsession with the fate of civilizations remained a constant factor in Sorel's thinking.

From 1894 to 1897 Sorel devoted his efforts to two Marxist journals that, as he himself tells us, were boycotted by the independent socialists under Millerand and never had much success:[24] *L'Ère nouvelle*, of which we have spoken, and *Le Devenir social*. *L'Ère nouvelle* was founded by Georges Diamandy, an émigré from eastern Europe, in July 1893, and appeared until November 1894. *Le Devenir social* included Gabriel Deville and Paul Lafargue among its founders, but was equally short-lived—it appeared from August 1895 to December 1898. The aim of these two journals was to introduce into France a form of Marxism that would be something other than the Guesdist vulgarization of that ideology.

The promotion of a deeper understanding of Marxism in France was indeed an urgent need at the end of the century, for at that time socialist thought in that country was at a very low ebb. The custom that prevailed of disseminating the works of foreign writers in abridged and simplified form was not limited to Marx: Michels in 1914 and De Man at the end of the twenties suffered the same treatment—they were known only through summaries, "digests." Marx, however, provides the most extreme example of this phenomenon. In 1889, when Sorel began his career, the only works of the founders of Marxism found in bookshops were the first volume of *Capital* and *Utopian and Scientific Socialism*, which Lafargue had extracted from Engels's *Anti-Dühring* in 1880. Throughout the 1880s, no book or pamphlet by Marx or Engels appeared in France: the socialist library sold only pamphlets by Guesdist leaders. It was not until 1885 that the *Communist Manifesto* was translated in France, appearing in serial form over a period of four months in *Le Socialiste*, the party's doctrinal publication.[25] It was only in 1895 that the *Communist Manifesto* was issued as a pamphlet by the socialist review *L'Ère nouvelle*.

Owing to their ignorance of foreign languages, the Guesdists had to gain their knowledge from translations—of the works of Marx and Engels, and those of foreign Marxists (Kautsky, Labriola, Georgi V. Plekhanov). There can be little doubt that Guesde himself had only a poor knowledge of Marx and only a superficial acquaintance with *Capital*. Even the works of Deville and Lafargue, the two economists of the Parti Ouvrier Français, are open to criticism on that account. In a letter of 11 August 1884 Engels urged Lafargue "to reread *Capital* seriously from beginning to end" to correct the many errors in his refutation of Paul Leroy-Beaulieu's criticism of Marxism.[26] Marx and Engels themselves were on several occasions obliged to point out the shortcomings of the vulgarization of Marxism. Engels complained that in France "a knowledge of the theory, even among the leaders, leaves much to be desired" and criticized the many errors in Deville's summary of *Capital*, and Marx, speaking of Marxism in France, went so far as to say, "What is certain is that I am not a Marxist."[27]

In their assimilation of Marxism, the Guesdists were hampered not only by their very incomplete knowledge of Marx's works but also by previous ideological influences. Moreover, the pedagogical nature of their mission led them to accept certain fundamental features of Marxism but to overlook, in part, the role of Marxism as an instrument of analysis and the importance of the dialectical method. The Guesdists tended to conceive of class struggle as the struggle of the proletariat alone, whose numbers and revolutionary significance were automatically increased by economic and historical evolution. The overthrow of the bourgeoisie was thus regarded as inevitable and near at hand, and the leaders of the Parti Ouvrier never tired of proclaiming that the revolution was imminent.[28]

The Guesdists left us no comprehensive account of their doctrines; their theoretical works were few. The Parti Ouvrier devoted little attention to the study and dissemination of Marxist philosophy; it offered no systematic exposition of dialectical materialism.[29] This observable weakness in doctrine helps, no doubt, to explain both the strong influence of the independent socialists under Millerand in the last decade of the century and the significance of Sorel's role in initiating a serious discussion of Marxism in France. To appreciate Sorel's role, there is no need to belittle that of Guesde or Lafargue;[30] one need only draw attention to Sorel's own efforts.

The collectivist doctrines of people like Lafargue were steeped in materialism. Lafargue insisted on the primacy of matter, of which thought was only a derivative, a reflection. In a controversy with Jaurès, he violently criticized Jaurès's Neoplatonic idealism. To Jaurès's contention that the natural, eternal concepts of justice and fraternity were the motive force of historical evolution, Lafargue replied that these ideas had come into being with the creation of private property and the division of society into opposing classes, and that society had developed only in consequence of the necessities of production.[31] "It is in the economic sphere, and there alone, that the philosopher of history must seek the first causes of social developments and revolutions," he wrote.[32]

Sorel began his career as a Marxist theoretician at a time when a vigorous campaign was in progress both in France and in Germany for the revision, modernization, and supersession of Marxism. This assault on orthodoxy was the outcome of an unprecedented political and economic situation in Europe. After the Franco-Prussian War, the international situation had been stabilized, and the Continent enjoyed a degree of calm hitherto unknown. Social relationships also lost some of their acerbity: it was in everyone's interests to avoid violent confrontations, and few of the proletarians for whom the memories of the Commune were still fresh were willing to risk an upheaval. Economically, the year

1895 marked the beginning of a period of expansion and prosperity. This new prosperity, which appeared to be durable, raised many questions regarding a political and economic situation very different from that which existed in Marx's day. Faced with this new situation, some socialist thinkers sought a new synthesis that would combine Marx's ideas with other doctrines.

La Revue socialiste, directed by Georges Renard, successor to Benoît Malon, had for a long time already propounded a dubious form of socialism combined with a violent anti-Semitism; it now accused Marxism of "holding things back," of not giving idealism its proper place. This journal advocated an "integral" socialism that would achieve a synthesis between a primitive idealistic socialism and Marxist realism.[33] Jaurès, who was closer to Marx, with whose ideas he was much better acquainted than the other socialists, was also seeking "a conciliation between economic materialism and historical and moral idealism."[34] This revival of idealist thought made inroads into Marxist orthodoxy and deeply influenced Sorel's thinking.

There was, however, a very great difference between Sorel and Jaurès, just as there was a world of difference between Sorel, the future theoretician of revolutionary syndicalism, and the independent syndicalists of Malon's school. As Sorel himself said, he did not come to socialism via the Jacobin tradition, and he never had much respect for the protagonists of the French Revolution.[35] He undoubtedly had even less respect (and here he was in agreement with the Guesdists) for the writers of La Revue socialiste. In his estimation, Malon was a mediocre personality, Rouanet and Eugène Fournière were mere journalists, and Millerand was a schemer and a humbug.[36] Moreover, he was of the opinion that "the Jacobins who had adopted the socialist label" were not particularly eager that the party should become interested in the philosophical aspect of socialism. None of the socialists, he claimed, was at all interested in a close reading of the texts: they thought that they had already obtained all that they needed from them. Sorel was entirely in agreement with those who reproached the French socialists for not making available to the public the works that the German social democrats had disseminated in thousands of copies.[37] He regarded as revealing Jules Guesde's statement, reported by Diamandy, that he "had conceived of Marxism before he knew anything about Marx."[38]

During the three years he worked for the two Marxist journals Sorel became convinced that official Marxism had serious shortcomings, and in late 1897, while preparing a preface to the works of Saverio Merlino, one of the initiators of revisionism, he came to the conclusion that henceforth he would have to work "outside any scheme connected with Marxist orthodoxy." He now devoted himself to the task of "renewing Marxism," but he wished to do so "by Marxist methods."[39] He remained, then, within the Marxist framework in the widest sense of the expression, and not within the framework of Marxist orthodoxy as it was practiced in France by the only official Marxists, the Guesdists.

There can be no doubt about the importance of Sorel's contribution to the introduction of Marxism into France. After Deville had left, no one in the Parti Ouvrier Français besides Lafargue had a really good knowledge of Marx's thought, and, outside the Guesdist ranks, hardly anyone besides Jaurès did. These three names thus summed up socialist thought in France at the turn of the century. However, from the start, Sorel's Marxism was much subtler and less dogmatically materialistic, and far more susceptible to outside influences and more easily affected by the changing political situation, than was the Guesdist ideology as a whole. It is not surprising that, alone of these three men, Sorel broke with Marxism and, after delving into Marx and Proudhon, Nietzsche, and Bergson, moved toward various forms of national socialism.

Sorel embarked on a revision of Marxism for reasons that were first and foremost ethical. In his first book, he reproached Socrates for having "confused morality, law and knowledge," and consequently for representing "only probabilism in morals, the arbitrary in politics."[40] This was Sorel's main accusation against Socrates: "That whole philosophy leaves us without moral certitude. The good is assessed according to a probabilistic scale of values."[41] For that reason, Sorel believed that Socrates' accusers were by no means wrong in claiming that he corrupted youth and undermined society:[42] his ethics "were detestable"[43] and socially destructive.[44] Indeed, the whole of Sorel's work was marked by a search for moral certitude, for a way of achieving a "moral reformation."[45]

Sorel's follower Édouard Berth was quite right in claiming in his article on Sorel in *Clarté* on the occasion of his death that, moralist that he was, Sorel's main concern was "to discover if any force existed that could save the modern world from a ruination similar to that which overtook the ancient world."[46] Sorel thought it natural for human nature to "slide toward decadence."[47] This drift toward catastrophe therefore had to be stopped; society had to be saved from death and regenerated. If the individual is to resist passions and temptations, if he is to preserve and develop a sense of duty and honor, he needs to find something outside himself that escapes the corrupting influence of modern life. It was to the search for this all-important element that Sorel devoted his entire existence. That is why his ideas changed so much, a fact that Sorel never attempted to conceal. He was first and foremost a moralist.

Because Sorel was a moralist who was haunted by the specter of decadence, there was no form of political life that was not for him a system of ethics. "Man is obliged," he wrote in the period when he was still close to Marxist orthodoxy, "by a fundamental law of his being, to justify his acts by his subjective reasoning just as he explains the phenomena of nature through the objective reasoning of the physical universe." Consequently, said Sorel, "no considerable change can take place in a stable manner without the presence of a *juridical concept*." [48]

Sorel claimed that socialism asserted that "*economic preformations* are the condition for any change." While socialism wished to avoid utopianism, "that is no reason to say that it is *amoral*." [49] Later, in an article of cardinal importance for an understanding of his thought and evolution, he insisted on "the ethical character of the class struggle," [50] and on the fact that, according to Marx, "the full development of a class" involves "a union of intelligence and heart." [51]

In the very last years of the century, Sorel began the revisionist phase of his development. In his preface to the works of Saverio Merlino, published in France as *Formes et essence du socialisme*, Sorel reflected a great deal on the ethical aspects of Marxism. "Socialism is a moral question," he wrote, "inasmuch as it provides the world with a new way of judging all human actions, or—to use Nietzsche's famous expression—with a total revaluation of things." [52] Sorel welcomed the return to Kant that was taking place in Germany; [53] there was a new awareness in that country that there was "a serious deficiency in socialist ethics"— namely, the belief that "environment had an automatic effect." [54] Today, he added, "nearly all Marxists strongly regret the exaggeration with which the beauties of materialism had been lauded." [55] Finally, Sorel went so far as to claim that, "originally, socialism was a *philosophical doctrine*," [56] and he defended Marx against the Marxists who failed to take into account the development of Marx's thought from the *Communist Manifesto* onward. [57] He even defended Marx against Engels, which bears witness to a knowledge of Marxism that was very deep for the period, especially among French socialists. [58]

When the Dreyfus affair broke out, Sorel threw himself enthusiastically into the fray. His conception of socialism quite naturally led him to do so, and he was convinced that, in taking a position, he was faithfully following Marx's teaching. "The International urges one to protest and to assert the rights of Justice and Morality," he wrote.[59] It was for that reason that when "the efforts of the proletariat have proven fruitless," the proletariat "gives its support to that element of the bourgeoisie that defends democratic institutions."[60] Sorel was well aware that when that happened, "the struggle took on a paradoxical character . . . and seemed to contradict the very principle of class warfare,"[61] but he nevertheless believed "that a temporary coalition for a specific, non-economic purpose between members of groups that the theoreticians of Marxism would regard as implacably hostile is not fatally injurious to the independence of socialist thinking."[62] The position adopted by the proletariat is not arrived at merely through theoretical analysis but represents a genuine popular reaction, for "when the people have been touched by the socialist spirit, they do not hesitate; they do not listen to the theoreticians. Without entering into any bargaining, they walk side by side with the bourgeoisie."[63] Sorel pointed out that in the Dreyfus affair it was the most authentically proletarian elements that adopted this position most enthusiastically: the Allemanists were the first to throw themselves into battle for "the defense of Truth, Justice and Morality. This is proof that in proletarian circles the ethical idea has not lost its importance."[64] The political conclusion that Sorel drew from this analysis was that "socialism in France is becoming more and more *a labor movement within a democracy.*"[65]

Thus, at the time of the affair, Sorel, justifying himself through his ethical concept of socialism, took the side of social democracy. He took his stand with the Allemanists, yet a few years later, in the name of the same ethical principles, Sorel supported the national-socialist synthesis of *L'Indépendance* and the *Cahiers du Cercle Proudhon*, and Jean Allemane gave his allegiance to a fascist group led by two former rebels of the extreme left, Hervé and Zévaès. After the First World War, the socialists of the generation of 1890 were still looking for a true socialism. The social-democratic amalgam of the turn of the century had proved short-lived. For a moralist like Sorel, the spectacle seen after the victory of Dreyfusism—"the terrific rush for spoils in which the parliamentary socialists were not the least cynical"[66]—could have no other consequence than to encourage him to return to the positions he held before the affair and concentrate on the development of the autonomous forces of the proletariat.

In his article "L'Avenir socialiste des syndicats," Sorel had already clearly stated that, according to the materialist conception of history, the struggle to assume power "is not a struggle to take over the positions occupied by the bourgeois and to rig oneself out in their cast-off garments. It is, rather, a struggle to divest the bourgeois political organism of life and to transfer all that is viable in it to a proletarian political organism, created in accordance with the requirements of the development of the proletariat."[67] The proletariat would be in a position to become emancipated only if it remained "exclusively working class"—if it excluded the intellectuals, if it refused to follow the example of the bourgeoisie,[68] and, summoning up "feelings of energy and responsibility,"[69] cut itself off from the democratic heritage.[70] Abandoning the democratic heritage meant first of all rejecting individualism, liberalism, and certain reforms such as the right to work that were among the most honored achievements of the French Revolution. The emancipation of the proletariat would therefore involve a restructuring of society according to principles opposite to those of liberal democracy: syndicalism regarded "the workers as a whole as constituting a single body,"[71] and the syndicates were "social authorities"[72] that "took the worker out of the control of the shopkeeper, that great elector of bourgeois democracy."[73] Thus, there would arise "a new organization independent of any bourgeois organization,"[74] which would develop workers' cooperatives[75] and replace the "government by all the citizens [that] has never been anything but a fiction,"[76] the "chaotic majority," and "a purely ideal and utopian equality" with "a real and just organized equality."[77] And, in the same way, there would arise a "proletarian spirit"[78] and autonomous labor organizations completely unlike the classical political organizations—the parties, the pressure groups, and the other instruments of bourgeois democracy. It is significant that already in 1897 Sorel invoked the authority of René Doumic, who became one of the main publicists of the Action Française, against parliamentary democracy.[79]

The new radical, nationalist right that rejected the established order could only be sympathetic toward this antiliberal, antibourgeois, anti-Jacobin proletarianism, this form of socialism that urged the organization of the proletariat into independent combat formations ("class struggle is the alpha and omega of socialism"),[80] that refused to honor the principles of the French Revolution and the "great forefathers," that "presented itself to the bourgeois world as an irreconcilable adversary,"[81] and that, by means of a new "organization that was both economic and ethical," set itself up against "bourgeois traditions."[82] Nothing could have been more to the taste of these nationalists than the Sorelian diatribes, immediately after the affair, against Jaurès, the "wealthy subscribers to his journal, [the] Dreyfusards of the stock exchange and [the] socialist countesses." [83] Nothing could have pleased them more than the idea that "the time of politicians' revolutions is over" [84] or the claim that "time has finally shown that such a coordination of socialism and democracy does not permit the revolutionary ideology to preserve the elevation that it ought to have if the proletariat is to accomplish its historical mission." [85]

Spiritualism and Activism

Soon after the "Dreyfusian revolution" in which he had placed such high hopes because he saw it above all as a moral issue, Sorel fell back on syndicalism, quoting Rosa Luxemburg to the effect that "proletarian socialism or syndicalism does not fully realize its nature unless it is voluntarily a labor movement directed against the demagogues." [86] He then began a revision of Marxism "that would ensure the conservation of whatever there is in it that has been fruitful for the study of societies," in order to rid it of external accretions such as those of Jaurès. This process of revision led him to the conclusion that, to understand "the true nature of the labor movement," one had to resort to experience, and to the idea of *direct action.*[87] Only by this means could syndicalism fulfill itself and finally achieve greatness.[88]

While rejecting all cooperation with the liberal bourgeoisie, refusing to involve himself in anything that might resemble a new Dreyfus affair (which he regarded as a kind of "political revolution" that had confused class relationships), and attempting to transform the proletariat into a weapon of attack against the bourgeois and liberal world as a whole, Sorel threatened the existing order not only with a "material catastrophe" but also with a "moral catastrophe." [89] He brandished this threat not after Dreyfusism had come to an end but already in the period when he was very close to social-democratic revisionism. The idea of a "moral catastrophe" is all-important for an understanding of Sorel's thought and, above all, his influence, for this concept underlies all his thinking, and if its maturest expression is in *Reflections on Violence*, it is no less present in all his work.

It was because, from the beginning of his intellectual development, he was preoccupied by decadence, by the factors that bring a civilization to an end and those that, instead, cause a regeneration and a new departure, that Sorel came to Marxism. Very soon, however, he began to reproach the vulgarization of Marxism for its materialism, its over-

simplification, its ignorance of what he regarded as authentic Marxism—
the Marxism of Marx as he defined it both before and after the affair,
in which the moral factor is always present: responsibility, voluntary
agreements, the status of the individual as a subject of history. It was
for that reason that he always stressed "the ethical nature of the class
struggle," [90] "the moral elaboration that sustains the class struggle," [91]
and the "ethical progress" [92] without which socialism cannot exist. For
Sorel, "the revolution is entirely imbued with the ethical spirit." [93] A few
years later, in *Reflections* and *La Décomposition du marxisme*, this idea
took the well-known forms of the general strike and of proletarian violence giving rise to a new world.

But the socialist ethics that Sorel propounded at the time of his *Reflections* was already quite far from Marxism, even if one adopts a mini-
malist definition of the term. Here, in fact, one has a different socialism,
one that has little in common with the eighteenth-century rationalist
tradition from which Marxism is derived. This new socialism was already imbued with a profound pessimism, "a doctrine without which
nothing very lofty is achieved in the world," [94] a "metaphysics of morals"
that is truly "the conception of a march toward deliverance." [95] Like
Barrès, Sorel was inspired by Eduard von Hartmann and Pascal; he stigmatized all forms of rationalist optimism, whether Greek philosophy or
the theory of the natural rights of man. [96] To the rationalist concept of
natural rights Sorel opposed the theory of myths. Myths are "systems of
images" that cannot be broken up into their component parts, but must
be accepted in their totality as historical forces. [97] "When one stands on
the ground of myths," said Sorel, "one is safe from all refutation": [98] a
failure "can prove nothing against socialism." [99] A general strike is a
myth; it "must be regarded as an undivided whole; consequently, no detail of its execution can contribute anything to an understanding of socialism. One should even add that one is always in danger of losing
something of that understanding when one attempts to split this whole
into parts." [100]

Socialism thus becomes a work of preparation, a mobilizing factor, a
source of energy. This, in fact, brings us back to the fundamental problem, the one that preoccupied Le Bon, [101] that De Man called the problem of motives, and that was at the heart of Déat's preoccupations: how
can one cause men to act so as to change the world? In the light of this
problem, immediate achievements hardly matter; what matters is the
conception of socialism as "creative movement." [102] Sorel referred to
Bergson's *Données immédiates de la conscience* at length [103] to show that

"movement is the main element in the life of the emotions," and it is "in terms of movement that one should speak of the creative consciousness." [104] The idea of class struggle fulfills this function of promoting movement; it is in fact a myth aiming at the maintenance of a state of continuous tension, scission, and catastrophe, [105] a state of covert war, a daily moral struggle against the established order. Only when that is achieved can the work of the socialists, that "grave, fearful and sublime" work, [106] fulfill its function of overthrowing the bourgeois, liberal, and democratic order and destroying not only its political and social structures but also its moral values and intellectual norms. To the idea of justice, that "vapor," as Maurras always called it, "that old lag, ridden for centuries by all the renewers of the world deprived of surer means of historical locomotion," as Rosa Luxemburg said, [107] Sorel opposed the idea of the strike, which is a "phenomenon of war." He concluded that "the social war for which the proletariat is continually preparing in the syndicates could create the elements of a new civilization proper to a people of producers." [108]

But what happened to these hopes of regeneration when the proletariat failed to respond to Sorel's expectations? What happened when he finally concluded, with Croce, that "socialism is dead"? [109] What became of his search for social and intellectual forms that could resist the decadence of the modern world when the day arrived when he said, again with Croce, that "Marx had dreamed up a magnificent epic," [110] which, however, was but a dream? To whom did he turn when he came to believe that this "heroic proletariat, creator of a new system of values, called to found, in a very short time, a civilization of producers on the ruins of capitalist society," did not exist anywhere, and that "the revolution foretold by Marx is chimerical"? [111] The answer is found in *L'Indépendance*, in the abortive plans for *La Cité française*, the national-socialist review that Sorel intended to found, in the *Cahiers du Cercle Proudhon*, and in the foreword to the *Matériaux d'une théorie du prolétariat*, in which the nation and tradition emerge as the only morally creative forces, the only ones that can arrest the progress of decadence. Thus one comes full circle and returns to the basic ideas of Sorel's first book, *Le Procès de Socrate*. At the end of this development, Sorel, too, like Barrès, might have spoken of the "smoke of all these lost battles that obscures the horizon."

The greatest of these battles was that for Marxism. It was after his attempt at saving Marxism that Sorel moved toward a synthesis of populism and nationalism in which the cult of Joan of Arc was mingled with the crudest anti-Semitism. Sorel tried to revive Marxism in a new, modernized form, adapted to the social and economic realities of the period. He accepted Bernstein's analysis of the evolution of capitalism, he was present at the death throes of Marxist orthodoxy in France and Germany, and he was enamored of revolutionary syndicalism, the form of the left-wing revisionism of the period that he then considered to be the last chance of saving the system as a whole.

However, this attempt at modernization and renewal had the effect of preserving the Marxist terminology, especially the idea of class conflict, while completely transforming the real meaning of the basic socialist concepts. By the time of *Reflections on Violence*, the label no longer describes the contents. The idea of class struggle henceforth served to indicate an ideology in which vitalism, intuition, pessimism, and activism, the cult of energy, heroism, and proletarian violence, generator of morality and virtue, replaced Marxist rationalism.

Marxism is a system of ideas deeply rooted in the mechanistic philosophy of the eighteenth century. Sorelian revisionism replaced the rational, Hegelian foundations of Marxism with Le Bon's new vision of human nature, with the anti-Cartesianism of Bergson, with the Nietzschean cult of revolt, and with Pareto and Michels's most recent discoveries in political sociology, with the result that a few years later Sorel had little difficulty abandoning the conceptual framework of Marxism and replacing the idea of the proletariat with that of the nation. This process was completed before the outbreak of the First World War, and was in no way connected with it. In the interwar period, De Man and Déat underwent a similar evolution.

This shift to the right appears all the more natural in that Sorel's ethical socialism—voluntarist, vitalist, and antimaterialist to a degree— utilized Bergson's doctrines as a weapon against rationalism, and unhesitatingly attacked reason because it "is in the nature of rationalism to eliminate, as far as possible, the psychological forces it meets on its path." [112] This form of socialism was above all "a philosophy of action that gave first place to intuition"; [113] it was based on a cult of energy and dynamism. It offered no resistance to the shock produced by the discovery, made by Le Bon and the generation of 1890, that the proletariat, too, is only a crowd, and a crowd is conservative by nature. To activate it, one needed a myth, and when it became clear that the myth of the general strike and of proletarian violence was ineffectual because the proletariat was incapable of fulfilling its revolutionary role, Sorel, like Lagardelle, Michels, Labriola, Déat, and De Man, fell back on the idea of the nation. The socialism of these people required the proletariat only to a limited degree.

Thus, the revolutionary syndicalist Michels, like De Man, Labriola, and even Spengler following the path opened up by Sorel, stated categorically, "It is not true that the capitalist system in giving birth not to the proletariat but to a new form of proletariat brought socialism into being. Socialism as an ideology existed before it." [114] One may conclude, then, that if need be, socialism can exist without a proletariat and is not necessarily linked to a system of production. Thus, there arises the concept of an "eternal" socialism, an ideal socialism that requires the proletariat only as long as it can act as an agent of political and social change and as a factor of moral regeneration. That form of socialism aimed at bringing about the creation of a new civilization, as different as possible from the bourgeois tradition. As Lagardelle wrote, "I confess that even if the dreams of the future of syndicalist socialism never come true—and no one foreknows the course of history—the fact that, at the time I am speaking, it is the main agent of civilization in the world would be reason enough for me to give it my full support." [115]

This whole structure collapsed when events gave rise to the first doubts concerning the capacity of the proletariat to fulfill the role assigned to it by the first generation of ethical socialists. The second generation, that of the revisionists of the interwar period, benefiting from the experience of Sorel, Berth, Lagardelle, Labriola, and all the revolutionary syndicalists both in France and in Italy, from the start had only limited confidence in the proletariat. If the first generation increasingly lost faith in the messianic potentialities of the proletariat, for the second generation the question did not even arise. It was willing to come to terms with its skepticism and construct its whole ideological edifice on the implicit assumption that socialism, in order to be realized, needed neither capitalism nor the proletariat. It soon became apparent that since it depended neither on a given historical situation nor on a social class but on a certain set of values, socialism could be not only national but also independent of political and social circumstances, of the character of a regime, and of the power relationships within a given society.

Cut off from historical realities, conceived only as an eternal aspiration toward justice (as with De Man, Labriola, Spengler, and also André Philip), or else, as in the case of revolutionary syndicalism, in terms of "duration," of energy extended toward an objective that perhaps will never be attained, of movement that may never be operative, this form of socialism can easily go astray. For, contrary to appearances, nothing is less real, less tangible than revolutionary syndicalism: the idea of the general strike, said Lagardelle, is "a spontaneous operation of the spirit" to which "no date or place can be assigned." [116] This form of socialism, though it aims at practicality, has no time for "utopian reveries," defines itself solely in terms of class struggle, and is interested in the working class only when it is "in combat formation," [117] seeks only a state of permanent tension that generates a clear will to confrontation. "It is enough," said Lagardelle, "for the combative faculties of the proletariat to be kept constantly on the alert and that it should never lose the adventurous energy that creates conquerors." [118]

What is most important, then, is the confrontation "between two worlds that have an opposite conception of life." [119] The purpose of revolutionary action is to "renew the world." [120] The working class is the only one that can accomplish this because it is the only one that can "isolate itself within its natural confines," the only one that can remain truly "foreign to bourgeois society" and refuse "the intellectual substance of the bourgeoisie." [121]

Roberto Michels, representing the German social-democratic "leftists" at the conference of April 1907, gave a similar interpretation to revolutionary syndicalism. The main thing, he said, was to "create a psychology of moral revolt" that would stir up the proletariat and endow it with "that revolutionary idealism that alone can lead it to victory." [122] The proletariat must be kept away from that "cowardly verbal socialism," "that heavy, bureaucratic hierarchical organization" that "estranges it from all virile effort, from every heroic act." [123] The importance of revolutionary syndicalism, said Michels, lies in "the grandiose union of the *idea* with the *class*." [124]

Michels repeated this formula—and idea—on many occasions in order to assert his conviction that "class egoism alone" was not enough to attain a revolutionary end. [125] The total transformation of the present society could be effected only through a labor movement having "ethical elements that raise brutal class egoism . . . to the level of a moral necessity" for such a transformation. [126] A concrete illustration of this point is the moral predicament of the workers of Krupp: "The economic egoism of the working masses employed by Krupp must necessarily lead them to militarism," he said. [127] The more orders for armaments Krupp received, the more the salaries of the metalworkers in the Krupp factories would tend to rise. "Without a good dose of ethical sentiment" that would make them see their duty of solidarity with their comrades in other industries, these workers would be lost for the cause of revolutionary class struggle. Consequently, "the economic factor is powerless without the coefficient of moral pedagogy."[128]

The most striking example of the impotence of a working class and a socialist party that lack a "moral thirst,"[129] thought Michels, was the German socialist party, which, with four hundred thousand members, was the largest in the world, and in general elections obtained more votes than all the other parties combined. The "innumerable unconscious and blind proletariat" that never received any "socialist and moral" education and possessed no "courageous will to action" was only one "of the grim consequences of an ill-understood historical materialism. Owing to the daily preaching of the strict subordination of man's feelings and ideas to economic fatality, one has finally denied the eternal truth that willpower and energy can also strongly influence our actions, sometimes in a manner contradictory to the material requirements of life."[130]

If the proletariat is to progress, it therefore has to be educated. An "ideological unity"[131] must be created, and that task falls to the intellectuals. Unlike Sorel and Berth, who for a short time sought to learn from the proletariat, Michels, even in the midst of his revolutionary-socialist period, thought that "the labor movement could not exist without a troop of intellectuals to serve it as guides."[132] He developed an elitism according to which the labor movement "was quite incapable of doing without intellectuals,"[133] for only the intellectuals were able to teach the proletariat to exert its willpower; only they could prepare it for its revolutionary role by giving it a sense of its final goal. And only they could make the proletariat understand that, as Engels said, the democratic political milieu is the most suitable for revolutionary class action.[134] The proletariat required a "free milieu" where there would be only "one obstacle to the development of proletarian forces: the ignorance—to be overcome—of the masses."[135]

However, it should be understood that if Michels believed that the proletariat needed democracy, for him it was only a means, a mere tool. The labor movement needed liberty: liberty of expression, of propaganda, of organization. But if it required liberty, it had no commitment to the institutions of a democratic regime. Everywhere in Europe, said Michels, "parliamentarianism kills socialism in the deepest sense by substituting a unilateral socialism of politicians."[136] In Germany, he said, you had the worst possible situation: there was no atmosphere of liberty, the people were not used to it and did not always seem to want it, and yet the corruption of socialism by parliamentarianism was rampant. The socialist party was full of the grossest opportunism, and people like Kautsky, Rosa Luxemburg, and Clara Zetkin constituted only a small minority.[137] Every conceivable concession and compromise was made to assure a few more seats and a few more votes: the bankruptcy of "socialist radicalism" in Germany was complete.[138]

Michels maintained, however, that all the socialist parties of Europe were endangered by liberal democracy, and the danger was everywhere the same. And there were also other dangers, such as the temptation to possess an organization just for the sake of having one[139] and the desire to enjoy material benefits, or, in Michels's words, "to have well-filled coffers shielded from all anxiety."[140] This danger of a "love of peace for one's coffers,"[141] said Michels, was compounded by defects inherent in every organization, in every form of representation.[142] Here it was no longer Michels the revolutionary socialist who was speaking, but Michels the future eminent political scientist and author of *Political Parties*. These dangers inherent in every organization, every form of representation, were the same, he maintained, as those that threatened the syndicates. It was not the masses themselves that were represented at the crucial moment of the strike, it was not the party that gave rise to bourgeois values and deviations, but the *organization* as such. The great problem, therefore, was to find an answer to the fact that the syndicate "also bears within itself its cruel contradiction."[143]

A few years later, Michels, like Sorel, came to the conclusion that the proletariat would never be a revolutionary factor and that socialism is consequently incapable of changing the world. At the beginning of the century, however, he still believed that a "revolutionary revisionism," a political trend based on "the clearest rigidity of principles . . . and on courageous willpower and offensive action,"[144] or, in other words, on a voluntarist and vitalist ethic, would succeed in breaking the inertia and conservatism of the masses. On the eve of the First World War, Michels, like nearly all the revolutionary syndicalists, finally came to acknowledge what he saw to be the true situation: capitalism does not drive a sufficiently large wedge between the bourgeoisie and the proletariat to provoke a workers' revolt. At the same time, it became clear to him that the sociological laws that he himself recognized and that determine the behavior of all men and organizations made illusory every hope of getting the proletariat to act as the revolutionary agent of which the syndicalists had dreamed.

When faith in the proletariat disappeared, one feature of revolutionary syndicalism still remained: the wish to overthrow liberal democracy.

"Socialism is not a derivative of democracy," said Arturo Labriola, addressing the Paris conference of 1907 on behalf of Italian revolutionary syndicalism.[145] Three years later, Labriola and Michels were already collaborating with Enrico Corradini, the theoretician of Italian nationalism, in founding *La lupa*, a review in which revolutionary syndicalists and nationalists joined forces.[146] Edited by Paolo Orano, it first appeared in October 1910. Soon afterward, Labriola became one of the most fervent supporters of the Libyan war, and through his advocacy of interventionism he helped to lay the groundwork for the Italian fascist movement.

It is perhaps not without interest to recall that it was in Labriola's review, *Avanguardia socialista*, that a young revolutionary syndicalist called Benito Mussolini made his debut. His biographer claims that for him, too, socialism was above all a state of soul; socialism was action, and it was through this weekly journal that Mussolini, exiled in Switzerland, took part in the intellectual ferment of the Italian extreme left.[147] Pareto and Croce also contributed to *Avanguardia socialista*, as well as writers of the next generation—Sergio Panunzio, Angelo O. Olivetti, Orano, and Agostino Lanzillo—who all reappeared in *La lupa* and later took part in the Tripoli campaign and were finally reunited around Mussolini. This convergence of ideas occurred in Italy at the same time as in France, before the First World War and even before the Tripoli expedition. It was the logic of a particular situation and intellectual development and not a conjunction of external circumstances that led to this new synthesis.

Activism—the wish to throw oneself into the battle, to reshape the world and remold history—led both the revolutionary syndicalists and the nationalists to assail the established order. In the political domain, the target of their attack could only be liberal democracy. At the beginning of the century, liberal democracy had become the guardian of the established order, a veritable citadel of conservatism. It was for that reason that Lagardelle received all manifestations of proletarian antidemocratic sentiment with such delight. "I must admit," he said, "that this disaffection of the French workers with the state, which has become republican, seems to me the culminating fact of the history of these recent years."[148]

Lagardelle claimed that what permitted "the proletariat to break with democracy was the very experience of democracy."[149] In the period of "spiritual confusion" that had followed the Dreyfus affair, participation in government had seemed to the labor activists a natural consequence of social democracy;[150] revolutionary syndicalism, on the other hand, set itself against both liberal democracy and "its substitute, parliamentary socialism," substituting "*direct action*, which is the principle of syndicalism"—revolutionary, warlike action—for "the debilitating atmosphere of social peace."[151] Thus, he claimed, the syndicalist movement became "even more an agent of moral progress than of economic progress. In a world in which the taste for liberty has been lost, in a period that lacks the feeling for dignity, it calls forth the living forces of humanity and provides a perpetual example of courage and energy."[152]

A few years later, however, the French and Italian revolutionary syndicalists—Sorel, Lagardelle, Labriola, Michels—increasingly discovered, well before the war, that the European proletariat had no desire for revolution and that the idea of playing the part of the "agent of moral progress" had never even entered its mind. Even less was it willing to make any sacrifices for this purpose. The former proponents of the idea of the moral regeneration of the world by the proletariat did not, however, abandon their desire to attack those forces that made progress impossible, namely, bourgeois society and liberal democracy. They very soon turned their eyes toward other horizons and with the same enthusiasm engaged in other battles, but always with the same objective in view: the destruction of the established order.

In a classic work of national socialism written at the end of 1912, Édouard Berth summed up the despair and feelings of revolt of the Sorelians. He condemned "the ignoble positivism" in which "the bourgeoisie seems to have succeeded in sweeping along both the aristocracy and the people."[153] "Pessimism, utilitarianism and materialism," he said, "are eating away at all of us, nobles, bourgeois and proletarians."[154] These words of Berth, a revolutionary syndicalist who was associated at that time with the integral nationalists, read like a text of Gentile. Did not the Italian philosopher also see fascism principally as a revolt against positivism? Against that positivism that created the "regime of money, the essentially leveling, materialistic and cosmopolitan regime" that delivers up France to "the essence and quintessence of bourgeois materialism, the Jewish speculator and financier"?[155] Thus, "one saw socialism and syndicalism successively pass into the hands of the Jews and become defenders of that nauseating and pestilential ideology of which Malthusianism, anti-Catholicism and antinationalism are the whole substance, . . . and it would seem, in fact, that the people now aspire only to the state of well-being of the man who has retired and is completely uninterested in anything except his pension, and lives in terror of social or international unrest and asks for only one thing: peace—a stupid, vacuous peace made up of the most mediocre material satisfactions." [156] Berth railed against "bourgeois decadence," against "the completely bourgeois pacifism" that infects "the people coming to birth with the corruption of the bourgeoisie coming to an end." [157] Bourgeois decadence bequeaths to the people "a hypertrophied state, the product of a beggarly and half-starved rural and urban democracy," and it creates a "universal stagnation" in which the proletariat borrows "the worst ideas of the decadent bourgeoisie." [158]

To counteract the effects of decadence, then as in the past, Berth saw but one solution: war. "War," he said, "is not always that 'work of death' that a vain people of effeminate weaklings imagines. Behind every powerful industrial and commercial development there is an act of force, an act of war." [159] War assures the progress of civilization and at the same time raises the question of the state and the nation. [160] Berth, who was Sorel's disciple, quotes Proudhon—"War is our history, our life, our entire soul"—and Arturo Labriola, who claimed that "the sentiment of national independence, like the religious sentiment, leads to the most incredible manifestations of sacrifice." [161] Only violence can save the human race from "becoming universally bourgeois," "from the platitude of an eternal peace." [162]

Six years before writing these words under the pseudonym of Jean Darville, Berth, returning to one of Sorel's main ideas, had said that he believed that the syndicalist movement and proletarian violence possessed "the capacity of regenerating the degenerate bourgeoisie and restoring its power of resistance so that it could fulfill its historical mission to the end." [163] In revolutionary syndicalism he had seen a fusion of the very Nietzschean idea of responding with "blows of the fist" to the self-interested benevolence of the bourgeoisie and the "Marxist precept" that if one wishes to resolve social antagonisms, they first have to be taken to an extreme. [164] If Berth was influenced by Nietzsche, that was certainly not accidental. Nietzsche had a considerable influence on the "new school," as he had formerly had on Barrès, [165] and it is therefore not at all surprising that their successors in the thirties should also be very preoccupied with him. Thierry Maulnier wrote a book about him, [166] and during the same period Drieu La Rochelle acknowledged his intellectual debt to Nietzsche's pessimism and his pragmatic philosophy of irrationality and action. [167]

However, Berth attempted a synthesis of Marx and Nietzsche, whereas Drieu rejoiced at the overthrow of Marxism by the Nietzschean spirit. [168] Berth could not conceive that the purpose of proletarian violence was merely that of setting two antagonistic classes against each other, but thought it was, rather, primarily that of creating the conditions in which a class could be formed, for "economic unity" (or "unity of situation"), he said, may be the *necessary* condition for the forming of a class, but it is not a *sufficient* condition. To this economic unity should be added "unity of will,"[169] and "unity of will" is created only through struggle. It is in struggle that the classes become conscious of themselves and of what Berth, apparently following Hegel's *Philosophy of Right*, called the collective self or complex personality.[170]

According to Berth, the concept most dangerous to the idea of a class was that of a party. The real difference, he believed, between a class and a party was not that a party was an ideological unit and a class an economic unit: a class, when it is fully developed, is also an ideological entity. The real difference, he said, is that a party is only a collection of individuals from various classes—something that does not allow class consciousness to awaken and to attain the full clarity of an idea. In a word, a party is an organ of democracy, and "democracy does not know classes, it only knows individuals."[171] Consequently democracy is fatal for socialism and the proletariat.

Berth claimed that liberal democracy and bourgeois society led to social atomization: "Society is brought to the point where it is only a market made up of free-trading atoms, in contact with which everything dissolves. There are now only individuals, dustlike particles of individuals, shut up within the narrow horizons of their consciousness and their money boxes."[172] Side by side with this disintegration "of the merchant, bourgeois, liberal and democratic world," however, one has the proletariat "restoring the scattered condition of things and minutes to the permanent unity of its will to power." Entrenched within "the strongholds of its syndicates," the proletariat alone is capable "of restoring to a dissolving world a meaning, a goal, a direction, an ideal." For, finally (here Berth quotes Sorel), "it is war . . . that engenders the sublime, and without the sublime there cannot be a lofty morality."[173] Consequently, setting off, like Sorel, on a crusade for the redemption of morality and civilization, Berth once again assailed the "international plutocracy" that "is pacifistic by instinct and interest," for this plutocracy fears "a revival of heroic values [that] could only hurt its purely materialistic domination."[174] Berth quotes at length a text that Pareto[175] had contributed to Sorel's journal *L'Indépendance*, in which the Italian sociologist accused this plutocracy of being "cowardly, as the Jews and the usurers had been in the Middle Ages. Its weapon is gold, not the sword: it knows how to scheme; it does not know how to fight. Thrown out on one side, it comes back on the other, without ever facing the danger; its riches increase while its energy diminishes. *Exhausted by economic materialism, it becomes increasingly impervious to an idealism of sentiments.*[176]

After having found inspiration in Pareto, Labriola, and Corradini, Berth turned to Nietzsche. Like Nietzsche, Berth wanted to destroy "*the power of the average,* or, that is to say, of democratic, bourgeois and liberal mediocrity (as Nietzsche said, the proper word to qualify whatever is *mediocre* is 'liberal')."[177] It follows, then, that "the dual, parallel and synchronized national and syndicalist movement must bring about the complete ousting of the regime of gold and the triumph of heroic values over the ignoble bourgeois materialism in which Europe is presently stifling. In other words, this revolt of Force and Blood against Gold, whose first signs were detected by Pareto, and the signal for which was given by Sorel in *Reflections on Violence* and by Maurras in *Si le coup de force est possible,* must end with the total downfall of the plutocracy."[178] To save civilization, one therefore had "to persuade one group that the syndical ideal does not necessarily mean national abdication, and the other group that the nationalist ideal does not necessarily imply a program of social pacification, for on the day when there will be a serious revival of warlike and revolutionary sentiments and a victorious upsurge of heroic, national and proletarian values—on that day, the reign of Gold will be overthrown, and we shall cease to be reduced to the ignominious role of satellites of the plutocracy."[179]

The intellectual evolution that we see here was not the result of chance, but followed naturally from the Sorelians' basic conception of the relationship between socialism and the proletariat. Ultimately, they looked on it not as a fixed relationship but as something circumstantial, arising out of a given historical situation. The relationship between socialism and the proletariat could even be regarded as accidental, and that explains the ease with which the proletariat could be integrated into the nation and lose its unique status as a revolutionary factor. It transpired that the revisionists, those "revolutionary revisionists" of the pre-1914 period, like the "néos" of the thirties, came to believe that this role could be played not only by the proletariat but also by the nation, and this was what connected the thinking of people like Sorel, Labriola, Berth, and Michels with that of the next generation's critics of Marxism and liberalism. Neither group really set as its goal the liberation of the proletariat and the liberation of the individual; both groups, rather, sought to save civilization through a negation of bourgeois and liberal values and a condemnation of the old Socratic tradition.

CHAPTER THREE

An Ingenuous Fascism: Georges Valois and the Faisceau

The Beginnings of the Movement

More than ten years passed before the ideological synthesis arrived at by the Sorelians and the Maurrassians of the Cercle Proudhon began to be reflected in French political life. In Italy, the situation was relatively straightforward. With a few exceptions, such as Ernesto Cesare Longobardi, Alceste De Ambris, and Enrico Leone, the revolutionary syndicalists, together with the nationalists, after having given their support to an out-and-out interventionism, fought side by side with Mussolini. Things were different in France, however. From the beginning of the war, Sorel had lapsed into silence. He died in August 1922. In 1920 Berth became a member of the Communist party and the *Clarté* group, whereas Lagardelle backed out and turned toward regionalism. The former director of *Le Mouvement socialiste* finally joined the Faisceau, but did not play an important part in it.

Only Valois, therefore, remained to pursue the aims of the Cercle Proudhon. Undoubtedly, many things had changed in the interim, but not the main goal: the war had demonstrated the existence of an upsurge of nationalism, but it had not resulted in a fusion of nationalism and socialism. It is precisely for that reason that Valois's new initiative, short-lived as it was, is so interesting: this time, one is dealing not with a mere political theory but with an attempt to put that theory into practice. For the first time in the postwar period, an organized political movement forced the "socially" oriented right to make a choice: would it accept the principle of a national and socialist synthesis? Would it agree to give up some of its privileges? Would it come around to the idea of an onslaught on capitalism, liberalism, and bourgeois society and culture? In other words, the question posed was, Was there any real revolutionary potential outside Marxism?

No one was better qualified than Valois to provide a concrete answer to this question, one that put to the test both the Maurrassian right and the "modernist" right—the great patrons of industry, avid for progress—for on the eve of the war it was Valois, the leading spirit of one of the most developed forms of a national-socialist synthesis in pre-1914 Europe, who had orchestrated a vast campaign to obtain the support of as large a section of the workers as possible.[1]

In the immediate postwar period, Valois—an infantry officer, wounded and decorated in the front line—pursued his political career in the Action Française, but from the start, it seemed, his heart was not really in it. The war, the Russian Revolution, and the march on Rome had transformed the world, but Maurras and his journalists did not seem to be aware of it. The men of action in the Maurrassian movement, however, began to feel that the time had come to change their approach. Valois, in particular, had been permanently influenced by his experience in the Cercle Proudhon and refused to be restricted to the role of specialist in war veterans or economist of the movement that Maurras had intended for him. He therefore took the initiative of launching a movement for the convocation of the States General, thus adopting a style of action that aimed at being "revolutionary" and that was to be very much developed in the following decade.

With Valois were two great industrialists: Eugène Mathon, a textile manufacturer, owner of Mathon et Dubrulle, one of the major firms of the Roubaix-Tourcoing region, and Gaston Japy, senator for the Doubs, who had been associated with Pierre Biétry and had been a leader and financial backer of the Jaune movement. Continuity was thus assured, and the way made clear for fascism. With regard to theory, Valois's monthly journal, *Cahiers des États généraux*, offered a new synthesis of the ideas put forward both by the "social" Catholics of *L'Accord social* and by Biétry's followers and the members of the Cercle Proudhon. Where its methods of action and alliances are concerned, the Faisceau was remarkable both for its modern quality and for its fidelity to the tradition of the French right.

Valois, who paid a fervent tribute to Christian corporatism on the occasion of the death of Colonel de La Tour du Pin,[2] was very conscious of this tradition: the *Cahiers des États généraux* claimed that, in its

modern form, it went back as far as Renan.[3] Thus, Valois endowed corporatism with the classic significance that continued to be attributed to
it for the next twenty years. It was, he said, the coming together of the
"scattered limbs of one and the same body in order to join them to the
head that is the state, to the torso that is the nation, with its heart,
which is the Family, so that the nation will really form a body in which
all the organs want nourishment, in accordance with the requirements
of necessity and justice, but are willing to act as a single entity, commanded by the same blood that flows through all of them, and the same
spirit that watches over the whole body of the nation and cares for it."[4]

Nevertheless, Valois was aware from the start that his social ideal,
translated into terms of corporatism, differed considerably from that of
other promoters of the movement. Corporatism, he said, is not "an internal reform for the purpose of satisfying the selfish interests of each of
us," but, on the contrary, "it represents the end of civic and economic
individualism and the long-prepared coming of a new social and economic regime, and the revelation, for the country that has prepared it
for long years, of the existence of an organized nation made up of mutually supporting bodies in place of a nation in which individuals live
juxtaposed."[5]

From a very early stage it was clear that the great industrialists associated with the enterprise saw things quite differently. For them, the general aims of corporatism, it social objectives, and the changes in human
relations that it implied were secondary if not contrary to their aspirations. Eugène Mathon said bluntly that the main purpose of the corporation "was economic and was first of all to assure the prosperity of
[the] industry." Accordingly, the principle was established "that only
employers should direct the economic corporation,"[6] for it was only on
this basis, it was believed, that a real cooperation between employers
and employed could be set up and joint ownership of industrial property
and workers' participation in the direction and profits of the enterprise
could be envisaged. The very strict discipline necessary for any social
organization (Mathon supported his argument with the authority of
Gustave Le Bon) required compulsory membership in the organization
and full compliance with its decisions.[7] However, this principle of the
supreme importance of discipline and the collective interest[8] could not
be carried over into the economic sphere. In that area, the principle that
"individual interest" must be "the basis of all economic organization"
could not be questioned.[9] The "ordered liberty" that would replace "the
present anarchic liberty"[10] while taking care that "the corporation does

not interfere with private initiative"[11] was based on the idea of the "divine right" of the employer and was primarily an employer's defense mechanism.

As had always been the case—as was the case with the first, unpracticed utterances of the radical right at the end of the nineteenth century and again with the Jaunes—an attempt was made to convince the workers of the fundamental error of class warfare, and of the need "to replace it with a freely entered collaboration."[12] Thus, Mathon's idea of corporatism was profoundly different from Valois's, inasmuch as the great woolen-goods manufacturer from northern France believed that "the state should limit its intervention to the role of counselor, guide and arbitrator,"[13] not imposing any real limitations on the employers' freedom of action but ensuring the necessary conditions for social peace. The corporation thus became a tool in the hands of the employers, which was assuredly something very different from what Valois had intended.

Mathon's version of corporatism had already been attempted a few years earlier by the Redressement Français, a propagandist organization financed by Ernest Mercier's group for the promotion of constitutional reform. Valois had taken part in this enterprise, which Drieu La Rochelle, who was also involved, was to describe a few years later as one more in the series of "idiotic attempts" of fascism in France.[14] Among its organizers was Raphael Alibert, who became Pétain's minister of justice and was responsible for the home policies of the Vichy government in its early stages. There can be no doubt that Valois viewed the development from the Redressement Français to the States General, followed by the creation of the Faisceau, as a constant progress toward a more militant, more radical, more "social," more left-wing political conception.

The role that Mathon wished to play in the movement for the convocation of the States General was precisely the one that Gaston Japy had played with Pierre Biétry. The conception of the role of the corporation put forward by the Roubaix factory owner was in no way different from that of the industrialist from Franche-Comté at the turn of the century.[15] In one respect, however, the two cases were very different. Whereas the association of Japy with Biétry lasted throughout the existence of the Jaune movement and influenced the development and determined the character of this form of national socialism, the association of Mathon with Valois did not last beyond the opening stages. In accepting a paternalistic conception of corporatism, after a few years the Jaune movement lost its proletarian character, its specific identity, and, with that, its raison d'être. It became increasingly subservient to the traditional right and finally disappeared. Valois, however, wanted to resist the attraction of the great factory owners and industrialists, and succeeded in doing so only through a violent rupture of relations. Eugène Mathon was with him long enough to help in the financing of the Faisceau and the launching of *Le Nouveau Siècle*, but he left very early on, and his departure was quite a shock. The same happened later with François Coty, the celebrated perfume manufacturer. Because Valois was an authentic fascist, because, from the beginning, he wanted to create a movement that would be "outside and above all parties," [16] because he had the feeling that "there is a revolution to be made in this country," [17] he took seriously the synthesis of nationalism and socialism that he was working out. He had no wish to place himself under the wing of the financiers, but he could not avoid getting entangled in a rivalry that had become permanent and had existed since the time of Boulangism—that between the radical and the conservative right.

A kind of prologue to the Faisceau episode, the movement for the convocation of the States General—that "corporative Boulangism," in the words of *Le Quotidien*, that "pedestrian Boulangism," as *Le Temps* described it [18]—had another aspect, much less known, that was also fundamental to fascist thought. In those postwar years, fascism, searching for a "third way" between capitalism and Marxist socialism, represented an earnest desire to modernize, adapt, and rationalize the national economy. The more the campaign for the reconvocation of the States General developed at the Faisceau (the left-wing, revolutionary terminology always being carefully retained), the more the "modernistic" aspect of fascism became apparent. The fascistically inclined elements and those who were to become fascist in the years ahead were the first to become aware of the need to introduce real structural changes, to see beyond the issues connected with small-scale exploitation, and to grapple with the threat presented by international capitalism. Eugène Mathon, for whom fascism was a protective mechanism, a lifebuoy for the French economy, advocated "a rational economic organization" that would be able to resist "the tyranny, the exploitation of international financiers." [19] Like all the other collaborators of the *Cahiers*, he had a very developed sense of the importance of technological progress and of the importance to the national life of gasoline, the petrochemical industries, and commercial aviation. The members of Valois's circle wanted to erect an effective barrier against the great international companies—Standard Oil, Shell, "those enormous industrial and commercial organizations" that ceaselessly sought "world hegemony," [20] and for whom all means were valid: financial pressure, political maneuvers, the manipulation of public opinion. Valois believed that only if they were organized into corporations would the body of producers have the means to resist the interference of the great trusts. Thus, the corporation was seen, at the time when the French fascist movement was just emerging, not only as something promoting social integration and the neutralization of the proletariat but also as a means of defending the national economy against international capitalism. Now more than ever before, it was necessary to prevail in this contest, to strengthen the national organism, and to prepare for the inevitable struggle for existence. In this respect, the corporatism of the interwar period was in keeping with the long tradition of national socialism, and its purpose was always the same: to resist the encroachments of cosmopolitan, large-scale capitalism and to create a means of protection capable of preserving the integrity of the national body.

At the same time as lashing out against large-scale national and international capitalism, Valois waged a fierce campaign against the values and way of life of the bourgeoisie and the bourgeoisie's moral and intellectual dominance. He never questioned the validity of private property or of profit as the motive force of the economy. (This was surely one of the most significant characteristics of fascism.) What he attacked was "the commanding of the state by the bourgeois spirit."[21] Accordingly, throughout his campaign, Valois displayed a contempt for the old bourgeois Europe, the old world of heirs and descendants. The fascist, he believed, would be the gravedigger of all the bourgeois virtues as of all the ills that the bourgeois order gave rise to: he would signify the birth of a new morality. Such was the nature of the coming "national revolution"—it represented not a collection of reforms but "an overturning of the values by which the bourgeois, liberal, democratic and parliamentary states have lived for a century."[22] The war, hailed as "the signal for a French and European renaissance," created the proper conditions for "giving the first place to blood, to sword," said Valois.[23] Even before the war, he said, in the time of the Cercle Proudhon, "we had the spirit of the combatant. Together we opposed the law of blood to the law of gold."[24] This glorification of the heroic virtues and desire to create a revolution that would free France and Europe from "the rule of the bankers and parliamentarians" opposed the "mercantile conceptions that depreciate and debase glory, art, thought, science, religion."[25] They dated back to before 1914, but it was only the war that had enabled the soldiers to get "the politicians by means of grenades,"[26] and that, having taken away political power from the bourgeois, who were "unsuited to run the state," permitted the foundation of the national state, that is, "a state based on the heroic values through which every society is founded, defended and brought to greatness."[27]

This lengthy disquisition, which at the same time was a refutation of René Johannet's celebrated book *Éloge du bourgeois français*, was a perfect expression of the traditional fascist view of the bourgeoisie. According to this view, the bourgeoisie was a useful social group that had performed great services in the past and could do so again, on one condition: that it go back to its place and consent to serve instead of command. As long as it governed the state, however, the bourgeoisie, or rather the bourgeois state, placed civilization in peril.[28]

The eradication of bourgeois values, the re-creation of the conditions necessary to French greatness—these were the aims of the national revolution, which already in November 1925 was called the fascist revolution. The idea of greatness or grandeur—"fraternity in grandeur," in Philippe Barrès's words[29]—was a constant preoccupation of the leaders of the movement. Valois believed that this "movement toward greatness that gives birth to all civilization"[30] was possible only if the "heroic spirit," the spirit of the combatant "armed with a sure doctrine,"[31] pervaded the entire life of the nation, and if the entire state and society were run by men who had this fighting spirit. In this situation, one would have a hierarchy of warriors with a "national leader," trustworthy elites, and new institutions, for the combatant who "places himself above parties and classes as in wartime"[32] has no wish to "belong to any one class any more than he wants to be the right hand of one of the bourgeois parties."[33] A unifying factor par excellence, the repository of all the virtues and all the hopes of the nation, the combatant, said Valois, wants to carry out a revolution, a total revolution that would be not a simple change of regime but "a negation of the whole political, economic and social philosophy of the nineteenth century."[34] To that end, "he wants to have the government of the country."[35]

Because he is a revolutionary, the combatant can be only a fascist or a bolshevist. In the opinion of the founder of the first fascist movement outside Italy, fascism and bolshevism were "one and the same reaction against the bourgeois and plutocratic spirit. To the financier, the oil tycoon, the pig breeder who consider themselves the lords of the earth and wish to organize it according to the laws of money, the requirements of the automobile, and the philosophy of pigs and to submit the people to the philosophy of the dividend, the bolshevist and the fascist reply by raising their swords. *Both of them proclaim the law of the combatant.*"[36]

Georges Valois was one of the first political thinkers in France to insist on the common basis of the left- and right-wing revolutionaries, of "those two inimical brothers, fascism and bolshevism, brothers because of their mutual contempt for the bourgeois regime, enemies because they occupy the two opposite capitals of Europe—fascism that of the sacred lake [the Mediterranean], bolshevism that of the land of barbarism."[37]

All authentic fascists in the following twenty years behaved in a similar manner. Up to the Second World War, and often during the war years themselves, their hatred of bourgeois Europe was stronger than their opposition to communism.

The Traditional Right versus Fascism

Georges Valois, like Déat and Bucard, saw the explosion of the First World War as part of a continuous revolutionary process. In Valois's opinion, the essentially antiliberal "revolution of August 1914," followed by the counterrevolutionary waves of 1919 and 1924,[38] had been temporarily arrested, and it was up to the combatants "who had the spirit of victory"[39] to carry it through. Valois, however, had a strong sense of continuity with the antiliberal and antibourgeois rebellions previous to 1914. The Cercle Proudhon, particularly, which was the real laboratory of the ideas that gave birth to the Faisceau, was always present in his thinking.[40] If the war and the victory had created the combatant, it had also had the effect of moderating the extremism of certain groups opposed to the liberal consensus and facilitating the integration of these groups into the established order. The Faisceau represented, precisely, a reaction of rebellion against this phenomenon. It rose up against the Action Française and the other nationalist movements in much the same way as the Maurrassian movement, a quarter of a century earlier, had expressed the reaction of the younger generation against the bankruptcy of bourgeois and conservative nationalism at the end of the century. The first French fascist movement as such in effect continued the work previously undertaken by the Action Française, which had now abandoned it owing to its shift toward the center.

The process whereby left- and right-wing radicals were absorbed by the center that had taken place in France in the 1880s now happened again, and the void that had been created by the shift in the position of the Action Française, which in practice had come to accept the idea of playing the game according to the rules of liberal democracy, was filled by the new fascist movement. Thus, Valois's movement was the creation of the activist—and generally young—elements both in the Action Française and in the other nationalist groups, for whom it represented a new weapon of combat.

If the movement itself was founded only on 11 November 1925, *Le Nouveau Siècle*, which became the organ of the Faisceau, had already appeared on 26 February of that year. This weekly journal had been founded by a group of industrialists led by the millionaires Franz Van den Broeck d'Obrenan, one of the chief shareholders of the Action Française publishing house, and Eugène Mathon, at that time president of the textile manufacturers' syndicate of Roubaix-Tourcoing. Most of the founding members of the journal came from circles close to the Action Française, and they included a few financial magnates, such as the ship owner Valentin Smith, and superrich industrialists like Serge André and Antoine Cazeneuve.[41] The presence of Eugène Mathon on the list of founders was regarded in Paris press circles as a guarantee of success for Valois—a success that became evident in the last two weeks of November, when *Le Nouveau Siècle*'s financial position seemed so secure that it could seriously consider becoming a daily.

The preparatory period thus lasted for about seven months, during which the financial infrastructure of the journal was set up. It was also a period in which ideological ambiguities—necessary for the founding of the movement and its journal—were maintained, and, first of all, that concerning the composition of the editorial staff.

The staff that was announced in mid-November, just before the launching of the daily, was outstanding for its richness of talent. It included some of the most brilliant names in right-wing journalism: Philippe Barrès, René Benjamin, Louis Béraud, Abel Bonnard, James de Coquet, René Johannet, Pierre Dominique, Jacques Maritain, Eugène Mathon, Henri Massis, André Maurois, Georges Suarez, Jérôme and Jean Tharaud, Xavier Vallat, and the famous nationalist cartoonist Forain. One can readily imagine the anxiety that such an editorial committee backed by the financial resources of the Roubaix textile industry must have caused the Action Française, but Maurras's strong reaction and the pressures brought to bear were so effective that when the new daily finally appeared the list of *Le Nouveau Siècle*'s collaborators included only one name known to the general public: Philippe Barrès. In the end, out of all these writers and journalists, the editorial staff comprised only Georges Valois, Jacques Arthuys, Hubert Bourgin of the Ligue des Patriotes, and Philippe Barrès. It was a notable moral and political defeat. The hostility of the Action Française and the inherent contradictions of the fascist ideology proved to be decidedly difficult obstacles to overcome.

Le Nouveau Siècle, moreover, soon began to run into an endless series of financial difficulties that rendered its existence precarious. A few weeks after the northern textile manufacturers withdrew their support, Maurras and Léon Daudet scored a new success in their campaign against the journal: François Coty, who had given Valois a grant of a million francs to start the daily, abruptly stopped his assistance to avoid being accused of participating in the polemic against the Action Française.[42] Valois attempted to learn something from this series of failed starts; henceforth, he tried not to attack or hurt anyone except, of course, Maurras and Daudet.

Le Nouveau Siècle experienced more than financial difficulties, however. In his attempt to accommodate different clienteles, opposing interests, and conflicting policies, Valois succeeded in giving his journal a dullness that even its most indulgent readers, the war veterans, complained of as early as the two last weeks in December[43]—only a week to ten days after its first appearance as a daily. This was immediately reflected in sales: the journal was a complete flop.

Originally, Le Nouveau Siècle was not intended to be the journal of a new political movement, but rather to provide a platform for the various political formations that gravitated around the Action Française. Its founders were all Maurrassians, or were close or related to that school of thought. Thus, in 1924, Valois, quoting Bernard de Vésins, who every morning thanked God for "having given us Charles Maurras," went so far as to say that the twentieth century, if it was named, would be named after Maurras,[44] and one year later, in July 1925, Léon Daudet described Valois as "the great monetary and financial talent of this period," the man "who saved French savings from immediate ruin by inflation."[45] This was four months after the foundation of the Faisceau, and there was as yet no hint of the outbursts of hatred, insults, and anger that were to characterize relations between fascists and Maurrassians, revolutionaries and conservatives.

At that moment, however, everything still seemed straightforward enough—at least to the members of the Action Française. As they saw it, Valois was to play a role vis-à-vis the war veterans similar to the one he had formerly played vis-à-vis labor circles, that of mobilizing an important section of public opinion with which he had particular affinities. Accordingly, not only did the leaders of the Action Française not oppose the makeup of the staff of *Le Nouveau Siècle*, but, on the contrary, they actively encouraged Valois and his friends to seek support for the movement in ever-wider circles and to disseminate Maurras's ideas.

The atmosphere at that time was particularly suitable for this campaign to mobilize the war veterans in support of the Action Française. The accession to power of the Cartel in May 1924 had the effect of provoking a defensive reaction among the "nationals." In fact, it was after this electoral victory of the left, and the demonstration of power achieved by the transfer of the ashes of Jaurès to the Panthéon, that the new militant groups came into being.

However, in the summer and fall of 1925 it began to become clear that the emergence of two such groups, the Légion of Antoine Rédier and the team of *Le Nouveau Siècle*, marked the beginning of a split in the Action Française. Certainly, both Valois and Rédier proceeded with great caution and always invoked Maurras's name,[46] but they were unable to maintain their ambiguous position indefinitely. It soon became apparent that the creation of the Faisceau resulted from a divergence that caused the breaking away from the Action Française not only of some of its most militant and zealous elements but also of quite a number of people further "to the left" than the leaders of the movement.

This was only to be expected. The total lack of any real will to action in the Action Française, its flavor of a literary salon, its royalism could only be repellent to the genuine fascists. The Action Française was singularly unattractive to them: from Valois in the days of the Cartel to Bucard, Déat, and Doriot in Paris under the Occupation, the fascists loudly proclaimed their profound contempt for the very narrow social power base of the Action Française, its association with one social class, its character as a movement that existed only in its journalistic publications, and its resulting incapacity for action. The fascists, or simply the men of action, were not deceived. They knew that the surly disposition, inflammatory style, and invectives of the Action Française ill concealed the truth, which was that, comfortably installed in their editorial offices, Maurras and his journalists were happy under a liberal regime—a regime that provided them with the perfect setting for the development of their talents. Not only did the Action Française not think of moving into action, but it was also totally incapable of it, never having envisaged the setting up of any structures other than those necessary for putting out its publications.[47]

There can be no doubt: in large part, the emergence of the Faisceau was due to the deep need for action felt by the younger generation in the old *ligues*, and for that reason the fascist movement represented a danger both for the Action Française and for the other national *ligues*, headed by the oldest—Déroulède's Ligue des Patriotes. All the police reports agree on this point: it was the immobilism of the existing organizations led by the old hands of parliamentary politics that aroused the anger of the youngest and most combative elements, most of whom had come out of the trenches. Of all the *ligues*, the Camelots du Roi and the Jeunesses Patriotes seem to have been most affected.[48]

According to police statistics, eighteen hundred members of the Paris sections of the Action Française resigned between December 1925 and April 1926 and joined the Faisceau. In the southwest of France, 30 percent of the members went over to fascism.[49] In December 1925 there was an atmosphere of panic at the Action Française headquarters in the rue de Rome. Over and above the ideological considerations, it is these figures and the need to dispel the malaise of their followers and to dissuade them from flirting with fascism that explain the persistent irascibility and resentment that Maurras and Daudet displayed toward Valois. Whatever the case, by the beginning of 1926 it became clear that the Action Française had to stem the tide that had brought in the Faisceau—the "Fesso" and the "fessistes," as Daudet called them. To be sure, the Faisceau eventually came to nothing, whereas the Action Française continued to exist, but this outcome was not obvious at the time. Far from it: if it had not been for the quick, violent reactions of Maurras, Daudet, and Maurice Pujo, one wonders whether the danger would have passed so quickly. The sheer violence of their vituperation shows that at the time the rise of this new movement was taken seriously.

This campaign of intimidation in which all means, fair or foul, were regarded as acceptable bore fruit rapidly: by the end of January 1926 *Le Nouveau Siècle* could no longer count on most of the writers and journalists who had promised their collaboration a few weeks earlier.[50] Maurras and Daudet had succeeded in surrounding Valois with a permanent atmosphere of defamation that undermined the confidence of his supporters and raised up a psychological barrier that those front-ranking figures who had been attracted by the dynamism of the new movement did not dare to cross for fear of compromising their respectability.

The Action Française, which by then was an experienced organization, had invented, as far back as the time of the Dreyfus affair, an art and technique of calumny hitherto unknown. In the postwar period as

at the turn of the century, accusations without proof and unfounded in-
sinuations and imputations were its most feared and effective weapons.
Having lost its heroic generation in the war (Octave de Barral, Henri
Lagrange, Léon de Montesquiou) and others of its best elements in the
following years, the Action Française now more than ever gave itself
over to defamation. In general the practice worked and the victim never
came out unscathed, and so it was with the Faisceau.

Of all the personalities who had left the Action Française to join the
Faisceau, the only ones to remain after the first few weeks were Maurice
de Barral, Bertrand de Lur-Saluces, and René de La Porte. Louis Dimier
and René Johannet retained their respect for Valois but never really stood
by him, while Xavier Vallat, like many others, submitted to the pressures and dictates of Maurras. In effect, those who joined the Faisceau
and stayed were the nonconformists of the Action Française and the
other national *ligues*. They were as yet not at all well known, and what
kept them in the Faisceau was their desire for action. As soon as they
realized that the new movement, like its rivals, was unlikely to topple
the regime, they left it.[51]

The Action Française, however, was not the only movement to regard the Faisceau as a threat. From the beginning, it aroused the hostility of the right as a whole—both the traditional, conservative, liberal
right and the right that had been "broken in," as one might say. Those in
command were opposed to Valois and were not at all displeased to see
Maurras leading the attack against him. Together with Maurras were
the heads of the Ligue des Patriotes: General Édouard de Currières de
Castelnau and Marcel Habert, Déroulède's former companion. The
Ligue des Patriotes, in fact, refused to sanction the principles of seizure
of power by force and dictatorship that underlay the fascist ideology.
How, indeed, could it have been otherwise when its steering committee
included people like Désiré Ferry, Édouard Bonnefous, and Louis Marin?
Under the leadership of the former president of the Republic, Alexandre
Millerand, these eminent republicans could only be opposed to fascism.[52]

If the actors kept changing, or if they simply changed their roles, the
script always remained the same. In the twenties, the Action Française
and the Ligue des Patriotes played the same role with regard to the
Faisceau that a generation earlier Jules Lemaître and François Coppée's
Ligue de la Patrie Française had played with regard to them, and a
few years later the Jeunesses Patriotes and the Croix de Feu were to play
with regard to the Francists, the Solidarité Française, the militia of the
neosocialist Adrien Marquet in Bordeaux, and Jacques Doriot's ex-

communists in Saint-Denis. The "centrist" right always had its own shock troops that served its own purposes, and took good care that they did not become confused with the fascists.

In the twenties, the pressures exerted by influential figures were decisive in preventing Pierre Taittinger from throwing in his lot with the Faisceau. Among the "nationals," Taittinger—leader of the Jeunesses Patriotes and at that time Paris deputy—was probably the strongest political personality, the one most likely to throw himself into the enterprise. He hesitated for a long time before associating himself with the views of the right-wing leaders, but finally his movement decided not to go so far as to question the legitimacy of the parliamentary regime. The breakaway of the activist elements thus became inevitable. The first to join the Faisceau were the members of Antoine Rédier's Légion. This was a great success for Valois, for the numbers involved were considerable, particularly in the provinces. They were estimated at about ten thousand people.[53]

Founded—like the Jeunesses Patriotes and the *Nouveau Siècle* group—after the elections of 1924, the Légion, independently of the Faisceau and well before Valois did so, rapidly developed a quasi-fascist style and program. On 1 July, the Légion merged with the Jeunesses Patriotes despite the fact that its authoritarianism and dictatorial tendencies were far more extreme than the vague right-thinking ideology that Taittinger's movement had just inherited from the Ligue des Patriotes. Appointed vice-president of this new entity, Rédier began a genuine radicalization of the Jeunesses Patriotes, and when the Faisceau came into being he wanted an immediate merger with Valois's movement. Supported by a number of leading members of the steering committee, Rédier represented a considerable danger for Taittinger and the other leaders of the Ligue des Patriotes. In mid-December the 131st "century" (company) of the Jeunesses Patriotes went over to the Faisceau with its cadres, followed, according to police reports, by several hundred other young Parisians.[54]

Taittinger, backed up vigorously by the steering committee of the Ligue des Patriotes, said to exert authority over the Jeunesses, intervened energetically. He refused to be drawn into a policy of revolt. Rédier was expelled, but that did not stop the slow hemorrhage caused by the fascist upsurge. While the cadres remained faithful and the leaders worked closely with the Action Française, only too happy to let Maurras, Daudet, and Pujo perform a task that they felt to be necessary but that was nevertheless distasteful, it was the simple rank and file that wandered away. A police report of 13 March 1926 stated that "many of them have recently joined the Faisceau." [55]

Thus, almost as soon as it was born, the first French fascist movement came up against the combined hostility of all the right-wing groups together. This was not merely an opportunistic reaction on their part. It is true that the Faisceau hardly did them a service by drawing away the best elements among their supporters, the subscribers to their journals, and above all their actual or potential backers. There was no end to the complaints at the headquarters of the old *ligues*—at the Ligue des Patriotes, where there was the hope of turning *Le Drapeau* of Déroulède and Barrès, formerly a daily, into a weekly, at the Ligue Millerand, where there was a constant shortage of money, and at the Fédération Nationale Catholique. Indeed, all the existing organizations often felt the drain on their resources, and their prospects for the future seemed seriously compromised. [56] But that was not the main point.

From the 1880s onward, the various opposition *ligues* became an integral part of the French political system. Led by senior politicians (all deputies eligible for office, former deputies, or potential deputies— faithful, despite appearances, to the parliamentary system), the *ligues* were in reality only small right-wing parties. Respectful of forms and legality, detesting agitators, particularly proud of their respectability, they were concerned above all with preserving the existing structures of society. It was to guarantee the survival of that society that they set themselves in opposition to fascism; the contradiction between their own aims and those of the Faisceau was such that they could not welcome its success. For the essential characteristic of the Faisceau was precisely that it was a genuine fascist movement with a national-socialist ideology, violently antibourgeois and anticonservative, seeking its support as much on the left as on the right. If the *ligues* attacked people who temporarily occupied a position, the Faisceau was in revolt against liberal democracy and bourgeois society as such.

To be sure, in France as elsewhere, the fascists were ultimately driven to the right by their hatred of a politics of class that their integral nationalism rejected. They were led, by the logic of positions that opposed them to the left, toward alliances that attenuated their radicalism and reinforced their anti-Marxism to the detriment of their nationalist collectivism. The revolutionary potential of the fascist movements, the Faisceau included, was thus largely obviated by the mechanism of the division between left and right that they could not avoid, but that they had tried so hard to eliminate.

What Is Fascism? "Nationalism
Together With Socialism"

Upon founding the Faisceau, Valois attempted to define the significance of the movement in relation to Marxism. He claimed that since it
was "a total conception of the national, political, economic and social
life," [57] "fascism had precisely the same aim as socialism set itself." Unlike Marxism, however, fascism did not abolish "individual or family
property, the generator of initiative." It could "oppose communism
through transcending it" and in this way corrected Marxism's most
glaring defect: instead of leading society to its ruin, it "utilized property
in the framework of national and social disciplines, within a general
conception of rational economic organization." [58] This "great constructive revolution" that would create "a new order," a "new society," [59]
would be, said Valois, "for the Europe of the twentieth century what
liberalism and parliamentarianism were for the nineteenth century." [60] It
signified the birth of a "new and progressive form of civilization" [61]
based on "a fusion of nationalism and socialism." [62] Valois never tired of
repeating this formula to make it quite clear that this was the very essence of the fascist ideology.

Both nationalism and socialism, he claimed, "sought to create or to
recreate the fundamental social forms destroyed by the individualism of
the last century." [63] Because it was a "social nationalism" or a "national
socialism," [64] fascism, a movement "of universal character," meant the
erection, on the ruins of the old bourgeois, individualistic, and liberal
society, of a completely "new political, economic and social structure,"
thus permitting a truly modern state—productive, efficient, and capable
of providing infinite riches—to come into being. The worker—who
"does not carry his country in his wallet" like the bourgeois, and for
whom "his country is not an abstraction, not an idea" [65]—would be the
main agent of renewal and of the creation of a new civilization, a civilization of abundance within the framework of a powerful and integrated nation. Because it sought to create a new, modern, efficient world,
a civilization of producers, fascism (here one sees the influence of Sorel)
required "a working class that is enthusiastic, eager for progress, headed
by bold captains of industry who will lead the whole national economy
toward a prosperity that today we can hardly imagine." [66]

However—and this is an important point—this stress on the necessity for leadership in industry in no way implies giving a dominant position to the bourgeoisie. "The Faisceau," said Valois, "is not a group of

extra policemen for the defense of the old order of things"; it is not "an auxiliary national police force" of the bourgeoisie.[67] This was a recurrent theme of fascism: the authentic fascists—those who defined themselves as such and those who, while not accepting the name, nevertheless exemplified the fascist spirit—always insisted on the gulf that separated them from the conventional, conservative, timorous right. The real competition in this race for modernization was not, according to Valois, between fascism and conservatism but between fascism and communism, for fascism, like communism, sought to represent the people: "Where the proletariat is concerned, fascism will play the role that liberalism and parliamentarianism played for the bourgeoisie,"[68] and it was through fascism that the proletariat would one day find a place in the life of the state.

Valois constantly repeated these ideas. On 14 July 1926 he insisted once more that there could be no greater mistake than to regard fascism as an extreme right-wing movement, as one of the forms of the counterrevolution, as a defense of the existing order against communism. Fascism, "which has a foothold both on the left and on the right," is in fact "much closer to what is called the left than to what is called the right in that it builds the authority, the state, on the needs of the people in order to defend them against the great and the mighty. Moreover, it is this alliance [of the state and the people] that is the condition for the survival of any state," and for that reason,

with regard to the movement of 1789, it is a tremendous mistake to think that fascism opposes it, misconstrues it and seeks to reverse it.

Fascism is completely in line with the movement of 1789; it feels a kinship with it; it continues it; it goes beyond it in providing it with a conclusion that the people have been seeking for a century—a conclusion that will give the historical period that began in 1789 its definitive form."[69]

Thus, "fascism—conclusion of the movement of 1789"—will lay the groundwork for a new morality, new relationships between people, and new power structures. It will produce:

A state that does not belong to one class but to all, and that is national;
A unified state with a leader;
A state in which the leader represents the action of authority, and the assemblies the organization of liberty;
A state of the industrial age that will raise up countless new riches out of the soil;
A state in which nationalism and socialism will finally be united. The parliamentary state and an exhausted, out-of-date elite, miscreations of 1789, attempt to oppose the creation of a modern state.

It is against this that we continue the movement of 1789 with the dual cry "Down with parliament! Long live the Nation!" [70]

These same ideas had been expressed by Barrès a generation earlier. Where ideology, historical reactions, and associations of ideas are concerned, there was complete continuity. Valois's arguments added very little to those advanced thirty-seven years before on the occasion of the centenary of the Revolution, when Boulangism seemed to have been carried forward by an irresistible tide. Barrès, too, associated the movement of revolt against liberal democracy with the liberating outbursts of the French Revolution, of 1848, and of the Commune, and he appealed to the old Jacobin and revolutionary tradition: "We are still the blessed rabble of 1789, 1830 and 1848!" he cried in July 1889. [71] In an article that could easily have been written by Hervé or Lagardelle, by Sorel just before 1914, by Valois just after the war, or by Jouvenel, Drieu, or Maulnier in 1936, Barrès accused the bourgeoisie of, since 1789, never having regarded the people as anything other than a mere means, a useful means, of establishing its own supremacy. Since the fall of the ancien régime, he wrote, "the bourgeoisie has constantly called on the revolutionary energy of the popular classes with the secret purpose of subjugating them. Hypocritically, it was willing to lure the masses with the bait of power, and, deluding them with false hopes, never really had any other intention than to subject them to its economic domination." [72]

Valois was thus quite correct in insisting that fascism was a "French product" whose origins went back not to Maurrassian nationalism as one might imagine but to Sorel and Barrès, who, each in his own way, helped to "fuse socialism and nationalism." The Boulangism and nationalism of the turn of the century, he said, were "forms of fascism." [73]

A few months later Valois recalled these origins by once again placing the Faisceau within the tradition of Sorel and Barrès, attempting to reconcile the "anti-Dreyfusard and nationalist" Barrès with the "Dreyfusard and socialist" Péguy and to combine the idea of patriotism with the idea of justice. [74] Valois's fascism was undoubtedly the truest and most ingenuous attempt to formulate an ideology that would be a genuine synthesis, a "social nationalism" or a "national socialism" that would put into practice "the Sorelian idea whereby, thanks to a vigorous, demanding proletariat, the bourgeoisie would be given back its creative energy." It was hoped that by placing the bourgeoisie "between a powerful national state and a vigorous working class" one might neutralize the most sordid aspects of capitalism without destroying its potential for energy. [75] Valois and the politicians with him—Philippe

Barrès, Philippe Lamour, Jacques Arthuys, Hubert Bourgin, and perhaps also the future Francist leader Marcel Bucard, the active propagandist of the Faisceau—regarded fascism as "the movement through
which the whole of European civilization sought to move to a higher
level,"[76] and as a revolution that would transform Europe as surely as
the French Revolution had done.[77] They saw it as a pan-European movement, destined to spread throughout the whole continent. They believed that fascism took different forms from one country to another,
just as there were various national forms of socialism, but its essential
purpose remained the same: the creation of a modern state on the ruins
of the old liberal and bourgeois order, a state that could mobilize the
producers—"the chief industrialists and technicians and the strongest
elements in the working classes"—and carry out "a policy of high wages
and large profits." This strong national state was the only kind that
could assure the prosperity of the proletariat and prevent "economic decay and subjection to American capital."[78] And, in accents familiar to
the contemporary reader, Valois added that the French soldier had
fought the war for quite another purpose than "submission to the plutocratic imperialism of the United States."[79]

Thus, "the economic revival of Europe and the independence of our
country"[80] required one to lay the foundations of a new economic system based on "the rational organization of production" and the intervention of a state in control of "the organs of economic command."[81]
This was one of the recurrent themes of fascism, and it had a flavor that
at the time was very modern and strangely "leftist." It was this quality
that allowed fascism to be a movement oriented toward the future, toward the rising classes, the technicians, and the industrial proletariat,
toward the man of the twentieth century and the "age of electricity."[82]

In the period of the Faisceau, Georges Valois launched most of the
ideas that formed the stock-in-trade of fascist ideology throughout the
thirties. "One age is going down into the grave," he wrote. "A new age is
calling us."[83] The idea of the "new" and "modern" is a key concept of
fascism. It is found in the notion of "new teams" that Valois introduced
in Le Nouveau Siècle of 30 July 1925 and that was to be so popular with
Déat, Drieu, Jouvenel, and Bergery. Two years later, the former anarchist
Charles Albert praised Valois for being the first to propose an alliance
"of renovating groups."[84] This taste for modernity was expressed as
much in the Faisceau's admiration for Le Corbusier[85] as in Valois's
enthusiasm for "the rational organization" of industrial production.[86]
Valois, again, started a political fashion that was to be very popular in

the following decade: the slogan "Neither of the right nor of the left," [87] followed by an appeal to the idea of coming together "above the parties" [88] and "beyond the old boundaries." [89]

In February 1927, when he organized the Single Front of Combatants and Producers for the elections to the Senate, Valois launched an idea that proved to be very popular, that of a "Bloc des Jeunes" (Youth Bloc). Valois saw this aspiration to transcend the old limitations as one of the components of fascism and one of its greatest virtues.

As one of the first to attempt to reach out toward a new order, Valois used another expression that turned out to be of cardinal importance in the fascist vocabulary: he called his journal a "total journal" and said that it propounded a "total doctrine" [90]—the only kind capable of bringing about a "total revolution." Like all those who came after him, Valois proclaimed the existence of "a revolutionary situation." [91] He made a stirring appeal for an elite, for "a national leader who would be above all classes, above all parties," and called on all men who wanted to engage in "a policy of the combatant." [92] The fascists, from Valois to Déat on the eve of the Liberation, always regarded the situation as revolutionary. For them, unlike the communists, whom they accused of having a wait-and-see policy, it was never too soon to make a revolution. [93] One only had to want it and to prepare the ground a little, especially by extending the social power base of the movement. These classic elements of fascism (the cult of the warrior being particularly important in the postwar period) recurred in many articles in *Le Nouveau Siècle* and in innumerable speeches, brochures, booklets, and posters.

This assessment of the situation led the Faisceau, from the beginning, to address itself to the workers in a long-drawn-out campaign. All the right-wing revolutionary movements did so, from the popular, Blanquist, and socialistically inclined Boulangists to the group of active communists surrounding Jacques Doriot. This constant attempt to reach the proletariat was fraught with ambiguities and always proved costly, for throughout the half century between Boulangism and the collapse of the Third Republic the problem persisted of choosing between attempting to appeal to the proletariat and attracting the middle classes, between social activism and the financial support without which political activity is quickly paralyzed. Another, often painful, choice had to be made between a "leftist" militancy and the "national" aspect of fascism, between a ferocious antiliberalism and the integration of all social classes that is fascism's raison d'être. Finally, one was faced with the classic problem of the discrepancy between ideological requirements

and those of political action. It was these contradictions that had paralyzed the attacks on liberal democracy before 1914, and they greatly
contributed to the failure of the movements of the interwar period. The
development of the Faisceau provides a perfect prototype of all the difficulties inherent in the fascist ideology, the first and not least being the
conflict between conservatives and revolutionaries.

From the beginning, the Action Française, for whom the Faisceau
represented a mortal danger, accused the latter of being "allied" to the
communists. This accusation, disturbing to the "nationals" in general,
turned especially the businessmen and industrialists against the movement; at any rate, it helped to drive Eugène Mathon away. Displeased
by Valois's appeal to the workers and frightened by his wish to recruit
the communists and socialists who might be attracted by fascist antiliberalism, the industrialist from the North soon withdrew his support
from the Faisceau.[94]

From the start of his campaign, Valois seized every opportunity to
assail "bourgeois Europe, rank with liberalism," to predict the demise
of the liberal state, and to proclaim the moral decay of the conservatives.[95] Valois's idea that fascism was "the outcome of a labor movement that, where the proletariat is concerned, . . . will play the role that
liberalism and parliamentarianism have played for the bourgeoisie" was
hardly calculated to appeal to Mathon and his friends, who finally realized how great a mistake they had made. Thinking that they were sub-
sidizing a conservative political group, a more stringent, efficacious, and
modern version of the national ligues, they found themselves taking part
in a movement that addressed itself to "you, above all, comrades of the
factories and the offices" and declared that "fascism wants the state to
be the best defender of the working classes." And when Valois went so
far as to state that "fascism is not particularly attached to any one system of production" and concluded that "the French workers today have
to choose between communism and fascism, which are the two forms of
labor revolt and will to construction,"[96] it was more than the Roubaix
industrialist could bear, especially as in the industrial regions of northern France fascism took on a truly revolutionary quality. Its recruitment
campaign was directed almost entirely at the workers, and not without
some success, especially among railway employees. Consequently a few
groups were set up in northern and eastern France by two specialists
in labor matters: Marcel Delagrange, formerly communist mayor of
Périgueux, and another fellow communist named Bardy, also from
the Périgord, and a former member of the Confédération Générale du

Travail.[97] In May 1926, the Intelligence Service of the Ministry of The Interior (the Renseignements généraux) found that Faisceau meetings among the workers were becoming better attended and that the working class was not as uninterested as one might have supposed.[98] But without doubt the efforts expended were incommensurate with the results: the communist recruits, at a time when the Communist party was expelling quite a number of its active members, were few, and as a result each of them was regarded as a great achievement.

And yet everything had gotten off to a good start. The kickoff of the recruitment campaign—drawing Delagrange into the ranks of the Faisceau—seemed in every way a masterstroke. The conversion of Delagrange, obviously a great success for the movement, was exploited as the theme of a long propaganda campaign. However, to say that the ex-communist was warmly welcomed by all the fascists would be an overstatement. Several wealthy tycoons in the Faisceau did not hide their disapproval of this man in their midst who constantly proclaimed his admiration for the methods of Lenin and seemed determined to apply them immediately in his new party. But this did not prevent Delagrange from getting quickly down to work and, in April 1926, emerging as the winner at the first session of the National Council of the Faisceau. At this meeting the former railway worker, who was said to be a gifted organizer, was given the role of the leader of fascist workers. It was at Delagrange's request that the movement created a committee for the Paris region in which he was responsible for propaganda and recruitment. The sum of a million francs was placed at his disposal.[99]

The aim of the Delagrange operation was clearly to take advantage of the difficulties that the Communist party was going through and the somewhat troubled situation in the SFIO to skim off the cream from the left-wing parties. The maneuver failed, both for objective reasons and because Delagrange himself did not have the necessary qualities. He quickly revealed himself as a man without initiative, who preferred to receive orders rather than to give them. If he attended a few meetings, it was because they had been arranged for him. Valois had presented him as a symbol, and he complacently accepted this role. Previously a permanent communist, he had become a permanent fascist with a salary of two thousand francs a month, rent included. That was at least preferable to returning to manual labor. The same applied to the ex-communist Bardy, who had joined the Faisceau with Delagrange. Bardy's salary was fixed at fifteen hundred francs a month.

These two turncoats worked together with Pierre Dumas, formerly a revolutionary syndicalist and activist of the CGT, a member of the Action Française, and secretary-general of the National Federation of Workers of the Clothing Industry. A close aide of Valois's, Dumas had set up and was in charge of the corporative section of the movement, which constituted the truly original achievement of the Faisceau. It was to the corporations that the Faisceau owed its greatest successes and much of its attractiveness. These corporations aimed to become the nucleus of the future social and economic organization of the country, which was to be opposed to both the liberal economy and the syndicalism of the class struggle.[100]

Other active communists joined the Faisceau, but they did not play an important role,[101] and the same was true of Hubert Lagardelle, who in 1926 joined the local organization in Toulouse. As we learn from the police officer in charge of political affairs in Toulouse, replying to Philippe Lamour, president of the Faisceau's university section and one of the pillars of the organization, "M. Lagardelle declares himself satisfied at having left the socialist party and assures the leaders that he is well disposed to help in working for the triumph of fascist ideas." [102]

As the Faisceau neared its end, the drive to the left became increasingly apparent. There were those who reproached Valois for "ganging up" with former members of the Bonnet Rouge, with Charles Albert and Joseph Caillaux's followers, whom he defended publicly. At that time, Valois was convinced "that there is nothing to be expected from the right, that nothing can be done without the producers." [103] "The Faisceau," he said, "intends to go into battle alone with proletarian nationalists." [104] In September 1926, Valois dwelt insistently on the Sorelian theme of a proletarian elite when urging local activists to make a particular effort to win over the workers.[105]

Yet, despite the tremendous effort made, the breakthrough to the workers never took place and the socio-economic composition of the Faisceau condemned it to having to wait for an economic crisis and inflation. As Valois said, addressing the National Council of the Faisceau, "There is no revolution that does not depend on a monetary and financial crisis." [106] He immediately understood the danger that the coming to power of the Raymond Poincaré government represented for him, and by October he knew that the momentum of his movement had broken.[107] Indeed, as soon as the government of national unity was formed, the local organizations began to become inactive, particularly in eastern France. Every attempt by Valois to oppose the financial policy of the new government met with the hostility of the provincial representatives, who began to hand in their resignations. Even in the Faisceau headquarters, Philippe Barrès, a Parisian to his fingertips yet one who aspired, like his father, to be a man from the eastern provinces of France, became the spokesman of those who condemned any attempt to oppose the "prince from Lorraine" who had finally come to power. Valois knew that his policies lacked coherence, but he also knew that any clear-cut action whatsoever would lead to a collapse. He hoped to be able to hold out long enough to see the left return to power, accompanied by the fall of the franc, inflation, and unemployment.[108]

No longer able to engage in a total opposition and having failed to gain the allegiance of the workers but wanting nevertheless to survive, Valois now tried to transform his movement into a political party—"a great party of order," as he said that November to the cadres of the Faisceau.[109] The Faisceau, to be sure, had never seriously envisaged seizing power by force, but, after all, it was written in its program, which also advocated dictatorship.[110] Of course, all this was postponed to an indefinite future, but the very raison d'être of the movement required faithful adherence to a revolutionary solution. Thus, when Valois decided to proclaim at the annual congress of the Faisceau—a skeletal Faisceau that had already lost three-quarters of its members—that, "in order to gain power, there is only one way: to engage in politics,"[111] he lost the support of his few remaining followers. In vain did he plead that to act in this manner would only be following the example of the Communist party, which also claimed to be revolutionary and antiparliamentary.[112] Those who had most recently come over to fascism had obviously done so precisely because it was not a party like the others and because they had hoped to find there a spirit of activism no longer found either in the Action Française or in the other national *ligues*. Those who declared themselves revolutionaries rebelled at the idea of taking the path of traditional politics.[113] Now the revolutionary principle of the Faisceau, for which its founder had fought so hard and used up so much money from so many financial backers, was invoked and turned against Valois. Thus, unable either to make a revolution or to survive, the Faisceau could only disappear.

With regard to ideology, the Faisceau provides a true prototype of fascism. It does so also with regard to political action, except for one important point: the Faisceau did not seek violence. That is not to say that it was frightened by a scuffle. Its body of officials responsible for order, however, was set up only when it became clear that the attacks and provocations of the Action Française were not about to end.

Their real enemies were the Camelots rather than the communists. The Faisceau really clashed with the extreme left only at the great gathering in Reims on 27 June 1926, when the fascists were confronted with a large communist counterdemonstration of about three to four thousand people. At the end of the two meetings, the columns met one another by the statue of Joan of Arc in the cathedral square. There was a violent confrontation: the police had to charge. Later, there were scuffles all over the town. It was thanks to the large security forces that had been brought in that by the end of the day only twenty people had been wounded.[114]

The gathering in Reims was a triumph, and it represented the climax of the movement. The eight to ten thousand people who took part, organized in delegations, arrived at eight in the morning by special trains. For the first time, there also came members of the Association Nationale des Anciens Combattants (National War Veterans' Association) and of the Jeunesses Patriotes.[115] The gathering in Reims followed one in Verdun, and it was the undeniable success of the gathering in Verdun on 21 February 1926 that persuaded Valois to organize another mass meeting. In the process of organizing these gatherings, Valois developed a new political style in France, involving grandiose settings, sumptuous decors, great ceremonies, "military" parades, and uniforms. Required dress was a blue or dark suit with a blue shirt, collar, and tie, a grey felt hat with a black ribbon, a badge, and a cane. The badge had to be constantly worn in one's buttonhole, while the uniform was worn for meetings and gatherings.

This taste for sumptuous gatherings undoubtedly recalls that of the Italian Fascio. It is only in this domain, however, that one can recognize the influence of the Italian movement on the French movement, for although Valois stayed in Italy in September 1926, and Philippe Lamour and a few other fascists of lesser importance declared themselves "jealous of the vitality, the prosperity of our Latin sister," the Faisceau had hardly any contact with Italian fascism.[116] By January 1928, Valois already accused Italian fascism of betraying its revolutionary origins and "becoming reactionary."[117] All the efforts of the French intelligence services to substantiate the claims made by the left of collusion between the two fascisms proved fruitless. The only indication of collusion that has come down to us is a police minute of 21 November 1925 in which the Duke of Comastra, vice-president of the Paris Fascio, is mentioned as a financial backer of Le Nouveau Siècle. The Intelligence Service apparently did not take this information very seriously. It was felt that there was no real evidence that the Italian government had employed funds to promote the propaganda of the French movement.[118]

The Intelligence Service, however, did not have to wait for the accusations of the left or the Action Française to watch over the activities of the Faisceau. From the start, the least words and actions of its leaders were followed up and reported, and a large quantity of information was gathered. The Faisceau received much attention. Today, all this seems quite incommensurate with the real importance of the Faisceau, but at the time things seemed different. Thus, at the end of November 1925 the Ministry of the Interior expressly asked the military governor of Paris to triple the picket services in the Department of the Seine.[119]

To exploit the success of the two large gatherings and extend the achievements of the Paris section of the movement to the provinces, in the spring and summer of 1926 the Faisceau mounted a large propaganda campaign. Special attention was paid to war veterans (especially officers and noncommissioned officers), to the staff of the war veterans' associations, to mayors and priests, and to family and syndical associations other than the communist-oriented Confédération Générale du Travail Unifiée (CGTU). To reach all these people, an enormous quantity of printed matter was put out in the rue d'Aguesseau. The cost of the operation launched following the gathering in Reims was estimated at a million francs for a relatively short period of three to four weeks. In addition to posters put up all over France, several hundred thousand copies of special issues of Le Nouveau Siècle were printed and the unsold copies distributed to sympathizers. Valois probably took the file of subscribers to L'Action Française with him when he left that organization, and that must have made his task of recruitment very much easier.[120]

In addition to this written propaganda, a considerable effort was made to train competent speakers. By September, ninety representatives trained in the Paris headquarters were ready to start campaigning.[121] The local Bordeaux section of the Faisceau, however, without waiting for this initiative of the leaders in Paris, set up its own school of oratory and a sports club whose obvious aim was to attract members, particularly from among young workers already belonging to the various suburban clubs and gymnastic societies.[122] Bordeaux was an important center for the Faisceau, just as it had been the great provincial center for Boulangism, and one can only wonder how many of the "Blue Shirts" of the twenties ten years later wore the grey shirts of the militia commanded by the mayor of Bordeaux, the neosocialist Adrien Marquet. It cannot be disputed that from the 1880s onward—from the socialist Ferroul, to Valois in the 1920s, up to Marquet, who became the first Vichy minister of the interior—the national-socialist tradition remained very strong in the Bordeaux area.

The campaign of propaganda and recruitment was prepared with enthusiasm, and in the provinces a tremendous effort was made, but even while organizing a third gathering, which this time was to take place in Meaux, they were aware at Faisceau headquarters of the need to develop the doctrinal aspect of the movement. From May onward, Valois had wished to publish, along with *Le Nouveau Siècle*, a weekly journal he intended to place under the editorship of a new deserter from the Action Française, René Johannet. This journal was intended to be to *Le Nouveau Siècle* what *La Revue universelle* was to *L'Action française*: a political, economic, and literary organ of doctrine.[123] By the end of 1926, however, little remained of these plans, for financial difficulties and the coming to power of the Poincaré government put an end to Valois's movement.

The disintegration of the Faisceau began at the end of 1926, at all levels. From the humblest party workers to the financial backers, and including the local and national leaders, the number of defections increased every day. December saw the departure of Jean de Lapérouse, the general delegate André d'Humières, Dr. Thierry de Martel, president of the medical corporation and son of the famous nationalist woman writer Gyp, and, finally, a wealthy jeweller named Brunet, who, some time before, had made considerable sacrifices for the movement. In January it was the turn of Maurice de Barral and Pierre Dumas, vice-president of the corporations. In February, the headquarters also began to disintegrate, the millionaires Franz Van den Broeck d'Obrenan and Serge André were the first to leave. For these people, the movement had had its day; the operation for the saving of the franc had sounded its death knell. During this period, Philippe Lamour was little to be seen, and he was finally expelled from the party in March 1928. In August 1927, the president of the building corporation, Pierre Darras, who had tried to launch a Jaune-type syndicalism,[124] also resigned. By then, the Faisceau had lost almost all its members.[125]

One year later, the remaining fascist faithful, true to the program approved at the great gatherings in Verdun and Reims, founded the Revolutionary Fascist party.[126] Valois himself began a return to the left that finally led him to the Popular Front, to the Resistance, and to his death at the camp at Bergen-Belsen. Apart from Édouard Berth, he is the only example of a returnee: having started at the extreme left with anarchist leanings, spent fifteen years in the Action Française, and created the

Faisceau, on 9 May 1928 he founded the Republican Syndicalist party. Among the principal leaders of the new party, Charles Albert and two former leaders of the Faisceau, Jacques Arthuys and Hubert Bourgin, are particularly worthy of mention. On 15 August, the first number of *Cahiers bleus*, the party organ, appeared. Among its contributors were Pierre Mendès France, Pietro Nenni, Emmanuel Berl, and Édouard Berth, as well as some people who later fell into fascism, Bertrand de Jouvenel, Marcel Déat, and Paul Marion, Doriot's future colleague and the future Vichy minister of information. At that time, their motive for gathering together around Valois was their desire to place themselves above and beyond the "old" parties that they felt no longer suited the real situation, and they therefore advocated "a new economic and social regime that will be essentially syndical." Like the Faisceau, the Syndicalist party attacked the "old state," the "institutions of the past." [127] They claimed that, to save Europe, "the modern world would have to be torn from the hands of the plutocracy." The only power that could give the world "its rational organization," they said, "and create a general prosperity that no capitalist system could provide" was socialism, but a socialism that was something other "than a doctrine that wished its orthodoxy to be respected," [128] a "mixture of science, fantasy and utopia" that ought not to be "revised" but "transcended." [129] Valois supported various efforts in that direction—those of Joseph Paul-Boncour, Charles Spinasse (future minister of economics in the Léon Blum government of 4 June 1936 and the first SFIO deputy to support Pierre Laval's constitutional reforms in Vichy), and Barthélemy Montagnon, one of the founders of neosocialism five years later. Thus, the idea of "transcending" socialism as a concrete political force took shape in French political life of the interwar period, in the wake of the collapse of the first organized fascist movement. The long ideological preparation before the First World War had not been in vain, and at the end of the twenties permitted a general mobilization of all revolutionary forces. The "new teams, very syndicalist in spirit," that represented the radicals' hopes of renewal [130] took part in this movement to pass "beyond" Marxism, and, together with Pierre Dominique's Camille-Desmoulins Club, Charles Albert's *L'Ordre*, and Émile Roche's *La Voix*, Valois praised the *Notre temps* group, which included Jean Luchaire and Bertrand de Jouvenel.

Thus, it was something external to the movement—the rectification of the country's economic situation—that brought about the fall of the Faisceau. It was to the Faisceau's disadvantage that it was active at a time when France was surely, though with difficulty, extracting itself from its financial and economic crisis. It was also to its disadvantage that while it existed, inflation and unemployment and fear of a communist revolution—the other element in the polarization that usually favored the burgeoning of fascist parties in Europe—never found a suitable climate in France. All the French fascist movements that followed the Faisceau encountered a similar situation.

But this was only one of the factors that worked to shorten the life of the Faisceau. Internal tensions, tactical indecision, the combined attacks of all the right-wing movements, and Valois's personality all played their part. The founder of the movement lacked the qualities of leadership necessary to the success of such an enterprise. The least that can be said is that he never succeeded in uniting under his leadership other groups with an authoritarian ideology and a similar membership. And—a last cause of failure—Valois thought he could succeed in an undertaking in which General Boulanger and his radical associates had failed, namely, getting the conservatives to finance a political movement with a revolutionary ideology but nonproletarian adherents. The makeup of French society did not allow this, just as it did not allow it later: the conservative right was—as it proved on both occasions—sufficiently strong to ensure its own security.

In this respect, the Faisceau illustrates a standard pattern found throughout Europe: fascism achieved its most striking successes whenever the traditional right was too weak to protect its own position. In that event, at times of acute crisis it placed itself in the hands of the new revolutionary movement, which it believed was the only force that could bar the way to communism, although at the same time it had only limited confidence in it. On the other hand, whenever it felt itself to be strong, or when, as in France, its position was assured and its social power base solid, it did everything possible to ensure that fascist tendencies were not taken too far. In such cases, the traditional right saw to the recruitment of its own troops and used its money for its own undertakings. It was not the power of the conservatives but, on the contrary, their weakness, their fears, and their readiness to panic that proved to be the essential precondition for the success of fascism. This situation, however, did not exist in France. Both with regard to voting power and sociologically, the conservative right was a force that fascism never succeeded in undermining. The crisis of the twenties thus proved to be soluble within the framework of the existing system: the right as a whole was so solidly based that there was no need to resort to extraparliamentary solutions.

CHAPTER FOUR

The Idealist Revision of Marxism: The Ethical Socialism of Henri De Man

The Negation of Marxism

From the beginning of this century, revisionism was an important factor in the rise of fascism, though historians have generally failed to recognize the importance of this factor. Indeed, one could hardly give a satisfactory explanation of the fascist phenomenon without reference to the stages of development of the crisis of socialism. From the Dreyfus affair until the time of Munich, the growth of the fascist ideology was the chief manifestation of the tremendous difficulty that socialism experienced in responding to the challenge of capitalism. One kind of revisionism—that of Bernstein and Jaurès—led to social democracy, while another kind—that of Sorel, Déat, and De Man—led to fascism. Both shared a desire to go "beyond" Marxism and both were agreed in regarding Marxism as an incomparable tool of historical analysis—an ideal conceptual framework for the arrangement of history—but not, unless radically altered, a real agent of political change.

In the interwar period, the revision of Marxism was associated in French cultural circles with the name of Henri De Man. The attack on Marxism found in the work of this Belgian writer was a reflection of the idealist revolt of the first decades of this century. In this respect, De Man's thought was a continuation and development of that of Georges Sorel. It deeply influenced Marcel Déat, who began to apply De Man's ideas in the sphere of French politics. At the other end of the political spectrum, the neo-idealist rebellion of Thierry Maulnier continued the tradition of Maurice Barrès, and these two streams of neo-idealism fused in a synthesis that, at the end of this second prewar period, assumed the form of fascism.

At the beginning of the thirties, De Man was regarded as one of the foremost theoreticians of European socialism. A true cosmopolitan who expressed himself with equal ease in Dutch, French, German, and English, this prolific writer wrote in whichever language seemed to him most appropriate to the subject and circumstances. He was one of the very few people in European politics—perhaps the only one—who had lived for a long time in foreign countries, including the United States, and was able to pass from one cultural environment to another and feel perfectly at home everywhere.

Born in Antwerp in 1885, this son of a great Flemish bourgeois family joined the socialist Jeune Garde on 1 May 1902. At that time, he was closer to Karl Liebknecht than to Jaurès, and unfavorably disposed toward Millerand. The young De Man threw himself body and soul into socialist activities. His studies were badly affected as a result, and his family was only too pleased to see him leave in 1905 for the University of Leipzig.

The following years were all-important for De Man's intellectual development. While pursuing his studies in Leipzig with distinction, he participated in the ideological ferment that the long struggle against revisionism had given rise to in the German social-democratic movement. After spending some time in England, where he gained a certain respect for bourgeois democracy, he accepted the invitation of Émile Vandervelde, the rising figure in Belgian socialism, to become the director of the new Workers' Educational Center. In August 1914, he took part as an interpreter and enthusiastic supporter in the mission of Hermann Müller and Camille Huysmans in Paris, sponsored by the Socialist International, to attempt—at the last minute—to prevent the war. Three years later, however, artillery lieutenant De Man, fresh from the trenches, went on another mission—to Russia, where, together with Vandervelde and Louis de Brouckère, he attempted to persuade the Kerensky government to continue fighting. Immediately afterward, he was sent by the Belgian government to the United States. These two experiences played an important role in his ideological evolution.

In the years before the war, De Man contributed to the formation of the Marxist left in Belgium as the leader of the Walloon (French-speaking) section. Here he came into contact only with Marxist orthodoxy in its strictest form, as represented by Kautsky. However, it should be pointed out as significant for his later development that, before becoming a "scientific" socialist, De Man passed through a phase of ethical socialism,[1] and later, during his stay in England, he published a series of articles in the celebrated German socialist journal the *Leipziger Volkszeitung* that Karl Radek described as already constituting the beginning of a heresy.[2]

There is no doubt that the first cracks in De Man's orthodoxy appeared before the war. The readjustments and modifications of position that were already noticeable around 1910 were the beginning of a prolonged process of change that lasted until 1926, when *Zur Psychologie des Sozialismus* was published. Already in the prewar period, De Man had questions about the schematic nature of the Marxist interpretation of social and cultural phenomena.[3] During the war and after, he became interested in psychology and acquainted himself with the new tendencies in psychoanalysis, and, as he himself said, well before the end of the war he had come to the general conclusion that the motives that underlie human nature, derived from instinct and only slightly modified by habit and education, are much broader than is allowed for by Marxist theory.[4] Thus, when he came to publish his comprehensive criticism of Marxism in 1926, he made his starting point the problem of motivation.

The war had a profound effect on De Man. As he wrote in his "fragment of spiritual autobiography," as he called it, the war had superimposed itself on "an intellectual crisis that lasted for about twenty years." Already before the war, he said, "the sharpest bones of my orthodoxy began to lose their edge."[5] His experience was similar to Sorel's. Like Sorel, he claimed to have moved toward revisionism under the influence of his practical contacts with the labor movement and especially the syndical movement.[6] "The developments of the last ten years have only brought to its culmination a crisis that has been in the making for a long time," he said.[7]

While the importance of the war as a factor in bringing about these changes ought not to be minimized, it should be pointed out that, on the one hand, post-1918 Marxism betrayed symptoms of crisis that are not to be explained solely by the difficulty of adapting to new conditions and that, on the other hand, if the war accelerated the process of the revision of Marxism, its influence was crucial only for people who already tended to nonconformity, such as Lagardelle, Hervé, and De Man.

It was the prewar "leftists," the people who throughout their careers remained on the fringes of the movement and the organized socialist parties, or born opposers like De Man, whose ideas were most affected by the war, just as later it was the nonconformists of socialism, communism, and the other left-wing factions who had the greatest difficulty coping with the intellectual crisis of socialism. Those who resisted best, on the other hand, were the most orthodox elements, the absolute die-hards, because they had no willingness to venture. However, in the case of De Man, it was not only the war that made him question Marxism but also the German experience of the twenties: he felt that Marxism, far from arresting the decline of the social-democratic movement, actually encouraged it with its materialism.[8]

Throughout the first thirty years of this century, the German Social-Democratic party played a crucial role in the history of European socialism. Its collapse and the breakdown of the Socialist International shed a new light on the Marxist phenomenon. This distressing experience widened still further the cracks of nonconformity that, even before 1914, had appeared on the polished surface of orthodoxy. De Man's theoretical writings thus reflect a revision of the philosophical principles of Marxism that went far beyond the experience of the war: the very essence of the system was questioned and not merely a given set of circumstances. Immediately after the war, De Man took the trouble to note down his reactions as he experienced them, producing a book of great interest, although one should always be conscious of his state of mind when he wrote it. He wrote the book in English, calling it *The Remaking of a Mind*. A more concise version appeared in French under the title *La Leçon de la guerre*.[9]

This book tells us that from that "tragic test" of an "ordeal by fire," the First World War, De Man learned one all-important lesson: the proletariat is not a revolutionary force and socialism is not an idea that can change the world, for it is not one of those truths for which people are willing to die. On the other hand, it must be recognized that millions of human beings unflinchingly risked and sacrificed their lives not only for the sake of the nation but also for other ideas of lesser importance. For De Man, one essential fact overshadowed all the others: the laboring masses in England, America, and France had consented to make far greater sacrifices for ideals such as the autonomy and inviolability of nations, justice in relations between states, and the self-government of peoples than they had previously made when material class interests had been at stake. From this he drew two major conclusions: that economic circumstances alone are not enough to explain every historical development, and that socialism cannot be realized outside the framework of political democracy. He wrote, "I no longer believe that to achieve socialism it is enough for us to appeal to the class interests of the industrial proletariat while ignoring the contribution we can receive from certain interests and certain ideas that are shared by the entire nation and the whole of humanity. I no longer believe that the struggle of the proletarian parties that remains the chief means of realizing socialism can be successful without certain forms of collaboration between classes and parties." [10]

Similarly, De Man declared that he was now convinced that socialism could not take the form of a simple appropriation of all the major means of production by the state without a profound change in the methods of management and without the stimulus for the whole economy represented by competition between independent enterprises and full remuneration for work. He said, "I believe in a socialism that is nearer at hand, more certain, more realistic, more pragmatic, more synthetic—in a word, more human." [11]

Well aware of the true significance of his criticisms, he concluded, "So that there should be no doubt about my apostasy, I shall call it: the revision of Marxism." [12]

This revision of Marxism comprised, on the one hand, a total support of liberal democracy, regarded as a *sine qua non* for the emancipation of the working classes, and, on the other, a repudiation of Marxism in the purest style of late-nineteenth-century national socialism. Marxism, he said, had been too strongly "imprinted with the socialism of Germany and Russia" [13]—two countries where the lack of democratic institutions had deeply affected the workers' mentality. As for bourgeois democracy, its present decadent condition, in which it gradually abandoned the traditions connected with its revolutionary origins as its fear of a labor revolution increased, should not lead, thought De Man, to a condemnation of the principles on which it was founded. [14]

Thus, De Man's socialism had now become inseparable from the idea of liberal democracy. In fact, it was already a new socialism, closely connected not only with the liberal ideology (De Man spoke enthusiastically about the "immortal principles of 1789") [15] but also with the existing social and political order. To the socialism of rebellion had succeeded a socialism of acceptance: the legitimacy of the bourgeois order was no longer seriously contested. The impression gained by the reader of *La Leçon de la guerre* is that the new socialism simply wished to take over the bourgeois order, improving it, modernizing it, and adapting it to the requirements of the period, but without any genuine revolutionary intention.

This retreat from Marxist orthodoxy took place in two stages. At first, in the name of liberty, revolutionary socialism withdrew to the most moderate positions of social democracy, and then, when Marxism was well and truly dead and buried, the old liberal principles were abandoned in favor of a strong state with a directed economy. The idea that private property and the profit motive were the generators of economic activity was retained, but everything was now placed under the control of an authoritarian government. This was the substance of the Pontigny proposals that accompanied the Labor Plan (Plan du Travail) in 1934; it was also the meaning of neosocialism.

The revisionism of the interwar period meant the end of the socialist utopia, or—to use the celebrated Sorelian expression—the end of the revolutionary myth. This was precisely the issue that, throughout the thirties, so deeply divided the socialists from the neosocialists, the orthodox from the revisionists. Claiming adherence to the facts—above all the fact of national existence—the new factions, readopting the positions of the national socialists of the 1880s, relinquished forever the dream of a proletarian revolution.

Did anything at all remain of Marxism? The element that, according to De Man, still gave Marxism some value was its usefulness as a method of scientific analysis. Its value, like that of any other instrument, depended on the way it was used. The method itself, said De Man, was "far from having become unusable," although if it was to retain its validity, it would have to be continually revised in the light of new circumstances.[16] This recognition of the necessity of adjusting the Marxist formulas to suit new conditions led, however, to the realization that changes would have to be introduced that would be as far-reaching as those that, for instance, the natural sciences had effected in the theories of Darwin. What remained of Marx was first, the idea, of lasting merit, of an evolution subject to scientific laws, and then, and most important, the method of using economic facts to explain the great forces of historical progress.[17]

Having stated this, De Man claimed that, after the First World War, his conception of Marxism developed in "a more liberal and realistic direction."[18] It was henceforth closely connected with parliamentary democracy, which he regarded as a necessary condition of socialism. Like Déat, De Man saw himself as belonging to the tradition of socialists such as Jaurès who never separated the cause of political liberty from that of economic emancipation and who sought for the proletariat the heritage of the great "bourgeois" revolutions.[19]

Such were the reflections that the end of the First World War suggested to De Man. In the fall of 1920, after a second stay in the United

States, he became principal of the École Ouvrière Supérieure (Workers' School of Higher Education), remaining in that post for less than two years. The leaders of the party were only too pleased to see the departure of this man who, known both for his personal worth and for his doctrinal nonconformity, could prove to be a dangerous rival.

De Man was constantly at odds with the leadership of his party over his disagreement with their belief that Belgian socialism should fall into line with Poincaré's *revanchisme* (a policy of "getting even" with Germany). In 1922 he once again left Belgium and went to live in Germany, where he remained for ten years. From 1922 to 1926 he taught at the Labor Academy at Frankfurt am Main. There he wrote his most famous work, *Zur Psychologie des Sozialismus*, known in French as *Au-delà du marxisme*. Translated into thirteen languages, this book was enormously successful, and made De Man the most talked-about and controversial political writer of the decade.[20]

The book had one fundamental objective: it envisaged quite simply "the liquidation of Marxism."[21] De Man demonstrated his "opposition to the fundamental principles of Marxist doctrine" by choosing, for the title of his book, "the formula *beyond Marxism*" rather than any of those "more lukewarm expressions, such as *revision, adaptation, reinterpretation*, etc., that attempt to run with the hare and hunt with the hounds."[22] At the same time, to forestall the criticisms of those who might hope to weaken the impact of his arguments by turning the discussion of fundamental issues into a criticism of classic Marxist texts, he declared himself uninterested in discovering Marx's original intentions, and he hardly cared what any given statement of Marx's had meant at any particular moment. What mattered now, he said, was not an evaluation of the "dead Marx" but of "living socialism." De Man made no attempt to avoid difficulties, and he was careful to make his intentions plain. What he had intended in this book, he said, was to make a comprehensive criticism not of Marx's doctrine[23] but of the whole collection of value judgments, affective symbols, collective wishes, principles, programs, and forms of action that constituted Marxism and still existed in the labor movement.[24] Since Marx, he said, had created his doctrine solely as a basis for action, any part of his thought that had not survived in Marxism could presumably be overlooked.[25] However, he continued, "in order to say *after* Marx, I must first say *against* Marx," and, in order to overcome the error that Marxism had turned into, "one should not go back to it; it is enough to go beyond it."[26] Finally, he said that this whole development would eventually lead to a "new synthesis."[27]

Au-delà du marxisme was, as De Man himself maintained, a "settling of accounts" with his Marxist past.[28] It was followed by a work that complemented his criticism of Marxism: *Le Socialisme constructif*, a collection of texts introduced by the report that De Man presented to the Conference of Heppenheim in 1928.[29] This conference, which was attended by many of the leading intellectuals of the day, including Paul Tillich, Eduard Heimann, Adolf Löwe, and Martin Buber, attempted to define the principles of a socialism characterized "by a deeper concern for spiritual values."[30] De Man summed up their conclusions in a series of propositions that have come to be known as the propositions of Heppenheim.

The book that De Man considered his best, however—and one whose importance in the history of ideas is at least equal to that of *Au-delà du marxisme*—was his last work, *L'Idée socialiste*, a positive exposition of his revision of Marxism. In many respects, this was his major work, the one in which he attempted to resolve the problems raised in *Au-delà du marxisme*. "It was an attempt," he said, "to situate socialism within the evolution not only of the economy and of institutions but of the ideas that make and unmake civilizations."[31]

This was a tremendously ambitious scheme, expressing a desire to find the very core of the socialist idea and to situate it in a vast philo- sophical, psychological, and historical canvas. *Au-delà du marxisme*, comprehensive criticism of Marxism though it was, did no more than state the problem—establishing, in particular, that beyond all consid- erations of class interests, movements, and institutions is some other ele- ment more deeply rooted in human nature, an element connected with our instinctive and emotional life before it ever reaches the state of con- sciousness. *L'Idée socialiste* was an answer to the question raised in the last chapter of *Au-delà du marxisme*: If socialism is a belief based on certain value judgments, from where do these value judgments proceed, what do they consist of, and to what do they conduce?[32]

If in spirit and intention *L'Idée socialiste* was quite similar to *Au-delà du marxisme*, in style and context it was vastly different. De Man's last book was written in the shadow of the rise of nazism, and the preface to the original edition was dated January 1933. The book was published by Diederichs, in Jena, at the time of the final collapse of the German left. As the Nazi movement had made anti-Marxism its rallying cry, De Man saw fit to answer with a challenge: "If anyone forces me to choose between Marxist and non-Marxist labels, giving the word 'Marxist' the sense that the opponents of the socialist labor movement give the term, he will receive from me an unequivocal answer: unhesitatingly, I take the side of the most decided Marxists." [33]

On 10 May 1933, this book was burned in front of the city hall of Frankfurt. By the summer of 1940, however, after ten more years of going "beyond" Marxism, such a reaction on De Man's part had become unthinkable. De Man now enthusiastically welcomed the conquest of Europe by Nazi Germany.

The Revisionist Philosophy

De Man's critique of Marxism did not question the importance of Marx in the development of the social sciences: without Marx's influence, he said, they would be half a century behind.[34] Nor, he said, should one deny the importance of Marx's contribution to the analysis of the capitalist system. However, De Man felt that if one wanted to move forward, one would have to accept the principle that the rule of the "relativity" of ideologies applies even to Marxism. One must therefore "go beyond Marxism," [35] and, to liberate oneself from it, one has to free oneself not only from Marxist conclusions but also from the Marxist way of thinking.[36] Accordingly, he attacked the very basis of the system: "economic determinism and scientific rationalism." [37]

Moreover, De Man believed that a truth is always bound up with its particular period, and that, like any other system of ideas, Marxism was conditioned by the circumstances of the period that gave rise to it. As those circumstances had radically altered, the conviction that Marxism had ceased to be true became part of the truth of our period.[38]

The starting point of De Man's critique of Marx was what he called Marx's "theory of motive forces," which "made the social action of the masses spring from a recognition of their interests." [39] All Marx's economic ideas and political and tactical opinions, said De Man, were based on the assumption that human actions are guided above all by economic interests. This "recognition of economic interests as the foundation of social activity" [40] underlay what De Man regarded as Marxism's most important and original achievement: "the creation of a doctrine that combines in one unique conception the idea of socialism and the idea of class struggle." [41] Thus, Marx assailed the legal and moral foundations of the present forms of society, using as his starting point the "motive forces of interest and power conditioned in industrial workers by the capitalist milieu." [42] Thus, the founder of scientific socialism could claim to have discovered a new justification for socialism, based, unlike utopianism, on the objective observation of reality.[43] Finally, claimed De Man, the economic hedonism that underlies the Marxist conception of class, of class interests, and of class struggle and the determinism that disregards the psychological process whereby economic necessities are transformed into human goals[44] give Marxism its "nonethical" character.[45]

But that, thought De Man, is precisely where the weakness of the system lies. For Marx, the very idea of socialism is brought into existence by class struggle, or, that is to say, by a necessary consequence of capitalism; it does not therefore represent a value judgment. Socialism, according to Marx, will come about not because it is just but because it is inevitable: it will result from the necessary victory of the proletariat in its class struggle.[46] Thus, one no longer needs any moral arguments to justify socialism; it is enough to recognize causes and effects. And the great question that then arises, said De Man, is whether socialism, basing itself on Marx's causal theory, is able to become what it seeks and ought to become. De Man gave a clear answer: socialism can only be the product of moral decisions that rest on foundations anterior to any historical experience.[47]

While rejecting Marxism on account of its "mechanistic," "automatic" character, De Man nevertheless recognized that "ethical judgment existed in Marx, and that he merely, so to speak, concealed it."[48] De Man claimed that Marx took great care to dissimulate his ethical intentions, for had he revealed them he would have undermined the scientific character of his system. Thus, one can find traces of his ethical convictions only in his writings dealing with the political events and problems of the day, where the expression of his feelings was essentially a concession on Marx's part to what he regarded as the immaturity of his fellow cofounders of the First International and to the presumed immaturity of many non-Marxist forms of European socialism. However, in the scientific works, where he exponded his doctrine without any thought of their immediate political effect, "his value judgments have to be looked for almost by psychoanalysis."[49]

If Marx's work has this character, said De Man, it was because Marx "borrowed from his master Hegel a belief in 'the cunning of reason.'"[50] Through its attempt to satisfy needs created by the capitalist environment, through its struggle for class interests, through its struggle for surplus value with the purchasers of the labor capacity of the industrial worker, the proletariat became subject to an inevitable process, created by the rise of capitalism and fostered by the development of the forces of production. If there was any room for choice, it was only that of recognizing the inevitability of that evolution, but—and here is where, according to De Man, the "cunning of reason" comes in—this same principle of inevitability, operating according to iron laws, directs historical progress toward a goal worthy of being pursued in itself: the abolition of classes and an end of exploitation and oppression. This, then, is how "the cunning of reason" operates: by means of material interests, power struggles, and conflicts of interest, the ideal comes to pass through a perfectly natural process.[51]

Such, said De Man, was Marx's general intention. The father of scientific socialism had a moral end in view, and his doctrine was a brilliant attempt to utilize to that end the efforts that capitalism had directed toward a material goal. In the heroic period of socialism, said De Man, this was a fruitful and reasonable approach, quite simply because "the motives of the combatants *were* in fact moral. Only fervent supporters of an eschatological ideal of justice then had the spirit of sacrifice necessary for the slightest struggle for the most immediate material goals."[52] That was why a spiritual end could be embodied in a material means: for the socialist who fought on the barricades, who schemed, or who made sacrifices or risked martyrdom simply by participating in the struggle for political power, the ends and means were the same. It was then both possible and logical to present socialism in the simple guise of a struggle for class interests while being fully aware that this was only a historical expedient.

Marxism, however, which "had counted on the cunning of reason, itself became victim of the ruse of interest."[53] De Man claimed that the socialist movement, having grown into a mass movement directed by a class of professionals and fragmented into national parties each defending the interests of its own members, now entered a phase in which the means increasingly became ends in themselves. He said that a spirit of opportunism threatened to transform the socialist conquest of the institutions of bourgeois society into a conquest of socialism by those institutions. This situation Marx could not have foreseen, just as he could not have foreseen the *embourgeoisement* of the proletariat. He could not have foreseen that, once it had reached maturity, Marxism would give way to "opportunistic reformism and an adoption of bourgeois culture,"[54] any more than he could have known that his deterministic philosophy would serve the interests of a "bureaucratic conservatism" and above all justify the resistance of the professional politicians to all tendencies of renewal within the movement.[55] In the same way, said De

Man, the theory of surplus value shows how futile it is to attempt to understand social realities through purely economic reasoning.[56]

The conclusion, then, is obvious: the modern world does not need a patched-up, reformed version of socialism, but a totally new socialism, one that can "emancipate us from this dependence of man on his technical and economic means of existence,"[57] that "abandons the fundamental Marxist position of determining all ideologies by the class to which one belongs,"[58] that ceases to be preoccupied with causes in order to concern itself with value judgments.[59] This new socialism could take the form of a "conciliation between Marxism and ethical socialism."[60] "Whatever is still vital of Marxist anticapitalism"[61] should be preserved, though it should not be forgotten that socialism is much more than anticapitalism,[62] for in all socialism there is "an impulsion—a striving toward an equitable social order—that is eternal"[63] and that belongs to the socialist way of thinking, just as it does to the spiritual origins of the bourgeoisie. De Man said that this impulsion could not be better described than by the term *humanism*.[64]

Accordingly, De Man defined socialism as "a manifestation, which varies according to period, of an eternal aspiration toward a social order in conformity with our moral sense."[65] De Man often returned to this definition, each time adding something new. Socialism, he said elsewhere, "is always justified by moral norms that claim universal validity. . . . All socialism is a morality applied to social phenomena, in which the moral principles are more or less deliberately borrowed from the beliefs of the civilization of the period."[66] Or, again, socialism is "the subordination of egoistical motives to altruistic motives."[67] And finally: "At the origin of every socialist concept is a moral judgment born of faith."[68] Thus, socialism is really a "way of feeling and thinking as ancient and as widespread as political thought itself."[69]

This was how the idealist revolt in European socialism expressed itself in the interwar period, with a socialism totally liberated from Marxism came into being. Regarded as totally independent of its historical context, of economic forces and social structures, and consequently of capitalism, socialism appeared as "a deep, powerful and eternal current"[70] whose history "began at least with Plato, the Essenes and the first Christian communities."[71] This history continued with the popular communistic movements of the Middle Ages and the Reformation and, passing through the utopias of the Renaissance and the eighteenth and nineteenth centuries, extended to the mass movements of the twentieth century.[72]

It should be pointed out that the idea of ethical socialism, of an "eternal" socialism, was widespread in the period 1920–35. De Man could not ignore Spengler, and it was the German historian who, just after the Great War, declared, "We are all socialists whether or not we know or desire it. Even the resistance to socialism takes a socialist form." [73] Spengler was speaking precisely of "ethical socialism," or, in other words, "the maximum generally accessible of a sentiment of life seen under the aspect of finality." [74] Elaborating his thought, he added, "Ethical socialism is not, despite its immediate illusions, a system of compassion and humanity, peace and solicitude, but of will and power." [75] This socialism, which, developed by Fichte, Hegel, and Wilhelm von Humboldt, "had its time of passionate grandeur around the middle of the nineteenth century," came to its end in the twentieth, when an "interest in current economic questions" was substituted for "an ethical philosophy." [76] De Man took the same line, and concluded that Marxism was responsible for that situation. Thus, his struggle for an ethical socialism in the name of an eternal socialism was not only a fight against Marxism but also an attempt to replace Marxism with another form of socialism. It was for the sake of an ethical socialism that De Man began the drift to the right that brought him, a few years later, to hail the Nazi conquests, which he saw as the greatest victory ever won over materialism.

Another exponent of an "eternal" socialism was the Italian syndicalist Arturo Labriola. It was in his journal *Avanguardia socialista* that in the first years of the century the violent opposition to the reformism of Turati took shape, preceding by a generation De Man's struggle against Vandervelde and Déat's attack on Léon Blum's old SFIO. Twenty years later, after passing, like De Man and Déat, through a phase of militant nationalism during the Great War and before returning to Italy as a display of solidarity with his country during its conquest of Abyssinia, Labriola, then in exile in Paris, acknowledged the special character of Italian revolutionary syndicalism: "We would consider socialism rather as an instrument for the transformation of the country than as an end in itself," he wrote, adding that "our point of view was strictly Italian, perhaps even a little nationalistic." [77]

In 1932, Labriola wrote a book with the revealing title "Beyond Capitalism and Socialism." In it, he too preached the doctrine of an eternal socialism: "All the societies that history has known have been the theater of manifestations of socialism," he said.[78] From the ancient world to Thomas More and Tommaso Campanella and modern socialism, said Labriola, we find "in the development of socialist thought a continuity that we have no right to deny."[79] Thus, "socialism is old": it is "old as a doctrine; it is old, terribly old as a movement; it is old in its aspirations."[80] Moreover, he claimed that "it is by no means established that there is a relationship between capitalism and socialism," and one must therefore conclude that "if socialism in its ideals, its movement and its politics is not a product of the capitalist phenomenon, the whole problem of the significance of socialism has to be reconsidered."[81]

There was thus a whole current of socialism in the thirties that envisaged a socialism without Marx, a socialism without capitalism, a socialism independent of every class consideration, a socialism that was simply an aspiration toward "a just society, a fraternal society."[82]

For De Man, then the most important representative of that school, the value of Marxism lay far more in its contribution to our understanding of capitalism than in what it actually brought to socialism,[83] for socialism is not, "properly speaking, a product of capitalism" but a "human disposition" characterized by "a certain determination of the meaning of judicial and moral values" that can be understood only by going back to the social experience of the feudal regime and the master craftsmen, to the morality of Christianity and the principles of democracy.[84] It involves not merely the question of salaries or the distribution of surplus value but a vast number of factors that create a "social inferiority complex" and pose a cultural problem.[85] The essential motivation of the labor movement, wrote De Man, "is the instinct of self-esteem." It is "a question of dignity at least as much as a question of interest."[86] In De Man's view, the determining factor is not the fact of selling one's market value but the social circumstances in which that sale takes place—the lack of cleanliness and social protection, the instability of the way of life, the insecurity and joylessness of the work, the dependence on employers.[87]

In other words, if living and economic conditions and social relationships can be established that assure the proletariat and other workers cleanliness, stability, security of employment, and dignity, socialism as understood by the Socialist International ceases to have any raison d'être, especially as De Man defined socialism "as the product of a personal will, inspired by a feeling for rightness and probity."[88] Socialism, he said, "existed before the labor movement, and even before the working class,"[89] and was not born "out of a victorious class struggle."[90] Socialist thought, like any other kind of thought, originated in an almost infinite variety of different intellectual, ethical, and aesthetic emotional reactions: "Ideas are created by people and are not the result of a parallelogram of social forces," said De Man.[91] As his thought matured, it developed in a direction commonly taken since the end of the nineteenth century: toward a conception of socialism that involves no change in social and economic relationships and aims not at revolution but at a "fraternal society," a social order based on the "altruistic instincts" of the "real man."[92]

Indeed, the idea that "the concept of exploitation is ethical and not economic"[93] played a major role in the development of the fascist philosophy both before and after the First World War. It underlay the negation of the "mechanistic and materialistic conceptions that have been an obstacle . . . to the ethical development" of the proletariat "and its sense of solidarity."[94] De Man considered a doctrine that bases workers' solidarity on class interests historically and psychologically indefensible and even practically harmful.[95] Class interests, he believed, "do not create ethical motives,"[96] and socialism cannot combat bourgeois egoism with labor materialism and hedonism.[97]

For, in the final analysis, socialism for De Man "is a faith. It is a passion,"[98] and not a science. ("Scientific socialism is as absurd as scientific love.")[99] Social science cannot predict the future, since it "*has no need* to know it except insofar as concerns present activities."[100] For that reason—and here one seems to be reading a text by Sorel—"it is enough that socialism should believe in its future."[101] One encounters here the kind of reasoning found in *Reflections on Violence*: socialism, thought De Man, cannot be a mere collection of abstract ideas or a mere logical deduction from the present state of the economy. Such a deduction, he said, "would give it no *image*," whereas it is precisely the capacity to provide an image that makes a socialist vision of the future conceivable.[102] De Man was well aware that he was invoking the Sorelian notion of a myth.[103] Just as the idea of a general strike was only a myth that symbolized the collapse of the capitalist order, so, he maintained, the basic notions of so-called "scientific" socialism—social revolution, the dictatorship of the proletariat—were mere myths, symbols of belief,[104] which constituted, precisely, the very foundation of politics: the "masses' need to believe."[105]

Sorel's revision of Marxism thus contained the seeds of the revision undertaken a generation later by De Man. If one reads it carefully, one finds that chapter 4 of *Reflections on Violence*, the central chapter of the work, anticipates several ideas expressed by the Belgian writer.

Openly declaring his intentions, Sorel, indeed, was the first to attempt a genuine revision of Marxism that touched the foundations of the system. De Man's position was in fact very close to that of Sorel and his school with regard to both theory and political action. Indeed, the French and Italian revolutionary syndicalists had traced exactly the same path that De Man was to follow. All the objects of De Man's criticism—determinism, opportunism, reformism, bureaucratization, bourgeois values, utopian verbalism, the disregard for humanistic values [106]— had already been attacked by the rebels of the turn of the century. Their criticism, too, was a functional criticism arrived at as a result of their own engagement in socialism, and they also concluded that the doctrine itself was responsible for these errors. Sorel, Michels, Lagardelle, and Labriola, before De Man, had associated the decadence of left-wing political movements with their doctrines.

Both Sorel and De Man, each in his own time and place, rebelled against the grotesque form of Guesdism and Kautskyism that forced Marxism into a mechanistic and narrowly economic straitjacket that at the same time concealed an opportunistic practical policy. Both objected to the transformation of socialism into a bureaucratic social-democratic movement, devoid of soul and grandeur: there was nothing they disliked more than politics as practiced by politicians—the politics of parties, of professionals, of electoral contests and parliamentary debates. However, if Sorel always succeeded in keeping his distance from anything that remotely savored of politics, De Man finally, at the age of fifty, accepted a ministerial post, though he never sought a parliamentary mandate. The struggle of these two men against a petrified Marxism, frozen into antiquated formulas, was only one aspect of their search for a new socialism that remained the great goal of their endeavors.

Thus, the true connecting link between the thought of Sorel and that of De Man was that form of revisionism that aimed at divesting Marxism of its materialism, determinism, and hedonism and replacing these with various forms of voluntarism and vitalism. Sorel was the first to seek to correct Marxism, placing at the heart of a system conceived as fundamentally mechanistic and rationalistic a voluntarist vision of the world and a new explanation of human nature. Sorel claimed that the deep forces guiding humanity were those of the unconscious, and that mankind moved forward in the light of myths and images.[107] In his *Reflections on Violence*, Sorel had been influenced by the psychology of Gustave Le Bon, and De Man, similarly, based his ideas on the authority of Freud. "The root of all our action is our instincts," he wrote,[108] repeating a formula that Barrès had coined a generation earlier. De Man was here echoing the words of the thinkers of the beginning of the century. "There is an emotional and affective current involved in the principle of the formation of an idea," he said again.[109] Further on, one seems to hear the voice of Vacher de Lapouge, the social Darwinist who had also been a socialist: "The moral consciousness," De Man wrote, "is an impulse of the subconscious. It is derived from a feeling of solidarity with the species that is as deeply rooted in our physical organization as the gregarious or maternal instinct in animals."[110]

De Man, however, included in his analysis another idea, unknown to the generation of 1890, namely, that the same experimental sciences that prove the dependence of our spiritual life and the processes of the conscience on the instincts demonstrate that the most powerful forces in man are his moral feelings. Thus, in the human subconscious is an irrepressible need for consideration and self-respect.[111] De Man could therefore claim that the findings of psychology allow us to conclude that socialism has a truly scientific foundation. Psychology thus corrects, complements, and sometimes, by divesting it of its material content, even replaces Marxism. In psychology, De Man finally found a discipline that he could successfully oppose to historical materialism.

Psychology, said De Man, provides an entirely new conception of man; it creates a veritable cultural and ideological revolution. The importance of Freud, he said, is comparable only to that of Marx, and the point of contact between the new psychology and socialism can be seen in the fact "that this psychology, with its individualization of man, has at the same time overcome his materialization."[112] From Freud De Man took the idea of the complex; from Adler he took two ideas, that of the importance of human society for the creation of the values that man requires, and that of the significance of the sense of inferiority.[113] As he wrote, "The chronic discontent of the working class . . . is only one particular aspect of a vast number of causes that bring about a social inferiority complex. . . . If one states the problem in this way, one realizes that the essential motivation of the labor movement is the sense of self-respect; or, to put the matter less prosaically, it is a question of dignity at least as much as a question of interest."[114]

Looking back some ten years later, De Man declared that in psychology he had discovered a discipline "that made the conscious ideal spring from the subconscious motive force, the doctrine from the will, the aim from movement, and the idea from suffering."[115] Even if, as has been argued, De Man's use of social psychology is ethically inspired,[116] even if it is his moral aspirations that lead him to make such an analysis and reach such conclusions, it must nevertheless be acknowledged that this development contributed greatly to the crystallization of the fascist ideology. A glorification of the "doctrine of the will" and the cult of "movement" was at the heart of the meaning of the intellectual revolution represented by fascism.

Already in *Au-delà du marxisme* De Man was well aware that the approach "that seeks behind the motives of economic interest the deeper psychological causes that inspire them . . . saps at the root . . . not only the Marxist interpretation of the labor movement but also the Marxist interpretation of political economy."[117] This is the heart of the problem: to Marxism, that "child of the nineteenth century" with its principle of "mechanical causality," De Man opposed "syndicalist voluntarism";[118] to a system characterized by "determinism, mechanism, historicism and economic hedonism" he opposed a "socialist science" that is "pragmatic, voluntaristic, pluralistic and institutionalistic."[119] As De Man pointed out, this conception went back to Proudhon, and he claimed that it was far more proletarian in its idea of revolution than was Marxism. For Marxism, said De Man, class struggle was in the final analysis only the realization of an idea conceived by intellectuals and imposed *a priori*, whereas "for Proudhonism, movement is itself the source of a constant *a posteriori* creation of ideas," and its concept of revolution was based on the idea of "direct action" by the workers in the social and economic spheres.[120] De Man often went back to Proudhon, to stress the great debt that socialism owed to Marx's pet aversion.[121] Like Sorel, the "social" Maurrassians, and all the socialists who moved toward fascism, he appreciated Proudhon's "socialism with an earthy flavor."[122]

It was no accident that, here again, De Man's development was very close to Sorel's before him. A revision of Marxism through the introduction of voluntarist, vitalist elements produced similar results in both cases. In the end, one obtained an ideology that still claimed to be socialist but whose meaning had changed profoundly. "What is all-important in socialism is the struggle to achieve it," wrote De Man in *Au-delà du marxisme*.[123] What really counts in socialism, he said, is movement, and if one really wants to move ahead, one should "simply say: in the beginning was action."[124] One should also, once and for all, jettison "the theory of superstructure," with its assumption "that ideas merely reflect interests."[125] One should make it quite plain that "egoistic enjoyment separates men, sacrifice unites them,"[126] and that, finally, "the aim of our existence is not paradisiacal but heroic."[127] No fascist ideologist has stated it better.

The idea of "joy in work" is important in De Man's thinking. For him, the fact that in modern times the major processes of production are in the hands of people who obtain no satisfaction from their work constituted a grave danger to civilization.[128] He considered this lack of satisfaction "a cause of discontent at least as important as the diminution—problematic in any case—of their resources,"[129] maintaining that factors such as personal satisfaction, "human dignity," and "professional capability"[130] are infinitely more important than those connected with the ownership of the means of production or the distribution of wealth. He gave psychological, affective, and emotional problems a greater role than economic problems, and held that aesthetics play at least as important a part in people's lives as economics. De Man's point of view seems to imply that it may be possible, by satisfying the workers' psychological requirements, to avoid having to tackle structural problems inherent in the modern economy.

De Man also maintained that man's foremost aspiration is to express in his work his most personal values. Thus, he claimed that all the social problems of history "are but different aspects of the eternal social problem that in the final analysis exceeds and epitomizes them all: how can a human being find happiness not only *through* his work but *in* his work?"[131] The full significance of this revision of Marxism is now clear: it merges quite easily into the fascist view of things.

There were other elements in De Man's revisionism that lent themselves even better to fascism. "The motive forces of the masses are essentially emotional," De Man wrote, taking up the old formula of Gustave Le Bon.[132] For that reason, the masses, like "Panurge's sheep," "will always feel the need to run after a leader, who represents in their eyes all that they would like to be."[133] This process of identifying with an ideal self, he felt, is quite natural, in the same way as the social difference between the leaders, with the status they necessarily have, and the masses is natural. It is therefore a mere fiction that the leaders of a socialist party, for instance, are simply representatives of the will of the members.[134] It follows that any society, whatever its structure, and any organization, needs leaders. A socialist society would not be different: it, too, would have its hierarchy, its powerful figures and natural inequalities. In a sense, De Man took up the tradition begun by Pareto, Mosca, and Michels at the beginning of the century: like the founders of the social sciences who had so deeply shaken the foundations of parliamentary democracy, De Man doubted the possibility of the existence of a socialist society in which the relationships between people would differ from those that prevail in capitalist society. The cardinal importance that De Man gives to psychological factors, to individual motivations, to all that is unchanging in human nature, considerably diminishes the difference between a socialist society and a nonsocialist one.

The same applies to the idea of equality. "The desire for equality and the need for inequality, far from being mutually exclusive, condition each other," De Man wrote.[135] Just as there is a "desire for equality," so there is a "need for inequality,"[136] and the most powerful of the forces pushing the masses toward socialism is "the instinctive and immediate need of the lower classes to diminish social inequality." This "socialist demand for equality," he said, "is at once the compensatory representation of an inferiority complex" inherent in the working-class condition[137] and the product of "the instinctive self-esteem" of Western man.[138] However, the social instincts of Western man at the same time require that every society "should have a *superior* class" that can provide an example of a desirable state, and it is for this psychological reason that "no society is possible without an aristocracy."[139] This aristocracy can take many forms: the European gentleman and the mandarin of ancient China and the Soviet party official are only different aspects of the same phenomenon.[140] In the final analysis, thought De Man, "the social inferiority of the working classes" is due neither to a lack of political equality nor to the existing economic structures "but to a psychological condition" arising out of a chronic feeling of insecurity and, above all, out of their own belief in this inferiority.[141] At the same time, De Man believed that it became increasingly clear that while engaging in a struggle of interests with the bourgeoisie, the workers considered bourgeois existence enviable and desirable, and, to the degree that they approached it, they came to resemble their adversaries.[142]

That, said De Man, is why there is no such thing as a proletarian culture. Such an idea is a mere fabrication, the product of the hostility against bourgeois culture that characterizes the socialism of the intellectuals. The way of life of the bourgeoisie has a great influence on the proletariat, and the desire for respectability leads the working classes to accept the moral norms of the privileged classes.[143] The specific character of the proletariat is thus only a delusion, an invention of the theoreticians. Was not Marxism itself the creation of a "haunter of libraries, a stranger to practical life and above all to the life of the workers"?[144] For

De Man, Marxism was exactly what democracy had been for Maurras: a "vapor."

A pronounced elitism was thus a major aspect of this revision of Marxism. De Man himself detested the bourgeoisie: he declared that the atmosphere of bourgeois society had "become unbreathable to him," [145] but he knew that in some spheres—in the formation of taste, for instance—there is generally no individual progress, "but a progress through generations in the course of which one inherits culture like property." [146] Alexis de Tocqueville might have spoken similarly, but then the author of *Democracy in America* did not claim to be a socialist. It is true that Michels also professed such ideas, as did Mosca and Pareto. When such an elitism is superimposed on a more or less pronounced negation of parliamentarianism and bourgeois values and on a contempt for a regime based on universal suffrage, there can be no doubt of the result.

Further, De Man claimed that for a very long time the proletariat had not lived in conditions resembling those of 1848. Today, organized in syndicates and enjoying universal suffrage, compulsory education, and an extensive social legislation, the workers, while permitting themselves to be beguiled by the Marxist illusion, "would have many things to lose by it that represent to them a part of the country." [147] First of all, he said, the workers had gained some influence in the state, and, still more important, "their influence has become more and more identified with the consolidation of the state itself." [148]

De Man thought that it was in fact the role of the working class, rather than the great industrial and financial monopolies, the stock exchange, or the banks, to be the support of the state. Here the Belgian socialist leader came once again to a conclusion of great significance: "The more that socialism becomes the vehicle of the idea of the state, the more it also becomes the vehicle of the idea of the nation that is embodied in the state." [149] Thus, the way was now clear for a new form of socialism. This new conception of socialism could lead to social democracy or to some kind of parliamentary labor movement, or it could lead to the position held by national socialism. This was all the more possible because, as De Man insisted, in modern times "all the interests of the workers are not necessarily opposed to those of the employers": [150] there is a solidarity of interests between workers and industrialists, and the fate of both depends on the policies of their political and military leaders, the international situation, and foreign competition. [151] On the other hand, said De Man, to the degree that the working class "increases in strength and assumes more responsibility,"[152] it finds itself increasingly drawn into conflicts between states. In this way, "the workers of different countries once more become competitors in this same sphere of immediate economic interests, which in the last century was expected to become more and more unified as a result of the continuous expansion of the world capitalist economy."[153]

Capitalism, then, had not played the role that Marx had assigned to it, and the world had not assumed the simple form that the father of scientific socialism had envisaged. Internationalism had remained an empty word; neither general pauperization nor polarization had taken place, and the middle class had not been driven into the proletariat by a concentration of capital. The social structure of the peasantry had remained essentially the same, and the rise of the new middle class had compensated for the decline of the old middle class of the precapitalist period. Numerically, the craftsmen and the independent merchants had been more than replaced by the office workers, the civil servants, and the people in the liberal professions. De Man showed that when one of these classes declined, it happened on a collective and not an individual basis. The loss of social independence affected the whole class: the peasants, for instance, ran into debt; the new middle class experienced increasing insecurity owing to a decrease in employment opportunities; and the former middle class lost its position through the melting of capital and large incomes.[154]

This was the new problem to which De Man addressed himself. He was extremely conscious of the diversity of classes and groups in modern society, of the pluralism of interests that could no longer be expressed in terms of the traditional Marxist dichotomy. He believed that the great issue of the thirties was the danger of the proletarianization of the middle classes, both urban and rural, and a revolt on their part against having to sink into the proletariat—a revolt that expressed itself "on the one hand in anticapitalistic sentiment and on the other hand in antiproletarian sentiment."[155] It was here, he claimed, that one could find the psychological key to this response to a growing proletarianization that comprised both a hatred of capitalism and a hatred of proletarian socialism.[156] Because reformist socialism in its existing form had little to offer them and communism seemed to them abhorrent, the middle classes went over to fascism.[157] This, then, was the new situation that had to be faced, as De Man saw it. He therefore proposed a third way between orthodox socialism, which excluded the middle classes, and the fascism into which they were slipping.

That third way was intended to provide an answer to the challenge posed by the European crisis—at once a crisis of the economic system, a crisis of the political regime, and a crisis of society. That answer was "planism"—the celebrated De Man Plan, which was followed by various similar schemes in France. Planism, however, went far beyond an *ad hoc* solution to a given problem, for in fact it constituted a dimension of revisionism, and the revisionism of De Man, followed by that of Marcel Déat, was, for the socialism of the time, the most thoroughgoing example of anticonformist thinking of the interwar period. Where political theory was concerned, it was an original experiment of great importance. Between the parliamentary, democratic socialism concerned with universal suffrage and the rules of the game on the one hand and liberalism on the other, this experiment envisaged a third solution: a socialism for all classes based at once on anti-Marxism, the negation of capitalism, and the integration of the proletariat into the national community. Planism, to be sure, can be combined with any political ideology that does not claim to be an extreme form of liberalism, and, essentially, there is no reason why it should lead to fascism. It did not do so after the Second World War, for instance, but in the thirties, when it was presented as an alternative both to democratic socialism and to liberalism at the same time as integrating corporatism and political authoritarianism, planism made an important contribution to the molding of the fascist outlook.

CHAPTER FIVE

A Socialism for the Entire Nation

The Problem of Continuity

Marcel Déat's ideas in *Perspectives socialistes*, his innumerable articles in *La Vie socialiste* and other journals, his speeches, interviews, and, finally, his electoral campaign in the twentieth *arrondissement* in 1936 already constituted an ideological totality that was essentially in no way different from the fascist system of ideas as these took shape from the time of the Popular Front and until the Liberation.

In this regard, it is worth drawing attention to a point of interpretation that occurs quite frequently in recent writings on the subject, and that raises a number of problems. In a recent article, one writer asks the question, How would Déat have gone down in history if he had died accidentally in 1936? He would probably, the writer answers, have been regarded as a reformist parliamentarian, eager to assume office, like the independent socialists at the beginning of the century, and he would probably have been forgotten like Pierre Renaudel and Alexandre Varenne.[1]

A similar argument has been put forward with regard to Michels. Suppose, says R. I. Bennett, that Michels had died immediately after writing *Political Parties*: would anyone then speak of his fascism?[2] Bennett, who refuses to see any connection between the theory of elites and fascism, attempts to distinguish Michels the author of pioneering works of political science from the Michels of the Mussolini period.[3]

Similarly, Ivo Rens and M. Brélaz, summarizing the conclusions of a symposium on De Man held at the University of Geneva in 1973, clearly distinguish between the man and his work.[4] It was De Man the individual, they say, who in June 1940 received with satisfaction the news of the defeat of the Western democracies, whereas the works of De Man the writer, revealing one of the most original minds of the period, had no connection, they claim, with the errors of political judgment of the socialist leader. The impression one receives from this collection of papers by fervent admirers of De Man is that his behavior in June 1940 was quite simply inexplicable and ought therefore to remain unexplained. The enigma of De Man's behavior, however, did not lead the participants in the symposium to consider the possibility that De Man's political thinking in the thirties had a quite different significance.

As for the more complex case of Déat—author of *Perspectives socialistes* and leader of the RNP—A. Bergounioux warns against a "substantialism of continuity,"[5] and S. Grossmann, at any rate, wonders about the nature of the forces that could have "produced a metamorphosis" in him.[6] Bergounioux comes to the conclusion that Déat's thought laid the foundations of a modern social democracy, and that consequently the equation "Neosocialism equals fascism" is exaggerated for 1932. He believes that it was not until May 1940 that Déat presented the figure of a politician "ripe" for fascism.[7]

In reality, however, these people never passed through any metamorphosis or underwent any inexplicable evolution. To see this it is not necessary, when reading them, to think only of the forties, any more than it is necessary to read what Michels and Labriola wrote in 1905 in the light of their development in the following two decades. One should simply read everything without emphasizing any particular period or work.[8] De Man's revision of Marxism, Michel's critique of social democracy, Déat's sociological analysis, and their disgust—from the time they wrote their major works—with both liberal democracy and democratic socialism are quite sufficient to explain both the evolution of their thought and their ultimate commitments.

Neither Déat nor De Man, in fact, said anything during the war that they had not said repeatedly throughout the thirties. Déat was quite correct in claiming, in a review of *Après-coup* in 1940, that De Man, "freed from the mechanical doctrine" of Marxism, had already, ten years previously, proposed "a revolutionary construction that, under pressure from producers belonging to all social strata, would impose profound structural reforms on bourgeois society."[9] In the fall of 1940, Déat analyzed De Man's June manifesto and declared that what applied to

Belgium was equally valid for France: the needed reforms, both men had always believed, could be carried out only by means of the state, that "indispensable instrument of the revolution." De Man, claimed Déat, had long since broken away "from the liberal conception of the democratic state. He demanded an 'authoritarian state,' he condemned the puerilities of antifascism and stressed the genuinely revolutionary inspiration of the German and Italian parties. It was *because he was a socialist, because he was a revolutionary*, that he also came around increasingly to an authoritarian conception of the state." De Man, he said, had wanted a state "that could shatter all the resistances," all the weaknesses of the political system—"the power of finance, the interference of the parties and the demoralizing influence of the press." [10]

These, indeed, were the major ideas of De Man's memoirs, which Déat faithfully summarized. De Man concealed nothing in *Après-coup*, and during the war, in Brussels and Paris, both under German occupation, he continued to proclaim his convictions. Speaking in April 1942 at the Cercle Européen, one of the great centers of ideological collaboration with nazism, De Man returned to the classic themes of the struggle against the power of finance and the necessity for a strong state,[11] and a year earlier, in an interview in *Le Petit Parisien*, he had expressed himself as follows: "You can say that the French have better luck than we have, since they have a government that has allowed them to enter into a policy of collaboration with Germany, which circumstances have prevented Belgium from doing until now." [12] It was these circumstances (i.e., the disappearance of the Belgian state), and also a different temperament—a tendency to detach himself from others, a "grand seigneurial" attitude—that prevented De Man from playing in Belgium the role played by Déat in France, despite the fact that where main policy guidelines were concerned, the former leader of the Parti Ouvrier Belge had by then no more doubts about the correctness of ideological collaboration with Germany than had the former *enfant terrible* of French socialism. During that same period De Man sponsored the foundation of a new journal, *Le Travail*, which, produced by the former staff of *Le Peuple* and printed by its presses, was intended to replace the old socialist newspaper. Its articles once again attacked liberal democracy, parliamentarianism, and the party system and proclaimed the birth of a new reality.[13] The time had come, said De Man, to "associate two ideas that till recently were held to be irreconcilable: the socialist order and the authoritarian state." [14]

If, during the Occupation, De Man was not an active collaborator like Déat, it was certainly not because of any ideological differences between the two men: the identity of their views was as great in the forties as it had been ten years earlier. Their critical attitude to Marxism and their detestation of liberal democracy and bourgeois society made them greet with delight the overthrow of a hated regime. Both regarded the defeat of democracy as proof of the moral and social superiority of the victor. As De Man said to the POB members in his June manifesto:

For years the brainwashing of the warmongers concealed from you the fact that this regime, despite its strangeness to our mentality, would have reduced class differences far more effectively than the so-called democracies where capital continued to be law.

Since then, everyone has been able to see that the superior morale of the German army is in large part due to the greater social unity of the nation and the greater degree of prestige that the authorities derive from it.

By contrast, the plutodemocracies offered us the spectacle of the authorities abandoning their post and the rich crossing the frontier by car without concerning themselves about what happened to the masses.[15]

There is no esssential point in these texts that De Man had not stated repeatedly throughout the thirties. Exceptional circumstances had led him to elaborate some of his ideas but had created none of them.

The same is true with regard to Déat. An examination of his editorials in *L'Oeuvre*, his many speeches and articles published in the RNP weekly bulletin *Le National populaire*, and his pamphlets—usually taken from his newspaper articles or expressing the same ideas—leaves no room for doubt: Déat's national socialism of the Collaboration period was the very same as that of the heyday of neosocialism and "planism." The leaders of the RNP quite rightly insisted that their policies in 1943 were directly descended from those of their campaign of 1933. They carried their concern for continuity—and they were careful to insist on this continuity—to the point of holding the plenary session of the National Council of the RNP on 17 July 1943 and in the Salle de la Mutualité, where, ten years earlier to the day, Déat, Marquet, and Montagnon had launched the now-famous slogan "Ordre, autorité, nation" at the SFIO conference. Jacques Guionnet, speaking on that occasion, said that it was then, ten years earlier, that "Marcel Déat publicly enunciated, for the first time, the principles of a national socialism that was more or less the same as that which we profess today." Guionnet, head of propaganda of the RNP, summarized the main ideas of *Perspec-*

tives socialistes, recalled Déat's attempt at reuniting all "anticapitalist" forces, and referred to the objectives that the present leader of the RNP had fixed for socialism: undertaking social, political, and economic reforms within a national framework, neutralizing and resolving class antagonisms in the general interest, and replacing parliamentary discussion with an authoritarian state. Once again, he correctly concluded, "Such were the essential principles of this neosocialism that—we can now say with pride—had many points in common with fascism and German national socialism. The foreign press of the period saw this clearly, and one can understand, after all, the horror of the Jew Blum at the speeches of Déat, Marquet, and Barthélemy Montagnon."[16]

It was quite true that the idea of a "socialist, national, authoritarian and popular France"[17] was contained both in the slogan we have referred to and in the three celebrated speeches of the founders of neosocialism. Naturally enough, these ideas recurred on innumerable occasions. Apart from the notion of the cult of the leader and a few other usual collaborationist themes, the writings of Déat and his group contained nothing of importance during this period that could not have been found ten years earlier.

Among the old ideas was the "planism" that attempted "to realize an intermediate regime between a capitalist and a communalistic economy."[18] This planism contained "the seed and sometimes more than the seed of national socialism, since it based national unity on social justice."[19] The RNP claimed the authority of Proudhon for the union of all social categories advocated by planism, for it was concerned in the thirties, as in the time of the Collaboration, with "bringing the country from a state of atomization to a state of socialist organization."[20] The RNP consequently proposed a program of national unity that would be, in the words of Georges Albertini, secretary-general of the RNP, a "new socialism," a "national socialism," a "communal socialism" that would renounce parliamentarianism, "the most formidable, because the most concealed, instrument of the domination of the plutocracy." But such a revolution "is not possible if it is not the revolution of the entire nation," and therefore "today it is up to the nation to tell this plutocracy that its time and its mission are ended." And Albertini concluded, "We do not have many things to deny in our doctrinal past."[21]

Déat himself, the "leader," seeking to revive the publication of *L'Oeuvre* under the Occupation, rightly claimed that he was only asking the German authorities for the right to express "the ideas that had always been ours."[22] Indeed, Déat's report of July 1940 advocating a single national party testifies to this continuity: it contained only familiar ideas, reiterated by Déat for exactly ten years,[23] including a consideration of the desirability for France of a planned economy integrated into a European economy.[24] After drawing up this report, which the new head of state, Marshal Pétain, apparently did not answer, Déat never wearied of painting the picture of a "new order" that would be the living antithesis of the "reactionary and conservative politics" that was still, he claimed, so much in evidence.[25] This new order, he said, would transcend both "capitalism and bolshevism"; it would, like the RNP itself, be "antidemocratic" in being "truly socialist and popular";[26] it would be based on "a positive socialism whose synthesis would transcend and unite" liberalism and bolshevism. All this would be controlled by a "strong, authoritarian state that would guarantee the whole man his development within an agreed discipline."[27] In place of the "old neutral state, indifferent and naturally impotent guardian of individual fantasies and anarchies," national socialism, said Déat, would build this "new order" that would express "an organic totality of aspirations and ideas."[28] Thus, in place of the old "socialism of demands," there would come into being "the constructive socialism"—the term was neither new nor original—of the national revolution, a revolution that, as Déat's supporters always insisted, still remained to be carried out.[29]

Like Déat's supporters in 1933, those of the war years did not attack "capitalist 'exploitation'" (they always put the word *exploitation* in quotation marks) but "the proletarian condition" that, they said, "*materialist* exploitation" did not fully explain.[30] They supported Déat's attempts to have the Charter of Labor applied,[31] but the former neosocialists did not wait for this question to come up to launch the idea of a syndicalist revival,[32] stating that "if a national socialism had developed in time in France, we would not be where we are now."[33] The logic of this point of view brought Pierre Thomas to look back to the revolutionary syndicalism of the beginning of the century. This expert on syndicalism, who was also one of the RNP's chief experts on the Jewish question, stated boldly that "whoever is concerned about the future is bound to look back to this period to attempt to discover the secret of an impetus that has since been lost."[34] The national socialism of 1940 extracted from the leftist revolt of the turn of the century its hatred of liberal democracy, parliamentarianism, and universal suffrage. Thomas referred to Pouget's and Griffuelhes's attacks against democracy, and recalled their cult of elites and of active minorities and their thirst for direct action. This faithful collaborator of Déat's also brought to light what he regarded as the two weak aspects of revolutionary syndicalism: the Marxist laborism that isolated the movement within the nation and the antistatism that ended by denying the nation.[35] He thought that if it remedied these two weaknesses, national socialism would be able to embody all the other elements of the syndicalist revolt against the established order and construct a new order, based on a fusion of the healthy elements in the syndicalist tradition and the planism of the prewar years.[36] Extending from Lagardelle to Déat, who in October 1940 still referred back to the old *Revue blanche* that Sorel had already condemned,[37] was a whole tradition of French socialism that, after half a century of rebellion and struggle, finally attempted to set up "an order that is called socialism"[38] under the protection of Nazi Germany.

An instrument was needed to initiate this new order. Accordingly, Déat, like De Man in Belgium, demanded the establishment of a single party—the true backbone of an authoritarian state—that would carry out the national revolution. In July 1940 Déat became the first French political figure to put forward an idea that stemmed directly from his traditional conception of authoritarian socialism. Throughout the second half of 1940 Déat waged a long campaign on behalf of the revolution and a "strong" state and against conservatives of all kinds, and especially the Action Française, whose doctrine, he said, "smelled of stale cream and dried-up cosmetics." The world, said Déat, did not need "an old France with white-powdered hair, flounces and crinolines" but "a robust sportswoman without lipstick."[39] This campaign followed naturally from his public activities of the previous decade. Déat's violence, his criticisms, his insults and threats, and his anti-Semitism were nothing new; they simply increased in proportion to "our misfortunes" and "our hopes."[40] The calls for new leaders, for the collective spirit as opposed to individualism, and for revolutionary ardor were nothing new to confirmed readers of Déat, Montagnon, Ludovic Zoretti, Gabriel Lafaye, and so many other activists of the neosocialist left who now also felt that its hour had come.[41] The RNP was founded in that spirit,[42] and, to initiate the first stage of the coming revolution, it declared its intention of transcending the old oppositions: "It is not a matter of knowing where one comes from, but where one is going," wrote Déat in the first issue of its bulletin.[43] "Neither right nor left," declared Albertini one week later in an article that revived the celebrated slogan of the thirties and seemed to come straight out of Jouvenel's *La Lutte des jeunes*, Maulnier's *Combat*, or one of the neosocialist publications of the preceding decade.[44]

Finally, like the neosocialism of the thirties, that of the war years wished not only to defend "the nation against the capitalist plutocracy"[45] but also to establish a new style of life. Confronted with the old bourgeois values, Déat, like De Man, urged his followers to "prove themselves men" and "live dangerously,"[46] for "without heroism, without this tension of soul, nothing has any meaning, everything returns to the lowest point."[47] One would seem to be reading a text by Berth, Lagardelle, or Michels: there was nothing here that had not been said not only by the same people ten years earlier but also by their predecessors—all those rebels who were forever searching for the best and most effective means of overthrowing the bourgeois order.

The Ideological Renewal of the Thirties and the Traditional Critique of Marxism

As at the turn of the century, the ideological renewal of the thirties gave rise, once more, to a critique of Marxism. Certainly, antimaterialism, antipositivism, and the other forms of negation of the established order did not necessarily lead to a fascist type of revolt. Ethical socialism was not always conducive to an anti-Marxist reaction that, while preserving the language of left-wing revolutionaries, considered the nation rather than the class to be the essential factor of change in the world. However, there is no denying that this desire to "pass beyond Marxism by substituting a method of psychological analysis for historical materialism, or, in other words, by seeking behind economic facts the psychic realities they express,"[48] was one of the main routes for going from left to right and from the extreme left to the extreme right. This did not happen with André Philip, but it did happen with Sorel, Berth, Michels, Labriola, and De Man. It makes no difference that during the Great War Sorel kept clear of the crude propaganda that flourished at the time of the Union Sacrée, or that Berth, immediately after the Soviet revolution, went over to the extreme left. Or, to take another example, Labriola, after having contributed to the rise of fascism in Italy, moved back to the left center in the thirties while, ideologically, the other Italian revolutionary syndicalists remained to the end the backbone of Italian fascism. However, that Labriola at a certain moment retreated in no way diminishes the importance of his contribution to the starting up of the mechanism. Georges Valois himself was in the left wing of the socialist movement in the thirties. For some Sorelians, going from left to right was undoubtedly a two-way journey; for others, it was a path without return. But these people all shared the same motivation, and that is what allows us to perceive the true nature of the phenomenon: to paraphrase Michels, they were all looking for the "grandiose union" of the revolutionary idea with the great revolutionary force of the moment. Revolutionary syndicalism had provided the idea, but it had not found a sociological group capable of putting that idea into action. The search for this "union" was the real history of protofascism, and in the interwar period it was the main preoccupation of the ethical socialists, the most authentic heirs of revolutionary syndicalism.

At the end of the twenties, it was André Philip who contributed more than anyone else to the popularization of De Man's ideas in France. Like the extreme left-wing nonconformists of the turn of the century, Philip told "a working class that had grown bourgeois" that socialism is "not only, as Marxism believed, an economic doctrine: it is above all a moral ideal that seeks to regenerate both society and individuals." [49] Socialism, he said, must therefore "transfer class struggle from the economic to the ethical sphere"; [50] to "selfish, pleasure-seeking bourgeois materialism" it must oppose "a *spiritualist realism*" and initiate "an ethical revival and a restoration of spiritual values." [51]

Philip's appeal was not in vain. De Man's ideas contributed a great deal to the revision of Marxism that created a new socialism—a socialism without a proletariat, a socialism that remained simply an idea and that easily became a socialism for the entire nation. Neosocialism and planism were the two main manifestations of this new wave of revisionism: two years after the appearance of Philip's introduction to his summary of *Au-delà du marxisme*, Déat published *Perspectives socialistes*, and an important article with the revealing title "Le Socialisme spiritualiste."

Déat's revisionism was in the classic tradition of the moralists who, from Sorel, Michels, and Lagardelle onward, were always the first to formulate the most violent criticisms of Marxism. "History, for the pure Marxists," wrote Déat, in a text that sometimes seems to have been produced by Sorel, "is foreign to every moral consideration, and evolution depends solely on power relationships created by the economy." [52] Déat joined De Man in his "vigorous protestation" against "this insufficiency of the Marxist psychology," and he challenged the right of Marxism to "enunciate laws." Historical materialism, he thought, belongs to a specific era, and is valid only for the capitalist period, when everything is subordinated to the search for profit and all the central values are polarized around economic relationships. The tendency of socialism, on the other hand, thought Déat, was to relinquish the present social order and to create a world in which historical materialism no longer applied. Déat denied Marxism "the right to provide the key to universal history."[53] Furthermore, according to one of his supporters, Déat believed that even in a capitalist regime the influence of these economic factors would be quite variable, and that, for all these reasons, Marxism could not be regarded as a permanently reliable criterion.[54]

François Gaucher, a member of the Central Council of the Parti Socialiste de France, founded by Déat immediately after the split, recognized De Man's basic contribution to the destruction of historical materialism, but he thought that his analysis, stripped of its Freudian envelope, was simply a systematization of what French socialism had always maintained.[55] However, even when they jealously insisted on the Frenchness of their ideological origins, the revisionists were delighted to discover in De Man, in a modernized form, the idea that it was the psychological reaction of the workers and not only the antagonisms within capitalism that caused capitalist exploitation to become the generator of class struggle. They agreed with him and with all of the first generation of ethical socialists that, on the one hand, the ideal of equality was precapitalistic and that, on the other hand, Marxism had only reinforced the tendency of the working classes to become increasingly bourgeois.[56] They also thought that the determinism of the economic conception of history, which had once been a stimulus, was now an obstacle.[57] To determinism, which necessarily reduced socialism to something passive, they opposed voluntarism. Gaucher could not help admiring both the bolsheviks and the fascists for changing the course of history.[58]

In this way, Gaucher expressed the desire of the French neosocialists to bring to heel a world that resisted the impatience of the right-wingers of the SFIO who, refusing "to wait for the hypothetical moment when the situation would be revolutionary," wanted "to dash forward."[59] He also pointed out that the voluntarist current in French socialism, imbued with the conviction that one ought to exert all one's energy to influence social developments, was associated with both the old revolutionary-syndicalist tradition and that of democratic socialism.[60] This rejection of determinism constituted a kind of ideological intersection bringing one to two parallel roads, one leading to social democracy and the other, by its very dynamism, to fascism.

The political controversy of the thirties was an intersection of this kind, recalling the situation of the first decade of the century. Within the socialist movement, within the already old SFIO, which had been sustained, said Gaucher, chiefly "by its battles and its conferences,"[61] they began once again to take up the study of fundamental problems, and they attempted to disengage themselves from the paradox, as Philip expressed it, "of a doctrine without practice joined to a practice without a doctrine."[62] If one listens to this new generation of SFIO nonconformists, one seems to hear the voices of those who, twenty years earlier, revolted against the dryness and poverty of the intellectual life and ideological debate within the party. It is therefore hardly surprising that when a new voice was heard (in Philip's modest popularization of *Au-delà du marxisme*), its main innovation was the idea that "class struggle" must be "transferred from the economic to the ethical sphere."[63]

The intellectual reawakening of French socialism produced several works of unequal value, none of which achieved the seriousness of De Man's writings. They all shared a critical attitude to Marxism. In 1929 Valois, whose publishing house in the place du Panthéon was at that time the center of an intense intellectual activity, put out *Grandeur et servitude socialistes* by Barthélemy Montagnon, later a neosocialist deputy for Paris. Though not an epoch-making work, this book is very characteristic of the ideological trend within the SFIO that led finally to fascism, and has the great merit of providing a kind of summary of the main revisionist ideas of the thirties.

In this work, Montagnon followed the classic procedure of first attacking Marxism and then, in a second part, putting forward the alternative solutions proposed by national socialism.[64] "The socialist doctrine no longer corresponds to the facts," he said. "The weakness of present-day socialism is due to the fact that its practice no longer fits its theories. It can only act in giving up its doctrine."[65] Montagnon criticized Marx's economic determinism, his theory of values, and his conception of history.[66] He condemned the idea of class struggle and even the idea of classes: class struggle, he thought, did not explain history.[67] Montagnon put forward an explanation of his own: "Some fantasies of kings," he said, "have had more influence on the development of history than many economic transformations. . . . It is the pride of kings and ministers that has constantly steeped the world in blood."[68]

Such was the level of the criticism of Marxism of one of the future leaders of the Parti Socialiste de France. And yet—perhaps because of the low level of its analysis—the work is characteristic: it represents a new awareness that gave rise to the search for a new direction.

Montagnon observed that, on the one hand, "class antagonism, far from increasing, has tended to lessen"[69] and, on the other hand, "the proletariat as an economic class has attained its maximum strength"[70] but is not in a position to make its revolution.[71] Socialism, he thought, could achieve power only through the liberal democratic system, and to do so it had to gain the support of the majority, and hence of other social strata besides the proletariat, for the implementation of a plan of governmental action that in essentials hardly differed, four years before the Christmas Congress of the Parti Ouvrier Belge, from the De Man Plan and the complementary Pontigny program.[72] He said that one had to gain the support of the mass of small-scale property owners and take them out of the clutches of the financial plutocracy; one had to attract "the middle and peasant classes," the technicians, and the junior cadres eager for progress.[73] One had especially to accept the idea of participation in government;[74] one had to work for the strengthening of the state[75] and the rationalization of the economy.[76] Socialism must endeavor to increase the authority of the state and at the same time encourage the scientific organization of labor that puts large quantities of goods on the market.[77] Montagnon expressed his admiration for the rational organization of production found in the United States, for Taylor and Taylorism.[78]

Montagnon was a worthy representative of the new, "planist" managerial and technocratic left that was enthusiastic about Taylorism and was opposed to the old world of liberals and orthodox socialists, all of whom were held to be incapable of understanding the needs of the modern economy and impervious to the idea of the fundamental solidarity that modern technology creates among all producers, among all the classes formerly regarded as antagonistic. People of the left moved toward fascism not because they wanted to return to a lost golden age but, on the contrary, because they wished to go forward, because they had come to view society as a workshop that had to be organized, rationalized, directed. They soon came to the conclusion that political power was the only real means of changing society; they quickly began to assume that to succeed one should above all get rid of democracy. A strong government was held to be essential for saving the world from the disaster that lay in store for society as a whole. The world crisis only encouraged this new vision of things, and added a special touch of urgency.

First of all, things must be arranged in such a way that, on coming to power, socialism would find "a methodically, rationally ordered economy."[79] This had always been the view of the revolutionary syndicalists, who believed that an economy that had reached its highest state of development was an essential prerequisite for a major leap forward. Only their method differed: for the neosocialists of the thirties, the movement had to be based on power—in a coalition government with a socialist minority or a socialist majority, or in a purely socialist government.[80] This meant, as Montagnon could not but see, taking over capitalist society for an indeterminate period without making any structural changes. The revisionism of the thirties implied a recognition of the legitimacy and endurance of bourgeois society.

Two famous Italian émigrés—Arturo Labriola, who was then in his reformist phase before returning, before the Abyssinian war, to militant nationalism, and Carlo Rosselli, who was murdered in the forest of Bagnoles-de-l'Orne—also engaged in lengthy criticisms of Marxism. "Socialism is old," wrote Labriola. "It is old as a doctrine; it is old, terribly old as a movement; it is old in its aspirations."[81] "The essential bases of the doctrine and not only its practical application are today in question," said Rosselli.[82] He advocated "a courageous revision of its moral and intellectual premises,"[83] and then launched into the routine ethical criticism of Marxism.[84] In a chapter called "Beyond Marxism"— a title that testifies to the care with which he had read De Man—Rosselli asked the question that he regarded as central for all reformist movements: "Does one seek a transformation of things or a transformation of the consciousness?"[85] His answer was hardly surprising: the transformation of things must take place together with the transformation of the consciousness. Rosselli asserted the need for a "moral integration that would correct the degeneration that too absolute an attachment to the idea of class struggle leads to,"[86] believing that the solution was a liberal socialism, a socialism in which the proletariat could "claim to be the heir of the liberal function,"[87] the guardian of liberty, and where one could say, "Proudhon is on his way back."[88] Proudhon did, in fact, come back, but not in the manner envisaged by Rosselli.

The "néos"—the neosocialists—were acquainted with the sources of their thinking and studied the origins of revisionism. Gaucher knew the works of Lagardelle and Sorel and carefully went over *Au-delà du marxisme*.[89] He used Jaurès against Blum, as well as Rosselli's revisionism.[90] Anything that helped to delegitimize Marxism was welcome.

A group of young intellectuals of the socialist party attacked the problem from a different point of view. It was Valois once again who published *Révolution constructive*, a collective work contrasting "the illusion of political power" with "the reality of socialist progress."[91] This rejection of the mystique of power[92] was motivated chiefly by the fact that, despite the establishment of socialist governments in several European countries in the years after the war, socialism had not been carried out anywhere.[93] It was for this reason that Georges Lefranc, Pierre Boivin, and Maurice Deixonne—the authors of this work—objected to Déat's policy of participation in government: it was impossible, they said, to resign oneself to a form of socialism that resulted only in a "disguised statism."[94] This group therefore directed its interest toward other institutions—the syndicates and the cooperatives—rather than the state.[95]

This confidence in the indigenous institutions of the working class did not, however, prevent the *Révolution constructive* group, and particularly Lefranc, from being enthusiastic advocates of "planism" (state planning). Planism, precisely, was the most perfect expression of a managerial, statist, technocratic left. To be sure, adherence to planism had been influenced by this group's earlier acceptance of Déat's concept of "anticapitalism": they said that all the rebellious anticapitalist movements could and should gather together around socialism.[96] In the years ahead, Lefranc was to become, together with René Belin, one of the main figures of French planism and one of those whose revolt against the established order would indeed lead to a revolution, but to a revolution not "constructive" but national; and the author of *Le Socialisme constructif* himself, through a profound logic that the similarity of vocabulary expresses perfectly, was also to take part in the same revolution.

The Revolution by the Center

The criticism of Marxism and the search for an alternative solution to the crisis of capitalism finally gave rise to Déat's *Perspectives socialistes*. To be sure, this work, also published by Valois, did not provide the revision of Marxism with as complete a conceptual framework as the works of De Man, but it was the need for immediate political action, the battle engaged in by the neosocialists that now occupied the foreground.

Marcel Déat was born on 7 March 1894 in Guérigny in the Nièvre. Accepted by the École Normale Supérieure in July 1914, he spent the First World War in the infantry. When the war ended he was a captain, decorated with the Légion d'honneur on the battlefield. He now entered the École Normale, graduating two years later. Lucien Herr, who noticed him, considered him one of the future hopes of French socialism and spoke about him to Léon Blum. Célestin Bouglé saw him as one of the future leading figures of French sociology.[97]

After the split in 1920 of French Socialists into two parties—a socialist party and a Communist party—Déat was an active member of the socialist party for four years in Paris, where he was secretary of the fifth section of the SFIO, and then in Rennes, where he taught in a high school. In February 1926, at the age of thirty-two, he was elected deputy for the Marne in a by-election on a joint list with a radical, Paul Marchandeau, who later became a minister. This was more than a personal success, for it had been achieved by a sort of private *Cartel des Gauches*: a coalition between socialists and radicals which at that time was still anathema to the party's leadership. Herr had disapproved of Déat's candidacy on these terms, and the National Secretariat of the SFIO had reproached Déat from the start for running on a joint list with a non-socialist.[98] Two years later, Déat was defeated in a general election on a one-member ticket, and he became administrative secretary of the socialist group at the Palais Bourbon. In 1932, however, he made a startling comeback: in the twentieth *arrondissement*, in the quarters of Belleville, Ménilmontant, and Charonne, the former constituency of Édouard Vaillant where Léon Blum had been defeated in 1928, he defeated the outgoing communist deputy Jacques Duclos.

When he won his victory, Déat had been well known for two years as the author of a work severely criticized by the leadership of the SFIO. The official response to Déat's campaign was given by Jean Lebas, the highly respected mayor of the workers' city of Roubaix. In an official party publication, he labeled the point of view expressed in *Perspectives socialistes* "neosocialism."[99] Thanks to the publicity he was given in *Le Populaire*, the term caught on. Déat and his friends finally adopted it as the name of their movement at the time of the split, just as Biétry's Jaunes had "adopted" that name when they realized they could never get rid of it.

At the twenty-eighth party congress of the SFIO held in Tours in May 1931, it became clear that Lebas's offensive was not just his own but represented the opinion of the entire Executive Committee: the ideas he expressed were the official thinking of French socialism.[100] The leaders of the party felt that they were dealing with a very serious deviation. And very soon, as the controversy became more bitter, conviction grew within the party that one day they would have, one way or another, to put an end to what they no longer regarded as a new attempt at revisionism but as a total revolution in socialist theory and tactics. In fact,

said Lebas, Déat had fully succeeded "in presenting us with an entirely
new socialism, previously unknown": of the original socialism—that of
1905, or that which had been revived immediately after the 1920 split—
"there was nothing left."[101]

Lebas attacked Déat's favorite concept of "anticapitalism." In his idea
of grouping together all anticapitalist forces, he saw only a vulgar alliance with the Radical party and other centrist forces for the sake not
of "a conquest of the state" but of "a penetration of the state."[102] Déat's
concept of the state was, in fact, the main object of his criticism. He
quite correctly saw the redefinition of the state as the very heart of neosocialism. To conceive of the government as a mighty institution that
would dominate the classes—all the classes—from above, as an essentially neutral mechanism that would force the bourgeoisie to yield each
time its interests were in opposition to those of the proletariat (assuming, that is, that the anticapitalist coalition would be victorious)—that,
he said, "is clearly a new socialist conception of the state."[103] Lebas recalled the traditional socialist conception of the state—the only one that
orthodox socialism recognized. According to socialist teaching, he said,
"the state had grown out of a society where class conflict had made it
necessary."[104] In spite of all its transformations and modifications, he
said, the state always remained a tool of the dominant class, which used
it to maintain for as long as possible a regime of which it was the sole
beneficiary. In a democratic country like France, the class character of
the state was not so clearly apparent, but its nature nevertheless remained unchanged: the state, represented by the government, is never
neutral; "the state, even when republican, is always a class state, and its
essential function is to maintain the bourgeois regime that rests on private property."[105] The same, he said, would be true under a neosocialist
regime, since—and this was Lebas's other main point in his criticism of
Perspectives socialistes—neosocialism had no intention of touching private property.[106] On the contrary: it is full of compromises and of as-
surances to the bourgeoisie that large-scale capitalist property and even
capitalist monopolies will not be touched.[107]

Lebas's pamphlet—scathing, ironic—was the official response of
the party to Déat's attempt at renewal. It is a remarkable example of the
Marxist orthodoxy of the SFIO at that time, and demonstrates the party's
firm determination to crush any form of nonconformism. This attitude
stemmed from a profound unwillingness to venture, from a conviction
that Marxism remained the only truly solid ground. This conservatism,
however, also explains the exasperation of the innovators, their feeling

that there was no longer anything to be done from within the movement, and their conviction that a party so incapable of adapting to an
ever-changing world had no future.

When Déat published *Perspectives socialistes*, the personality with
whom he would have liked to have engaged in a debate replied with silence if not contempt. His intellectual and moral rupture with Blum, he
noted in his unpublished memoirs, went back to the appearance of this
book.[108] Before it was published, nothing suggested an imminent break:
Déat spoke to Blum and about Blum with deference and respect and
remained within his role of disciple. He hoped that his book would give
rise to a great debate that would enable him, if not to conquer the party
from within, then at least to play the role of the leader of a faction that
one would have to reckon with. In 1930, Déat thought he could dominate an intellectual renewal within the movement, perhaps even within
the Socialist International; he hoped he could give the debate an ampli-
tude that Pierre Renaudel, the leader of the "participationists" and formerly Jaurès's deputy at *L'Humanité*, a respected but limited party
worker, had never been able to give the right wing of the party. Déat
thought he was producing a shock, giving a sudden jolt that, in shaking
the edifice, would change the direction of French socialism. His challenge, indeed, was sufficient for that purpose, but, contrary to what he
had hoped and expected, Blum answered Déat with silence. He did not
even take the trouble to acknowledge receipt of *Perspectives socialistes*;
he never said a word about it in private, and *Le Populaire* never reviewed it. "Blum had well understood," wrote Déat in his memoirs,
"that I had overturned all his artful decors and invented a machine to
deossify the brain, and that if these subversive ideas spread it would
mean the end of his great policy of procrastination and his learned
immobilism."[109]

From the time of the appearance of *Perspectives socialistes*, Déat regarded himself as Jaurès's successor, as the new leader of a democratic
and patriotic socialism that would seek to storm the citadel of the old
Guesdist socialism. He explained Blum's hostility as a desire on the part
of the leader of the party to rid himself as quickly as possible of a nui-
sance or even a potential rival.[110] Whatever the case, however, after the
elections of 1928 he stated his policy plainly: he sought a union of all
groups of the left and the center-left, without the communists, and participation in government. He thought that the socialists should already
have participated in the government of the Cartel and "fought the war"
with Clemenceau.[111] He reproached Blum for his subtle "*distinctions*"

between "*the exercise of power in a capitalist regime* and the *assumption of power* . . . ; although having the appearance of a doctrine," he said, they amounted only to a "deliberate refusal to accept one's responsibilities." [112]

However, this matter of participation in government, which was the main issue of the controversy within the SFIO, was in fact only a secondary question, or, rather, it was part of a far broader objective, for Déat was proposing nothing less than the "launching of a revolutionary offensive by the center." [113] He envisaged neosocialism as the generator of "a real revolution in stages, carried out by a resolute and clear-headed government," [114] and *Perspectives socialistes* was intended to provide the conceptual framework of this revolution from above, planned and executed by the state.

Perspectives socialistes contained three main ideas. First, one had to recognize that Marxism was only a method and not a dogma, a form of metaphysics. Second, one had to gain the support of the middle classes who also suffered from capitalist exploitation without having sunk into the proletariat. And, finally, socialism had to be reconciled with the nation and, within the national framework, refashion the state and make extensive use of the state. By using the formidable instrument of a transformed and modernized state, socialism would be able to carry out this "planned revolution," [115] which in the present circumstances was the only one possible.

The argument of the book was summed up in one fundamental concept that in fact replaced the idea of socialism: anticapitalism. Déat took this term, as he admitted, from Werner Sombart, but he gave it a very different significance. In Sombart, it was socialism, because it was regarded as Marxist and proletarian, that was considered most authentically "anticapitalist." For Sombart, who denied capitalist ideology and practice any positive quality, this term had a purely negative connotation. Déat, on the other hand, adopted a much broader conceptual framework, far transcending the limits of the proletariat. He argued from the assumption that the proletariat was far from being the only anticapitalist force. Although undoubtedly the main one, it was clearly not the only one, especially as numerically it seems to have reached its maximum development without having become an absolute majority of the population. One therefore had to reckon with other social categories—with the middle classes that, in France, constituted, if not the driving force, then certainly the decisive factor. In the front rank of these middle classes were the peasant proprietors, [116] followed by the artisans, the functionaries, and other still less clearly defined categories. Déat even included in his anticapitalist grouping the consumer, who was hardly less victimized than the wage earner.[117] Action by groups of consumers was regarded as anticapitalist, and, taking place within the regime, it could transform it from top to bottom.[118]

All this meant, as Déat admitted, that "anticapitalism cannot appear to be very homogenous."[119] He was also careful to distinguish between anticapitalism and socialism. There exists, he said, replying to criticisms from the extreme left of the party, a "virtual socialism" in anticapitalism,[120] and it was socialism's task to organize the anticapitalist forces. Déat therefore advocated a coordination of the efforts of all the victims of the crisis "within the flexible framework of a socialism as rich and varied as life itself,"[121] "in touch with concrete realities" and pursuing a "realistic and positive policy."[122] These ideas of flexibility, realism, and pragmatism were constantly repeated by the members of this school.

In opposition to traditional socialism, which turned "easily to utopia"—and Déat insisted that "we are not legislating for the year 2000"—the pragmatists waved this banner of an anticapitalism that "goes far beyond the socialist boundaries."[123] They were convinced of the possibility of finding a third way between "the American evasion" and "the catastrophic crisis." Déat believed it was possible to follow in the tracks of capitalism "in order to make it change direction with the use of all the anticapitalist forces combined." But everything depended on "the reconciliation . . . between democracy and revolution," and consequently "everything here converges toward the state."[124] Thus, one is faced with the problem "of the independence of the state being threatened by economic groupings," for "the capitalist authority" is opposed not only by the working class but also by the middle classes as a whole.[125] According to Déat, the true left began wherever one took up a position against capitalism, and its struggle took place wherever the popular will confronted "the power of finance."[126] Anticapitalism thus went beyond the limits of socialism and, in Déat's opinion, replaced it. The author of Perspectives socialistes called on all those who, regardless of party affiliation, were willing to encourage the grouping together of all the anticapitalist forces. The socialist party would have to lead the assault, but it could not claim a monopoly of the anticapitalist struggle,[127] any more than the proletariat alone could today claim to provide the total alternative to capitalism. Déat thus denied the proletariat any specific role, any special social function in this battle against capitalism.[128]

For Déat it followed that "henceforth there is anticapitalism without proletarianization,"[129] and that the real struggle was between "all the producers and all the profiteers"[130] rather than between the industrial proletariat and the bourgeoisie. An alliance between the latter two sections of the population had become possible owing to the changes that had taken place within capitalism itself. Jouvenel expressed a similar conclusion in an article in *La Tribune des fonctionnaires* in which he described anticapitalism in two formulas: as an alliance between the proletariat and the middle classes and as a planned economy in a reformed state.[131] In effect, the people of this school all accepted De Man's idea that capitalism had passed from a progressive to a regressive phase and from a competitive stage to a stage of monopoly, the main cause of this evolution being the increased power of capital represented by high finance. It was the domination of the credit system by high finance that produced the conflict of interests that determined the attitude of most of the middle classes. The independence of the middle classes was thus threatened and their fear of sinking into the proletariat increased. De Man claimed that for this reason the middle classes were opposed to large-scale capitalism and capitalist monopolies, and the common interest of the middle classes and the working class in opposing financial capitalism thus made possible the creation of a vast anticapitalist front.[132]

However, De Man had no illusions concerning the real character that such a coalition would have. He knew that it would necessarily be accompanied by a certain antiproletarianism,[133] and that it would finally lead to a revolution of the middle classes. "The middle classes?" he asked. "Let us be revolutionaries for them in the sense understood by those who want a structural reform of the regime." The French neosocialists also wished to exploit the potential of the middle classes, the only ones, said Montagnon, to possess "revolutionary ferment today."[134] Bergery and Doriot's supporters took the same view: all the factions of a certain nonconformist left tried to capture the middle classes. It is true that the "néos," at least, spoke of "diverting" that enormous reservoir of energies "to the left,"[135] whereas in other quarters it was chiefly the wretched condition of the middle classes that was emphasized. "The middle classes are suffering," insisted the néos, the writers of *La Flèche*, and Doriot, who spoke of "the ruin of the middle classes."[136] Very soon, they began to sing the praises of "that great rising force"[137] and to regard it as the cornerstone of the French revival.

Georges Izard spoke of "the idea of individuality and the idea of liberty" carried "to its maximum" in the middle class,[138] and Doriot painted a picture of the "soldier-peasant," victim of liberalism and of Marxism.[139]

In many cases, the historical role of the proletariat was questioned. Its time appeared to have passed: now the middle classes seemed to hold the key to the future. It was they who were responsible for the successes of fascism, and it was they who would determine the fate of Europe.[140] If the future no longer belonged to the proletariat, it was because technical evolution, rationalized methods of production, and automation had gradually transferred the functions of the worker to machines and to intellectual cadres within the middle classes. The era of industrialization had been that of the proletariat; that of automation, in advanced industrial countries, would be that of the middle classes between the capitalist class and the proletariat. This, essentially, was the point of view of De Man, Jouvenel, Doriot, and the writers of *La Flèche*.[141] All were agreed that, instead of destroying the middle classes as Marx had predicted, technological progress had worked in their favor—something that obviously necessitated a revision of the very notion of class warfare.

The Integration of the Classes and National Solidarity

From a very early stage, Henri De Man had had serious doubts concerning the proletariat's capacity to act as the only instrument of social transformation. Immediately after the First World War he was already of the opinion that, in spite of their effectiveness as a theme of propaganda, the class interests of the proletariat would not lead to decisive changes. De Man, Déat, and the néos in France, like the supporters of the Belin faction in the CGT, were only being true to their own convictions when, in the hour of decision, they refused to base their political actions on the proletariat. The proletariat, said De Man, did not have a monopoly of wisdom and disinterested motivation. It had not succeeded in wresting the monopoly of higher culture from the bourgeoisie, or in annexing the social groups responsible for the processes of management and coordination essential for industrial production. And, on the other hand, said De Man, no one can claim that the worker's mentality is exclusively the product of the class condition of the proletariat. The workers have the same intellectual foundations, the same cultural heritage, and the same national institutions as all the other members of society. They carry the imprint of the religious and moral beliefs of their period and

cannot be reduced to the abstract concept of a *homo oeconomicus* who
has nothing except hands to produce and a stomach to be filled.[142] It is
wrong, therefore, to appeal only to the class interests of the industrial
proletariat and to disregard the positive value of certain interests and
ideas common to all the nation and all humanity. Unless allowance was
made for some forms of collaboration between different classes and parties, thought De Man, the proletarian class struggle could not succeed.[143]

What De Man, Déat, and Jouvenel were in fact suggesting was that
progress did not work in favor of socialism. Technological evolution, the
sociological structures it had created, and modern war undermined the
very foundations of Marxism. They demonstrated the interdependence
of the social classes, their actual solidarity, their common interests as
members of the same national collectivity. In De Man's opinion, the
most miserable of unskilled workers was linked in his daily existence by
as many bonds of solidarity with the national community as with the
class to which he belonged.[144]

For people of this school, the notion of class solidarity also had a different connotation from that traditionally given to it. De Man believed
that proletarianization of the middle classes had increased, but, contrary to the beliefs of the socialists who clung to the old formulas, this
proletarianization differed from that of a century before. Instead of involving individuals sinking into the proletarian condition as in the nineteenth century, proletarianization now applied to the social situation of
sections of the middle classes as a whole, for the essential characteristic
of the proletariat is precisely the situation of dependence in which it
finds itself owing to its not possessing its own means of production. The
situation of the proletariat in relation to the owners of capital was
the same as that of the middle classes, and more especially of the new
middle classes. That is why the new middle classes can be described as
undergoing proletarianization, and De Man considered this process infinitely more significant than that whereby particular individuals, becoming genuine proletarians, ceased by that very fact to form part of the
middle classes. Whether it involved farmers up to their ears in debt, ship
owners become branch managers, or technicians or engineers become
junior employees in limited companies, proletarianization always affected the entire social category.[145]

So there came into being—to use a favorite expression of the twenties—a "solidarity of fact" among all the producers: there is no greater
solidarity, it was believed, than that produced by economic insecurity[146]
in the face of "hypercapitalism."[147] Like the national socialists of the

turn of the century, like the Jaunes or the collaborators of the Cercle Proudhon, the interwar generation made a distinction between "good" and "bad" capital, exploited and exploiters, "little" and "big" people. What the néos, the frontists, and the future members of the PPF led by Jouvenel wanted was a vast popular upsurge based on "this solidarity in distress,"[148] this "union before the peril of the same shipwreck."[149] In 1935, Georges Izard put forward "the great and uplifting idea of union" in La Fléche, and frontism "extended the revolutionary front to the exploited as a whole—that is to say, to the vast majority of the population."[150] Déat pointed out in 1934 that in 1930 he had put forward the idea that "the front of the existing classes and interests was stabilized in accordance with the line on which the forces were balanced." That line, "always changing and variable," was determined only "through the complex influence of its constant internal modifications."[151] Déat added that his ideas were immediately condemned as pure and simple corporatism,[152] especially as the néos, through their representative Barthélemy Montagnon, speaking in the Chamber of Deputies, had already officially repudiated the principle of class warfare.[153]

This solidarity of the classes seemed all the more natural to the members of this school in that economic developments had created "sharper and sharper antagonisms between the nations."[154] Thus, the néos addressed themselves to the entire nation,[155] and on the eve of the Second World War La Flèche did the same with particular clarity: "In order to liberate France from the tyranny of finance and the interference of foreign governments," it wrote, "for the sake of peace with all peoples, whatever their regime, Frenchmen of all classes, unite!"[156]

This very characteristic text, which carries the personal hallmark of Gaston Bergery, later the Vichy government's ambassador to Moscow, was the result of several years of reflection. In 1935, for instance, in an important doctrinal article, Izard had been careful to use the word socialism—defined as orthodox—only between quotation marks to proclaim clearly the refusal of the middle classes to take orders from the proletariat. The middle classes, he said, were not willing to pay the costs of a dictatorship of the proletariat, and the proletariat, in seeking to isolate itself from the rest of society, was everywhere heading for defeat.[157]

The idea of collaboration of the classes was at the end of the thirties one of the main principles of the Doriotist school of thought. More than anyone else, the adherents of the Parti Populaire Français returned to the old Jaune ideology, and their works seem to have been written by Biétry and his supporters. "We are among those who demand harmo-

nious relations between capital and labor," wrote Doriot.[158] The whole
Doriotist ideology rested on this principle of solidarity: "There is the
solidarity of the family, there is that of the community, of the region, of
the firm, of the profession, and, above them all, the expression and synthesis of all the others, there is national solidarity."[159] The PPF saw it as
its task to restore these "true communities," to create social structures
that could favor their development so that one would finally achieve a
new reality—the nation as a "harmonious aggregate of natural communities."[160] One therefore had to create institutions where people "will
feel what unites them rather than what divides them";[161] one had to establish, said Doriot, reviving Biétry's old formulas, "a living collaboration between producers, workers, technicians, and employers."[162]
Doriot took up the defense of the small- and middle-scale employers and
insisted on the solidarity between these employers and their workers.[163]
In sympathy with this view, Robert Loustau urged that present-day
capitalist enterprise, "which concretizes the subordination of classes,"
be replaced with a new form of enterprise that would achieve "a collaboration of the three factors of production: capital, creation, labor."[164]

Similarly, Drieu La Rochelle demanded that one stop misusing "this
word worker. We too are workers. The peasants and bourgeois are also
workers—exactly like the industrial laborers."[165] Like all the fascists,
Drieu began by declaring that the postulate that there are only two
classes was fundamentally false. The social arena, he said, had never
been filled exclusively by the duel between the bourgeoisie and the nobility, and then the bourgeoisie and the proletariat; the class structure,
once established, had never been unchangeable.[166] Today more than in
any other period, wrote Drieu, a one-dimensional class warfare has
been rendered impossible by the indefinite multiplicity of classes. In this
chaos, the proletariat is unable to constitute a genuine class party, and
as a result of the lack of homogeneity "in the so-called working class"
the proletariat in France, following Italy and Germany, where the socialist and communist parties were crushed, is once again heading for
defeat.[167] One class can therefore never replace another—that has never
happened. Nor can one class seize political authority, which, in any
case, always belongs to an elite independent of the social classes. The
only way to succeed, thought Drieu, is to have what one had in Italy,
Germany, and the Russia of Lenin—a combined revolution of all the
classes together. The Russian Revolution, said Drieu, was not the work
of the proletariat. It contributed, just as it contributed to all revolutions.
It rose up against absolutism, but it was not alone. Incipient large-scale

capitalism, the bourgeoisie, the intellectuals, the nobility, the peasants—all these, no less than the proletariat, found the existing order
intolerable.[168]

If Drieu and Déat sought to blur the specificity of the proletariat,
Doriot, using the language of Biétry, proclaimed his desire to "overcome
the social war."[169] Like the Jaunes a generation earlier, the adherents of
the PPF considered that "the essential characteristic" of their movement
"was to have been born at a time of great social battles."[170] Consequently, they declared, "all our party is in these words: social Peace and
Justice."[171] Doriot continued, almost exactly in Biétry's words, "Our
mystique is justice and social peace. . . . And we think, moreover, that,
without social peace, France will disappear. Social peace is the only
ground on which France can be reconstructed."[172]

These declarations from the end of the thirties could easily have been
made at the beginning of the century. Like the Jaunes, born in the turmoil of the great strikes of the beginning of the century, the PPF bore the
mark of the confrontation of the period of the Popular Front. Doriot,
who had probably never heard of Biétry but who, like him, had come
from a genuinely proletarian background and found himself, at least at
the beginning, at the head of an authentic workers' movement, had the
same preoccupations and reactions. Neither of the two was a Marxist
theoretician; neither indulged in a criticism of Marxism comparable to
that of Sorel or De Man; but both of them had the same rebellious reaction, which expressed itself in the founding of proletarian, anti-
Marxist, social, and national movements separated by some thirty
years. These movements rejected social polarization and class confrontation and aimed at a fraternal, united France of little people. These
people, said Loustau, needed a hope. "The hope is that of another
France, freed from the errors that divide it, the hatreds that torment it—
a France in which people will no longer be alone, lost in melancholy
herds, haunted by the anxiety of a vague yet certain catastrophe, but one
where, at every hour of their life, in every position that they occupy, they
will have a place within a family; one where, at every stage of their
earthly existence, they will be able to lean on other men who will participate in their joys and alleviate their sufferings."[173]

If Doriot and Loustau used the language of Biétry and Japy, Jean de
Fabrègues echoed the language of Barrès. "One ought not to suppress
nations," he wrote. "One should create a nation that belongs to everyone, and first of all to the proletarian. One cannot achieve this without
giving the proletarian his share of ownership of the national assets, his

share of responsibility in their administration and his share of emotional involvement in their enhancement. For that reason, the problem of the national integration of the proletariat cannot be separated from that of its economic integration any more than from that of its cultural integration." [174]

"The integration of the proletariat into the national community, the restoration of the proletariat to participation in national life and spiritual values" [175]—that was at all times a basic objective of national socialism. For Barrès in 1890, for Sorel in 1910, for the writers of *Combat* in 1936, this was the sole answer to the decadence of France. National socialism, or social nationalism, was conceived not just as a means of national salvation but as a life buoy for an entire civilization that was perishing.

One of the classic lines of argument taken by revisionists of Marxism had always been the defense of democracy. Déat took this line, and never ceased, while fighting a constant battle against Marxism, to refer to Jaurès and the "democratic spirit." [176] Unlike Jaurès, however, Déat was not afraid to question the fundamental assumptions of socialism, for this apologia for democracy based on the conception of a pragmatic socialism "able to adapt the doctrine to the facts" [177] and intimately linked to liberal democracy in fact represented, in the years after the Great War, an attempt to link the fate of socialism to that of the established order in western Europe. To do this, however, one first had to eradicate the connection between democracy and capitalism in the popular mind.

Accordingly, in *Perspectives socialistes*, Déat, adopting an idea from De Man, stated that democracy "is the very prototype of institutions that derive from an ideology not only anterior to capitalism in its inspiration, but in some way transcendent to it in its evolution." [178] Déat objected to the materialist explanation of democracy common to the theoreticians of both Marxism and capitalism, and to that school of thought within socialism that had always suspected the Republic or regarded it as a deception. [179] He insisted on the fact that, so far, political democracy has never succeeded in freeing itself from capitalism, and in the same way as capitalism manipulates the pseudodemocracy of shareholders' meetings, so it manipulates democracy through the press, through corruption, through economic threats that at the right moment frighten the population. It is easy to allow oneself to be convinced by the enemies of democracy and to arrive at Marx's familiar conclusion that democracy is simply an instrument created and utilized by capitalism. The bourgeoisie, said Déat, used democracy as a mere tool, and the equivocal liberalism with which it covered the operation was a useful camouflage. This, he said, allowed the orthodox socialists to condemn all the methods of democracy and to maintain that violence is unavoidable and that the dominance of one class would have to be replaced, through dictatorship, with the dominance of another. Because it considered political power to be only a disguise or an extension of economic power, so that the first without the second had no significance, orthodox socialism, said Déat, refused to dissociate the idea of the revolutionary seizure of power from that of the total nationalization of the means of production and exchange.[180] And, on the other hand, orthodox socialism condemned what it regarded as the absolute impotence of democracy and its incapacity to realize socialism. Déat was thus led to ask the following question, which he considered fundamental: "What is the value of democracy as a method of socialist construction?"[181] This question applied as much to the period preceding the working class's accession to power as to the period succeeding it.[182]

So, once again, one met with the great problem that the European left could not escape at any decisive stage in its evolution from the Dreyfus affair onward: is the fate of European socialism tied to that of democracy, or does its entire significance not reside, on the contrary, in class struggle? Is the state anything other than an instrument for the exploitation of the proletariat by the bourgeoisie? Does not political equality, to which so much importance is normally attached, seem abstract, formal, unsuitable, lamentably insufficient? Is it not nullified, in fact, by a tremendous economic inequality?[183] To these questions, which he knew had been asked long before by the German social democrats, by Sorel, by the revolutionary syndicalists, and, since the war, by the Communist party, Déat did not hesitate to reply: democracy was not formal in its original conception; it became so only *a posteriori*, after the event.[184]

It was in these terms that Déat defended democracy against Marxism, and for this purpose democracy had to be seen to have a value in itself, and not only in the special political context of social conflicts. At the beginning of the thirties this was an essential element in all revisions of Marxism, enabling most socialist principles to be discredited and the very foundations of the socialist consensus to be undermined.

However, in that period of crisis and chronic instability, Marxism appeared to the leaders of French socialism to be, now more than ever, the only solid ground to stand on. And, indeed, what else was left to these people in distress in a Europe in which the working class and the socialist parties, grappling with hitherto-unsuspected difficulties, lost their foothold when they did not get completely crushed? The situation was made more difficult by the appearance of new ideological models that confused the traditional scheme of things: surrounded by the various forms of "planism," "dirigism," and Keynesianism, socialism became diluted and lost its way. Faced with these new manifestations, these "intermediate forms," the French socialist leaders stated their position unequivocally: "It is not for us," said Léon Blum to Adrien Marquet, the neosocialist mayor of Bordeaux, "to take the direction of the movements intermediate between socialism and capitalism, even if we have to suffer for years on account of it. We must remain true to the conception we have always had." [185]

In view of this intransigence, it was not enough, in order to discredit Marxism, to address oneself to tactical questions and coalition problems: it was no longer possible to advocate union. In view of the party's determination to preserve its Marxist identity at all costs, Déat had no choice but to attack fundamental principles. He began by analyzing his opponents' position, and stating that those who interpreted class struggles and social antagonisms as a clash of incompatible, irreconcilable, and mutually exclusive forces could never solve the problems of modern society. No solution was possible as long as it was believed that because they could be connected to no common ideology, because they existed in a different moral atmosphere, social classes could engage only in relationships of conflict. Anyone who saw things in this way, said Déat, would have to regard the penetration of the bourgeois state by socialism as a "conquest of socialism by the government." If this was so, one could only bitterly reject this defiling and catastrophic relationship: any socialist who accepted this view would have to envisage reform as something imposed on the bourgeoisie from the outside. Consequently, added Déat, democracy itself could only seem a negotiated concession without any intrinsic value, and any argument put forward in its favor a hypocritical self-justification of the propertied ruling class.[186]

Déat claimed that most of the members of the socialist party, holding such views, still believed in the imminent collapse of capitalism. On the other hand, they believed that the only solution to the crisis was the total, ruthless substitution of socialism for capitalism. They could not conceive of any possible intermediate situations; they did not believe that the bourgeois state could be influenced in a positive direction or that democracy had a constructive potential or that the capitalist economy, under the influence of the crisis and under the pressure of the organized working class, could evolve toward a progressively freer and more structured economy.[187] This, then, is what Déat reproached the SFIO for: comfortably entrenched in its doctrinal purity, the party simply seemed to be waiting for a miracle. It rejected all compromises, all coalitions, all alliances. In fact, it advocated, in the guise of Marxist purity, a most absolute immobilism.

To get beyond this impasse, one had to go beyond Marxism itself, and thus Déat sought to replace the traditional concept of a total war of the proletariat against the bourgeoisie with a point of view that amounted to an acceptance of the principle of the reconciliation of the classes and the legitimacy of the "bourgeois state." This state, he said, "is that of a democracy that itself is not only illusion and hypocrisy."[188] Déat concluded, "That, indeed, is why the state should not appear to the working class as a bloc to destroy or an idea to be disproved. It is, rather, an as yet dim mirror in which it is nevertheless beginning to discern its idealized image. There are already, in the 'bourgeois' but democratic state, principles and values that the proletariat recognizes as its own, and that the bourgeoisie, for its part, cannot avoid taking into consideration."[189]

However, this progress "beyond" Marxism soon turned into a violent anti-Marxism. Just before the split in the socialist party, Déat declared his point of view quite plainly: "I don't like the Marxism of Pontius Pilate," he told "certain comrades" whose heads "rested irresistibly on the 'soft doctrinal pillow.'"[190] One year later, Adrien Marquet, the most hard-line of the néos, was plainer still: he asked his party to involve itself unfailingly "in the anti-Marxist, anti-Guesdist struggle." He said that accordingly, after having rejected "parliamentary politics," it had resolutely to assume "the leadership of the movement that will rid the slumbering working class of Marxism."[191] To certain hesitant spirits, to all those who had naively imagined they were only setting up another socialist party, Marquet replied brusquely, "What reason would we have to be a French socialist party—we who have broken with the Marxist ideology, with the erroneous Guesdist interpretation of the facts—if we are not the anti-Marxist, anti-Blumist, anticommunist party?"[192]

One was therefore dealing with something quite different from a renewal of socialism, from the greater flexibility of tactics and approach that Renaudel had advocated, from a synthesis of revolutionary, proletarian socialism and democratic socialism, or, again, from the integration of modern sociology within socialism that Déat had spoken of.[193] In 1935, after the 6 February street riots, which the néos considered to be the beginning of a revolutionary situation, the tone hardened, they grew more ambitious, and "in the general confusion and the panic of the old cadres" Déat and the néos prepared to replace "the faltering parties."[194]

The rupture, however, did not come easily. Since the appearance of *Perspectives socialistes*, Déat had tried to convince the party that "the new reformism" that he advocated, learned "in the school of facts and under their pressure,"[195] was in reality shared by the whole of the Socialist International. He claimed that Tony Sender and Otto Bauer were of the same opinion: in fighting to maintain its standard of living, in seeking the realization of socialism through democracy, the proletariat was not refurbishing capitalism. On the contrary, it was creating a new economy by orienting the present economy in the direction of socialism.[196] And, moreover, the great advantage of this wager on reformism that, according to Déat, had Bauer's tacit approval was the choice it gave the bourgeoisie: it was up to the bourgeoisie to assume its responsibilities and to decide if it wanted to collaborate with the proletariat or fight it[197]—which was another way of saying that if the bourgeoisie opted for peaceful relations and collaboration between the classes, socialism would not do otherwise.

Essentially, this choice stemmed from an acute consciousness of the collapse of socialism. Indeed, this feeling of bankruptcy had existed in the movement since the beginning of the century, and revolutionary syndicalism had been, in France and Italy, the strongest and clearest expression of this rebellion against official socialism. Revolutionary syndicalism had represented an attempt by the left to "go beyond" official socialism, while neosocialism was an attempt to extend socialism to the right. In both cases, however, the nonconformists developed toward a national, activist, and authoritarian form of socialism. Déat, De Man, Lagardelle, and Michels were united in their common condemnation of liberal democracy and Marxism.

All of these men had, throughout their careers, the feeling of living in a period of crisis of unprecedented magnitude, but, for the generation of the thirties, the collapse of German social democracy, the trial of strength in Austria, and the impotence of the French party before the massive upsurge of extraparliamentary forces created an especially dramatic situation: "Yes, crisis everywhere . . . Yes, crisis of socialism, certainly! But also a crisis of parliamentarianism and democracy, a fearful crisis that is manifested in all the countries of Europe and even in the whole world!" cried Montagnon at the Socialist Party Congress of 1933, and, with regard to that crisis, he observed, "I do not have the

impression that it works in favor of socialism." [198] It was a political crisis, certainly, he said, but it was also an economic crisis that gave rise to
unemployment and poverty, and the unemployed worker, "abased by
. . . his moral torpor," is not "a revolutionary element." [199] This "general
abasement," he added, is liable at a given moment to attract the unemployed "not to our side, where they will only receive distant promises,
but to wherever they, too, will be given an immediate hope." [200]

This sense of extreme urgency was at that time widespread within the
party, but the question always remained, What to do? There were many
different answers. That of the néos allowed no room for misinterpreta-
tion: the path that had been followed up to the present having led nowhere, one would have to try another path. Confronted with the majority of the party, which had nothing else to propose than fidelity to
traditional socialism, Marquet, the deputy for Bordeaux and its mayor,
summed up thirty years of socialist action, efforts, and daily sacrifices.
In 1914, he said, the party had 104 deputies and 100,000 members,
while in 1932, when wars and revolutions had changed the face of the
Continent, it had 130 deputies and 120,000 members. "One does not
give one's life in order to win thirty seats in the Chamber," he told the
people at the Paris congress. [201] To a distraught youth that official socialism, according to its critics, would surely sacrifice, as it had sacrificed the first two generations of party workers, neosocialism offered
more interesting prospects.

A National Revolution
Directed From Above

In a particularly lucid passage in his memoirs, Marcel Déat characterized the outline of the great party he had dreamed of already in 1934,
after 6 February:

There should have been a mighty movement, at once popular, national and revolutionary, to train and mold the best elements, the most intelligent, the most
capable of constructing—even though they may have come from different
spheres—and these forces, all together, should have been capable of conquering
the state, of rejuvenating it, of transforming it under the auspices of a vigorous
French socialism, self-confident, capable of spreading order within and without,
sufficiently sure of itself to consider the facts in Europe without ideological
prejudice, and to look for points of agreement with anyone—even with fascism
and national socialism. The difficulty of such a project, however, was immense:
one would have had to close up the two sides of a wound that was still fresh. And

already France was beginning stupidly to cut itself in two, everyone following the facile bent of his passion and his political routines.[202]

Such was the true nature of neosocialism, as some clear-sighted observers perceived. Very soon, what Renaudel had regarded as merely another socialist party—less dogmatic, more flexible—began to profess a relatively clearly articulated fascist ideology.

The Parti Socialiste de France was founded on 5 November 1933, following a long period of agitation that had culminated in July of that year at the SFIO Congress. Tension had been high since the congress in Tours in May 1931, and parliamentary incidents had occurred in which the two camps had confronted each other. However, over and above the problem of participation in government that preoccupied the party, the main question at issue was undoubtedly the nature of socialism itself. The intellectual rebellion caused by Déat since the publication of *Perspectives socialistes* came to a head in the summer of 1933 and created a split, but already, after the Tours congress in 1931, a declaration had been published by twenty-five parliamentarians of the *Vie socialiste* group stating openly that a split had just been averted.[203] That tensions existed was undeniable, but if it had not been for Déat's strong personality and his desire to break with the past, they would certainly never have led to the creation of a new party. Indeed, Renaudel, once Jaurès's associate and always true to Albert Thomas's school of thought, who had done everything in his power to prevent the break, would never have resigned himself to leaving the "old home," and, similarly, the other malcontents, the out-and-out "participationists," would not have been capable of forming an independent organization.

Nineteen thirty-three was a year of acute crisis in the SFIO. In February, polls revealed that its group of parliamentarians was divided between those who favored the measures proposed by the government of Edouard Daladier and those who did not. Differences appeared between the majority of the group, who were generally favorable to the idea of providing the government with a certain form of support, and the permanent executive committee, custodian of the official party line. Indeed, it soon became clear that the majority of the party and its parliamentary majority had lost confidence in each other and would henceforth be at loggerheads, for the minority in the parliamentary group that rejected participation in government represented a majority in the party, and, accordingly, Léon Blum and Vincent Auriol resigned from their posts of president and secretary of the parliamentary group.[204] The party congress held in Avignon on 16 and 17 April declared itself by a large majority in favor of a motion defended by Blum and against a motion proposed by Renaudel,[205] but nevertheless failed to dispel the malaise. When Parliament reconvened, the same conflicts reappeared: the party minority would not agree to accept the lesson in socialism imposed on it by the decision adopted in Avignon; those defeated at the Easter congress refused to yield. On 24 May, the parliamentary group decided to vote in support of the budget at its second reading. The executive committee immediately called on the deputies to comply with the resolution passed at the recent congress, and Paul Faure informed them brusquely that he intended to ask for sanctions.[206]

A new congress was held in Paris on 15 and 16 July. Once again, a large majority voted against a motion proposed by Renaudel, but this time three important speeches were given—by Déat, Marquet, and Montagnon—that left no doubt about the nature and the depth of the ideological differences that were rending the party. It was during Marquet's speech, in which he said that "today we must enter into a new national reality," that Blum cried out, "I must confess I am horrified!"[207] and on the next day he accused the néos of fascism.[208] He lashed out against the new slogans "Authority" and "Order," against the importance that the néos attached to the attainment of political power, and against the race that they seemed to have entered into with fascism, adopting fascist methods and the fascist ideology. "Simple, elemental slogans—socialism has never had them," Blum said to the néo leaders.[209] In his answer to Marquet, later minister under Gaston Doumergue and Pétain, Blum asked if it was not the program of a new "national-socialist" party "that had just been presented to the congress."[210]

Blum resumed his attack in *Le Populaire* throughout July. He had already expressed his anxiety over the emergence of neosocialism in three long articles published just before the congress, devoted to problems of power.[211] Faithful to his distinction between the conquest and the exercise of power, Blum attacked what he considered the fundamental error of the "participationists"—the illusion that there is an intrinsic value in political power and a confusion between political and social revolution.[212] He claimed that neosocialism exemplified the "unconscious fascination" that fascism now held for socialist thought.[213] If one regards the conquest of power as an end in itself, if one competes with fascism for the attainment of power, if one tries to fight fascism with its own weapons,[214] one can only end by imitating fascism, he said.[215] If one wants action at any price, to get something done no matter what, one becomes responsible for those intermediate forms between capitalism and socialism that fascism and nazism claim to have created.[216] In this way, said Blum, the néos were developing a coherent body of doctrine that was in every respect opposed to traditional socialist doctrine,[217] for "there do not exist two kinds of socialism, one of which is international and the other of which is not. . . . A national socialism would no longer be socialism and would soon become antisocialism."[218]

Finally, Blum, in turn, also quoted Jaurès. Since the time of Marx, he said, who "united idea and fact, thought and history . . . , socialism and the proletariat are inseparable: socialism cannot realize its full conception except through the victory of the proletariat and the proletariat cannot realize its full being except through the victory of socialism."[219] Blum told the new socialist party that placed itself under the banner of the former leader and called itself the Union Jean-Jaurès that Jaurès would never have agreed to "situate socialist action outside the class organization of the proletariat." Whoever did so necessarily placed himself "outside socialist life and thought."[220]

In July 1933, the challenge represented by the speeches of Déat, Montagnon, and Marquet reverberated far and wide. They were attempting to reach opinion beyond the limits of the congress, and they received enormous publicity. This success contributed to their decision to break with the party, as did their feeling that they represented a considerable force among the party members. This feeling was encouraged by the fact that, in July, sixty-nine deputies and ten senators, or seventy-nine parliamentary representatives out of 147, opposed the executive committee and voted for the Daladier cabinet. The three men did not hide their contempt for the Paris congress and acted in such a way that their expulsion became inevitable. On 24 October, the néo deputies voted in favor of the Daladier government and the other socialist deputies voted against. The split became official.

A few days before the National Council of 5 November that declared their expulsion, the rebellious deputies had already stated that they were setting up a new party. Seven parliamentarians were expelled, including the three who had spoken at the congress and Pierre Renaudel. Others left the SFIO of their own accord—twenty-eight deputies in all, including Paul Ramadier, a future prime minister of the Fourth Republic, and seven senators, representing the federations of Aveyron, the Charente, the Hautes-Alpes, and the Var.[221] These numbers, however, were far smaller than they had been in July: the stigma of the Paris congress, Paul Faure's skill in isolating and reducing the level of néo opposition, and above all the fear of many of the "participationists" of cutting themselves off from the old party had borne fruit, with the result that, in its heyday, the Parti Socialiste de France seems to have had no more than twenty-two thousand members.[222] It never succeeded in getting off the ground, and in its very first year of activity, the malaise that always characterized the party caused Déat to ask in his address to the annual congress whether they were not drawing up the balance sheet of an action that had failed.[223]

There was deep confusion among the members. Those who, like Renaudel and Adéodat Compère-Morel, thought they were simply founding a new socialist party immediately found themselves confronted with a new radical wing led by Marquet and Déat. Following 6 February, Marquet became a minister—not, however, without having first threatened his friends with setting up a real neosocialist party. He finally left the Parti Socialiste de France at the head of the important Gironde Federation. Marquet's participation, on his own initiative but with the authorization of the parliamentary group, in a government of national unity gave rise to lively protestations. The Renaudel faction opposed it, and the majority grouped around Déat pretended to resign itself to it. The genuine néos, however, indulged in a violent antisocialist campaign and enthusiastically welcomed the chance to participate in government.[224] Déat himself never condemned Doumergue's new minister of labor, and in his Paris journal, *Paris-Demain*, even gave the Marquet Plan much publicity and tended to take Marquet's part.

Between this "100 percent néo"[225] tendency and that of Renaudel ("I don't like to pick up my flag in the gutter")[226] coexistence became increasingly difficult. It became clear that the party would have to choose between those who considered themselves only "socialists and democrats"[227] and those who, to be able to "act—act swiftly and vigorously, give France a spurt"—"would like to see a mighty movement like the Hitlerian movement."[228] This analogy aroused a storm of protestation, but that did not prevent Marquet from conceiving of the neosocialist movement as a rallying point not only for the proletariat and the middle classes but also for "certain capitalist elements,"[229] and it was in that spirit that Déat wished to launch "a preventive, planned revolution, as thoroughgoing as you like."[230] This formula had a disagreeable ring even at that time, but it was much favored in Déat's circle because they always sought to widen the rift with the SFIO. The néo pamphlets of the eighteenth and twentieth *arrondissements*, especially, were particularly fond of it. For *Néo*, a bulletin written solely by Montagnon, and for

Paris-Demain, Déat's weekly in the twentieth *arrondissement*, the very name *neosocialist*, because of this desire to burn one's bridges, was something to be proud of.

The rejection by the Socialist International of the request for affiliation of the Parti Socialiste de France, whose positions the International judged to be in opposition to its fundamental principles,[231] helped to push the party to the right. Renaudel's refusal to associate himself with an anti-Marxist bloc and simply repudiate Marxism and espouse instead certain watchwords that already had a somewhat dubious history[232] met with a sympathetic response from party workers like Compère-Morel, Perrin, and Perceau, who was in charge of the important group in Clignancourt. All these people formed an internal opposition to Déat, and finally went back to the left.[233]

Despite very great efforts, the Parti Socialiste de France did not succeed in enlarging its membership. Quite the contrary. The optimism of November 1933 did not justify itself in the following year: membership did not increase, internal differences became more pronounced, and financial difficulties became more and more pressing. In February 1934 Déat admitted that the resources he had announced as forthcoming had remained a mirage.[234] A year later, Renaudel said that, having gone through great crises in July and December of the preceding year, *La Vie socialiste* was threatened with having to close down.[235] In fact the number of subscribers to the journal never reached three thousand:[236] the considerable influence of the néo ideology was exerted via the national press—daily or weekly newspapers that informed the general public of the theoretical debates in which only a minority of party members took part.

From March 1935, *La Vie socialiste* appeared only fortnightly, and in July of that year it came to an end. Meanwhile, Renaudel's death permitted Déat to sever the last remaining links connecting neosocialism with its Marxist past, and, believing that the Parti Socialiste de France had run its course, he founded a new political party,[237] the Union Socialiste Républicaine, which was a fusion of the néo movement with two other small groups, the Parti Socialiste Français and the Parti Républicain Socialiste. The new party came into being on 3 November 1935, exactly two years after the expulsion of the *Vie socialiste* group from the sfio. Its parliamentary representation included forty deputies,[238] and, in spite of the violent anticommunist campaign of its secretary-general, Déat, the Union Socialiste Républicaine participated in the Popular Front.[239] Déat himself became minister of aviation in the Albert Sarraut cabinet that, for a few months in 1936, assured the transition to the elections in May.

In the weeks before the new elections, the loyalty of the néo members of the Union Socialiste Républicaine to the Rassemblement Populaire was unfailing. Déat presented the Popular Front as a genuine concretization of his 1933 political program and a retaliation for his defeat at the Paris congress: he claimed that the Popular Front had in fact taken up the watchwords of neosocialism.[240] "Under the pressure of events," he said, one is compelled "to extend one's hand to the most moderate of republicans and the middle classes, and socialism can no longer be separated from the nation."[241] Its weekly, *Le Front*, even published, after the great demonstration under the auspices of the Rassemblement Populaire that went from the Panthéon to the place de la Nation, an article by Montagnon that would not have been out of place in *Le Populaire*.[242] Its electoral defeat (of the forty deputies who belonged to the parliamentary group of the Union Socialiste in December 1935 only twenty-five remained the following May)[243] did not prevent it from participating in the government of the Popular Front. Under the influence of Ramadier and in opposition to Paul Marion, the Union Socialiste Républicaine took up a position in support of Blum: it was unimportant compared to the SFIO, and its leaders realized that not taking this stand would have been tantamount to signing the party's death warrant.[244] A short time afterward, Marion, taking the youngest and most dynamic elements of neosocialism with him, went over to the Parti Populaire Français,[245] while Déat continued his campaign for a pacifistic, and frankly pro-German, national socialism, until in 1940 he launched a campaign to transform the Vichy regime into a totalitarian single party system.

Although the Union Socialiste Républicaine participated in the Popular Front, Déat pursued a vigorous anticommunist and antisocialist campaign for which neither party forgave him. His narrow defeat by the communist Adrien Langummier was especially welcome to the socialists.[246] Indeed, for the traditional left, which wished to remain faithful, at least in theory, to Marxism, Déat represented a policy that meant the end of socialism. The political program of the neosocialist party expressed a desire to "take over from the old parties"[247] and, "placing oneself at the head of the general discontent,"[248] make "a great union" that would bring about a "directed revolution."[249] Accordingly, without being "in any way basely empirical,"[250] the program should leave aside "doctrines that have grown cold"[251] and capture the "enormous community of discontent" that burst forth on 6 February in the place de la Concorde.[252] To "gather up these anticapitalist forces," to satisfy the expectations of the unemployed, more, said Déat, was needed than "ideological garglings. France," he said, "is saturated with political philosophy; it is sick of great machines and programs without end. It wants something immediate, positive, simple and effective."[253] A few months later, Déat asked his followers to "cure themselves, once and for all, of false humanism, of false freedom of thought."[254] He said that he wanted to protect the new party "against dogmatism and against sclerosis," and he reminded his critics that "it was because they were ferociously doctrinal that the old parties turned aside from action and are now effectively bankrupt."[255] To these "men turned toward action," Montagnon suggested abandoning the old "conceptions of *right* and *left*," for "if you want the left one day to triumph, it will have to bite into the right."[256] For Déat, what was really important in action was "movement,"[257] "a practical convergence around a certain number of immediate formulas"[258] that will enable an enormous mass of people from all political horizons—people, he said, who drift undecidedly not only among the groups and parties of the left but also between the left and the right, and who understand today that philosophical similarities and doctrinal affinities are less important than agreement on an immediate program—to gather around a "center of attraction" in an "upsurge of youth and hope."[259]

The only possible framework for such a "massive union,"[260] Déat thought, was the national state. He expressed the gist of his thought in a text to which he would subsequently have nothing to add:

The character of the battle is changing, we say, because the driving force is no longer class interest but purely and simply an imperious desire for collective salvation. One does not have—that would be too simple—a bourgeoisie and a proletariat disputing the shreds of power to safeguard their conditions of existence during the crisis. What one has is a bourgeoisie, a proletariat, and a middle class variously affected by the crisis, contained within the same national framework, and obliged to save themselves, or to attempt to save themselves, together. In the name of what, however, and in accordance with what principle? Not that of class, which generates irreconcilable antagonisms. Not in the name of humanity, a superior principle, but abstract. In the name of the nation, in the name of national solidarity, *in the name of the general interest.*

Consequently, said Déat—and here he reached a crucial stage in his argument—"*in the present period it is unquestionably the nation, it is unquestionably the general interest that are the revolutionary principles. It* is in the name of the nation, it is in the name of the collective interest, that the revolution, undoubtedly begun, will be carried to its conclusion." [261]

The revolution can thus be carried out only by means of and on behalf of the collectivity as a whole, which means that the proletariat finds itself in competition with the bourgeoisie, and one has to show it that it is able, better than the bourgeoisie, to express "this general and national interest." [262] Accordingly, said Déat, the working class has to recognize that in the situation of crisis that exists in Europe "national solidarity must prevail over class oppositions." [263] In consequence, a "rallying of the proletariat becomes impossible," [264] and no one can afford "to fail to take into account the fact of the nation." [265] The fact that human beings are grouped first of all "in their national frameworks" [266] forces anyone who wishes to leave his mark on history to accept not only the primacy of the nation but also "the transcendence of the nation over individuals" [267] and, finally, to set up within the national framework "a strong authority that will replace the failing bourgeoisie." [268]

These néo ideas were taken over word for word by the intellectuals and leaders of the Parti Populaire Français, people like Loustau and Doriot. Loustau considered the self-contained existence of the national unit an irrevocable fact, [269] and Doriot spoke of "sacred national egoism." [270] This former communist now spoke in a way that would not have been unworthy of Déroulède, [271] and "working within the national framework" became one of Doriot's favorite expressions, suggesting the principle that "the national idea has to be coupled with a new organization of the country." [272] The neosocialists and their allies called for a return to the "old French socialism of Saint-Simon and Proudhon," [273] to "the true tradition of French socialism," [274] to a national, anti-Marxist, "truly French" [275] socialism. This socialism would truly be a "revolutionary idea": it alone would be capable of "guiding the nation toward salvation"; [276] it alone could save democracy, for "democracy is weakened and is replaced by dictatorship to the degree that class antagonisms prevail over a concern for cooperation in a common rescue action." [277]

In this way, Déat developed his idea of democracy. In itself, he said, "normal democracy is not and cannot be a regime for revolutionary periods"; it does not exist, in the usual, traditional sense of the word, in times of acute crisis, but democracy nevertheless exists "insofar as the nation really cooperates in the work undertaken bravely, heroically, in the face of the common disaster, in the face of the common misery." Democracy always exists "if the recovery takes place nationally, through and on behalf of the nation, through a brutal negation of class oppositions and interests and a harsh imposition of collective discipline." He added, "It is almost by instinct that the masses aspire to a concentration of power, demand to feel *governed*." [278]

Convinced that this aspiration to a strong authority is deeply rooted in human nature, Déat suggested that socialism "appropriate for its own benefit the idea of order, the idea of authority, the idea of the nation." [279] "Order," said Max Bonnafous in his commentary on the three speeches-cum-programs collected in one volume, "has always seemed to me to have an objective value in various societies, relatively independent of the end that that order pursued." [280] For a long period, he said, democracy and socialism had undermined some of these fundamental values without which no society is possible. [281] Jouvenel, similarly, expressed a "passion for order," [282] while Marquet, Montagnon, and other neosocialists spoke of their desire "for a strong state, a powerful state, a state of order." [283] For, finally, said Montagnon, "order, today, is a revolutionary idea." [284]

As early as 1930, Déat had said that "henceforth the revolution passes through the state" and that "the realization of socialism passes through the exercise of power." [285] Déat attached so much importance to the state that he thought that, "in practice, the social problem tends to become a political problem," and that "one way or another" the state should overcome "the unfettered and pernicious political forces." [286] This faith in the intrinsic virtues of political power was rooted in the conception of the state that Déat expounded in *Perspectives socialistes*. He rejected the "Marxist idea that the state, forged by the dominating class, is merely an instrument of dictatorship in the hands of the bourgeoisie," and insisted that "the state belongs neither to the bourgeoisie nor to the proletariat" and can be used in various ways. [287] The "democratic state," he said, is very different from the "class state," [288] and once one has succeeded in effecting "a separation of capitalism from the state" [289] and affirming the sovereignty of the state, it can be made into an instrument for the service of the majority that can be identified with anticapitalism. [290]

In their fight against Marx and the orthodox Marxists of their own generation, the néos liked to invoke the authority of Jaurès. "Our conception of the state," wrote Déat, "is not that of an instrument of bourgeois domination, that of a fortress where the exploiters of the proletariat would be ambushed. Our conception of the state is progressive, democratic, like Jaurès's. We believe that one can reform, transform that state without first having to create a *tabula rasa*." [291]

It was on this conception of political power that the neosocialists based their policy of attempting to participate, at almost any price, in the exercise of power. Déat stated the problem unequivocally. From the period of *Perspectives socialistes,* he told the party members to have the courage to choose either to give up any attempt to penetrate the cadres of bourgeois society and prepare a violent, total, desperate revolution or to be present everywhere and do battle everywhere, including in the government.[292]

This was also how Henri De Man viewed the situation. Indeed, a refusal to identify the state with the domination of a class was a fundamental characteristic of the revisionism of the interwar period: De Man claimed that "the state is a philosophical formation *sui generis.*"[293] Capitalist domination and the state are different concepts, said De Man. The state carries out its function not in the sphere of production but in the much broader sphere of political and judicial relations. The will of the state is different from the desire for gain of the capitalist, and embodies, in fact, the immediate total effect of the will of all the human beings who have a permanent part in the destiny of the state. The state, said De Man, is made up of people—it is a distinct being with a will of its own.[294] What consequently prevents the labor movement from understanding the fundamental nature of government is the initial error of seeing the state only as an instrument of class domination.[295]

Undoubtedly, neosocialism saw the state as the chief agent of economic and social transformation. The state, in its view, if it succeeded in restoring its sovereignty, could play its role of arbiter between the classes: it could become an incomparable tool in the hands of anticapitalism. For this reason, it was believed, the problem of the state was the essential problem for socialism.[296] The state, said Déat, could exercise authority on behalf of the general interests of the community;[297] it had its own nature and was capable of independent action: its conquest, its neutralization, its penetration, and its utilization by socialism constituted for all the reformers an essential condition of the great battle against capitalism.[298] If this battle was to be won, the state had to play its role, and its role, said Jouvenel, was to direct the national economy and defend the general interest.[299] Accordingly, one needed a strong state, a regenerated, renewed state, in possession of all the commanding positions of the economy and finances. One needed, in other words, a different state, a modern state.[300]

One must therefore restore the state, but above all, thought Déat, one must reform democracy, for "parliamentarianism as we have experienced it since 1875 is not in itself democracy."[301] The néos—some of whom, notably Marquet's followers in Bordeaux, were becoming increasingly contemptuous of democracy[302]—were attracted, like the Boulangists half a century earlier, to the idea of a Constituent Assembly.[303] Their projects for reform were not very clear in their details, but in their broad outlines they consisted of a form of corporatism based on a "universal suffrage of producers" together with a *"horizontal,* that is to say regional, representation."[304] Each individual would thus have a triple vote: as a citizen, as the member of a profession, and as a producer in a particular economic region. Déat thought it was impossible to establish a system for balancing the interests of employers and workers apart from laying down the principle of an equitable representation of each element "with due regard to its numerical importance, its volume of interests and the place it holds in the general framework of the national life."[305] This is a good exposition of the basic principles of corporatism as a genuine alternative to liberal democracy as well as to socialism.

Jouvenel put forward a slightly more detailed plan. He opposed the dictatorship of Parliament and wanted to introduce a new form of ministerial responsibility and the practice of dissolution to assure the stability and continuity of the executive.[306] As for the legislature, it would be divided into three bodies: the Chamber of Interests, the Chamber of Departments, and the Chamber of Deputies. The first two would be "advisory Chambers" that would submit to the Chamber of Deputies questions to which it would reply with a yes or a no like a jury.[307] Seven years later, *La Lutte des jeunes,* edited by Jouvenel, proposed a revision of the constitution based on the following principles: the president of the Republic would be replaced by a premier as head of state and appointed for two years; a Council of Corporations would pass laws and take the place of the Chamber of Deputies; and technical directors, responsible to the premier, would take the place of ministers.[308]

Before Jouvenel, however, before Bergery and Doriot, Déat had organized his party on the lines of the parties of the totalitarian countries. He thought some benefit could be gained from the type of organization and techniques used by both the Nazis and the Soviets. These techniques, he thought, could be used for different ends, and he saw no reason not to draw some practical conclusions from the Nazi experience.

Déat claimed that the Nazi party "had been conceived at one and the same time as an army capable of imposing itself by force and as the prefiguration of a new state."[309] To be able to take over the government, the

Nazis had carefully trained all those who would be responsible for carrying out the revolution. The party had to appear to the electors as a force commanding all the technical and political personnel necessary for governing society once it came to power. This new type of party would make possible the mobilization of public opinion, facilitate its accession to power, and enable it to remain in power.[310]

The second lesson that Déat drew from the experience of the parties of the totalitarian systems was to regard the party as a prefiguration of the state. "The party will become the state as soon as you want it to," he told his supporters.[311] He wanted, in fact, to create a "party-state" and organized "technical groups" and "action groups" for that purpose. The action groups were there not only to keep order but also as a possible source of assistance "in probable moments of difficulty, which would compensate for a certain foreseeable negligence on the part of the regularly constituted forces of the state."[312] In other words, he wanted to prepare a paramilitary force that, when the time came, could take the place of the old mechanisms of the state as it collapsed.

It was in the Gironde *département*, Marquet's area, that the action groups were most in evidence, but they were also active in the Seine *département*. During the second national congress, a formation of the Girondin action groups appeared dressed in gray shirts, with arm bands, flags, and pennants bearing the sign of the ram. This apparition aroused a vehement protest from Renaudel. In reply, the leaders of the Gironde and Seine groups explained the nature and purpose of their formations, giving, without being aware of it, a perfect description of fascist shock troops. The purpose of these groups, they said, was not only to stick notices on billboards, to distribute tracts, and to assure order at party gatherings but above all to "create a new youth." The shirt was a symbol, and "the symbol is as important as the word," and the same was true of the sign of the ram, which symbolized youth, springtime, vigor. The groups existed to give the youth a sense of discipline and to teach the whole party "the team spirit: the party must be a large team," as one of the leaders of the Seine Federation put it, while another, eyeing with envy the Jeunesses Patriotes and other right-wing movements, "with their symbols, their fanfares, their flags," asked, "Why can't we have our own troops?"[313]

Side by side with the "action groups" were "technical groups" whose essential purpose was "to penetrate the state instead of trying to overthrow it." If the party was to infiltrate the government, it needed information; it needed people who would be able to set the planned economy on its feet. It therefore needed special economic and technical cadres. The technical groups were thus a kind of school for government—for a rejuvenated, revitalized, and reformed government.[314]

While setting up these various groups, Déat declared his desire to "limit certain anarchic and dangerous liberties."[315] He was aware of the accusation of fascism that was increasingly leveled at his movement, and of the praise he received in the Italian press.[316] At the same time, he employed a classic technique of fomenting excitement by creating the atmosphere of a *coup de force*. He even fixed the date of that much hoped for *coup*—8 July—and named the forces that were to overthrow the regime: the CGT, the War Veterans' Association, and various planist groups directed by the Parti Socialiste de France, which was to hold a meeting of its Central Council precisely on that day. That 8 July finally proved to be no more fateful than similar attempts by Déroulède and the Boulangist leaders made little difference. For several weeks, Déat exerted himself to create a climate that, coming after 6 February and while Marquet was in the government, was by no means as inoffensive as it might seem in retrospect.

Like revolutionary syndicalism before the First World War, neosocialism was not a simple phenomenon. Unquestionably, the revisionism of the interwar period represented an attempt at modernizing socialism, at adapting it to new realities. Very often, it was simply a matter of matching theory with practice. There can be no doubt that, at the beginning of the thirties, socialist praxis was no longer in keeping with the traditional conception of a class state. And it moved farther and farther away from this conception: the néos in France and De Man in Belgium were quite correct in claiming that, in Europe, socialism was increasingly becoming the vehicle of the idea of the state and that the socialists had become the true supporters of the state. Where the fundamental principles of socialist theory are concerned, neosocialism gave ideological expression to the fact that, for a long time, it had no longer been possible to regard political power solely as an instrument of class domination. If the state, thanks to universal suffrage, was one day to fall into the hands of socialism, it could be regarded as an instrument that could be used against the regime that it sought to replace. The state thus became a mighty tool of social transformation.

Déat's thinking on this point was not, perhaps, particularly original: it represented a banal social democracy and a commonplace desire to gain office. However, if one places this cult of political power in its context, one immediately realizes that Déat's neosocialism was already well beyond socialism. The anti-Marxism and idealism that were basic to neosocialism, the principle of the solidarity of the classes within the national framework, the refusal to regard the proletariat as the principal agent of social transformation, the return to a pre-Marxist French socialism, and, finally, the wish to found a new political system on corporatist lines added up to an original ideological whole, at once innovative and almost traditional.

Georges Valois, who in this period had already returned to socialism, was scathing. He regarded neosocialism, essentially based on anti-Marxism, as "the crudest national socialism,"[317] dominated by an "aspiring dictator" who dreamed "of a *coup de force*."[318] The violent anti-Marxism of neosocialism rendered it suspect even to those adherents "of the third party"[319] who, while rejecting orthodoxy, nevertheless did not want to slide into fascism. They refused to subscribe to the idea that only the proletariat practiced class warfare. They accepted the principle of the reconciliation of the classes, but only on condition that it be loyal to the interests of all social classes, that it not be detrimental to the proletariat, and that relations between employers and employees be subjected to the control of an organism reflecting the general interest.[320]

Such were the reactions to the néo phenomenon of various dissidents eager to agree on the meaning of words, for, in the context of the thirties, a revisionism that soon became an anti-Marxism, an anti-materialism that, to liberate itself from Marxist ideology, threw itself into a cult of youth, vitalism, and energy and sang hymns to life, movement, and discipline, entailed the revision not only of a political ideology but also of a whole set of basic values and finally of an entire civilization.

CHAPTER SIX

Planism, or Socialism Without a Proletariat

The De Man Plan was adopted almost unanimously amid general enthusiasm at the Christmas Congress of the Parti Ouvrier Belge in 1933. Earlier, the "planist" ideas had been discussed in Germany by the Hamburg section of the German Socialist Party, which was to put them forward at the party congress in March 1933.[1] If the German social democratic movement had not collapsed, the new program would therefore have first been presented before the most famous of socialist parties.

When the Nazis came to power, De Man returned to Belgium. In the spring of 1933, he became director of the Bureau of Social Studies, which was responsible for working out the Plan. Two years of preparation had preceded the return of the prodigal son. Indeed, Émile Vandervelde, president of the Parti Ouvrier Belge, had invited him to return in 1931. Despite the differences of opinion that had existed between them since the appearance of *Au-delà du marxisme*, Vandervelde considered De Man one of the best minds of the period.[2] Without actually saying so, he clearly regarded De Man as the leading intellectual of the party, and suggested to him that he set up a Bureau of Social Studies for the formulation of the party's policies. De Man accepted eagerly, in a letter that Vandervelde was happy to publish in March 1935 when he wanted to claim paternity for the idea that the party needed a new strategy. Vandervelde took the opportunity to tell De Man that the Plan, whose origination was henceforth to be attributed to the entire party and not to a single individual, was the result of a collective effort inspired by classic socialist doctrine. It was simply that and nothing more, he said.[3]

The bureau, in whose name De Man spoke at the congress, included members of all the party's factions, and among those on the bureau's Scientific Committee were the party's leading figures, Vandervelde, Louis de Brouckère, and Arthur Wauters.[4] At the end of October, when the syndicates gave it their support, the Plan gained unanimous acceptance: all the party authorities accepted the principles of a program of action that had the great advantage of avoiding, for once, the classic dilemma resulting from always wanting to make electoral platforms embody great revolutionary programs. For the first time, the party possessed a program of government and administration that could immediately be carried out in terms of legal action.[5]

To stress the novelty of his conception, De Man deliberately used the term *plan* rather than *program*. The Plan, he said, "is a precise commitment," a "plan of action" that could be put into effect as soon as one came to power.[6] The classical programs of socialist parties always remained in the sphere "of the ideal," but the Plan, he said, was "a program that could *immediately* be applied as a governmental program,"[7] and that, indeed, was how it was perceived by the party members, whom this new concept fired, in that winter of crisis, with an enthusiasm unknown for some time. The great virtues of the Plan were simply that it existed and addressed itself to the main problem, the only one that really mattered: how to deal with the terrible distress resulting from the present economic crisis.

And yet, the adoption of the Plan by the POB involved, from the start, a fundamental ambiguity. It soon became clear that its promoter, in putting forward the Plan, had objectives much broader than those envisioned by the party. De Man, in the year following the Christmas congress, regarded it as a genuine revolution in socialist thought of great theoretical and practical significance, whereas the vast majority of the POB, which, unlike the SFIO, was a truly proletarian party, regarded it only as a vigorous and practical program of political action that could solve a problem crucial to the proletariat—unemployment—in accordance with socialist principles. De Man understood this view, and admitted in the conclusion of his major speech that it was necessary to "concentrate action on a limited but sharply and clearly defined objective."[8] He returned to this idea in another text characteristic of his attempts to convince the Belgian proletariat. "My friends," he said, "as you know, the Labor Plan is a plan for overcoming the crisis by curing

unemployment. When one has said that, one has described all it contains. It contains only the conditions necessary for attaining that objective. It contains them all and it goes no further."[9] In reality, however,
things were much more complicated, and the fundamental differences
between De Man's attitude and that of the majority of the party were
soon revealed.

To be sure, in this fight against economic distress, the first step was
to attack the unemployment—and resulting low consumption—that
De Man considered the basic cause of the crisis. The main idea of the
Plan, accordingly, was the creation of a planned economy that would
end the crisis. But the Plan would work only if it had the support of the
majority of the population, and could never be effective—especially in
the mixed economy De Man envisaged—without the support of a massive
majority. Such a majority, however, would require the adherence of the
middle classes. One had therefore to bring together all the social classes
affected by the crisis, propose an alliance with the "proletarianized
middle classes," and so rally all the "anticapitalist and non-working-class
forces."[10] This alliance of the working class with non-working-class elements would embrace all the victims of "financial capital"—both the
proletariat and "the middle classes in revolt against the hypercapitalism
of high finance."[11]

The use of the term *hypercapitalism* was characteristic. Introduced
by the "Rex" fascists,[12] it was a kind of password used by all those—and
especially the "Rex" fascists—who hoped to bring together everyone
affected by the crisis and maintained that the intended reforms, including those that De Man, for party reasons, described as "a general transformation of society,"[13] did not have to change the structures of capitalism, the principles of private property, or the laws of the market
economy. It was no longer capitalism as such that was now attacked, but
only supercapitalism, high finance, and the great financial magnates
who from the end of the nineteenth century had been opposed by all the
critics of the bourgeois order who, like De Man, had found the atmosphere of bourgeois society "unbreathable" but nevertheless had refused to undermine its economic foundations. De Man's attitude was
thus in no way surprising: it had become commonplace since the time of
the national socialists of the turn of the century.

To bring this great anticapitalist coalition into being, De Man addressed himself, in the best national-socialist tradition, to "men of
goodwill, sincere men" in all parties, including "parties that at present
are our adversaries."[14] Indeed, his Plan, he felt, could satisfy all, and

had something for everyone. To the liberals, who had seen the limits that capitalism, in its present stage of evolution, had imposed on the development of free competition, De Man presented the Plan as a synthesis of individual freedom and enterprise on the one hand and social solidarity on the other. In presenting the Plan to the Catholics and Christian democrats, he said he was only asking them to take the papal encyclicals seriously and to put their own programs into practice. De Man likewise claimed to respect "all that was clean" in the Communist party, to whom he said that he was only asking them to follow Trotsky's advice. According to him, the communist leader in exile had told the Belgian communists and socialists that the only way out of the present impasse was to rally to the Plan.

De Man believed that the Plan was the only means of preventing the formation of a nonlabor alliance directed against the working classes. He thought that, by harnessing the discontent of the middle classes, the farmers, the intellectuals, and the young, the Plan would keep them from attempting fascism as a solution.[15] The collapse of social democracy in Germany had left an indelible impression on De Man: it was the defection of the middle classes, he thought, that had made possible the rise of nazism. the middle classes had turned their backs on social democracy not because it had seemed too revolutionary but because socialism had appeared to be "a movement of conservation for immediate reforms that now interested only one class of the population."[16]

Thus, the class egoism of German socialism—its inability to place itself at the head and center of a vast coalition and to understand the new situation—had contributed to its own destruction. In modern, crisis-ridden Europe, the working class, he said, now found itself sandwiched between an unemployed subproletariat and the "revolutionary middle classes."[17] The unemployed no less than the tradesmen and farmers felt the attraction of fascism, and the only way to counteract it was to show them that the Plan's intention of eliminating unemployment was in everyone's interests, and that the Plan was the only way of dealing with the sickness undermining the national economy as a whole. Because it shrank the market by creating chronic underconsumption, unemployment was the fundamental cause of economic depression.[18]

The Plan, therefore, originated in the idea that, instead of passively undergoing the crisis, one should formulate a program of governmental action. Accordingly, the Plan envisaged the creation of a planned mixed economy, the nationalization of credit and of basic industries that had already become monopolies, and, in the political field, a reform of the state and the parliamentary regime in order to lay "the foundations of a genuine economic and social democracy."[19] Its immediate aim, however, was to eliminate unemployment, to change the present situation, to end the policy of deflation that benefited only the banks, and to replace it with a policy of producing more money and providing cheaper credit.[20]

However, what is most significant about the Plan is not what it contained but what it omitted. Its long-term objectives and the political means it envisaged for achieving them throw the most light on the profound changes in socialist thinking that were taking place at the time. First of all, De Man had from the start an attitude of detachment toward all the existing political parties, one that did not make a real difference between the socialist movement and other political trends ready to accept his solutions. His memoirs make it quite clear that, as opposed to the "out-of-date partisan groups," De Man wanted to create an alliance of all the victims of the crisis, "a government of little people."[21] He chose to work through the socialist party because the leaders of the other parties he had invited to join him in his project had rejected his initiative, and he did not try to found a new party because, in the Belgium of his day, such an attempt would have led to disaster. As a means of realizing the Plan, the POB, said De Man, was "far from perfect, but it at least had the merit of existing, and of being of some use."[22] This ideological neutrality explains why the Plan lacked a specifically proletarian character, just as it helps us to understand the hostility toward De Man—open in some cases, implicit in others—of nearly all the major socialist leaders.

In reality, the Plan had far vaster ambitions than simply the elimination of unemployment. It represented nothing less than the completion, in practical terms, of the demolition of Marxism begun in *Au-delà du marxisme*, continued in *Le Socialisme constructif* and *L'Idée socialiste*, and pursued further in the mass of articles of 1933–35. Thus, the Plan replaced the old principle of class struggle with a common front "of all the productive social groups against parasitic high finance."[23] As this front was an alliance of the "small" against the "great," there was no longer any need for the celebrated principle of "nationalization of the means of production." The Plan was based on another principle, one more modern and more realistic but fraught with grave implications for the socialism of the thirties: it replaced the concept of "transference of property" with the concept of "transference of authority." The main concern was no longer to change society but to ensure state control of the economy, no longer to develop a new relationship between people in

an egalitarian society but to prevent banking monopolies and the owners of essential industries from taking charge of the economy.

To be sure, these were aims that any socialist party might have found
acceptable, but on condition that such a plan should be—to employ the
jargon of the period—a "minimum program," a first step toward a different kind of society. For De Man, however, the Plan was an end in itself, the final goal of all his efforts, especially insofar as the Plan not only
respected the private sector of the economy but even sought to develop
it. This sector, he said, was important to the "vast majority"; far from
condemning private ownership of the means of production, he held that
"one had, on the contrary, to protect it and move toward the union of
labor and property within the same hands." [24]

De Man's attitude toward the free sector of the economy was not, as
someone ill acquainted with his ideas might think, a form of opportunism dictated by the politics of the day, but derived from his "personalist and pluralistic concept of socialization." [25] The policies he advocated were designed to lead to far-reaching and fundamental changes,
and not merely to solve a given number of situational problems. The desire to "transcend divergent interests" through an appeal to the "general
interest" [26] was an essential aspect of De Man's revisionism; it gave rise
to the notion of a mixed system of economy midway between the capitalist and socialist systems. This intermediate system was a key concept
of neosocialism, and played an essential role in the slide toward fascism.

Another important element of the revisionism of the thirties was the
idea that socialism ought to deal with the causes of the economic crisis
without going outside the national framework. In insisting on the supreme importance of national solutions to the problems of the day, revisionism abandoned once and for all the hope of an absolute reversal of
the existing social order. [27] Unquestionably, with De Man socialism profoundly changed its nature and objectives.

This development culminated in the fourteen propositions expounded
by De Man, then vice-president of the POB, at the symposium of planist
groups held at the Abbey of Pontigny in September 1934 and in a series
of ten articles published in Le Peuple between July and October 1934
under the general but significant title "Corporatism and Socialism." [28]
On 10 December 1934 De Man returned to the ideas presented at Pontigny in a lecture on "Socialism Facing the Crisis" given at the Sorbonne
under the auspices of the Nouvelle École de la Paix, which had been
founded by Louise Weiss. [29] The lecture eliminated all doubt: this "planist socialism," De Man said, this "anticrisis socialism," was a new kind

of socialism.[30] Marcel Déat, René Belin (Marshal Pétain's future minister), and Georges Lefranc gave the vice-president of the POB their enthusiastic support.

The fourteen propositions expounded at Pontigny developed and clarified the ideas of planism in a way that had not been possible when the Plan had been presented to the POB congress. They laid stress, once again, on the "voluntarist policy" that ought to replace the old "deterministic doctrine" (proposition 3) and result in the setting up, within the national framework (proposition 8), of a mixed economy (propositions 6 and 7) in which "the problem of administration would be more important than that of possession" (proposition 8). The socialist movement had sought to accomplish these objectives because it had come to realize that capitalism had ceased to bring about a continuous increase in the size of the proletariat. Therefore, one had immediately to create a majority that would include, in addition to the proletariat, as large a section of the middle classes as possible (proposition 10). Such a majority was not only a political necessity but, first and foremost, an economic necessity (proposition 12). Consequently—and this was one of the main principles of planism—the composition of this alliance would require that it be directed not against capitalism as a whole but against monopolistic capitalism and first of all against the capitalism of high finance (proposition 11).

All these elements were already present in the plan approved by the Christmas congress, but at Pontigny it became clear that planism was a stage in the evolution of socialism whose significance went far beyond that of a mere economic program. Indeed, two other important conclusions followed from the abandonment of the fight against capitalism. Not only did De Man seek to create "an autonomous corporative organization of the enterprises that have been nationalized or controlled by the state," but he wanted "a new economic state whose forms differed from those of the old political state." Here, then, was the new doctrine in a nutshell:

The classic doctrine of bourgeois democracy, which no longer applies to the present situation, must be replaced by a new doctrine based on a different conception of the separation of powers: the executive governs, the representative bodies control. Similarly, in the new economic state in the process of being formed, the representative bodies—those, that is, founded upon the individual right of suffrage—will have only the right of supervision and control; the exercise of the right of administration will stem from a delegation of powers by the executive and control by a representation of corporative interests.[31]

Soon afterward, again speaking at the Sorbonne, De Man advanced another step along the same road. He laid emphasis on his idea of the "strong state," saying that the old Marxist struggle against the state had become nonsensical, and that "one can no longer achieve power through revolution, but one can achieve a revolution through the exercise of power." [32] A few years later, in 1938, he said, "In the future one will have to be more bold in establishing a socialist order while setting up an authoritarian state—the one being conditional on the other." [33] According to his account in *Après-coup*, it was in this way that he attempted, through a break with Marxism ("the ideology of class struggle") and with democracy ("the maintenance of the parliamentary regime"), to arrest "the downward path of socialism." [34] In fact, what De Man proposed to the POB was the adoption of a different kind of socialism—"planist socialism." [35] He not only regarded the Plan as "the expression and symbol of the new phase of socialist action," [36] but he believed that its "revolutionary character" [37] made it the "program of a new socialism," [38] a socialism that "must be as different from recent socialism as Marxist socialism was from socialism before 1848." [39]

Corporatism, Modernism, and the Planned Economy

The De Man Plan, having become the official program of a great socialist party, was triumphantly received in Paris. In reality, however, it was not the Labor Plan as Vandervelde and the party leadership conceived of it that was hailed in Paris but "planism" as a replacement for Marxism. Thus, speaking on behalf of the first "planists," Georges Lefranc thanked the Belgian theoretician "for having said that an apocalyptic and paradisiacal socialism should be succeeded by an essentially heroic socialism." [40] Commenting on the "planist" ideas, Marcel Déat declared, "The Plan is a mystique," and he described planism, which he put "above the Plan," as "a great upsurge, as much moral as intellectual." [41] Planist "voluntarism," he said, had replaced the "fatalism" and the "belief in absolute determinism" that characterized Marxism. [42] That was also how Jouvenel's and Maulnier's circles saw planism, with the result that this "new socialism" that sought not to divide the cake differently but to "make another cake" was favorably received by *La Lutte des jeunes* and *Combat*. [43] Jouvenel's collaborator Henri Lefort regarded the Plan's popularity as "the triumph of revolutionary action." [44] Jouvenel himself already saw a "néo—war veteran—syndicalist combination" coming to power, thanks to Déat, that would change the face of the regime.[45]

It was, in fact, with Déat and the people of *La Vie socialiste*, which had just been disowned by the SFIO, that the adoption of the Plan by the Parti Ouvrier Belge took on its truly political significance, for it both strengthened their stand and provided them with excellent justification. In his confrontation with the leadership of the French socialist party, Déat insisted on the similarity between his own ideas and De Man's. The Labor Plan, he said, "was born under the sign of *neosocialism*."[46] He pointed out, quite correctly, that in 1930 he had already advocated some of the main principles of planism, especially those involving the creation of an anticapitalist alliance and a front of the middle classes[47] and the substitution of structural reforms for reforms of distribution.[48] Planism, he said, meant not the "total subversion" of the existing regime but "the construction of a mixed economy."[49] In other words, for the Belgian planists as for the French neosocialists, "it was not a matter of achieving socialism completely at once, it was not a matter of nationalizing the means of production and exchange; it was a matter of curing unemployment and reviving the economy."[50] This aim, he thought, could not be accomplished without the support and the alliance of the middle classes, and this involved setting up an "intermediate regime" within the "national framework."[51]

Déat took from De Man the idea of "the economic majority, the social majority, sometimes distinct from the political majority," but insisted that this was identical to his own idea of an "anticapitalist grouping."[52] Like De Man, he said that the time had come to speak on behalf of the "general interest,"[53] to show "concern for the nation"[54] and plainly declare the need for a revision of the parliamentary system, an adaptation of the executive, and a reform of the state, for it was necessary to create "*a strong state*."[55] Déat was naturally enough gratified by De Man's lecture at the Sorbonne on his fourteen propositions, in which he advocated a reform of the state in an authoritarian direction. "This is not the time for integral socialism," said Déat finally,[56] to make it quite clear that with the split in the SFIO and the adoption of the Plan by the POB a new period had begun in the history of European socialism.

Indeed, for Déat, as for De Man and all the revisionists, planism represented "a new socialism" that would be able to deal with the present crisis "but also, even more," was an attempt "at spiritual rescue."[57] For Georges Roditi, editor of *L'Homme nouveau*, the neosocialist journal par excellence, there was no room for doubt: "The ideal of planning that will triumph will be a national planning, foreign to the materialist spirit."[58] Antimaterialism was the very essence of this attempt at the renovation, the moralization of economic relationships; in concrete terms, it expressed itself as corporatism.

De Man was the first to make a long defense of corporatism. A disciple of Henri Pirenne, he began by dwelling on "the analogy between medieval guilds and modern syndicalism," and sought to rehabilitate "a movement that for centuries had been creative and progressive."[59] Did not the flowering of the guilds, or corporations, coincide with the height of the humanist phase of the Middle Ages, a period that historians consider worthy of comparison with the finest periods of ancient civilization?[60] But this flowering was followed by several centuries of decline, and, on the eve of the French Revolution, the guilds, which in the Middle Ages had aimed at enabling all workers to attain the status of master, exercised exactly the opposite function. After the Revolution, the guilds, corrupted by capitalism as it emerged, were finally extinguished by capitalism triumphant.[61]

De Man attempted to demonstrate that the greatest enemy that capitalism had ever known was the corporatism of the guilds, a corporatism that never ceased to represent class interests and that acted exactly like the modern syndicalist movement, a corporatism one of whose principal concerns was preventing the emergence of the capitalist system. De Man also claimed that in the period of pure corporatism there were no conflicts of interest like those that developed under the capitalist regime.[62] Finally, De Man took up an idea expounded from the beginning of the century by La Tour du Pin and the Action Française, and particularly by the adherents of the social movement headed by Firmin Bacconnier, namely, that the French Revolution, in opposing the guilds, aimed at making all autonomous labor organization impossible.[63]

Corporatism, De Man claimed, was thus fundamentally opposed to this bourgeois and liberal revolution, symbol of the victory of capitalism. In the nineteenth century, however, corporatist organization began to develop once more under the auspices of syndicalism and socialism: "After capitalism had killed corporatism, socialism revived it."[64] De Man attempted to show that "the syndicalist and corporative ideas, far from excluding one another, condition one another,"[65] and he employed the term *corporative socialism*, which he considered equivalent to *Sorelian syndicalism*.[66]

After thus attempting to rehabilitate corporatism in the eyes of the left, De Man made it the key element in the plan of reform he was proposing, the "planned mixed economy" that, he said, was "the present aim of the labor movement, and that implied a mixed organization of the regime of production."[67]

In the summer of 1934, he stated, "The vital principle of syndical corporatism is that the state intervenes only to consecrate and coordinate activities resulting from the initiative of those who are freely organized on a professional basis."[68]

Soon enough, however, De Man began to move toward paternalistic and authoritarian solutions, engaging, as always, in violent attacks on Marxism. Hence the Pontigny propositions and the concepts of anti-parliamentarianism and the "strong" state, which gave the notion of a planned economy based on corporatism a quite different significance; for as soon as one abandoned the other possibility—the idea of revolutionary socialism—the rejection of liberal democracy led inevitably to the formula of the authoritarian state.[69] In a liberal democratic regime, a rejection of the rules of the parliamentary game goes together with a rejection of the Marxist theory of classes and an acceptance of the theory of elites that De Man, like the Italian sociological school, adopted. The resulting system constituted a clear and consistent whole.

In France, that ideological system found its strongest expression in *L'Homme nouveau*. This monthly review edited by Roditi, who, together with Paul Marion, was one of the prominent activists of the young néo generation, was intended as a tool of political combat rather than an organ of doctrinal theory. Better than any other journal of the period, it represented the authentic neosocialist spirit, and was already quite fascist in flavor.[70] In it Roditi published two important articles that were really manifestos of a hard-line neosocialism centered on a violent criticism of the "Marxist spirit" and its "materialistic conception of man and history." "By its inhuman and repellent quality," said Roditi, Marxism had "sterilized the labor movement."[71] Roditi reproached Marxism for its "*scientific* fatalism, its lack of hierarchical sense, its inability to arouse and utilize personal qualities in individuals," opposing to it "the socialist and national outlook."[72] In his attack on Marxism, Roditi invoked the authority of Proudhon, Sorel, and Péguy, "the constructive spirit of French pre-Marxist socialism," ideas "of order and responsibility," and, at the same time, the "heroic socialism" or "Nietzschean socialism" to which the Révolution Constructive group and their Belgian counterparts like Léo Moulin aspired.[73]

These ideas, which were certainly nothing new and looked back to Sorel, giving him a place of particular importance,[74] found concrete expression in planism and corporatism. It was by De Man, La Tour du Pin, "who gave a lesson in revolutionary corporatism," Luigi Fontanelli, and Ugo Spirito that the young neosocialists claimed to be inspired in wishing to create "an extreme left-wing social revolution."[75] In a passage worthy of inclusion in any anthology of fascist writings, Roditi added, "Any true revolution is itself a reconciliation, the birth of a new human community, of a new principle of love and kinship between men. It is impossible to imagine a mighty revolutionary current without this new fraternity."[76] And he concluded, "To all these outworn ideas of the conservatism of the right and the conservatism of the left, youth, like Proudhon, should answer: reconciliation is revolution."[77]

Thus, Andreu, another neosocialist, spoke of "a meeting of socialism and corporatism," declaring that he no longer saw any difference between "Christian corporatism" and "fascist corporatism."[78] Andreu, to be sure, was deeply distrustful of a materialistic tendency present in official corporatism in Italy, fearing that corporative bodies, "which have not only economic functions but also political and even ethical ones,"[79] might become enmeshed in purely material functions. True fascists were always motivated by an ethical concern, and, reading Andreu, one often has the impression that the official fascism practiced in Italy still left much to be desired from the point of view of an ideal fascism as conceived by the idealistic and combative younger generation. For that reason, Andreu and Roditi, stressing their debt to Spirito, the spiritual leader of the young corporatists—more hard-line than the corporatists of the revolutionary-syndicalist generation before 1914—preached a return to the sources. By comparing texts they demonstrated "the real interrelationship between those very different authors"[80] La Tour du Pin, De Man, Fontanelli, Spirito, and, as was only proper for French socialists, Jaurès on "the corporatism of Count de Mun and socialism."[81]

In a more guarded way, without referring directly to Spirito, Fontanelli, or Lieutenant Colonel de La Tour du Pin, Louis Vallon[82] and Déat launched a similar campaign on behalf of corporatism in La Vie socialiste. Déat adopted Georges Lefranc's idea that at the present time one had to consider "the creation of *work communities* bringing together, in proportions to be determined, representatives of *employers*, technicians, the workers and the state," and went on to ask, "The work community, the German formula of the *Arbeitsgemeinschaft*, what is it if not a *corporative body*?"[83] He was aware that this formula constantly recurred "in all the speeches of Hitler and Dollfuss," but that did not worry him unduly: "I am not disturbed by it," he said.[84] On the other

hand, he insisted that "it was not Mussolini who invented corporations": they were part of the French syndicalist tradition. Moreover, he
claimed, "between the corporation as conceived by the socially minded
employers of the north of France and the CGT there is only a difference of
degree and not of nature." [85] In a similar spirit, Vallon reconsidered the
social ideas of the great northern-French woolen-goods manufacturer,
Mathon.[86] Ten years earlier, in the time of the Faisceau, his ideas had
been categorically rejected by Valois on account of their reactionary
character.[87]

All the néos invoked the authority of De Man and appropriated the
ideas expressed in *L'Homme nouveau* on the equilibrium of forces between employers and workers that the corporation represented.[88] The
corporation thus played a decisive role in the neosocialist system. It was,
in fact, the key element in the "intermediate regime" that neosocialism
sought to create. Corporatism assured the ascendancy of the state: "It is
under its authority that a corporative organization must be set up," said
Vallon.[89] Corporatism combated individualism and assured harmony
and collaboration between the classes. It permitted the creation of a new
political and social order—the intermediate regime, based on the idea
that "the total expropriation of capitalism is a foolish dream." [90] Déat
already regarded this intermediate regime as a fact, concerning which
he admitted, "I do not know how one is going to get out of it, if one will
get out of it," for "we know where we come from; we do not know
where we are going." [91] What one does know, at any rate, he said, is that
this intermediate regime will contain a flourishing capitalist economy.[92]
Doriot took this idea still further: according to the program of the Parti
Populaire Français, the corporation, based on "solidarity of enterprise,"
the foundation of "the harmonious society, would deliberately protect
the free sector." [93]

The fascists never objected to private ownership, or to profit. "Individual profit remains the motor element of production," said Doriot,[94]
while Déat rejected nationalization and made subtle distinctions between various forms of profit.[95] Doriot, the former communist, declared
that he refused to indulge in "anticapitalist demagoguery." [96] In this he
resembled the national socialists of the interwar period who continued
an already well established tradition, for if the dissidents were violently
opposed to capitalism, trusts, banks, and plutocracy in all its forms,
they touched neither private property nor individual profit.[97] On this
point the national socialists—De Man, Déat, Bergery, and Jouvenel—
and the "social" nationalists—Brasillach, Maulnier, and the Sorelian

Andreu—were entirely in agreement. Conscious though they were of the ravages wrought by capitalism—of "the frightful order of this frightful capitalist society," as Brasillach put it[98]—they nevertheless did not hold private property responsible. They did not believe it should be suppressed; what was necessary, they thought, was to destroy the rule of finance. One did not have to eliminate capital and its private ownership—which, according to Maulnier, was quite simply impossible—but to deprive money of the capacity to create and control productive enterprises.[99] But this had already been done, wrote Déat as early as 1930, and "the excesses of capitalist ownership have been reduced to such a degree that there no longer seems to be an urgent need to intervene," for "this capitalism no longer possesses any activity, any virulence, although it still has enough of an internal motive force."[100] Dire poverty, he said, had disappeared, and one now had to reach "a compromise that would be to the advantage of both parties."[101] In other words, one had to put order into production, management, and the organization of enterprises as well as into social relationships. Reforms were needed in technical organization, but above all one had to increase the consumption of the masses. One consequently required "a planned economy."

Jouvenel had come to this conclusion in 1927. His book called, precisely, L'Économie dirigée (The Planned Economy), which appeared the following year, contained a first chapter in which he spoke of "a passion for order." His book Le Réveil de l'Europe, which came out ten years later, in 1938, ended with "a recall to order." Undoubtedly, the term planned economy signified a third way, an idea, said De Man—himself the author of Réflexions sur l'économie dirigée (Reflections on the Planned Economy)—intermediate between liberalism and socialism.[102] Planism, in fact, represented a rationalization of the economy and constituted a reform of capitalism that would turn it into a "productive and antiparasitic" system.[103] Presenting, in 1934, the main outlines of the neosocialist program based on "economic reorganization," Déat spoke of the need for "discipline": for the sake of the well-being of France, whose industrial infrastructure was "about to burst from so much liberty," one should put an end to "the traditional anarchy" and "liberal capitalism."[104] One had to create what Loustau, in his report to the second national congress of the PPF, called "a conscious economy" in "an organized society."[105] In order to achieve that, however, one needed a state—a state that wanted, that was able, to intervene, or, that is to say, a different kind of state and a different form of politics.[106] Jouvenel claimed that modern politics "is a science" that lacks only its scholars.[107] Had

not Valois already wanted to lay the foundations of the "syndicalist republic"—the political form of the "new age," the age of electricity?
This State of technicians would replace the State of politicians [108] just as
the "scientific organization of labor" and the cult of "efficiency" and
"scientific management" [109] had replaced the old factory of the nineteenth century.

This new political and economic conception naturally implied a new
pattern of social relationships. Déat and Jouvenel claimed that in a
"truly rationalized national economy," an industrial society based on
the principles of Ford and Taylor—that is to say, on an organization that
tends to raise the salaries and the living standards of the workers and at
the same time lower the prices of products and increase profits—the interests of the industrialist, the worker, the consumer, and the collectivity
would be identical. [110]

Drieu had the same idea when he expressed his dislike of the "useless
debris that is stirred up" by both capitalists and socialists, and that is
called liberty. [111] "I want to defend the worker as a part of my blood, as a
part of the people," he said. [112] Déat, too, thought one could contribute
to "molding institutions already oriented toward socialism" [113] by defending the have-nots, the people as a whole, but four years later he admitted that what he really had in mind was an "intermediate equilibrium," an "unprecedented economic system" that, however, would be
"integrated into the nation." [114] This, then, was the significance of the
"composite economy" [115] advocated in the thirties by all those who rejected both socialism and liberalism. Undoubtedly, this regime was based
on a compromise with capitalism and an acceptance of its principles.

At the root of this compromise, however, was the desire for a modernization and rationalization of the system. With Valois's supporters
began, in 1925–27, the wish to put all the might of a reorganized,
powerful, and authoritarian state at the service of a rationalized economy, creator of a technological civilization and a society of producers.
This ideological tendency persisted and increased after the collapse of
the Faisceau. Around 1930, the foundations of a complete refashioning
of the economy and society were laid in the ideas of the people associated with the "new teams." These ideas thus came into existence before
the Great Depression: the rationalist, technocratic, "managerial" aspect
of fascism was not the product of a simple combination of circumstances,
of a transitory catastrophic situation, but one of the answers to the
many questions raised by the modernization of France and Europe. [116]

By 1930 the Librairie Valois, which, together with *Cahiers bleus*, provided the forum for the intellectual activity of the Republican Syndicalist party, had already published most of the theoretical works underlying left-wing fascism. After Jouvenel's *L'Économie dirigée*, Valois published Montagnon's *Grandeur et servitude socialistes* and Déat's *Perspectives socialistes*, as well as works of lesser importance by Hubert Lagardelle and Jean Luchaire. (The former editor of *Le Mouvement socialiste* began to go in for regionalism at that time, while Luchaire praised the merits of *Une Génération réaliste*—"A Realistic Generation.") Together with the works of people who were preparing a revision of socialism that was to lead directly to fascism and collaborationism, Valois published *L'État moderne* by his former anarchist companion Charles Albert, and a work by Mendès France entitled *La Banque internationale*. Valois saw in this modernistic and rationalistic tendency the continuation of the "revolutionary fascism" that he had founded and that would lead to the creation of a "syndicalist state," whereas the Mathon-Coty group represented a "reactionary fascism." [117] The revolutionaries of the earlier period had wanted a fascism that would be, as in Italy in the beginning, "a form of socialism." [118] That was what Valois still wanted in 1928 when he fell back on a syndicalist socialism of Sorelian inspiration, advocating the creation of a new type of state, [119] a rationalization of the economy, and the taking over of the country by the "new generation," the "young teams," and the "technicians": in April 1929, the *Cahiers* sounded a "call for the entry of the technicians into public life." To retrieve the state from capitalism and to set up a "rational and just organization of production" [120]—such was the purpose of the campaign launched by *Cahiers bleus* and continued by *Chantiers coopératifs* at the beginning of the thirties. In this new publication, and subsequently in *Le Nouvel Age*, Valois engaged in a struggle for a new society, a new economy, and a new culture. He was thus one of the first to hail the "abandonment of Marxism" and the "awakening of socialism" announced by De Man, [121] but if, later, he enthusiastically welcomed his Labor Plan, [122] he soon became aware of the danger represented by the compromise between democracy and plutocracy advocated by the planists and neosocialists. [123] Valois then returned to the left, [124] leaving it to Lagardelle, his fellow traveler from the time of the revolutionary syndicalism of the beginning of the century until the period of the Faisceau, to advance further on the path of planism, modernism, and syndicalism allied with antiliberalism and anti-Marxism.

The first issue of the monthly journal *Plans* appeared in January 1931. Philippe Lamour, formerly of the Faisceau, was chief editor, but it was the personality of Lagardelle that dominated this modernistic, avant-garde publication, an almost perfect example of a technically oriented fascism that was enamored of skyscrapers, the work of Walter Gropius and Le Corbusier, and the art of Fernand Léger and at the same time aspired toward an organic, harmonious society—the society of the "real man." For there were undoubtedly two tendencies in fascism: on the one hand that of Drieu, who wished to protect the worker "against the big city"—"I say that the big city is capitalism"[125]—and on the other hand the tendency to glorify ultramodern urban developments and the new aesthetics.[126] This taste for modernist aesthetics was, of course, not limited to architecture. *Plans*, for instance, published Filippo Tommaso Marinetti, who explained "the elements of the futuristic sensibility that gave birth to our pictorial dynamism, our unharmonic music, our Art of noises and our Words of liberty."[127]

Apart from this avant-gardism, the doctrinal aspect of Lagardelle's publication was not particularly original. There was the familiar criticism of capitalism, democracy, and the parliamentary system, and the idea that the present crisis demonstrated the inability of the individualistic society to adapt itself to the conditions of modern life. Democracy, Lagardelle complained, "only recognizes the individual: it ignores the group"; it divests "the individual of his sensitive qualities" and makes him into "a theoretical man."[128] Thus, "the fault of individualistic democracy," he said, was that it "left the producer defenseless."[129] The real break with the established order and the "abstract man" would come about only through syndicalism, "which has offered the most striking example of the real man brought by the group to the surface of society."[130] With the advent of the "real" man, not only a new society but also a new culture would come into being.

The review stopped appearing in 1933, when Lagardelle joined the French embassy in Rome. He was very warmly welcomed in the Italian capital: in his famous article in the *Enciclopedia italiana* written in collaboration with Gentile, Mussolini mentioned Lagardelle and *Le Mouvement socialiste*, together with Sorel, as among the major sources of fascism.[131]

Planism Versus Orthodox Socialism

The immediate treatment by the various parties of their would-be innovators or revolutionaries varied a great deal. Vandervelde, the leader of the Belgian socialist party, was well aware of the difficulty of explaining an anomaly of this kind to the party members. So put it plainly, one might even gain the impression that he did not mind casting a certain amount of discredit on De Man, the vice-president who had been imposed on him by circumstances. Vandervelde pointed out the intellectual affinity between De Man and Déat. In the history of socialism, he said, they will be regarded as the most representative figures of the revolt of the "under-forty-year-olds" of the postwar era against a certain form of Marxism that they reproached for having lost contact with life.[132] He even conceded that the Pontigny propositions, which he said the Belgian socialists did not support as wholeheartedly as Déat[133] or even support at all,[134] were already found in *Au-delà du marxisme*.[135] He insisted, however, that there were two essential differences between these men. In the first place, he categorically denied that De Man had introduced "any essentially new elements" into socialism—quite the contrary.[136] Vandervelde claimed that De Man's ideas in no way represented a "neosocialism"; they were not a revolt against Marxism, and Déat was wrong to suggest that they represented a new doctrine that was as violently opposed to Marxism as Marxism had been opposed to the utopian socialism of before 1848.[137] According to Vandervelde, De Man's *L'Idée socialiste* was, in fact, a return to Marx in reaction against the vulgarization of his doctrines.[138] Moreover, he insisted that the situation in France differed from that in Belgium: in France, Déat and his group could produce a "planism," concerning whose general implications he had grave reservations, whereas in Belgium there was only a specific plan for dealing with a particular crisis, which was limited to that purpose and left the party program intact.[139] In Belgium, said Vandervelde, De Man was "a factor of unity," while in France Déat was responsible for a split.

Vandervelde, however, was not deceived by this reassuring image that, because of his anxieties, which after the Christmas congress were constantly increasing, he was attempting to put across. The purpose of his articles in *Le Peuple* and his polemic with Renaudel and Déat was not to describe the real situation but, by defending De Man against the praise of his compromising allies, to make clear just what the Belgian party would not stand for.[140]

To be sure, the general distress in 1933 was so great that it was agreed to commit to the famous but embarrassing academic just arrived from Frankfurt the task of steering Belgian socialism through a difficult period and to entrust him with the preparation of a plan of action that could be carried out in the near future. He was permitted to launch a new, original formula—one that could mobilize the party and convince the masses, so soon after the collapse of German social democracy, that socialism still had something to offer. He was even allowed, it seems, to attempt a renewal of socialist thought. But "another" socialism was not wanted. Even if the POB was willing to accept him as a stimulating thinker whose original ideas could arouse interest,[141] it refused to regard him as a savior who could force the party to accept a new doctrine.

On this point of principle Vandervelde was intransigent. There could be a plan, but there would be no planism. There could be a program of action, but there would be no new socialism. Vandervelde constantly attempted to demonstrate that nothing in De Man's ideas contradicted those found since the turn of the century in democratic socialism, or "reformism," as he preferred to call it.[142] The demonstration of this continuity seemed enough to exorcise the demons of neosocialism with which Déat had rightly tried to associate De Man's thinking. The French and Belgian socialist leaders were aware of the danger represented by the enthusiasm for reform of these younger men, whose freedom of action they feared. They were likewise conscious of the responsibility they bore for ensuring the survival of socialism, especially after Hitler's rise to power. Thus, to keep their bearings, they clung to the Marxist foundations of their doctrines. Vandervelde affected to see only a return to Marx in what is obviously a demolition of Marxism, and Léon Blum, during the attacks of the Déat faction, could only make the touching admission, "Believe me, I too sometimes feel my reason taking me further than I thought I would go. Every day, it seems to me that we enter new planetary systems in which we have only the Marxist doctrine to serve as a compass."[143]

This refusal to venture was precisely what the socialist leaders were reproached for by the nonconformists—all those on the left who wanted to move forward, to find new formulas and original answers to the challenge of the crisis of liberalism. On this point the official leaders of European socialism wholeheartedly followed Blum, who wanted to preserve the revolutionary character of the movement. They advocated an absolute rejection of the bourgeois order, an unswerving fidelity to the essential principles of Marxism, and a translation of those principles into operational terms in the form of a constant refusal to participate in government. In practice, their rigor gave rise to an almost complete immobility, but there was no escaping the fact that this was the price of preserving the ideological identity of the movement. For Blum, any attempt at updating socialist doctrine in the face of the crisis that enveloped

France and Europe was an adventure that the movement could not afford. Henceforth, the split between official socialism—or, rather, the left
as a whole—and those who sought innovation at any price could only
grow wider.

The adoption of the De Man Plan by the Brussels congress thus constituted a real challenge for Blum. A few weeks earlier, the SFIO had expelled Déat and the *Vie socialiste* group from the party for expressing
the same ideas embodied in the Plan. Blum knew that Déat was quite
correct in claiming that his ideas resembled those of the Plan, and he
was also aware of the danger that the adoption of the Plan by the POB
represented for socialism as he understood it. On the other hand, he
could not very well maintain that the Belgian section of the Socialist
International ought to expel a man who, despite the tensions he caused,
had just been appointed vice-president of the party. He therefore had to
adopt another line of defense, and, to avoid having to deal with the contradiction with which the Belgian socialists had confronted him, he decided to concentrate on two points. First he attempted to demonstrate
that the De Man Plan and neosocialism had nothing in common, and
then, like Vandervelde, he pretended to believe that there was nothing
particularly new or original in De Man's ideas. He wrote a series of
ten articles on this theme, under the general title of "Au-delà du réformisme"; they were published in *Le Populaire* in January 1934.

In these articles, Blum claimed that the great difference between the
néos and De Man was that the Plan was a collective enterprise and its
adoption a collective decision of the POB. Unlike Déat, De Man had
convinced his party that circumstances required a change, but, Blum
said (apparently quite seriously), this was "not precisely a change in the
orientation of his approach, but rather a change in its presentation, or, if
you will, in its emphasis."[144] Nothing, he said, prevented a member of
the French party from coming before the party authorities and suggesting that, without changing anything in its program, it should concentrate all its efforts on the nationalization of banking. This would amount
to telling the party to improve its propaganda and not to proposing another form of socialism. Blum pretended to believe that this was the purpose of the Plan, claiming that the equivalent of the De Man Plan in
France was not the neosocialist program but the resolutions of the 1932
national congress,[145] or, in other words, that French socialism had already received its plan thanks to the "Cahiers d'Huyghens" and had
even preceded the Belgians. The French equivalent of De Man's work,
said Blum, was the fiscal counterproject or the plan for the protection of

public savings drawn up under the direction of Vincent Auriol.[146] This absurd comparison, which minimized the importance of the Plan, reducing its content to that of a few routine documents, ended with an equally surprising conclusion: armed with the Labor Plan, said Blum, "it is to a class battle that the Parti Ouvrier Belge is summoning the proletariat."[147]

In all the articles after the third Blum harped on the idea that "the party modifies nothing, revises nothing, renounces nothing. From its general program it simply extracts, isolates a single article: the nationalization of banking."[148] It was this article, said Blum, that became the Plan, and, owing to the discussions it aroused and the publicity surrounding it, it struck the imagination. The Labor Plan thus became "a plan of offensive for the conquest of political power."[149]

Thus far, Blum had tried to convince his party that the Plan contained nothing new, but he was nevertheless obliged to concede that the Plan was directed not against the capitalist system as such but only against "*capitalist monopoly*." Blum also realized that not only did the Plan not envisage the total elimination of the free sector, but it even tended to preserve and develop it;[150] and, as for the nationalized sector, instead of being gradually extended until it embraced the whole, it was limited and isolated from the start.[151] Therefore, after praising the Plan chiefly on the grounds that it contained nothing original, Blum issued a final warning: the Plan was of value as a strategic tool, but had no value in itself.[152] Once in power, socialism would have to take its own path: "It should follow its destiny," he concluded.[153]

As a result of the positions adopted by Blum, planism in France never gained the respectability within the socialist movement that it had in Belgium, and one should add that De Man's entry into the Paul Van Zeeland government in 1935 did little to restore faith in the socialist character of planism. By 1935, it had become clear that all the worst fears of the opponents of planism were about to be confirmed.

The success of planism in Belgium until 1935 was due to a number of factors that never came together in France. First, the POB, which, unlike the SFIO in France, was the party of the industrial proletariat, was much closer to reaching an electoral majority, and, from its point of view, the elaboration of a plan of combat that could contribute to a victory was worth a few sacrifices. Second, the adoption of the Plan as an electoral program facilitated improved relations between various tendencies within the POB.[154] Finally, Vandervelde's inability to lead the party through the present crisis obliged him to call on De Man, who not only provided the party with a new ideology but also de facto replaced the aging leader. The fatalistic attitude of Vandervelde became clear at the May 1933 congress, where he admitted that he had no solution to the crisis and the misery it engendered.[155]

In 1933, the situation in France was quite different. In the first place, the SFIO could not hope to govern alone, but only as an auxiliary to a large center-left coalition. It therefore had little reason to make concessions, modify its program, or replace it with a plan. On the other hand, French socialism under Blum, the central figure whose position was accepted by the most important people in the party, did not suffer from a lack of leadership. It felt itself to be perfectly well equipped to meet the crisis and did not regard its doctrine as outmoded or ill adapted to the new realities, and it was consequently little inclined to welcome innovators. When Déat tried to present the party with a new ideology, he was met by silence, and when he tried to give it a new strategy, he was excluded from its ranks. Déat's progress toward national socialism began when he was still a member of the SFIO, but it continued within the framework of a new socialist party whose application for membership was refused by the Socialist International.

The neosocialism of the members of this new party—the Parti Socialiste de France—was not identical with planism, but all neosocialists were planists and planism was an element of neosocialism. De Man's planism, resulting from his revision of Marxism in the twenties, takes on its full significance only if one understands its long-term implications. Belgian planism, and then neosocialist planism, represented a total alternative to Marxism and to social democracy: as a form of rebellion against Marxism, planism contributed greatly to the creation of a national, authoritarian, antiparliamentarian form of socialism, a socialism for the entire nation over and above the divergent social classes and opposed interests. Planism did more than advocate a planned and rationalized economy: far from being the harbinger of a renewal of socialist thought, it prepared the way for, it already was, a national socialism.[156] It makes no difference that some sincere socialists failed to understand this from the beginning, or that people like André Philip, Léon Jouhaux, and young Hugh Gaitskell (who thirty years later headed the British labor party) worked together at that time with future Nazis like G. Oltramare, notorious collaborators like Déat, Marion, and Ludovic Zoretti, and Vichyists like Belin, Lefranc, and Fabre-Luce.[157] The important point is that planism, although it never succeeded in conquering the SFIO or the CGT, played a major role in the long process of fascist impregnation and the progressive destruction of socialism and democracy in France in the thirties.

First of all, in planism there was not only a virulent anti-Marxism: in fact planism intended to replace socialism. This was its main justification and the reason for its novelty and attraction. Planism made it possible to oppose capitalism and high finance in the name of the general interest, and by creating a common front of the proletariat and middle class sought to reestablish the compromised unity of the nation. Thus, class warfare could be eliminated, and the entire nation under an authoritarian state could go off in conquest of the citadel of high finance, held from the time of Proudhon to be the source of all evil.

From the national socialism of the end of the nineteenth century to the planism of the 1930s, the diagnosis of the trouble, and the proposed remedies, never altered. "A planned economy . . . on behalf of the general interest . . . is a form of socialism," said Déat, presenting the French Plan in his capacity as secretary-general of the Plan Committee, "but what kind of socialism—that is what we must now investigate." And he answered immediately: this socialism was the "old French socialism" of Saint-Simon, of Fourier, of Proudhon.[158] Invoking this tradition, Déat elaborated a national socialism that was to become the ideology of the collaborationist Rassemblement National Populaire.

It was no accident that corporatism was part of De Man's "planist" ideology as adopted by the French neosocialists or as conceived by the "9 July" group dominated by the néos. Indeed, the Plan Committee envisaged the setting up of a corporative type of regime whose cornerstone would be the creation of a banking corporation.[159] It was no accident, either, that planist conferences held at the Abbey of Pontigny from September 1934 onward were no longer in any way socialist in the original sense of the term.[160]

Within the sFIO was one school of thought, the "Redressement" (Rehabilitation) faction, that had largely come over to planist ideas.[161] Two of its leading figures later became members of the Rassemblement National Populaire: Ludovic Zoretti of the Calvados Federation, who was secretary of the Teachers' Federation, and Georges Albertini of the Aube Federation, who during the war became Déat's closest collaborator.

Within the cGT, René Belin's "Syndicats" faction was a major nucleus of planism.[162] From 1937 onward, two planist tendencies developed within the cGT that met up with those that had existed since the time of the Faisceau in the "modernist" circles of the great industrialists. Meetings and discussions took place between Belin (regarded as the unofficial successor of Jouhaux), Robert Lacoste, Ernest Mercier, and Auguste Detoeuf. The journal *X Crise*, which was the medium for the expression of the views of the planist and authoritarian tendencies among the great industrialists, published an article and then a lecture by Belin,[163] which were followed by a reply by Detoeuf in which he advocated a single, apolitical syndicalist structure with compulsory membership within the framework of an authoritarian state.[164]

In June 1938, a Franco-Swedish meeting was held at Pontigny.[165] Planism had now led to a corporatism that no longer even attempted to conceal itself behind an appearance of neutrality between the opposite interests of workers and employers. In many respects, it was a return to the kind of corporatism that the great industrialists in the Faisceau had defended against Valois in the twenties. Valois himself, the former fascist who at the end of the thirties had become one of the acutest observers of the political currents of the day, after having displayed a great deal of interest in planism in its early stages, now raised a cry of alarm: the Pontigny meeting, he said, was nothing other than a plot against the proletariat.[166] Where De Man was concerned, Valois's judgment was no less severe: De Man, he said, "had made the Parti Ouvrier Belge into an agent of international capitalism." [167] Though his language was exaggerated, Valois was not entirely mistaken: planism as it emerged at the end of the decade allowed capitalism to achieve legitimacy in the eyes of its victims.

Also in 1938, at the CGT congress in Nantes the abandonment of the doctrine of class warfare was defended by certain figures of planist inclination—by André Delmas of the Teachers' Federation, who claimed that "everything is not bad in the example provided by certain totalitarian states and certain democracies more active than our own," and by Raymond Froideval, an administrator of *Syndicats* and future private secretary of Belin, who urged the movement to "keep away from certain formulas that have grown old with use and no longer mean very much." [168] By the end of 1934, Déat had come to the conclusion that "the antifascist front" that had led to the Popular Front "was the antithesis" of planism.[169]

It should be pointed out, however, that though the Plan was not accepted by the SFIO, by Blum and Paul Faure, just as it had not found favor with Vandervelde, it was received quite differently by the CGT. At the congress of September 1935 the CGT adopted the Plan, as adapted by Georges Lefranc and the Révolution Constructive group, but did not succeed in having it accepted as the program of the Rassemblement

Populaire. The Plan was again adopted by a majority of the CGT at the congress of syndical unity in Toulouse in March 1936, but the opposition of the communists and the revolutionary syndicalists inside and outside the CGT, and of the radicals, put an end to this new endeavor.[170]

The repudiation of Marxism by the planists—all the planists who had come from the left—represented not only the repudiation of a past common to all socialists but also the rejection of a certain future. Except in one single case, planism was not a rejection of the principle of exploitation; nor did it oppose a society devoted to the search for profits. Planism did not seek to build a new society; it had no intention of changing the relationships of production. It accepted the fundamental principles governing the existing bourgeois order, and simply improved, modernized, and rationalized it.[171] The planist ideology thus helped to stabilize the existing order with its advocacy of class collaboration, and with its frequent championship of corporatism it became the guardian of that order. Planism did not consider touching the essential decision-making power of capitalist society; it envisaged only the transfer of a more or less important part of this power to the state. Planists of all kinds wanted to increase demand and investments simultaneously, and for that purpose they needed the control of credit and the great commercial banks. This was the basis of the De Man Plan.

A corporatism of this kind, linked with the advocacy of a reform of the state in a clearly authoritarian, antiparliamentary direction, hostile to any form of internationalism, and imbued with a deep contempt for "materialism," could only contribute to the fascist impregnation of French political thought, for the main point of planism was not the rationalization of the national economy but rather the galvanization of all classes within the framework of a "strong" state, freed from the shackles of democracy. Planism expressed the triumph of politics over economics, of willpower and energy over matter. It was no accident that De Man replaced the materialistic interpretation of history with a psychological and voluntarist explanation. For a man who knew the German school of socialism and had a complete knowledge of Marxist theory, it was not a matter of correcting the excesses of vulgar Marxism but of substituting a new conceptual framework for Marxism itself.

Here one should draw attention to a further element in this move toward fascism of a whole school of thought of French-speaking socialism. De Man saw planism as the only weapon capable of opposing the rise of nazism. He dwelt on this theme at the POB Christmas congress, and his doing so was probably much more than a matter of expedience. Déat, too, declared his belief that planism—that is, the official Belgian Plan, as interpreted by De Man, plus the Pontigny propositions—was the only solution in "this race between democracy and socialism on the one hand and fascism on the other." [172]

De Man's planism and its French neosocialist equivalent were intended as alternatives to fascism. By winning over the middle classes and uniting them to the proletariat, planism hoped to deprive fascism of its sociological foundations; and, by laying the basis for a new socialism, planism hoped to undermine its doctrine and present itself as an alternative ideological solution. However, in seeking to fight fascism with its own methods and on its own ground, the new socialism, owing to the logic of the current situation and the exigencies of the ideological confrontation in the thirties, itself came to resemble fascism. In being so eager to outstrip fascism, De Man and Déat came to develop a system of ideas that quickly became a fascist ideology.

All in all, planism provided a "total" alternative to liberalism and Marxism, both of which were regarded as materialist systems embodying permanent social conflict. From the planist viewpoint, Marxism was based on class warfare, and liberalism on the daily battle of each individual against all others. The planists hoped that by bringing authoritarianism and corporatism together they could create a new and harmonious system that alone would be capable of meeting the need for class solidarity before the harsh realities of the modern world.

Yet, on the other hand, the revision of socialism by the French and Belgian socialist rebels itself developed into fascism for one essential reason—the same reason that underlay the move toward the extreme right of the generation of 1910. For the revolutionary syndicalists at the beginning of the century as for the exponents of the new socialism twenty years later, the proletariat had ceased to be a revolutionary force and Marxism no longer provided a suitable answer to the problems of the modern world. This loss of faith in the vitality and capacities of the proletariat, joined with an unhesitating denunciation of the essential principles of Marxism and social democracy, this desire to achieve quick results by utilizing the full force of political power but without undertaking structural changes, this need to come to terms with the existing social order because one has come to regard it as natural and immutable, this replacement of Marxism by a national socialism, and of the revolutionary impulse of Marxism by a planned, organized, rationalized system of economy, led, through a natural inner logic, to fascism. Thus, in the thirties, fascism often appeared to be the only system of thought that answered to the logic of the twentieth century.

CHAPTER SEVEN

Spiritualistic Fascism

Against the Right and
Against the Left

Antimaterialism was the dominant trait and common denominator of all the movements of revolt between the two world wars. It brought together, in a single opposition to capitalism and liberalism, currents of thought that had arisen from the right and left but that were in conflict with both the right and the left. It was in the name of antimaterialism that men with different ideological backgrounds condemned Marxism, liberalism, and the political, social, and cultural characteristics of the traditional left and right. They all shared a common hatred of money, speculation, and bourgeois values, and condemned the exclusion of the proletariat from intellectual and cultural life and the life of the nation.

Pierre Andreu, a young fascist of the thirties (and one of those who, unlike Drieu, Brasillach, and Déat, never went all the way), rightly stated, twenty years later, that it was wrong to apply the term *personalism* exclusively to the ideas expressed in the review *Esprit* simply because it appeared so much in its columns.[1] In reality, a form of personalism underlay the general condemnation of materialism of all these movements of revolt, and the resulting political and philosophical consequences created the atmosphere of openness, of readiness for new ideas, characteristic of the thirties. The dissidents hoped that the revolution they spoke so much about would lead not only to profound cultural changes but above all to the creation of a new caliber of man. Even the leading "dirigists" (advocates of controlled planning)—De Man, Jouvenel, Déat—expected the reform of the economy to entail the moral transformation of man.

If planism was to bring about a revolution, this revolution was to be above all a moral one. "I no longer believe in the revolution as the Last Judgment," wrote De Man, "but I believe all the more firmly in a revolution that will transform us."[2] The members of the PPF held a similar view. "Since the crisis is in man before it is in things," wrote Loustau, playing on the title of Maulnier's first book, "we must first carry out the revolution in ourselves so that it will then be extended to things."[3] Finally, for Déat, state planning was a form of socialist humanism. "What we want to construct," he said, "is not only an economic system that will procure everyone the means to live decently and to the full but also a climate of civilization, a work of spiritual renewal."[4] With the revisionists of the interwar period as with those of the turn of the century, ethics and aesthetics were interconnected, and politics was an expression of ethical values.

The belief in the "primacy of the spiritual" was common to the fascists and to the nonconformists who never were, and never were to become, fascists—to the writers of *Combat* as well as to those of *Esprit*. The prospectus of February 1932 announcing the first issue of *Esprit* contains the ideas for which "social," antibourgeois, anticapitalistic, and anti-individualist nationalism had always fought. Once again one finds the same revulsion toward a society that has lost sight of any goal except capitalist profit and sullied itself with a sordid materialism, toward a humanity without a transcendent aim, without a hope.

There exists no form of thought or activity that is not enslaved to materialism. Everywhere man is subjected to systems and institutions that neglect him: he destroys himself in submitting to them. . . . Our hostility is as great toward capitalism, as at present preached and practiced, as toward Marxism and bolshevism. Capitalism, by means of poverty or prosperity, reduces an increasing number of people to a state of servitude incompatible with the dignity of man. It directs whole classes and one's whole personality toward the acquisition of money: that is the only desire that fills the modern soul. Marxism is a rebellious son of capitalism from which it received its faith in matter. Revolting against an evil society, it has some justice on its side, but only until it triumphs. As for bolshevism, alone among the manifestations of the modern world does it possess a breadth of doctrine and a heroism that are equal to the occasion, but it achieves its greatness through a simplification of the human considerations, within a system and through means that derive entirely from the tyranny of matter.[5]

This disgust for capitalism is always the expression of a contempt for a materialism that degrades the human soul. In this catholic vision, Marxism is seen to be in the tradition of liberal heresies—a mere extension of capitalism whose materialism it inherits.[6]

In the issue of *Esprit* of March 1933, one reads that there ought to be a rupture between the Christian order and the "established disorder": the gospel should be taken out of the hands of the bourgeois.[7] Yet, at the same time as expressing a wish to break the alliance between Catholicism and conservative forces, *Esprit* was severe in its criticism of Marxism.[8] Liberal, bourgeois materialism and Marxist, proletarian materialism, it felt, were one and the same. This classic conclusion, which Sorel and the revolutionary syndicalists of before 1914, the ethical revisionists of Marxism like De Man and Déat, and the social nationalists of the young Action Française and of the Maulnier-Brasillach-Drieu group had all come to, likewise resulted from an attempt to moralize politics.

It is not certain whether Mounier, *Esprit*'s editor, had read Sorel, although, as Michel Winock demonstrates, one can assume that he was acquainted with Péguy and Bergson. Concerning De Man, however, there is no doubt: Mounier described *L'Idée socialiste* as "the culminating work of the postwar period."[9] *Esprit*'s chosen enemies,[10] like those of *Combat* and all the rebels and dissidents—all the "princes of youth," to use Barrès's favorite expression—were always the same: individualism, capitalism, liberalism, Marxist determinism, democratic "disorder," and bourgeois mediocrity. For all these revolutionary currents of thought, revolution had to be separated from materialism.

This being the case, anything became possible, and great confusion resulted: pre-1914 fascism, like that of the interwar period, was the youngest, most nonconformist, and at the same time most unforeseeable ideology of the twentieth century. Because it rejected capitalism as well as Marxism, democracy as well as social democracy, and replaced them with a national socialism, because it attacked all the weaknesses of the existing political and social system, because it aimed at destroying bourgeois culture, fascism had a strong fascination for large segments of a whole generation, and particularly for the young intellectuals searching for a solution to the crisis of liberalism.

Consequently, the antimaterialism inherent in fascism, fascism's ethical and aesthetic preoccupation, and its desire to reform the world by transforming the individual satisfied a widespread aspiration, which helps to explain the fascist impregnation of the 1930s. In consequence of what later seemed to be a series of simple misunderstandings and an improbable if not accidental mismatching of ideas, in May 1935 Mounier accepted an invitation to attend a congress at the Institute of Fascist Culture, and, together with André Ulmann, represented *Esprit* in the Italian capital. The French delegation, consisting of about fifteen young intellectuals, included Robert Aron of *L'Ordre nouveau*, Jean de Fabrègues, representative of the Jeune Droite, and Georges Roditi and Paul Marion of *L'Homme nouveau*. The congress was organized on the French side by Roditi and Andreu, and its purpose was to acquaint the representatives of the French opposition movements with the social concepts of the Italian fascist left.

In his autobiography, Andreu perfectly evokes the atmosphere of the period in describing its ambiguities.[11] Things were by no means simple in 1935, and the journey to Rome—at the end of which, Andreu writes, "we were all caught up in a wave of sentiment. The congress ended in a sort of friendly enthusiasm"—was far from being, on Mounier's part, merely the result of "an obvious lack of political sense."[12] But even more interesting than the fact that Mounier's group participated in the Rome symposium were the texts that subsequently appeared in *Esprit*. In June 1935 was published a long and sympathetic account of the symposium, and in September the text of Mounier's speech following Ugo Spirito's report. The June article was unsigned, but it appears in the bibliography of Mounier's articles and reports at the end of the fourth volume of his *Oeuvres* and is unmistakably in his style, so we may assume that he was the author.[13]

In his article, Mounier first paid tribute to the youthfulness, ardor, and fighting spirit of the "active fraction of the fascist world" that possessed an "authentic anticapitalistic élan" and that undoubtedly had "deep roots in the proletariat."[14] Mounier, to be sure, pointed out the differences between fascism and personalism—"They place the state, we, the person, at the apex of human values"[15]—but at the same time expressed an understanding of the function of the totalitarian state in Italy. "Born essentially out of a need to create an Italian model of society," he said, "this historical situation endowed this statism with a significance that we cannot overlook."[16]

The friendly tone of this text recurred in Mounier's address to the symposium.[17] In these pages, one senses that a "family" atmosphere prevailed, and Mounier insisted that the discussions of the symposium involved people engaged in the same anticapitalist, antiliberal, and antibourgeois struggle. Mounier's address, it should be pointed out, was not improvised. Delivered in May, it was published in September: Mounier considered this exchange of views between himself and the fascist left sufficiently important to merit publication four months later. In his address, Mounier first sought to define the common ground between all the members of the symposium, and immediately put his finger on the salient point: the rejection of bourgeois values. Next he tried to define the difference between fascism and personalism. While fascism, he said,

asserted the primacy of the state, personalism sought "to build a pluralistic state." [18]

Yet, at the same time, because he regarded liberalism, bourgeois society, and the democratic system as negations of personal commitment,
Mounier was willing, at the Rome symposium, both to condemn "the
democratic totalitarianism of the unilateral protection of individuals by
the majority" and to join the fascists in their rejection of "false liberties." [19] In this connection, he went as far as reproaching the Italian fascists for their intellectual links with the old Jacobin tradition:

Some of your formulas seem to me to renew, certainly, but also to return to our
old myth of the democratic general will such as we find in Rousseau. I am struck
by the fact that fascism sometimes goes in for the mystique of the leader, and
sometimes, also, for a sort of culmination of democracy in a unanimity of assent.
We, however, since 1789, have revised our conception of tyranny. We no longer
believe that the majority is the tutelary divinity that our fathers worshiped. We
know that the majority is more commonly an oppressor today than tyrants are.
We see, finally, that the formation, through individualist corruption, of those
large and amorphous masses that overturn old political ordinances is the favored terrain of the anonymous dictatorships on the one hand and the personal
dictatorships on the other. [20]

Thus Mounier, speaking to the Italian Fascist party, placed "the
anonymous dictatorships"—the democracies—and the "personal dictatorships"—the fascist regimes—in the same category. He concluded:

There is no need for us to continue arguing about formulas: democrats, antidemocrats, liberals, antiliberals—the greatest confusion always goes on under
their cover. A French radical socialist who dreams of imposing *his* conception of
liberty through the exercise of power is a "fascist" and even a theocrat: "absolute" majorities succeed absolute governments, it all amounts to the same thing.
A dictatorship that places the same confidence in the subjective infallibility of a
man or a party that democracy places in the subjective infallibility of the majority has the same claim to be liberal in that it hypostatizes the relative. [21]

Such were Mounier's preoccupations in 1935, and they were always
part of his thought. He was fascinated by the great revolutionary movements in Germany and Italy. A year earlier, for example, between January and May 1934, *Esprit* had published a long essay, spread over four
issues, by Otto Strasser called "L'Allemagne est-elle un danger ou un
espoir pour l'Europe?" (Is Germany a Danger or a Hope for Europe?). [22]
Strasser was considered a representative of national-socialist nonconformism, just as *Esprit* regarded Ugo Spirito and the Italian fascist
left as the rebels of Mussolini's movement.

In July 1936, Mounier participated in a dialogue at the Belgian seaside resort of Zoute with representatives of the Hitler Youth, a meeting organized by Édouard Didier. John Hellman has shown that the Didier circle in Brussels was frequented by Otto Abetz, the Nazi party propaganda specialist who would later advise Ribbentrop on French affairs.[23] Didier published the journal *Jeune Europe*, for which Mounier had written an article condemning the League of Nations[24] before going to Zoute to take part in this "International Youth Meeting," on which Raymond de Becker, a Catholic activist with increasingly pro-Nazi sympathies, reported in *L'Avant-Garde*, a daily close to *Esprit*. At the meeting, we read in this account, Mounier engaged in a long discussion with the German representatives—a discussion that fully reflected the ambiguities of *Esprit*. One receives the impression that between these two movements—the personalist and the Nazi—discussion was possible and had some significance.[25] While the two movements proposed different solutions, they appeared to have similar preoccupations. During the same period, Mounier published a summary of his philosophical ideas under the title "Was ist der Personalismus?" (What Is Personalism?) in Otto Abetz's journal, and he supported the initiatives of de Becker, who rapidly moved toward a more and more open espousal of national socialism. Indeed, Mounier seems never to have given up his deep attachment to de Becker.[26] It should be pointed out, however, that Mounier tended to allow the local groups of *Esprit* free expression: the Brussels group was somewhat right-wing, whereas the Spanish group under J.-M. Semprun y Gurrea was the most liberal and fought vigorously on the anti-Franco side.

But *Esprit* in the thirties was more than a laboratory of ideas—it had a purpose: to discover a third way between the left and the right, opposed to both the left and the right, opposed to Marxism, whether communist or social-democratic, and opposed to democracy, whether liberal or conservative. That is why Mounier never identified himself entirely with the Popular Front or fully supported Blum's experiment, just as he never wholeheartedly supported the Spanish Republic. To be sure, he preferred the Popular Front to its opponents and the Spanish Republicans to the insurgents. Undoubtedly, his refusal to adopt the positions that prevailed among the majority of Catholics with regard to the Spanish Civil War and the Popular Front was in itself an act of great significance. *Esprit* thus played an important role in the liberalization of French Catholicism, but in the period of the Popular Front this role was far from unambiguous.

A careful examination of the two numbers of *Esprit* published in

April and May 1936 (a critical period for the Popular Front) reveals no
clear or definite support of the left-wing coalition. All Mounier's writings in *Esprit*, including a long editorial of April 1936 signed "Esprit"—"Adresse des vivants à quelques survivants" (Address of the Living to a Few Survivors)—betray the same attitude to both the right and
the left.[27] Mounier deeply deplored the preponderance of Marxism in
the left-wing coalition. He stated his position quite unequivocally: he
saw the "materialist" evil as always constituting the main enemy, and
everything else was subordinate to the struggle against it.[28] That is why
Mounier never really took a stand in favor of the Popular Front.[29] He
and his close companions, who set the tone of *Esprit*,[30] refused to associate themselves with a political experiment within the framework of a
system that was based on "materialism" and that had issued from the
French Revolution, for Mounier opposed not only the practices of the
regime and its functional weaknesses but also its philosophical foundations and its essential structures. In his view, it was the very essence of
liberal democracy and of democratic socialism that rendered the regime
fundamentally corrupt. In an article of March 1938, Mounier passed
judgment on the French Revolution, which, according to him, "consecrated the triumph of juridical individualism."[31] Mounier did not deny
that the French revolutionaries had "some splendid achievements" to
their credit, but he thought that these were "more connected with the
necessities of history than with the conceptions of the period." He saw
in the Revolution "the permanence of a Christian sentiment,"[32] but, finally, he said, "its weak spot, which today is causing the collapse of a
particular form of democracy," was individualism.[33] This indictment of
the "left-wing mythos" ended with an invocation of Dostoyevsky and
Nietzsche, "two references that are all-important to us," and with the
declaration that "this 'static' country that has had three revolutions in a
century is preparing a fourth."[34]

In October 1937, Mounier expressed the feeling that he was living in
the death throes of a world, and drew the following conclusion, of para-
mount importance for an understanding of his thought, writings, and
activities: "We have already made a mark in the history of ideas and in
the interplay of forces through a dissociation from the spiritual (especially Christian) and the established disorder, but we have not yet made
a mark, as we should do, through an equally great dissociation of the
law, of civilization, of the reality of the people from the lamentable left-
wing ideologies. . . . I call upon all our friends to undertake this task."[35]

The problem, clearly, was not a simple one,[36] and even a historian as sympathetic to *Esprit* as Michel Winock was aware of its complexity when, to explain Mounier's behavior, he pointed out how Julien Benda, the opponent of the nationalist writers and the champion of universalism, praised Drieu's *Socialisme fasciste*.[37] The author of *La Trahison des clercs* well understood the meaning of Drieu's fascism, and precisely because he understood it so well he showed himself well disposed if not sympathetic toward it. Drieu's fascism, wrote Benda, "is less a political statement than a moral attack, being a Nietzschean will always to surpass oneself in contempt of all stagnation, everything static, all peaceful enjoyments, of which democracy seems to him symbolic."[38] The fact is that fascism had a fascination for men who did not admire the Italian regime but for whom any attempt to transcend bourgeois mediocrity and democratic flaccidity was highly praiseworthy.

Thus, if Benda the moralist so well understood Drieu, who was equally a moralist, why should it be otherwise with Mounier when he went to Italy to study the advantages of corporatism? Was not corporatism a new, unconventional approach, able to resolve old contradictions and provide an alternative to the class struggle, to vulgar Marxist materialism, to uncontrolled liberalism, to inhuman capitalism? In the spring of 1934, when he expounded the principles of a personalist and communal revolution directed simultaneously against individual and collective tyrannies,[39] Mounier, always open to new insights, published a few articles by Andreu, of which one, "The True Face of La Tour du Pin," represented the search for new solutions transcending both Marxism and liberalism. The fascist impregnation was so deep precisely because it was a new ideology, proposing original solutions—a living ideology, product of the twentieth century, proclaiming an ethical concern to which neither historical materialism nor liberal democracy had accustomed a younger generation thirsty for morality.

That is why men of different political backgrounds came to regard with a certain benevolence this ideology eager to transcend all the others—this ideology that, as Brasillach said, "took its benefits where it found them."[40] A whole generation wished to do the same. In 1925 young Hubert Beuve-Méry was attracted by Georges Valois's Faisceau,[41] and four years later young Mendès France declared himself entirely in agreement with the basic ideas of the man who had just become known as the leader of French fascism.[42] Even today, Maurice Duverger, looking at Doriot with the eyes of the young man he was in 1938, said that at that time the head of the PPF seemed a man of the left and his party a party of the left. In his opinion, the program of the PPF in 1936, "as a whole, seemed to be a moderate, up-to-date Keynesian interventionism. Some might say Mendèsist." [43]

All these people, then, were animated by a strong desire to create something new. This desire, shared by a whole generation, was a kind of common denominator for the fascists and their fellow travelers, and also for all those who simply could not resist the attraction of fascism—its ethics, its dynamism, its youthfulness. Fascism had a heroic, virile aspect that attracted people who detested the police state in Italy and the racial repression in Germany. In people like Mounier—who saw France as "sick and exhausted," as a country prey to "decomposition," stricken with a paralysis of the will, with people who asked, "Is France finished?" [44]—the message of Maulnier or Brasillach could not fail to find an echo.

For the image of France that one finds in *Esprit* at the end of the thirties hardly differs from that found in *Combat*. Mounier's diatribes against liberal democracy and bourgeois society closely resemble that enormous literature of condemnation that began with Barrès and Sorel and ended with Drieu, Maulnier, and Brasillach. It was precisely because the representatives of schools of thought at the opposite extreme from fascism saw the weaknesses and sicknesses of France in the same way as the fascists that the penetration of the fascist ideology in France was so deep and so easy. Mounier's criticism of France resembled Maulnier's and Brasillach's in all essential points. He made a similar attack on its political regime, its social structures, its intellectual and moral condition; he had the same sense of decadence, of decrepitude, the same conviction that an intellectual and moral, political and social revolution was necessary for the salvation of the French soul. And this no doubt helps to explain why, in the critical moments of 1940, French democracy found many fewer zealous defenders than one might have expected.

Indeed, there was far too much common ground between the critics of the "system" and the rebels of every stripe for the regime to have been able to resist. Nothing was more usual among the young than a rejection of the Third Republic, and intellectual prestige went to those who sought out nonconformist solutions. Among these, the fascists often represented only the most advanced, most extreme elements, but they nevertheless expressed a way of thinking that was widespread. To be sure, not everyone who wants to create something new is a fascist, but no one has ever had a stronger taste for renewal than a fascist in the making. No one has ever considered himself the bearer of a future more promising, more different from the present order, more radically opposed to that which exists: "We are against everyone," said Drieu in July 1934. "We fight against everyone. That is what fascism is." [45]

Because, in the final analysis, it thought only in political terms, that "realistic generation" [46] began its revolt in opposing both the right and the left. From Valois, who said that fascism, being the only movement to reconcile authority and freedom, "is neither of the right nor of the left," [47] to Drieu, Jouvenel, and Maulnier, to Bergery and Déat, the néos, and the members of the PPF, fascism regarded its refusal to accept traditional divisions as its greatest contribution to contemporary politics. Drieu and the writers of *La Lutte des jeunes* rode up against "the old right and the old left" in the name of all those who were "both anticapitalist and antiparliamentarian" [48] and, like Bergery, regarded the very idea of right and left as a gigantic deception. [49]

"In saying *neither right*," wrote Andreu in a characteristic passage, "we reject the open alliance between the right-wing parties and capitalism to safeguard the spiritual values of which the right-wingers are the false custodians. In saying *nor left*, we reject the covert alliance of the left-wing parties with capitalism and the false values (democracy, individualism) that they defend." [50]

After the events of 6 February, Drieu commented on what had taken place in the place de la Concorde. On that day, he said, "social elements had marched that belong neither to the right nor to the left, and confounded these two equal and impotent old formations with the same distrust and the same reproval." [51] A few months later he said, "The only merit of fascism is to tear off these masks, all these masks. One no longer speaks of left and right in fascist territory. There is only capitalism against socialism, locked in a fight to the death." [52]

The same idea was expressed by Déat. For him, too, the only true political reality was the opposition of the revolutionaries and the conservatives. "I must confess that all this is of little significance to me," wrote the secretary-general of the PSF. "Henceforth, there are on one side political conservatives who are as much to be found on the left as on the right, and as much on the extreme left as on the extreme right. And then there is an enormous, still-confused mass that will order itself through our efforts and that is tired of the established order, deeply wants it to change, and is capable of changing everything through its pressure. There are the fossils and there are the revolutionaries, who are also the builders." [53]

Being neither of the right nor of the left meant for some that "we join (and sometimes overtake) the left by our programs and the right by our methods,"[54] while for others it meant that "these men, these doctrines, these parties, whether of the right or the left . . . , are all equally odious."[55] Thierry Maulnier proclaimed his rejection of the established scheme of things in a passage that reads like a classic expression of the revolt of these young people in search of a third way between the left and the right, between capitalism and socialism:

We believe neither in capitalism which creates the class struggle, nor in socialism which exploits it; neither in presidents of boards of directors who enrich themselves from the people's labor, nor in politicians who make a career out of its resentment; neither in those who pay commissions, nor in those who receive them; neither in conservative blindness, nor in demagogic impudence; neither in egoism, nor in humanitarianism; neither in cowardice, nor in arrivism; neither in the left, nor in the right.

We do not say that the words right and left no longer have a meaning. We say that they still have one, and that it should be taken away from them, for they signify routine and utopia, death through paralysis and death by decomposition, Money and Figures: antagonistic tyrannies, possibly, but equally detestable, and liable to come together at the expense of the mystified onlooker. For we know from experience—and it is as well to remember it now that the right and the left seem quite close to coming together around the Jacobin flag for another "union sacrée" with a thousand dead a day—we know that a war for Principles can also be good for Business, and the interests of armaments manufacturers can easily be reconciled with the liberation of oppressed peoples.[56]

Everything is already present in this passage—the rejection not only of liberalism and socialism but also of ideological struggle, of war against dictatorial regimes. A war on behalf of certain values, in a bourgeois system, can only, it is claimed, be a war of the bourgeois, a war of Money for the sake of Money.

In the struggle between "the forces of routine and the forces of renewal"[57] the rebels called for an alliance "of the dissidents,"[58] dissidence alone having the power to stand against both left and right. True dissidence, however, can abandon a position without ceasing to manifest the same hostility toward the opposite position. Maurice Blanchot, who was to become in postwar France a famous writer and literary critic, provided a perfect definition of the fascist spirit in claiming that it is a synthesis between a left that forsakes its original beliefs not to draw closer to capitalist beliefs but to define the true conditions of the struggle against capitalism and a right that neglects the traditional forms of nationalism not to draw closer to internationalism but to combat internationalism in all its forms.[59] One finds innumerable variations of this idea among the néos, the members of the PPF, and the Drieu-Jouvenel group. "This is not a politics of equilibrium, of weights and balances; it is a politics of fusion," wrote Drieu, who asked both sides to give up their old obsessions and anxieties and acknowledge that they were of the same opinion. La Rocque had to show that he was ready to break with "the old civilization of profit," and Doriot had to show that he was not ashamed to "discover that Saint-Denis is in France"[60]—a sentiment echoed by Doriot himself, the former leader of Communist Youth, when he said that he had lived through too much French politics to attach much importance to the difference between the right and the left.[61]

For this generation of fascist intellectuals, which was perfectly represented by Drieu, Maulnier, and Déat, to be against both right and left meant first of all to recognize that "the worlds of the right and left go together and cannot be separated. Both of them . . . spanning all classes, they form part of the politico-economic system of capitalist democracy."[62] The Action Française and the Communist party, the people of the right and the people of the left were all held to be equally attached to the system—to the democratic parliamentary regime, to the freedom of the press and of opinion—which meant that, in defending democracy, they were also defending capitalism.[63] Consequently, said Maulnier, a new world could be constructed only by waging a struggle against the true enemy—the political and economic forces of democracy.[64]

These ideas had already been put forward by the Cercle Proudhon in the period just before 1914, and they were to underlie the ideology of collaboration with the Nazis. The problem described by the young fascists of the interwar period had already existed at the beginning of the century. For Maulnier and Jouvenel, the Popular Front was the equivalent of Dreyfusism. Once again the proletariat had been mobilized in the service of democracy; once again the bourgeoisie had been able to mobilize its distress and anger in the service of the established order.[65] The left, said Jouvenel, had reached the point where it no longer regarded social justice as an end in itself: to defend parliamentary democracy, the leaders of the CGT accepted "a coalition that paralyzed them in the struggle against capitalism and even against its abuses."[66] Socialism's "concern to defend republicanism" was "overriding,"[67] and Maulnier, on Sorel's authority, stated that "socialism's alliance with democracy . . . wounded it in its depths, because it felt it to be the end of any greatness it had hoped for."[68] Maulnier exemplified the convergence of the Maurrassian school of thought that had taught the French to dissociate "the idea of nationalism from that of bourgeois social conservatism" and the Sorelian school of thought that had attempted to separate "the idea of social revolution from the idea of democratic progress."[69] Finally, he tried to revive the spirit of the former "theoreticians of proletarian violence" to draw out in the proletariat "whatever Marxism and its democratic corruptions have left in the people of that violence."[70]

Maulnier had no doubts: if one wants to create a new system "that will put an end to the mad dictatorship of money and restore to the workers, who have been deprived of it, an organic place in the nation,"[71] "one must appeal to the proletariat"; one must call on "disciplined and powerful elites."[72] Barrès and Sorel would not have changed a word of these statements. For them, too, "the true violence in ideas, the real power of rupture is where the struggle against the present society is constantly going on, without sparing its political forms."[73]

True fascists hated politics and abhorred the conservative right, the liberal right—the "regimist" right, one might say—no less than the moderate left. Valois at the end of the twenties and Déat a few years later denounced the "old parties" and all those who belonged to the "cartel of the established order,"[74] while Drieu heaped scorn on both Blum and Maurras, who were perfectly satisfied "in their passive opposition, in their journalistic chairs."[75] Drieu accused Maurrassism of having "subtle but deep connections with the present republican system,"[76] and his young friend Andreu reminded Maurras that in 1908 he had defended the people, the "laboring mass" on which the Republic had opened fire, just as it had in his day in the place de la Concorde.[77] For this Maurrassian right, this right of the Croix de Feu, this right of Louis Marin—"that spluttering fellow, encumbered and bedecked with tearful idiocy and spotted fabrics"[78]—Brassilach, Drieu, and Maulnier felt only disgust. Faced with these "old cuckolds of the right, these eternal deceived husbands of politics," Brasillach stated that "the enemies of all national restoration are not only on the left but first and foremost on the right."[79]

The generation of Drieu and Maulnier, like that of Barrès and Sorel, proclaimed loudly that "the nation is not made out of a union of money bags and checkbooks,"[80] or, in Drieu's words, that "a vague nationalism is a form of capitalist defense."[81] They claimed that capitalism uses nationalism as a mystique, even though nationalism is external to capitalism, independent of all social and political forms.[82] In the hands of the French right at the end of the thirties, however, nationalism deviated "toward the fetid marshes of the old right," wrote a contributor to Combat. "It fits very well into the framework of Marxist definitions: it is a capitalism with a Boulangist superstructure."[83] The editor of the review added, "The essential task of a true 'nationalism' must be not only to dissociate the national idea from the present political and economic structure of the nation but also to provoke or precipitate the disintegration of this dual structure so that a new national organization will come into being. . . . A democratic state, a society dominated by money, the present institutions no longer express what unites the nation and perpetuates it, but what consumes and divides it."[84]

Thierry Maulnier expounded this basic idea common to all the nonconformists in innumerable articles and several books, which began to appear in 1932, when his first work, *La Crise est dans l'homme*, was published.[85] He belonged to the school that found in fascism a logical and rational third alternative—the only one that could bring about a deep change in society. Why should not "a third party that, being social, was also national and, being national, was also social"[86] appeal to that class of young people who, in any period, are able to demonstrate a remarkable detachment toward old differences? In the days of Boulangism, Barrès was already thinking in this way. "What are all these old quarrels—republicans, royalists, Bonapartists—to us newcomers?" he wrote. "We feel that there are good people in all factions."[87] A half century later, Déat took up the same idea and tried to "cut short old quarrels."[88] It was then that this conceptual framework of politics in a democracy was characterized as "neither right nor left."

At the end of the twenties, Valois defined fascism and Marxism as "varieties of socialism."[89] A few years later, Montagnon said that "we are aware that . . . our way is not the only way to come to socialism, that there can be another—the fascist way."[90] Trying to visualize the future of fascism in his country, Maulnier concluded that France could "move either toward a fascism of the right or toward a fascism of the left."[91] Jouvenel used the term *fascist socialism*,[92] and one of his collaborators examined "the socialist possibilities of fascism."[93] Jouvenel had no doubts about the nature of fascism: "Socialism contains something else than material requirements—a hope, a desire for progress within man himself. This 'something else' passed into the anti-Marxist movements known as 'fascist.'"[94]

Drieu was also well aware of this "socialist" aspect of fascism. "Fascism is always a party of the 'left,'" he wrote,[95] and elsewhere he spoke of "bolshevik fascism,"[96] "socialism in fascist costume,"[97] and "socializing fascism."[98] "Not everyone who wants to be a fascist is one," he said. "A mere nationalist cannot be one, because he has not the slightest idea of socialism."[99] Brasillach had a similar attitude. "We have no interest in the capitalist universe," he declared,[100] while Andreu warned against "the governmental fascism, without youth and without liberty," into which the néos were slipping.[101]

Never, it seems, were political concepts in France subject to more ambiguity, and precisely this ambiguity explains the depth of the fascist impregnation. It was because Valois could claim that "there is a fascism of the plutocracy and popular fascism"[102] and because Drieu could say that he wanted to abandon the "word fascism" if that "meant reaction"[103] that the young Duverger felt in 1937 that to join the PPF would be to "swing to the left."[104] He knew that Jouvenel's circle refused "conservative bourgeois" the right to call themselves fascists—none of their groups "deserved that accusation."[105] In *Combat*, among the friends of Brasillach and Jouvenel, the hatred for the moderates could be stronger than that for the Popular Front. "The famous 'gust of wind of May 1936'—we have not always felt hostile toward it," wrote Brasillach.[106] In May 1938, when the left commemorated the Commune in Père Lachaise cemetery, the editors of *Je suis partout* published a list of those who had "died for the national revolution," and went to the Wall of the Federates with a wreath "for the first victims of the regime."[107]

One of the most revealing expressions of the "fascicization" of the nonconformist elements of the right and left was Gaston Bergery's frontism. Bergery was one of the great hopes of the generation of 1930. A brilliant soldier in the Great War, Édouard Herriot's chief of staff in 1924, deputy for Mantes in 1928, he was situated at the extreme left of the Radical party. Rebellious intellectuals delighted in him as a new type of politician. Slim and athletic, despising city clothes and the bourgeois tie, for which he substituted a simple strap of leather, he was regarded as a "star."[108]

In 1933 Bergery founded *Front commun* to bring together radical dissidents, socialists, and communists on an individual basis.[109] Jouvenel remembers being present at a meeting in March 1933 at which Bergery expounded his program and to which Déat brought a socialist greeting and Doriot a communist greeting.[110] Previously, Bergery, who had never been asked to participate in any of the radical governments that succeeded the legislative elections of 1932, had been defeated at the Radical party's Toulouse congress and forced to resign.[111] After 6 February, Bergery appeared—and not only in the eyes of Jouvenel, who had been a Radical party member—to be the "natural leader of a left of direct action. . . . Let us hope," wrote Jouvenel, "that he is able to summon to revolutionary action not only the youth of the left but all the youth."[112]

To avoid confusion after the creation of the Popular Front, Bergery's *Front commun* was renamed *Front social*. In November 1937 *La Flèche* began to receive contributions from Déat, and in February 1939 it opened its columns to Georges Scapini. In the meantime, frontism had lost first Paul Langevin and then Georges Izard. Owing to his nonconformism, Bergery also gravitated toward the national revolution.

First Izard lashed out against the existing political, social, and economic system—the trusts, the two hundred families, and all the "old phenomena" from "capitalist orthodoxy" to the "bolshevik revolution." [113] Then Bergery himself, taking up a position that by now had become classical, rejected not only "Marxism governing in the guise of social democracy" but also the categories "left and right," advocating "a socialism free from foreign directives that would be supported by all classes in opposition to the tyranny of money." [114] Similarly, in May 1935, Izard stated, without realizing the real meaning of his words, that "frontism appropriates from fascism the terms union, nation, honor as well as the terms justice, order, comradeship." [115] This slide toward fascism was noticed by contemporaries. Valois's new journal *Le Nouvel Age* accused frontism of fascism, [116] and even more revealing were the reactions of the militant Doriotists present at a meeting held by Bergery in Saint-Denis in March 1938. Their spokesman observed—wrote a police inspector on duty at the time—"that the ideas expressed by Bergery were close to those of the PPF, and he was surprised that he did not join the party." [117]

The evolution of frontism illustrates the inner logic of a process that explains why the idea of a "fascism of the left" was so widespread between the wars. It was spoken of first by Valois's supporters [118] and then by the néos, [119] the writers of *La Lutte des jeunes*, [120] and Maulnier. [121] From 1934 onward, Drieu and Valois described frontism in these terms. [122] Anticipating one of the modern theories of fascism by half a century, Drieu wrote, "Today, what does one see in the world? Communists and fascists, or, more exactly, red fascists and white fascists." [123] And he concluded, "Fascism is a universal title extending from Stalin to the Japanese, passing through the Chinese." [124]

Democracy Against the Spirit

For all the dissident elements in revolt against the established order, adherence to a fascist ideology represented the wish to break with a particular society, with a particular way of life, with ideologies that every day demonstrated their incapacity to change the world. Fascism satisfied both a longing for revolution and a desire to preserve the past, the national history, and the cultural paraphernalia of society. Fascism wanted to do away with democracy, liberalism, and Marxism; it wanted to end the immobility and materialism of bourgeois society, yet without endangering the national collectivity. One of the most striking and instructive examples of this approach, and one of the least known, was the journal *Combat*, created and directed by Jean de Fabrègues and Thierry Maulnier.

At the end of the thirties, *Combat* constituted a laboratory of ideas of great influence, for though the review could lay claim to only a thousand subscribers in November 1936, ideas developed in small reviews of limited circulation soon found their way into the national press and became common currency. *Combat* developed a subtler political ideology than that of the self-declared fascists, but it is hard to see any real basic difference between them. Certainly, in its expression the ideology of *Combat* was less blatant, less vulgar perhaps than that of *Je suis partout*, but one finds in *Combat* the same vehemence, the same intensity, and, above all, the same intellectual content. The invectives also have a similar intention, but the campaigns of defamation and cries for murder of the Brasillach group are generally toned down and appear in a more refined fashion. To the young who were, in Brasillach's words, "caught between social conservatism and the Marxist rabble" [125] *Combat* offered a relatively attractive alternative. The review combined "the antidemocratic and the anticonservative spirit," [126] and, thanks to the place that its contributors held in the world of letters, it exerted an influence that went far beyond the restricted circle of its readers.

Maulnier's journal attacked democracy and materialism while taking up the defense of the spirit. This was one of the main ideas put forward by the rebels, and formed the basis of their common campaign against democracy: they all presented democracy as the natural enemy of spiritual values. On this point the fascists, quasi-fascists, and other "nonconformists" were all in complete agreement because they all had the same goal—to save the spirit and to regenerate the body of modern society. *Combat* therefore defended Italian fascism, and when it expressed reservations about the Hitler regime, it was only to deplore the antitranscendental aspect of nazism. [127] The hatred of the existing regime in France sometimes bred a sympathy for its enemies. Thus, one watched with interest, sometimes with indulgence, always with strong feelings, the rise of that antimaterialism par excellence that was fascism. In July

1939, Jean de Fabrègues, who founded *Combat* with Maulnier, summed up the aims of the review: it was to fight "materialistic socialism," defend "interior, personal values," and develop a "discipline of ourselves."[128] These aims, obviously, were not very different from those of *Esprit*.

Maulnier had high ambitions. He was not content merely to practice literary criticism, or to defend "true" culture against bourgeois or proletarian barbarity, or to become the leader of a little group of intellectuals: Maulnier sought to lay the foundations for the regeneration of the ailing body that France had become 150 years after the Revolution. Clearly, Maulnier was attempting to play the role of Barrès for his own generation. His first book, *La Crise est dans l'homme*, was obviously written in imitation of the young Barrès: it has his impertinent tone, his way of looking down on his elders, his affected mannerisms, his nationalism.

Like Barrès, Maulnier preached "disobedience to the laws." One must "despise the laws, violate the laws and destroy them: there is no other method of action and no other way."[129] Nearly half a century earlier, the young Barrès had published his own manifesto of revolt. In his book *L'Ennemi des lois*, he declared that he was "drawn to destroy all that exists," and he advised against acts of violence only because he did not believe that by "dynamiting a bourgeois" one could destroy "the social order that brought him into being," and "good lectures, clearly written booklets . . . would appear to be a more effective form of propaganda."[130] He believed that it was the "instinct for revolt disseminated around the world" that "created the perpetual and necessary revolution."[131] The mouthpiece for Barrès in *L'Ennemi des lois* was a twenty-eight-year-old *agrégé*, the author of a seditious article calling legality into question. This character in the novel, André Maltère, could easily have been called Thierry Maulnier, who likewise preached revolution, "illegal violence," and "subversion of the regime,"[132] or Drieu La Rochelle, who also rebelled against the established order, which he associated with reaction: "Reaction thinks that revolutions are purposeless. We joyously believe that they are necessary."[133]

This revolt was accompanied by a violent rejection of what Barrès had called machinism.[134] From the last decade of the nineteenth century, in his newspaper, *La Cocarde* (and *Combat* often seemed like a scarcely modernized version of the Boulangist deputy's daily), he railed against the crimes of industrial civilization. Barrès was categorical: modern man was the victim of a situation that made him "the slave of the rela-

tions between labor and capital." He denounced a "harsh society," a situation of incessant struggle.[135] The future theoretician of *La Terre* and
Les Morts held responsible for the sickness of his period not the iniq-
uities of the social order but industrial society itself, and it was on
behalf of the individual that he attacked industrial society: "The educational machinery no less than the industrial machinery arrests the harmonious development of the individual, the expansion of his powers, of
his propensities."[136] He claimed that the "industrial machine" oblit-
erates the individual's identity and originality; it dehumanizes man, and
therefore industrial society and the bourgeois liberal state by their very
nature produce revolts.

The fascists took up this idea with little alteration. Drieu claimed
that one of the main virtues of fascism was its "defense of man against
the city and against the machine,"[137] while Maulnier believed that "at
the height of the machine civilization we shall find ourselves more oppressed by matter, by our needs, than primitive men. . . . That, indeed,
is the new barbarism."[138] Like Barrès, Maulnier attacked all the consequences of the industrial revolution, which promoted a single school
system, a technical and vocational education, and an "every day more
intimate association of capital and science, of the plutocrat and the engineer, which will give rise to a sort of economic determinism" perfectly
expressed by democracy.[139] Materialism had taken on the sinister forms
of a barbarous "Americanism" or of a Marxism "that had betrayed itself
in the Russian construction."[140] "The Marxist society coming to birth
and the Fordist society in decline have been revealed to us in their insane
inhumanity, sacrificing souls to machines."[141] Thus, one was faced with
"the extraordinary spectacle of a society taking complete possession of
man," a society where "man subjected to economics not only had to . . .
produce; he also had the duty to consume."[142] "American civilization,"
the "American spirit," tended toward "universal enslavement,"[143] but in
this, American society in no way differed from Soviet society: "All this
well deserves the name of collectivism, the barbarous name for a barbarous thing."[144] Collectivism can assume different forms: the Rousseau-
esque form or the Marxist form, which is only "the transposition of
Rousseau into economics," for "democracy devours man body and soul
and sacrifices him to its political sovereignty, while Marxism devours
him and sacrifices him to its economic sovereignty."[145] The same is true
with regard to democracy, capitalism, and socialism: "Democracy is a
collective Caesarism; socialism is a collective capitalism."[146] However,
the productive, rationalized societies of Ford and Stalin go even further

in the spiritual destruction of the individual: they constitute "an irre-
mediable enslavement to the most brutal forces of matter."[147] Thus, it is
all one: with "Hoover on the one side, Stalin on the other side,"[148] democracy, liberalism, capitalism, socialism, and Marxism are only different aspects of one and the same evil—materialism.

The victory of materialism brings about a "spiritual crisis," a "crisis
of values," an "almost unprecedented spiritual bankruptcy,"[149] and to
confront the "peril that threatens the spirit"[150] there is no alternative
but to "defend the unquestionable primacy of the spirit."[151] Maulnier,
throughout the thirties, fought materialism with unflagging vigor. His
new political work, *Mythes socialistes*, published in 1936, was a long
indictment not only of Marxism but also of "individualistic disorder"
(note the similarity to Mounier's terminology), "individualistic" and
"bourgeois" idealism, and "socialist materialism."[152] Maulnier was
quite clear: "Idealism is the true father of materialism."[153] All these elements are interchangeable—one of the key chapters of *Mythes socialistes* is called "Materialistic Idealism"[154]—and all are symptomatic of
the "decline of spiritual values."[155] Maulnier claimed that, for the materialist, "the spirit ceases to be . . . a means of gaining knowledge of the
world. . . . All true materialism reaches the conclusion that it is impossible for man to pass beyond the limits of the utilitarian, and that the
spirit is philosophically powerless with regard to reality."[156] That is why
Maulnier, the intellectual leader of the Jeune Droite, welcomed the
revisionism of Henri De Man so enthusiastically, seeing it as a "self-
examination of the socialist conscience."[157] Maulnier appreciated De
Man's "revolutionary *voluntarism*," his criticism of "revolutionary
quietism," "*mechanism*," and determinism.[158] He understood very well
the ideas that De Man had expressed at Pontigny—his desire to overtake fascism in order to fight it with its own weapons.[159] He was aware
of the significance of this process: the right, to triumph over socialism,
had borrowed its terminology and many of its ideas, and there existed,
said Maulnier, a "*socialistic fascism*" that was "the only still-living form
of socialism."[160] Maulnier, however, criticized De Man's timidity, his advocacy of that compromise "between the old bourgeois liberalism and
socialism . . . that is a directed economy," for "what has to be recreated
is the very idea of economy." Liberalism and Marxism "can be opposed
only by some method of subordinating the economy."[161]

This hostility toward materialism in all its forms finally brought
Maulnier to look favorably on the fascist experience in Italy and the
Nazi experience in Germany. For both, Maulnier used the term *neo-*

nationalism, and he attempted to provide this neonationalism with the element that, in his opinion, the movement lacked: a solid conceptual framework.[162] Long before the end of the decade, Maulnier displayed an interest in and a sympathy for this dynamic new movement. As early as 1933, he wrote an introduction to Arthur Moeller van den Bruck's celebrated work *The Third Reich.* These pages are a document of great importance, and reveal a very characteristic attitude. Dedicated to the memory of "that young, enthusiastic and somber writer [who], believing that the policy of Stresemann, the policy of mildness, the policy of Locarno, humiliated and dishonored Germany, committed suicide," [163] this panegyric was the manifesto of a new morality. Maulnier wished to "draw a lesson of energy and pride" [164] from this act of "heroism," this "superhuman" gesture. He proposed it as an example to French youth, saying that "one has to recognize that from 1918 to 1933 the German nationalist youth taught us very great lessons." [165] After the Great War, he added, there were in Germany "generations virile enough not to shrink from murder or death." [166]

Moeller van den Bruck, whose gesture "resembled the battles, the conspiracies, the assassinations in which the 'Outlaws,' Ernst von Salomon's fighting companions, sought to give form to their despair and vengeance," [167] thus became, in the eyes of the Jeune Droite, a "teacher of energy," to use Barrès's celebrated expression. Nearly half a century earlier, some other young people, the seven young Lorrains of *Les Déracinés,* had also learned a "lesson of energy," [168] but the psychological distance that separates Napoleon's tomb from Moeller van den Bruck's was equaled by the extent of the changes that had taken place in the interim. The national pride of Barrès and Déroulède had given way to the inferiority complex of Maulnier, Brasillach, Drieu, Jouvenel, and Déat.

Maulnier envied young Germany the quality of Moeller van den Bruck's work—the "quivering tension that inspires even the argument, a proud and harsh passion, this desire for grandeur, this sense of the tragic" that enabled the author of *The Third Reich* to evoke "the slightly primitive violence and rude nobility . . . of these companions-in-arms of Ernst von Salomon who stripped naked to fight in the light of dawn." [169] This young German became a symbol for Maulnier, because "he was one of the first of those serving heroes, perfectly forgetful of themselves, completely devoted to the grandeur and the mission of the race, which the new German morality wishes to create with the men of tomorrow." [170] Maulnier was perfectly aware of the significance of *The Third*

Reich in the context of postwar Germany. He presented it to the French public precisely because he considered it "one of the essential works of national-socialist doctrine," one that belongs to the "domain of social morality and the criticism of ideas," "halfway between the one [Rosenberg] and the other [Hitler], between philosophy and politics."[171] In speaking of Moeller van den Bruck, Maulnier, in fact, presented his own vision of nazism. "The racist doctrine," he claimed, found its "scientific foundations" in Alfred Rosenberg's works, while the "political program and the tactical possibilities of the new party" were defined in Hitler's *Mein Kampf*.[172] Moeller van den Bruck's work was situated between the two.

Maulnier considered one element of the book to be particularly deserving of the reader's attention. Even more than by its analysis of the contemporary history of Germany, "one is drawn by the call that emerges from this book, a call of pride and distress, a call of generations deeply wounded and yet virile, ready to harden themselves against decay not only through a fierce will to courage and violence but through the choice of a difficult, exacting and perfectly disinterested task."[173] The book thus expressed "a deep and tragic virility, a natural tendency to heroism, a contempt for happiness, a search for sacrifice through the natural volition of one's being and not through a passively endured discipline, an abstract imperative."[174] These were the exemplary qualities that Maulnier recommended to French youth.

Moeller, to be sure, had not been sparing of attacks against France, but, said Maulnier, "why should a well-born German necessarily be a friend of ours? . . . Here is a generous, violent, lucid, implacable enemy, no doubt the very type of those heroes that national socialism wishes to fashion against us."[175] French nationalists, thought Maulnier, do not have to love Germany, nor do German nationalists have to love France. National socialism is a form of German nationalism, and it is "specifically anti-French."[176] And yet, he said, "even if we have to be separated from the new Germany by a conflict against which no sense of fraternity can prevail, I feel it is opportune to say quietly that we feel closer to— and more readily understood by—a German national socialist than to a French pacifist."[177] This was so essentially because "the dispute between Germany and us is not a quarrel about principles. If we question the German principle that a superior form of humanity has the right to subjugate an inferior form, why do we have colonies?"[178] Not only did Maulnier accept the Nazi ideology, but he wished to use it as an example for the regeneration of France. He wanted to be rid of "the petit bourgeois politics that claims to assure us of the possession without risk of that which it is the destiny of the people to acquire and maintain only with continual risk." [179] All the fascists said something similar: Déat urged his followers to "live dangerously," [180] Degrelle, the leader of Belgian Rexism and hero of Brasillach and Jouvenel, defined fascism as a *Revolution of Souls*,[181] and Brasillach himself deplored the "anarchist spirit becoming bourgeois" of a France that was fast asleep.[182]

If Maulnier was fascinated by nazism—and he, as easily as Brasillach, could have spoken of the "brusque grace" of Hitlerism [183]—it was not only because of the "Faustian and demonic side . . . of national-socialist doctrines . . . born of the apotheosis of blood and of the vital instinct" but also because of certain criticisms of Marxism and democracy by Moeller van den Bruck that he found "singularly acute and pertinent." [184] The Nazi criticism "of the primacy of economics" seemed to him "perfectly justified," as did "the parallel criticism of the abuses of capitalism and those of Marxism" and "the important place given to willpower in history." [185] Moeller van den Bruck's pertinent criticism of Marxism, so much appreciated by Maulnier, was based not only on a rejection of materialism [186] but also simply on the fact that Marx "was Jewish, and so a stranger to Europe," and one can understand him "only by assuming a Jewish point of view," and yet "he concerned himself . . . with the affairs of the European peoples. It would seem that he wished to gain the right of hospitality among them by showing them their wretchedness and the means of getting rid of it. But he was not one with their history, their past was not his, and the legacy of former times to the present was not the one he carried in his blood. He had not lived with them throughout the ages; he did not feel like them, he did not think like them." [187]

All the principal themes of his introduction to *The Third Reich* were taken up again and developed by Maulnier in a more guarded manner in *Combat* and *Au-delà du nationalisme*. The latter work is Maulnier's main contribution to political thought. It provides a theoretical framework for the revolt against materialism, and a comprehensive critique of Marxism, capitalism, and liberalism. *Au-delà du nationalisme* ends with the following passage, which sums up the significance of the entire work:

Separated from each other, confronting each other, neither the national consciousness nor the revolutionary consciousness is the dialectical creative force of the future; they are only the sterile products of disintegration of a society coming to an end. The national consciousness becomes conservative; that is to say, it stupidly combines the effort to preserve the national entity with an attempt to preserve the strength of those forces in it that destroy it. The revolutionary consciousness becomes antihistorical and antinational; that is to say, it works for the destruction of the very thing that it wishes to liberate. The very words "national" and "revolutionary" have both been so much dishonored by demagoguery, mediocrity and verbalism that they are now received in France with an indifference bordering on disgust. The problem today is how to transcend these political myths based on the economic antagonisms of a divided society, how to liberate nationalism from its "bourgeois" character and the revolution from its "proletarian" character, and how to interest totally and organically in the revolution the nation that alone can carry it out and to interest in the nation the revolution that alone can save it.[188]

Announcing the publication of *Au-delà du nationalisme* in March 1938, *Combat* described its contents in the form of a slogan: "True nationalism against the power of money, true socialism against democracy."[189] Maulnier's point of departure was class struggle. "National-socialist or fascist neonationalism" had the great merit, in his eyes, of having "attenuated the economic rivalries of the classes, very correctly reminding the parties concerned that life should not be devoted to a search for material benefit."[190] The nationalist movements had, "up to a certain point, diverted the attention of individuals from the material interests that had divided them, and united them in the cult of honor, service to the fatherland and a disdain for riches."[191] But "this refusal of the new nationalism to consider the conditions of life created by capitalism as a real issue," this tendency "to substitute on this point, for a real solution of the economic antagonisms, a heroic will to ignore them," cannot replace the necessity of finding a solution to these antagonisms.[192] This is the only adverse criticism that Maulnier has to make of nazism and fascism. As we read: "The deep desire for transformation that underlies neonationalism seems to waver and hesitate between real reforms on the one hand, sometimes admirable, but partial and empirical, and, on the other hand, a general attitude hostile toward capitalism, the economic system of the old society, but mystical and sentimental,"[193] for "no moral, patriotic, mystical or heroic negation of the class struggle can finally weigh against the fact that the class struggle really exists, and the only way to really abolish the class struggle is to transform the economic conditions that have created the classes."[194]

Indeed, Maulnier claimed that fascism and nazism were subject to a particular danger: the two movements had a "greater historical value, a greater grasp of reality on the emotional level and on the level of instructive energy than on the level of lucid intelligence."[195] These movements therefore remained "inferior in their positive creations to their creative possibilities." Neonationalism "was still searching for its general ideas; it did not yet go any further than the general unity of the nation," the product of "a sentimental reconciliation of the classes." [196] They had to "raise their consciousness to the level of possibly justified historical pretensions" and find "constructive solutions" based on a "true understanding of the world." [197] In other words, fascism and nazism lacked a philosophy of history and a realistic operational ideology that took the existing economic forces and social structures into account. Maulnier attempted to fill this gap, and *Au-delà du nationalisme* aimed precisely to provide "neonationalism" with both a system of historical analysis and concrete political solutions.

Maulnier's analysis was based on the idea that social antagonisms exist and constitute a reality that it is as absurd as it is dangerous to ignore or to try to cover up by means of a "moral reconciliation" or "sentimental effusion." [198] The class struggle was a historical reality that expressed the struggle for power, in the Nietzschean sense of the term, of two segments of society. One could not, therefore, end the class struggle "in people's will and consciousness without first overcoming it in the social structure itself." [199] However, if the classical conservative interpretation of the class struggle was absurd, so was the Marxist interpretation. They were both forms of "political fetishism." [200]

In Maulnier's view, "individualistic idealism" and "collectivistic determinism" were related in their interpretation of history, in their simplification of infinitely complex realities. [201] Marxism, which defined the history of human societies as the history of economic relationships, supposed that the classes produced by economic relationships were, of all human groupings, the ones possessing the most reality, but to Maulnier it was obvious that "the association of men according to a community of economic interests was neither an original nor the most complete form of the human community." [202] Class antagonisms cannot therefore be the real "motive force of history"; they are merely the product of history. The division of people into classes has less reality than their division into organized historical communities. The real problem, therefore, is to understand how the nation came to be divided into classes, how society formed economic relationships, and how it endeavors to overcome the struggle of its classes. For "the division of society into antagonistic economic classes" is only "a particular case of the divisions that come into being in every society," so that if "it is no longer possible to question the role of material factors" in history, it is necessary "to give the economic facts of human history and the actual problems raised by the economy their true importance and their true limits." [203] Maulnier felt that it must be acknowledged that "economic power, far from being the origin of all forms of social power, is only one of the many forms in which social power has been exercised in the course of history," but the peculiarity of modern society was that antogonisms produced by purely material circumstances constituted a menace for the "historical and biological solidarity" that was the nation. [204] However, these peculiar conditions of the modern period in no way altered the fact that the "first principle of the explanation of historical phenomena is the unity of the constituted historical community and not the struggle of the classes." [205]

Indeed, the nation, wrote Maulnier, "is a community formed of the whole human substance, representing all forms of life." It would "therefore be absurd to imagine that antagonisms created by conditions of life and labor would be enough in themselves to destroy . . . the common social bond that, although threatened and hurt, nevertheless retains an almost invincible force, the common soil, blood, and language continuing to mingle their voices with the voices of the conflicting factions." [206] In this vision of history, human society "is not an economic society but a biological society," and "in their forms and developments, economic relationships obey the biological law of life in society." [207]

One can readily understand why Maulnier felt so much affinity with the Nazi philosophy. Like the German "neonationalists," he believed that the forces of division were always accompanied by "other visible and invisible forces that embodied the community and the perpetuity of the superior interests of the group." [208] The fact that the new economic forces, however powerful, had not been able to attain their perfect form, and that nowhere had capitalism been able to overcome "the powerful structure of national societies," proved that, far from being only the "superstructure and political form of the capitalist class domination, in the capitalist world the organized nation has represented the living heritage bequeathed by a previous society." [209]

This is an important point in the interpretation of history of the school of thought to which Maulnier belonged. Attacked by capitalism, the national entity had defended itself successfully, and in modern Europe it defended itself ever more successfully. For the revolutionary right, that was the historical significance of fascism and nazism. The national state, "the depository of values that are not always limited to economic riches alone," had always endeavored to place capitalism at its service, and in contemporary Italy and Germany it had opposed a national organization of the economy to capitalist economics.[210] But this did not apply only to liberalism; Marxism, too, was held in check by the nation, as the evolution of the Soviet Union definitively proved.[211]

However, Maulnier thought that the economic forces had always been held in check by those historical and biological entities that are the national structures not only because of the solidity of those structures but also because of the very nature of social conflict. In all societies, conflicts arise out of the desire of the various groups "to affirm their predominance in all forms of life and activity."[212] Here one hears the voice of Nietzsche, on whom Maulnier had written a book in 1935:[213] in Maulnier's view, the struggle for social and economic power was only an aspect of an eternal power struggle. For the "revolutionary proletariat," said Maulnier, "the conquest of the means of production" was only a means of "attaining social power." The proletariat simply wished in its turn "to attain a *master's* liberty, a *master's* morality, a *master's* pride, a *master's* pleasures."[214]

Though history constitutes an eternal "competition for social power" between antagonistic groups,[215] there is a form of power that is the possession of the national community and whose purpose is to safeguard its unity and its survival. That form of power is sovereignty and its organ is the state. The state represents society conceived in its totality and organized as such, and therefore cannot be regarded as an instrument of class domination: "It is the juridical and political form of the community conceived in its historic continuity."[216] Even when a victorious faction takes over the state, the state cannot be created by it but only "occupied" by it.[217] This occupation of the state incurs a weakening of society; as soon as "new and formidable instruments of social power" appeared with the industrial revolution, the old national state, the result of a "magnificent effort of the Western communities," was dethroned "by a newer and more powerful force than science"[218]—capitalism. The weapon of this new power was liberalism: liberalism set itself up "against the organic forces of the old national community"[219] and set out to conquer the state. The "new caste" that held the economic power succeeded first in relegating the state to a subsidiary position and then in overcoming it.[220] In the eighteenth century, the new economic system achieved an independent position in society and demanded the right to govern society: the subordination of the state by these masters of the economy signified their subordination of the nation.[221] Capitalist society was the first "in which the power of the dominant economic class was exercised not as a government of the entire community but for the benefit of the

dominant class alone." [222] Thus, said Maulnier, "the fate of national societies for the last two centuries has been to pass from a form of government that expressed the unity and totality of their historical existence to
a form of government that expressed only their dissociation." [223] This
conception of the state and the national community is the fascist view
par excellence. In this respect Maulnier's thought is very close to the
ideal model of a fascist ideology.

Maulnier maintained that the destruction of the old society in the
name of liberty and equality had, since the Revolution, benefited only
the new wielders of power. The people had been the victims of a gigantic
hoax: in destroying the old social organization in the name of liberty
and equality, they had only played into the hands of those in power.
Thus, "an essentially economic form of oppression and inequality was
substituted for the essentially noneconomic constraints and hierarchies
that had now disappeared." [224]

At this stage of his argument, Maulnier identified liberalism with democracy and thereafter used the terms interchangeably. He spoke first of
"governments of liberal and democratic form" [225] and then of a "liberal
democratic state" or, more simply, a "democratic state." [226] Finally, he
adopted the Marxist definition of a "democratic" state as a "bourgeois"
state that still pretends to be "the emanation of the national community
when it is only the emanation of the dominant caste and crushes proletarian revolts in the name of the nation." [227] Under the cover of "parliamentary democracy" had taken place "an annihilation of all power and
of all social discrimination other than the powers and discriminations
resulting from the rise of industry," for, while "affirming and glorifying
the nation, the liberal society destroyed the nation as an autonomous
manifestation of the life of the community," and "'bourgeois' nationalism basically expressed nothing other than the pride and euphoria of a
class instinctively certain that the nation had become its chattel." [228] As a
result, when "the lower classes . . . obtained a revolutionary doctrine
with which to oppose the 'bourgeoisie,'" it could "only take the form of
an internationalism." [229]

Not only did the new caste subjugate the state while benefiting "from
the national character of the former state"; it also "subjugated civilization." The power of the spirit, as a living force of the human community
that created civilization, disappeared from modern society. The new
masters "imposed upon society a style of life in which the values of civilization had no part." [230] The spirit, said Maulnier, acted "as the servant
of the rising power in society . . . , it did not create civilization." [231] The

transformation of modern society thus condemned "the activities of the spirit to a mortal dissociation."[232]

The conclusion was obvious: to save the nation and hence civilization, one has to destroy capitalism, liberalism, and democracy, which are only aspects of sordid bourgeois society. But civilization and the nation have another enemy, also a product of capitalism—Marxism. Capitalism created "the mercenary army of industrial workers" that in fact lived excluded from the community and did not participate in the creation of the values of civilization.[233] The proletarian condition is less a cause of material insecurity than a sign of "social decadence."[234] In a capitalist regime, the worker "is cut off from the highest values of civilization and separated from the historical substance of the nation."[235] As a result, all the power of modern industrial society "depends on servants who are strangers to it," a situation that gives rise to Marxism, an "ideological parasite of liberalism" that is also opposed to the national community.[236]

Marxism, thought Maulnier, claimed for the producer of the material substance of civilization the right to be sole master and to impose on all of society a way of life derived from the present life-style of the proletariat. Because it has no property owners, the proletariat creates a world without property; because it is no longer attached to national traditions, it creates an internationalist world; because it is wage earning, it forces on all walks of life a condition analogous to that of the wage earner. The essentially proletarian life-style envisaged by Marxism implies that communal settlements will be fostered and collectivization imposed.[237] Maulnier recognized that Marxism had the immense virtue not only of having "shed a most pitiless light on democratic liberalism" but also of having "drawn attention to the real facts of history and condemned the lamentable impotence of bourgeois thought."[238] Marxism had drawn the attention of the "theoretical citizen, the citizen who was 'free and had the same rights' as the other citizens," to "the man of the suburbs and factories, the real man."[239] Marxism, however, is at the same time destructive of the "organic reality of the community," since it regards the national state and the national community as mere "hypocritical masks" of the "new economic power."[240] Marxism invites the proletariat to "oppose not only the 'bourgeois' state but all forms of national life, land ownership and the products of labor, the secular heritage of civilization, for the sole reason that they had been appropriated by the bourgeoisie."[241] In fact, the Marxist revolution completes the destruction of "the social, human infrastructure of the economy"; it ac-

242 Neither Right nor Left

cepts and completes "the devastation . . . of the historical frameworks of human existence, and the substitution, as the basis of society, of economic organization for the biological and social community." [242] Thus, Marxism and liberalism both attack the biological community of the nation, even though they are enemies. The fight between capitalism and Marxist socialism is always grounded in a shared acceptance of "the subordination to economic activity of all the slowly elaborated forms of social life and all the values of civilization." [243]

Thus far the main obstacle to Marxism, said Maulnier, has been "the resistance of noneconomic elements to a doctrine that refused to take them into account." [244] Like Déat and De Man, Maulnier discovered "intermediate categories," the "nonproletarian classes of the nation"— those social groups on which the liberal system had imposed conditions of life that were hardly superior to those of the proletariat, but which nevertheless refused to be assimilated to the proletariat. Their standard of living was the same, but their way of life was essentially different, [245] and their relationship with the organized national community was not limited to a purely economic exchange of labor for money. [246] These nonproletarian social groups, by their participation in the national community and in civilization, rejected "the joint capitalist and proletarian destruction of the national community" and so found common ground with syndicalism. Syndicalism, said Maulnier, represented the workers' attempt to regain, through their own social organization, the power and the place in the community of which they had been deprived by the development of the liberal society. Syndicalism, for the workers, was therefore much more than a way of dealing with the owners of the means of production as equals; it was an "alternative community," the only place "where they could regard themselves as the subjects and not the passive objects of historical evolution." [247] And for that reason, said Maulnier, despite the snare and diversion of reformism and revolutionary Marxism, "the modern nationalist movements . . . have found themselves naturally drawn to incorporate syndicalism . . . in the new structure of society." [248] Finally, the growing awareness of these two forces "liberated by liberal fragmentation of the community" of their "real, their only struggle against a single form of subjugation" could play a tremendous role in "the community's unique effort of liberation." [249] Thus, Maulnier came to the now-classic conclusion reached earlier by the Cercle Proudhon: "Syndicalism liberated from its materialist and proletarian deviations and nationalism liberated from its sentimental and idealistic tendencies, which make it a weapon for the use of the present masters of the state, can both pass beyond their present stage of sterility in the positive creation of a new form of human community." [250]

However, an idea that, around 1912, was somewhat speculative took on, a quarter of a century later, when the antiliberal and anti-Marxist tide was irresistibly rising in Italy and Germany, a totally different significance. And, in the middle of the thirties, Maulnier knew exactly where he stood: "The only political path for nationalism," he wrote, "is the revolutionary path." "A revolution can only be national," for "the struggle to liberate the national community from its present masters concerns almost all the members of that community." [251] Accordingly, "it is henceforth impossible to justify nationalism within the democratic framework of the state. It is impossible to justify nationalism within the capitalist framework of society. Today there can be no nationalism—that is, a consciousness of the living continuity of the nation—that is not at the same time *revolutionary*." [252]

The instrument of that revolution can only be the state, "a new, non-democratic state," [253] an organ of "synthesis and transcendence" of "particular antagonisms," [254] for "the liberation of all the social groups that suffer the economic tyranny can only be effected by the construction of a new state and the destruction of democracy. The new state can only be constructed by men who directly feel the weight of the economic tyranny, and can only be conceived as the instrument of their liberation. The liberation of the nation will be accomplished in the same revolutionary movement as the liberation of the proletariat and the other subjugated classes." [255]

To be sure, there are "natural antagonisms in community life" that cannot be eliminated, and Maulnier insisted that a "valid political creation" had to be "pluralistic and equilibrated," [256] but the task of "giving back the national community its unity, its vitality, its grandeur is identical to the task of constructing a new society." [257] This could be accomplished only by revolutionary action, for, as Maulnier said in an important passage, only revolutionary action could realize "a 'totalitarian' unity . . . between the community and the individuals responsible for its destiny." [258]

It was therefore quite natural that Maulnier should finally turn toward fascism. Had not the fascist movements realized the main objectives and aspirations of the new nationalism—a revolutionary nationalism, a nationalism that rebelled against the "historical blindness" of "reactionaries" and "conservatives" [259] and revealed the biological foundations of the community? In an interesting passage that explains both the attraction of fascism and the depth of the fascist influence in France, Maulnier justified his position:

The "nationalist" and "fascist" movements of the last years, in an empirical, imperfect and sometimes dangerously verbal and impassioned way, undoubtedly represent, first of all, a tremendous attempt to impose a communal unity upon the striving classes so as to put an end to the period of class divisions, and to restore to the community control of the tools of economic power that have become the only-too-effective instruments of social power in the hands of a caste. Whatever the future of these movements may be, it is clear that they have brought the organic or biological infrastructure of human communities back into the forefront of the historical scene, which had been abandoned for a moment to class competition, and thus revealed the only synthesizing factor sufficiently powerful to resolve the formidable antagonism produced by the rise of industry between the instrument of economic power and the world of ancient human relationships.[260]

Despite everything, Maulnier never made a direct political commitment. In this he differed from Barrès, and still more from Drieu and Brasillach. When Maulnier's book appeared, Drieu reproached the author for "deliberately remaining on a philosophical plane" and "increasingly refusing to make any specific profession of faith, embodied in a group of men."[261] This refusal to take part in active politics makes Maulnier's work even more significant.

Maulnier belonged to that group of fascistically inclined intellectuals who played a major role in undermining democracy in prewar France without assuming any direct responsibility for membership in a fascist party or organization. Maulnier's role in disseminating a national-socialist, antiliberal, and anti-Marxist ideology in intellectual and political circles in no way differed from the influence exerted by *Je suis partout* or the intellectuals of the PPF. While Drieu became, along with Jouvenal, a militant member of the PPF, giving the party its intellectual respectability,[262] Maulnier seemed to confine himself to political thought. This lent credibility to ideas concerning which moderate, traditionalist, and Christian elements might have had serious doubts. Unlike Drieu and Jouvenel, Maulnier assumed the role of a theoretician who, without indulging in party politics, nevertheless regarded himself as engaged in revolutionary political activity. In transcending "abstract ideologies," he felt that he was "defining a truly realistic political action."[263] During the Occupation, Maulnier continued his educative task, taking care, however, never to participate in active collaboration.

Thus, in 1942, Maulnier was still saying that "liberal and capitalist democracy had weakened the French state and delivered up French politics to financial interests, to international intrigues and to popular passions";[264] he still attacked the "old left" and the "old right," and finally proclaimed that "one of the essential aims of the national revolution is to free the nation from the materialism that the former regime had made its law."[265] Thus, one always returns to the same point: the fight against materialism is the alpha and omega of this school of thought.

The admiration for fascism and nazism displayed by Maulnier's *Combat* in the years before the war was equal to that shown by Drieu and Brasillach. In December 1938, Maulnier declared that he had "no preconceived hostility against the authoritarian or 'fascist' regimes of Europe." On the contrary: "I admire many of the reforms they have undertaken, and even some of those that have aroused the most indignation. (I am by no means convinced, for example, that every individual has the right to procreate degenerate children at will.)"[266]

If Maulnier responded to even the most detestable aspects of nazism in so favorable a manner, it is hardly surprising that he had little to say against the system as a whole. Maulnier does condemn the contemptuous attitude of the "European nationalist societies" toward the refinements of culture, and deplores their dangerous tendency toward a "subjugation of the individual to the purposes of the community" and a "predominance of military values over civil values," but all these weaknesses, however dangerous, are small compared to the tremendous achievements of the "profound and irresistible phenomenon"[267] of fascism and nazism, such as the anticapitalistic restructuring of the economy, the integration of the proletariat into the national community, and the creation of a new form of state. As Maulnier says in a passage in which every word has weight:

There are some facts that cannot be questioned. The totalitarian regimes have restored to the state as a political instrument, a servant of the national destiny, an extraordinary efficacy. In various forms more or less real (although sometimes dangerously verbal and *misleading*) they have given the proletariat an organic participation in the life of the community. They have devised an economic technique that, despite its imperfections, has made nonsense of the theories of classical economics and defeated capitalism even where it proclaimed itself undefeatable—in the domain of productivity. They have invented a social morality that, in more than one way, is far superior to the "morality" of the democratic states. Their methods of subjugating the misleading public opinion are not more outrageous than those practiced in the democratic states, and it is difficult to see on the basis of what superior values *proper to themselves* the democratic states could look down upon them.[268]

Therefore, he concludes, "it would be absurd to judge the importance or the historical value of what is at present coming into being in Europe from anecdotal phenomena such as the looting of Jewish shops or the Roman step. We should not waste too much time devoting our attention to this mere froth upon the waves of history."[269]

Jean de Fabrègues held a similar view of nazism. In an article on "Hitlerian democracy," he expressed his appreciation at seeing "the primacy of the political (which is an ordering of the spirit) over the economic (which is simply the expression of matter)." He was delighted with the hierarchy of values set up by Hitler, and he welcomed his sound conception of democracy. The chancellor, he said, had "found the right formula" when "he called for a government that desired the happiness of the German people at the same time as being independent of it." Thus, Hitler governed "in the name of the General Will and its sovereignty" and rejected "a democracy in which the Jew can find a place, calling into being a democracy of men of pure blood."[270]

As a Catholic, Fabrègues could not gladly countenance Nazi racial determinism, or the fact that the racial revolution prided itself on not being interested in the "hereafter" and on not having to justify itself spiritually. At the same time, however, he demonstrated a strong sympathy for Hitler's political regime and social system: "If the ultimate justifications for his policies are democratic and materialistic" (something not at all to the liking of the future director of *La France catholique*), the foundation of these policies was nevertheless "the real sovereignty of the common good." Therefore, without wanting to turn it into a Hitlerian society, he accepted for France the principles of political and social organization of the Third Reich. Fabrègues wished to combine "a condemnation of democracy with a condemnation of Marxist economics" and to join "a proclamation of the necessity for a coherent national and social community" to one favoring "a strong state."[271]

While admitting that the Nazi way of thinking was entirely foreign to "the Christian horizon," Fabrègues acknowledged that "behind national socialism there was a fine movement of human rectification: that ought not to be denied." "Like the fascist reaction, like the despair of the surrealists," he said, nazism demonstrated "the insufficiency of a period and of a way of life that offered only peace and a search for material satisfactions." This protest against "bourgeois quietude" also, found expression, he thought, in "the heroism of the Komsomols and in the crack teams of Stakhanovites," but "national socialism has undoubtedly taken this further still. Demonstrating the necessity of subordinating the life of the individual to the life of the nation, it has revealed the grandeur of the nation, and has shown that this grandeur does not reside only in the better material conditions that people are offered by a national community."[272]

Finally, Fabrègues described the quality that he especially appreciated in nazism: "There is not an atom of liberalism in national-socialist thought. Hitler himself has always said that 'the individual who appears free' is in reality 'the defenseless plaything of the harsh struggle for existence.' A 'boundless liberty,' in preventing the formation of a community, seems to him to exclude all grandeur from human life."[273]

This is how a Christian whose respectability was never questioned in the postwar period viewed nazism in the thirties.

This "new right," this "party of movement" whose coming, in Maulnier's words, "the phalanxes of the Action Française had heralded at the beginning of the century," admired in fascism "the moral revolution it represented" and "its profound transformation of everyone's outlook."[274] In this respect there was no difference between Brasillach and Drieu on the one hand and Maulnier, Fabrègues, Massis, and René Benjamin on the other. We must see this clearly if we are to understand the fascist impregnation of France in the interwar period: its instruments were not only the men and movements stigmatized by collaboration with the Germans but also some of the most eminent French intellectuals of the second half of the twentieth century. And we should not allow this fact to becloud our understanding of the fascist phenomenon or to restrict us in our attempt to measure its importance in the history of France and of Europe.

Maulnier and Brasillach differed only in the place they gave ideology in fascism and nazism. Maulnier had written *Au-delà du nationalisme* to provide a conceptual framework for this revolt of the instincts, of blood, and of race. He felt that, without a solid philosophical foundation, "neonationalism" would be incomplete and at a disadvantage in relation to Marxism. Maulnier's fascism was more intellectual, and, without losing its corporeal dimension, it also complemented the work of Brasillach, the friend of his youth. For Brasillach, "Fascism was a spirit. For us, he said, it was not a political doctrine, nor was it an economic doctrine. . . . It was first of all an anticonformist, antibourgeois spirit, in which disrespect played its part. It was a spirit opposed to prejudices—to class prejudices, as to all others. It was the very spirit of friendship, which we would have liked to have raised to the level of the friendship of the whole nation."[275]

This dimension of fascism was of great importance. All the revolutionaries—the pure fascists, such as Drieu and Brasillach, who described themselves as such,[276] and fascists like Maulnier, Jouvenel, and Déat, who shrank from the appellation—were agreed on this point: fascism was a revolt against materialism, a revolt of the spirit, the will, the instincts; it was a revolt of youth. Fascism, Mussolini told the French in 1934, was a will to create a "new civilization,"[277] and Brasillach, after seeing "a new human type being born" in Nuremberg,[278] returned to France a convinced Nazi. Ultimately, the fascination exerted by fascism and nazism was primarily the fascination of the coming into being of the "fascist man."[279]

The right-wing press, like most of the dissident reviews, developed at that time a cult of fascism and nazism that affected large sections of public opinion and bore witness to the depth of the fascist penetration of France. Drieu was "converted" to fascism in 1934,[280] as was Andreu, who returned a fascist from a journey to Rome and Milan, won over by the enthusiasm for social revolution of the intellectuals of *Caminare* and *Cantiere* and of Giuseppe Bottai and the *Critica fascista*, and by the possibility of transcending both left and right in a vast dialectical synthesis.[281] Brasillach declared himself a fascist a little later, deeply fascinated by the uplifting experiences "that the totalitarian regimes offer their own youth."[282] During the same period, Massis published an interview with Mussolini in which the latter enumerated "the ideologies that weaken and debilitate the organism of the West," namely, "liberalism, democracy, socialism."[283] At the end of 1936, when the radical right was preparing to resist the Popular Front and a "national union" coalition that would be under the tutelage of the left, the doctrinal journal of the Action Française devoted a series of six articles to "Mussolini and His People" by René Benjamin.[284] This was also the period of the *Cadets de l'Alcazar* by Massis and Brasillach, praising the Spanish Nationalist uprising.[285] Earlier, Brasillach had attended one of the famous Nuremberg rallies, and gave an account of it in his "Hundred Hours with Hitler."[286] A year later Jouvenel's interview with Hitler appeared.[287]

Most dissident and revolutionary circles paid constant attention to fascism and nazism. In December 1934, the néo deputy Montagnon accused his colleagues in the Chamber of misjudging "present-day Germany. You have not understood what is curious and profound in the

Hitlerian movement."[288] Two months later, attacked by his party's left wing, he explained what he had meant in an address to the French socialist party: "Yes, in the Hitlerian movement there *is* something curious and profound. In this movement there is an upsurge of socialism and an upsurge of brutality. Is it not curious to see men seek out their destiny in this way? Is it not profound to see forty million men hurl themselves into the same movement?"[289]

Socialism and brutality were the two key elements of the fascist and Nazi equation as seen by its French sympathizers. Drieu, author of *Socialisme fasciste*, confirmed the opinion of Déat's colleague. After first declaring himself a fascist—"For my part, I felt a need to say I was a fascist"[290]—he then made a second declaration of faith: "I know and declare myself to be a socialist."[291] Finally, Drieu explained the difference between a fascist and a mere reactionary, making a comparison with the Maurrassians: "A monarchist is never a true fascist. . . . A monarchist is never a modern: he does not have the brutality, the barbaric simplicity of a modern."[292]

The cult of youth was another basic element of the fascist ideology. Youth meant physical vigor and intellectual nonconformism, physical virility and moral readiness—a will for renewal of body and spirit. "The deepest definition of fascism," wrote Drieu, "is this: it is the political movement that goes the most directly, the most radically toward a great revolution of morals, toward a restoration of the body—toward health, dignity, plenitude, heroism."[293]

That, said Drieu, is the great innovation of the twentieth century, and therein lay the originality of fascism: fascism is a revolution "that gives an important place to the spontaneous forces of life, of health, of the blood," that saves people by permitting them to leave the cities and give themselves up to sport and the open air.[294] For the right-wing revolutionaries, fascism was both an ethic and a system of aesthetics, "a universal revolution,"[295] whose devotees, said Brasillach in an important passage, "wanted a pure nation, a pure race. They liked to be together in great gatherings of people where the rhythmic movements of armies and throngs seemed like a single heartbeat. They did not believe in the promises of liberalism, in the equality of mankind, in the will of the people. . . . They did not believe in the justice that is expressed in words, but inclined toward the justice that rules by force, and they knew that this force could give birth to joy."[296]

No one has better expressed the deep significance of this mystical and poetic aspect of fascism, or better described the attractions of national unity, or better conveyed the fascination of nazism. Brasillach retained an impression of Hitler's Germany as "the suprising mythology of a new religion," and "a call to youth for faith, sacrifice and honor."[297] The fantastic spectacle of the nocturnal ceremonies, like the electoral campaign of 1932—"a river of bells, drums and violins"[298]—had shown Brasillach that the success of nazism derived "from its power of suggesting images to the masses, and its being, first of all, for better or worse, a poetry,"[299] for, as he said, quoting Sorel,[300] "only revolutionaries have understood the meaning of myths and ceremonies."[301] He insisted on the religious element in fascism and nazism;[302] this was deeply felt by all the "dissidents," and its social function was perfectly understood.

Two articles glorifying fascist youth in *La Lutte des jeunes* showed the place given to religion in its most pagan form in the fascist system of education. According to the first of these articles, the regime was undoubtedly based "on a system of moral values. After half a century of materialism, it rejected materialism"; it pursued "a struggle against commercial values in the name of ideal values" and endowed education with the quality of a crusade.[303] The second article compared fascist youth organizations to monastic orders.[304] Fascism thus answered a need: it was what youth was looking for, wrote De Man (a man very different from Brasillach); it was "less a new theory of economics or a new interpretation of history than a new conception of life, a new religion."[305] A French account of the German work camps in *1933* had described the construction of a "magnificent road" by workers "stripped to the waist, with muscled torsos." "Those handsome boys with blonde hair and bronzed skin" gave "the impression of performing a priestly rite."[306]

Thus a complete break was seen to have occurred between the old world and the world of the revolutionaries. Materialism—Marxist or liberal—was opposed by a sense of the spiritual (the fascists "entered religion, so to speak," wrote Jouvenel);[307] the united and disciplined national collectivity replaced fragmented bourgeois society; and the young, athletic fascist replaced the flabby-muscled bourgeois. Fascism represented a physical and spiritual renaissance, a moral revolution that gave a new meaning to the dignity of the individual, who, after centuries of decadence, was recreated in body and soul.

A New Civilization

From the end of the nineteenth century, the nonconformists, and particularly the nationalists, had always painted the darkest picture of

France. Meditations on national decadence had accompanied the analyses of the French political and social malaise of the 1880s. Barrès, Bourget, and Lemaître, following Renan, pondered the intellectual and moral rottenness of the period. Many intellectuals, in an atmosphere of malaise that sapped their vitality, felt that they were living in the twilight of a civilization. The writings of the young Barrès and the works of other nationalistic intellectuals give the impression that there were no guiding principles or solid values or truths to fall back on. This feeling of corruption and decadence found its most striking expression in a terrible remark made by Renan to Déroulède: "France is dying, young man. Do not disturb it in its death throes."[308]

The generation of 1890 also made its own case against positivism, science, technical progress, and industrial development: modern civilization was associated with corruption, vice, decadence. The reaction against the sense of helplessness, of sinking into the mire, of political and moral decadence, the rejection of materialism and the way of life created by materialism, was a key element in the development of the nationalist movement. To pessimism and doubt were opposed the certitudes of history, of the national collectivity, of the race; to the artifice so prevalent in the cultural life of the period was opposed a cult of energy and vitality; to an aging civilization, a cult of youth; to disintegration and individualism, a sense of discipline and the powers of the instinct.

The reaction of the generation of the thirties was similar, but its criticism of French society was much more extreme than that of the generation of 1890. If Renan, Taine, Bourget, Barrès, Sorel, and Lemaître had "philosophized" about the fate of civilizations, or condemned a particular way of life, culture, or regime, the next generation manifested a real hatred of all that existed, including, over and beyond particular political and social structures, the very nation itself. The only late-nineteenth-century writer to achieve the vindictiveness of Maulnier or Drieu was Drumont. "Will we be able to emerge from the French state of abjection?" asked Maulnier in November 1936 in an article on "the French decadence." The answer was not at all self-evident, for Maulnier was worried about France itself and not only the bourgeois society or the democratic regime. The sad reality, he felt, was that the France of Saint Louis, the Crusades, and Versailles had turned into "a nation of swindlers, of eunuchs and street urchins." In this connection, thought Maulnier, it was worth pointing out "certain irrefutable facts." A France "sunk in its baseness and exulting in it with a sort of lewd bravado, . . . incapable any longer of playing any role in the world, [and regarding] as enemies of civilization all those who do not take her own decadence as a model—a France, hate-filled and trembling, proclaiming Democracy and Human Rights throughout the world, but sweating with fear at the slightest action of its neighbors, disturbing the peace of the mighty with vain abuse, with a kind of provocative cowardice—that France is the France of today." [309]

These ideas occurred repeatedly in the writings of all the revolutionaries. It was in this image of "a certain France of innkeepers and procurers," [310] of an "atmosphere of facility," [311] which prevailed "in the French swamp," [312] that the nonconformists found the justification for their revolt. Possibly without knowing it, Doriot, too, returned to Barrès's ideas: he deplored the "decadence" of a "socially . . . dislocated country"; [313] Barrès had described France as "disunited and brainless." [314]

However, it was argued, the gravity of this sickness of the "triumph of materialism" [315] should not make us lose sight of the fact that the direct responsibility for this state of affairs lies with democracy, liberalism, and the bourgeoisie. "The regime has corrupted the country to the core," we read in an editorial in *Combat*. "Democracy has degraded us." [316] And elsewhere we read that "capitalist democracy" [317] ruins the country: democracy and capitalism are merely "the economic and political aspects of the same evil," [318] and the damage caused by liberalism, that ideology imported from abroad, is, "so to speak, immeasurable." [319] Democratic institutions, we are told, betrayed the most important values of civilization, [320] parliamentarianism degraded the country and accentuated its decadence, [321] and the bourgeois spirit that had governed the nation had produced "a civilization of pretense, of lamination, of stucco and plaster." [322] One must therefore get rid of bourgeois culture, but, at the same time, it would be absurd to rebuild France on the foundation of the "slovenly vulgarity" of the people. One must at all costs avoid subjecting our civilization to proletarian values. [323] One must create another civilization, and therefore one must make a revolution.

This revolution for the salvation of the nation and of civilization would have to be a total revolution—a cultural revolution, [324] an anti-bourgeois revolution, [325] "a revolution of the community," [326] a "spiritual revolution" [327] that "is commensurate with the drama of our period and that in our souls," [328] and an anti-Marxist revolution "that will outstrip Marxism in the destruction of the regime." [329] It would be brought about by "all the 'right-wingers' who have understood the shame of capitalism" and "all the 'left-wingers' who have understood the shame of democracy." [330] Because the present social and political systems "had brutalized and degraded the people,"[331] they had to be replaced with new structures. "What one must do," wrote Maulnier, "is create an authority, a hierarchy, an order—a harmonious, coherent and noble society."[332] Such a society could be achieved only through a "national" revolution, that is, a revolution at once antiliberal and anti-Marxist. The idea of a national revolution was taken up repeatedly by all the fascistically inclined French writers of the period,[333] and was therefore widespread several years before it became the aim and slogan of all those who sought to recreate France under the aegis of Nazi Germany.

Fascism thus appeared to be the only real and credible revolutionary movement. In the period of the Popular Front, when communism— "one of the great hopes of humanity," as the fascists of *Combat* put it[334]—had appeared to take "the path of democratic corruption" and "join the language of Jaurès to the language of Déroulède," the inevitable conclusion was reached that henceforth it was others who (as Sorel had taught) had the duty not only of saving "socialism . . . from democracy" but also of fostering among the enemies of the existing order "the vocation of civil war."[335] A form of socialism divested of democracy, reuniting, as Jouvenel said, all "anticapitalist elements"[336]— such, exactly, was the fascist synthesis. It is not surprising that it was precisely these theoreticians of fascism who were beginning to weigh, with Jouvenel, "the necessary acts of violence."[337] Drieu even declared that "without this violence we shall not get out of the present vicious circle,"[338] and Maulnier could already hear the "heavy footsteps" of revolutionary justice. The crimes of the present regime, Maulnier said, would really be repaid only on the day when "a whole flock of cattle with Légions d'honneur in their buttonholes, administrators, cops and judges, will be kicked toward the legitimately inhuman justice or revenge of those who await their day."[339]

The fascists were the first to advocate a complete rupture—not simply to hate the personalities, institutions, and authorities of the regime but to "totally repudiate them."[340] They were also the first to preach a contempt for their country for the purpose of saving it. Maulnier claimed that this "kind of healthy and creative . . . scorn" was really a form of patriotism, for "to accept, love, venerate, serve France as it is, is to make oneself the active accomplice of its abasement."[341] In France of the thirties, "the national will and the revolutionary will come together . . . in a liberating metamorphosis."[342] Only an upsurge of energy, only a "historic act of creation" in which the French community, "in a new synthesis, will triumph over the antagonisms that tear it apart,"[343] could save it from "the

invasion of justice that lies in wait for it." [344] The revolt against both liberal and socialist democracy is thus justified in the name of the salvation
of the nation and of civilization, and the collapse of the regime can
therefore never mean a defeat either for the nation or for civilization.
The ideological collaboration with Germany and lack of ideological resistance to nazism are thus easily explained: the fascists, the antiliberal
nonconformists, and the revolutionary anticapitalists could only watch
the rise of German national socialism with sympathy. During the war,
De Man still described nazism as a reaction against the "dissolution
of a civilization" and "the progressive disintegration of the morality
of youth." [345]

As elsewhere in Europe, fascism was seen in France as a phenomenon
of the younger generation—as a revolt of youth for the sake of youth, in
the name of a system of values that was the antithesis of that of the established order. In fact, from the period of Boulangism onward the revolutionary right had constantly risen up against the bourgeois order in
the name of the special values of the younger generation. A comparison
with Barrès, the representative par excellence of the generation of 1890,
is particularly instructive because it reveals an unfaltering ideological
continuity.

From the moment he became politically active, Barrès brought General Boulanger the support of the younger generation. [346] He regarded
Boulangism as first and foremost a revolt of the younger generation, a
message brought to the nation by "living France, the young part"—the
one that is "the whole of the future." Boulangism, he claimed, expressed
the rising generation's protest against "the parliamentary tumult"; [347] it
was also a call for "a strong man who will open the windows through
which the garrulous will be precipitated and which will let the air in." [348]
Barrès hoped that Boulanger's appearance on the scene would have the
effect of breaking apart the traditional political structures and wiping
out established ideas and old divisions. Barrès insisted on Boulanger's
affinities with the younger generation: united in their disgust at the opportunistic ways of the Republic, enlightened youth and its natural
leader would together launch the decisive attack against the established
order.

In his novel *Les Déracinés*, Barrès wonderfully described the state of
mind of this new generation that longed to construct a world in its own
image. The book illustrates a thesis, but it is also *the* novel of action; it is
the story of a failure, but also the account of a battle against the established order. [349] It is by no means surprising that, in his confrontation

with Déat's group, Léon Blum, who knew and liked the work of Barrès (especially *Le Culte du moi*),[350] scoffed at his critics who demanded action from him, calling them "stuck-up teachers of energy."[351] However, the generation of 1930 had neither the literary qualities nor the substance nor the depth of that of 1890, and, above all, it lacked a leader. And yet, imprisoned as it was within a world it despised, that generation, like that of the end of the nineteenth century, represented a tremendous explosive force. Its thirst for action prompted it to engage in an out-and-out struggle against all forms and aspects of the established order.

It was their "need for action" that led the dissidents of French socialism to rebel against the party.[352] Their rejection of the path chosen by Blum was, in their eyes, "an attempt to mold destiny."[353] They wanted to achieve the "dynamism" that was the secret of fascism's success,[354] to respond to the desires of "the masses," who had voted, as Déat wrote after the left had come to power in 1932, "in order that one should act, in order that one should dare, in order that one should risk, in order that one should build."[355] "Our ideal is a short-term one and our certainties [are] provisional," declared the néos at the time of the split.[356] Adopting De Man's formula, they described themselves as "voluntarists."[357] They were sure where they stood: "Planism and voluntarism are very close to each other."[358] Undoubtedly planism, as a new kind of socialism, was a form of activism, and the néos were not wrong to insist on what separated them from socialism and liberalism.

Planism and néo voluntarism were perfectly in keeping with the activist themes that recurred constantly in the writings of the rebels. These themes are found in Jouvenel,[359] and also in Drieu La Rochelle, who declared himself always in favor of "those who get down to it."[360] He admired Lenin and praised "the philosophy of mobility and action" advocated by Pareto and Sorel.[361] None of these writers had any use for Blum, that "intellectual who doesn't betray":[362] they had a "taste for service" and wanted "to serve under a clearly defined and strong order."[363] In Bonnafous's writings, this basic element of fascist ethics is naturally enough associated with his memories of the Great War and the virtues of physical conflict—"the joy of living dangerously, the taste for risks, the assurance of physical courage."[364]

It is not surprising that Jouvenel, who coined the term *directed economy*, was among those who most enthusiastically espoused the principles of the new morality. He claimed that the thirties had seen a blossoming of this morality, whose legitimacy he had implicitly asserted.

In Jouvenel's opinion, it represented a revival of the principle of force that had been praised by Proudhon and that, from the tenth century onward, had enabled Europe to set out and conquer the world. "Nothing but the high tension of their wills" had predisposed the rough and ignorant barons of western Europe to this destiny.[365] From the time when Europe first began to bristle with castles at the end of the tenth century until Henry II of France was killed in a tournament in 1552, Europe produced a type of man that assured its supremacy: the head of a family and of a clan, a warrior and a landowner, who enjoyed a great deal of authority over his own people and a great deal of independence toward the state. As long as a society produces this type of man, thought Jouvenel, as long as it admires it, it is a society in progress, but as soon as this type of man ceases to be admired and disappears, decadence sets in. According to Jouvenel, the salient historical fact of the sixteenth century was the decline of this type, a decline that increased in the seventeenth century. In the eighteenth century they smiled at *Le Cid*, at the end of the nineteenth Cyrano became a comic character, and in the twentieth Kipling is for children.[366]

This evolution, thought Jouvenel, is like that which took place in the later Roman Empire. Taking up a theme that had been fully elaborated by Bourget, Jouvenel asserted that in that era also a certain security and ease, favoring the development of a certain intellectual agility, had destroyed the ancient criteria whereby a man was judged by his personal prowess.[367] The human quality declined, and the Romans of the decadence regarded man as unchangeable.[368] The same was true in the modern world, which was dominated by a "childish optimism" perfectly expressed by the view of human nature put forward by Jaurès. Jaurès, said Jouvenel, founded his "individualistic society" on "the postulate of the natural goodness of man." For him, the human individual was "the measure of all things." One could understand why European youth had been drawn by the antithesis of this vision of the world, by "austere Nietzschean pessimism." The Nietzschean concept of man, wrote Jouvenel, "restored the energies that had been waning." According to Nietzsche, "man is something that has to be overcome."[369] This "heroic remedy" had been used by "all the statesmen who had been restorers of society: the Augustuses and the Napoleons had attempted to revive the manly virtues—the sense of initiative, responsibility and command." Jouvenel concluded, "The similarity of what Mussolini and Hitler are attempting today is striking."[370]

Thus, Jouvenel believed that under the tutelage of "our modern restorers"—Hitler and Mussolini—"a kind of Judgment of God" was taking place in Europe, and for youth "the thirties meant something special: the liquidation, throughout the whole of Europe, of those who hate effort by those who like it."[371] They also meant the victory of force, about which Jouvenel said, "One cannot help admiring it, acknowledging its rights, hailing its creative and ordering virtue."[372] He claimed that it was this "taste for effort," for creating mankind anew—this renaissance of the manly virtues—that, having contributed "to the formation of fascist parties," was responsible for the process whereby "regimes of faith replace regimes of opinion," for, in the end, it is always "faith that creates force."[373] Once again, it was no accident that, in the summer of 1940, Jouvenel hailed the German victory as a triumph of the spirit.[374]

Fascism thus appeared as a rejection of comfort, as a "need for a certain intensity of life." The world, wrote a collaborator of Jouvenel's, "is disgusted with ease, just as it is disgusted with economics."[375] Fascism, said Mussolini to Henri Massis, "is a horror of a comfortable life."[376] According to Drieu, fascism meant replacing "the incentive of lucre by the incentive of duty"; it required "as the foundation of moral force . . . a disposition to sacrifice, a will to fight" that cannot be denied.[377]

Indeed, Jouvenel viewed this revolution of the twentieth century that he longed for as "the coming of an aesthetic power." He proclaimed the "primacy of the ethical" and declared, just before the war, that the major problem of our time "is the relationship between the temporal and the spiritual."[378] Similarly, Déat advocated "a spiritual revolution,"[379] and Doriot came to the conclusion that the causes of the "lamentable" situation in France "were primarily moral."[380] Even the Solidarité Française—a movement that was launched by the perfume manufacturer Coty in 1933 and that, from its first apparition on 6 February, brought together a few honest rowdies and many doubtful elements as well as unemployed Arabs paid for the evening[381]—preached a return to "spiritual values."[382]

Already at the end of the twenties, the intellectual of the Solidarité Française, Jean-Pierre Maxence,[383] had published a series of Cahiers whose main theme was that "the only definite misery was that of the soul."[384] In 1934, in collaboration with Robert Francis and Thierry Maulnier, Maxence, deploring the "industrialization of intellectual values,"[385] produced a book called Demain la France, dedicated to the "dead of 6 February, first witnesses of the coming revolution, fallen beneath the bullets of an antinational, antisocial and inhuman regime."[386]

This book, which heralded Maulnier's *Au-delà du nationalisme*, attacked "the materialistic society," [387] and concluded that "democratic ideals lead to Marxist materialism." [388] In other words, all materialisms were basically the same, and to overcome them one needed nothing less than a total revolution.

It was precisely this revolution that fascism and nazism were carrying out. The fascists and Nazis, wrote Drieu, "are moving toward a spiritual, aesthetic concept of society." [389] In the context of the long struggle against materialism—against capitalism, Marxism, and liberalism—such a vision of society was a revolutionary vision, and for that reason Jouvenel mourned "these young German comrades whose naive ardor aroused such friendly feelings in me." [390] Their death, he felt, had signified the end of all revolutionary hopes: "The man who they had expected would call them to the social revolution has turned against them the automatic pistols of the police." [391] Jouvenel was unequivocal: "The brown uniforms in the streets of Berlin were the external signs of a proletarian dictatorship." [392] The revolutionaries whose death the brilliant young French journalist, recently resigned from the Radical party, [393] was bewailing were none other than the storm troopers liquidated by Hitler on 30 June 1934 in the famous feud within the Nazi movement.

The dissidents' admiration for fascism and nazism was actually only an aspect of their "disgust" for the existing regime. The word *disgust* was used continually by the rebels of the thirties, [394] as it had been by the Boulangists, who adopted it as a slogan. Generally, this disenchantment with the existing order was expressed, again as at the end of the nineteenth century, by a rejection of "ease" and by a demand for a "clean sweep": reading Jouvenel, Abel Bonnard, Montagnon, or Déat, one has the impression that one is reading the Boulangist leaders. [395] All these rebels lived in a world that they despised, and that they wanted to reform physically, morally, and intellectually. "Down with bourgeois culture!" cried Maulnier, [396] while Drieu, who regarded fascism as a "renewal of human life," [397] called for passion "in order to attain grandeur." [398] René Vincent, like Barrès who, half a century earlier, had rejected "reason, that little thing on our surface," was replacing reason with the living forces of instinct and the unconscious. [399] Finally, if these men were conscious of the necessity for a "national mystique" [400] for France, if they wished to get the people to take part in magnificent manifestations in which "the spectacle is for everybody, and delirium, fervor, and dignity are also for everybody," if they realized that "France must find some faith in honor, in grandeur, in creation and in adventure,"[401] they knew also that it would be necessary to "reduce the French stomach" and give the French back "physical joy."[402]

The sense of an urgent need for the physical renewal of the nation was very strong at that time. An idolatry of sport and physical activity, a love of life in the open air, together with the cultivation of the team spirit and life in groups, created an almost physical barrier between bourgeois, liberal society—sedentary, conformist, and individualistic—and the virile, powerful new world of the fascists, based on the collective values par excellence of the nation and race. "A nation is *one*, just as a sports team is *one*," wrote Brasillach.[403] The fascists were fond of this image, which permitted them to draw a contrast between two types of men, two types of society, two types of civilization. "One has only to look at them," wrote Drieu. "Go to a socialist congress and see all those beards, all those paunches, all that tobacco, all that anxious waiting for the hour of the apéritif."[404] This image of corpulent politicians, of great, sedentary bourgeois who "live physically like the monks they have so much reviled," continued Drieu, symbolizes "an intellectualistic and rationalistic conception of life that is quite out-of-date."[405] This "old gaga world of the left-wing intellectuals," he concluded, proves only one thing: "the ideas of the socialist party are even older than its leaders."[406]

In contrast to this senile world, one had the "party of the living body," the bearer of a "religion of salvation through sport."[407] The fascist revolution restored to validity "all kinds of values that men had forgotten: dignity, pride in the body"; it encouraged "collective celebrations" and "splendid and intoxicating physical ceremonies."[408] To the fat, "pot-bellied intellectual" Drieu opposed the "good athlete" represented by Doriot.[409] Through him, "the France of camping" would "overcome the France of apéritifs and congresses."[410] All the rebels were agreed on this, and all had great admiration for Italy and Germany, where "whole generations of athletes with magnificent muscles" were coming into being. "Life there," said Maulnier, could "be considered happy and straightforward."[411] Was not fascism the "party of good humor?"[412] Like Drieu, Brasillach reproached the opponents of fascism for their "total ignorance of fascist joy."[413] "The young fascist," he said, "exulting in his race and in his nation, proud of his vigorous body, his clear mind, scorning the cumbersome goods of this world . . . , is first of all a joyful being."[414] He is a person who, like Hitler's Germany or the staff of *Je suis partout*, lives a group life in joy and partnership.[415] The unity and comradeship that he admired in the Nazis Brasillach also found when he spent the day working on *Je suis partout*: there was "a feeling for better or worse of forming a band, and what might be called, to shock the bourgeois, the gang spirit." [416] Jouvenel also thought of the victory of fascism as "that of the team," and he expressed the thinking of his generation of dissidents perfectly when he brought the physical and moral aspects of fascism together in the statement "It is through sport that the concept of duty will return to Western society." [417] The regeneration of the body, moral rebirth, and political regeneration constituted a totality that could be realized only by the part of society that had not yet been affected by bourgeois decadence.

Never in any earlier period was such an effort invested in youth as in the thirties. The dissidents were young men, and they were well aware that their revolt was a generational phenomenon. With the possible exception of Drieu, [418] all of them had broken away from other movements, and their entry into political life represented the radicalization of younger men unhappy with the static quality of those movements. Valois broke with the Action Française; Maulnier and Brasillach came out of the Maurrassian movement, but went further; Jouvenel and Bergery, and Déat and his colleagues, were defectors from the radical and socialist movements, respectively. They all discovered in youth a potential that they felt to be revolutionary, and they all produced a body of writings that proclaimed their disgust with the world as it was. And all of them declared themselves ready for action.

"Down with the old and long live the revolution!" exclaimed Jouvenel's weekly [419] in an attempt to mobilize the young men whom Maulnier considered resistant to the "comforts of decadence," to inertia, and able to tackle the "hard and virile tasks" that events offered. [420] For this "available youth," [421] avid for "movement" and "a life of rapidity" and "action," [422] the rebels proposed innumerable "plans for youth." They suggested convening a "States General," [423] and proposed that the French emulate José Antonio's Falange, the Romanian Iron Guard, and Degrelle's Rex. [424]

Undoubtedly, the thirties witnessed a revolt against the cultural conformity that dominated not only life in school and in the family but also social and political life. More and more frequently, young people felt that the accepted norms, the traditional means by which one "got ahead," were conventional, artificial, and contrary to nature. De Man explained what worried that generation: it regarded the overestimation of the importance of money "as a contradiction of the natural order of values, sexual taboos as a violation of the natural process of individual and social formation, the utilitarian platitude of an education directed exclusively toward profit as an oppression of the heroic instincts of struggle, adventure and sacrifice, and the constraints of scholastic life and urban civilization as a hindrance to the natural instinct for travel and sport." [425]

Drieu said that "fascism is the coalescing of European man around the idea of manly virtue," [426] and sports and parades, exercise and dance were essential means to that end. Young people attempted, by means of voluntary acts of asceticism, to rid themselves of the standards imposed by culture. Brasillach hitchhiked and thought that all those "grave people" who objected to this new way of seeing the world "obviously lacked the fascist spirit" [427]—that spirit most clearly expressed, perhaps, in the spontaneously desired communal culture to which that section of youth in revolt against the bourgeois order aspired. This, surely, was the "fascist atmosphere" referred to by Drieu, [428] and it was also Brasillach's "immense red fascism," "with songs, parades, the conquest of power, José Antonio, a virile youth, the nation." [429]

Everywhere in Europe one found the same thing: fascism was an affair not of veterans but of a younger generation that rose up against the established order—against society generally, but also against the family, against school, against sexual restrictions, against a way of life whose constraints that generation rejected. It was no accident that the fascist leaders, like their followers, belonged to a much younger age group than most political leaders. This fact earned them a good deal of sympathy.

The more tensions in Europe rose, the more did the admiration for fascism and nazism increase. The dissidents despised the existing regime, and had confidence neither in their country nor in its institutions; and, at the same time, they professed a profound admiration for the neighboring dictatorships. The sense of horror aroused by the memory of the Great War, and the complexity of the international situation, do not explain everything: a sympathy for a regime diametrically opposed to the bourgeois democracy the dissidents so reviled played a major part. And, moreover, had not the dissidents, since the day Hitler came to power, constantly proclaimed the desire for peace expressed by the Nazi youth and its führer? [430] But the vindication of nazism did not stop there. In February 1939, Félicien Challaye, member of the National Council of the Frontist party, returning from a study tour in Germany sponsored by the Labor Front, reported on his mission. He praised the "national-socialist achievements in teaching," in political education, in town planning. He particularly liked "the party's college for the formation of the national-socialist elite."[431] The year before, Challaye had already declared his refusal to go to war "for the sake of Czechoslovakia."[432]

This refusal to go to war was above all a rejection of ideological war, of war for the sake of democracy. Maulnier spoke of "the annoying taste that the democracies sometimes have for wars of principle";[433] one of his collaborators described Czechoslovakia as "an ideological republic,"[434] while Challaye condemned that "center of intrigues where too many German refugees spread false reports that poison the moral atmosphere of Europe."[435] Jouvenel, too, made his contribution to this chorus of opinion. He said that when he met Hitler he found him "very careful to act according to reason" but that he "suddenly lost all moderation on the question of *Judeo-Marxist bolshevism*."[436] The reader can draw his own conclusion, as did several of the quasi-fascist writers: is it worth risking a war—a "democratic war,"[437] "an ideological war"[438]— just for that? Is it right to give way to "an 'antifascist' war fever,"[439] especially as an external war can only mean the victory of the trusts? All of the dissidents insist that "the defense of the nation is not the defense of the trusts."[440] Everyone who wants "the necessary revolution"[441] within the country must totally reject the outcome proposed by the advocates of ideological war—"the union of the people of France with its masters; the union of the robbed and the robbers."[442] Once again, all the rebels use the same argument: an external war only obscures the real problems, which are internal. Only now the challenge comes from a different quarter than it did twenty years ago.

There was another category of instigators of ideological war: the Jews who were coagitators with the Marxists. A pacifistic attitude combined with a sympathy and understanding of Italian fascism and German nazism created a new channel for anti-Semitism. Déat, for instance, writing his memoirs after the war in the Italian convent where he was in hiding, still maintained that it was Blum's desire to "be done with Hitler, the Jew killer," that prompted him to return to power in 1938.[443] Similarly, in *Après-coup*, De Man declared that he had long been convinced of the necessity of eliminating "from our political organism the foreign body constituted by all the residues or embryos of the Ghetto."[444] De Man believed that there was a real "historical conflict between German thought and Jewish thought."[445] Déat and De Man never changed their opinion, and on the eve of the outbreak of the Second World War they found themselves in agreement not only with Maulnier and the writers of *Combat*[446] but also with Bergery, Claude Mauriac, and the writers of

La Flèche. The attitude of these former militants of the League for the Rights of Man is the clearest manifestation of the extent of the changes that had taken place in France.

Attempting to explain anti-Semitism, Bergery, editor of *La Flèche*, reflected on its causes: "I cannot better explain this reaction of the public than by quoting the remark made to me by one of my friends who is beyond suspicion of anti-Semitism but who, returning from some offices where he had been sent from Rosenthal to Rosenfels and from Rosenfels to Blumenthal, told me, 'A Jewish Frenchman is a Frenchman like any other, but if one goes to see ten Frenchmen and they turn out to be ten Jews, they are no longer Frenchmen like any others.'" [447]

This theme recurred constantly, in various forms, from the period of the first Blum government. The worse the European crisis became, the more was attention drawn to the presence of Jews in public life. Reading Claude Mauriac [448] or Bergery makes one better able to understand the view of the Statut des Juifs expressed in 1941 by the brilliant jurist Duverger, formerly a PPF student. He felt that it was quite natural that the new authoritarian and national regime in France should forbid public office to naturalized Frenchmen and Jews. [449]

Bergery, however, claimed that the deepest and most serious cause of anti-Semitism lay in the attitude of the Jews during the Munich crisis. To be sure, said this man of the left, the Jews did not form separate communities in France as they did in eastern Europe, but "neither were they mixed with the other nationals," and "many also form a bloc that refuses to intermingle through mixed marriage." Bergery recalled that "the first racists were the Jews, an elected race and people. Their persecutions have only confirmed them in this error." It was thus only natural that, put to the test, they chose a policy that would lead to war, "and a war, as public opinion sensed, less to defend France's direct interests than to defeat the Hitler regime in Germany—which means the death of millions of French and Europeans to avenge a few dead Jews and a few hundred thousand unfortunate Jews." [450] A few months later, Bergery, taking up the title of a celebrated article by Déat, said he refused to "die for Danzig." [451]

It is in *Combat*, however, that one sees, in the clearest and most cohesive form, all the contradictions of the revolutionary right. Nationalism, to be sure, had been since the 1890s a factor generating civil war, but in the interwar period, when its radical wing together with the left-wing dissidents, in a common revolt against Marxism, developed in a fascist direction, its contradictions became particularly evident. Thus, fascism was an international ideological movement, a movement in which ideology played an essential role and according to which the country was worth defending only to the degree that it possessed an acceptable regime. Seen in this aspect, fascism is not simply an extreme form of nationalism. Indeed, fascism is sometimes not a form of nationalism at all, for the nation is held to be of value only insofar as it embodies the fascist ideal of society and civilization.

In April 1936, in an eloquent editorial "A France That Disgusts Us," *Combat* utterly rejected the idea of a national union. Just before the victory of the Popular Front, when tension in Europe was rising after the reoccupation of the Rhineland by Hitler's forces, these brilliant intellectuals who had emerged from Maurrassism reacted strongly: "Down with the Union Sacrée!" said Maulnier's review.

Once again, patriotic verbiage is joined with democratic verbiage in order to persuade us. Once again, it is a matter of Democracy and the Rights of Man and Liberty versus Despotism, and, no doubt, of the War to End Wars also. Once again, the regime claims to defend its principles and pay its bills with French blood.

We feel that we have had enough. We wish to denounce the horrible piece of trickery that in dangerous times unites the communist agents of a foreign power, radicals whom the crusade of 1792 prevents from sleeping, and stupidly patriotic conservatives in the same democratic cult and the defense of the regime in the name of the Union Sacrée.[452]

And the obvious conclusion: "Down with the Union Sacrée! On no account *will we support the France of today*. It is in opposition, in rejection, and, when the time comes, it is in revolution that our only hope of dignity is to be found. We agree to defend France, but only on condition of regaining or rebuilding a France worthy of being defended."[453]

The problem was of great importance. If, as Fabrègues thought, it was "necessary to Western civilization" that "armed conflict with Hitler's Germany" should be avoided,[454] and if, as Jouvenel believed, Hitler and Mussolini, far from being "despots who can do everything . . . , rather resemble the founders of dynasties of whom our Capetians provide a splendid example,"[455] it was clear that a mobilization of energies, resources, and means such as was represented by the Union Sacrée became impossible.

Maulnier was well aware of the impasse presented by the contradictions of French nationalism. He was convinced, for instance, that war should not have been declared in September 1938, because a defeat "would undoubtedly have been a defeat for France," while "a victory for

France would have been less a victory for France than a victory for principles justifiably considered as leading straight to the ruin of France and of civilization itself." [456]

Maulnier refused to take "the side of the nationalisms against the declining democracies" so as not to "play into Germany's hands," but at the same time he opposed with all his might the "'antifascist' crusade that would mean the victory of everything that French nationalism has taken upon itself the mission of fighting." [457] For, finally, wrote Maulnier in a text of great clarity,

a war in which France's victory, which would also be the victory of its repugnant allies, would quickly efface from the earth the most precious values of human civilization, would efface from the earth, by an inevitable repercussion, France itself. . . . This war, if by any chance it was victorious, would finally benefit only what we hate most; and . . . thus, for perhaps the first time in their history, the French are compelled to say that the destiny of the highest civilization has ceased, through France's fault, to coincide with France's destiny, and that a victory for France is in danger of being a defeat for the human race. [458]

This explains not only the active ideological collaboration in France in the following years but also the lack of a large-scale, active ideological resistance. However, of particular significance for an analysis and definition of fascism and for the history of ideas is the fact that nationalism, far from being a factor that brings fascists and conservatives together, is precisely the factor that divides them. Around 1940, fascism was not just the only truly revolutionary—not radical—doctrine but also, with the exception of communism, the only authentic internationalist doctrine. Pure, quintessential nationalism was a doctrine of moderates: the radical right, for whom nationalism was the revolutionary factor par excellence, engaged in a war that was an ideological war par excellence—a war in which the defeat of the nation would not be too high a price to pay for the victory of certain ideas. Dissociated from conservatism, this form of nationalism accepted the idea of a France that, though diminished by comparison with its revolutionary neighbors, was regenerated, virile, living dangerously, a France that was the guardian of civilization and charged with a historic mission: to engage in the great antimaterialist revolution.

Conclusion

The 1930s were perceived by contemporaries—as they still are today by many historians—as a time of exceptional intellectual ferment.[1] People as different as Georges Valois and Daniel-Rops had the sensation of being involved in "a great intellectual turmoil"[2] and living through "years that were a turning point."[3] Statements like these abound. Jean Touchard, attempting to describe "the spirit of the 1930s," distinguishes between the spirit of 1930 and that of 1936, and sees them as very different.[4] J.-L. Loubet del Bayle went so far as to limit his work on the "nonconformists" of the thirties to 1930–34.[5]

Historians as well as those who personally recall them agree that those "fresh years"[6] had a specific and very special quality. Déat was aware of this quality, and described these years as the period "that was born dolorously in the painful birth of the depression."[7] Twenty-five years later, Andreu spoke of the period as the moment when "the twentieth century began to turn."[8] The First World War, said Loubet del Bayle, had undermined the faith in progress and confidence in reason that had characterized the nineteenth century.[9] Without a doubt the generation of 1930 felt that it was passing through a period of deep malaise—through a moral crisis, an economic crisis, a crisis of civilization.[10] It is necessary, however, to investigate the causes of this situation and to describe the evolution of ideas in the thirties as it really occurred, for what generation since the time of Taine and Renan has not had the feeling of living at the end of an age? Which group of men did more than the generation of 1890 to undermine belief in reason and progress? How can one hold the First World War responsible for something to which

Bergson and Sorel, Barrès and Le Bon, Michels and Pareto had already contributed so much some years before 1914?

Indeed, the same kind of intellectual and moral crisis, the same sense of decadence, the same revolt against materialism, the same desire for moral regeneration that characterized the generation of 1930 had typified the generation of the turn of the century. The same critical attitude toward bourgeois society and its values, toward liberalism and democracy, the same wish to overthrow the existing order, imbued the thoughts and deeds of these two generations separated by the Great War. Even the strong dislike for certain aspects of industrial civilization—"Fordism," "Taylorism," and the "American cancer," as Robert Aron and Arnaud Dandieu were to call it[11]—was already present, to a large extent, in the last decade of the nineteenth century, when Barrès called it *machinism*. There was hardly any important aspect of the intellectual ferment of the thirties that was not paralleled in this earlier period—also a period of unprecedented economic expansion.

This last point is an important one. Toward the middle of the last decade of the nineteenth century there began in Europe—and particularly in Germany and France—a period of rapid economic growth, and this situation contributed to the stagnation of orthodox Marxism and to the emergence, in France and Italy, of the two characteristic forms of revisionism: that of the right (the schools of Merlino, Bernstein, Jaurès, and Turati) and that of the left (the schools of Sorel, Lagardelle, and Arturo Labriola). Reformism and Sorelian syndicalism were thus the consequence of the ideological inadequacy of Marxism and its inability to provide a realistic theoretical response to the questions raised by the new economic situation. Hence, the radicalism represented by revolutionary syndicalism resulted not from an economic crisis but from a situation of relative prosperity.

At the other end of the political spectrum, the Action Française, which emerged at that time, represented a similar process of radicalization. The Maurrassian movement filled the gap left by the collapse of Déroulède's Ligue des Patriotes, of Lemaître and Barrès's Ligue de la Patrie Française, and of Drumont and Guérin's Ligue Antisémitique. The Action Française did not result from either a military defeat or an economic recession. Its integral nationalism and the variety of socialism represented by revolutionary syndicalism were both a reaction to the inability of the movements from which they originated to fulfill their essential function of acting as a revolutionary force against the liberal and bourgeois order. The economic situation of bourgeois society therefore served only as a catalyst—it did not create the rebellion, although it did provide it with its combatants. The revolt of the end of the century consequently arose neither from a disastrous international situation nor from an economic recession: it represented a rejection of the bourgeois, liberal order as such and was thus independent of that order, which explains why though the Great War created conditions favorable to the emergence of fascism as a political force, it made no real difference to the evolution of fascist ideology.

That ideology was above all a rejection of "materialism"—that is, of the essence of the European intellectual heritage from the seventeenth century onward. It was precisely this revolt against materialism that permitted antiliberal and antibourgeois nationalism and that variety of socialism that, while rejecting Marxism, still remained revolutionary to come together. That kind of socialism was also, by definition, antiliberal and antibourgeois, and its opposition to historical materialism made it the natural ally of radical nationalism. This synthesis represented the rejection of a certain type of civilization of which liberalism and Marxism were simply two aspects. It represented a complete rejection of the eighteenth century, of which liberalism and Marxism were the heirs, and was founded on a quite different view of the relationships between man and nature and man and society. But, above all, this synthesis was based on an antimechanistic explanation of human nature and a new conception of individual motivation.

Thus, there is an unbroken continuity between the period before the First World War and the interwar period. The idealism of the thirties, with its ideas of transcendence and of the union of opposites, of "going beyond" the classical ideologies and systems, simply took over from the movement of revolt of the beginning of the century. Henri De Man's *Au-delà du marxisme*, Thierry Maulnier's *Au-delà du nationalisme*, Arturo Labriola's *Au-delà du capitalisme et du socialisme*, and Hubert Lagardelle's "Au-delà de la démocratie" could make no claim to originality with readers of Sorel, Pareto, and Michels. Writing in 1935, Labriola and Lagardelle, both theoreticians of the revolutionary syndicalism of 1905, would have had less difficulty than one might think in recognizing themselves in their own writings of a quarter of a century earlier. The contribution of that generation and its journals to the revolt against "materialism," against liberalism and democratic socialism, against the class struggle and capitalism, parties and parliaments, conservatives and Marxists, preceded that of the interwar generation by some thirty years.

This criticism of the established order—in its political and social aspects as well as its ethical and moral aspects—in the period before the First World War had a depth and a comprehensiveness not easily found some twenty or thirty years later, for France in the twenties was relatively unproductive and lived chiefly on its cultural heritage. Proust, Durkheim, Barrès, Péguy, and Sorel were dead, and the truly productive period of Gide, Valéry, and Maurras was over. Though Bergson had undoubtedly been the main figure in philosophy, there were practically no more Bergsonians in France. Neither Barrès nor Maurras nor Péguy had any real heir among the younger generation; for all their qualities, neither Maulnier nor Brasillach nor Mounier could claim to play the same role or to have the same position in the history of ideas or in modern French letters. The Marxism of the Left Bank was only in its infancy and Sorel's legacy was spread out among several people. And, once again, Sorel's only true successor, De Man, was a cosmopolitan—born in Belgium, influential in France, but more active in the development of ideas in Germany than in that of the Latin Quarter. While Paris had been, at the turn of the century, the undisputed capital of arts and letters and a world center for philosophy and the social sciences, the Paris of the interwar period turned inward on itself. Freud and Weber were little known there,[12] and the city was chiefly distinguished for its circles of "journalistic-political apprentices"[13]—to use a phrase of Jouvenel's that well describes the new situation. This phrase also describes perfectly both the moral fragility of that generation and its exceptional fluidity, for the intellectual ferment of the thirties above all involved political journalists or politicians who were also journalists, which explains why the Resistance and the collaborators alike never had any real intellectual leadership.

The revival that took place during those years could not obscure the fact that, for the first time in many generations, Paris had lost its intellectual preeminence in the world. The new generation, which was much less interested in basic questions than in topical affairs, and whose intellectuals were no longer pioneers, is nevertheless of great interest to the historian. The participation in active politics that was then practically the rule, the search for new formulas and unconventional solutions that was so common, the endeavor to transcend and to pass "beyond"—all this bore witness to a state of great confusion before a world that was rapidly changing, and that one was not too sure one understood or was able to master.

Of all the major countries of continental Europe, France was the only one, until the beginning of the Second World War, where liberal democracy had withstood the impact of fascism and nazism. The liberal revolutions of the nineteenth century and the failures of Boulangism and anti-Dreyfusism had borne fruit; moreover, victory in the Great War had spared the French enormous psychological tensions, and the slow pace of the country's economic development had forestalled serious social problems. Fascism, in France, consequently remained theoretical, and never had to make the inevitable compromises that to some degree always falsify the official ideology of a regime. Thus, in studying French fascism, one is able to apprehend the true significance of the phenomenon of fascism in general, and in examining its ideology in its origins, in its stage of incubation, one obtains a clearer understanding of fascist thought and behavior, as well as a clearer perception of the complexity of the circumstances and attitudes that form the fabric of the 1930s.

Not every form of antimaterialism can be described as fascism, but fascism was a form of antimaterialism, and it canalized all the main currents of antimaterialism in the twentieth century. In this sense, fascism was an authentic revolutionary movement: it wished to make a clean break with the established order, and politically, ethically, and aesthetically provided a clear alternative option. Fascist spiritualism and idealism provided the basis for a total revolution, the only one that did not depend on a class struggle. This revolution of the spirit, of the will, of the instincts constituted a totality: it sought to create a new type of man connected in his very flesh with a new society. Society would no longer be a kind of battlefield where individuals and social groups challenge one another, but a collectivity in which all the strata and classes of society would work together in harmony. The natural framework of such a harmonious, organic human collectivity is the nation—a purified, revitalized nation, in which the individual would count only as a cell in the collective organism, and which would enjoy a moral unity that could never be provided by Marxism and liberalism, both of which were consequences of fragmentation and war. The embodiment of this unity is the state, and its power derives from the spiritual unanimity of the masses; but the state is at the same time the protector of that unity, which it fosters by every available means, including the party, propaganda, and education.

In addition to a political revolution, fascism sought to bring about a moral revolution, a profound transformation of the human spirit. Not only the fate of the nation was at issue, but also the destiny of civilization: the problem of decadence was one of the major preoccupations of fascism, which was animated by a desire to create a new type of man, characterized by the classically antibourgeois virtues of heroism, energy, alertness, a sense of duty, a willingness to sacrifice, and an acceptance of the idea of the preeminence of the community over the individuals who compose it. First and foremost of fascist qualities, however, was a faith in the power of will—of a will that could reshape the world of matter and shatter its resistance.

The moral unity of an organic society requires the creation of a new physical environment and new forms of social organization and cultural expression. The virile, vigorous fascist, spending his leisure hours on the sports field and the racetrack, is the very antithesis of the bourgeois. Fascist aesthetics also had an antibourgeois character. Because fascism was a form of antimaterialism, it had an antimercantilist, antimechanistic aspect; but at the same time it was in awe of modern technology. Fascism was related to the futurist movement in literature and architecture, for fascism had a modernistic side that helped to set it apart from the old conservative world. A poem by Marinetti and a building by Le Corbusier were both immediately accepted by the fascists, for, better than any literary dissertation, they embodied everything that distinguished the revolutionary future from the bourgeois past.

The revision of Marxism in the interwar period (as undertaken, for example, by De Man and Déat) and the Sorelian revisionism of the beginning of the century both expressed a desire to shatter and remold history and an attempt to discover a means of doing so. Corporatism was found to be the tool par excellence of this struggle to change the existing order of things, a struggle that always took the same course: Sorel, Michels, and Berth, like the planists and neosocialists rejecting historical materialism, replaced it with psychological arguments, finally arriving at a form of socialism in which the proletariat ceases to have any particular importance. Thus, socialism, from the turn of the century onward, developed into a socialism for all, for the whole collectivity—a socialism that opposes capitalism not in the name of a single class but in the name of the entire nation.

Thus, a perfectly natural alliance occurred between this form of socialism and the new-born nationalism—a radical nationalism that also set itself against the old world of the conservatives, against the aristocrats and bourgeois, and against social injustice, and that believed that the nation would be truly whole only when the proletariat became an integral part of it. A socialism for the whole collectivity and a nationalism that, dissociated from conservatism, aimed to be the vehicle of unity and unanimity together formed an engine of war against capitalism of unprecedented power. Corporatism and the strong state, having all the resources of the economy at their disposal and liberated once and for all from the trammels of universal suffrage, parliamentarianism, parties, and committees, were to be the instruments of this assault against the capitalist citadel, against a society fragmented into antagonistic classes, against the national decadence and the disintegration of a whole civilization.

In the France of the interwar period, such a message could not fail to find a favorable response among large segments of the public. Many young intellectuals—an important part of the world of letters—could not remain unaffected by this way of thinking, or at least by certain elements of it. The self-declared fascists were never more than a tiny minority among all those who responded to this call for youth, ardor, dignity, and unity, to this rejection of determinism and materialism, this affirmation of the primacy of the spiritual. Far more numerous than the confirmed fascists were the supporters of a new, anti-Marxist, non-proletarian type of revolution—a revolution of the spirit. The response to the ideas of the fascist intellectuals was thus much greater than is often thought.[14] But even more numerous than the fellow travelers were those who regarded with a benevolent neutrality that resurrection of antibourgeois values that Maurice Duverger called "the revolution of 1940"[15]—a revolution for the entire nation. Men and movements that were hostile to the Nazi repression were nevertheless forced to pause and reflect before what seemed, in July 1940, to be an opportunity to save the nation by taking advantage of the fall of the regime—that hated regime based on capitalist exploitation and inimical to spiritual values.

This point is all-important for an understanding of fascism. Fascism was not merely an extreme form of nationalism, nor was it simply a return to a primitive tribalism. It had a solid conceptual framework, and could provide answers to questions much greater than those posed by particular historical circumstances. Consequently, in the hour of testing, fascist ideology did not fail and appeared to be the perfect type of political ideology—a system of ideas that could guide political action, prescribe choices, and reshape the world. Insofar as it possessed internal contradictions, these were no obstacle to action. In the final analysis, fascism, contrary to Brasillach's description, was not only a "spirit" but also a "political doctrine."[16] It was also a system of ethics and aesthetics. One could say that fascism was a complete ideological system,

rooted in a comprehensive vision of the world and having its own philosophy of history and its own criteria for immediate political action. In
all this, fascism hardly differed from the other great modern ideological
systems. Like any other ideology, it had its operational aspect.[17] Insofar
as it was put to the test in France, this ideology showed that the distance
between its basic principles and its praxis was less great than had been
the case with the ideologies that preceded it. In June 1940 the hard core
of French fascists remained true to their principles and consistent in
their analysis of the situation and their choices.

Between the nationalists—for whom the concept of fatherland was
an absolute, not subject to any condition—and the fascists—who no
longer represented a form of nationalism but were part of a universal,
deeply ideological movement—were situated the other nonconformist
political forces and currents of thought, all in a state of great confusion.

Once again, it is in its period of incubation that one can most clearly
perceive a political phenomenon. Thus, if one is to judge people's behavior during the Occupation accurately, one must confine oneself to the
period between June 1940 and June 1941. For the noncommunists and
those not haunted by the shade of Napoleon, one might extend this period to the time of the Soviet counteroffensive in the winter of 1941–42,
but it was only until June 1941 that the best laboratory conditions
existed. Later, to a greater and greater degree, people's actions were influenced by opportunism.

The political and moral collapse of the ruling elites in the summer of
1940 and the setting up of an alternative regime owed a great deal to the
discredit into which liberal democracy had fallen. The official fascists,
the avowed fascists, were only a radical minority, but they were backed
by the great battalions opposed to "materialism," and it was precisely
because it was not only capitalism that was attacked but also liberalism—not only the bourgeois world but also certain universal principles readily associated with the bourgeoisie—that the harsh criticisms
to which the regime had been subjected during the previous decade now
took on their full weight and significance. Indeed, these criticisms were
directed less at a system of government that, in a fragmented society,
considerably weakened the power of the executive than at the very principle of democracy. Thus, a combination of circumstances existed that
contributed much to undermining the foundations of democracy, of pluralism, and of a certain view of the world generally associated with the
heritage of the Enlightenment and the French Revolution.

As an illustration of this point, the case of Mounier is particularly interesting, first of all because he was a figure of exceptional moral rectitude, whose influence in the immediate postwar period was considerable. His behavior under the Occupation demonstrates the deep moral malaise, the disgust with the regime, and the longing for change that existed in France. That someone like Mounier could choose to work for more than a year within the framework of the Vichy regime shows that almost anything seemed preferable at that time to a return to the former situation.

Mounier, the philosopher of personalism, was a worthy representative of all the nonconformist intellectuals of the thirties who, searching for some non-Marxist form of revolution, automatically rejected the liberal and social-democratic consensus. Mounier also rejected fascism, but it cannot be denied that his violent criticism of the "established disorder" was similar to that of the fascists. His solutions to the problem were different, but his criticisms were practically identical. It is not surprising that, after Mounier's *Esprit* was banned in August 1941, Jean de Fabrègues, coeditor of *Combat*, tried to offer Mounier's readers a Vichyist Catholic journal.[18]

Analyzing his leader's motivations in 1940, Jean-Marie Domenach wrote, "Mounier is not sorry to see bourgeois liberalism come to grief. The situation is open: beyond the disaster he hopes a new world will come into being."[19] It is this very willingness to consider various possibilities that makes Mounier's choice so problematic. His reaction was shared by all the rebels of the thirties, and his rejection of "bourgeois liberalism" led to acceptance of the legitimacy of Vichy, "to which," he wrote, "my position as a French citizen attaches me for better or for worse.[20] Mounier worked for more than a year for the "national revolution." In February 1941 he reproached the Christian-democratic leader Étienne Borne for totally rejecting the regime. He wrote (this was not a banal statement at the time) "that some of our friends, more or less connected with *L'Aube*, are once again starting to engage dangerously in the formula of a *defense of democracy*."[21] To a certain extent he could understand the behavior of Maritain, for whom "that had American associations, very different from ours. . . . But in France, where one had to create something new at all costs, it blocked up the very spirit of creativity."[22] Mounier explained what he meant by that in an interesting passage:

The antifascist defensive reaction in all its negative characteristics, like the anticommunist reaction that paralyzed *La Flèche*, turned into a dangerous stain on the Christian democrats. We do not doubt for an instant the vigor of the genuine *no* that one must oppose to all spiritual infiltration of the spirit of the victor, but here, as in military matters, defensive, even heroically defensive, positions are bad and kill the creative spirit. When, after the armistice, we saw a number of these same Christian democrats . . . do nothing but sigh over past times as if the "Popular Democratic party" had really brought France something in the past twenty years, we reacted vigorously.[23]

Mounier's rejection of the republican defensive reflex, which, from the time of Boulangism, to the Dreyfus affair, and up until the Popular Front, had assured the survival of French democracy, hardly differed from Maulnier's or Bergery's reaction in the same circumstances. Mounier rejected out of hand Borne's policy of "all or nothing," which he criticized for casting discredit on "all that is being done now," and particularly on those "real islands of sanity," those "truly free corners of France"— "the École d'Uriage" and "Jeune France."[24] And, on the other hand, Mounier made it clear by referring to *L'Aube* in the context of his rejection of Borne's criticisms of *Esprit* that he did not believe "that an obsolete journal can bear witness more honorably than another one that is attempting to struggle. It's a fallacy: the pornographic booklets have also disappeared from the shop windows."[25]

In March 1941 Mounier stated that "we are still in an open situation" and that the legitimacy "of an action declaring our presence" could not be doubted.[26] He was then very active as a lecturer and educator in Uriage, "that fine rock of French fidelity," "in the 'Chantiers' and in the Movements."[27] Mounier derived satisfaction from the fact that people like Henri Massis associated Uriage with *Esprit*, and that in the youth movements and the Chantiers, where "they at last felt the need for a doctrine," only two things met the need: the "Action Française and *Esprit*."[28] He worked out his doctrine in the course of lectures on "The Present Positions of Personalism" and "The Christian Sense of the Community," as well as on "The End of the French Bourgeois" and "Our Cultural Revolution."[29]

In fact, Mounier's participation in the attempt at intellectual and spiritual renewal that took place within the context of the regime in the summer of 1940 was a consequence of the ambiguity of his positions in the period when *Esprit* was founded. The editor of the new review then shared all the uncertainties of the rebels and dissidents of whom he was one, and who were headed by the members of the *Ordre Nouveau* group. For a short time Mounier even broke with the Aron-Dandieu group, and his opposition to the Hitlerian terror, as to the totalitarianism of Mussolini's state, was to remain unwavering.[30] But one finds in

Mounier, as in most of the dissidents, a certain indulgence toward fascism, a certain appreciation of it, sometimes even a certain admiration for it, which derived from their common perception of the weaknesses and drawbacks of liberal democracy. The weaknesses, pettiness, and fragility of the French democracy seemed to them quite tragic compared to the decisiveness, energy, and willpower displayed by the regimes of Italy and Germany.

In December 1933 Mounier attempted to define his position. He refused fascism the right to claim the preeminence of spirituality. He denounced fascism as a "pseudohumanism, [a] pseudospiritualism that weighs man down beneath the tyranny of the heaviest 'spiritualities' and the most ambiguous 'mysticisms': the cult of race, of the nation, of the state, of the will to power, of an anonymous discipline, of the leader, of successes in sports and economic achievements." [31] He concluded that fascism was a "new materialism," and could find no words harsh enough to say about the "*agents provocateurs* of the spiritual revolution." [32] Yet at the same time he wrote, "We have no intention of being summary. We do not deny that the fascist regimes bring, with respect to those that they replace, an element of health and a loftiness of tone that are manifestations of energy that ought not to be despised. We know what very great differences there are between them. We do not doubt that a study of their institutions, transposed into our own terms, would provide us with valuable suggestions." [33]

And, simultaneously, he lashed out at the established order: "We are no less severe toward liberal and parliamentary democracy. *Jam foetet.* A democracy of slaves in liberty, deprived in their souls and in their livelihoods, subjected to the brutal force of money that has affected even their revolt. . . . Let us have the courage to say it: the problem of democracy and the problem of authority are new, as yet unresolved problems caused by the conditions that the modern world has imposed on them." [34]

Mounier's conclusion was somewhat curious: "We ought not to try and conceal the fact: a dictatorship is indispensable for any revolution, particularly a spiritual one, in order to neutralize and overcome evil forces." To be sure, "this dictatorship could only be a provisional and limited one." Mounier immediately ruled out the possibility of a fascist dictatorship, saying that the regime he was proposing "could not set up the dictatorship of a state or of a party, and consequently, together with the regime of falsehood, spiritual sterilization and the supremacy of renegades and courtesans." He finally provided his own solution to the dilemma: "Our formula is: a material dictatorship, controlled as far as is necessary, together with integral spiritual liberty"; and he added, "Liberalism is the grave digger of liberty."[35]

This important text clearly reveals the internal tensions, the contradictions, and the search for new directions that characterized the thinking of the dissidents of the thirties. Mounier shows himself here to be closer to Maulnier, in many respects, than one might think.[36] He was also closer than is generally thought to Pierre Dominique, the future head of censorship of the Vichy government, who protected him against the local censor in Lyons.[37] Mounier's subtle distinctions are singularly lacking in clarity and definition. Statements like "Yes, organic and functional hierarchy, but be careful,"[38] or "Order, discipline, authority, yes" (which takes up the néos' famous formula), or "Youth, energy, awakening, yes—and may there be an end to the rule of old men, dead ideas and faintheartedness," even when qualified by statements like "But may the call to youth be a call to ardor of faith, to simplicity of heart, and not to brutality and the complacent confusion of vital forces or the dangerous puerilities of armed schoolboys,"[39] could only add to the general confusion. This lack of precision in political thought weighed heavily on the thirties and undermined not only a certain "bourgeois liberalism" (to use J.-M. Domenach's phrase) but also, in Mounier's own words, "liberal and parliamentary democracy."[40]

Mounier's rejection of the old order of things finally brought him to accept the principle of the "national revolution." To be sure, he bitterly regretted its excesses, but his only practical response was a sort of game of hide-and-seek with the Lyons censorship. On 19 October 1940 "the shameful Statut des Juifs" was enacted, and Mounier felt himself "aged, as though by a sickness." Six days later, he noted, "This morning, permission to start republishing Esprit arrived, with Montigny's signature, at the same time as the news of the Hitler-Laval, Hitler-Pétain meetings."[41] Mounier was aware of the profound ambiguity of the situation that was emerging and, with full knowledge of that situation, made his choice. The task of building a new order on the ruins of liberal democracy was in his view the overriding necessity.

Though it is absurd to see Mounier as one of the "Young Turks" of fascism,[42] at the same time it is important not to underestimate Esprit's contribution to the intellectual confusion so characteristic of the interwar period. In the creation of the intellectual climate that made the "national revolution" possible and encouraged the rise of fascism this team of writers undoubtedly played their part. Throughout the thirties,

Mounier expressed his sympathy for attacks on materialism made from the most varied quarters. He praised De Man's "critique of determinist materialism" and his "spiritualism so close to being Christian."[43] At the same time, he expressed satisfaction at the revolt of the Jeune Droite, declaring his "complete agreement with Jean de Fabrègues on the spiritual reality of the problem, happy, moreover, to see him condemn capitalist disorder more radically than some of his friends."[44] He was also sympathetically inclined toward the little fascist group L'Assaut, whose ideas, he thought, had been recently "very well explained."[45]

These views are confirmed by certain other texts we should examine; these are among Mounier's most revealing writings, and include his reviews of some important books. Thus, presenting Maulnier's *Au-delà du nationalisme* to his readers, Mounier wrote, "Most of those who collaborate on this review could sign their names to almost the whole of his last book."[46] He drew a comparison between Maulnier's analysis of the situation and De Man's, giving a perfect summary of their ideas—"Liberalism and Marxism have dealt convergent blows to the national community and to the state, which must take on its defense from above"— and concluding, "Thus far we agree entirely."[47] The only criticism that the theoretician of personalism could make of the theoretician of the new nationalism was that he had disregarded "that republican French soul, so profoundly sensed by Péguy."[48] Otherwise he had no objections: analyzing Maulnier's ideas, Mounier declared that he "would not change a line of his criticism of 'democracy.'"[49] Maulnier's great mistake, he thought, was simply that he failed to see "that this word contained another possibility, another tradition apart from bourgeois, capitalist and parliamentary democracy, of which there is not one of us who is not sickened."[50] It is interesting that Mounier was well aware of the dangers presented by Maulnier's ideas if "taken out of the small circle of just and thoughtful people and put into an area where indeterminate forces and approximate ideas are operating,"[51] but nevertheless was willing to take up a tradition, going back to the time of Boulangism, of dissociating the "democratic" from the "republican." Claiming that there was a "certain French sensibility that, if it is not always democratic, remains deeply republican," he recommended that Maulnier take that sensibility into account, and, addressing him, concluded:

That we should extirpate from the French soul the radical canker and its Croix de Feu surgeons; that we should proclaim loud and clear that the Third Republic was only a caricature of democracy; that we should restore the significance of organic communities in the face of petit bourgeois distrustfulness (while providing the counterweight of a greater wariness of their pitfalls); that we should revise completely what empirically, for a short period of French history, has been the so-called "democratic" notion of the state, of the social system, of political life and of institutions; and that we should rid the very sources of the democratic idea of certain pretentious and deadly ideologies, we agree wholeheartedly.[52]

Mounier's review of Maxence's *Histoire de dix ans*[53] and his later account of Drieu La Rochelle's *Gilles*[54] were written in a similar spirit. Drieu, he said, "had come to diagnose the French prewar political sickness as a sickness of willpower, of vitality,"[55] and Mounier thought he was right. If he did not endorse Drieu's belief in "the necessity to do something, no matter what,"[56] the sentiments he expressed in a text written in full wartime help to explain the atmosphere of uncertainty that existed in November 1940, the month when *Esprit* reappeared:[57]

It is nonetheless true that prewar France needed some muscle and a bit of savagery: "Put together socialism, religion and a virile spirit," as one of Drieu's spokesmen stated. The great lesson of the fascist regime that he echoed was to set against the impotent and pretentious idealist rhetoric with which the democracies were so deeply impregnated the preeminence of Being and of affirmation (from a taste for affirmation, however, one slips imperceptibly into a vindication of force). It is not the attraction of ease that Gilles seeks in fascism; it is a sense of monasticism that reasserts itself far more forcefully after a period of too easy achievement. Drieu recently deplored the lack of suitability to present circumstances of the ideas of more than one defender of the democracies. Indeed, if the point of this war were to return, once the dangers have passed, to the charms of an age recently gone by, and to revive waltzing Vienna, slum-ridden Naples, Baroque Munich and glittering Paris, we should very soon lose face. "Turn fascism against Italy and Germany" remains an ambiguous, ill-balanced formula, but, yes—turn against the monstrosities of fascism the virtues of fascism and whatever living history it has given birth to in aberration and terror, and there can be no durable victory, adapted to the world as it is, without such an integration.[58]

This philosophy of history led Mounier to decide, in the summer of 1940, to seek permission to revive *Esprit* in southern France. His desire not to be excluded from the activities that shaped the destiny of the French nation prompted him to write a programmatic article in February 1941, "On Intelligence in Times of Crisis."[59] In this article, after condemning the "wild and decadent intelligentsia," he reflected on the spiritual causes of the defeat: "A certain Gidean climate, a certain Valerian detachment, a certain Bergsonian pathos, a certain political conformism on the opposing sides and a certain de luxe literature have helped to bring about the decomposition of the French soul."[60] This, he said, was one of "the few fundamental truths" that it was "one of the tasks of the national revolution, now that the measures of first aid have been taken," to understand.[61] Mounier was really encouraging people to participate in the national revolution: he unambiguously rejected the "temptation of all or nothing" and condemned "the fanaticism of the opposition"—"those unhappy spirits, agitated by a demon of disputation, who are fruitful only in an ever-destructive criticism."[62] It is difficult to see this text as a call to resistance.

One may also wonder about the significance of the following text of Mounier's, which appeared in November 1940, when the oppressive legal measures of the Vichy government were already in force: "From the beginning, we have not ceased to condemn liberal democracy, but that was a kind of act of politeness rendered to a secondary truth, if not to a truth of the second order. We thought it was parasitic on France, like some kind of dust or lichen: we did not realize that it ate away at it like vermin, as surely as a spiritual sickness or social disorder. We had conserved the hope that a real democracy would overcome a formal democracy, an organic democracy would overcome an anarchic demagogy."[63]

The November 1940 issue of *Esprit* also contained a number of other attacks on the democracy of the Third Republic. In those dark days, the judgment of a man like Mounier of a past that could only be assessed in relation to the present is very striking:

Not being an elector or a representative for a number of months, the Frenchman is going to find himself deprived of a distraction that has preoccupied him a great deal: a bit too much in fact. By not indulging in political actions for some time, the French have a chance to learn the value of an activity that has been devalued by use, and a reflectiveness that has been swamped in verbiage. They will also be in the best position to deal directly with their activities and problems, their work, literature and religion, abandoning the erroneous perspectives in which these had been seen in the light of the political obsession. Who can assert that this forced retreat had not become necessary to true culture, to healthy labor, to true religion?[64]

In this connection, Mounier coined a new formula. He said he wanted to see, within "the framework of the new regime," "a mentality of the active vanquished,"[65] which he felt to be the only possibility for the French in 1940.

With the satisfaction of a prophet who has been justified by history, Mounier recalled the special issues of *Esprit* of before the war devoted to "the death of the parties" and "the problem of representation." When the war came, he said, *Esprit* posed "in new terms the *problem of liberty* and the *problem of the leader*."[66] As for the struggle against liberal democracy, Mounier now addressed himself to the Action Française: "We still keep in store a few discussions with the Action Française for a time when the French will have the heart to discuss things. But now we must give in." [67]

In the same issue, Mounier lashed out at individualism, the bourgeois, and "the revolution of '89," which "was not a popular revolution but a bourgeois revolution." [68] Like the Maurrassians, he attacked both bourgeois mediocrity and communism. Indeed, bourgeois liberalism and communism, whose "bottled-up virulence has not yet been eliminated from the French organism," between them, he said, bore the responsibility for French decadence. [69] Thus, in July 1941, a few weeks after Hitler's invasion of the Soviet Union, Mounier, speaking of communism, expressed the hope that it would at last be possible "to sterilize with hot irons the political and social wound that had developed in the weakened body of Europe," for, he said, there was "nobody who is not ready to hail the downfall of the somber Stalin regime, when it takes place, as a deliverance for Europe, for it is not accompanied by equally evil consequences. Among the faces of the Antichrist, that of the cunning, vain, and bloodthirsty little tyrant who for years has cut off Europe from Holy Russia, and from all the power of the new Russia, has been one of the most odious." [70] And, finally, quoting *L'Action française* of 2 July 1941, Mounier stated that since "all crusades are not pure . . . , for the sake of Europe's honor its 'crusade' against communism ought not to be a crusade of Pharisees." [71]

In July 1941, this way of speaking and this terminology—the many references to ideas that then constituted code words for collaboration with the new regime and a recognition of German hegemony over the Continent—could only signify a de facto recognition of the new order of things.

Another point must be strongly made here. The fascination of fascism in the thirties had resulted primarily from a search for new values. The attractiveness of fascism at that time was far greater than is today admitted by the people who felt that attraction, their political colleagues, or their followers. There can be no doubt that fascism, because it was to be the instrument of a profound moral and spiritual revolution, made an impression on the nonconformist circles of the thirties. Even people who in the immediate postwar period became symbols of the new France that had grown out of the Resistance had been favorably disposed toward fascism at the time. Their criticism of democracy, of the heritage of the French Revolution, had been directed not against the practices of the regime and its institutional weaknesses but against its very principles.

Speaking in May 1935 at the famous symposium organized in Rome by representatives of the Italian fascist left, Mounier stated that "even those in the French delegation who by their training had been staunch opponents of fascism publicly admitted the close kinship they felt with the constructive vigor of the new generation."[72]

This revealing text gives a good idea of the feelings of certain nonconformist circles toward fascism: this sentiment of "close kinship" among the revolutionaries—all those up in arms against the old liberal and bourgeois civilization—united fascists and some nonfascists in one and the same attitude of rejection. Mounier praised the left wing of Italian fascism, that "lively and audacious wing, radically anticapitalist and daringly constructive."[73] Soon after the Nazis seized power in Germany, one of his colleagues, Alexandre Marc, had expressed his agreement with the harsh criticism of the Weimar regime advanced by its opponents,[74] and three years later Georges Duveau, after proclaiming his disgust for the methods of Hitler's regime, nevertheless admitted "that the führer's tone, his alacrity, his brutal, plebeian, brisk way of saying these words—peace, war—give rise to an emotion that is not entirely devoid of sympathy."[75] In December 1938, François Perroux, in his turn, expressed both his conviction that Europe had rejected the principles of 1789 and his faith in the future of national socialism.[76] Mounier likewise saw the French Revolution as the origin of totalitarianism.[77] He expressed his rejection of the entire "bourgeois civilization" that was now being challenged by the "fascist civilizations,"[78] and although he recognized and understood the totalitarian character of fascism, he could not help but feel attracted by its total rejection of the liberal and bourgeois world—the total repudiation, without any shadow of compromise, signified by "fascism in its broad sense," that "revolutionary negation of bourgeois rationalism."[79] He admired the moral qualities of the fascists: "devotion, sacrifice, virile friendship," "the authentic spiritual energy that sustains these men violently uprooted from bourgeois decadence, filled with all the ardor that one possesses when one finds a faith and a meaning in life."[80]

The temptation of fascism thus was not felt only by people like Brasillach or Drieu La Rochelle. A particularly instructive example of the attraction exerted by fascism and nazism is provided by *L'Ordre nouveau*. From the time it appeared in May 1933, this journal, edited by Robert Aron and Arnaud Dandieu, expressed some reservations about national socialism and at the same time showed a great deal of sympathy toward it. The reservations concerned the practice of nazism, while the sympathy was for the Nazi revolt that was simultaneously directed against liberalism, socialism, and communism. Alexandre Marc even suggested "leaving aside for the moment the question of national-socialist excesses and brutalities," claiming that "every insufficiently prepared revolution is accompanied by brutalities and excesses." [81] He then outlined national-socialist ideology, which, he said, was "aimed in its entirety against the doomed liberal and Marxist ideologies." [82] Marc's text perfectly expresses the view of nazism current in the mid-thirties among the Parisian nonconformists—even those who were to become totally alienated from the Vichy regime or who were to become its first victims.

In the sphere of *home policy*, national socialism has violently rebelled against parliamentary democracy. It has regarded parliamentary democracy, quite correctly, as a survivor of a period that has forever passed, as a political conception that is abstract, atomistic, and hopelessly obsolete. National socialism has fought against the egotism, the corruption, and the impotence of political parties and has triumphantly exposed the fatal disorder of a regime dominated by the rapacity of party politicians "devoid of character or capability" and supported by a press willing to do anything!

In the sphere of *foreign policy*, how can one fail to approve of the revolt of national socialism against the myths of decadent liberalism? The Treaty of Versailles, which accumulated injustices and blunders and sought to hide fierce egotisms beneath a third-rate sentimentality, wrapping everything up in puritan hypocrisy and democratic rhetoric, could arouse nothing but scorn and anger in a well-born soul. National socialism has also risen up against the internationalism that denied human diversity, against Geneva-type pacifism—that religion of eunuchs!—and against the falsehood of capitalist "solidarity," the League of Nations, and other publicistic rubbish. . . . And when Goering boldly declares that the Disarmament Conference is merely a cynical farce, it is not we who will contradict him.

In the *economic* sphere, national socialism represents a reaction against the occult dictatorship of anonymous and wayward finance. The Nazis are not the only ones to pass a severe judgment on the "slavery of loans to interest." Not without reason do they attack the disorder of the liberal economy, the excesses of the industrialism to which Weimar Germany surrendered itself, out-and-out productivism. . . . And at the same time they refuse—at least in theory—to fall into the statist trap and transfer all economic functions to the state. They are opposed to capitalist disorder and the super-industrialization it fosters and to economic absolutism of the Stalinist type. How can one not approve of this rejection?

The *social* policy of national socialism is antagonistic to both capitalism and Marxism, which uproot people, tear them away from a living tradition, turn them into proletarians. The national socialists deplore the servile condition of this artificial man, this "man in the street," and advocate a return to a natural equilibrium and the restoration of human frameworks—family, profession (*Stand*), region (*Landschaft*)—the rehabilitation of small-scale ownership and of man's direct relationship to his work and to the land.

Finally, in the *cultural and spiritual* sphere, national socialism manifests a desire to break with materialism. Not that it has the slightest intention of denying material factors; rather it refuses to accept the primacy of matter. It is opposed to all the "by-products" of "free thought" and vehemently attacks decadent immorality, license, and moral degradation.[83]

This rejection of materialism is a central point in the long "Letter to Adolf Hitler, Chancellor of the Reich" which, as Mournier himself said, "contained fourteen phrases of reservations and thirty pages of apologies." Moreover, according to Mounier, Dandieu "was not without an inclination for certain other leading tendencies of Hitlerism."[84] Signed "Ordre Nouveau," this profession of faith is a document of rare interest. With regard to nazism as an ideological system and a body of doctrine, Dandieu and Aron boldly declared: "Your work is courageous: it has grandeur."[85] They went on to say: "Your movement possesses in its foundations an authentic grandeur,"[86] one that "consists in being, through the heroism, the sacrifice, and the self-abnegation that it instills, a protest against contemporary materialism."[87] The writers of the letter insisted repeatedly on this idea.[88] Since, in their opinion, it constituted a "legitimate revolt against modern materialism,"[89] they maintained that "in its spiritual origins, if not in the tactical development of the national-socialist movement, there are the seeds of a new and necessary revolutionary position."[90]

For, first of all, the writers of *L'Ordre nouveau* told Hitler, "You have put an end to a lie, that of liberal democracy."[91] In overthrowing "this maleficent regime . . . you have done something salubrious,"[92] especially since "in the same way that you have deflated the lie of political freedom, you have deflated that of moral freedom. . . . In the state of decadence into which a world to which all discipline is odious is slipping because the inner order no longer corresponds to the outer order, your protestation is highly valid. With a significant gesture, it demonstrates your theoretical attitude, which we respect."[93]

They concluded: "You have engaged in a struggle against the occult dictatorship of economics."[94] "You have understood what a danger the myth of the proletariat propagated by the Marxists represents for man. . . . You have understood and made it understood that American-

Bolshevik gregariousness and democratic-capitalist individualism must be opposed with the sentiment of the organic collectivity, rich in fraternity and love. Your dead young heroes bear witness to this great truth. Have you succeeded in bringing it into the political structures of the country? That is another matter." [95]

That, indeed, was the great question that concerned the writers of *L'Ordre nouveau*, for if the Aron-Dandieu group entertained any doubts about nazism, it was not because of the essence of the system nor even its methods, but because of the institutional application of its principles and also a certain ideological confusion: "In the fight against materialism," they wrote, "you will find us all in agreement, and yet we do not belong to you. An abyss divides us." [96]

What was this abyss? The writers of *L'Ordre nouveau* reproached nazism for a certain doctrinal weakness. If the greatness of nazism consisted in its revolt against materialism, its inadequacy was due to the fact that this revolt "never gave rise to a new, sane, and fruitful conception of the spirit." [97] However, in order to avoid any misunderstanding, *L'Ordre nouveau*, addressing Hitler, dissociated itself from the reproaches "heaped on you by democrats of every kind and by defeated and discontented Stalinists"; [98] "as for us, it is with a *total Revolution, a Revolution of order* on which the future of humanity depends, that we identify first. It is while supporting whatever is most authentically revolutionary in national socialism itself that we have a few questions to put to you. It is in the name of the Revolution that we do not hesitate to criticize you, to judge you." [99]

Aron and Dandieu told Hitler that "if you have perhaps carried out a revolution, Mr. Chancellor, you have not carried out *the* Revolution. There can only be a universal revolution: you have not succeeded in raising yourself to a broadly human ideal. You stopped on the way; you have been content with half measures." [100]

This, then, was the essential objection of the nonconformists of *L'Ordre nouveau* to Hitler: all their other criticisms derived from this basic point. Nazism did not carry out its ideas to the end; it did not draw all the conclusions of its revolt against materialism. "Destroyer of parliamentary parties" though it was, it never became "the revolutionary destroyer of the party": [101] it fell back "into familiar grooves" and showed "a lack of audacity and a conflict of ideas." [102] Antimaterialist as it was, it instituted "a new religion, that of work. Once more, Mr. Chancellor," they said, "flagrante delicto of materialism." [103] What was even more serious, however, was that in the final analysis Hitler was unable to avoid the pitfall of behaving like a democrat. His starting point was the mass rather than the individual, and he had liquidated "a regime of parliamentary oligarchy only to replace it with a Caesarian democracy." [104]

To be sure, the writers of *L'Ordre nouveau* did not approve of "the murders, the imprisonments, the beatings which," they told Hitler, "you have not known how to avoid or have not been able to," but, at the same time, they refused to associate themselves with "liberal opinion" that condemns "your 'tyranny' and your 'atrocities'" [105] (note the quotation marks enclosing *tyranny* and *atrocities*). Their stance was natural enough for those, like themselves, who judged national socialism "not from the point of view of foreigners or immigrants like your opponents, but from a profound viewpoint, a revolutionary viewpoint." [106] The writers of *L'Ordre nouveau* had no difficulty understanding how different Hitlerian nationalism was from the former "tradesmen's nationalism" or from "Pan-Germanism, of unhappy memory." [107] It was not hard for them to condemn as inhuman a policy "which forces your people to suffocate, stamping up and down in a territory which is too small for them." [108] Finally, Aron and Dandieu had little doubt about the essential community of sentiment between the Nazi movement and the ideas professed by the young intellectuals in whose name they claimed to speak. They addressed themselves to Hitler and Mussolini with a tone of great assurance: whether problems of civilization or international European politics were in question, they believed that because of this affinity, because of this essential agreement, they and their school were the only valid partners in dialogue. "Mr. Chancellor," they said, "we know that what we are saying here, few people are capable of understanding, but we think that you who have come to power supported by the enthusiasm of youth will be able to understand. *Mussolini has understood.* He does not conceal the fact that if he considers it useless to enter into a deep engagement with the present French government, it is because he believes it to be temporary, vain, and ineffectual. He awaits the time when a real government with political responsibility will take on the mission of France. When that time comes, one will be able to speak." [109]

Where principles were concerned, the personalists of *L'Ordre nouveau*, like most of the rebels, were hardly able to resist the attraction of the revolutions that had succeeded while they themselves were continually frustrated. These revolutions, after all, had been able to overcome liberalism and social democracy. All these people recognized in one way or another the superiority of the political cultures that flourished beyond the Rhine and on the other side of the Alps. They all admired what Jouvenel called "the great historical phenomenon of our time: the seizure of power by young groups animated by an anti-bourgeois spirit."[110]

Jouvenel enthusiastically hailed this "rise of a generation morally divorced from those preceding it"; the ideal type of this new youth, according to him, was "Ernst von Salomon, who, in *Les Réprouvés*, had celebrated the fate of those who had not taken root, who lived the years from 1919 to 1923 violently, who spent the years of ease in prison or in exile."[111] Von Salomon, one should recall, was a member of the Freie Korps, which sprang up in the immediate postwar period and revolted against the Weimar Republic, and he personified the rebel against liberal democracy: the members of the Freie Korps engaged in terrorism and von Salomon was implicated in the assassination of Walter Rathenau. Imprisoned for five years, he was finally pardoned. It was during his years in prison that he wrote his famous book "The Outlaws," in which he related the history of that revolt that was in many ways a prelude to the Nazis' seizure of power.

It was in these terms that Jouvenel explained the rise of Hitler. For the first time in the recent history of Europe, he maintained, events had begun to work in favor of the "dynamic elements." Unlike France, Germany was a country in which "the static element was dying."[112] Thus, a "revolution of youth" had taken place that had culminated in nazism: "On 30 January 1933, this German youth came to power and seized the reins of command." The conclusion to be drawn from this development he thought was obvious: "Victory comes to the man who attaches to his standard the leading idea of his time, which henceforth fights with him and on his behalf."[113]

This sentiment seems to have been shared in many different quarters, and it explains the ease with which the national revolution could be set in motion in the summer of 1940. Seen in the context of half a century of continuous history, the national revolution appears to be the logical consequence of an intellectual trend that, though a minority tradition, was always vigorous and on the lookout for a suitable opportunity. France successfully met the terrible trial of 1914 and something of that victory did credit to the regime. Owing to its slow economic development and its relative backwardness, France escaped the great economic and financial crises of the beginning of the thirties, and so the Republic won a certain respite. But with the great collapse of 1940 an ideology that had infiltrated society for half a century rose to the surface and became a force of profound influence upon the holders of political power.

It was not only the confirmed fascists who wished to participate in the construction of a new France. In this respect there was little difference between Mounier, Hubert Beuve-Méry, Pierre Brisson, and Jouvenel. With the perspective of another half century, we can see that the positions adopted by the founders of *Esprit* and *Le Monde*, like those of the editor of *Le Figaro*, enable us to perceive the real significance of the regime that was being set up. The defeat had rid France of liberal democracy, and the nonconformists would have been very untrue to themselves if they had failed to avail themselves of the opportunity that was offered.

Mounier's ideas contained nothing that had not been said constantly throughout the thirties. In the summer of 1940 he thought that the hour of the great nonconformist confederation had come, and he addressed himself once more "to those young Frenchmen who, *for the last ten years*, coming from everywhere (or waiting everywhere, no matter), have reflected on their period and have committed themselves to the necessary revolution." [114] Mounier invited these "young intellectuals . . . coming '*from the right*' and '*from the left*'" to engage once more in battle against "that form of liberal intelligence that was prevailing yesterday, in order to preserve the values of the spirit." Only now, he said, the fight had to take place in different circumstances, for "one cannot row against the stream of history, and even if one wishes to straighten its contours, it is only by first embracing it that one can influence its direction. More precisely, this means that Europe is taking a totalitarian [word effaced], if one understands by this term the quite vast variety of regimes that have come into being, from Mr. Salazar's regime to the Nazi regime." [115]

Mounier was convinced during that period that Germany's victory would last for a very long time, and he concluded, therefore, that it was "our duty to be present at the event." [116] Hitler's perspective of a thousand years even seemed to him "a bit narrow." [117]

At the very moment when, with the permission of the Vichy authorities, he was relaunching *Esprit*, Mounier, in an interesting article for his American readers, attempted to analyze the causes and significance of the collapse of France. First of all, he insisted on the fact that "our defeat is a defeat for France rather than for the French army; at least for a certain France, and behind her a certain form of Western civilization." [118] The ultimate cause of the disaster, he thought, was the bourgeois spirit, of which he wrote, "That invisible and open wound in the body of the modern world, had completed its work of decomposition," and further

on he said that "individualism is at the root of the evil."[119] Individualism and the bourgeois spirit, then (defined in a manner very familiar
to Mounier's readers), were held by Mounier to have been responsible
for the decline of France, and he added that "a certain form of parliamentary and libertarian democracy heightened this disorder through its
incompetence, irresponsibility, slovenliness and vulgarity—all perennial
evils, but a little too prevalent in our country in the last few decades."[120]
He concluded that "what we condemn is more than a single event, it is
an epoch, and more than a nation, it is a sector of civilization."[121]

Once again, Mounier looked at the recent past to determine the nature of the trouble, what remedies ought to have been applied, and what
direction should be taken from now on. In a text that could easily have
been written by Drieu La Rochelle, he wrote:

A few young Frenchmen for a long time have been saying this in vain to their
own country: the war which shakes Europe to its foundations is not imperialist
but revolutionary. Europe divided against itself is giving birth to a new order,
not only perhaps for Europe but for the whole world. Only a spiritual revolution and an institutional rebirth of the same scope as the fascist revolution could
perhaps have saved France from destruction. The totalitarian countries present a frenzied image of the outlines of a civilization in which we will have
to discover, after them and better than they have discovered, the profound
essence. . . .

After a century of bourgeois languor, the adventurous life again claims its
place in the world. I see the twentieth century as a century of great stature, after
a century that has inaccurately been called stupid, and which was perhaps
worse, mediocre. There is no place in such an era for those who think only of
defending the quiet of their own garden, their own home, their own coun-
tryside, their own habits. The vital question for every nation is to enter into this
epoch with a high and valid purpose. For times of conquest are never easy times.
I do not say that they cannot be times of joy. Our duty is to save the joy of life
from the wreck of pleasure.[122]

Finally, Mounier compared his own period to the Renaissance. He
was certain that enormous changes would happen: the great revolution
of the twentieth century would take place on the ruins of individualism.
"It is the discontent with this individual and with his narrow and deso-
late life which the revolutions of the masses in the twentieth century
express. Napoleon was conquered, the French revolution disappeared;
whatever outcome Americans can imagine for the present conflict, this
century will bring about throughout the world an anti-individualist and
communitarian revolution."[123]

Such was the conceptual framework of Mounier's thinking in 1940.

He regarded the national revolution as the natural conclusion of his long ideological conflict with liberal democracy. He saw the new regime as providing a unique opportunity, and his reactions not only illuminate the deep significance of the nonconformism of the thirties but also help make it clear that the Vichy regime was part of a continuous development. He relaunched *Esprit* not to fight the regime from within but to participate in the building of a new France within a new Europe. He was convinced that an era had died, and he was the last to regret it.

However, as the Vichy regime evolved, Mounier evolved also. Soon enough, it became obvious that the "anti-individualist and communitarian" revolution that he had hailed enthusiastically in October 1940 was developing in a direction quite different from the one he had foreseen. At the same time, Mounier was becoming acquainted with other aspects of national socialism. Göring's sallies of wit that he had once found attractive [124] and the spiritualistic, young, virile side of nazism that had appealed to his imagination assumed a darker cast in the light of the harsh realities of the war and the Collaboration. The outcome of the conflict also appeared to be far more uncertain. On 6 December 1941 the Red Army launched its first great counteroffensive and the German army as it approached Moscow was in danger of collapse: the years of easy conquests and spectacular advances were over. All this was perhaps not fully grasped in the regions of Lyons and Vichy, but, still, it was clear to everyone that the days of the blitzkrieg were past, and that Moscow, Leningrad, and Stalingrad had not fallen. These events no doubt encouraged Mounier to modify his vision of a Hitlerian Europe that fifteen months earlier he had thought he could see lasting a thousand years.

The rest of the story is much better known. In August 1941 *Esprit* was shut down by the Vichy authorities: cooperation was no longer possible between a regime that was becoming increasingly harsh and a team of young intellectuals that was becoming increasingly aware. After the publication of Marc Beigbeder's "Supplements to the Memoirs of an Ass" in the July 1941 issue, the order of prohibition finally arrived, signed by another nonconformist of the thirties, Paul Marion. On 15 January 1942 Mounier was arrested: he figured on a list of names and addresses carried by an agent of the Resistance movement Combat. Provisionally released, he was nevertheless kept under house arrest in Clermont. Finally, on 1 May, he was interned in the residential prison of Le Vivarais, where he began a hunger strike made famous by the BBC. In October, the case of Combat was judged and Emmanuel Mounier became a great figure in the Resistance. Released, he settled in the Drôme, where he lived until the Liberation under the name of Leclerc.[125]

The Resistance drew many recruits from the members of Mounier's group. Their story, and especially that of the school of Uriage, belongs now to the history of fighting France. Yet these events should not obscure our view of the situation that existed in 1940–42, or the fact that the Uriage school had been founded to form the elites of the new regime and not a combat unit of the Resistance, or the fact that Mounier turned to the Resistance only after committing himself to the national revolution. Seen in this perspective, Mounier's development is a good illustration of the ideological continuity represented by the intellectual renewal undertaken by the Vichy government. The dissidents' objective in 1940 was exactly what it had been ten years earlier: to destroy the intellectual and political structures of liberal democracy.

Nearly all the nonconformist groups shared an implicit recognition of the moral superiority of fascist Italy and Nazi Germany in relation to bourgeois and decadent France. "Germany versus the West is Sparta versus Athens, the hard life versus the pleasant life," wrote Mounier in October 1940,[126] and Jouvenel—a great liberal in the postwar period—saw the German victory as a triumph of the spirit. He expressed this opinion in one of his major works, *Après la défaite*. Published in 1941, this book was a classic condemnation of liberal democracy, of the intellectual heritage of the French Revolution, of the political culture opposed by fascism and nazism. He described the Nazi victory as the triumph of youth, of a young people with "communitarian tendencies," over a bourgeois society steeped in liberal values and destroyed by the French Revolution: "The youthful character of Germany and Italy is to be attributed to the fact that, in these countries, youth has been given importance, and that the top has been blown off institutions that, twenty years ago, weighed heavily on it as they still weigh heavily on French youth today." Jouvenel also sang praises to Mussolini and the "brawlers who like to make the bourgeois turn pale" who came to power with him, and waxed enthusiastic about fascist education, which stimulated violence, swept aside the old bourgeois customs, and "encouraged as virtues the blossoming forth of what were formerly called vices." [127]

Jouvenel viewed nazism as part of the continuity of German history, and regarded the conquest of Europe by Nazi Germany as perfectly natural. "The thrust of the German revolution has carried German might far beyond the limits intended by the thought of the nation," he said, "but that is exactly what happened to us at the time of our own

Revolution."[128] The Nazi revolution was thus equated with the French Revolution and Hitler once more compared to Napoleon.

It is not surprising that *Après la défaite* was very popular among the Nazi propaganda specialists. The Germans correctly understood the true significance of this book, and saw its value as a tool of propaganda. After its appearance in 1941, it was immediately translated into German and was published that same year by Herbig in Berlin as *Nach der Niederlage*. Important passages from *Après la défaite* were included in *Phönix oder Asche?*, a large anthology prepared by Bernhard Payr, a close associate of the Nazi ideologue Alfred Rosenberg, and published in 1942 by Volkschaft Verlag in Dortmund. Finally, the book was regarded as so important that the German propaganda services—the Propaganda Abteilung Frankreich-Gruppe Schrifttum—placed it on their list of works to be promoted. *Après la défaite* was recommended together with another important work by Jouvenel, *La Décomposition de l'Europe libérale*.[129] As Gérard Loiseaux has demonstrated, Jouvenel was one of the six French writers particularly favored by the German propaganda services in France.[130]

To be sure, the attraction of fascism and the acknowledgment of the moral superiority of Germany do not in themselves explain the defeat of France. The responsibility for the outcome of the Battle of France does not rest with the rebels but with the most extraordinary war machine in modern history. And yet this was not how the nonconformists saw the situation: to the rebels the defeat of France represented the overthrow of a certain way of life, of a certain political culture, both in France and elsewhere. In France in 1870 and in 1940, in Germany in 1918, in Italy in 1896 after the battle of Adowa, and again in 1919–20, following the psychological sense of defeat engendered by the peace treaties, the blame was attached to the same cause: it was the values of democracy that were responsible for the disasters that overtook the country. These sentiments do not in themselves explain the military defeat, but they help us to understand the ease, the naturalness with which the alternative regime was set up in France and the wide consensus it enjoyed. It was only then that half a century of ideological preparation was able to bear its fruits.

In June 1940 the new France, freed from the enemy without, was able to turn its attention to the enemy within. The aim was not just the survival of the country but also its purification. The accession to office of the new governing elites was made possible by the German victory, but the relatively broad consensus enjoyed by the national revolution was a consequence not only of weariness and a desire to return to normality as soon as possible but also of the long "antimaterialist" impregnation. The discredit that overcame democracy, liberalism, and socialism was rooted in a long tradition—previously a minority tradition, often marginal, but always existing and awaiting its turn.

The new regime did not issue from an ideological vacuum. Where the history of ideas was concerned, Vichy was neither an accident nor an aberration but the logical sequel to the nonconformist attempts at renewal of the whole half century that preceded the collapse of 1940. The antimaterialist rebellion, to be sure, never succeeded in attaining power in a period of peace and stability. As long as no major crisis threatened the country, as long as economic growth, however slight, provided the workers with employment and the petite bourgeoisie with a reasonable purchasing power, the nonconformists were forced to vegetate. As long as the country was not shaken by a military defeat, the republican consensus condemned the revolutionaries to impotence.

With the national disaster of 1940, however, the long antimaterialist impregnation of France finally became effective, for it is always conditions of crisis, confusion, frustration, and humiliation that give revolutionary ideologies the mass support they need. The same was true in Italy and Germany: in each of these three countries, a long-standing ideology of revolt succeeded in occupying the political stage only with the onset of a profound national crisis.

An economic crisis with unemployment is never in itself sufficient to cause such a complete break with the past. The rise of fascism in Italy and nazism in Germany is explained not by the number of unemployed but by the fact that the economic crisis was part of a general condition of distress. In such circumstances, an ideology of revolt can easily fuel a political movement and sustain a regime. It was a crisis of this kind that occurred in France in the summer of 1940. The crisis situations in these three great European countries—France, Italy, and Germany—were quite similar. Allowing for differences in circumstances and in regional traditions, the remedies adopted were also quite similar. In France they involved doing away with the principles of 1789 and the political structures based on the "materialism" of the Enlightenment. Once again the rebels insisted that the responsibility for the defeat rested with individualism and liberalism; once again a national, antimaterialist, antiliberal, and anti-Marxist revolution was carried out in the wake of a great crisis.

Just as in Germany and Italy, it was effected in a country that possessed all the ideological equipment necessary for the application of alternative solutions.

In this respect France, Italy, and Germany were similar—but only in this respect. France differed from its neighbors in two important ways: it had carried out the only liberal revolution on the Continent, and it already enjoyed national unity, and had for a long period. Why, then, was France not automatically immunized against fascism by the liberal vaccine? Does not the example of France in 1940 compel one to reflect on the fact that in none of the three great countries of western Europe that had undergone a long impregnation by a fascist-type ideology was the liberal order able to withstand the shock of a major convulsion? And do not the cases of Britain and the United States confirm the fact that considerable economic difficulties and widespread misery and unemployment are not enough to sweep away democracy?

To bring about a fascist or fascist-type revolution, two conditions are necessary and perhaps even sufficient: there must be an ideology and there must be a major national crisis. In the three major countries where these conditions were met, alternative structures were set up, all of which shared one common denominator: their purpose was to eliminate, once and for all, materialism and its by-products—liberalism, Marxism, individualism, and democracy. The fascist revolution in Italy, the Nazi revolution in Germany, and the national revolution in France all had the same objective: to overthrow a political culture based on the idea of the primacy of the individual. The application of the alternative principle of the primacy of the collectivity varied in accordance with local conditions, but common to all three countries was the belief that only a great spiritual revolution, an antimaterialist, anti-Marxist, antidemocratic, and antiliberal revolution, could save the nation from decadence. These three great antimaterialist revolutions each possessed a different degree of intensity and each necessarily developed in a different manner. The national revolution in France was not always the least violent. The anti-Semitism under Vichy, for instance (not to speak of the behavior of the collaborationists in the occupied part of the country), was far greater than in Mussolini's Italy.

Here we must make one point quite plain: most Frenchmen unquestionably hated the repression that occurred in their country and under the auspices of their government. One might say the same about the Germans and the Italians. And yet, just as fascist Italy and Nazi Germany belong to the history of Italy and Germany as such, so the Vichy

regime is part of the history of France. It was more than simply a parenthesis. Considered strictly on its own, without taking the thirties into
account, the Vichy regime is incomprehensible. While the aspirations
toward a "national," "spiritual" revolution that one found in France
were similar to those that existed in Italy and Germany, the new French
regime had only a very short time in which to act; and yet it needed only
a few months to lay the groundwork of a genuine revolution—the most
significant since 1789. Whereas the setting up of the fascist regime in
Italy took up the whole of the third decade of the century, and Mussolini
had to overcome a great deal of resistance, the Vichy regime required
only one summer to sweep away most of the inheritance of the French
Revolution.

The extent of the changes and the speed with which they took place
can no longer be laid to the charge of the conqueror. Thanks to Robert
Paxton, we have known for more than ten years that the Collaboration
was an option freely chosen by the French and not one imposed by the
Germans. Both the foreign policy of Vichy and its home policy were
freely adopted. Throughout the first year of Vichy's existence, the German authorities hardly intervened at all in French internal affairs,[131] and
1940–41 therefore constitute a kind of test period and the only true criterion for understanding the real nature of the changes that took place.

The revolution would probably never have been possible without the
fascist impregnation and the respectability acquired by antidemocratic
ideas throughout the half century between Boulangism and the Vichy
regime. To be sure, the pure fascists in France, as everywhere else in Europe, were never more than a minority, but fascism owed its real success
to the support it received from outside its ranks, to the fact that its main
concepts—as opposed to its methods—aroused the sympathy of vast
sections of the public. Many different nonconformist circles found it
difficult to remain impervious to the appeal of fascism, or at least to
some of its elements. Far more numerous than is generally admitted
were those who were well disposed toward this revolution for the entire
nation, this cleansing revolution, this opportunity to save the nation by
taking advantage of the fall of the hated regime. From Drumont and
Barrès to Brasillach and Maulnier, from Rochefort to Jouvenel, and
from the Maurras of the affair to the Maurras of Vichy, the rebels did
not confine their activities to a restricted intellectual coterie: they formed
an essential part of French society as a whole. Their books were often
best-sellers, and their journals and newspapers were sometimes widely
popular. After half a century, the cumulative effect of all this made itself

felt. Drumont's *La France juive* was one of the best-selling books of the nineteenth century, while the Dreyfusard press, at the time of the affair, was patronized by only 11 percent of the reading public in Paris and 17 percent in the provinces.[132]

Between the two world wars, however, the situation was different. Drumont, Barrès, and Rochefort were gone, and Maurras had outlived his great period, and yet their successors were by no means marginal figures. If the readership of *La Libre Parole* had been four times that of *L'Aurore* (one hundred thousand versus twenty-five thousand), in 1933 *L'Ami du peuple* still had twice as many subscribers as *Le Populaire*. *L'Ami du peuple* was a typical medium of expression for the popular right of the suburbs that had waged a long campaign against the "fat, the plump, the well endowed" and against monopolies, foreign workers, free education in high schools, and inviting Albert Einstein to join the College de France. With its circulation of four hundred thousand and its eighty thousand subscribers, Coty's newspaper had gained, in the words of Léon Blum, "a kind of emotional hold over its readers and consequently over a considerable portion of public opinion."[133] In 1933 *L'Ami du peuple* sold six hundred thousand copies. Writing after Coty had left the scene, Blum was well aware of the role played by the popular press in the formation of the political climate of the period, and he gave it the importance it deserved. Now, the ideology of the popular press was forged in small reviews of limited circulation like *Combat*, *L'Ordre nouveau*, *Plans*, J.-P. Maxence's *Revue française*, and Jean de Fabrègues's *Revue du siècle*. These intellectual publications effectively served their function, which was to generate the materials for political debate and for the mass media of the period. Taken together, they had not more than twelve thousand subscribers, but the right-wing *Candide* had three hundred thousand readers and *Gringoire* had six hundred thousand. No publication of the left or of the center could compete with *Gringoire*.

During the war, one million Frenchmen freely chose to watch the well-known Nazi movie, *Jud Süss*.[134] This famous piece of racial propaganda was distributed on a purely commercial basis: people had to pay to see it. Similarly, nobody was forced to buy the fascist papers every morning—and they sold by the hundreds of thousands. Nor was anyone forced to make a best-seller of Lucien Rebatet's *Les Décombres*. No French publisher was obliged to sign the censorship agreement with the German authorities in Paris, yet all the major publishers decided to do so.[135]

Without a great deal of sympathy for the antimaterialist revolution beyond the Rhine, collaborationism would never have started up with such success. In October 1940, no pressure was brought to bear on the new regime to make it fall in line with the Nazi racial legislation: because of its intellectual origins, the national revolution took measures comparable to those in force in the two neighboring countries, and particularly in Germany, not for "reasons of state" but to put into practice a policy advocated in France itself for half a century. Far more than the presence of the occupying power, it was the delegitimization of French democracy that explains Vichy legislation. The small amount of resistance this legislation encountered cannot be explained only by the shock of the disaster. One wonders if the very favorable view of the measures taken by Vichy expressed by Pierre Brisson in his paper, *Le Figaro*, did not represent a fairly widespread attitude. "June–December 1940: SIX MONTHS IN THE HISTORY OF FRANCE—The Political, Economic and Social Achievements of Marshal Pétain"—this was the headline of a whole page of *Le Figaro* dealing with the new legislation. The initial paragraphs introducing this page, signed "P. B.," are of particular interest:

On 17 June 1940 Marshal Pétain assumed power. We have thought it worthwhile to draw up a list here of the reforms carried out under his guidance. They are far-reaching, some of them are of great importance, all of them reveal a realistic sense of what is required. They reveal a desire for strengthening and moral recovery worthy of the most decisive trials of our history.

For 180 days, without sparing himself any time, the marshal has devoted himself unflinchingly to saving the country. It would be superfluous to pay him a tribute. He has understood that the conditions for an alliance with the victors depend on mutual respect, and that the first requirement for such an agreement can only be the spiritual union and confidence of all Frenchmen.[136]

Brisson was to become one of the leading opinion makers and one of the most outstanding figures in postwar Paris, as was that other great "molder" of public opinion who came out of the Resistance, Hubert Beuve-Méry, who for a quarter of a century following the Liberation commanded an unprecedented authority among the French intelligentsia. In 1941 the founder of *Le Monde* was not as disapproving of the new regime as a well-established legend would have it. How, for instance, is the reader, even taking the existence of censorship into account, to understand the following declaration made by Beuve-Méry in March 1941? "Consequently, it is a human revolution, as much as a national one, that cannot remain isolated. It allows, it even postulates a daring rationalization of Europe, which the peace of Versailles had ridiculously divided up." [137] Beuve-Méry concluded with the following observation: "That is to say that principles that long determined the fate of Europe—the absolute sovereignty of states, large and small, the European balance of power, the right of neutrality—must give way to a more ordered arrangement of the continent." [138]

Like Mounier, Beuve-Méry attacked the very sources of the trouble: the "150 years of individualism" that had "emptied" man "of all substance," and the "Marxist solvent" that attacks "national communities . . . in their very heart and soul." [139] Thus, "a profound crisis for the whole of civilization" had arisen: the national communities "had reacted strongly" to this crisis, and, "in its turn, which was practically the last, France entered the arena and was late in carrying out its revolution." [140] This reaction to the crisis of civilization, he said, this revolution that France "does not want to, ought not to, miss," was the "national revolution." [141] What were the necessary conditions for the success of such a revolution? Beuve-Méry's ideas on the subject deserve to be quoted at length:

The national revolution in France can be neither radical nor quick, for a number of reasons.

A revolution must have a leader, cadres, troops, a faith or a myth.

The national revolution has a leader and, thanks to him, the main outlines of a doctrine, but it is looking for its cadres. Many old cadres, still solid—too solid—try to persist and to mold the revolution to their own requirements. The new ones often feel the effects of their improvisation.

The revolution is recruiting its troops, but the aging of the population, the softening up resulting from a long prosperity, the stupor following great defeats, the absence of two million prisoners, and the occupation of the greater part of the territory are all reasons why the new spirit can penetrate the masses only very slowly.

The revolution has its ideal, but the trilogy Family, Work, Fatherland cannot immediately attain the explosive force of a revolutionary myth. The binomial formula Person and Community is not yet sufficiently detached from its philosophical matrix. None of these expressions, as François Perroux says, "catches you in the throat" or "hits you in the diaphragm." A long-drawn-out effort, heroic testimonies will be required in order to give insipid or obscure words an immediate resonance for everyone, the value of dogma or a talisman. [142]

For this school of thought, the revolution would thus be a "total revolution," a total "spiritual and material revolution," [143] which would enable "an organic significance to be found in this national union that for years was only a subject for speech and a profitable illusion." [144]

Mounier felt that "France had reached the crisis point where only a conversion can save a man or a country." [145] Accordingly, he said, "we shall have no other concern in the months to come except to help in the delivery of the new world that must gradually be born on the ruins of the old. In the situation in which France finds itself, our readers will understand that we are concentrating our energies on this creative task." [146] It is difficult to see how even the cleverest reader could have regarded these texts as an encouragement to resistance.

In 1941 the national revolution appeared to be the natural outcome of a process that seemed worth exploiting, and that was regarded very favorably even by people who later threw themselves enthusiastically into the Resistance. Of course, we must always be aware of the context in which all this took place. If we look at these events in the context of the collapse of France, we can see that the natural reaction of these people to the disaster was not to rally to Gaullism or the Resistance but to join Marshal Pétain in participating in the national revolution. The reactions of people like Mounier, Beuve-Méry, and Brisson are particularly significant because they help us not only to explain the attitude of a large section of the public but also to understand why the structures of the French state did not collapse in the summer of 1940 and why its personnel—the administration, the police, the army, the church, and other official bodies—for the most part chose to serve the new regime at a time when its sinister character was already apparent.

One must insist on the revolutionary nature of the Vichy regime. Contrary to a well-established idea, the national revolution was anything but "eminently reactionary." [147] The Vichy authorities aimed neither at conserving the status quo nor at returning to the past. Quite the opposite: they forged ahead even faster than the Italians, although, even so, their reforming zeal did not entirely satisfy the Paris-based collaborators. They vigorously dismantled all the structures that had existed for seventy years and unhesitatingly demolished all the 150-year-old principles. At the end of 1940 a new order was established and France changed more radically in a few months than at any other time in its history since the summer of 1789.

The alternative structures that were set up were of a particularly modern character and relatively close to those of the totalitarian systems. Even the importance attached to certain traditional values—as reflected, for example, in the veneration of the family and the village—was paralleled in Mussolini's Italy and was part of the general war against "individualism." As for the benevolent attitude toward the

French church: there again it was a matter of undoing the French Revolution and opposing "materialism." The measures of repression (beginning with the racial legislation), the recruitment of the young, the
reforms in the school system, the propaganda, the manipulation of information, and the attempt to impose a kind of corporatism—were all
aimed at creating a new consensus and a new type of unity. None of
these reforms attests to the conservative nature of the regime, and neither does, finally, the institution of the dictatorship of a charismatic
leader. The peaked cap and old age of the marshal should not deceive us.

Finally, one must bear in mind that, in the situation that existed on
the eve of the Second World War and just after the defeat, this rejection
of the established order posed an insoluble problem. If the Third Republic was a regime that was hard to defend, it was nevertheless the regime of democracy. Thus, a rejection of the evils of capitalism led to a
rejection of democracy itself. The rebels threw aside the last barrier of
democracy, which since the time of Boulangism had consisted of an alliance of all the moderates—of all those who, whatever their revolutionary rhetoric, had been willing to abide by the rules of the game as played
within the context of the republican consensus—and set out in search of
a fourth possibility beyond liberalism, Marxism, and democratic socialism. This path inevitably led to a form of fascism.

The dissidents were far from being marginal figures. Luchaire,
Bergery, Marion, and Jouvenel were regarded by their colleagues as the
most brilliant members of their generation. Jouvenel spoke of Drieu as a
legendary personage,[148] and Brasillach and Maulnier considered themselves Barrès's successors. Who could ever think of Déat or De Man as
only a marginal figure?[149] A dissident is not necessarily marginal. All
these people represented a way of thinking that was widespread; their
relentless criticism of capitalism, always associated with liberalism and
democracy, of the regime of egoism and irresponsibility, their permanent
struggle not only against the weaknesses of the system but also against
its very principles, met with a deep response. The attack on liberal democracy enjoyed a measure of legitimacy because many segments of the
public, beyond the fascists themselves, were actively engaged in criticiz-
ing the established order, so that the fascists appeared to be merely the
radical vanguard of a great army united in one battle against the same
wrong.

Here we can perceive the banality of fascism. In the thirties, fascism
was a political ideology like any other, a legitimate political option, representing a fairly common way of thinking that extended far beyond the

limited circles that described themselves as fascist or, like Brasillach, insisted on the unique national characteristics of French fascism.[150] Fascism formed part of the general interaction of ideas and shared all the ambiguities of the political life of the period. Some of the people and movements that, in 1942, resisted fascism, nazism, and the German occupation ten years earlier could easily have professed ideas that the present-day historian identifies as partly or wholly fascistic, while others who called themselves fascists in the twenties later joined the Resistance (for instance, Valois, and also Jacques Arthuys, cofounder of the Faisceau, who in the fall of 1940 created the Organisation Civile et Militaire, was arrested, and, like Valois, died in a German concentration camp). Thierry de Martel, a well-known rightist, son of the famous anti-Semitic *femme de lettres* Gyp, who was also a militant of the Faisceau, committed suicide when the German army entered Paris. Philippe Barrès joined the French forces in London, while Marcel Bucard was executed for treason on 19 March 1946. Both had been active supporters of Valois. Among the members of the Resistance were also some néos and planists—people like Louis Vallon and André Philip, who refused to accept the defeat of France.

There were pure nationalists who saw the country as separate from the social order or political system that it possessed at any given moment in its history. These were only a tiny minority. And there were also the dissidents and rebels, some of whom (notably Brasillach, Drieu, Déat, and Doriot) were also very bold in their thinking, believing that, to save civilization, one had to impose a new political and social order on the nation and endow it with a fresh spirit. The whole nation, they maintained, had to be drawn into the great crusade against liberalism and Marxism. The point of view of this hard core of fascists went far beyond nationalism, and its true significance lay elsewhere. What was now at stake, from the fascist point of view, was the fate of civilization itself, and, in this gigantic confrontation, nationalism took on a quite different meaning. The members of this school—Brasillach, Déat, Doriot, Marion—never thought of changing sides during the German invasion and occupation. Even when the outcome of the conflict was no longer in doubt, it never occurred to them to betray the cause, for, in this huge confrontation between good and evil, the national interest as narrowly understood, the sectarian egoism of yesterday, had become anachronistic.

Fascist ideology in France extended far beyond the restricted and ultimately unimportant little groups that described themselves as fas-

cist. It was not people like Bucard and Jean-Renaud, or the vague
Cagoulards, who endangered liberal democracy: the most dangerous
enemies of the dominant political culture were the intellectual dissidents
and rebels, of both the new right and the new left. From the end of the
nineteenth century this new right—which was distinguished from the
conservative right not only by its violence, its radicalism, and its rejection of the rules of the game but also by its social concern—was embodied first in Barrèsian nationalism, then in the Maurrassian movement,
and finally in the Jeune Droite, whose philosopher Thierry Maulnier
wanted to be. The new left, on the other hand, entered the dissident
movement with revolutionary syndicalism. In its revolt against historical materialism, it found strong support in the philosophical ideas of
Nietzsche, Bergson, and Croce, as well as in the political sociology of
Pareto and the psychology of Le Bon and Freud. In the post-First World
War period this dissident left, which, since before 1914, had also refused
to be integrated into the liberal-democratic consensus, was represented
by the new revision of Marxism of Henri De Man, Marcel Déat, the
"planists," the "dirigists," and the "futurists," of whom there were then
a great many in western Europe. The new right and the new left together forged that brilliant and seductive ideology of revolt that the historian identifies as fascism, many of whose adherents never wore a
brown shirt.

Many intellectuals could thus be fascists without admitting it, although some, like Drieu or Brasillach, declared themselves as such.
Others preferred not to declare themselves. However, to a large extent,
fascism owed its influence to the wide diffusion of ideas that became a
generally accepted currency. It was not until the end of the Second World
War that the rebels, whether of the right or of the left, were able to recognize that to condemn political liberalism and economic liberalism, so-
called bourgeois liberties and so-called bourgeois virtues, democracy,
Marxism, and "established disorder" at one and the same time meant to
open the way to fascism. No other ideology so depended on the ambiguity and vagueness of thought prevalent in the interwar period.

Thus, the growth of the fascist idea can ultimately be attributed to
the presence of a favorable environment. The pure fascists were always
small in number and their energies were scattered. However, the existence of quasi-fascist channels of transmission—people, movements,
journals, study circles—devoted to attacking materialism and its by-
products—liberalism, capitalism, Marxism, and democracy—created a
certain intellectual climate which was to undermine the moral legiti-

macy of an entire civilization. This ideology of revolt advocated a revolution of the spirit and the will, of manners and morals. It offered not only new political and social structures but also new types of relationships between man and society, between man and nature. In periods of economic growth, abundance, peace, and stability such an ideology has only a limited hold on society, but in times of severe crisis the revolutionary potential of such a system of thought becomes clearly evident, and it can fuel mass movements of an exceptional destructive force. To a world in distress, fascism represents a heroic opportunity to dominate matter once more, and to subdue through an exertion of power not only the forces of nature but also those of society and the economy.

Notes

Preface to the Paperback Edition

1. R. Wohl, "French Fascism Both Right and Left: Reflections on the Sternhell Controversy," *The Journal of Modern History* 63 (March 1991), 91–98. See also A. Costa-Pinto, "Fascist Ideology Revisited: Zeev Sternhell and His Critics," *European History Quarterly* 16 (1986), 465–83.

2. P. Ory, "La nouvelle droite de la fin de siècle," in *Nouvelle Histoire des Idées politiques,* ed. P. Ory (Paris: Hachette, 1987), 362.

3. E. Renan, "La Monarchie constitutionnelle en France," reprinted from *La Revue des Deux Mondes* 84 (1 November 1869), in *Oeuvres Complètes de Ernest Renan* (Paris, Calmann-Lévy, 1947), 505.

4. Ibid., 479, 483, 508, 513, 519.

5. E. Renan, *La Réforme intellectuelle et morale de la France* (Paris: Union Générale d'éditions, coll. 10/18, no date), 25, 46.

6. Ibid., 32, 79, 89, 90, 93–94.

7. Ibid., 29.

8. Ibid., 88, 92.

9. Ibid., 26.

10. E. Renan, "Qu'est-ce qu'une nation? Conférence faite en Sorbonne le 11 mars 1882," in *Discours et Conférences* (Paris: Calmann-Lévy, 1935), 307.

11. B. Mussolini, "Fascismo: Dottrina Politica e Sociale," *Encyclopedia Italiana* 14 (1932), 849.

12. When writing *Neither Right nor Left,* I was unacquainted with John Hellman's excellent study, *Emmanuel Mounier and the New Catholic Left* (Toronto: University of Toronto Press, 1981). This study confirms my general analysis and in questions of detail has taught me a great deal.

13. On those so-called nonconformist movements of the interwar period, see P. Andreu, "Les Idées politiques de la jeunesse intellectuelle de 1927 à la

guerre," *Revue des travaux de l'Académie des sciences morales et politiques,* 4th ser. (2d semester, 1957), 17–35. Andreu's work was not so much an analysis as a testimony by an involved contemporary who looked back with affection on the years of his youth. A Sorelian and a member of the Parti Populaire Français, Andreu describes himself as having been "half a fascist" during that period. See P. Andreu, *Le Rouge et le Blanc* (Paris: La Table Ronde, 1977), 72. The first academic study on this issue was J. Touchard, "L'Esprit des amnées 1930: Une Tentative de renouvellement de la pensée politique française," in *Tendances politiques dans la vie française depuis 1789,* ed. G. Michaud (Paris: Hachette, 1960), 90–120. This work inspired J. L. Loubet del Bayle, *Les Non-conformistes des années 30: Une Tentative de renouvellement de la pensée politique française* (Paris: Éditions du Seuil, 1969).

14. B. Comte, *Une Utopie Combattante. L'École des Cadres d'Uriage 1940–1942* (Paris: Fayard, 1991), 13. In spite of its highly apologetic character, this work constitutes a mine of useful information.

15. J. Hellman, *The Knight-Monks of Vichy France: Uriage 1940–1945* (Montreal: McGill-Queen's University Press, 1993), 94, and see also p. viii. The ethnologist Paul-Henri Chombart de Lauwe analyzed the Italian and German youth movements, and Hubert Beuve-Méry, the Portuguese. Beuve-Méry was Director of Studies at Uriage and Segonzac's *de facto* deputy.

16. For an analysis of that text see the conclusion to this book.

17. Comte, *Une Utopie Combattante,* 202.

18. Ibid., 205.

19. Ibid., 508.

20. Ibid., 535, and Hellman, *The Knight-Monks of Vichy France,* 210ff.

21. Comte, *Une Utopie Combattante,* 213–15; 528–30.

22. Hellman, *The Knight-Monks of Vichy France,* 196.

23. Ibid., 197.

24. Ibid., 305.

25. G. Heller, *Un Allemand à Paris, 1940–1944* (Paris: Éditions du Seuil, 1981), 90. The best political biography of Brasillach is William R. Tucker, *The Fascist Ego: A Political Biography of Robert Brasillach* (Berekeley and Los Angeles: University of California Press, 1975). This work contains an excellent bibliography. The team of *Je suis partout,* with which the name of Brasillach is associated, is the subject of a study by P. M. Dioudonnat, *"Je suis partout": Les Maurrassiens devant la tentation fasciste* (Paris: La Table Ronde, 1973). For a treatment of the subject as a whole, see A. Hamilton, *The Appeal of Fascism: A Study of Intellectuals and Fascism, 1919–1945* (New York: Macmillan, 1973). See also P. Sérant, *Le Romantisme fasciste* (Paris: Fasquelle, 1959). The most recent and illuminating work on these questions, however, is D. Carroll, *French Literary Fascism, Nationalism, Anti-Semitism and the Ideology of Culture* (Princeton: Princeton University Press, 1995).

26. B. de Jouvenel, *Un Voyageur dans le siècle* (Paris: Laffont, 1979), 250–56.

27. B. de Jouvenel, interview with Hitler, *Paris-Midi,* 28 Feb. 1936, 1, 3.

28. Jouvenel, *Un Voyageur dans le siècle,* 250–56.

29. R. Brasillach, "Cent Heures chez Hitler: Le Congrès de Nuremberg," *La Revue universelle* 61, 13 (1 Oct. 1935), 55–74.

30. Berlin Document Center, Abetz file/00814-5. When *Paris-Soir* refused to publish the article, Jouvenel managed to place it with *Paris-Midi*. For the discovery of this letter, I am indebted to Mr. Philippe Burrin.

31. G. Loiseaux, *La Littérature de la défaite et de la collaboration d'après "Phönix oder Asche?" (Phénix ou cendres?) de Bernhard Payr* (Paris: Publications de la Sorbonne, 1984), 70. This thesis for the Sorbonne casts an entirely new light on the issue of the literary collaboration.

32. Jouvenel, *Un Voyageur dans le siècle*, 31.

33. Jean Longuet, "Audacieuse propagande," *Le Populaire*, 29 Feb. 1936.

34. B. de Jouvenel, "A propos de mon interview du chancelier-führer," *La Flèche*, 7 Mar. 1936. It is interesting to note that in the same issue of this journal Gaston Bergery clearly expressed his disapproval of the apologetic character of this interview (see "Il faut répondre à Hitler").

35. P. Andreu and F. Grover, *Drieu La Rochelle* (Paris: Hachette, 1979), 273. On Drieu, see also R. Soucy, *Fascist Intellectual: Drieu La Rochelle* (Berkeley and Los Angeles: University of California Press, 1979).

36. See the conclusion to this book.

37. T. Maulnier and G. Prouteau, *L'Honneur d'être juif* (Paris: Laffont, 1971), 22.

38. Ibid., 19, 12.

39. T. Maulnier, "Notes sur l'antisémitisme," *Combat*, June 1938.

40. G. Heller, *Un Allemand à Paris*, 83–86.

41. H. R. Lottman, *La Rive Gauche* (Paris: Éditions du Seuil, 1981), 298–301.

42. For this aspect of the intellectual collaboration in France, see an excellent study by P. Assouline, *Gaston Gallimard: Un Demi-siècle d'édition française* (Paris: Balland, 1984), 268ff.

43. See G. Loiseaux, *La littérature de la défaite*, 96–98.

44. Ibid., 500.

45. R. Aron, *Mémoires* (Paris: Julliard, 1983), 205. It is interesting to note that in 1979 Fabre-Luce published a text that aroused a violent polemic: *Pour en finir avec l'antisémitisme* (Paris: Julliard, 1979). As we see in Jeffrey Mehlman, *Legacies of Anti-Semitism in France* (Minneapolis: University of Minnesota Press, 1983), 113, "Fabre-Luce's argument in large part is that anti-Semitism is horrendous and would long since have disappeared in France were it not for the annoying habit of the Jews to insist that Vichy's attitude toward them was anything less than benign."

46. P. Péan, *Une Jeunesse Française. François Mitterrand 1934–1947* (Paris: Fayard, 1994).

47. Ibid., 179, 220–21, 288ff, 475.

48. Interview with J.-P. Elkabbache on France 2 T. V. Network, 9 September 1994. See also Péan, *Une Jeunesse Française*, 210.

49. Péan, *Une Jeunesse Française*, 314–15.

50. H. Rousso, *Les années noires. Vivre sous l'occupation* (Paris: Gallimard, 1992), 92–93, 100–101.

51. Ibid., 93.

52. Quoted in Péan, *Une Jeunesse Française*, 315. See also R. Poznanski, *Être Juif en France Pendant la Seconde Guerre Mondiale* (Paris: Hachette, 1994), 415ff.

53. H. Rousso, *Le Syndrome de Vichy de 1944 à Nos Jours* (Paris: Éd. du Seuil, 1990), 174, and Péan, *Une Jeunesse Française*, 314–15.

54. H. Rousso, *Le Syndrome de Vichy*, 174.

55. Péan, *Une Jeunesse Française*, 315.

56. Ibid., 18.

57. Ibid., 77, 99.

58. Rousso, *Le Syndrome de Vichy*, 136–45.

59. Quoted in ibid., 145.

60. See E. Conan and H. Rousso, *Vichy, Un Passé Qui ne Passe pas* (Paris: Fayard, 1994), 292.

61. "L'arrêt de la chambre d'accusation: 'La Milice, auxiliaire des services publics . . . ,'" *Le Monde,* 15 April 1992.

62. P. Milza, *Fascisme Français. Passé et Présent* (Paris: Flammarion, 1987), 8.

63. R. Rémond, "La Complexité de Vichy," *Le Monde,* 5 October 1994.

64. Z. Sternhell, "Ce Passé Qui Refuse de Passer," *Le Monde,* 21 September 1994.

65. P. Birnbaum, "Sur un Lapsus Presidentiel," *Le Monde,* 21 October 1994. This is one of the most important contributions to the debate that took place in the autumn of 1994. See also T. Judt, "Entre le Tabou et l'Obsession," *Le Monde,* 21 September 1994, and M. Ophuls, "Le Prince et le Professeur," *Le Monde,* 22 September 1994.

66. M. Agulhon, *La République* (Paris: Hachette, 1990), 2 vols., J.-F. Sirinelli and E. Vigne (ed.), *Histoire des Droites en France* (Paris: Gallimard, 1992), 3 vols. On Vichy in particular see two recent collective volumes edited by J.-P. Azéma and F. Bédarida, *Vichy et les Français* (Paris: Fayard, 1992) and *La France des années noires* (Paris: Éd. du Seuil, 1993), 2 vols.

67. R. Rémond, *Les Droites en France* (Paris: Aubier-Montaigne, 1982), 231–38 and *Notre Siècle de 1918 à 1991* (Paris: Fayard, 1991), new ed., 259–79.

68. On some aspects of that continuity, cf. Z. Sternhell, *Maurice Barrès et le Nationalisme Français* (Paris: Presses de la Fondation Nationale des Sciences Politiques, 1972; paperback ed. Complexe, 1985) and *La Droite Révolutionnaire. Les Origines Françaises du Fascisme 1885–1914* (Paris: Éd. du Seuil, 1978; paperback ed. 1984).

Introduction

1. I cannot provide full references to everything of importance in this field. To gain an idea of the present state of research on the subject one should refer to the following works, all of which provide a very complete bibliography.

First, there is the most recent study, Stanley G. Payne, *Fascism: Comparison and Definition* (Madison: University of Wisconsin Press, 1980). At the present, this is the best reference work.

A neglected and practically unknown area, the sociology of fascism, has recently been treated in a work edited by Bern Hagtvet, Stein Ugelvik Larsen, and Jan Petter Myklebust, *Who Were the Fascists? Social Roots of European Fascism* (Oslo: Universitetsforlaget, 1980). Concerning France, see Z. Sternhell, "Strands of French Fascism," ibid., 479–500.

One can also profitably consult a number of older and by now classic works: A. James Gregor, *The Ideology of Fascism: The Rationale of Totalitarianism* (New York: Free Press, 1969); Ernst Nolte, *Three Faces of Fascism: Action Française, Italian Fascism, National Socialism*, trans. from German by Leila Vennewitz (New York: Holt, Rinehart, and Winston, 1966) (originally published as *Der Fascismus in seiner Epoche: Die Action française, der italienische Faschismus, der Nationalsozialismus* [Munich: R. Piper and Co. Verlag, 1963]); Eugen Weber, *Varieties of Fascism* (New York: Van Nostrand, 1964); and Juan J. Linz, "Some Notes toward a Comparative Study of Fascism in Sociological Historical Perspective," in *Fascism: A Reader's Guide: Analyses, Interpretations, Bibliography*, ed. W. Laqueur (Berkeley and Los Angeles: University of California Press, 1976), 3–121. See also another collective volume, George L. Mosse, ed., *International Fascism: New Thoughts and New Approaches* (London and Beverly Hills: Sage Publications, 1979), which has an introduction by Mosse, "Toward a General Theory of Fascism," 1–45. Mosse has collected a number of his more important articles in *Masses and Man: Nationalist and Fascist Perceptions of Reality* (New York: Howard Fertig, 1980).

With regard to the different interpretations of fascism, see particularly Renzo de Felice, *Interpretations of Fascism* (Cambridge: Harvard University Press, 1977), and Ernst Nolte, *Theorien über den Faschismus* (Cologne: Kiepenheuer und Witsch, 1967).

Excellent examples of modern Marxist interpretations are Nicos Poulantzas, *Fascisme et dictature* (Paris: Seuil-Maspéro, 1976), and Mihaly Vajda, *Fascisme et mouvement de masse*, trans. from English by Gerard Valland (Paris: Le Sycomore, 1979). The latter is based on Lukács's ideas in *History and Class Consciousness: Studies in Marxist Dialectics*, trans. Rodney Livingstone (London: Merlin Press, 1971).

The problems arising from the study of ideologies are treated in M. Seliger, *Ideology and Politics* (London: Allen and Unwin, 1976). This detailed, often brilliant, not at all facile work gives an excellent comprehensive picture of the subject.

Finally, some aspects of the question with which we are particularly concerned here are treated in Eugen Weber's classic study "Nationalism, Socialism, and National-Socialism in France," *French Historical Studies* 2, no. 3 (Spring 1962), 273–307.

2. See for instance, H. Seton-Watson, "Fascism, Right and Left," in *International Fascism, 1920–1945*, ed. W. Laqueur and G. L. Mosse (New York: Harper Torchbooks, 1966), 183.

3. In its most primitive and extreme form, this approach is expressed by Gilbert Allardyce in "What Fascism Is Not: Thoughts on the Deflation of a

Concept," *The American Historical Review* 84, no. 2 (Apr. 1979), 376–78. Allardyce denies that there is a concept of fascism or a fascist ideology or a "fascist minimum" or even a fascist "spiritual family." As for the various political manifestations that are said to be fascist, he believes that it would be better to call them simply by their names. Thus, there are Fascists in Italy, National Socialists in Germany, Falangists in Spain, and so on, but according to Allardyce there is no general fascist phenomenon. For a much more sophisticated point of view, which, however, also differs from my own, see H. R. Trevor-Roper, "The Phenomenon of Fascism," in *European Fascism*, ed. S. J. Woolf (London: Weidenfeld and Nicolson, 1970), 18–38.

4. The expression is from Ernst Nolte's masterly *Three Faces of Fascism*, 9.

My definition of fascism is a broad one, even broader, in many respects, than Nolte's. It lays the main emphasis on the rejection of "materialism," while Nolte insists on the character of fascism as a "resistance to transcendence" (pp. 429–34).

5. See Sternhell, "Fascist Ideology," 316ff.

6. B. de Jouvenel, *Le Réveil de l'Europe* (Paris: Gallimard, 1938), 148.

7. Quoted in P. Andreu, "Fascisme, 1913," *Combat*, Feb. 1936. See also Andreu's "Demain sur nos tombeaux," ibid., Apr. 1936.

8. See, for instance, P. Andreu, "Textes à relire: Capitalisme et démocratie," *Combat*, May 1936 (texts from Maurras).

9. P. Andreu, "Si j'étais Charles Maurras . . . ," *La Lutte des jeunes*, 20 May 1934.

10. T. Maulnier, "Les Deux Violences," *Combat*, Feb. 1936.

11. G. Valois, *Le Fascisme* (Paris: Nouvelle Librairie Nationale, 1927), 6.

12. Ph. Barrès, "Les Signes du succès," *Le Nouveau Siècle*, 30 Jan. 1927.

13. Valois, *Le Fascisme*, 6.

14. See especially Valois, *Le Fascisme*, 25, 29.

15. R. Vincent, "Retour à Barrès," *Combat*, Mar. 1939.

16. J. de Fabrègues, "Barrès, Péguy, Claudel" and "La Préoccupation de l'essentiel devant les menaces du monde," *Combat*, Mar., July 1939.

17. P. Drieu La Rochelle, *Chronique politique, 1934–1942* (Paris: Gallimard, 1943), 89.

18. J. Doriot, *Refaire la France* (Paris: Grasset, 1938), 127.

19. Valois, *Le Fascisme*, 5.

20. Ibid., 12. See also pp. 7–9, 73. Valois often refers to Sorel.

21. Ibid., 22.

22. Maulnier, "Les Deux Violences."

23. Ibid.

24. Ibid.

25. "Déclaration," *Cahiers du Cercle Proudhon*, Jan.–Feb. 1912, 1.

26. G. Valois, "Notre première année," *Cahiers du Cercle Proudhon*, May–Aug. 1912, 157. The *Cahiers* appeared from January 1912 to January 1914; it was planned as a bimonthly.

27. G. Valois, "Sorel et l'architecture sociale," *Cahiers du Cercle Proudhon*, May–Aug. 1912, 111–12. This issue was devoted mainly to Georges Sorel. See Édouard Berth (under the pseudonym of J. Darville), "Satellites de la ploutocratie," ibid., Sept.–Dec. 1912, 209, and "Déclarations du Cercle," ibid., 174.

The founders of the Cercle were two former revolutionary syndicalists, Berth and Marius Riquier, and six "social" Maurrassians, Valois, Henri Lagrange, Gilbert Maire, René de Marans, André Pascalon, and Albert Vincent.

28. G. Maire, "La Philosophie de Georges Sorel," *Cahiers du Cercle Proudhon*, Mar.–Apr. 1912, 62–74.

29. É. Berth, *Les Méfaits des intellectuels*, quoted in G. Valois, *La Monarchie et la classe ouvrière* (Paris: Nouvelle Librairie Nationale, 1914), cxvii.

30. T. Maulnier, "Le Seul Combat possible," *Combat*, June 1936.

31. Ibid.

32. See, for instance, "Congrès national du parti socialiste de France," *La Vie socialiste*, 9 Feb. 1936, 2, and F. Gaucher, "Sur un programme qualifié de contre-révolutionnaire," ibid., 3 Feb. 1934, 9.

33. See Z. Sternhell, *La Droite révolutionnaire, 1885–1914: Les Origines françaises du fascisme* (Paris: Éditions du Seuil, 1978), 33–76.

34. See Allemane's letter on joining the Parti Socialiste National in G. Hervé, "Le PSN et l'adhésion d'Allemane," *La Victoire*, 8 Aug. 1919.

35. B. Mussolini to H. De Man, 21 July 1930, "Lettres d'Henri De Man," *Écrits de Paris*, no. 184 (July–Aug. 1960), 79.

36. Ibid., 80.

37. H. De Man to B. Mussolini, 23 Aug. 1930, "Lettres d'Henri De Man," 81.

38. H. De Man, "Un Manifeste du POB," *La Gazette de Charleroi*, 3 July 1940, 4.

39. M. Déat, "Rassemblement national-populaire: La Politique générale" (speech at the First Congress of the Rassemblement National Populaire, Paris, 14, 15 June 1941), 20.

40. Ibid.

41. M. Déat, *Pensée allemande et pensée française* (Paris: Aux Armes de France, 1944), 107–9.

42. Ibid., 110–11.

43. Déat, "Rassemblement national-populaire," 19.

44. Déat, *Pensée allemande et pensée française*, 60–62, 65.

45. Ibid., 63, 62.

46. See René Rémond, *Les Droites en France* (Paris: Aubier, 1982); first published, under the title *La Droite en France*, in 1954. In a reference to my *La Droite révolutionnaire*, Rémond (p. 44) sees the revolutionary right as a mere extension of Bonapartism.

47. The great weakness of Bernard-Henri Lévy's *L'Idéologie française* (Paris: Grasset, 1981), a work of popularization, is that it overlooks this essential fact. Lévy, who ill understood the works he used as sources and ignored the requirements of scientific research, makes the absurd statement that there is an ideology common to all Frenchmen that is close to fascism.

Chapter One

1. H. De Man, *L'Idée socialiste* (Paris: Grasset, 1935), 285.

2. Ibid., 284.

3. Ibid., 455.

4. On the intense intellectual activity of the period, see H. S. Hughes, *Consciousness and Society: The Reorientation of European Social Thought, 1890–1930* (New York: Knopf, 1961); J. Weiss, ed., *The Origins of Modern Consciousness* (Detroit: Wayne State University Press, 1965); G. Masur, *Prophets of Yesterday: Studies in European Clture, 1890–1914* (New York: Harper and Row, 1966); and two works edited by W. W. Wagar, *European Intellectual History since Darwin and Marx* (New York: Harper and Row, 1966) and *Science, Faith, and Man: European Thought since 1914* (New York: Harper and Row, 1968).

5. See Berth, "Satellites de la ploutocratie," 202. This text is very representative of this outlook. Édouard Berth was the best-known disciple of Georges Sorel.

6. G. Gentile, "The Philosophic Basis of Fascism," in *Readings of Fascism and National Socialism* (Denver: Swallow Press, n.d.), 53–54.

7. G. Vacher de Lapouge, *Les Sélections sociales: Cours libre de science politique professé à l'université de Montpellier* (Paris: Fontemoing, 1896), 191.

8. Nothing can replace a reading of the texts themselves, and we must therefore refer the reader to these writers' chief works. See V. Pareto, *Traité de sociologie générale* (Paris: Payot, 1919) and *Les Systèmes socialistes*, 2d ed. (Paris: Giard, 1926); G. Mosca, *The Ruling Class*, trans. Hannah D. Kahn, ed. Arthur Livingston (New York: McGraw-Hill, 1939) (originally published as *Elementi di scienza politica* [Rome: Fratelli Bocca, 1896]); and R. Michels, *Political Parties: A Sociological Study of the Oligarchical Tendencies of Modern Democracy*, trans. Eden and Cedar Paul (London: Jarrold, 1915) (originally published in 1911 as *Zur Soziologie des Parteiwesens in der modernen Demokratie*); and the articles in *Le Mouvement socialiste*, in which Michels published many important pieces.

Pareto's writings as a whole are well represented in his *Sociological Writings*, ed. S. E. Finer (London: Pall Mall Press, 1966).

Informative works on Pareto are R. Aron, *Les Étapes de la pensée sociologique* (Paris: Gallimard, 1967), 409–94, and S. E. Finer's introduction. Works dealing with these three writers, their theory of elites, and its implications are James H. Meisel, *The Myth of the Ruling Class* (Ann Arbor: University of Michigan Press, 1962); A. James Gregor, *Roberto Michels e l'ideologia del fascismo* (Rome: Giovanni Volpe, 1979); and D. Beetham, "From Socialism to Fascism: The Relation between Theory and Practice in the Work of Robert Michels," *Political Studies* 25, no. 1 (Mar. 1977), 3–24; no. 2 (June 1977), 161–81. See also R. I. Bennett's reply to Beetham's article, claiming that the theory of elites is as much a part of socialism as of fascism: "The Elite Theory as Fascist Ideology: A Reply to Beetham's Critique of Robert Michels," ibid., 26, no. 4 (Dec. 1978), 474–88.

9. See below, chap. 3.

10. G. Le Bon, *Les Lois psychologiques de l'évolution des peuples* (Paris: Alcan, 1894), 54. See also pp. 54–58, 167–68. The only comprehensive work on Le Bon to this day is N. A. Nye, *The Origins of Crowd Psychology: Gustave Le Bon and the Crisis of Mass Democracy in the Third Republic* (London: Sage, 1975).

11. Le Bon, *Les Lois psychologiques*, 11.

12. Ibid., 6.

13. G. Le Bon, *Psychologie du socialisme* (Paris: Alcan, 1898), 40. "To ignore the role of race is to condemn oneself to never understanding history," he adds (p. 40n).

14. G. Le Bon, *Psychologie des foules* (Paris: Alcan, 1895), 70.

15. M. Barrès, *Mes cahiers*, 14 vols. (Paris: Plon, 1929–57), 2:58. On Barrès and his school of thought, see C. S. Doty, *From Cultural Revolution to Counterrevolution: The Politics of Maurice Barrès* (Athens: Ohio University Press, 1976); R. Soucy, *Fascism in France: The Case of Maurice Barrès* (Berkeley and Los Angeles: University of California Press, 1972); and Z. Sternhell, *Maurice Barrès et le nationalisme français* (Paris: Colin, 1972). There is no lack of apologetic works on Barrès. Good examples are P. de Boisdeffre, *Maurice Barrès* (Paris: Éditions Universitaires, 1962); J.-M. Domenach, *Barrès par lui-même* (Paris: Éditions du Seuil, 1954); and H. Massis, *Barrès et nous* (Paris: Plon, 1952).

16. Barrès, *Mes cahiers* 1:39.

17. Ibid., 14:191.

18. Le Bon, *Psychologie des foules*, 3.

19. On Boulangism, see the works on Barrès (n. 15) and two unpublished works by Jacques Néré, "La Crise industrielle de 1882 et le mouvement boulangiste" and "Les Élections Boulanger dans le département du Nord." Several copies of his three volumes were presented to the Faculty of Letters of the University of Paris in 1959. See also F. H. Seager, *The Boulanger Affair: Political Crossroad of France, 1886–1889* (Ithaca: Cornell University Press, 1969), and P. H. Hutton, "Popular Boulangism and the Advent of Mass Politics in France, 1886–1890," *Journal of Contemporary History* 11, no. 1 (1976), 85–106. The book that was long regarded as the standard work on the subject, Adrien Dansette, *Le Boulangisme*, 15th ed. (Paris: Fayard, 1946), only repeats the accounts of two contemporaries: Barrès, in *L'Appel au soldat* (Paris: Fasquelle, 1900), and the Boulangist deputy Mermeix (pseudonym of Gabriel Terrail), in *Les Coulisses du boulangisme* (Paris: Éditions du Cerf, 1890).

20. Sternhell, *La Droite révolutionnaire*, 33–57, 75–76.

21. G. Rouanet, "Le Matérialisme économique de Marx et le socialisme français," *La Revue socialiste*, no. 29 (May 1887), 395. This is the first of a series of three articles published from May to July 1887 containing a most distressing analysis of Marxism. First, there is Rouanet's attitude to his sources: "We therefore have no need, in order to study Marx's thought, to quote him or his disciples directly, since the role of conscientious translators that his disciples have taken on themselves guarantees the perfect exactitude of their résumés" (p. 402). Moreover, his sources were more or less limited to the *Communist Manifesto*, sometimes at second or third hand. In this connection, see Benoît Malon's series of articles "Les Collectivistes français (les précurseurs théoriques)," *La Revue socialiste*, no. 25 (Jan. 1887): 39–58; no. 26 (Feb. 1887): 107–30; no. 27 (Mar. 1887): 221–43; no. 28 (Apr. 1887): 306–27, which aimed to demonstrate that French socialism preceded Marx's and had its own roots. A few months earlier, the Boulangist deputy Mermeix had already claimed that "this idea, Marxism, which did not originate in France, is not an idea congenial

to our temperament" (*La France socialiste: Notes d'histoire contemporaine* [Paris: Fetscherin et Chuit, 1886], 47). And Rouanet stated in his third article of July 1887 that "to an equal, and even greater, extent than Blücher's soldiers, German philosophy met its rejoinder in France" (p. 83).

22. G. Rouanet, "Le Matérialisme économique de Marx et le socialisme français," *La Revue socialiste*, no. 30 (June 1887), 581. See also 582, 589–99.

23. Ibid., 583.

24. Ibid., 599.

25. Sternhell, *La Droite révolutionnaire*, 77–145. On the Ligue des Patriotes, see also P. M. Rutkoff, "The Ligue des Patriotes: The Nature of the Radical Right and the Dreyfus Affair," *French Historical Studies* 8, no. 4 (Fall 1974), 585–603.

26. M. Barrès and Ch. Maurras, *La République ou le roi: Correspondance inédite, 1883–1923*, ed. H. and N. Maurras, intro. by G. Dupré (Paris: Plon, 1970), 374 (letter of 17 May 1902).

27. "Lettre d'Édouard Drumont à Jules Guérin," *Bulletin officiel de la Ligue antisémitique de France*, no. 1 (1 Jan. 1898), 1. Drumont returned here to an idea he had expressed eight years earlier: "The truth is that in no period, in no country, has the Jewish question been a religious question, but always and everywhere an economic and social question" (*La Dernière Bataille: Nouvelle Étude psychologique et sociale* [Paris: Dentu, 1890], xi–xii).

The standard reference work on anti-Semitism in France before the Dreyfus affair remains R. F. Byrnes, *Anti-Semitism in Modern France*, vol. 1, *The Prologue to the Dreyfus Affair* (New Brunswick: Rutgers University Press, 1950). The best work on anti-Semitism in the following period is Michael Marrus, *Les Juifs de France à l'époque de l'affaire Dreyfus* (Paris: Calmann-Lévy, 1972). See also the following important articles: M. Winock, "Édouard Drumont et l'antisémitisme en France avant l'affaire Dreyfus," *Esprit* 38, no. 5 (May 1971), 1085–1106, and S. Wilson, "The Ligue Antisémitique Française," *The Wiener Library Bulletin* 25, nos. 3–4 (1972), 33–38; "The Anti-Semitic Riots of 1898 in France," *The Historical Journal* 16, no. 4 (1973), 789–806; and "Le Monument Henry: La Structure de l'antisémitisme en France, 1898–1899," *Annales*, Mar.–Apr. 1977, 265–91.

28. "La Ligue antisémitique de France," *Bulletin officiel de la Ligue antisémitique de France*, no. 1 (1 Jan. 1898), 2.

29. J. Morin (pseudonym of Albert Monniot), "Pas d'équivoque," *L'Antijuif*, 18 Feb. 1900. *L'Antijuif*, the weekly journal of the Ligue Antisémitique, appeared from 21 August 1898 to 27 December 1902. Two more numbers appeared in March and April 1903. Directed by Jules Guérin, *L'Antijuif* bore the epigraph "In defense of all the workers" and "Against all speculators."

30. Drumont, *La Dernière Bataille*, 39. See also *L'Antijuif*'s first editorial, "*L'Antijuif* et la Ligue antisémitique de France," 21 Aug. 1898, and J. Guérin, "Les Juifs fusilleurs," ibid., 16 Oct. 1898.

31. Barrès, *L'Appel au soldat*, 465.

32. Marquis de Morès, *Rothschild, Ravachol, et Cie* (Paris: 38, rue du Mont-Thabor, 1892), 39. The most recent work on Morès is D. J. Tweton, *The Marquis de Morès, Dakota Capitalist, French Nationalist*, (Fargo, N.D.: Insti-

tute for Regional Studies, 1972). See also Steven S. Schwarzchild, "The Marquis de Morès: The Story of a Failure (1858–1896)," *Jewish Social Studies* 22, no. 1 (Jan. 1960), 3–26; R. F. Byrnes, "Morès, the First National Socialist," *The Review of Politics* 12 (July 1950), 341–62; and Ch. Droulers, *Le Marquis de Morès, 1858–1896* (Paris: Plon, 1932).

33. Morès, *Rothschild, Ravachol, et Cie*, 46, and see his *Le Secret des changes* (Marseille: Imprimerie Marseillaise, 1894), 78.

34. Morès, *Rothschild, Ravachol, et Cie*, 39.

35. H. Vaugeois, "Notes politiques: Nos trois proscrits," *L'Action française*, 15 Jan. 1900.

36. H. Vaugeois, "Notes politiques," *L'Action française*, 15 May 1902, 823.

37. Morès, *Le Secret des changes*, 84, and see H. Vaugeois, "Notre antisémitisme," *L'Action française*, 15 Aug. 1900, 263: "We wish to assert unambiguously once again that anti-Semitism is essential to any truly French action." Speaking of the electoral alliances that were being envisaged, he added, "There is no better criterion than the Jewish question to test the solidity of the alliances that are being proposed to us."

38. Morès, *Le Secret des changes*, 84.

39. Cited in C. Capitan, *Charles Maurras et l'idéologie d'Action française* (Paris: Éditions du Seuil, 1972), 75. The classic work on the Action Française remains Eugen Weber, *L'Action française* (Paris: Stock, 1962).

40. G. Rouanet, "La Crise du parti socialiste," *La Revue socialiste*, no. 176 (Aug. 1899), 212.

41. There are many examples of the adoration of Biétry. To obtain an exact idea of the cult around him see the issues of *Le Jaune* of 2 and 16 July, 10 Sept., 15 Oct., and 12 Nov. 1904, and of 19 May 1906, in which the poet of the movement, Paul Harel, sang the praises of Biétry.
The only studies of the Jaunes are Sternhell, *La Droite révolutionnaire*, chaps. 6, 7, and George L. Mosse, "The French Right and the Working Classes: Les Jaunes," *Journal of Contemporary History* 7, nos. 3–4 (July–Oct. 1972), 185–208.

42. H. Valary, "Socialisme français," *L'Union ouvrière*, 5–12 Apr. 1902.

43. P. Biétry, "Biétry," *Le Jaune*, 19 Mar. 1904.

44. P. Biétry, "Les Propos du Jaune," *Le Jaune*, 5 Mar. 1904.

45. P. Biétry, *Le Socialisme et les Jaunes* (Paris: Plon, 1906), 320.

46. Ibid., 14.

47. See Sternhell, *La Droite révolutionnaire*, 299–310.

48. On this important subject, see E. Weber, *The Nationalist Revival in France, 1905–1914* (1959; reprint, Berkeley and Los Angeles: University of California Press, 1968), and R. Wohl, *The Generation of 1914* (Cambridge: Harvard University Press, 1979), 5–41.

49. Agathon was the pseudonym of Henri Massis and Alfred de Tarde, authors of *Les Jeunes Gens d'aujourd'hui: Le Goût de l'action; la foi patriotique; une renaissance catholique; le réalisme politique*, 12th ed. (Paris: Plon-Nourrit, 1919), a study of youth that was first published in 1913 and quickly became famous. See also their *L'Esprit de la nouvelle Sorbonne: La Crise de la culture classique; la crise du français*, 3rd ed. (Paris: Mercure de France, 1911).

50. See J. Julliard, *Clemenceau briseur de grèves* (Paris: Julliard, 1965).

51. R. Louzon, "La Faillite du dreyfusisme ou le triomphe du parti juif," *Le Mouvement socialiste*, no. 176 (July 1906). On this whole question, see Sternhell, *La Droite révolutionnaire*, chaps. 8, 9.

52. The proceedings of the symposium were published in H. Lagardelle, ed., *Syndicalisme et socialisme: Discours prononcés au colloque tenu à Paris le 3 avril 1907* (Paris: Rivière, 1908). Boris Kritchewsky and Victor Griffuelhes spoke there, as well as Lagardelle, Labriola, and Michels.

53. H. Lagardelle, *La Grève générale et le socialisme* (Paris: E. Cornély, 1905), 12, 7–11.

54. Ibid., 417, 420.

55. R. Michels, *Le Prolétariat et la bourgeoisie dans le mouvement socialiste italien* (Paris: Giard, 1921), 336–37.

56. Ibid., 337.

57. Hervé's journal, *La Victoire*, is of considerable interest. To sample its contents, one might refer to the following editorials by Hervé for July and August 1919: "Pour la revanche d'Amsterdam," 7 July; "Notre socialisme est national," 9 July; "Zévaès et le parti socialiste national," 4 Aug.; "Socialisme national," 16 Aug.; and "Le Parti socialiste national," 17 Aug. After Giacomo Matteotti's assassination, Hervé wrote, "There is no point in denying, in this journal, where we are basically in favor of Mussolini and Italian fascism, that this Matteotti affair is an ugly affair" ("L'Epreuve de fascisme," 22 June 1924).

58. R. Michels, *Political Parties* (London: Jarrold, 1915), 407. The French edition published in 1914 is an abridgment, as is the edition published by Flammarion in 1971 with a preface by René Rémond.

59. É. Pouget, *La Confédération générale du travail* (Paris: Rivière, 1909), 35–36.

60. G. Sorel, *La Décomposition du marxisme* (Paris: Rivière, 1908), 61–62. (See also 58–60.) The most recent work on Sorel and his school is Jack J. Roth, *The Cult of Violence: Sorel and the Sorelians* (Berkeley and Los Angeles: University of California Press, 1980). See also R. Vernon, *Commitment and Change: Georges Sorel and the Idea of Revolution: Essay and Translations* (Toronto: University of Toronto Press, 1978); M. Charzat, *Georges Sorel et la révolution au XXᵉ siècle* (Paris: Hachette, 1977); I. L. Horowitz, *Radicalism and the Revolt against Reason* (London: Routledge and Kegan Paul, 1961); and R. Humphrey, *Georges Sorel, Prophet without Honor* (Cambridge: Harvard University Press, 1951). Good examples of fascistically slanted interpretations of Sorel in the Maurras tradition are P. Lasserre, *Georges Sorel, théoricien de l'impérialisme* (Paris: L'Artisan du Livre, 1926), and P. Andreu, *Notre maître M. Sorel* (Paris: Grasset, 1953).

61. V. Griffuelhes, *L'Action syndicaliste* (Paris: Rivière, 1908), 37. (See also 6.)

62. H. Lagardelle, "Le Syndicalisme et le socialisme en France," in *Syndicalisme et socialisme: Discours prononcés au colloque tenu à Paris le 3 avril 1907*, ed. Lagardelle (Paris: Rivière, 1908), 36–37.

63. Sorel, *La Décomposition du marxisme*, 58; see Pouget, *La Confédération générale du travail*, 10, 37–38, and H. Lagardelle, foreword to *Syndi-*

calisme et socialisme: Discours prononcés au colloque tenu à Paris le 3 avril 1907, ed. Lagardelle (Paris: Rivière, 1908), 5, where we read that syndicalism endeavors to destroy "hour by hour, as it is created, the mendacious work of the union of the classes sought by democracy."

64. Pouget, *La Confédération générale du travail*, 25.

65. É. Berth, *Les Nouveaux Aspects du socialisme* (Paris: Rivière, 1908), 3.

66. Pouget, *La Confédération générale du travail*, 34.

67. Ibid., 34–35.

68. Ibid., 35.

69. Ibid.

70. Berth, *Les Nouveaux Aspects du socialisme*, 3.

71. Ibid., 54.

72. Ibid., 55–56. On the idea of "social myths" see Sorel, *La Décomposition du marxisme*, 54–55, 62–63; on p. 62, Sorel supports his argument with a reference to Bergson's *L'Évolution créatrice*.

No general work exists on the influence of Bergson on political ideas in France. The only article on this subject deserving of attention is E. Kennedy, "Bergson's Philosophy and French Political Doctrines: Sorel, Maurras, Péguy, and de Gaulle," *Government and Opposition* 15, no. 1 (Winter 1980), 75–91.

73. "Nos maîtres," *L'Action française*, 1, 15 July 1902, 63–75, 145–52. Among the *maîtres* is Voltaire because of his anti-Semitism, Charles Fourier because of his nationalism, and Baudelaire because of his contemptuous attitude toward progress and modernity (15 Jan. 1901, 147–53; 1 May 1901, 730–32; 1 Sept. 1902, 394–98).

74. Ch. Maurras, "Besançon," *Cahiers du Cercle Proudhon*, Jan.–Feb. 1912, 4.

75. P. Galland, "Proudhon et l'ordre," *Cahiers du Cercle Proudhon*, Jan.–Feb. 1912, 31–33; H. Lagrange, "Proudhon et l'ordre européen," ibid., Mar.–Apr. 1912, 97.

76. G. Valois, "L'Esprit proudhonien," *Cahiers du Cercle Proudhon*, Jan.–Feb. 1912, 34–43.

77. É. Berth (under the pseudonym of J. Darville), "Proudhon," *Cahiers du Cercle Proudhon*, Jan.–Feb. 1912, 190–92.

78. G. Maire, "La Philosophie de Georges Sorel," *Cahiers du Cercle Proudhon*, Mar.–Apr. 1912, 80.

79. Ibid., 62.

80. See, for instance, G. Sorel, *Réflexions sur la violence*, 11th ed. (Paris: Rivière, 1950), 8–9, 41–42, 173, 186–88, and review of *La Philosophie de M. Bergson*, by P. Lasserre, *L'Indépendance*, 1 May 1911, 190–92.

81. Concerning Le Bon, see Sorel's enthusiastic review of *Psychologie de l'éducation*, *L'Indépendance*, 11 Apr. 1911, 109–10, and an article in praise of Le Bon, "Sur la magie moderne," ibid., 1 Sept. 1911, 1–11. Le Bon and Pareto also contributed to *L'Indépendance*; see 1 May 1911 and 1 Mar. and 1 May 1912, 155–66, 15–18, 209–16.

82. Berth, "Satellites de la ploutocratie," 187; Valois, *La Monarchie*, xlvii–xlviii.

83. É. Berth (under the pseudonym of J. Darville), "La Monarchie et la classe ouvrière," *Cahiers du Cercle Proudhon*, Jan.–Feb. 1914, 29, 15.

84. Valois, *La Monarchie*, xx, xxvii, lxv, cxvi, 4–8, 63, 152, 348, 356.

85. Berth, "Satellites de la ploutocratie," 209. See the references to Pareto in this article.

86. H. Lagrange, "L'Oeuvre de Sorel et le Cercle Proudhon," *Cahiers du Cercle Proudhon*, May–Aug. 1912, 129; Valois, "Notre première année," 158–59.

87. Berth, "Satellites de la ploutocratie," 201.

88. Ibid.

89. G. Sorel, "Aux temps dreyfusiens," *L'Indépendance*, 10 Oct. 1912, 51–56.

90. A Toussenel, *Les Juifs, rois de l'époque: Histoire de la féodalité financière*, 3d ed. (Paris: Marpon et Flammarion, 1886), 1–3.

91. Morès, *Le Secret des changes*, 79.

92. É. Drumont, *Le Testament d'un antisémite* (Paris: Dentu, 1891), 2.

93. Chronique du mois, *L'Indépendance*, Apr.–May 1913, 114.

94. Berth, "La Monarchie," 12. See also V. Pareto, "Rentiers et spéculateurs," *L'Indépendance*, 1 May 1911, 164–65. The article argues that against the power of money one can only use force.

95. Berth, "Satellites de la ploutocratie," 189; see also Berth, "La Monarchie et la classe ouvrière," 13, and 179: "War is the supreme factor in the making and unmaking of nations."

96. Berth, "Satellites de la ploutocratie," 192, 194.

97. Ibid., 194.

98. A. Vincent, "Le Bilan de la démocratie," *Cahiers du Cercle Proudhon*, Mar.–Apr. 1912, 102.

99. J. Laurent, "Le Cri du jour," *Terre libre*, 15–30 Mar. 1910.

100. Berth, "La Monarchie," 10. See also pp. 27–32.

101. J. Saillenfest, "Fascisme et syndicalisme," *Combat*, Oct. 1936. See also P. Drieu La Rochelle, *Socialisme fasciste* (Paris: Gallimard, 1934), 130.

102. T. Maulnier, "L'État des forces en face de la société libérale," *Combat*, Jan. 1938.

103. Ibid.

104. Ch. Maurras, "Introduction to Aphorismes de politique sociale," *L'Action française*, 15 Oct. 1900, 527.

105. Ch. Maurras, "Politique mortelle et société renaissante," *Gazette de France*, 21 Dec. 1906. See also his "Lectures et discussions: Socialistes et royalistes," *L'Action française*, 1 Dec. 1903.

106. Ch. Maurras to M. Barrès, 3 Feb. 1899, Barrès and Maurras, *La République ou le roi*, 207.

107. Ch. Maurras, "Liberté d' esprit," *L'Action française* (daily newspaper), 4 Aug. 1908.

108. J. Rivain, "L'Avenir du syndicalisme," *L'Action française*, 15 Sept. 1908, 468–69.

109. Ch. Maurras, "Sur le nom de socialiste," *L'Action française*, 15 Nov. 1900, 685.

110. G. Valois, "Patriotes et révolutionnaires," a report presented on 28 Nov. 1912 to the Fifth National Congress of the Action Française, in *Histoire et philosophie sociales* (Paris: Nouvelle Librairie Nationale, 1924), 563.

111. G. Valois, "La Propagande dans les milieux syndicalistes," a report to the Second National Congress of the Action Française, held from 17 to 20 June 1909, *L'Action française*, 15 July 1909, 71–72. Valois recommended to those present at the congress a thorough, careful reading of the "*Mouvement socialiste* library series" and, more generally, all the works of Pouget, Griffuelhes, Lagardelle, Janvion, Berth, and Sorel.

112. Valois, *La Monarchie*, 4.

113. J. Rivain, "Les Socialistes antidémocrates," *L'Action française*, 15 Mar. 1907, 472. See his "L'Avenir du syndicalisme," 477: "The development of syndicalism seems to us an essential element in an economic reorganization of society."

114. G. Sorel, "L'Avenir socialiste des syndicats," in *Matériaux d'une théorie du prolétariat* (Paris: Rivière, 1921), 103. See also p. 107.

115. F. Bacconnier, "La Monarchie de demain," *L'Action française*, 15 Oct. 1902, 15 Sept. 1902, 472 (see also p. 474).

116. Ibid., 15 Oct. 1902, 652; 15 Sept. 1902, 472.

117. Ibid., 15 Sept. 1902, 472–73.

118. L. Thoyot, "Le Salaire d'association dans la corporation," *L'Accord social*, 10 Nov. 1907.

119. F. Bacconnier, "Les Bienfaits du régime corporatif," *L'Accord social*, 15 Dec. 1908.

120. F. Bacconnier, "Conclusion de l'ABC du royalisme social," *L'Accord social*, 20 June 1909.

121. F. Bacconnier, "La Monarchie de demain," *L'Action française*, 1 Aug. 1902, 238. See also L. Thoyot, "Salaire d'association et libéralisme," *L'Accord social*, 20 Oct. 1907.

122. F. Bacconnier, speech to the Learned Societies, *L'Accord social*, 16 June 1907; "Une Année d'action sociale," ibid., 23 Nov. 1907.

123. "Quinzaine sociale," *L'Accord social*, 11 Sept. 1907, and "Un Nouveau Panama," ibid., 13 Mar. 1910; J. Hélo, "La Réforme morale," ibid., 13 June 1909; F. Bacconnier, "La Réunion du 26 mai à la salle des Sociétés savantes," ibid., 16 June 1907; L. Thoyot, "Le Sentiment de force dans les syndicats," ibid., 7 July 1907.

124. Hélo, "La Réforme morale."

125. Ibid.

Chapter Two

1. In *La Décomposition du marxisme*, Sorel mentions Lafargue's observations on "the metaphysical and ethical harlots, Justice, Freedom, Fatherland, which walk the streets in academic and parliamentary speeches, electoral programs and commercial advertisements" (p. 21).

2. H. De Man, *Au-delà du marxisme* (Paris: Éditions du Seuil, 1974), 435.

3. De Man, "Un Manifeste du POB," 4.

4. See his letter to the editor, *La Revue philosophique* 35 (Jan.–July 1893), 509–11.

5. This series of essays, published in *L'Ère nouvelle* from March to June

1894, was reprinted in book form under the title *D'Aristote à Marx* (Paris: Rivière, 1935).

6. The three articles bearing this title in *L'Ère nouvelle*, published from August to October 1894, were republished as *La Ruine du monde antique: Conception matérialiste de l'histoire*, 3d ed. (Paris: Rivière, 1933; 1st ed. 1901), with a foreword by Édouard Berth.

7. Ibid., 159. J. J. Roth, on the other hand, thinks that this article shows Proudhon's influence rather than Marx's (*The Cult of Violence*, 7).

8. G. Sorel, *Le Procès de Socrate: Examen critique des thèses socratiques* (Paris: Alcan, 1889).

9. Sorel, *La Ruine du monde antique*, 44.

10. Ibid., xviii, 44.

11. Ibid., 44.

12. Ibid., 57, 142–43. See also p. 154.

13. Ibid., 143.

14. Ibid., 132–33.

15. Ibid., 132.

16. Ibid., 134.

17. Ibid., 133. See also p.136.

18. Ibid., 133.

19. Ibid., 138.

20. Ibid.

21. Ibid., xix. See also p. 159.

22. Ibid., xiii (quoted by Édouard Berth).

23. Ibid., 177.

24. G. Sorel, "Mes raisons du syndicalisme," in *Matériaux d'une théorie du prolétariat* (Paris: Rivière, 1921), 249. This essay was written in 1910.

25. C. Willard, *Le Mouvement socialiste en France, 1893–1905: Les Guesdistes* (Paris: Éditions Sociales, 1965), 28.

26. F. Engels to P. Lafargue, 11 Aug. 1884, F. Engels and P. and L. Lafargue, *Correspondance*, ed. Emile Bottigelli, 3 vols. (Paris: Éditions Sociales, 1956), 1:235. In 1884, Leroy-Beaulieu had written a work opposing the economic conceptions of Marxism, entitled *Le Collectivisme: Examen critique du nouveau socialisme* (Paris: Guillaumin, 1884).

27. This quip of Marx's quoted by Engels in a letter to Bernstein of 2–3 Nov. 1882 was published in *Le Mouvement socialiste*, no. 45 (1 Nov. 1900), 523.

28. Willard, *Le Mouvement socialiste en France*, 30.

29. Ibid., 160.

30. See Sorel's introduction to his *Saggi di critica del marxismo* (Milan: Sandron, 1903), 5–6. The question of Sorel's role in the beginnings of Marxism in France was taken up again by his first biographer, the Italian revolutionary syndicalist A. Lanzillo (*Giorgio Sorel* [Rome: Libreria Romana, 1910]). See also N. McInnes, "Les Débuts du marxisme théorique en France et en Italie, 1880–1897," Cahiers de l'Institut de science économique appliquée, no. 102 (June 1960), 5–51, and Willard, *Le Mouvement socialiste en France*, 31.

31. See Willard, *Le Mouvement socialiste en France*, 160.

32. P. Lafargue, "Idéalisme et matérialisme dans l'histoire," *L'Ère nouvelle*, 1 July 1893.

33. G. Renard, *Socialisme intégral et marxisme* (Paris: Librairie de *La Revue socialiste*, 1896). See also B. Malon, *Le Socialisme intégral*, 2 vols. (Paris: Alcan, 1890–91), and *Le Socialisme réformiste* (Paris: Derveaux, 1886), and E. Fournière, "L'Idéalisme social," *La Revue socialiste* 23 (Mar. 1896), 257–84.

34. Quoted in Willard, *Le Mouvement socialiste en France*, 167.

35. Sorel, "Mes raisons du syndicalisme," 248. This is not the case, however, in *La Ruine du monde antique*, where the tone is different (see pp. 138–41).

36. Sorel, "Mes raisons du syndicalisme," 250–51.

37. Ibid., 251–52.

38. Ibid., 252. Sorel was referring to Diamandy's article in *L'Ère nouvelle*, 1 Nov. 1893.

39. Sorel, "Mes raisons du syndicalisme," 253. Sorel was writing a preface to Merlino's *Pro e contra il socialismo*.

40. Sorel, *Le Procès de Socrate*, 9.

41. Ibid., 92.

42. Ibid., 13, 9.

43. Ibid., 16.

44. Ibid., 13.

45. G. Sorel, foreword to *Matériaux d'une théorie du prolétariat* (Paris: Rivière, 1921), 39. This text was written in 1914 and first published in 1918.

46. Quoted in Jean Prugnot's foreword to *Lettres à Paul Delesalle, 1914–1921*, by G. Sorel (Paris: Grasset, 1947), 92. Berth's article was in the issue of 15 Sept. 1922.

47. G. Pirou, *Georges Sorel* (Paris: Rivière, 1927), 15.

48. G. Sorel, "Superstition socialiste," *Le Devenir social*, 1st year, no. 8 (Nov. 1895), 753.

49. Ibid., 757.

50. G. Sorel, "L'Éthique du socialisme," *Revue de métaphysique et de morale* 7 (Mar. 1899), 286, 291ff.

51. Ibid., 288.

52. G. Sorel, "Bases de critique sociale," in *Matériaux d'une théorie du prolétariat* (Paris: Rivière, 1921), 170.

53. Sorel, "L'Éthique du socialisme," 292.

54. Ibid., 294. In "L'Avenir socialiste des syndicats," written in 1897 (in *Matériaux d'une théorie du prolétariat* [Paris: Rivière, 1921]), Sorel said that "the weak aspect of socialism is the moral aspect" (p. 124). Further on, he said, "No doubt it is wrong to say that the social question is a moral question in the sense that this statement is given by certain philosophers, but, on the other hand, it must also be said that economic transformations cannot take place if the workers have not attained a superior degree of moral culture. The very idea of the interdependence of phenomena, which is the foundation of historical materialism, makes this quite obvious, yet one often sees the disciples of Marx showing a surprising indifference where moral questions are concerned, and that is because they have realized that the main remedies proposed by the philosophers are not very effective" (p.125).

55. Sorel, "L'Éthique du socialisme," 292.

56. G. Sorel, "Préface pour Colajanni," in *Matériaux d'une théorie du prolétariat* (Paris: Rivière, 1921), 178. This preface was written in 1899 for *Le Socialisme*, a work by the Italian deputy Napoleone Colajanni published in Paris in 1900.

57. Sorel, "Préface pour Colajanni," 177. Sorel follows Bernstein on this point.

58. G. Sorel, "Y a-t-il de l'utopie dans le marxisme?," *Revue de métaphysique et de morale* 7 (May 1899), 167, 174–75. An enormous amount has been written about the problems of interpreting Marx. Two works on the subject are classics, each in its own way: S. Avineri, *The Social and Political Thought of Karl Marx* (Cambridge: Cambridge University Press, 1966), and M. Seliger, *The Marxist Conception of Ideology: A Critical Essay* (Cambridge: Cambridge University Press, 1977).

59. Sorel, "L'Éthique du socialisme," 294.

60. Ibid., 293. See also p. 300.

61. Ibid., 293.

62. Sorel, "Mes raisons du syndicalisme," 263.

63. Sorel, "L'Éthique du socialisme," 293.

64. Ibid., 301. See also Sorel, "Préface pour Colajanni," 177-78.

65. Sorel, "Préface pour Colajanni," 179.

66. G. Sorel, *La Révolution dreyfusienne* (Paris: Rivière, 1909), 36.

67. Sorel, "L'Avenir socialiste des syndicats," 123.

68. Ibid., 131–32.

69. Sorel, "L'Éthique du socialisme," 299.

70. Sorel, "L'Avenir socialiste des syndicats," 123.

71. Ibid., 102.

72. Ibid., 118. See also p. 120.

73. Ibid., 113.

74. Ibid., 105.

75. Ibid., 113–14.

76. Ibid., 118.

77. Ibid., 120.

78. Ibid., 114.

79. Ibid., 119 n. 2.

80. G. Sorel, "Préface de 1905," in *Matériaux d'une théorie du prolétariat* (Paris: Rivière, 1921), 67.

81. Sorel, "Bases de critique sociale," 171.

82. Sorel, "Y a-t-il de l'utopie?," 125.

83. Sorel, "Préface de 1905," 59.

84. Ibid.

85. Sorel, "Mes raisons du syndicalisme," 263.

86. Ibid., 268. See also p. 269 n. 1.

87. Ibid., 284–85 (italicized in the original text). Sorel, one must point out, was a great admirer of Fernand Pelloutier, whom he regarded as "the greatest name in the history of syndicates"; see J. Julliard, *Fernand Pelloutier et les origines du syndicalisme d'action directe* (Paris: Éditions du Seuil, 1979), 9.

88. Sorel, "Mes raisons du syndicalisme," 277. See also Sorel, *La Décomposition du marxisme*, 52ff.

89. Sorel, "Bases de critique sociale," 171. This idea recurs in Sorel's "Préface pour Colajanni," 188.

90. Sorel, "L'Éthique du socialisme," 286.

91. Ibid., 291.

92. Ibid.

93. Ibid., 289.

94. Sorel, *Réflexions sur la violence*, 13.

95. Ibid., 17. See also pp. 18–24.

96. Ibid., 24–28.

97. Ibid., 33.

98. Ibid., 49. See also p. 46.

99. Ibid., 50.

100. Ibid., 185. See also p. 189.

101. Sorel had been one of the first to hail the appearance of *Psychologie des foules*. See his review in *Le Devenir social*, 1st year, no. 8 (Nov. 1895), 765–70.

102. Sorel, *Réflexions sur la violence*, 41.

103. Ibid., 40–43. See also pp. 186–88.

104. Ibid., 43. Bergson's influence on Sorel is very striking; it is particularly strong in his works of the first decade of the century. See Sorel's *De l'utilité du pragmatisme* (Paris: Rivière, 1921), 357–451, an analysis of *L'Évolution créatrice*, as well as his lengthy study of this major work, "Études et critiques: L'Évolution créatrice," in *Le Mouvement socialiste* of Oct. and Dec. 1907 (nos. 191, 193), pp. 257–82, 478–94, and Jan., Mar., and Apr. 1908 (nos. 194, 196, 197), pp. 34–52, 184–94, and 276–94.

105. Sorel, *Réflexions sur la violence*, 279.

106. Ibid., 202. See also p. 315.

107. R. Luxemburg, "Démocratie industrielle et démocratie politique," *Le Mouvement socialiste*, 15 June 1899, 649.

108. Sorel, *Réflexions sur la violence*, 434–35.

109. Sorel quotes Croce in his foreword to *Matériaux*, 4. From 1895 until his death, Sorel maintained a warm friendship with Croce. He wrote him 343 letters, which were published between 1927 and 1930. See Roth, *The Cult of Violence*, 9, 281.

110. Sorel, foreword to *Matériaux*, 4.

111. Ibid.

112. Ibid., 35.

113. Lagardelle, "Le Syndicalisme et le socialisme en France," 8.

114. R. Michels, "Controverse socialiste," *Le Mouvement socialiste*, no. 184 (Mar. 1907), 282.

115. Lagardelle, "Le Syndicalisme et le socialisme en France," 52.

116. Ibid., 50–51.

117. Lagardelle, foreword to *Syndicalisme et socialisme*, 3–5, 8.

118. Ibid., 8.

119. Ibid., 3.

120. Ibid., 5.

121. Ibid., 4–5.

122. R. Michels, "Le Syndicalisme et le socialisme en Allemagne," in *Syndicalisme et socialisme: Discours prononcés au colloque tenu à Paris le 3 avril 1907*, ed. H. Lagardelle (Paris: Rivière, 1908), 26, 28.

123. Ibid., 27, 25.

124. Ibid., 23. See the same formula in Michels, "Controverse socialiste," 280.

125. Michels, "Controverse socialiste," 280–81.

126. Ibid., 281.

127. Ibid.

128. Ibid.

129. R. Michels, "Les Dangers du parti socialiste allemand," *Le Mouvement socialiste*, no. 144 (Dec. 1904), 202.

130. Ibid., 199–200, 202.

131. Michels, "Controverse socialiste," 286.

132. Ibid., 283.

133. Ibid.

134. R. Michels, "Le Congrès des socialistes de Prusse," *Le Mouvement socialiste*, no. 149 (Feb. 1905), 250–51. Michels quotes Engels, who in *La Critique sociale*, wrote to Turati, in 1892, "Marx and I have for forty years repeated *ad nauseam* that a *democratic republic* is the only political form within which the struggle between the working class and the capitalist class can develop to the point where it can achieve its aim, which is the complete victory of the proletariat" (p. 250).

135. Michels, "Les Dangers," 212.

136. Ibid., 201. See also p. 203.

137. R. Michels, "Le Socialisme allemand après Mannheim," *Le Mouvement socialiste*, no. 182 (Jan. 1907), 7–9, 13.

138. Ibid., 14.

139. Ibid., 20.

140. R. Michels, "Le Congrès syndical de Cologne," *Le Mouvement socialiste*, no. 158 (July 1905), 314.

141. Ibid.

142. Michels, "Controverse socialiste," 282.

143. Ibid.

144. Michels, "Le Congrès des socialistes," 251.

145. A. Labriola, "Le Syndicalisme et le socialisme en Italie," in *Syndicalisme et socialisme: Discours prononcés au colloque tenu à Paris le 3 avril 1907*, ed. H. Lagardelle (Paris: Rivière, 1908), 10. Together with Enrico Leone, Sergio Panunzio, Agostino Lanzillo, and many others, Labriola represents the Italian Sorelians. In Italy, the theories of Sorel, mingled with Italian elements, had taken root among the university youth. The followers of Sorel were above all young university students, specialists in political economy and law. In many respects, Sorel was more influential in Italy than in France. In December 1902 Labriola founded the review *Avanguardia socialista*, which soon became the center of intellectual activity of Italian revolutionary syndicalism. Labriola was then

spokesman for the extreme left of the Italian socialist movement that was opposed to the reformist policies of Turati. The opinions of Labriola during this period can be found particularly in *Riforme e rivoluzione sociale*, 2d ed. (Lugano: Società Editrice Avanguardia, 1906), *Sindacalismo e riformismo* (Florence: G. Nerbini, 1905), *Storia di dieci anni 1899–1909* (Milan: Casa Editrice Il Viandante, 1910), and his articles in the syndicalist review *Il divenire sociale*, founded by Leone in 1905, and in *Pagine libere*, a review Labriola ran between 1906 and 1910. Excellent summaries of the history of revolutionary syndicalism in Italy are found in Gian Biagio Furiozzi, *Il sindacalismo rivoluzionario italiano* (Milan: Mursia, 1977) and *Sorel e l'Italia* (Messina and Florence: G. D'Anna, 1975), and Alceo Riosa, *Il sindacalismo rivoluzionario in Italia* (Bari: De Donato, 1976). The work of Leo Valiani on Italian socialism of the period is especially important: *Il partito socialista italiano nel periodo della neutralità* (Milan: Feltrinelli, 1977) and "Il partito socialista italiano dal 1900 al 1918," *Rivista storica italiana* 75, no. 2 (June 1963), 269–326.

146. See E. Santarelli, "Le Socialisme national en Italie: Précédents et origines," *Le Mouvement social*, no. 50 (Jan.–Mar. 1965), 41–70.

147. R. de Felice, *Mussolini il rivoluzionario, 1883–1920* (Turin: Einaudi, 1965), 42–43. See also J. A. Gregor's excellent work on the young Mussolini, *Young Mussolini and the Intellectual Origins of Fascism* (Berkeley and Los Angeles: University of California Press, 1979), 23ff.

148. Lagardelle, "Le Syndicalisme et le socialisme en France," 36.

149. Ibid., 37.

150. Ibid., 37–38.

151. Ibid., 44, 45, 53.

152. Ibid., 53.

153. Berth, "Satellites de la ploutocratie," 195.

154. Ibid., 202.

155. Ibid., 195.

156. Ibid., 195–96.

157. Ibid., 198.

158. Ibid., 201–2.

159. Ibid., 202.

160. Ibid., 203.

161. Ibid., 204–5.

162. Ibid., 206.

163. É. Berth, "Les Revues socialistes allemandes," *Le Mouvement socialiste*, no. 179 (Oct. 1906), 179.

164. Ibid. See also É. Berth, "Prolétariat et bourgeoisie dans le mouvement socialiste italien," *Le Mouvement socialiste*, no. 179 (Oct. 1906), 179.

165. See Sternhell, *Maurice Barrès*, 16–18.

166. T. Maulnier, *Nietzsche* (Paris: Gallimard, 1935).

167. Drieu La Rochelle, *Socialisme fasciste*, 63–65, 68–72, 111.

168. Ibid., 65–71.

169. Berth, "Prolétariat et bourgeoisie," 169.

170. Berth, here, was quite close to Gentile. See Berth, "Les Revues socialistes allemandes," 176. Here Berth refers to Hegel's *Philosophie de l'esprit*,

misquoting, of course, *Philosophie du Droit*. Berth's argumentation has obvious flaws and his notation system is inadequate for purposes of scholarly research. Concerning the Italian philosopher, see especially Gregor, *The Ideology of Fascism*, 210–16, and H. S. Harris, *The Social Philosophy of Giovanni Gentile* (Urbana: University of Illinois Press, 1966).

171. Berth, "Les Revues socialistes allemandes," 176.

172. Ibid., 180.

173. Ibid.

174. Berth, "Satellites de la ploutocratie," 206.

175. Here we must refer the reader to an important article by S. E. Finer, "Pareto and Pluto-democracy: The Retreat to Galápagos," *American Political Science Review* 62, no. 2 (June 1968), 440–50, in which Finer disagrees with the view that Pareto was a protofascist.

176. Berth, "Satellites de la ploutocratie," 296. One should not overlook the fact that some of the basic problems of Marxism raised by Sorel and his school were again raised, immediately after the First World War, by Lukács. During 1918–22 the Hungarian philosopher was close to the syndicalist tradition, and in 1967, in his preface to the new edition of his celebrated collection of essays *History and Class Consciousness*, he acknowledged his debt to Sorel (p. x).

It is not possible, within the scope of the present work, to examine the extremely interesting points of similarity between Sorel and certain of his followers on the one hand and Lukács and the Frankfurt school on the other. It would be especially worthwhile to make a comparative study of the introduction of idealist and voluntarist elements into orthodox Marxist ideology and to examine the idea of the primary importance of cultural rather than economic factors.

On Lukács, see N. McInnes, *The Western Marxists* (London: Alcove Press, 1972), 105–29; Seliger, *The Marxist Conception of Ideology*, 45ff.; and G. Lichtheim, *Lukács* (London: Fontana, 1970). For a criticism of Lukács by the "new left," see a collection of articles from the *New Left Review* published in book form under the title *Western Marxism: A Critical Reader*, ed. G. S. Jones (London: *New Left Review*, 1977), 11–139.

177. Berth, "Satellites de la ploutocratie," 180.

178. Ibid., 209.

179. Ibid., 210.

Chapter Three

1. In addition to *La Monarchie et la classe ouvrière*, see especially Valois's reports to the national congresses of the Action Française from 1909 to 1913, published in the review *L'Action française* and as an appendix to his *Histoire et philosophie sociales* (Paris: Nouvelle Librairie Nationale, 1924).

On this aspect of the development of ideas in the pre-First World War period, see Sternhell, *La Droite révolutionnaire*, chap. 9.

On Valois's intellectual development, see Y. Guchet, "Georges Valois ou l'illusion fasciste," *Revue française de science politique* 15, no. 6 (Dec. 1965), 1111–44, and *Georges Valois, l'Action française, le Faisceau, la République syndicale* (Paris: Albatros, 1975). See also J. Levey, "Georges Valois and the Faisceau: The Making and Breaking of a Fascist," *French Historical Studies* 8, no. 2 (Fall 1973), 297–304, and Z. Sternhell, "Anatomie d'un mouvement fasciste: Le Faisceau de Georges Valois," *Revue française de science politique* 26, no. 1 (Feb. 1976), 5–40.

2. G. Valois, "Le Colonel de La Tour du Pin," *Cahiers des États généraux* 3, no. 17 (Dec. 1924), 481. Mathon also referred to La Tour du Pin: "La Corporation, base de la représentation des intérêts," ibid. 2, no. 6 (Oct. 1923), 27.

3. See, for instance, the passage from *La Réforme intellectuelle et morale* quoted as a heading in *Cahiers des États généraux* 2, no. 6 (Oct. 1923).

4. G. Valois, "La Coordination des forces nationales," *Cahiers des États généraux* 2, no. 6 (Oct. 1923), 132.

5. Ibid.

6. Mathon, "La Corporation," 10–11.

7. Ibid., 17–20.

8. Ibid., 32.

9. Ibid., 22.

10. Ibid., 32.

11. Ibid., 28.

12. Ibid., 32–33.

13. Ibid., 27.

14. Drieu La Rochelle, *Socialisme fasciste*, 226.

15. Ibid., 32–33. On the Jaunes, see Sternhell, *La Droite révolutionnaire*, 245–317, and Mosse, "The French Right."

16. G. Valois, "Sommes-nous des démolisseurs ou des architectes?," *Cahiers des États généraux* 1, no. 3 (June 1923), 234. See also Valois, "La Coordination des forces nationales," 151.

17. G. Valois, "Les Relations de l'État et des diverses classes sociales," *Cahiers des Etats généraux* 3, no. 18 (1st semester, 1925), 696.

18. See the press reviews in *Cahiers des États généraux* 1, no. 2 (May 1923), 261; no. 3 (June 1923), 140–41. It is clear that at that time the movement had gained a certain importance and that the national newspapers spoke about it a great deal.

19. Mathon, "La Corporation," 14, 26.

20. Ibid., 19, 29–30.

21. G. Valois, *La Révolution nationale* (Paris: Nouvelle Librairie Nationale, 1924), 11.

22. Ibid., 162–63.

23. Ibid., 9.

24. Ibid. Concerning the Cercle Proudhon, see Sternhell, *La Droite révolutionnaire*, 391–400.

25. Valois, *La Révolution nationale*, 189, 34.

26. Ibid., 27.

27. Ibid., 49. See also 43, 48, 155.

28. Ibid., 13, 61–63, 98.

29. Ph. Barrès, "Il est bien vivant l'esprit de la victoire," *Le Nouveau Siècle*, 17 Dec. 1925.

30. Valois, *La Révolution nationale*, 59. On the theme of greatness or *grandeur*, see pp. 12, 33–34, 55–56, 59.

31. Ibid., 12, 13.

32. Ibid., 163. See also pp. 12, 50.

33. Ibid., 13.

34. Ibid., 50.

35. Ibid., 13.

36. Ibid., 151–52.

37. Ibid., 153.

38. Ibid., 33, 34, 48.

39. Ibid., 33.

40. Ibid., 9.

41. AN F^7 13208, report of Nov. 1925. The Société Française d'Informations Politiques, Économiques, et Sociales was created for a period of ten years with a capital of fifty thousand francs divided into five-hundred-franc shares. The registered capital was subscribed by:

Franz Van den Broeck d'Obrenan	33 shares
Eugène Mathon	20 shares
Antoine Cazaneuve	20 shares
Serge André	20 shares
Valentin Smith	4 shares
Hubert Bourgin	1 share
Jacques Roujon	1 share
Pierre Masquelier	1 share

On 26 June 1926, the members of the society decided to make a new issue of capital and to bring it progressively up to twenty million francs. The composition of the board of directors was then as follows: president, Franz Van den Broeck d'Obrenan; secretary, Antoine Cazaneuve; directors, Serge André, Count Bertrand de Lur-Saluces, Count Jean de Lapérouse, Eugène Mathon, Jacques Arthuys, and Georges Valois.

42. F^7 13208, 4 Jan. 1926; F^7 13210, 15 Feb. 1926.

43. F^7 13208, minute of 20 Dec. 1925.

44. Valois, *La Révolution nationale*, 140.

45. L. Daudet, "Caillaux contre Valois," *L'Action française*, 8 July 1925.

46. See, for instance, F^7 13208, report of the special representative in Marseilles. Rédier attempted to convince the Constituent Assembly of the Légion that he had "the approval of Maurras for this work of national reconciliation and defense."

47. Ernst Nolte, on the other hand, is of the opinion that the Action Française represented an authentic form of fascism (see *Three Faces of Fascism*). An acquaintance with the work of Nolte, whose views are very different from those expressed here, is essential for the study of the Action Française. Also important is Eugen Weber, *L'Action Française* (Paris: Stock, 1962), the first real history of the movement.

48. F⁷ 13208; see particularly the two major comprehensive reports of 6 Dec. 1925 and Jan. 1926, and F⁷ 13210, 20 Jan. 1926, Nov. 1925: members of the Jeunesses Patriotes helped the Faisceau to maintain order at its meetings in Paris. See also F⁷ 13208 of 10 Dec. 1925, which mentions defections from the Corps des Commissaires and the Camelots du Roi, which, although not numerous, happened every day. Those who left, or were simply attracted by the Faisceau, according to police sources, said they were "fed up." "For years, they say, the Action Française has promised to overthrow the Republic, and has never made the slightest move. If Valois really intends to proceed as he says, we will follow him" (F⁷ 13209, 12 Nov. 1925). The comprehensive report of 6 Dec. (F⁷ 13208) notes that those who had left claimed to be "tired of speeches and tired of policies that come to nothing."

49. F⁷ 13208, 10 Apr. 1926.

50. F⁷ 13210, 20 Jan. 1926.

51. From April 1926, the activist elements who had joined the Faisceau in the hope of some quick action began to show impatience (F⁷ 13210, 21 Apr. 1926).

52. F⁷ 13208, Jan. 1926; F⁷ 13210, 3 Mar. 1926.

53. F⁷ 13208, Jan. 1926; F⁷ 13209, 18 Dec. 1925.

54. F⁷ 13209, 16 Dec. 1925.

55. F⁷ 13210, 13 Mar. 1926.

56. F⁷ 13208, 6 Dec. 1925.

57. G. Valois, "Erreurs et vérités sur le fascisme," *Le Nouveau Siécle*, 24 Apr. 1926. See also Valois, *Le Fascisme*, 15, 16.

58. G. Valois, "Sur la voie glorieuse et rude de la pauvreté et de la réussite," *Le Nouveau Siècle*, 5 June 1927.

59. Ibid.

60. G. Valois, "Nationalisme et socialisme," *Le Nouveau Siècle*, 25 Jan. 1926.

61. From a tract of the Faisceau called "Qu'est-ce que le fascisme?"

62. G. Valois, "Nationalisme et socialisme," *Le Nouveau Siècle*, 25, 26 Jan. 1926.

63. Valois, "Nationalisme et socialisme," *Le Nouveau Siècle*, 26 Jan. 1926.

64. Ibid. See also G. Valois, "Les Nations, laboratoires politiques et sociaux de l'humanité," *Le Nouveau Siècle*, 28 Jan. 1926.

65. G. Valois, "Nationalisme et socialisme," *Le Nouveau Siècle*, 27 Jan. 1926.

66. G. Valois, "Aux travailleurs français," *Le Nouveau Siècle*, 1 May 1926.

67. Valois, "Sur la voie glorieuse."

68. G. Valois, "La Politique ouvrière du Faisceau," *Le Nouveau Siècle*, 26 Sept. 1926.

69. G. Valois, "Le Fascisme, conclusion du mouvement de 1789," *Le Nouveau Siècle*, 14 July 1926.

70. Ibid.

71. M. Barrès, "Les Violences opportunistes," *Le Courrier de l'Est*, 28 July 1889.

72. M. Barrès, "La Lutte entre capitalistes et travailleurs," *Le Courrier de l'Est*, 28 Sept. 1890.

73. Valois, "Erreurs et vérités."

74. G. Valois, "Nous honorons la mémoire de Maurice Barrès," *Le Nouveau Siècle*, 26 Nov. 1926.

75. G. Valois, "Origines françaises du fascisme," *Le Nouveau Siècle*, 27 Apr. 1926.

76. Valois, *Le Fascisme*, 16.

77. Ibid., 19.

78. Ibid., 76–77.

79. Ibid., 106.

80. Ibid., 81.

81. G. Valois, *La Politique économique et sociale du Faisceau* (Paris: Éditions du Faisceau, 1926), 18.

82. Valois, *Le Fascisme*, 18.

83. G. Valois, "La Victoire en chantant," *Le Nouveau Siècle*, 2 Aug. 1926.

84. C. Albert, "Tribune libre: Par le coeur et par l'esprit vers l'ordre nouveau," *Le Nouveau Siècle*, 14 Dec. 1927.

85. P.-C. Biver, "L'Esprit nouveau," *Le Nouveau Siècle*, 20 Mar. 1927.

86. G. Valois, "Chantiers 1928," *Cahiers bleus*, no. 1 (15 Aug. 1928), 14.

87. Valois, *Le Fascisme*, 67, 139.

88. Ibid., 143.

89. The title of an article by Valois in *Le Nouveau Siècle*, 11 Jan. 1928.

90. G. Valois, "Notre journal et notre mobilisation financière," *Le Nouveau Siècle*, 9 Apr. 1926, and *La Révolution nationale*, 162.

91. See the editorial so entitled in *Le Nouveau Siècle*, 23 June 1926, and Valois, "Les Relations de l'État," 696.

92. Valois, "Les Relations de l'État," 691–92, 695.

93. Accused of collusion with the communists, the Faisceau continually reproached them for their lack of revolutionary ardor. See P. Dumas, "La Crise du communisme francais: Il a perdu toute physionomie révolutionnaire," *Le Nouveau Siècle*, 18 Dec. 1925.

94. F^7 13208, reports of 14 and 20 Dec. 1925; F^7 13209, report of 3 Dec. 1925. On 10 February 1926, Valois publicly described the financial pressures that were brought to bear on him to make him change his policies (F^7 13210, report on a public meeting of the Faisceau).

95. G. Valois, "Le Drame monétaire ou l'agonie de l'État libéral," *Cahiers des États généraux* 3, no. 18 (1st semester, 1925), 612, and *Le Fascisme*, 47, 77, 147.

96. G. Valois, "Appel aux travailleurs français," tract 8 published by the Faisceau.

97. F^7 13209, 18 July 1896; F^7 13210, 13, 21, 31 Oct. 1926.

98. F^7 13209, 26 May 1926.

99. F^7 13210, 3, 9, 24 Mar., 8, 30 Apr. 1926; F^7 12950, 6 Feb. 1926.

100. On the structures of the Faisceau, see Sternhell, "Anatomie d'un mouvement fasciste," 21ff.

101. F^7 13210, 8, 27 Aug., 23 Oct., 26 Apr. 1926; F^7 13209, 27 Nov., 7 June 1926, 6 Apr. 1927.

102. F^7 13212, 26 July 1926.

103. F⁷ 13210, 24 June 1927, speech by Valois at the club of *Le Nouveau Siècle*.

104. F⁷ 13212, summer 1926, speech by Valois in Toulouse.

105. F⁷ 13210, 30 Sept. 1926, speech by Valois in Strasbourg.

106. F⁷ 13209, 18 July 1926.

107. F⁷ 13210, 28 Oct. 1926.

108. F⁷ 13210, 6, 15, 24 Nov., 27 Dec. 1926, 22 Jan., 22 Feb. 1927.

109. F⁷ 13212, 22 Nov. 1926.

110. F⁷ 13210, 9 May, 19 Jan., 1 Apr. 1926. The identity of the proposed dictator was never revealed publicly, but within the ranks of the Faisceau General Maxime Weygand's name was the one most frequently mentioned. At the same time, the members of the Faisceau remembered General Charles Mangin, who they believed would have made the ideal leader. The fascists' duty, while waiting for the dictator to appear, was to prepare the ground so that the savior could spring forth at the appropriate moment.

111. F⁷ 13212, 26 Feb. 1928.

112. Ibid.

113. Ibid.

114. F⁷ 13210, 3 July 1926; F⁷ 13208, 3, 9 June 1926. Bardy had the task of keeping order and of running a sort of counterespionage service to defend the movement against penetration by the police. Concerning the gathering in Rheims, see the large dossier prepared by the Security Services. Most of the documentation is found under the classification F⁷ 13211.

115. F⁷ 13210, 1 July 1926.

116. F⁷ 13210, 21, 24, 27 Sept., 24 Nov. 1926.

117. G. Valois, "Réponse à Georges Guy-Grand," *Le Nouveau Siècle*, 9 Jan. 1928.

118. F⁷ 13210, 15 Feb. 1926. There was never really a question of a Fascist International either. It is true that, while in Italy, Valois spoke with the president of the fascist corporations and with the undersecretary of state, Rostoni, with the purpose of organizing an international conference that would bring together all the fascist economic organizations (F⁷ 13210, 21 Sept. 1926). Such a conference, however, never took place. Only once did Valois attempt to establish an international organization: at the beginning of November 1926 he tried to create a "Latin Bloc" that would bring together the representatives of the nationalist movements of Belgium, Spain, Portugal, and Italy, the last represented by Filippo Tommaso Marinetti (F⁷ 13210, 3, 15 Nov. 1926).

119. F⁷ 13209, 23 Nov. 1925.

120. F⁷ 13210, 3, 6 July 1926; F⁷ 13209, 10 July 1926.

121. F⁷ 13210, 27 Sept. 1926.

122. F⁷ 13210, 15, 23 Dec. 1926.

123. F⁷ 13210, 13 Mar., 27 Sept. 1926.

124. F⁷ 13210, 16 Feb., 25 Apr. 1927, 29 Nov., 1 Dec. 1926, 3 Aug. 1927.

125. F⁷ 13208, 1 Nov. 1926. From that moment, it was feared in the Faisceau that the great majority of members would not renew their memberships for 1927.

126. P.P.B./prov. 344, July 1928, report on the structures of the new party.

127. Valois, "Chantiers 1928," 4.

128. Ibid., 11.

129. Ibid., 10.

130. Ibid., 9.

Chapter Four

1. H. De Man, *Après-coup* (Brussels: La Toison d'Or, 1941), 41.

2. Ibid., 91.

3. Ibid., 101.

4. Ibid., 118.

5. De Man, *Au-delà du marxisme*, 35–36.

6. Ibid., 36.

7. Ibid., 43.

8. De Man, *Après-coup*, 88.

9. *The Remaking of a Mind* was published in 1919 by Scribner in New York and Allen and Unwin in London. The best intellectual biography of De Man is Dodge's *Beyond Marxism*. More recently, Dodge has published an excellent anthology, *A Documentary Study of Hendrik De Man, Socialist Critic of Marxism* (Princeton: Princeton University Press, 1979). An intellectual symposium on De Man of a somewhat apologetic character was held in Geneva in June 1963; its transactions were published in three volumes in 1974 by the Faculty of Law of the University of Geneva and in *Revue européenne des sciences sociales et Cahiers Vilfredo Pareto* 12, no. 31 (1974), 1–303.

10. De Man, *La Leçon de la guerre* (translation of *The Remaking of a Mind*) (Brussels: Librairie du Peuple, 1920) 8–9.

11. Ibid., 9.

12. Ibid.

13. Ibid., 18.

14. Ibid.

15. Ibid., 19.

16. Ibid., 15.

17. Ibid., 13–15.

18. Ibid., 12.

19. Ibid., 23.

20. *Zur Psychologie des Sozialismus*, which might be translated "Contribution to the Psychology of Socialism," was published in French in 1927, under the now-famous title *Au-delà du marxisme*, by Éditions de l'Églantine in Brussels. A complementary work, *Der Kampf um die Arbeitsfreude*, appeared in 1927; the French translation, *La Joie au travail*, was published in 1930. A further work, *Die sozialistische Idee*, appeared in 1933, and the French version, *L'Idée socialiste*, in 1935.

21. H. De Man, *Au-delà du marxisme*, preface by M. Brélaz and I. Rens (Paris: Éditions du Seuil, 1974), 35.

22. Ibid., 38. See also p. 418: "I am no longer a Marxist," said De Man in presenting his final conclusions.

23. Ibid., 357.

24. Ibid., 39–40. See also p. 354: "Unlike all previous criticisms of Marx, mine starts with the premise that it is Marxism and not Marx that has to be questioned."

25. Ibid., 357.

26. Ibid., 354, 351.

27. Ibid., 354.

28. De Man, *Après-coup*, 195.

29. *Le Socialisme constructif* (Paris: Alcan, 1933) was the French translation of De Man's *Sozialismus aus dem Glauben*, published in 1929.

30. De Man, *Le Socialisme constructif*, 199.

31. De Man, *Après-coup*, 195.

32. De Man, *Au-delà du marxisme*, 418–22; *Après-coup*, 195–96.

33. De Man, *L'Idée socialiste*, 8. It is quite possible that the publication of Marx's youthful works in 1932 also led De Man, if for only a brief period, to take a milder view of Marx. We know the important role played by these works in influencing the interpretation of Marx in a more humanistic and nondeterministic direction. This conscious reattachment of Marxist thought to the humanist tradition occurred at a crucial moment in European history.

34. De Man, *Le Socialisme constructif*, 181.

35. Ibid., 50.

36. De Man, *Au-delà du marxisme*, 289.

37. De Man, *Après-coup*, 191. According to Guy Desolre, De Man's view of Marxism was based on his experience of Marxist orthodoxy. This orthodoxy was dominated by Karl Kautsky, the leading German social-democratic theoretician, whom most socialists regarded as the proper model to follow. Desolre claims that the Marxism that De Man attacked was really Kautskyism, "an optimistic fatalism" with a mechanistic conception of classes, that reduced Marxism to a form of positivism ("Henri De Man et le marxisme: Critique critique de la critique," *Revue européenne des sciences sociales et Cahiers Vilfredo Pareto* 12, no. 31 [1974], 36–43).

38. De Man, *Au-delà du marxisme*, 420–21. See also De Man, *Le Socialisme constructif*, 50: "We should liberate ourselves from Marxism, not because it is unworthy of its task, but because it has accomplished it."

39. De Man, *Au-delà du marxisme*, 49.

40. Ibid.

41. De Man, *Le Socialisme constructif*, 20. On this theme, see also De Man, *Au-delà du marxisme*, 20.

42. De Man, *Le Socialisme constructif*, 20.

43. Ibid.

44. De Man, *Au-delà du marxisme*, 317.

45. De Man, *Le Socialisme constructif*, 21.

46. Ibid., 21, 23.

47. Ibid., 28–29.

48. Ibid., 40.

49. Ibid., 41.

50. Ibid., 23.

51. Ibid., 23–24.

52. Ibid., 25.

53. Ibid., 24.

54. Ibid., 86–87.

55. De Man, *Au-delà du marxisme*, 346.

56. Ibid., 328.

57. Ibid., 350.

58. De Man, *Le Socialisme constructif*, 127.

59. Ibid., 32, 37–38.

60. Ibid., 40.

61. Ibid., 178.

62. Ibid., 155.

63. Ibid., 157.

64. De Man, *L'Idée socialiste*, 341.

65. De Man, *Au-delà du marxisme*, 419.

66. De Man, *Le Socialisme constructif*, 17.

67. De Man, *Au-delà du marxisme*, 176.

68. De Man, *Le Socialisme constructif*, 59.

69. De Man, *Au-delà du marxisme*, 176.

70. Ibid.

71. De Man, *Le Socialisme constructif*, 9. See also De Man, *L'Idée socialiste*, 374–76.

72. De Man, *Le Socialisme constructif*, 9–10.

73. O. Spengler, *Le Déclin de l'Occident*, trans. M. Tazerout, 2 vols. (Paris: Gallimard, 1931), 2:558.

74. Ibid., 559.

75. Ibid.

76. Ibid., 561.

77. A. Labriola, *L'État et la crise: Étude sur la dépression actuelle* (Paris: Rivière, 1933), 281–82, 297.

78. A. Labriola, *Au-delà du capitalisme et du socialisme* (Paris: Librairie Valois, 1932), 281.

79. Ibid., 16. See also p. 15.

80. Ibid., 22, 15.

81. Ibid., 17.

82. De Man, *L'Idée socialiste*, 374.

83. De Man, *Le Socialisme constructif*, 48–51.

84. De Man, *Au-delà de marxisme*, 54–55.

85. Ibid., 68. See also p. 192.

86. Ibid., 68.

87. Ibid., 192.

88. Ibid., 214.

89. Ibid., 50.

90. De Man, *Le Socialisme constructif*, 90. See also pp. 23, 91–92, and De Man, *Au-delà du marxisme*, 331.

91. De Man, *Le Socialisme constructif*, 51.

92. De Man, *Au-delà du marxisme*, 124.

93. Ibid., 329.

94. Ibid., 123. See also p. 125.

95. Ibid., 126. See also p. 121.

96. Ibid., 126.

97. De Man, *L'Idée socialiste*, 435.

98. De Man, *Au-delà du marxisme*, 424. See also p. 406, and De Man, *Le Socialisme constructif*, 60.

99. De Man, *Au-delà du marxisme*, 374.

100. Ibid., 424.

101. Ibid.

102. Ibid., 155.

103. Ibid.

104. Ibid., 149, 155.

105. Ibid., 433.

106. Adriaan M. Van Peski lists these targets of his criticism, but greatly exaggerates De Man's originality ("La Critique du marxisme chez Henri De Man et chez quelques néo-marxistes," *Revue européenne des sciences sociales et Cahiers Vilfredo Pareto* 12, no. 31 [1974], 13–16).

107. Sorel, *Réflexions sur la violence*, 173–85.

108. DeMan, *L'Idée socialiste*, 287. De Man was also acquainted with Le Bon (*Au-delá du marxisme*, 205) and with Bergson, who had played such an important role in Sorel's intellectual formation (*L'Idée socialiste*, 412–16).

109. De Man, *L'Idée socialiste*, 32.

110. Ibid., 288.

111. Ibid. On the place of psychology in socialism, see also De Man, *Le Socialisme constructif*, 53–54.

112. De Man, *L'Idée socialiste*, 328. See pp. 324–27 on Freud and Marx. On Freud, see also De Man, *Au-delà du marxisme*, 60–68. As De Man himself said, he was the first in Europe to teach social psychology, in Frankfurt in 1929. Others besides De Man concluded, during the same period, that there is no such thing as an automatic, homogeneous reaction of the masses in defense of threatened material interests, but only a conflict between old, preexisting values and new ones. Madeleine Grawitz greatly exaggerates the revolutionary, innovative character of De Man's use of social psychology ("Henri De Man et la psychologie sociale," *Revue européenne des sciences sociales et Cahiers Vilfredo Pareto* 12, no. 31 [1974], 75–76, 84).

113. Grawitz, "Henri De Man," 83–84. See De Man, *Au-delà du marxisme*, 63: "I call a complex—to adopt Freud's increasingly popular terminology—a lasting association of representations colored by a given emotive state and thus tending toward a volition of a given direction."

114. De Man, *Au-delà du marxisme*, 68.

115. De Man, *Après-coup*, 194.

116. Grawitz, "Henri De Man," 76, 84–85.

117. De Man, *Au-delà du marxisme*, 381. See also pp. 160–61, on Freudian psychology, and 137–68, on Adler and Jung.

118. Ibid., 290, 380.

119. Ibid., 48, 384. On voluntary motivation, see also pp. 298, 380, and De Man, *L'Idée socialiste*, 469.

120. De Man, *Au-delà du marxisme*, 384–85.

121. See, for instance, De Man, *Au-delà du marxisme*, 250–51, 333; *L'Idée socialiste*, 174–75, 180; and *Le Socialisme constructif*, 182.

122. De Man, *Après-coup*, 57. De Man says here that what he found in Proudhon was not so much answers to his questions as the stimulus "of the passionate élan of his thought."

123. De Man, *Au-delà du marxisme*, 402. See also De Man, *L'Idée socialiste*, 470.

124. De Man, *Au-delà du marxisme*, 390.

125. De Man, *L'Idée socialiste*, 388.

126. Ibid., 435.

127. De Man, *Au-delà du marxisme*, 402.

128. Ibid., 78.

129. Ibid., 76.

130. Ibid., 85.

131. Ibid., 75.

132. Ibid., 45.

133. Ibid., 109.

134. Ibid., 144–45, 185. See also p. 366, where De Man refers to the ideas of Roberto Michels.

135. Ibid., 107.

136. Ibid., 110.

137. Ibid., 101.

138. Ibid., 107.

139. Ibid.

140. Ibid.

141. Ibid., 103.

142. Ibid., 110.

143. Ibid., 220, 233–34.

144. Ibid., 350.

145. Ibid., 426–27.

146. De Man, *Le Socialisme constructif*, 115.

147. Ibid., 274.

148. Ibid.

149. Ibid., 275.

150. Ibid., 270.

151. Ibid., 270–71.

152. Ibid., 262.

153. De Man, *L'Idée socialiste*, 479. See also pp. 476–77, where De Man shows that in a period of crisis there is a difference in attitude between the unemployed and the employed workers. According to him, they constitute two different classes of workers with different immediate economic interests.

154. Ibid., 477–78. See also De Man, *Le Socialisme constructif*, 200–201.

155. De Man, *L'Idée socialiste*, 478–79.

156. Ibid.

157. Ibid., 495–96.

Chapter Five

1. A. Bergounioux, "Le Néo-socialisme: Marcel Déat: Réformisme tradi-tionnel ou esprit des années trente," *Revue historique* 260, no. 2 (Oct.–Dec. 1978), 389.

2. Bennett, "The Elite Theory," 477.

3. Ibid., 474–75.

4. I. Rens and M. Brélaz, "Introduction," *Revue européenne des sciences so-ciales et Cahiers Vilfredo Pareto* 12, no. 31 (1974), 7–10.

5. Bergounioux, "Le Néo-socialisme," 389.

6. S. Grossmann, "L'Évolution de Marcel Déat," *Revue d'histoire de la Deuxième Guerre mondiale*, no. 97 (Jan. 1975), 3.

7. Bergounioux, "Le Néo-socialisme," 392, 399, 402, 411. This was also the opinion of R. Lasierra and J. Plumyène; in their view, Déat, who was minister of aviation in the Albert Sarraut cabinet from January to June 1936, remained a classic parliamentarian until January 1939 (*Les Fascismes français* [Paris: Édi-tions du Seuil, 1963], 89).

8. R. I. Bennett, for example, overlooks Michels the militant revolutionary syndicalist of *Le Mouvement socialiste* and concerns himself only with the po-litical scientist of *Les Partis politiques* ("The Elite Theory," 474–88).

9. M. Déat, "De l'État libéral à l'État autoritaire," *L'Oeuvre*, 2, 3 June 1941. Throughout their careers, the two men often crossed paths, and they spoke about each other in their works. See, for instance, M. Déat, "Mémoires politi-ques," 5 vols. (manuscript in the Bibliothèque Nationale), vol. 2, chap. 11, p. 15, and chap. 12, p. 5, and De Man, *L'Idée socialiste*, 387.

10. M. Déat, "Solidaires dans l'épreuve," *L'Oeuvre*, 20 Oct. 1940.

11. "M. Henri De Man a parlé de 'la Belgique devant l'Europe,'" *L'Oeuvre*, 24 Apr. 1942.

12. H. De Man, interview by Philippe Frez, *Le Petit Parisien*, 6 Mar. 1941.

13. See the following articles by H. De Man in *Le Travail* of 1941: "Vers la démocratie autoritaire," no. 2 (13 Sept.); "Illusions et réalités de la démocratie," no. 3 (20 Sept.); "Les Mobiles de la démocratie," no. 4 (27 Sept.); "Le Contenu social de la démocratie," no. 5 (4 Oct.); "Échec à la peur," no. 6 (11 Oct.); "Li-bertés concrètes," no. 7 (18 Oct.); and "La Liberté change de camp," no. 8 (25 Oct.).

14. H. De Man, "La Liberté ou des libertés," *Le Travail*, no. 1 (6 Sept. 1941).

15. De Man, "Un Manifeste du POB," 4.

16. J. Guionnet, "A propos d'un anniversaire," *Le National populaire*, no. 54 (10 July 1943).

17. See Déat's speech at the Palais de Chaillot on 26 Sept. 1943, *Le National populaire*, no. 65 (9 Oct. 1943). See also M. Déat, "Principes et méthodes d'une action révolutionnaire," ibid., no. 30 (23 Jan. 1943).

18. J. Guionnet, "Où sont les socialistes?," *Le National populaire*, no. 31 (30 Jan. 1943).

19. L. Rebeix, "Socialismes et socialistes," *Le National populaire*, no. 99 (10 June 1944). Rebeix was formerly a leading member of the Parti Socialiste de France.

20. Ibid.

21. "Le RNP et le parti unique: Le Rapport de Georges Albertini au Conseil national du 12 juillet 1942," *Le National populaire*, no. 10 (8 Aug. 1942).

22. M. Déat, "Librement," *L'Oeuvre*, 21–24 Sept. 1940. The cult of the leader around Déat often took ridiculous forms and was expressed in a pompous manner that is rather rare among the French. This was the only new element in the national-socialist ideology. See, for example, R. Benedetti, "Marcel Déat, notre chef," *Le National populaire*, no. 6 (11 July 1942), or G. Albertini, "Le Chef avait raison," ibid., no. 45 (8 May 1943), and all the reports on the RNP meetings of which the bulletin is full. We even learn of the existence, in October 1943, of "cadets Marcel-Déat"—an organization for ten- to sixteen-year-olds (ibid., no. 67 [23 Oct. 1943]).

23. This report had been commissioned by Marshal Pétain on 3 July 1940. On this matter, see A. Prost, "Le Rapport de Déat en faveur d'un parti national unique (juillet 1940): Essai d'analyse lexicale," *Revue française de science politique* 23 no. 5 (Oct. 1973), 933–65, and J.-P. Cointet, "Marcel Déat et le parti unique," *Revue d'histoire de la Deuxième Guerre mondiale*, no. 91 (July 1973), 1–22.

24. This favorite theme of the ideological collaborationists appears in Déat's articles throughout the thirties, as does discussion of the Déat-Bergery project of "making France a national community in which the salaried elements would be completely integrated, where the farmers would be the backbone, where the family would again become the social unit par excellence, and where the state would take complete control of all the great economic and financial forces. One should add that there should be a purely French foreign policy that would free our country from pernicious alliances and aim at winning it its true place in the Europe of tomorrow" (Prost, "Le Rapport de Déat," 935).

25. Summary of Déat's speech to the Third National Council of the RNP, *Le National populaire*, no. 56 (24 July 1943).

26. G. Albertini's speech to the Third National Council, *Le National populaire*, no. 56 (24 July 1943).

27. Full text of Déat's speech of 18 July 1943, *Le National populaire*, no. 57 (31 July 1943).

28. Ibid.

29. Déat, "Le Discours du chef," *Le National populaire*, no. 94 (6 May 1944). The questions raised by the problem of collaboration—ideological collaboration and political collaboration, voluntary collaboration and forced collaboration—have been treated in a masterly manner by Stanley Hoffmann and later by R. O. Paxton and M. R. Marrus: Hoffmann, "Aspects du régime de Vichy," *Revue française de science politique* 6, no. 2 (Jan.–Mar. 1956), 44–69, and "Collaborationism in France in World War II," *Journal of Modern History*

40, no. 3 (Sept. 1968), 375–95; Paxton, *La France de Vichy, 1940–1944* (Paris: Éditions du Seuil, 1973); and Marrus and Paxton, *Vichy et les juifs* (Paris: Calmann-Lévy, 1981).

30. G. Lemmonier, "La Condition prolétarienne," *Le National populaire*, no. 90 (8 Apr. 1944). Lemmonier was a former neosocialist.

31. "Le RNP et la Charte du travail," *Le National populaire*, no. 67 (23 Oct. 1943).

32. See the unsigned editorial in *L'Oeuvre* of 8 Dec. 1940, as well as R. Château, "Un Syndicalisme sans syndicalistes," ibid., 9 Dec. 1940, and L. Rebeix, "Mort et transfiguration du socialisme," ibid., 10 Nov. 1940. The latter article, which summarizes the main principles of neosocialism, Déat's "Destin du socialisme" (ibid., 6 Oct. 1940), and Montagnon's "D'abord voir clair" (ibid., 26 Sept. 1940) could easily be articles in *La Vie socialiste*.

33. Déat, "Destin du socialisme."

34. P. Thomas, "Servitudes et grandeur du syndicalisme révolutionnaire," *L'Oeuvre*, 10 Nov. 1940.

35. Ibid.

36. P. Thomas, "D'où vient, où va le syndicalisme ouvrier?," *L'Oeuvre*, 4 Dec. 1940. In this connection, we learn from Georges Albertini that the very name of another collaborationist left-wing journal, *L'Atelier*, "was taken from that of the first French syndicalist journal founded in 1840 by the Saint-Simonian Buchez" ("La Maçonnerie et nous," *Le National populaire*, no. 44 [1 May 1943]).

37. M. Déat, "Le Tournant de la liberté," *L'Oeuvre*, 31 Oct. 1940.

38. M. Déat, "Ordre et justice sociale," *Le National populaire*, no. 89 (1 Apr. 1944).

39. M. Deát, "De l'Action française au parti unique." *L'Oeuvre*, 15 Dec. 1940.

40. Ibid. See, for instance, the following articles by Déat in *L'Oeuvre* of 1940: "Le Parti unique de la réconstruction," 8 July; "Révolution nationale," 10 July, 13 Oct.; "Révolution dans tous les cas," 26 Dec.; "Le Parti et l'État," 21 Dec.; "Le Parti fera la Révolution," 22 Dec.; "Structure et fonction du parti," 23 Dec.; and "La Révolution nationale est dans l'opposition," 14 Dec.

41. B. Montagnon, "Horizons révolutionnaires," *L'Oeuvre*, 4 Oct. 1940; M. Déat, "Mais où sont les hommes nouveaux?," ibid., 1 Oct. 1940, and "L'Individu et la nation," ibid., 7 Oct. 1940.

42. See M. Déat, "Vers le parti unique," *Le National populaire*, no. 1 (6 June 1942).

43. Ibid.

44. G. Albertini, "Ni droite, ni gauche," *Le National populaire*, no. 2 (13 June 1942).

45. Ibid.

46. Report of the Central Council of 5 June 1943, *Le National populaire*, no. 50 (12 June 1943).

47. Speech of Déat, *Le National populaire*, no. 64 (2 Oct. 1943).

48. A. Philip, *Henri De Man et la crise doctrinale du socialisme* (Paris: Librairie Universitaire J. Gamber, 1928), 49–50.

49. Ibid., 49.

50. Ibid.

51. Ibid., 48–49.

52. M. Déat, "Le Socialisme spiritualiste," *L'Étudiant socialiste*, 6th year, no. 2 (Nov. 1930). This is an account of a lecture given during a study week at Uccle organized by the socialist students of Belgium.

53. M. Déat, "Notes pour l'action," *La Vie socialiste*, 21 July 1928, 10.

54. F. Gaucher, *Contribution à l'histoire du socialisme français (1905–1933)* (Paris: Les Presses Modernes, 1934), 132 (originally a thesis for a doctorate in law).

55. Ibid., 138.

56. Ibid., 138–42.

57. Ibid., 145.

58. Ibid., 147–48.

59. Ibid., 149.

60. Ibid.

61. Ibid., 116.

62. Philip, *Henri De Man*, 20.

63. Ibid.

64. Like the vast majority of French socialists, Montagnon based his criticism of Marxism on secondhand sources (*Grandeur et servitude socialistes* [Paris: Librairie Valois, 1929], 16ff.). However respectable these sources were (Montagnon followed Jaurès), one is nevertheless dealing with a vulgarization of Marxism, and ideas that were commonplace or "in the air" at that time.

65. Ibid., 10.

66. Ibid., chaps. 2, 3, 4.

67. Ibid., 39–40.

68. Ibid., 41.

69. Ibid., 57.

70. Ibid., 72.

71. Ibid. See also pp. 87–88.

72. Ibid., 90–92.

73. Ibid., 162–63.

74. Ibid., 101.

75. Ibid., 118–21.

76. Ibid., 126.

77. Ibid., 127.

78. Ibid., 126–27.

79. Ibid., 127.

80. Ibid., 101.

81. Labriola, *Au-delà du capitalisme*, 14.

82. C. Rosselli, *Socialisme libéral*, trans. from Italian by Stefan Priacel (Paris: Librairie Valois, 1930), 5.

83. Ibid., 6.

84. Ibid., 9–45.

85. Ibid., 114.

86. Ibid., 115. See p. 116ff. on De Man.

87. Ibid., 131.

88. Ibid. See also p. 137ff.

89. Gaucher, *Contribution à l'histoire du socialisme français*, 30, 120–23, 136–43, 261–64.

90. Ibid., 128, 143–47, 163.

91. G. Lefranc, P. Boivin, and M. Deixonne, *Révolution constructive* (Paris: Librairie Valois, 1932), 27.

92. Ibid.

93. Ibid., 29. See also p. 121 on "the mirage of power."

94. Ibid., 174. See also pp. 175–76.

95. Ibid., 178.

96. Ibid., 218.

97. G. Lefranc, *Histoire des doctrines sociales dans l'Europe contemporaine* (Paris: Aubier, 1960), 235. *Le National populaire* of 19 Sept. 1942 published an exact and detailed *curriculum vitae* of Déat.

98. Lefranc, *Histoire des doctrines sociales*, 235.

99. J. Lebas, *Le Socialisme, but et moyen: Suivi de la réfutation d'un néo-socialisme* (Lille: Imprimerie Ouvrière, 1931).

100. Statutory reports: twenty-eighth congress of the socialist party, Tours, 24–27 May 1931, *La Vie socialiste*, 6 June 1931, 12. See also Henri Siriez, "Deux conceptions socialistes de l'État: Le Néo-socialisme en bonne compagnie," ibid., 25 Apr. 1931, 9–11.

101. Lebas, *Le Socialisme*, 35–36.

102. Ibid., 42.

103. Ibid., 48.

104. Ibid.

105. Ibid., 49–50.

106. Ibid., 50. See also p. 60ff.

107. Ibid., 63.

108. Déat "Mémoires politiques," vol. 2, chap. 11, p. 6. The first part of these memoirs is entitled "The Massacre of the Possibilities," the second "The Fight for the Impossible."

Déat's "Mémoires politiques" is a remarkable work. To a careful reader who comes to them after gaining a good knowledge of Déat's writings—his books and the enormous mass of his journalistic pieces—they do not really reveal anything new, but they are written with a cogency and readability that never flag. Admirably written and obviously intended for publication, this manuscript is neither an apology nor an *a posteriori* reconstruction but rather a testimony that faithfully reflects the realities of Déat's period.

109. Ibid., 5.

110. Ibid. See also chap. 9, p. 31, where Déat complains of not having been supported by Blum in the parliamentary elections of 1928. He accuses the party leader of having refused his support and aided his rival, who had helped Blum's son, an engineer, to obtain a position with Hispano-Suiza.

111. Ibid., chap. 4, p. 21; chap. 7, p. 28; chap. 8, p. 26.

112. Ibid., chap. 11, p. 1.

113. Ibid., vol. 3, chap. 18, p. 3.

114. Ibid., vol. 2, chap. 13, p. 13.

115. M. Déat, "Après deux ans," *Le Front*, 2 Nov. 1935. See also his "Mémoires politiques," vol. 2, chap. 11, p. 3, and chap. 13 of vol. 2.

116. M. Déat, *Perspectives socialistes* (Paris: Librairie Valois, 1930), 47–49.

117. Ibid., 60.

118. Ibid.

119. Ibid.

120. M. Déat, "Réflexions sur quelques critiques," *La Vie socialiste*, 31 Jan. 1931, 5. *Perspectives socialistes* had been reviewed by Séverac in *La Bataille socialiste* of 23 Dec. 1930.

121. Déat, *Perspectives socialistes*, 10. On p. 135, Déat speaks of the "flexible framework of a broad doctrine."

122. Ibid., 62, 9.

123. Ibid., 62.

124. Ibid., 8–10.

125. Ibid., 133–34.

126. Ibid.

127. Déat, "Réflexions sur quelques critiques."

128. On the other hand, Renaudel, a former associate of Jaurès's, continued to insist on the socialist character of anticapitalism. The coming together, he said, of the proletariat, "all the forces of peasant democracy," and all the other victims of capitalist exploitation was "socialism that is expanding and not socialism that is retreating or diminishing" ("Les Difficultés et les tâches," *La Vie socialiste*, 6 Jan. 1934, 1).

129. Déat, "Réflexions sur quelques critiques," 6.

130. M. Déat, "Après la constitution du cabinet Doumergue: Sang-froid et raison," *La Vie socialiste*, 17 Feb. 1934, 2.

131. B. de Jouvenel, "Qu'est-ce que l'anticapitalisme?," *La Tribune des fonctionnaires*, 16 Dec. 1933. See also L. Vallon, "Points de vue et façons de voir: Économie contrainte ou économie consciente," *La Vie socialiste*, 13 Jan. 1934, 7.

132. H. De Man, "Pour un socialisme renouvelé: L'Anticapitalisme des classes moyennes," *La Vie socialiste*, 4 Nov. 1933, 9.

133. R. Bobin, "L'Adoption du Plan De Man au Congrès du POB: Le Discours d'Henri De Man au Congrés du POB," *La Vie socialiste*, 6 Jan. 1934, 10.

134. B. Montagnon in Montagnon, A. Marquet, and M. Déat, *Néo-socialisme? Ordre, autorité, nation*, preface and commentary by Max Bonnafous (Paris: Grasset, 1933), 26.

135. L. Capdeville, "Points de vue et façons de voir," *La Vie socialiste*, 3 Feb. 1934, 6.

136. B. Montagnon in Montagnon, Marquet, and Déat, *Néo-socialisme?*, 25–26; editorial, *La Flèche*, 27 Mar. 1937; Doriot, *Refaire la France*, 22–25, 30.

137. G. Izard, "Classes moyennes, votre union est indispensable à la rénovation française," *La Flèche*, 27 Mar. 1937.

138. Ibid.

139. Doriot, *Refaire la France*, 22.

140. See De Man, "Pour un socialisme renouvelé," 7.

141. See especially De Man, "Pour un socialisme renouvelé," 7–8, and Jouvenel, *Le Réveil de l'Europe*, 122–24.

142. De Man, *La Leçon de la guerre*, 37–39.

143. Ibid., 32.

144. Ibid., 39.

145. Ibid., 9–10.

146. B. de Jouvenel, *L'Économie dirigée* (Paris: Valois, 1928), 28–29, 43, 127.

147. R. Bobin, "Henri De Man et le nationalisme économique," *La Vie socialiste*, 14 July 1934, 4.

148. Ibid., 6.

149. M. Bonnafous in Montagnon, Marquet, and Déat, *Néo-socialisme?*, 135–36.

150. G. Izard, "Notre doctrine: L'Idée frontiste libérera tous les peuples," *La Flèche*, 11 May 1935. On this theme see P. Birnbaum, *Le Peuple et les gros: Histoire d'un mythe* (Paris: Grasset, 1979).

151. M. Déat, "Syndicalisme et corporation," *La Vie socialiste*, 17 Mar. 1934, 2.

152. Ibid.

153. M. Déat, "La Vie politique: Présentation du cabinet Doumergue," *La Vie socialiste*, 17 Feb. 1934, 10.

154. Bobin, "Henri De Man," 6.

155. M. Déat, "Vers une nouvelle économie: Actualité de la corporation," *La Vie socialiste*, 7 Apr. 1934, 1–3.

156. *La Flèche*, 3 Mar. 1939.

157. Izard, "Notre doctrine."

158. Doriot, *Refaire la France*, 42.

159. R. Loustau, *Un Ordre social français: Rapport de Robert Loustau* (Paris: Éditions du PPF, n.d.), 3–4 (report to the second national congress of the PPF, 12 Mar. 1938).

160. Ibid.

161. Ibid., 5.

162. Doriot, *Refaire la France*, 45.

163. Ibid.

164. R. Loustau, *Notre doctrine devant le problème social* (Paris: Éditions du PPF, n.d.) (PPF propaganda pamphlet).

165. Drieu La Rochelle, *Socialisme fasciste*, 108.

166. Ibid., 23, 28–29.

167. Ibid., 47–48.

168. Ibid., 49–50.

169. Doriot, *Refaire la France*, 107.

170. Ibid.

171. Ibid., 108.

172. Ibid., 107–8. For a textual comparison see Sternhell, *La Droite révolutionnaire*, chaps. 6, 7.

173. Loustau, *Un Ordre social français*, 5.

174. J. de Fabrègues, "Libérer le prolétariat," *Combat*, July 1937.

175. Ibid.

176. M. Déat, "Démocratie et salariat," *La Vie socialiste*, 15 Feb. 1930, 9. The writers of *La Vie socialiste* liked to present Jaurès as the true spiritual progenitor of neosocialism, as the only socialist leader of his period to possess, like Déat in 1930, a sense of the national interest; see Montagnon, Marquet, and Déat, *Néo-socialisme?*, 136–37. Concerning Déat's devotion to Jaurès, see especially "Mémoires politiques," vol. 1, chap. 4, p. 15; vol. 3, chap. 8, p. 4. In fact, all the issues of *La Vie socialiste* attest to it.

177. M. Déat, "Jaurès et la conception socialiste de l'État," *La Vie socialiste*, 25 Jan. 1930, 9.

178. Déat, *Perspectives socialistes*, 137.

179. Ibid., 139.

180. Ibid., 139–41.

181. M. Déat, "De Marion à Zyromski," *La Vie socialiste*, 10 Jan. 1931, 7.

182. Ibid.

183. Déat, *Perspectives socialistes*, 143.

184. Ibid. See Déat, "Démocratie et salariat," 4.

185. Speech of Léon Blum, with comments by R. Bobin, *La Vie socialiste*, 29 July 1933, 53.

186. Déat, "Jaurès et la conception socialiste de l'État," *La Vie socialiste*, 25 January 1930, 8.

187. M. Déat, "L'Internationale et sa section française," *La Vie socialiste*, 13 May 1933, 5.

188. Ibid., 9.

189. Ibid.

190. M. Déat, "Méditations sur les problèmes du jour: La Tactique socialiste et la marche au pouvoir," *La Vie socialiste*, 13 May 1933, 5.

191. Speech of Adrien Marquet at the Second National Congress of the Parti Socialiste de France, *La Vie socialiste*, 2 Mar. 1934, 18.

192. Ibid., 17.

193. P. Renaudel, "Nous attendons sans peur la décision suprême," *La Vie socialiste*, 4 Nov. 1933, 3; Déat, *Perspectives socialistes*, 87 and 8.

194. Déat, "Après deux ans."

195. Déat, "Mémoires politiques," vol. 2, chap. 9, p. 21.

196. Déat, "L'Internationale et sa section française," 7–8.

197. Ibid.

198. B. Montagnon in Montagnon, Marquet, and Déat, *Néo-socialisme?*, 22, 44.

199. Ibid., 44.

200. Ibid., 29.

201. A. Marquet, ibid., 43.

202. Déat, "Mémoires politiques," vol. 2, chap. 14, p. 2.

203. "Déclaration," *La Vie socialiste*, 6 June 1931, 5–6.

204. See Déat's interpretation of these moves in "Méditations sur les problèmes du jour: La Tactique socialiste et la marche au pouvoir," *La Vie socialiste*, 11 Mar. 1933, 9.

205. There were 2,807 votes for Blum's motion and 925 for Renaudel's.

206. See M. Prélot, "Le Socialisme français: Le Néo-socialisme," *Politique*, Feb. 1939, 135.

207. See Blum's interruption of Marquet's speech in Montagnon, Marquet, and Déat, *Néo-socialisme?*, 60. See also pp. 10, 88, as well as M. Déat, "Crise de réadaptation," *La Vie socialiste*, 20 Jan. 1934, 10.

208. Speech of Léon Blum, *La Vie socialiste*, 20 July 1933, 53.

209. Ibid.

210. Ibid. The same idea is expressed in Blum's "Parti de classe et non-parti des déclassés," *Le Populaire*, 19 July 1933, and "Le Double Danger," ibid., 20 July 1933. These articles are included in *L'Oeuvre de Léon Blum*, ed. J. Léon-Blum, J. Cain, L. Fancon, and J. Texcier, 6 vols. (Paris: Albin Michel, 1972), vol. 3, pt. 2, pp. 543–45, at the beginning of a section on "The Neosocialist Deviation."

211. L. Blum, "Le Problème du pouvoir," *Le Populaire*, 13 July 1933; "Le Pouvoir total," ibid., 14 July 1933; "La Mesure du pouvoir," ibid., 15 July 1933. These articles are not included in *L'Oeuvre de Léon Blum*.

212. Blum, "Le Pouvoir total."

213. Blum, "Le Problème du pouvoir."

214. Blum, "La Mesure du pouvoir"; "Le Pouvoir total."

215. *L'Oeuvre de Léon Blum*, vol. 3, pt. 2, pp. 543–46.

216. Ibid., 548, 550, 557.

217. Ibid., 561.

218. Ibid., 572.

219. Ibid., 580.

220. Ibid., 581.

221. See the issues of *La Vie socialiste* devoted to the split and the founding of the new party, particularly those of 2, 9, 16, and 23 Dec. 1933 and those of 9 Feb. 1934 (p. 21), 19 May 1934 (p. 8), and 26 May 1934 (pp. 14–15).

222. Grossmann, "L'Évolution de Marcel Déat," 15. Grossmann does not give his sources; he may simply be citing the figure given by Marcel Prélot in 1939 (twenty thousand) ("Le Socialisme français," 139).

223. Speech of M. Déat at the PSF congress, *La Vie socialiste*, 9 Feb. 1939, 139.

224. See *La Vie socialiste* of 10, 17, and 24 Feb., 17 and 24 Mar., 12 and 19 May, 9 June, and 7 and 14 July 1934—articles and speeches by Renaudel, Déat, Montagnon, Perceau, unsigned articles, decisions of the party . . . material abounds.

At the second national congress, Montagnon expressed his point of view in a logical manner: "We want to enter the government. Very well, then! When, in a revolutionary period, one has—as we have—someone in the government, one leaves him there!" (ibid., 2 June 1934, 17).

225. Speech of B. Montagnon at the national congress of the PSF, *La Vie socialiste*, 9 Feb. 1935, 12–14.

226. P. Renaudel, "Plaidoyer *pro domo*," *La Vie socialiste*, 2 Mar. 1935, 3. See also J. Texcier, "Pas d'équivoque!," ibid., 17 Mar. 1934, 9; Renaudel, "Les Difficultés et les tâches," 1.

Renaudel found himself in this situation almost involuntarily, and stayed there out of loyalty to his commitments but above all out of weakness. It was a terrible wrench for him. Déat used Ranaudel's influence with the Socialist International for his own benefit.

227. P. Renaudel, "Mon sentiment vrai, profond . . . ," *La Vie socialiste*, 26 May 1934, 6. See also his "Pour notre Congrès national: Difficultés d'hier, tâches d'aujourd'hui," ibid., 12 Jan. 1935, p. 5.

228. L. Capdeville, "Un Message d'espérance," *La Vie socialiste*, 3 Feb. 1934, 8.

229. Speech of A. Marquet at the second national congress of the PSF, *La Vie socialiste*, 2 June 1934, 18.

230. M. Déat, "Autour d'une Constituante: Précisons notre tactique," *La Vie socialiste*, 13 Oct. 1934, 7.

231. "Le Projet de résolution Adler-Vandervelde," *La Vie socialiste*, 16 June 1934, 3.

232. Renaudel, "Mon sentiment vrai, profond . . . ," 6.

233. For the conflict between these two major tendencies, see especially the issues of *La Vie socialiste* of 19 May (on the Congress of the Federation of the Paris Region) and 2 June 1934 (on the second national congress of the PSF).

234. M. Déat, "Avant le Conseil central: Problèmes politiques et questions pratiques," *La Vie socialiste*, 24 Feb. 1934. On the various kinds of difficulties encountered by the party, see especially the issues of *La Vie socialiste*, for February, May, and September 1934 and July 1935.

235. P. Renaudel, "Changements intérieurs à *La Vie socialiste*," *La Vie socialiste*, 16 Feb. 1935, 2.

236. In September 1934 the number of subscribers rose to 2,794. There were 2,862 in December 1933 and 2,015 in April 1930. See P. Renaudel, "Aux amis de *La Vie socialiste*," *La Vie socialiste*, 29 Sept. 1934, 1, and "A nos lecteurs," ibid., 19 Apr. 1930, 1.

237. Renaudel opposed too close a collaboration with the "centrists" of the left, fearing that the PSF might lose whatever specifically socialist character it had. See Renaudel, "Pour notre Congrès national," 4.

238. The best-known figures apart from the néo deputies were Paul-Boncour, Euguène Frot, and, later, Paul Ramadier.

239. This participation was made possible by a common declaration by the three parties (M. Déat, "L'Union socialiste est réalisée," *Le Front*, 16 Nov. 1935). This declaration did not represent the true néo ideology of Déat, Marquet, and Montagnon.

240. Remarks by M. Déat at the beginning of the electoral campaign, *Le Front*, 4 Apr. 1936.

241. Speech by M. Déat, *Le Front*, 16 Nov. 1935.

242. B. Montagnon, "La Belle Riposte du peuple de Paris aux menaces des troublions," *Le Front*, 22 Feb. 1936. See also, in the same issue, Émile Favier, "Espérance d'hier, réalité de demain."

243. In all of France, the Union Socialiste Républicaine received only three hundred thousand votes (the socialists received 1.8 million). One obtains the impression from *Le Front* that the Union Socialiste was active mainly in Paris and the Seine (département).

244. See *Le Front* of 23 and 30 May and 16 June 1936.

245. See Déat, "Mémoires politiques," vol. 3, chap. 18, p. 2, and Andreu, *Notre maître M. Sorel*, 81–83. Communist, socialist, then néo, Marion was the prototype of an available "revolutionary" in search of action.

246. Langummier was elected in the second electoral district of the twentieth *arrondissement* by 13,621 votes as against Déat's 12,766. The communist had defeated Déat in the first round by 10,642 votes versus 10,034. The SFIO candidate received only 1,819 votes. See Paul Faure's article in *Le Populaire*, 14 May 1936. Montagnon's defeat in the twenty-eighth *arrondissement* should also be noted. See also M. Déat, "Lignes de rupture," *La Vie socialiste*, 23 June 1934, 4; "Devoirs de vacances," ibid., 14 July 1934, 4; "Quand Moscou tient les fils," ibid., 21 July 1934, 2; and "Fronts et rassemblements," ibid., 3 Nov. 1934, 4; and R. Bobin, "L'Unité d'action socialo-bolchéviste n'est plus qu'une question de jours," ibid., 7 July 1934, 6, and "L'Unité d'action est chose faite entre la SFIO et les communistes," ibid., 21 July 1934, 5. On the campaign against Déat, see "L'Immonde campagne personnelle contre Déat," *Le Front*, 2 May 1936, and "Les Remerciements de Déat aux 12,766 électeurs de Charonne-Père-Lachaise," ibid., 9 May 1936. After Déat's defeat *Paris-Demain* stopped publication and its subscriptions were taken over by *Le Front*.

247. Déat, "Devoirs de vacances," 3.

248. Capdeville, "Un Message d'espérance," 3.

249. M. Déat, "Pour notre Congrès: Positions nettes et devoir clair," *La Vie socialiste*, 24 Mar. 1934, 2.

250. Ibid. See also Déat, "Fronts et rassemblements," 4.

251. P. Lafue, "La Révolution est-elle pour le 8 juillet? Entretien avec M. Déat," *1934*, 13 June 1934. See also Montagnon's response to P. Lafue's survey "Sommes-nous en période révolutionnaire?" (ibid., 14 Feb. 1934): "L'homme de gouvernement ne se laisse lier par aucun principe" (The man of government should not let himself be bound by any principle).

252. Déat, "Pour notre Congrès," 4.

253. M. Déat, "La Fin d'une controverse," *La Vie socialiste*, 7 Apr. 1934.

254. Déat, "Fronts et rassemblements," 6.

255. Déat, "Pour notre Congrès," 2.

256. Speech of B. Montagnon at the second national congress, *La Vie socialiste*, 2 June 1934, 17.

257. Déat, "Pour notre Congrès," 2.

258. "Discours de Déat au Congrès national du PSF," *La Vie socialiste*, 9 Feb. 1930, 20.

259. M. Déat, "Gros problèmes et lourdes tâches," *La Vie socialiste*, 13 July 1935, 4. See the attack on Déat's ideas by Jean Texcier, of Renaudel's group, in "Pas d'équivoques!," 10–11, and "Point final d'une controverse: La Chasse aux grues métaphysiques," *La Vie socialiste*, 7 Apr. 1934, 7: "On the pretext that orthodoxy is sclerosis, are we going to wander about singing hymns to life and proclaiming that *facts* are supreme?"

260. Déat, "Fronts et rassemblements," 4.

261. M. Déat, "Épreuve de la démocratie," *La Vie socialiste*, 10 Mar. 1934, 2–3.

262. Ibid., 3.

263. Ibid., 2.

264. Ibid.

265. M. Déat in Montagnon, Marquet, and Déat, *Néo-socialisme?*, 90.

266. A. Marquet, ibid., 57.

267. Déat, "Syndicalisme et corporation," 1.

268. A. Marquet in Montagnon, Marquet, and Déat, *Néo-socialisme?*, 61. The same idea is expressed by M. Bonnafous (pp. 128, 134–35).

269. Loustau, *Un Ordre social français*, 15–16.

270. Doriot, *Refaire la France*, 95.

271. Ibid., 94–97.

272. Ibid., 97.

273. B. Montagnon in Montagnon, Marquet, and Déat, *Néo-socialisme?*, 35.

274. G. Vaillant to the Congress of the Federation of the Paris Region of the PSF, *La Vie socialiste*, 19 May 1934, 12.

275. G. Bergery, statement in the Chamber of Deputies, *La Flèche*, 22 May 1937.

276. Déat, "Syndicalisme et corporation," 1–2.

277. Déat, "Épreuve de la démocratie," 3.

278. Ibid.

279. M. Déat, "Retour sur nous-mêmes," *La Vie socialiste*, 13 Apr. 1935, 2.

280. M. Bonnafous in Montagnon, Marquet, and Déat, *Néo-socialisme?*, 123. See also pp. 124–26.

281. Ibid., 123.

282. Jouvenel, *L'Économie dirigée*, 7.

283. B. Montagnon in Montagnon, Marquet, and Déat, *Néo-socialisme?*, 24. See also Marquet's speech, pp. 52–55, and L. Capdeville, "Nous ne renonçons pas," *La Vie socialiste*, 16 June 1934, 6–7, as well as Déat, "Mémoires politiques," vol. 2, chap. 13, p. 6.

284. Montagnon's answer to P. Lafue's survey "Sommes-nous en période révolutionnaire?," *1934*, 14 Feb. 1934.

285. M. Déat, "Qu'est-ce qu'un programme d'action?," *La Vie socialiste*, 5 Apr. 1930, 7.

286. Déat, "Démocratie et salariat," 5.

287. Déat, *Perspectives socialistes*, 157, 159.

288. Ibid., 161.

289. Ibid., 180. Déat gave this expression great importance and repeated it on many occasions. See, for example, "Les Trois Formes de la socialisation," *La Vie socialiste*, 2 Aug. 1930, 5, and "La Tactique socialiste," 7.

290. Déat, *Perspectives socialistes*, 183–84.

291. Déat, "Syndicalisme et corporation," 1. With regard to Déat invocation of Jaurès's authority, see, for example, "Examen semi-critique d'un texte quasi officiel," *La Vie socialiste*, 18 Apr. 1931, 1–5; *Perspectives socialistes*, 157–59, where Déat quotes from *L'Armée nouvelle* at length; "La Tactique socialiste," 7; and "Jaurès et la conception socilaste de l'État," where Déat says, invoking Jaurès against Blum, "It is good to be heretical in his company." The writers of *La Vie socialiste* regarded Jaurès as the spiritual progenitor of neosocialism.

292. M. Déat, "Bouillie doctrinale et charte en lambeaux," *La Vie socialiste*,

11 Jan. 1930, 9. This issue also included a letter from Karl Kautsky supporting participation in government (p. 6). See also *La Vie socialiste*, 8 Feb. 1930, 6, and Déat, "Qu'est-ce qu'un programme d'action?," 5.

293. De Man, *Au-delà du marxisme*, 181.

294. Ibid., 181–82.

295. Ibid., 191.

296. M. Déat, "Avenir socialiste et destins radicaux," *La Vie socialiste*, 28 June 1930, 4; "Récidive et diversion," ibid., 25 July 1931, 6; U. Stale, "Le Socialisme et le problème de l'État," ibid., 9 June 1930, 10; Siriez, "Deux conceptions socialistes de l'État," 12.

297. Déat, *Perspectives socialistes*, 195.

298. Déat, "Les Trois Formes," 5; "L'Internationale et sa section française," 7. On "the conquest of the state," see also H. De Man, "Les Causes essentielles du fascisme," *La Vie socialiste*, 4 Nov. 1933, 6.

299. Jouvenel, *L'Économie dirigée*, 84–85, 107–8, 170.

300. B. Montagnon in Montagnon, Marquet, and Déat, *Néo-socialisme?*, 23–24, 32–33; H. De Man, speech at the POB congress, *La Vie socialiste*, 6 Jan. 1934, 10; Marquet's speech at the second national congress of the PSF, ibid., 2 June 1934, 17–18; Jouvenel, *L'Économie dirigée*, 132.

301. Déat, "Pour notre Congrès," 2.

302. See, for instance, the speeches given at the second national congress of the PSF, *La Vie socialiste*, 2 June 1934, 8–9.

303. Resolution of the Central Council of the PSF, *La Vie socialiste*, 8 July 1934, 2.

304. Déat, "Autour d'une Constituante," 3.

305. Ibid.

306. Jouvenel, *L'Économie dirigée*, 175–76, 185–86.

307. Ibid., 188–89.

308. "Réforme de la Constitution," *La Lutte des jeunes*, 24 Feb. 1934. The creation of a "strong state" was the aim of Bergery's adherents and the members of the PPF. See P. Drieu La Rochelle, "Sous Doumergue," *La Lutte des jeunes*, 27 May 1934; Doriot, *Refaire la France*, 104; Loustau, *Un Ordre social français*, 21, and *Notre doctrine*; G. Bergery, "La Faiblesse de l'État est une menace pour les libertés du peuple," *La Flèche*, 3 Jan. 1938; and Jean Maze, "Vers la seconde révolution française: Frontisme, espoir d'un peuple," ibid., 24 Feb. 1939.

309. Quoted by Grossmann, "L'Évolution de Marcel Déat," 21, from an article by Déat in *La Montagne* (Puy-de-Dôme), 26 Jan. 1934.

310. Grossmann, "L'Évolution de Marcel Déat," 21.

311. Ibid.; quoted by Grossmann from *L'Appel*, 7 Mar. 1934.

312. Quoted by Grossmann, "L'Évolution de Marcel Déat," 21, from an article by Déat in *La Montagne* (Puy-de-Dôme), 26 Jan. 1934.

313. "Notre Congrès de la Mutualité," *La Vie socialiste*, 2 June 1934, 8.

314. Ibid. See also Déat's "Rapport moral" (Moral Report), *La Vie socialiste*, 12 Jan. 1935, 12–13.

315. Conversation with Déat in connection with P. Lafue's survey "La Révolution est-elle pour le 8 juillet?," *1934*, 13 June 1934.

316. Ibid.

317. G. Valois, "Congrès et rassemblements," *Chantiers coopératifs*, 30 May 1934.

318. G. Valois, "A propos de l'échéance du 8 juillet," *Chantiers coopératifs*, 30 May 1934.

319. P. Norgeu, "Néos et Croix-de-feu," *La Lutte des jeunes*, 24 June 1934.

320. Ibid.

Chapter Six

1. See De Man, *L'Idée socialiste*, 8–9.

2. E. Vandervelde, *Études marxistes*, 2d ed. (Brussels: L'Églantine, 1930). Vandervelde deplored De Man's increasing distance from Marxism (see pp. 9–10, 15–18, 97–142), but nevertheless regarded *Au-delá du marxisme* as "perhaps the most important work on socialism to have been published since the war" (p. 15).

3. E. Vandervelde, "L'Exécution du Plan du travail," *Le Peuple*, 24 Mar. 1935.

4. Dodge, *Beyond Marxism*, 130.

5. See the 444-page volume produced by De Man and the Bureau of Social Studies of the POB, *L'Exécution du Plan du travail* (Paris: Alcan, 1935), which identifies the members of the General Committee for the Plan (p. 7) and of the committees whose reports appear in the volume (p. 431ff.), and, most important, includes a detailed study of the problems at issue and concrete proposals for reviving the national economy. This austere, detailed document is remarkable in every way.

6. See the complete text of De Man's speech at the POB Christmas congress in Georges Valois's *Chantiers coopératifs*, 21 Mar. 1934.

7. De Man, *L'Idée socialiste*, 507.

8. Ibid.

9. H. De Man, "La Résorption du chômage et le Plan du travail," *Mouvement syndical belge*, no. 7 (20 July 1934), 12, quoted in Dodge, *Beyond Marxism*, 132.

10. De Man, "Discours au Congrès de Noël."

11. Ibid.

12. See J. Denis, *Principes rexistes* (Brussels: Éditions Rex, 1936), 28. See also another excellent account of the Rexist ideology by one of the leaders of the movement, J. Streel, *Ce qu'il faut penser de Rex* (Brussels: Éditions Rex, 1936).

13. De Man, "Discours au Congrès de Noël."

14. Ibid.

15. Ibid.

16. Ibid.

17. Ibid.

18. Ibid. De Man's speech at the Christmas congress provides a concise summary—perhaps too concise—of the main planist ideas. These were elaborated in articles in newspapers and journals published by De Man in 1934–35. See particularly the series of articles published before the Christmas congress in *Le*

Peuple, the POB daily, between October and December 1933. On 4 November 1933 *La Vie socialiste*, the organ of the right wing of the SFIO, published, under the title "Pour un socialisme renouvelé," a series of five articles that had previously appeared in *Le Peuple*. In 1934–35, De Man pursued his campaign in a long series of articles in *Le Peuple*; hardly a week went by without an article on the Plan by De Man. See also his *L'Exécution du Plan du travail*, and the following pamphlets derived from his articles in *Le Peuple: Réflexions sur l'Économie dirigée* (Paris and Brussels: L'Églantine, 1932); *Pour plan d'action* (Brussels: L'Églantine, 1933); *le Plan du travail* (Brussels: Lucifer, 1933); *La Réforme bancaire du gouvernement et le Plan du travail* (Brussels: L'Èglantine, 1934); and *Le Plan du travail et les communistes* (Paris and Brussels: Labor, 1935).

19. See the complete text of the Plan in *Chantiers coopératifs*, 1 Mar. 1934. It is also found in *L'Idée socialiste*, 536–42, and at the end of Dodge, *Beyond Marxism*, 232–36.

20. De Man, *Après-coup*, 210.

21. Ibid., 209–11.

22. Ibid., 245.

23. Ibid., 209–10.

24. Ibid. On this subject, see Birnbaum, *Le Peuple et les gros*.

25. De Man, *L'Idée socialiste*, 514. See also pp. 512–13.

26. Ibid., 480.

27. See H. De Man, "Le Plan national d'abord," *La Vie socialiste*, 6 Jan. 1934.

28. Se *Le Peuple*, 25 July, 1, 8, 15, 22, 29 Aug., 5, 13, 19 Sept., 3 Oct. 1934. These articles were republished in the pamphlet *Corporatisme et socialisme* (Paris and Brussels: Labor, 1935).

29. H. De Man, "Les Thèses essentielles du planisme," *La Vie socialiste*, 22 Dec. 1934.

30. H. De Man, "Le Socialisme devant la crise," *La Vie socialiste*, 22 Dec. 1934, 5. Despite this declaration, Pierre Renaudel still tried to convince himself that the De Man Plan was "a specifically socialist plan" ("Pour notre Congrès national," 4).

31. De Man, "Le Socialisme devant la crise," proposition 9.

32. H. De Man, "Planisme et réformisme," *La Vie socialiste*, 22 Dec. 1934. On the theoretical basis of De Man's conception of the state, see *Au-delà du marxisme*, 120–21, 180–82, 184–85.

33. De Man, *Après-coup*, 302.

34. Ibid., 194.

35. De Man, "Planisme et réformisme.

36. De Man, *L'Idée socialiste*, 405.

37. De Man, "Planisme et réformisme."

38. De Man, *Après-coup*, 214.

39. Quoted by G. Lefranc in his statement following De Man's lecture at the Nouvelle École de la Paix, *La Vie socialiste*, 22 Dec. 1934, 10.

40. Ibid.

41. Statement by M. Déat, *La Vie socialiste*, 22 Dec. 1934, 11.

42. Ibid.

43. P. Andreu, "Capitalisme et corporatisme," *Combat*, Aug.–Sept. 1936. See also various articles in *La Lutte des jeunes* of 25 Feb., 18 Mar., and 22 Apr. 1934. The first issue of *La Lutte des jeunes* appeared on 25 February 1934. The journal stopped publication after eighteen issues, owing to lack of funds, on 14 July of the same year.

44. H. Lefort, "Si j'étais Henri De Man," *La Lutte de jeunes*, 20 May 1934.

45. B. de Jouvenel, "Mes cinq points," *La Lutte des jeunes*, 27 May 1934.

46. M. Déat, "Le Plan belge et nous," *La Vie socialiste*, 6 Jan. 1934, 5. See also Déat, "Crise de réadaptation," 10.

47. M. Déat, "Pour l'élaboration d'un plan . . . d'un plan unique," *La Vie socialiste*, 24 Nov. 1934, 9. See also Déat's statement following De Man's lecture at the Nouvelle École de la Paix, ibid., 22 Dec. 1934, 11.

48. Déat, "Crise de réadaptation," 11.

49. Déat, "Le Plan belge et nous," 3, 4.

50. Ibid., 4.

51. Déat, "Pour l'élaboration d'un plan," 9; "Crise de réadaptation," 10–11.

52. Déat, "Pour l'élaboration d'un plan," 9.

53. Déat, "Crise de réadaptation," 11.

54. Ibid.

55. Déat, "Le Plan belge et nous," 4. See also Déat, "Crise de réadaptation," 11.

56. M. Déat, "Avant le Congrès national: Si vous voulez un beau Congrès," *La Vie socialiste*, 26 Jan. 1935, 5.

57. M. Déat, "Le Planisme et la tradition française," *L'Homme nouveau*, no. 12 (1 Jan. 1935) (unpaginated).

58. G. Roditi, "Du néo-marxisme au néo-socialisme, *L'Homme nouveau*, no. 14 (1 Mar. 1935).

59. De Man, *Corporatisme et socialisme*, 5, 4.

60. Ibid., 6.

61. Ibid., 7.

62. Ibid., 11–16.

63. Ibid., 7.

64. Ibid., 8.

65. Ibid., 25.

66. Ibid., 29.

67. Ibid., 18.

68. Ibid., 34–35.

69. See Desolre, "Henri De Man," 54.

70. The journal appeared from January 1934 to April 1935. On *L'Homme nouveau*, see Andreu, *Le Rouge et le blanc*, 103–5. For a different point of view, see also A. G. Slama, "Henri De Man et les néo-traditionalistes français, 1933–1936," *Revue européenne des sciences sociales et Cahiers Vilfredo Pareto*, 12, no. 31 (1974), 179ff.

71. Roditi, "Du néo-marxisme au néo-socialisme."

72. Ibid.

73.´ G. Roditi, "Mort ou naissance du néo-socialisme?," *L'Homme nouveau*, 1 Sept. 1935 (special issue).

74. See, for instance, P. Andreu, "Le Socialisme de Sorel," *L'Homme nouveau*, no. 17 (June 1935).

75. G. Roditi, "La Solution corporative," *L'Homme nouveau*, no. 18 (July 1935). On the corporatist ideas of the Action Française at the beginning of the century, see Ch. Maurras, "Sur le nom de socialiste," *L'Action française* (journal), no. 34 (15 Nov. 1900), 859–67, and a selection of texts by La Tour du Pin, "Aphorismes de politique sociale," ibid., no. 32 (15 Oct. 1900). Maurras describes La Tour du Pin as "a monarchist and a socialist" (p. 859). He was also regarded as the father of corporatism in *La Lutte des jeunes* (B. Feuilly, "Corporatisme ou capitalisme?," 10 June 1934), and in June 1934 *Esprit* published an article by P. Andreu entitled "La Vraie Figure de La Tour du Pin" (The True Face of La Tour du Pin).

76. Roditi, "La Solution corporative."

77. Ibid.

78. P. Andreu, "Corporatisme chrétien, corporatisme fasciste," *L'Homme nouveau*, special issue (July 1935).

79. Ibid.

80. Roditi, "La Solution corporative."

81. See the special July 1935 issue of *L'Homme nouveau*.

82. Vallon contributed many articles to *La Vie socialiste*. In 1930 he wrote one of the most serious and succinct accounts of neosocialism, "La Tâche des jeunes. Dépasser? Non! Prolonger le marxisme," 20 Sept. 1930, 5. In his opinion, socialism needed to "broaden the idea of class struggle. Class struggle, thus broadened, becomes the struggle of the whole collectivity against a well-to-do minority, wielders of financial power, masters of the major means of production, controllers of the markets."

83. Déat, "Syndicalisme et corporation," 3.

84. Ibid.

85. Déat, "Vers une nouvelle économie," 1. See also Déat's speech at the Congress of the Federation of the Paris Region of the PSF, *La Vie socialiste*, 19 May 1934, 13–14.

86. L. Vallon, "L'Organisation économique du secteur industriel libre," *La Vie socialiste*, 26 Jan. 1935.

87. See chap. 3.

88. Déat, "Syndicalisme et corporation," 2–4; "Vers une nouvelle économie," 1–3. See also Montagnon's speech at the national congress of the PSF, *La Vie socialiste*, 9 Feb. 1935, 13.

89. L. Vallon, speech at the national congress of the PSF, *La Vie socialiste*, 9 Feb. 1935, 15.

90. Déat, "Pour notre Congrès," 4; "Autour du Plan belge: La Nouvelle Épouvante de M. Blum," *La Vie socialiste*, 27 Jan. 1934, 6; "Syndicalisme et corporation."

91. Déat, "Autour du Plan belge."

92. Ibid. See also B. de Jouvenel, *L'Économie dirigée*, 98–99.

93. Doriot, *Refaire la France*, 99–100. See also Loustau, *Un Ordre social français*, 9, 11–15, and P. Marion, *Programme du parti populaire français* (Paris: Les Oeuvres Françaises, 1938), 72ff. (Marion summarizes Loustau's work).

94. Doriot, *Refaire la France*, 98.

95. Déat, *Perspectives socialistes*, 122–23, 128–33; "Syndicalisme et corporation"; "Le Socialisme et la question agraire," *La Vie socialiste*, 19 July 1930, 5.

96. Doriot, *Refaire la France*, 8–9. Of the dissidents Jouvenel was the only one to attack the profit motive, but only during the short period when he published *La Lutte des jeunes* (see "Mes cinq points").

97. It is unnecessary to refer to the hundreds of articles on this subject. One need only study the series of journals like *Chantiers coopératifs, Combat, La Lutte des jeunes, L'Insurgé, La Flèche, L'Homme nouveau,* and *La Vie socialiste.* The same ideas constantly recur, though the writers may differ.

98. R. Brasillach, "Anticipations: Quand L. Blum fait tirer sur le peuple," *Combat*, June 1936.

99. T. Maulnier, "Libérons-nous du capitalisme," *Combat*, Dec. 1936.

100. Déat, *Perspectives socialistes*, 220, 215.

101. Ibid., 210. See also Déat, "Syndicalisme et corporation."

102. De Man, *Réflexions sur l'économie dirigée*, 5.

103. Ibid., 9.

104. Déat, "Syndicalisme et corporation," 1–2.

105. Déat, "Vers une nouvelle économie," 2; Loustau, *Un Ordre social français*, 19.

106. "Un Plan d'action économique immédiate," *La Lutte des jeunes*, 18 Mar. 1934.

107. Jouvenel, *L'Économie dirigée*, 172.

108. "Échos du monde moderne et des jeunes équipes," *Cahiers bleus*, no. 27 (17 Aug. 1929), 26.

109. Jouvenel, *L'Économie dirigée*, 31–34.

110. M. Déat, "Propagande rurale et propagande agraire," *La Vie socialiste*, 10 May 1930, 6; Jouvenel, *L'Économie dirigée*, 31–33.

111. Drieu La Rochelle, *Socialisme fasciste*, 104–5.

112. Ibid., 108.

113. Déat, "Propagande rurale et propagande agraire," 6.

114. Déat, "Syndicalisme et corporation," 1.

115. Ibid.

116. This is one of the least-known aspects of fascism. The first scholar to study fascism as a factor of modernization was A. James Gregor in *The Ideology of Fascism* (1969). He further developed the theme in *Italian Fascism and Developmental Dictatorship* (Princeton: Princeton University Press, 1979). See also H. A. Turner, "Fascism and Modernization," *World Politics* 24 (July 1972), 547–64; A. James Gregor, "Fascism and Modernization: Some Addenda," ibid. 26 (Apr. 1974), 370–84; and A. J. Joes, "On the Modernity of Fascism: Notes from Two Worlds," *Comparative Political Studies* 10 (July 1977), 259–78. See also in the same issue of the latter journal a discussion on this question between A. L. Greill, "The Modernization of Consciousness and the Appeal of

Fascism" (pp. 213–38), and A. James Gregor, "Fascism and the Countermodernization of Consciousness" (pp. 239–57). An article by Mancur Olson, Jr., "Rapid Growth as a Destabilizing Force," *Journal of Economic History* 23, no. 4 (Dec. 1963), 529–52, is also of great interest. Finally, on France, Klaus-Jurger Müller's article "French Fascism and Modernization," *Journal of Contemporary History* 11, no. 4 (1976), 75–107, provides pertinent information.

117. G. Valois, "A longueur d'ondes," *Cahiers bleus*, no. 6 (1 Dec. 1928), 20.

118. G. Valois, "Commentaires," *Cahiers bleus*, no. 114 (22 Aug. 1931), 23.

119. Valois, "Chantiers 1928," 3–5.

120. "Échos du monde moderne et des jeunes équipes," *Cahiers bleus*, no. 38 (30 Nov. 1929), 24.

121. G. Valois, "Au-delà du marxisme," *Le Nouveau Siècle*, 27 Jan. 1928.

122. G. Valois, "A bas la dictature des banquiers! Vive la République syndicale!," *Chantiers coopératifs*, 1 Mar. 1934. *Chantiers coopératifs* appeared in June 1932. Two years later *Le Nouvel Age* took over from *Chantiers*, and soon revealed itself as a sometimes "leftist" but always perspicacious publication. Valois's journal took the part of Trotsky against Stalin, condemned the Moscow trials, championed republican Spain, and opposed nazism, anti-Semitism, the Munich agreements, and the policy of appeasement and capitulation to Germany.

123. G. Valois, "Contre tout fascisme," *Chantiers coopératifs*, 28 Mar. 1934.

124. In 1935, Valois's request to join the SFIO, sponsored by Marceau Pivert, was accepted by the forty-fifth section but refused by the Federal Council of the Seine (see *La Révolution prolétarienne* of 25 Dec. 1935, *Le Populaire* of 17 Dec. 1935, and *Le Nouvel Age* of 21 Dec. 1935). Valois's request to join the Comité Antifasciste de Vigilance, founded by Paul Rivet, was likewise refused. On 5 March 1935, *Le Nouvel Age* had published a long article by Édouard Berth on "Le Cas Valois" that *La Révolution prolétarienne* had rejected. This article was a reply to an attack on Valois by Louzon, to whose celebrated anti-Semitic article "La Faillite du dreyfusisme ou le triomphe du parti juif" in *Le Mouvement socialiste*, no. 176 (July 1906), 193–99, Berth referred to show how everyone can make mistakes: the Cercle Proudhon, the product of an "extraordinary, unprecedented historical situation," was also, he believed, a mistake. In Berth's opinion, however great, however bewildering Valois's shifts of position were, he "always pursued but one goal, obstinately and passionately, and that was the emancipation of the working class."

After he joined the *maquis* in the Haute-Savoie during the Second World War, Valois continued attacking high finance in his writings. The Valois dossier in the Archives Mennevée, now at the University of California, Los Angeles, includes a booklet signed "Adam" but undoubtedly written by Valois. Sold "for the benefit of the Maquis of the Resistance," this booklet is entitled *La France trahie par les trusts* (France Betrayed by the Trusts). According to a Dr. Fréjafon, who returned from Bergen-Belsen, Valois was the spiritual leader of the members of the Resistance there (*Le Nouvel Age*, no. 17 [1 Feb. 1947]).

125. Drieu La Rochelle, *Socialisme fasciste*, 108.

126. See Le Corbusier's articles "Une Nouvelle Ville remplace une ancienne ville," *Plans*, no. 8 (Oct. 1931), 49ff., and "Descartes est-il américain?," ibid.,

no. 7 (July 1931), and the following issues of *Plans* for 1931: nos. 1, 2, 5, 7, 8, and 9, where Le Corbusier's articles begin on p. 49; no. 6, p. 65ff.; and no. 3, p. 33ff.

127. F. T. Marinetti, "La Nouvelle Sensibilité," *Plans*, no. 7 (July 1931), 91. See also P. Latercier, "Éthique de l'automobile," ibid., no. 1 (Jan. 1931), 9ff.

128. H. Lagardelle, "Au-delà de la démocratie: De l'homme abstrait à l'homme réel," *Plans*, no. 1 (Jan. 1931), 24–25.

129. H. Lagardelle, "Au-delà de la démocratie: L'Homme réel et le syndicalisme," *Plans*, no. 3 (Mar. 1931), 12.

130. Ibid., 17. See also H. Lagardelle, "Supercapitalisme," *Plans*, no. 10 (Dec. 1931), 7ff.; and "Capitalisme," ibid., no. 9 (Nov. 1931), 16ff.; and "La Fin d'une culture," ibid., no. 5 (May 1931), 9ff.

131. B. Mussolini, *La Doctrine du fascisme* (Florence: Valecchi, 1937), 24.

132. E. Vandervelde, "Après le Congrès du POB: Henri De Man and Marcel Déat: Analogies nombreuses et saisissantes," *La Vie socialiste*, 19 Jan. 1934.

133. E. Vandervelde, "Le Marxisme et le planisme," *Le Peuple*, 3 Feb. 1935.

134. E. Vandervelde, "Retour à Marx et analyses marxistes," *Le Peuple*, 17 Feb. 1935.

135. Ibid.

136. Vandervelde, "Le Marxisme et le planisme."

137. Ibid.

138. Ibid.

139. E. Vandervelde, "Planisme, néo-socialisme ou néo-réformisme?," *Le Peuple*, 6 Jan. 1935.

140. See, for instance, Vandervelde's articles in *La Vie socialiste* of 13 and 20 Jan. 1934 and 12 Jan. 1935.

141. As C. Harmel suggests in "A propos d'Henri De Man et de Léon Blum," *Le Contrat social*, July–Aug. 1965, 261.

142. Vandervelde, "Planisme, néo-socialisme ou néo-réformisme?"

143. L. Blum, speech of 16 July 1933 at the SFIO national congress, *La Vie socialiste*, 29 July 1933, 53.

144. L. Blum, "Au-delà du réformisme: Le Plan de travail et le parti français," *Le Populaire*, 6 Jan. 1934. Note that Blum spoke of a "Plan de travail" (Working Plan) instead of a "Plan du travail" (Labor Plan); it was only a few days later that he saw his error. It is interesting, moreover, that these articles in which Blum analyzed the Plan were judged not important enough to be included in pt. 2 of vol. 3 of his *Oeuvres*.

145. Blum, "Au-delà du réformisme." These resolutions were called the "Cahiers d'Huyghens" after the hall (Salle Huyghens) in which the 1932 national congress took place.

146. Ibid.

147. Ibid. See also L. Blum, "La Résorption du chômage," *Le Populaire*, 19 Jan. 1934.

148. L. Blum, "'Plan' et 'programme,'" *Le Populaire*, 17 Jan. 1934.

149. L. Blum, "Le Sens véritable du Plan du travail," *Le Populaire*, 21 Jan. 1934.

150. L. Blum, "Le Secteur privé," *Le Populaire*, 25 Jan. 1934.

151. L. Blum, "La Socialisation par étapes," *Le Populaire*, 27 Jan. 1934.

152. L. Blum, "Socialisation et socialisme," *Le Populaire*, 26 Jan. 1934.

153. Blum, "Le Secteur privé."

154. See S. Ph. Kramer, "Neo-Socialism: The Belgian Case," *Res Publica* 18, no. 1 (1976), 65.

155. Ibid., 6.

156. This, however, was certainly not the opinion of G. Lefranc in his detailed article tracing the history of the planist movement, "Le Courant planiste de 1933 à 1936," *Le Mouvement social*, Jan.–Mar. 1966, 69–89.

157. For a list of the planist groups, see Lefranc's "Le Courant planiste" and his contribution to the volume on De Man, "La Diffusion des idées planistes en France," *Revue européenne des sciences sociales et Cahiers Vilfredo Pareto* 12, no. 31 (1974), 151–64.

158. M. Déat, "Préface," in *Le Plan français: Doctrine et plan d'action* (Paris: Fasquelle, 1935), 15–18.

159. Concerning the "disturbing waverings" of the 9 July group, see Lefranc, "Le Courant planiste," 84, and Andreu, "Les Idées politiques," 26.

160. Concerning the planist meetings at Pontigny, see the two chapters on the subject by Ralph Nordling and Georges Lefranc in *Paul Desjardins et les décades de Pontigny: Études, témoignages, et documents inédits*, ed. Anne Heurgon-Desjardins (Paris: PUF, 1964), 215–32.

Paul Desjardins, a fellow student of Bergson and Jaurès at the École Normale, was an extraordinary figure. André Siegfried considered him "the last humanist" (p. 397). When he acquired the Abbey of Pontigny, Desjardins made it a renowned meeting place of European intellectuals from 1910 onward. From 1922 to 1939, three ten-day "sessions" were held each summer, each session devoted to a different subject. In 1929, Desjardins was won over by *Au-delà du marxisme*, and from that time did his best to make De Man known. In June 1936, the Second Conference of Labor Plans was held in Geneva, no doubt because of the political tensions in France. The third conference was held at Pontigny, in October 1937.

161. See Françoise Laurent, "Le Gouvernement de Vichy et la Révolution nationale" (paper presented at the symposium on "The Vichy Government and the National Revolution, 1940–1942," held at the National Foundation of Political Sciences on 6 and 7 March 1970), 41. The Redressement group was composed largely of former members of "Révolution constructive" (see chap. 5).

162. In 1936, Belin founded the weekly journal *Syndicats*, assuming the position of chief editor. He became a member of the National Bureau of the CGT in September 1933, and after the reunification led the so-called "independent" trend in the CGT.

163. R. Belin, "La Position du syndicalisme français devant les problèmes économiques actuels," *X Crise*, no. 35, Feb. 1937, 39–46; "Quelques réflexions sur l'orientation du syndicalisme français," ibid., no. 66, Jan. 1938, 23–26.

164. Auguste Detoeuf, *Construction du syndicalisme* (Paris: Gallimard, 1938).

165. The Franco-Swedish encounter was conceived by Detoeuf, then president of the Alsthom and of the Electrical Construction Syndicate. Its purpose was to determine, on the basis of the Swedish model, a method of permanently

avoiding social conflicts and to establish employer-worker contractual relationships on a new foundation. On the French side were Ernest Mercier, president of the Union of Electricity, Lambert Ribot, director of the French Heavy Industries Association, and Barnand, director of the Worms Bank. (See R. Nordling and G. Lefranc, "La Rencontre franco-suédoise de Pontigny en 1938," in *Paul Desjardins et les décades de Pontigny*, ed. Heurgon-Desjardins [Paris: PUF, 1964], 224–25.) One can readily imagine how, in the then-prevailing atmosphere, the French left reacted to such an encounter, in which the CGT refused to participate.

166. G. Valois, "La Trahison de Pontigny et le complot pour l'automne 1938," *Le Nouvel Age*, 27 Aug. 1938, 3:

> An unprecedented betrayal has been taking place: Pontigny could be the prelude to a Sedan of the international proletariat; a gigantic capitulation has been prepared there of labor syndicalism and socialism to the employers and the plutocracy. . . .
> The class spirit and the very idea of class have been used to bring the syndicalist fighters to recognize the definitive right of the capitalist class over the means of production, and to place this right, henceforth inviolable, outside the labor struggle.
> The Pontigny meeting was an enormous swindle: in exchange for a definitive recognition of the right of syndicates to regulate the conditions of labor, capitalism wishes to obtain a definitive recognition of the right of capitalism to the ownership of the factory and to undisputed control of the factory.

167. Ibid., 7.

168. Quoted in Laurent, "Le Gouvernement de Vichy," 42.

169. M. Déat, "Offensive générale sur le front du Plan," *La Vie socialiste*, 22 Dec. 1934, 3.

170. See G. Lefranc, "Le Courant planiste de 1933 à 1936," *Le Mouvement social*, Jan.–Mar. 1966, 83ff. On the neosocialist point of view, see Déat, "Offensive générale," 1–3.

It is interesting to note that Georges Izard, "Socialisme, planisme, et frontisme," *La Flèche*, 13 Apr. 1935, was also opposed to planism for reasons similar to those advanced during the same period by Valois's *Le Nouvel Age*: "In whittling down, even in doctrinal matters, its starting positions, planism has created and maintained a psychology of abdication, a tendency to excessive conciliation, an atmosphere of reformism."

171. See Déat, *Perspectives socialistes*, 215–16, as well as "Le Congrès du Parti Socialiste de France," *Le Front*, 16 Nov. 1935, an account of the congress of the Parti Socialiste de France held in November 1935: "The general idea of the Plan" is to demonstrate "how the notion of the planned economy and the law of the general interest can replace capitalist anarchy in a practical and smooth manner." See also André Bailland, "La Pensée socialiste dans le Plan français," ibid., 7 Dec. 1935.

· 172. Déat's statement following De Man's lecture at the Nouvelle École de la Paix, *La Vie socialiste*, 22 Dec. 1934.

Chapter Seven

1. Andreu, "Les Idées politiques," 27.
2. De Man, *Au-delà du marxisme*, 300.

3. Loustau, *Un Ordre social français*, 25.

4. M. Déat, "Organisation sociale et philosophie," *Bulletin de la Société française de philosophie* 37–38, no. 2 (Mar. 1938), 49, quoted by Grossmann, "L'Évolution de Marcel Déat," 17. See also an article written by Pierre Renaudel following the neosocialist split in which he asserts that underlying all "the problems that arise in modern society, one inevitably finds these two obligations: the reform of the state and its moral transformation. . . . The state will never be reformed if it is not made moral" ("L'État ne sera pas réformé s'il n'est moralisé," *La Vie socialiste*, 20 Jan. 1934, 3).

5. E. Mounier, *Oeuvres*, Intro. P. Mounier, 4 vols. (Paris: Éditions du Seuil, 1961–62), 4:490.

6. See P. de Senarclens, *Le Mouvement "Esprit," 1932–1941: Essai critique* (Lausanne: L'Age d'Homme, 1974), 20–21.

7. M. Winock, *Histoire politique de la revue "Esprit"* (Paris: Éditions du Seuil, 1975), 71.

8. Ibid., 73.

9. E. Mounier, "Henri De Man: *L'Idée socialiste*," *Esprit*, no. 31 (Apr. 1935), 90.

10. Winock, *Histoire politique*, 76–80.

11. Of all the works of its kind published in recent years, *Le Rouge et le blanc* is the most trustworthy, insofar as it is the least apologetic and the most faithful to the realities of the period it describes.

12. Winock, *Histoire politique*, 84. See also Andreu, *Le Rouge et le blanc*, 111–12. Winock's account is highly apologetic.

13. E. Mounier, "*Esprit* au Congrès franco-italien sur la corporation," *Esprit*, no. 33 (June 1935), 474–80. See Mounier, *Oeuvres* 4:844.

14. Mounier, "*Esprit* au Congrès franco-italien," 480, 476.

15. Ibid., 479.

16. Ibid., 476.

17. E. Mounier and G. de Santillana, "Dialogue sur l'État fasciste," *Esprit*, nos. 35–36 (Sept. 1935), 725–36.

18. Ibid., 734.

19. Ibid., 735.

20. Ibid., 732.

21. Ibid.

22. O. Strasser, "L'Allemagne est-elle un danger ou un espoir pour l'Europe?," *Esprit*, no. 16 (1 Jan. 1934), 651–70; no. 17 (1 Feb. 1934), 750–80; no. 18 (1 Mar. 1934), 996–1009; no. 20 (1 May 1934), 270–83.

23. Hellman, *Emmanuel Mounier*, 115.

24. E. Mounier, "Tentation," *Jeune Europe*, no. 3 (1936), 3.

25. R. de Becker, "Le Camp international de Zoute," *L'Avant-Garde*, 16 July 1936. Reinhold Schulze led the German group. John Hellman is responsible for the rediscovery of this article. *Esprit* announced this "Youth Meeting" (no. 46 [July 1936], 632), but did not give an account of it.

26. Hellman, *Emmanuel Mounier*, 123, cites *Monatshefte* 11 (1936). See also Hellman, p. 124ff.

27. E. Mounier, "Adresse des vivants à quelques survivants," *Esprit*, no. 43 (Apr. 1936), 3–4. See also Mounier, "Les Deux Grandeurs," ibid., no. 44 (May

1936), 152, and "Rassemblement populaire," ibid., no. 45 (June 1936), 444.

28. Mounier, "Rassemblement populaire," 446.

29. Ibid., 447–49; R. Leenhardt, "Le Vin nouveau et les vieilles outres," *Esprit*, no. 54 (Mar. 1937), 982–85.

30. It should be pointed out once again that writers with other points of view were published in *Esprit*. They were not many, but they existed. See, for example, P.-Henri Simon, "Équivoques de l'antiparlementarisme," no. 75 (Dec. 1938), 394–95.

31. E. Mounier, "Court traité de la mythique de gauche," in *Oeuvres* 4:58.

32. Ibid.

33. Ibid., 61.

34. Ibid., 75.

35. E. Mounier, "Note sur la tactique et l'attitude politique d'*Esprit*," *Journal intérieur*, no. 19 (1 Oct. 1937), 6. See also Hellman, *Emmanuel Mounier*, 128–29.

36. For a more detailed study of these questions, see Z. Sternhell, "Emmanuel Mounier et la contestation de la démocratie libérale dans le France des années trente," *Revue française de science politique* 34, no. 6 (Dec. 1984), 1141–80.

37. Winock, *Histoire politique*, 85.

38. Quoted in Winock, *Histoire politique*, 85 n. 1.

39. See E. Mounier, "Révolution personnaliste et communautaire," in *Oeuvres* 1:129–219.

40. R. Brasillach, "Lettre aux cocus de la droite," *Combat*, Mar. 1936.

41. J. Thibau, *"Le Monde": Histoire d'un journal: Un Journal dans l'histoire* (Paris: Jean-Claude Simoën, 1978), 19.

42. See the exchange of views between P. Mendès France and G. Valois following Valois's lecture, "Lever de rideau avant les tragédies mondiales," *Cahiers bleus*, no. 26 (3 Aug. 1929), 17, 29.

43. M. Duverger, *L'Autre Côté des choses* (Paris: Albin Michel, 1977), 42.

44. See Senarclens, *Le Mouvement "Esprit,"* 230–31.

45. Drieu La Rochelle, *Socialisme fasciste*, 10, 114.

46. This was the title of a book by Jean Luchaire published by Valois in 1929.

47. G. Valois, "L'Autorité et la liberté ou la souveraineté et la représentation," *Le Nouveau Siècle*, 1 Feb. 1926. See also *"L'Ami du peuple,"* ibid., 30 July 1936.

48. Drieu La Rochelle, "Sous Doumergue"; "Les Deux Premiers Mois de *La Lutte des jeunes*," *La Lutte des jeunes*, 27 May 1934.

49. G. Bergery, "Bilan politique de 1937," *La Flèche*, 1 Jan. 1938.

50. P. Andreu, "La Troisième Force, parti de *gauche*," *La Lutte des jeunes*, 20 May 1934.

51. P. Drieu La Rochelle, "Contre la droite et la gauche," *La Lutte des jeunes*, 11 Mar. 1934.

52. Drieu La Rochelle, "Allons voir Staline au Pavillon de l'URSS," *Socialisme fasciste*, 101–2. "The two most obsolete, idiotic, and mendacious words are *left* and *right*," he said in the time of the PPF (*L'Émancipation nationale*, 19 June 1937).

53. M. Déat, "Rapport moral" (Moral Report) for the second national con-

gress of the PSF, *La Vie socialiste*, 5 May 1934, 10. See also Déat, "La Fin d'une controverse," 8–9.

54. H. Lefort, "Comment faire la révolution," *La Lutte des jeunes*, 20 May 1934.

55. Maulnier, "Le Seul Combat possible."

56. Ibid.

57. M. Déat, "Extrême urgence," *La Vie socialiste*, 3 Feb. 1934, 5.

58. M. Blanchot, "On demande des dissidents," *Combat*, Dec. 1937.

59. Ibid.

60. Drieu La Rochelle, *Socialisme fasciste*, 102; "La République des indécis," *La Lutte des jeunes*, 10 June 1934; "Sous Doumergue"; P. Andreu, "Et à la rentrée," ibid., 14 July 1934; Lafue, "La Révolution est-elle pour le 8 juillet?," *1934*, 13 June 1934; Loustau, *Un Ordre social français*, 5.

61. Doriot, *Refaire la France*, 124–25. For examples of the same ideas as expressed by the néos, see Montagnon's speech in *La Vie socialiste*, 9 Feb. 1935, 13–14, and "Le Congrès du parti socialiste," *Le Front*, 16 Nov. 1935. There was a difference of opinion between the Renaudel group and the other néos on whether the left and right still existed; see Renaudel, "Pour notre Congrès national," and Texcier, "Pas d'équivoque!"

62. Drieu La Rochelle, *Socialisme fasciste*, 88.

63. Ibid., 86–87, 89, 90.

64. Maulnier, "Les Deux Violences."

65. Ibid.

66. B. de Jouvenel, "Les États généraux du travail et la défense républicaine," *La Lutte des jeunes*, 15 Apr. 1934.

67. Ibid.

68. T. Maulnier, "Le Socialisme antidémocratique de Georges Sorel," *La Revue universelle* 64, no. 21 (1 Feb. 1936), 373.

69. Ibid., 374. On the "social" aspect of the Maurrassian right, see also T. Maulnier, "Charles Maurras et le socialisme," *La Revue universelle* 68, no. 19 (1 Jan. 1937), 169: "It would not be an exaggeration of the thought of Charles Maurras to say that before anyone else in Europe, and long before the war, he had thought of the formula of 'national socialism' that, under different forms, was to assume such a singular form in Europe."

70. Maulnier, "Les Deux Violences."

71. T. Maulnier, "La Fin d'un ordre," *Combat*, July 1936.

72. Maulnier, "Les Deux Violences."

73. Ibid.

74. G. Valois, "A la recherche du parti nouveau," *Le Nouveau Siècle*, 19 June 1927. When he began his return toward the left, Valois became an important political innovator. Not only did he initiate the idea of a "parti nouveau" (a few years later Sir Oswald Mosley was to call the British fascist movement the New Party), but he organized study and discussion groups called clubs (see Valois's "L'Organisation des clubs," ibid., 26 June 1927). On the néos' attitude to the "old parties," see Capdeville, "Nous ne renonçons pas," 9, and Déat, "Pour notre Congrès," 2; "Fronts et rassemblements," 6; and "Après la constitution," 3.

75. P. Drieu La Rochelle, "Si j'étais La Rocque," *La Lutte des jeunes*, 20 May 1934. "The Action Française has one function in history, which is that of looking back," wrote Drieu.

76. P. Drieu La Rochelle, "Verra-t-on un parti national et socialiste?," *La Lutte des jeunes*, 4 Mar. 1934.

77. Andreu, "Si j'étais Charles Maurras. . . ."

78. Brasillach, "Lettre aux cocus."

79. Ibid. See Brasillach once again on "the trembling liberals," the political figures of the right: "One will have to get rid of these self-righteous marionettes, these tender-hearted fools, these funks and imbeciles who are called the deputies of the right."

80. J. Roumanès, "La Tradition nationaliste," *La Lutte des jeunes*, 15 Apr. 1934: "We cannot be satisfied with the egotistical patriotism or mean nationalism of people for whom there are no social problems. *How can one ask the workers who are so shamefully oppressed by the capitalist system to love a nation that cannot promise a human existence for its citizens?* How can one love one's country when one is not even sure of having work every day, when one is not even assured of one's daily bread?" See also Jouvenel's article "Où cours-tu camarade avec ta matraque?," ibid., 24 June 1934. Jouvenel addresses an imaginary Croix de Feu: "And yet, if you do not desire to overthrow the great financial dynasties, you are not a revolutionary. You are only a little boy with a bludgeon, and very few brains under your beret."

81. Drieu La Rochelle, "Sous Doumergue."

82. Drieu La Rochelle, *Socialisme fasciste*, 175–76.

83. F. Gravier, "Deux démocraties: Une Seule Révolution," *Combat*, Dec. 1937.

84. T. Maulnier, "Pour un examen de conscience du nationalisme," *Combat*, Feb. 1938.

85. T. Maulnier, *La Crise est dans l'homme* (Paris: Librairie de *La Revue française*, 1932). Two years earlier, in the spring of 1930, a young student named Jacques Talagrand, having heard that the few students who wrote the royalist journal *L'Étudiant français* had suddenly left *L'Action française*, proposed to write the next issue. So that there should be no hiatus, the journal was put together in forty-eight hours by himself, Brasillach, José Lupin, and Maurice Bardèche. It was on this occasion that Talagrand took on the pseudonym of Thierry Maulnier. See R. Brasillach, *Notre avant-guerre* (Paris: Plon, 1941), 89.

86. Drieu La Rochelle, "Contre la droite." See also Drieu La Rochelle, "Verra-t-on un parti national et socialiste?," and *Socialisme fasciste*, 206, 221–24. Jean de Fabrègues took up this same formula in *Combat* to sum up the main argument of Maulnier's *Au-delà du nationalisme* ("Libérer le prolétariat"). In *Un Voyageur dans le siècle*, Jouvenel noted that it was Drieu's close association with the journal that gave it its fascist quality (p. 184), but in fact quite a number of its articles, especially those on Italy and Germany (see below), had a markedly fascist and Nazi character. *La Lutte* was a fascist journal not because Drieu was a contributor but because that was the aim of its editor and writers.

87. M. Barrès, "M. le général Boulanger et la nouvelle génération," *La Revue indépendante* 8 (Apr. 1888), 31.

88. Déat, *Perspectives socialistes*, 10.

89. G. Valois, "Les Socialistes découvrent le socialisme," *Le Nouveau Siècle*, 15 Jan. 1928.

90. B. Montagnon in Montagnon, Marquet, and Déat, *Néo-socialisme?*, 30–31.

91. T. Maulnier, "Le 'Fascisme' et son avenir en France," *La Revue universelle* 64, no. 19 (1 Jan. 1936), 22.

92. B. de Jouvenel, "Bilan," *La Lutte des jeunes*, 14 July 1934.

93. "Les Possibilités socialistes du fascisme," *La Lutte des jeunes*, 22 Apr. 1934.

94. Jouvenel, *Le Réveil de l'Europe*, 147.

95. Drieu La Rochelle, "Verra-t-on un parti national et socialiste?" See also B. de Jouvenel, "Deux opinions sur *Front commun*," *La Lutte des jeunes*, 3 June 1934, and G. Valois, "Appel pour le front unique," *Chantiers coopératifs*, 8 Mar. 1938.

96. Drieu La Rochelle, *Socialisme fasciste*, 179.

97. Ibid., 231. See also pp. 52–57, 205, 215, 230–32.

98. Ibid., 172. See also pp. 110, 163, 202–10.

99. Drieu La Rochelle, "Verra-t-on un parti national et socialiste?" See Drieu La Rochelle, *Socialisme fasciste*, 233–34.

100. Brasillach, *Notre avant-guerre*, 184.

101. P. Andreu, "Réformisme pas mort," *La Lutte des jeunes*, 27 May 1934.

102. G. Valois, "Il y a fascisme et fascisme," *Le Nouveau Siècle*, 25 Feb. 1928.

103. Drieu La Rochelle, "La République des indécis."

104. Duverger, *L'Autre Côté des choses*, 20.

105. C. Maldor, "Nullité d'une politique de complot et de commissions," *La Lutte des jeunes*, 25 Mar. 1934.

106. Brasillach, *Notre avant-guerre*, 184. See also Saillenfest, "Fascisme et syndicalisme."

107. Brasillach, *Notre avant-guerre*, 221.

108. Jouvenel, *Un Voyageur dans le siècle*, 79–81. See also Brasillach, *Notre avant-guerre*, 177–78.

109. The first issue of *Front commun*, fortnightly journal of the "frontist" movement, appeared on 1 December 1933. It was succeeded by *La Flèche*.

110. Jouvenel, *Un Voyageur dans le siècle*, 174.

111. Jouvenel, "Deux opinions sur *Front commun*."

112. Ibid.

113. Izard, "Notre doctrine"; "Du Front populaire au front des Français," *La Flèche*, 13 Mar. 1937.

114. G. Bergery, "Dans les ornières de l'orthodoxie," *La Flèche*, 22 May 1937.

115. Izard, "Notre doctrine."

116. See "Néo-fascisme!," *La Flèche*, 28 Oct. 1938.

117. Archives de la Préfecture de Police, document 79.501.1845, third frontist meeting, 25 Mar. 1938.

118. See G. Valois, "A la recherche du 'parti nouveau,'" *Le Nouveau Siècle*, 19 June 1927, 3, where an article by Georges Hoog in *La Jeune République* is mentioned.

119. Renaudel used the expression "left-wing fascism" when speaking to the militants of the PSF ("Défense d'un 'démocrate fossilisant' et 'proportionaliste,'" *La Vie socialiste*, 9 June 1934, 1–2).

120. H. Dubief, "Front rouge ou faisceaux," *La Lutte des jeunes*, 27 May 1934; Maldor, "Nullité d'une politique."

121. See Maulnier, "Le 'Fascisme,'" 22.

122. Drieu La Rochelle, "La République des indécis"; Valois, "Contre tout fascisme."

123. Drieu La Rochelle, *Chronique politique*, 69.

124. Ibid., 71. See Gregor, *Italian Fascism and Developmental Dictatorship*.

125. Brasillach, *Notre avant-guerre*, 184.

126. Ibid., 185.

127. See André Monconduit's series of articles "Qu'est-ce que le fascisme?," *Combat*, June, Nov. 1937, Jan. 1938. See also Brasillach's article in the Dec. 1936 issue in honor of José Antonio Primo de Rivera.

128. J. de Fabrègues, "Devant l'esclavage de la civilisation," *Combat*, May 1939; "La Préoccupation de l'essentiel."

129. T. Maulnier, "Pour un complot contre la sûreté de l'État digne de ce nom," *Combat*, Dec. 1937.

130. M. Barrès, *L'Ennemi des lois* (Paris: Perrin, 1893), 19, 25–26.

131. Ibid., 22.

132. Maulnier, "Pour un complot."

133. Drieu La Rochelle, *Socialisme fasciste*, 52.

134. M. Barrès, "Le Problème est double," *La Cocarde*, 8 Sept. 1894.

135. M. Barrès, "Opprimés et humiliés," *La Cocarde*, 14 Sept. 1894.

136. Barrès, "Le Problème est double."

137. Drieu La Rochelle, *Chronique politique*, 50. See also p. 54.

138. Maulnier, *La Crise est dans l'homme*, 93.

139. Ibid., 96, 180.

140. Ibid., 181–82. See also pp. 60–61.

141. Ibid., 9.

142. Ibid., 59, 58.

143. Ibid., 180.

144. Ibid., 183.

145. Ibid., 193.

146. Ibid., 194.

147. Ibid.

148. Ibid., 10.

149. Ibid., 8–9, 15.

150. Ibid., 96. See also p. 95.

151. Ibid., 182. See also p. 8: "It is spiritual values that must first be reestablished."

152. T. Maulnier, *Mythes socialistes* (Paris: Gallimard, 1936), 20–21.

153. Ibid., 14.

154. See Maulnier, *Mythes socialistes*, esp. 127ff.

155. Ibid., 11.

156. Ibid., 129–30.

157. Ibid., 157.

158. Ibid., 157–62.

159. Ibid., 165–67.

160. Ibid., 168.

161. Ibid., 174–76.

162. T. Maulnier, *Au-delà du nationalisme* (Paris: Gallimard, 1938), 28–29, 33–35.

163. T. Maulnier, introduction to *Le Troisième Reich*, by A. Moeller van den Bruck (Paris: Librairie de *La Revue française*, 1933), 5.

164. Ibid., 6.

165. Ibid., 5.

166. Ibid., 6.

167. Ibid., 5. *The Outlaws*, translated from the German by Ian F. D. Morrow (London: J. Cape, 1931), is the English translation of Ernst von Salomon's book *Die Geächteten* (Berlin: E. Rowahlt, 1930).

168. M. Barrès, *Les Déracinés* (Paris: Fasquelle, 1897), 232.

169. Maulnier, introduction to *Le Troisième Reich*, 8, 9.

170. Ibid., 7.

171. Ibid.

172. Ibid.

173. Ibid., 8.

174. Ibid., 9.

175. Ibid., 9–10.

176. Ibid., 15.

177. Ibid., 16.

178. Ibid., 13.

179. Ibid., 11.

180. See above, chap. 5.

181. L. Degrelle, *Révolution des âmes* (Paris: Éditions de France, 1938).

182. Brasillach, *Notre avant-guerre*, 3, 101.

183. Ibid., 273.

184. Maulnier, introduction to *Le Troisième Reich*, 9, 7.

185. Ibid., 8.

186. A. Moeller van den Bruck, *Le Troisième Reich*, trans. from German by Jean-Louis Lenault (Paris: Librairie de *La Revue française*, 1933), 62–67.

187. Ibid., 68. See also further on: "It is not accidental that all his characteristics are Mosaic, Maccabean, Talmudic, and that they possess all the features of the ghetto. He is very far from Christ; and yet, in a way, he kept close to him, like a Judas who wished to expiate his betrayal of his Lord. In all his work one does not find a single word on the love of man, but only a somber passion informed by hatred, vengeance, the desire for retaliation. Christ's mission was beyond all national sentiment, and for that reason it could reach the peoples of the North. Marx's doctrine was international, and for that reason it could dissociate Europe and lead the Europeans astray."

On Moeller, see Fritz Stern's fine book *The Politics of Cultural Despair*, 183ff.

188. Maulnier, *Au-delà du nationalisme*, 249.

189. *Au-delà du nationalisme* was undoubtedly the most representative and complete work produced by the "social right" in the interwar period. A thirty-page booklet summarizing its main arguments was published before the work itself. See T. Maulnier, *La Société nationale et la lutte des classes* (Paris: Combat, 1937). This was the first of the *Cahiers de Combat*.

Some of the basic ideas of Maulnier's work, especially the idea that capitalism destroys the nation, may also be found in Drieu La Rochelle's *Socialisme fasciste*, 175–78.

190. Maulnier, *Au-delà du nationalisme*, 34.

191. Ibid.

192. Ibid., 35.

193. Ibid. See also p. 37.

194. Ibid., 35.

195. Ibid., 35–36.

196. Ibid., 37.

197. Ibid., 36.

198. Ibid., 40.

199. Ibid., 41.

200. Ibid., 42.

201. Ibid., 50.

202. Ibid., 56.

203. Ibid., 57, 75, 67.

204. Ibid., 94, 59.

205. Ibid., 61.

206. Ibid., 62.

207. Ibid., 65.

208. Ibid., 63.

209. Ibid., 70–71.

210. Ibid., 72.

211. Ibid., 73.

212. Ibid., 85.

213. Maulnier, *Nietzsche*.

214. Maulnier, *Au-delà du nationalisme*, 86.

215. Ibid., 89–94.

216. Ibid., 97.

217. Ibid. See also p. 98ff.

218. Ibid., 104–5.

219. Ibid., 106.

220. Ibid., 107ff.

221. Ibid., 110–11.

222. Ibid., 114.

223. Ibid.

224. Ibid., 121.

225. Ibid., 120.

226. Ibid., 133, 120.

227. Ibid., 133.

228. Ibid., 121, 135, 136.

229. Ibid., 136.

230. Ibid., 137–38.

231. Ibid., 138.

232. Ibid.

233. Ibid., 149ff.

234. Ibid., 157.

235. Ibid.

236. Ibid., 164, 182.

237. Ibid., 176.

238. Ibid., 180.

239. Ibid., 181.

240. Ibid.

241. Ibid., 182.

242. Ibid.

243. Ibid.

244. Ibid., 194.

245. Ibid., 193.

246. Ibid., 194–95. Here Maulnier takes up E. Goblot's well-known ideas; see *La Barrière et le niveau: Étude sociologique sur la bourgeoisie française moderne* (Paris: PUF, 1967; first published 1925).

247. Maulnier, *Au-delà du nationalisme*, 196.

248. Ibid., 197.

249. Ibid.

250. Ibid., 197–98.

251. Ibid., 224, 226–27, 231.

252. Ibid., 227.

253. Ibid., 241.

254. Ibid., 242.

255. Ibid., 237.

256. Ibid., 239.

257. Ibid.

258. Ibid.

259. Ibid., 203–7.

260. Ibid., 198. See also p. 218.

261. Quoted in T. Maulnier, "A propos d'*Au-delà du nationalisme*: Réponse à Drieu La Rochelle," *Combat*, May 1938.

262. On Drieu in the PPF, see Andreu and Grover, *Drieu La Rochelle*, 365ff.

263. Maulnier, "A propos d' *Au-delà du nationalisme*."

264. T. Maulnier, *Révolution nationale: L'Avenir de la France* (Hanoi: Éditions du Gouvernement Général de l'Indochine, 1942), 7. See also his *La France, la guerre, et la paix* (Lyon: Lardanchet, 1942).

265. Maulnier, *Révolution nationale*, 84, 117.

266. T. Maulnier, "Notes sur le fascisme," *Combat*, Dec. 1938.

267. Ibid.

268. Ibid.

269. Ibid.

270. J. de Fabrègues, "Une Mystique matérialiste: La Démocratie hitlér-ienne," *Combat*, Jan. 1937.

271. Ibid.

272. Ibid.

273. Ibid.

274. Maulnier, "Le 'Fascisme,'" 17, 20.

275. Brasillach, *Notre avant-guerre*, 283.

276. Ibid., 193.

277. See B. Mussolini, "L'Aurore d'une civilisation nouvelle," *1934*, 12 Dec. 1934. Launched in 1933 by the Librairie Plon, this elegantly designed and pro-fusely illustrated weekly, edited by Henri Massis, had the current year as its title, as had J.-P. Maxence's *Cahiers* at the end of the twenties. Brasillach was editorial secretary, and Maulnier collaborated on the page "Jeunesse du monde." This publication was intended as a counterpart to Emmanuel Berl's *Marianne*.

278. Brasillach, *Notre avant-guerre*, 235.

279. Ibid. See also M. Déat, *De l'école d'hier à l'homme de demain* (Paris: Éditions du RNP, 1943).

280. See Drieu La Rochelle, "La République des indécis."

281. Andreu, *Le Rouge et le blanc*, 96–97.

282. Brasillach, *Notre avant-guerre*, 193.

283. H. Massis, "Quand Mussolini n'est plus devant la foule," *1933*, 1 Nov. 1933.

284. R. Benjamin, "Mussolini et son peuple," *La Revue universelle* 67, nos. 16–18 (Oct.–Dec. 1936), 385ff., 529ff., 678ff.; nos. 20–22 (Jan.–Mar. 1937), 237ff., 363ff., 468ff.

285. R. Brasillach and H. Massis, "Les Cadets de l'Alcazar," *La Revue uni-verselle* 67, nos. 15, 16 (Oct.–Dec. 1936), 257ff., 407ff.

286. Brasillach, "Cent heures chez Hitler." (This article is included in *Notre avant-guerre*.)

287. A. Hitler, interview by B. de Jouvenel, *Paris-Midi* 28 Feb. 1936. See above, Preface.

288. Statement of B. Montagnon in an account of a foreign-affairs debate in *La Vie socialiste*, 8 Dec. 1934, 12.

289. "Débat sur l'orientation générale du parti: Discours de B. Montag-non," *La Vie socialiste*, 9 Feb. 1935, 12.

290. Drieu La Rochelle, "La République des indécis." See also Drieu La Rochelle, *Socialisme fasciste*, 235, and Jouvenel, "Deux opinions sur *Front commun*."

291. Drieu La Rochelle, *Socialisme fasciste*, 238. Drieu declared himself a fascist in June 1934; he declared himself a socialist in August of the same year.

292. Drieu La Rochelle, "Verra-t-on un parti national et socialiste?"

293. Drieu La Rochelle, *Chronique politique*, 50.

294. Ibid., 52, 49.

295. Brasillach, *Notre avant-guerre*, 236.

296. Ibid., 282.

297. Ibid., 277, 278.

298. Ibid., 131. See also p. 269ff. on the ceremony at the Nuremberg stadium, "sacred site of the national mystery."

299. Ibid., 246.

300. Ibid., 237.

301. Ibid., 151.

302. Ibid., 237.

303. D. Ollivier, "Éducation fasciste: Culte de la révolution," *La Luttes des jeunes*, 10 June 1934.

304. B. de Prévaux, "Demoiselles en uniforme," *La Lutte des jeunes*, 18 Mar. 1934.

305. De Man, *Au-delà du marxisme*, 46–47.

306. L.-D. Girard, "Camps de travail," *1933*, 1 Nov. 1933.

307. Jouvenel, *Un Voyageur dans le siècle*, 46–47.

308. P. Déroulède, *L'Alsace-Lorraine et la fête nationale* (Paris: Blond, 1910), 7. See P. Bourget, *Essais de psychologie contemporaine*, 4th ed. (Paris: Lemerre, 1885), 14–16, 24–25, and M. Barrès, "Le Sentiment en littérature," *Les Taches d'Encre*, Jan. 1885, 10–11, 33. See also A. E. Carter, *The Idea of Decadence in French Literature, 1830–1900* (Toronto: University of Toronto Press, 1958).

309. T. Maulnier, "Sortirons-nous de l'abjection française?," *Combat*, Nov. 1936.

310. Drieu La Rochelle, *Socialisme fasciste*, 201.

311. Jouvenel, *Le Réveil de l'Europe*, 229. See also pp. 12–13, 227–28.

312. J. de Fabrègues, "Les Nouveaux Bellicistes et la vraie dignité de l'homme," *Combat*, Apr. 1938.

313. Doriot, *Refaire la France*, 53. See also pp. 10, 93, and Loustau, *Un Ordre social français*, 25.

314. Barrès, *Les Déracinés*, chap. 9.

315. Jouvenel, *Le Réveil de l'Europe*, 147.

316. "Une France qui nous dégoûte," *Combat*, Apr. 1936. See also Charles Mauban, "Les Bons Sentiments," ibid., Dec. 1937.

317. P. Drieu La Rochelle, "Congrégations," *La Lutte des jeunes*, 22 Apr. 1934. See also B. de Jouvenel, "La Crise du capitalisme et la fin des démocraties," ibid., 1 Apr. 1934.

318. T. Maulnier, "Un Régime ennemi des arts," *Combat*, Apr. 1936.

319. G. Blond, "Liberté de la presse et réalisme politique," *Combat*, Dec. 1937. See also D. Bertin, "Notes politiques," ibid., Feb. 1939.

320. T. Maulnier, "Les Nouvelles Conditions imposées à l'action politique en France," *Combat*, July 1937.

321. J. Chaperon, "Pour ou contre Stavisky," *Combat*, 25 Mar. 1934; Jouvenel, *L'Économie dirigée*, 177–80.

322. Maulnier, "Un Régime ennemi des arts."

323. T. Maulnier, "A bas la culture bourgeoise," *Combat*, Oct. 1936.

324. G. Valois, "Pour la Révolution culturelle," *Chantiers coopératifs*, June 1932.

325. P. Norgeu, "L'Esprit bourgeois," *La Lutte des jeunes*, 22 Apr. 1934.

326. B. de Jouvenel, *Après la défaite* (Paris: Plon, 1941), 191.

327. J. Roumanès, "Révolution marxiste ou révolution spirituelle?," *La Lutte des jeunes*, 20 May 1934. See also P. Andreu, "L'Opinion du groupe l'Assaut," ibid., 8 Apr. 1934. The little fascist group L'Assaut had taken as its slogan Péguy's saying "The social revolution will be a moral one, or it will not take place."

328. J. de Fabrègues, "Une Révolution justifiée," *Combat*, Jan. 1938.

329. Maulnier, "Pour un complot." See also M. Péguy, "Révolution," *L'Assaut*, 2 May 1935. *L'Assaut*, written by Péguy, Roumanès, and Andreu, had only three issues. On the little national-syndicalist front, see also Andreu, *Le Rouge et le blanc*, 93.

330. Maulnier, "Le Seul Combat possible."

331. Maulnier, "Sortirons-nous de l'abjection française?" Democracy and capitalism must be overthrown, says Maulnier, "for capitalism is only the social form of democracy."

332. T. Maulnier, "Désobéissance aux lois," *Combat*, Jan. 1937.

333. For the néos, see Déat, "Épreuve de la démocratie" and an editorial in *Néo*, 19 Dec. 1934, and Jouvenel, *Le Réveil de l'Europe*, 62, and "Mes cinq points." Articles in *La Lutte des jeunes* of 15 and 22 Apr., 6 May, and 24 June 1934 should also be consulted, and the following articles by J. de Fabrègues and T. Maulnier in *Combat*: Fabrègues, "Où sont vos principes?," Apr. 1936, and "Une Révolution justifiée"; Maulnier, "Désobéissance aux lois" and "Sortirons-nous de l'abjection française?"

334. D. Bertin, "Oraison funèbre du communisme," *Combat*, May 1936.

335. Ibid.

336. Jouvenel, "Mes cinq points."

337. Ibid.

338. Drieu La Rochelle, "Congrégations."

339. Maulnier, "Pour un complot." See also Maulnier, "Le Seul Combat possible."

340. Maulnier, "Désobéissance aux lois."

341. Maulnier, "Sortirons-nous de l'abjection française?"

342. Maulnier, "Pour un examen."

343. Ibid.

344. Maulnier, "Sortirons-nous de l'abjection française?"

345. De Man, *Après-coup*, 187–88.

346. See Barrès, "M. le général Boulanger" and "La Jeunesse boulangiste," *Le Figaro*, 19 May 1888.

347. See Barrès, "M. le général Boulanger" and "La Jeunesse boulangiste"; see also Barrès, "Aux parlementaires du quartier Latin" and "Éloge de nos adversaires," *Le Courrier de l'Est*, 22 Jan., 9 Mar. 1889.

348. Barrès, "M. le général Boulanger."

349. Barrès, *Les Déracinés*, 232ff.

350. *L'Oeuvre de Léon Blum*, vol. 3, pt. 2, pp. 616–18.

351. Quoted by M. Bonnafous in Montagnon, Marquet, and Déat, *Néosocialisme?*, 140.

352. A. Marquet, ibid., 140.

353. M. Déat, ibid., 97–98.

354. Déat, "Méditations," 5.

355. M. Déat's reply to a question in *La Vie socialiste*, 28 May 1932, 6.

356. M. Bonnafous in Montagnon, Marquet, and Déat, *Néo-socialisme?*, 141. See also pp. 10, 93–97, 107–17, 162, and M. Déat, "Les Conditions de Léon Blum," *La Vie socialiste*, 16 Apr. 1932, 3.

357. "La Voix de l'Union socialiste et républicaine se fait entendre par TSF," *Le Front*, 25 Apr. 1936.

358. G. M., "En avant les volontaires socialistes!," *Le Front*, 16 June 1936.

359. Jouvenel, *L'Économie dirigée*, 7.

360. Drieu La Rochelle, *Socialisme fasciste*, 112.

361. Ibid., 66–67.

362. M. Bonnafous in Montagnon, Marquet, and Déat, *Neo-socialisme?*, 114.

363. Ibid., 127–28.

364. Ibid.

365. Jouvenel, *Le Réveil de l'Europe*, 241. See p. 232, where Jouvenel quotes Proudhon extensively.

366. Ibid., 243–44.

367. Ibid.

368. Ibid., 245.

369. Ibid., 248–49.

370. Ibid., 245–46.

371. Ibid., 234.

372. Ibid., 233. See p. 231.

373. Ibid., 234–36.

374. Jouvenel, *Après la défaite*, 4.

375. J. Roullier, "Ceux qui s'en vont," *La Lutte des jeunes*, 14 July 1934.

376. Massis, "Quand Mussolini n'est plus devant la foule."

377. Drieu La Rochelle, *Socialisme fasciste*, 211, 202.

378. Jouvenel, *Le Réveil de l'Europe*, 251, 262, 269.

379. Déat, "Qu'est-ce qu'un programme d'action?," 6.

380. Doriot, *Refaire la France*, 51.

381. See Brasillach, *Notre avant-guerre*, 161, and H.-P. Molinier, "Le Torchon brûle à la Sidilarité française," *La Flèche*, 1 Aug. 1934. Bergery's journal used the name that *Le Canard enchaîné* had given to Coty's movement.

382. J.-P. Maxence, "Pour l'avenir de l'intelligence," *La Solidarité française*, Oct. 1935, 28–29. See also, in the same issue, a remarkable interview with the leader of the movement, Commandant Jean-Renaud, by Robert Francis (pp. 16–17), as well as Thierry Maulnier's tribute ("Témoignage," p. 27).

383. Maxence's real name was Pierre Godmé. He first used the name Jean Maxence, then J.-P. Maxence. At the end of the thirties, he published an authentically fascist little review, *L'Insurgé*, of a national-socialist and anti-Semitic character. See, for instance, the issue of 28 Apr. 1937, in which, just before 1 May, Maxence summarized his ideas.

384. "Manifesto," *Cahiers 1929*, third booklet of the second series, p. 4.

385. Ibid., 1.

386. R. Francis, T. Maulnier, and J.-P. Maxence, *Demain la France* (Paris: Grasset, 1934), 7.

387. Ibid., 212ff.

388. Ibid., 353ff. See also p. 224ff.

389. Drieu La Rochelle, *Socialisme fasciste*, 211.

390. In *Un Voyageur dans le siècle*, 189, Jouvenel quotes his own article published in Luchaire's journal, *Notre temps*, no. 159 (4 July 1934).

391. Jouvenel, *Un Voyageur dans le siècle*, 189.

392. Ibid. Jouvenel claims that Gregor Strasser had always considered national socialism a very socialist doctrine.

393. See his letter of resignation in *La Lutte des jeunes*, 25 Feb. 1934.

394. See Jouvenel's letter of resignation, *La Lutte des jeunes*, 25 Feb. 1934, and Francis, Maulnier, and Maxence, *Demain la France*, 142ff.

395. See B. de Jouvenel, "Aveuglés," *La Lutte des jeunes*, 4 March 1934; A. Bonnard, "Pour une France propre," *1934*, 4 Feb. 1934; M. Déat in *La Vie socialiste*, 20 Jan. 1934, 8–9; and P. Norgeu, "Contribution catholique à la révolution," *La Lutte des jeunes*, 3 June 1934. See also *La Flèche* of 13 Apr. 1935, which proposed cleaning up France "from top to bottom."

396. T. Maulnier, "A bas la culture bourgeoise!," *Combat*, Oct. 1936.

397. Drieu La Rochelle, *Socialisme fasciste*, 113.

398. P. Drieu La Rochelle, "Mesure et démesure de l'esprit français," *Combat*, July 1937.

399. R. Vincent, "Le Miroir du siècle: Nécessité d'un surréalisme," *Combat*, Apr. 1937.

400. B. Montagnon, "Bon courage," *Néo*, 14 Dec. 1934.

401. Maulnier, "A bas la culture bourgeoise!"

402. Drieu La Rochelle, "La République des indécis."

403. Brasillach, *Notre avant-guerre*, 282.

404. Drieu La Rochelle, *Chronique politique*, 53.

405. Ibid., 52. The same image—of smoke-filled rooms and pot-bellied orators—appears in Jouvenel, *Le Réveil de l'Europe*, 234.

406. Drieu La Rochelle, *Chronique politique*, 52, 41.

407. Ibid., 48, 52.

408. Ibid., 56, 51.

409. Ibid., 54.

410. Ibid., 55.

411. T. Maulnier, "Les Trois Grandes Démocraties," *Combat*, Oct. 1937.

412. Drieu La Rochelle, *Chronique politique*, 58.

413. Brasillach, *Notre avant-guerre*, 58.

414. Ibid., 282–83.

415. Ibid., 214, 220, 270–73.

416. Ibid., 222. The same ideas are in P. Copeau, "J'avais un camarade," *1933*, 20 Dec. 1933, and G. Tourmakine, "La Jeunesse hitlérienne," *La Lutte des jeunes*, 4 Mar. 1934.

417. Jouvenel, *Le Réveil de l'Europe*, 233–34. See also pp. 148–49, and Drieu La Rochelle, *Socialisme fasciste*, 107.

418. On Drieu's Maurrassian leanings, see Andreu and Grover, *Drieu La Rochelle*, 154ff. See also Drieu's *Socialisme fasciste*, 220, concerning the "vague relations with the AF with which my journey began."

419. G. Zuccarelli, "Dégonflage des anciens combattants," *La Lutte des jeunes*, 24 June 1934.

420. See Maulnier's *Révolution nacionale*, 7.

421. T. Maulnier, "Une Jeunesse disponible," *1933*, 20 Dec. 1933.

422. Déat, *Perspectives socialistes*, 8; B. Montagnon in Montagnon, Marquet, and Déat, *Néo-socialisme?*, 26–28, 34–35.

423. See especially *La Lutte des jeunes* of February–March 1934.

424. See, for example, the survey of the "youth of the world" which Maulnier began in *1933* and which was continued in *1934*; Barrès, Claude Popelin, and Pierre Lamy sang the praises of German youth, the Spanish Falangists, the followers of Mosley in England, and the young Portuguese fascists (see nos. 1 [11 Oct. 1933], 16 [24 Jan. 1934], and 26 [4 Apr. 1934]).

425. De Man, *L'Idée socialiste*, 269–70.

426. Drieu La Rochelle, *Socialisme fasciste*, 179.

427. Brasillach, *Notre avant-guerre*, 193.

428. Drieu La Rochelle, *Socialisme fasciste*, 234.

429. Brasillach, *Notre avant-guerre*, 234.

430. See, for example, the editorial in *La Lutte des jeunes*, 8 Apr. 1934; F. O. Wrede, "La Jeunesse allemande veut la paix," ibid., 8 Apr. 1934; Girard, "Camps de travail"; and Jouvenel's interview with Hitler. Even Bergery, who was inclined to an extreme pacifism, deplored the partisan tone of Jouvenel's interview with Hitler ("Il faut répondre à Hitler," *La Flèche*, 7 Mar. 1936).

431. Archives de la Préfecture de Police, document 79.501.1845.3, conference of the frontist party, 8 Feb. 1939.

432. F. Challaye, "Pas de guerre pour la Tchécoslovaquie," *La Flèche*, 25 Mar. 1938.

433. Maulnier, "Les Trois Grandes Démocraties."

434. F. Gravier, "Nécessité de l'Autriche-Hongrie," *Combat*, Feb. 1938.

435. Challaye, "Pas de guerre."

436. Jouvenel, "A propos de mon interview."

437. R. Vincent, "Perspectives de la grande guerre prochaine," *Combat*, Apr. 1938.

438. Maze, "Vers la seconde Révolution française." See also L.-E. Galey, "Non, rien, pas même l'antifascisme, ne justifie la guerre," *La Flèche*, 29 Aug. 1936.

439. Maze, "Vers la seconde Révolution française."

440. J. Maze, "Non, M. Daladier, la défense nationale n'est pas la défense des trusts," *La Flèche*, 26 Aug. 1938.

441. Ibid.

442. G. Izard, "Pour la vraie réconciliation française," *La Flèche*, 14 Mar. 1936.

443. Déat, "Mémoires politiques," vol. 3, chap. 19, p. 1. On anti-Semitism in France, see Michel Winock's recent work, *Édouard Drumont et Cie: Antisémitisme et fascisme en France* (Paris: Éditions du Seuil, 1982).

444. De Man, *Après-coup*, 84. See also pp. 132–33, 187.

445. Ibid., 46.

446. See Maulnier, "Notes sur l'antisémitisme," and R. Brasillach, "Un

Vieux Gaulois," *Combat*, Apr. 1936. Georges Blond wrote an article on the celebrated Schmeling-Louis boxing match that Nazi propaganda had presented as a symbol of the white man's struggle ("Un Noir vaut un blanc," *Combat*, July 1938). Blond was replying to an article in *Droit de vivre* ("Un Noir vaut un blanc"), and protested this display of "antifascist satisfaction": "The active elements of Jewish agitation attempt and will attempt to activate this particular form of democratic egalitarianism that, to some degree, becomes purely and simply an action against the whites. That is not without danger."

447. G. Bergery, "L'Antisémitisme renaît, pour le combattre enlevons-lui ses prétextes," *La Flèche*, 11 Nov. 1938.

448. C. Mauriac, "Les Tremplins de l'antisémitisme: Réponse à Bernard Lecache," *La Flèche*, 28 Oct. 1938.

449. M. Duverger, "La Situation des fonctionnaires depuis la révolution de 1940," *Revue du droit public et de la science politique* 57 (1940–41), 277–332, 417–539. On this matter see Marrus and Paxton, *Vichy et les juifs*, 17–18, 138–39. The Statute on the Jews constituted a legislative assault on Jews living in France. It assigned, on the basis of race, an inferior position in French civil law and society to a whole segment of French citizens as well as to non-citizens and foreigners living on French soil.

450. Bergery, "L'Antisémitisme renaît."

451. G. Bergery, "Malfaisance des slogans," *La Flèche*, 2 June 1939. See M. Déat, "Mourir pour Dantzig?," *L'Oeuvre*, 4 May 1939.

452. "Une France qui nous dégoûte," *Combat*, Apr. 1936.

453. Ibid. See also T. Maulnier, "La Mode est à l'Union sacrée," *Combat*, Apr. 1938.

454. Fabrègues, "Une Mystique matérialiste."

455. Jouvenel, *Le Réveil de l'Europe*, 236.

456. T. Maulnier, "Après les accords de Munich: Les Nouvelles Conditions imposées à l'action politique en France," *Combat*, Nov. 1938.

457. Ibid.

458. T. Maulnier, "Il faut refaire un nationalisme en dépit de la nation," *Combat*, Apr. 1937.

Conclusion

1. See Pierre Andreu, "Les Idées politiques" and *Le Rouge et le blanc*, or J.-L. Loubet del Bayle's *Les Non-conformistes des années trente*, 11–31.

2. Valois, "Au-delà du marxisme."

3. This was the title of a book by Daniel-Rops published in 1932 by Éditions du Siècle. Loubet del Bayle used this title as the "motto" of his introduction to *Les Non-conformistes des années trente*.

4. Touchard, "L'Esprit des années 1930," 89.

5. To call a movement or ideology "nonconformist" in the thirties was to use a current "technical term." See Mounier, *Oeuvres* 1:422.

6. Andreu, *Le Rouge et le blanc*, 72.

7. Déat, "Fronts et rassemblements," 6.

8. Andreu, "Les Idées politiques," 177.

9. Loubet del Bayle, *Les Non-conformistes des années trente*, 21.

10. On the idea of a generation and the "spirit of a generation," see Jouvenel, *Un Voyageur dans le siècle*, 76ff., and R. Wohl, *The Generation of 1914* (Cambridge: Harvard University Press, 1979), 1–4, 203–37.

11. Aron and Dandieu used this phrase as the title of their book published by Rieder in 1931.

12. See H. Stuart Hughes, *The Obstructed Path: French Social Thought in the Years of Desperation* (New York: Harper and Row, 1968), 9.

13. Jouvenel, *Un Voyageur dans le siècle*, 467.

14. For a different view of these problems, see R. Girardet, "Notes sur l'esprit d'un fascisme français, 1934–1940," *Revue française de science politique* 5, no. 3 (July–Sept. 1955), 529–46, and R. Rémond, "Y a-t-il un fascisme français?," *Terre humaine*, nos. 7–8 (July–Aug. 1952), 45–47. These articles were pioneering works on the question, but their conclusions are very different from those of the present study. See also R. Rémond, *La Droite en France: De la première Restauration à la Ve République* (Paris: Aubier, 1963), p. 224, in which Rémond returns to his 1952 article and says, "France, in fact, only knew wretched imitations of fascism, uninteresting counterfeits, plagiarisms without talent or honor. It had its Mosley. It never found a Mussolini. This failure of fascism, however, stemmed from a still more important cause: there was no French fascism because it was difficult for it to gain a foothold in France."

15. In Duverger's study of "La Situation des fonctionnaires depuis la révolution de 1940," pp. 306–9 are devoted to "the Jews' incapacity for office." "The measure to which they are subjected thus has the character of a measure fo public necessity," wrote the young lecturer at the University of Bordeaux (p. 317). At the end of his long article, Duverger listed the "major reforms carried out since June 1940: expulsion of the Jews and of naturalized subjects, the reinforcement of discipline, political purification through relieving of functions, a new regime of associations, etc." (p. 539). This analytical, scientific study of "the law of 3 October 1940 concerning the status of the Jews" can cause even the least intransigent reader to wonder. To treat in this unemotional manner a subject involving such changes in French society requires an uncommon degree of detachment from the realities of the period. When it is found in a "political animal" like Duverger, a political theorist and militant journalist who, after the war, spent the rest of his life preaching the need for morality in politics, suh a detachment seems to represent a kind of legitimization of the most sordid aspects of the regime resulting from the "revolution of 1940." It is true that Duverger was writing in the *Revue de droit public et de la science politique*, a publication whose political line had been fixed by its editor, Roger Bonnard, dean of the Faculty of Law of the University of Bordeaux. In presenting the first issue of the journal after the defeat of France, Bonnard said that although it would naturally be scientific in character, "its science would not be neutral, for at the present time one must take sides before 'setting off.' . . . Besides with our 'leader,' M. le maréchal Pétain, France now has a guide of an incomparable, almost superhuman wisdom and mastery of thought, who will prevent it from going astray and will lead at along the path of truth" (R. Bonnard, "A nos lecteurs," *Revue de droit public et de la science politique* 57 [1940–41], 142). What follows is in the same vein.

16. Brasillach, *Notre avant-guerre*, 283.

17. See Seliger, *Ideology and Politics*, 175. Chapter 6 of this remarkable work is entitled "Fundamental and Operative Ideology."

18. See R. W. Rauch, Jr., *Politics and Belief in Contemporary France: Emmanuel Mounier and Christian Democracy, 1932–1950* (The Hague: Martinus Nijhoff, 1972), 216. The journal in question was *Demain*, a "weekly of French society," which appeared from February 1942 to June 1944.

19. J.-M. Domenach, *Emmanuel Mounier par lui-même* (Paris: Éditions du Seuil, 1972), 112.

20. Mounier, *Oeuvres* 4:677 (10 Nov. 1940).

21. Ibid., 694 (22 Feb. 1941).

22. Ibid.

23. Ibid.

24. Ibid., 695. See also p. 702, on the total independence of groups like "Jeune France" or Uriage.

25. Ibid., 695.

26. Ibid., 699ff.

27. Ibid., 711, 703.

28. Ibid., 712.

29. Ibid., 693.

30. Mounier reproached *L'Ordre nouveau* in the following sentence in the Dec. 1933 issue of *Esprit*: "At the origins of the national-socialist movement are the germs of a new and necessary revolutionary position" (*Oeuvres* 1:228).

31. Mounier, *Oeuvres* 1:255.

32. Ibid., 255, 226.

33. Ibid., 224.

34. Ibid., 226.

35. Ibid., 227.

36. See Maulnier, "Le 'Fascisme,'" 13–26, and "La France entre deux destins," *La Revue universelle* 64, no. 24 (14 Mar. 1936), 747–58.

37. For an example of Dominique's thinking, see a text quoted by Maulnier in "La France entre deux destins," 755: "If France needs a moral unity, and like Bergery I believe that, how far should that unity go? Should we give it a philosophical or religious basis? What basis? And who ought to give it that basis? Which person, or what group of people? Which party? These are simple questions, aren't they? However, I confess myself incapable of answering them except through the hypothesis of a strong government, but one that, unlike the governments of Berlin and Moscow, would not interfere in the philosophical domain and would allow each person the free play of that inner power and that secret life that are the very essence of our personality."

38. Mounier, *Oeuvres* 1:227.

39. Ibid., 226.

40. See above, p. 274.

41. Mounier, *Oeuvres*, 4:675.

42. Lévy, *L'Idéologie française*, 49.

43. See Mounier on "Henri de Man: *L'Idée socialiste*" in *Esprit*, no. 31 (Apr. 1935), 90–91.

44. "Le Point de vue des mouvements de Jeunes," *Esprit*, no. 21 (1 June

1934), 475 (unsigned but obviously written by Mounier).

45. Ibid.

46. E. Mounier, "Thierry Maulnier: *Au-delà du nationalisme*," *Esprit*, no. 69 (June 1938), 442.

47. Ibid., 443.

48. Ibid., 446.

49. Ibid., 445.

50. Ibid.

51. Ibid., 446.

52. Ibid., 445–46.

53. E. Mounier, "J.-P. Maxence: *Histoire de dix ans*," *Esprit*, no. 79 (Apr. 1939), 127–29: "Maxence's '*Cahiers 1928*' was one of the endeavors in which *Esprit* sought itself before it realized itself" (p. 129).

54. E. Mounier, "P. Drieu La Rochelle: *Gilles*," *Esprit*, no. 91 (Apr. 1940), 87–90. On Drieu's work, see M. Winock, "Une Parabole fasciste: *Gilles* de Drieu La Rochelle," *Le Mouvement social*, no. 80 (July 1972), 29–47 (republished in *Édouard Drumont et Cie*).

55. E. Mounier, *Esprit*, no. 91 (Apr. 1940), 89.

56. Ibid.

57. In January 1945, Mounier attempted to explain "*Esprit* 40–41" (*Esprit*, n.s., no. 2 [1 Jan. 1945], 303–6). He gave a somewhat prettified account that distorted the realities of the period. For instance, speaking of the issue of Mar. 1941, Mounier wrote, "The notes attack Massis, the AF, the Paris press, etc." (p. 305). Now, in the issue of Mar. 1941 (pp. 337–39), there is indeed a review by Mounier of Massis's last book, *Les Idées restent*, but it is very difficult, even taking into account Mounier's need to evade the censor, to see this review as an attack on the ideology expounded by Massis, one of the chief thinkers of the new regime. If Mounier's expression of his conviction that Massis's intentions are pure and his declaration of his desire to be open to Massis's ideas ("this dialogue in which I wish to engage with Massis": p. 339) are intended as an attack, one can only wonder (as Rauch did in *Politics and Belief*, 212) about the "resistant" effectiveness of the ten issues of *Esprit* published between November 1940 and August 1941, especially in view of the problems involved in operating within the framework of the regime. The interpretation of Mounier's role under Vichy is only one of the issues on which the brilliant study by Michel Winock (*Histoire politique de la revue "Esprit"*) is not convincing. On this subject, see the contrary interpretation of P. de Senarclens (*Le Mouvement "Esprit"*), which is not without merit, and which claims that "Mounier demonstrated his warm support of the marshal's regime" (p. 272). The fact remains that Mounier decided to revive *Esprit* four months after the armistice, after having approached Laval, although he was already aware of the repressiveness of Vichy legislation. After the Liberation, Mounier said that he was pleased that he had published a veiled criticism of the film *Jud Süss*. In fact, Marc Beigbeder's review did no more than accuse this famous Nazi propaganda film of "besmirching individuals" instead "of giving serious consideration to the Jewish problem whose existence nobody would think of denying" ("*Le Juif Süss*," *Esprit*, no. 101, June 1941, 598–99). Mounier considered this review an act of resistance, something to be proud of. (See his reply to a partisan attack by Garaudy in 1950 in

Winock, *Historie politique*, 394.) In view of the tragedy that was then overtaking France and Europe, one can only question the value of this "foxes' war," as Winock calls it (p. 218). One should note, finally, that in his latest book Winock admits not only that Mounier lacked "the elementary reflex of Edmond Michelet in June 1940" but also that *Esprit* bore "the old, profound imprint of Catholic antiliberalism" (*Édouard Drumont et Cie*, 150).

58. E. Mounier, "P. Drieu La Rochelle: *Gilles*," *Esprit*, no. 91 (Apr. 1940), 89–90.

59. E. Mounier, "Sur l'intelligence en temps de crise," *Esprit*, no. 97 (Feb. 1941), 201–15.

60. Ibid., 202.

61. Ibid., 215.

62. Ibid., 208, 205, 206. See also p. 207 concerning those people "who for twenty years and more have shown themselves incapable of rethinking or transforming their period, and who today are grinding their teeth and hurling sarcasms at all and sundry, full of self-confidence and satisfaction."

63. E. Mounier, "D'une France à l'autre," *Esprit*, no. 94 (Nov. 1940), 4–5.

64. E. Mounier, "Les Nouvelles Conditions de la vie publique en France," *Esprit*, no. 94 (Nov. 1940), 62.

65. Ibid.

66. Mounier, "D'une France à l'autre," 5.

67. Ibid., 4.

68. E. Mounier, "Fin de l'homme bourgeois," *Esprit*, no. 102 (July 1941), 614–15.

69. Ibid., 612.

70. Ibid., 611, 609.

71. Ibid., 611. Mounier uses the word *crusade* several times here. Only once is it put in quotation marks.

72. Mounier, "*Esprit* au Congrès franco-italien," 475.

73. Ibid., 476.

74. A. Marc, "Jeunesse allemande," *Esprit*, no. 5 (1 Feb. 1933), 723–24.

75. G. Duveau, "Le Dialogue franco-allemand," *Esprit*, no. 43 (Apr. 1936), 22.

76. F. Perroux, "Intelligence de la nation," *Esprit*, no. 75 (Dec. 1938), 344, 353.

77. Mounier, *Oeuvres* 1:614.

78. Ibid., 499ff.

79. Ibid., 500.

80. Ibid., 501.

81. A. Marc, "Hitler ou la révolution manquée," *L'Ordre nouveau*, no. 2, June 1933, 28–29.

82. Ibid., 30.

83. Ibid., 29–30.

84. E. Mounier, "Réponse à *L'Ordre nouveau*," *Esprit*, no. 19 (Apr. 1934), 199.

85. "Lettre à Adolf Hitler, Chancelier du Reich," *L'Ordre nouveau*, no. 5 (Nov. 1933), 12.

86. Ibid., 14.

87. Ibid., 13.

88. Ibid., 13–14, 16, 19–20.

89. Ibid., 16.

90. Ibid., 4.

91. Ibid., 8.

92. Ibid., 9.

93. Ibid., 12–13.

94. Ibid., 10.

95. Ibid., 11.

96. Ibid., 14.

97. Ibid., 16.

98. Ibid., 15.

99. Ibid.

100. Ibid.

101. Ibid., 9.

102. Ibid., 20. See also pp. 5–6.

103. Ibid., 18.

104. Ibid., 17.

105. Ibid., 6.

106. Ibid., 5.

107. Ibid., 19.

108. Ibid., 25.

109. Ibid., 31.

110. Jouvenel, *Après la défaite*, 41–42.

111. Ibid., 41.

112. Ibid., 40.

113. Ibid., 45.

114. E. Mounier, "A l'intelligence française," *Marianne*, 21 Aug. 1940.

115. Ibid.

116. Ibid.

117. On 25 October 1940 the American Catholic journal *The Commonweal* published a message from Mounier under the title "Letter from France: A Personalist Leader, Editor of *Esprit*, Sends This Message to America from France" (pp. 8–11). John Hellman discovered this article (see *Emmanuel Mounier*). This is what is written in the original: "The first step to take is to place oneself on the scale of vision of the man who at this moment has taken the initiative in the history of Europe. Herr Hitler on several occasions has declared that he envisions his policies on the scale of a thousand years. The 'realists' smile. But on reflection this perspective would seem a bit narrow" (p. 8).

118. Mounier, "Letter from France," 8.

119. Ibid., 9.

120. Ibid.

121. Ibid.

122. Ibid., 10.

123. Ibid.

124. E. Mounier, "Le Monde moderne contre la personne," in *Oeuvres* 1:500.

125. Winock, *Histoire politique*, 235–37.

126. Mounier, "Letter from France," 10.

127. Jouvenel, *Après la défaite*, 38–39.

128. Ibid., 112, 165, 216.

129. These books figure on the two published lists, of 31 Dec. 1942 and 1 Mar. 1944. Copies of these lists (DLIV-60) are in the archives of the Centre de Documentation Juive Contemporaine in Paris.

130. G. Loiseaux, "Collaboration littéraire au service de l'Europe nouvelle," *Lendemains 29: Zeitschrift für Frankreichforschung und Französischstudium*, 1983, 17–19. See also the important book by G. Loiseaux, *La Littérature de le défaite et de la collaboration d'après "Phönix oder Asche?" (Phénix ou cendres?) de Bernhard Payr* (Paris: Publications de la Sorbonne, 1984), 95–98.

131. See the classic work of Robert O. Paxton, *Vichy France: Old Guard and New Order* (New York: Knopf, 1972), 142–43.

132. J. Ponty, "La Press quotidienne et l'affaire Dreyfus en 1898–1899: Essai de typologie," *Revue d'histoire moderne et contemporaine* 21 (Apr.–June 1974), 201, 214. See also the recent, justly acclaimed work by J.-D. Bredin, *L'Affaire* (Paris: Julliard, 1983), 472ff.

133. L. Blum, "*L'Ami du peuple* et Coty," *Le Populaire*, 30 Dec. 1933.

134. A. Grynberg and C. Singer, "Le Pouvoir de l'image: Les Pérégrinations du *Juif Süss*," *Les Nouveaux Cahiers*, no. 75 (Winter 1983–84), 41–43.

135. On the publishing business and literary production under the German occupation, see Assouline, *Gaston Gallimard*, 313–26.

136. *Le Figaro*, 19 Dec. 1940.

137. H. Beuve-Méry, "Révolutions nationales, révolution humaine," *Esprit*, no. 98 (Mar. 1941), 284.

138. Ibid. On the idea of a unified Europe, see also Mounier, "D'une France à l'autre," and "Fin de l'homme bourgeois," 611–12.

139. Beuve-Méry, "Révolutions nationales, révolution humaine," 281.

140. Ibid., 281–82.

141. Ibid., 283.

142. Ibid., 282–83.

143. Mounier, "D'une France à l'autre," 2. See also J. Lacroix, "Nation et révolution," *Esprit*, no. 94 (Nov. 1940), 16: "No doubt we have not sufficiently understood that the revolution is a unity, a totality. The French tradition will fortunately keep us from all spiritual totalitarianism, but in the political, economic and social spheres today it is the nation that commands."

144. Mounier, "Les Nouvelles Conditions," 63.

145. Mounier, "Sur l'intelligence," 207.

146. Mounier, "D'une France à l'autre," 7.

147. See, for example, J.-P. Azéma, review of Z. Sternhell, *Ni droite, ni gauche: L'Idéologie fasciste en France*, in *L'Histoire*, no. 61 (Nov. 1983), 112–13.

148. Jouvenel, *Un Voyageur dans le siècle*, 468–69.

149. In *Un Voyageur dans le siècle*, Jouvenel says that Léon Blum told him that he had seen Déat as his successor as leader of the party (p. 174).

150. Brasillach, *Notre avant-guerre*, 283.

Bibliography

This bibliography is divided into two main sections: contemporary sources (books and articles from reviews and journals) and critical studies written after 1944. The second section conveys an accurate, although necessarily selective, picture of the present state of research; it is restricted to works directly pertinent to the subject of this book. The Bibliography lists all the works used for this study, except for articles in contemporary journals and reviews. Where primary sources are concerned, only particularly important and representative articles are cited. The reader will find references to all the other articles in the notes.

Contemporary Sources

BOOKS

Barrès, M. *L'Ennemi des lois*. Paris: Perrin, 1893.
———. *Les Déracinés*. Paris: Fasquelle, 1897.
———. *L'Appel au soldat*. Paris: Fasquelle, 1900.
———. *Mes cahiers*. 14 vols. Paris: Plon, 1929–57.
———. *Leurs figures*. Paris: Plon, 1932.
Barrès, M., and Ch. Maurras. *La République ou le roi: Correspondance inédite, 1883–1923*. Paris: Plon, 1970.
Benda, J. *La Trahison des clercs*. Paris: Grasset, 1927.
Berson, H. *L'Évolution créatrice*. Paris: PUF, 1962; first published 1907.
Berth, É. *Les Nouveaux Aspects du socialisme*. Paris: Rivière, 1908.
———. *Les Méfaits des intellectuels*. 2d ed. Paris: Rivière, 1926.
Biétry, P. *Le Socialisme et les Jaunes*. Paris: Plon, 1906.
Bourget, P. *Essais de psychologie contemporaine*. 4th ed. Paris: Lemerre, 1885.
Brasillach, R. *Notre avant-guerre*. Paris: Plon, 1941.
Colajanni, N. *Le Socialisme*. Paris: Giard et Brière, 1900.
Déat, M. *Perspectives socialistes*. Paris: Librairie Valois, 1930.
———. *Le Plan français: Doctrine et plan d'action*. Paris: Fasquelle, 1935.

———. *Le Front populaire au tournant*. Paris: Éditions du Journal *La Concorde*, 1937.

———. *Perspectives françaises*. Paris: Éditions de *L'Oeuvre*, 1940.

———. *De l'école d'hier à l'homme de demain*. Paris: Éditions du RNP, 1943.

———. *Le Parti unique*. Paris: Aux Armes de France, 1943.

———. *Pensée allemande et pensée française*. Paris: Aux Armes de France, 1944.

———. "Mémoires politiques." 5 vols. Manuscript in the Bibliothèque Nationale.

Degrelle, L. *Révolution des âmes*. Paris: Éditions de France, 1938.

De Man, H. *The Remaking of a Mind: A Soldier's Thought on War and Reconstruction*. New York: Scribner, 1919.

———. *Au-delà du marxisme*. Paris: Éditions du Seuil, 1974; first published 1927.

———. *La Joie au travail: Enquête basée sur des témoignages d'ouvriers et d'employés*. Paris: Alcan, 1930.

———. *Nationalisme et socialisme*. Paris and Brussels: L'Églantine, 1932.

———. *Réflexions sur l'économie dirigée*. Paris and Brussels: L'Églantine, 1932.

———. *Le Plan du travail*. Brussels: Lucifer, 1933.

———. *Pour un plan d'action*. Brussels: L'Églantine, 1933.

———. *Le Socialisme constructif*. Paris: Alcan, 1933.

———. *La Réforme bancaire du gouvernement et le Plan du travail*. Brussels: L'Églantine, 1934.

———. *Corporatisme et socialisme*. Paris and Brussels: Labor, 1935.

———. *L'Exécution du Plan du travail*. Paris: Alcan, 1935.

———. *L'Idée socialiste*. Paris: Grasset, 1935.

———. *Le Plan du travail et les communistes*. Paris and Brussels: Labor, 1935.

———. *Après-coup*. Brussels: La Toison d'Or, 1941.

Denis, J. *Principes rexistes*. Brussels: Éditions Rex, 1936.

Déroulède, P. *L'Alsace-Lorraine et la fête nationale*. Paris: Blond, 1910.

Detoeuf, A. *Construction du syndicalisme*. Paris: Gallimard, 1938.

Doriot, J. *La France ne sera pas un pays d'esclaves*. Paris: Les Oeuvres Françaises, 1936.

———. *La France avec nous*. Paris: Flammarion, 1937.

———. *Le Front de la liberté face au communisme*. Paris: Flammarion, 1937.

———. *Refaire la France*. Paris: Grasset, 1938.

———. *Discours prononcé le 11 juin 1939 à Niort*. Poitiers: Imprimerie Poitevine, n.d.

———. *Réalitiés*. Paris: Éditions de France, 1942.

Drieu La Rochelle, P. *Socialisme fasciste*. Paris: Gallimard, 1934.

———. *Avec Doriot*. Paris: Gallimard, 1937.

———. *Chronique politique, 1934–1942*. Paris: Gallimard, 1943.

Droulers, Ch. *Le Marquis de Morès, 1858–1896*. Paris: Plon, 1932.

Drumont, É. *La Dernière Bataille: Nouvelle Étude psychologique et sociale*. Paris: Dentu, 1890.

———. *Le Testament d'un antisémite*. Paris: Dentu, 1891.

Engels, F., and P. and L. Lafargue. *Correspondance*. Edited by Emile Bottigelli. 3 vols. Paris: Éditions Sociales, 1956.

Francis, R., T. Maulnier, and J.-P. Maxence. *Demain la France*. Paris: Grasset, 1934.

Gaucher, F. *Contribution à l'histoire du socialisme français (1905–1933)*. Paris: Les Presses Modernes, 1934.

Goblot, E. *La Barrière et le niveau: Étude sociologique sur la bourgeoisie française moderne*. Paris: PUF, 1967; 1st ed. 1925.

Griffuelhes, V. *L'Action syndicaliste*. Paris: Rivière, 1908.

Johannet, R. *Éloge du bourgeois français*. Paris: Grasset, 1924.

Jouvenel, B. de. *L'Économie dirigée*. Paris: Valois, 1928.

———. *Le Réveil de l'Europe*. Paris: Gallimard, 1938.

———. *Après la défaite*. Paris: Plon, 1941.

Labriola, A. *Sindacalismo e riformismo*. Florence: G. Nerbini, 1905.

———. *Riforme e rivoluzione sociale*. 2d ed. Lugano: Società Editrice Avanguardia, 1906.

———. *Storia di dieci anni 1899–1909*. Milan: Casa Editrice Il Viandante, 1910.

———. *Au-delà du capitalisme et du socialisme*. Paris: Librairie Valois, 1932.

———. *L'État et la crise: Étude sur la dépression actuelle*. Paris: Rivière, 1933.

———. *Le Crépuscule de la civilisation: L'Occident et les peuples de couleur*. Paris: G. Mignolet et Storz, n.d.

Lagardelle, H. *La Grève générale et le socialisme*. Paris: E. Cornély, 1905.

———, ed. *Syndicalisme et socialisme: Discours prononcés au colloque tenu à Paris le 3 avril 1907*. Paris: Rivière, 1908.

Lanzillo, A. *Giorgio Sorel*. Rome: Libreria Romana, 1910.

Lasserre, P. *Georges Sorel, théoricien de l'impérialisme*. Paris: L'Artisan du Livre, 1926.

Lebas, J. *Le Socialisme, but et moyen: Suivi de la réfutation d'un néo-socialisme*. Lille: Imprimerie Ouvrière, 1931.

Le Bon, G. *Les Lois psychologiques de l'évolution des peuples*. Paris: Alcan, 1894.

———. *Psychologie des foules*. Paris: Alcan, 1895.

———. *Psychologie du socialisme*. Paris: Alcan, 1898.

Lefranc, G., P. Boivin, and M. Deixonne. *Révolution constructive*. Paris: Librairie Valois, 1932.

Leroy-Beaulieu, P. *Le Collectivisme: Examen critique du nouveau socialisme*. Paris: Guillaumin, 1884.

Loustau, R. *Notre doctrine devant le problème social*. Paris: Éditions du PPF, n.d.

———. *Un Ordre social français: Rapport de Robert Loustau*. Paris: Éditions du PPF, n.d.

Luchaire, J. *Une Génération réaliste*. Paris: Librairie Valois, 1929.

Malon, B. *Le Socialisme réformiste*. Paris: Derveaux, 1886.

———. *Le Socialisme intégral*. 2 vols. Paris: Alcan, 1890–91.

Marion, P. *Programme du parti populaire français*. Paris: Les Oeuvres Françaises, 1938.

———. *Leur combat: Lénine, Mussolini, Hitler, Franco*. Paris: Fayard, 1939.

Massis, H., and A. de Tarde. *L'Esprit de la nouvelle Sorbonne: La Crise de la culture classique; la crise du français*. 3d ed. Paris: Mercure de France, 1911.

———. *Les Jeunes Gens d'aujourd'hui: Le Goût de l'action; la foi patriotique;*

une renaissance catholique; le réalisme politique. 12th ed. Paris: Plon-Nourrit, 1919.

Maulnier, T. *La Crise est dans l'homme*. Paris: Librairie de *La Revue française*, 1932.

——. *Nietzsche*. Paris: Gallimard, 1935.

——. *Mythes socialistes*. Paris: Gallimard, 1936.

——. *La Société nationale et la lutte des classes*. Paris: *Combat*, 1937.

——. *Au-delà du nationalisme*. Paris: Gallimard, 1938.

——. *La France, la guerre, et la paix*. Lyon: Lardanchet, 1942.

——. *Révolution nationale: L'Avenir de la France*. Hanoi: Éditions du Gouvernement Général de l'Indochine, 1942.

Merlino, S. *Formes et essence du socialisme*. Preface by G. Sorel. Paris: Giard et Brière, 1898.

Mermeix [G. Terrail]. *La France socialiste: Notes d'histoire contemporaine*. Paris: Fetscherin et Chuit, 1886.

——. *Les Coulisses du boulangisme*. Paris: Éditions du Cerf, 1890.

Michels, R. *Political Parties*. Trans. E. and C. Paul. London: Jarrold, 1915.

——. *Le Prolétariat et la bourgeoisie dans le mouvement socialiste italien*. Paris: Giard, 1921.

Moeller Van den Bruck, A. *Le Troisième Reich*. Introduction by T. Maulnier. Trans. J.-L. Lenault. Paris: Librairie de *La Revue française*, 1933.

Montagnon, B. *Grandeur et servitude socialistes*. Paris: Librairie Valois, 1929.

Montagnon, B., A. Marquet, and M. Déat. *Néo-socialisme? Ordre, autorité, nation*. Preface and commentary by M. Bonnafous. Paris: Grasset, 1933.

Morès, Marquis de. *Rotschild, Ravachol, et Cie*. Paris: 38, rue du Mont-Thabor, 1892.

——. *Le Secret des changes*. Marseille: Imprimerie Marseillaise, 1894.

Mussolini, B. *La Doctrine du fascisme*. Florence: Valecchi, 1937.

Pareto, V. *Traité de sociologie générale*. Paris: Payot, 1919.

——. *Les Systèmes socialistes*. 2d ed. Paris: Giard, 1926.

——. *Sociological Writings*. Ed. S. E. Finer. London: Pall Mall Press, 1966.

Philip, A. *Henri De Man et la crise doctrinale du socialisme*. Paris: Librairie Universitaire J. Gamber, 1928.

Pirou, G. *Georges Sorel*. Paris: Rivière, 1927.

Pouget, É. *La Confédération générale du travail*. Paris: Rivière, 1909.

Renard, G. *Socialisme intégral et marxisme*. Paris: Librairie de *La Revue socialiste*, 1896.

Rosselli, C. *Socialisme libéral*. Trans. S. Priacel. Paris: Librairie Valois, 1930.

Sorel, G. *Le Procès de Socrate: Examen critique des thèses socratiques*. Paris: Alcan, 1889.

——. *Saggi di critica del marxismo*. Milan: Sandron, 1903.

——. *Réflexions sur la violence*. 11th ed. Paris: Rivière, 1950; first published 1907.

——. *La Décomposition du marxisme*. Paris: Rivière, 1908.

——. *La Révolution dreyfusienne*. Paris: Rivière, 1909.

——. *De l'utilité du pragmatisme*. Paris: Rivière, 1921.

——. *Matériaux d'une théorie du prolétariat*. Paris: Rivière, 1921.

————. *La Ruine du monde antique: Conception matérialiste de l'histoire.* 3d ed. Paris: Rivière, 1933.

————. *D'Aristote à Marx.* Paris: Rivière, 1935.

————. *Lettres à Paul Delesalle, 1914–1921.* Paris: Grasset, 1947.

Spengler, O. *Le Déclin de l'Occident.* Trans. M. Tazerout. 2 vols. Paris: Gallimard, 1931.

Streel, J. *Ce qu'il faut penser de Rex.* Brussels: Éditions Rex, 1936.

Toussenel, A. *Les Juifs, rois de l'époque: Histoire de la féodalité financière.* 3d ed. Paris: Marpon et Flammarion, 1886.

Vacher de Lapouge, G. *Les Sélections sociales: Cours libre de science politique professé à l'université de Montpellier.* Paris: Fontemoing, 1896.

Valois, G. *La Monarchie et la classe ouvrière.* Paris: Nouvelle Librairie Nationale, 1914.

————. *Histoire et philosophie sociales.* Paris: Nouvelle Librairie Nationale, 1924.

————. *La Révolution nationale.* Paris: Nouvelle Librairie Nationale, 1924.

————. *La Politique économique et sociale du Faisceau.* Paris: Éditions du Faisceau, 1926.

————. *Le Fascisme.* Paris: Nouvelle Librairie Nationale, 1927.

————. *L'Homme contre l'argent: Souvenirs de dix ans 1918–1928.* Paris: Valois, 1928.

Vandervelde, E. *Études marxistes.* 2d ed. Brussels: L'Églantine, 1930.

ARTICLES

Albertini, G. "Ni droite, ni gauche." *Le National populaire,* no. 2 (13 June 1942).

Andreu, P. "Si j'étais Charles Maurras. . . ." *La Lutte des jeunes,* 20 May 1934.

————. "La Troisième Force, parti de *gauche.*" *La Lutte des jeunes,* 20 May 1934.

————. "Le Socialisme de Sorel." *L'Homme nouveau,* no. 17 (June 1935).

————. "Corporatisme chrétien, corporatisme fasciste." *L'Homme nouveau,* special issue (July 1935).

————. "Fascisme 1913." *Combat,* Feb. 1936.

————. "Demain sur nos tombeaux." *Combat,* Apr. 1936.

————. "Capitalisme et corporatisme." *Combat,* Aug.–Sept. 1936.

Bacconnier, F. "La Monarchie de demain." *L'Action française,* 1 Aug., 15 Sept., 15 Oct. 1902.

————. "Les Bienfaits du régime corporatif." *L'Accord social,* 15 Dec. 1908.

————. "Conclusion de l'ABC du royalisme social." *L'Accord social,* 20 June 1909.

Barrès, M. "M. le général Boulanger et la nouvelle génération." *La Revue indépendante* 8 (Apr. 1888).

————. "La Lutte entre capitalistes et travailleurs." *Le Courrier de l'Est,* 28 Sept. 1890.

————. "Le Problème est double." *La Cocarde,* 8 Sept. 1894.

————. "Opprimés et humiliés." *La Cocarde*, 14 Sept. 1894.

Barrès, Ph. "Il est bien vivant l'esprit de la victoire." *Le Nouveau Siècle*, 17 Dec. 1925.

————. "Les Signes du succès." *Le Nouveau Siècle*, 30 Jan. 1927.

Benjamin, R. "Mussolini et son peuple." *La Revue universelle* 67, nos. 16–18 (Oct.–Dec. 1936); nos. 20–22 (Jan.–Mar. 1937).

Bergery, G. "Dans les ornières de l'orthodoxie." *La Flèche*, 22 May 1937.

————. "Bilan politique de 1937." *La Flèche*, 1 Jan. 1938.

————. "La Faiblesse de l'État est une menace pour les libertés du peuple." *La Flèche*, 3 Jan. 1938.

————. "L'Antisémitisme renaît, pour le combattre enlevons-lui ses prétextes." *La Flèche*, 11 Nov. 1938.

————. "Malfaisance des slogans." *La Flèche*, 2 June 1939.

Berth, É. [J. Darville, pseud.]. "Proudhon." *Cahiers du Cercle Proudhon*, Jan.–Feb. 1912.

———— [J. Darville, pseud.]. "Satellites de la ploutocratie." *Cahiers du Cercle Proudhon*, Sept.–Dec. 1912.

———— [J. Darville, pseud.]. "La Monarchie et la classe ouvrière." *Cahiers du Cercle Proudhon*, Jan.–Feb. 1914.

Bertin, D. "Oraison funèbre du communisme." *Combat*, May 1936.

Beuve-Méry, H. "Révolutions nationales, révolution humaine." *Esprit*, no. 98 (Mar. 1941).

Biétry, P. "Les Propos du Jaune." *Le Jaune*, 5 Mar. 1904.

Blanchot, M. "On demande des dissidents." *Combat*, Dec. 1937.

Blond, G. "Liberté de la presse et réalisme politique." *Combat*, Dec. 1937.

Blum, L. "Le Problème du pouvoir." *Le Populaire*, 13 July 1933.

————. "Le Pouvoir total." *Le Populaire*, 14 July 1933.

————. "La Mesure du pouvoir." *Le Populaire*, 15 July 1933.

————. "Au-delà du réformisme: Le Plan de travail et le parti français." *Le Populaire*, 6 Jan. 1934.

————. "'Plan' et 'programme.'" *Le Populaire*, 17 Jan. 1934.

————. "La résorption du chômage." *Le Populaire*, 19 Jan. 1934.

————. "Le Sens véritable du Plan du travail." *Le Populaire*, 21 Jan. 1934.

————. "La Socialisation par étapes." *Le Populaire*, 22 Jan. 1934.

————. "Le Secteur privé." *Le Populaire*, 25 Jan. 1934.

————. "Socialisation et socialisme." *Le Populaire*, 26 Jan. 1934.

Bobin, R. "L'Adoption du Plan De Man par le POB: Le Discours d'Henri De Man au Congrès du POB." *La Vie socialiste*, 6 Jan. 1934.

————. "Henri De Man et le nationalisme économique." *La Vie socialiste*, 14 July 1934.

Brasillach, R. "Cent heures chez Hitler: Le Congrès de Nuremberg." *La Revue universelle* 61, no. 13 (1 Oct. 1935).

————. "Lettre aux cocus de la droite." *Combat*, Mar. 1936.

————. "Un Vieux Gaulois." *Combat*, Apr. 1936.

————. "Anticipations: Quand L. Blum fait tirer sur le peuple." *Combat*, June 1936.

Capdeville, L. "Un Message d'espérance." *La Vie socialiste*, 3 Feb. 1934.

———. "Points de vue et façons de voir." *La Vie socialiste*, 3 Feb. 1934.

Challaye, F. "Pas de guerre pour la Tchécoslovaquie." *La Flèche*, 25 Mar. 1938.

Déat, M. "Notes pour l'action." *La Vie socialiste*, 21 July 1928.

———. "Jaurès et la conception socialiste de l'État." *La Vie socialiste*, 25 Jan. 1930.

———. "Démocratie et salariat." *La Vie socialiste*, 15 Feb. 1930.

———. "Qu'est-ce qu'un programme d'action?." *La Vie socialiste*, 5 Apr. 1930.

———. "De Marion à Zyromski." *La Vie socialiste*, 10 Jan. 1931.

———. "Réflexions sur quelques critiques." *La Vie socialiste*, 31 Jan. 1931.

———. "Méditations sur les problèmes du jour: La Tactique socialiste et la marche au pouvoir." *La Vie socialiste*, 11 Mar. and 13 May 1933.

———. "Le Plan belge et nous." *La Vie socialiste*, 6 Jan. 1934.

———. "Crise de réadaptation." *La Vie socialiste*, 20 Jan. 1934.

———. "Extrême urgence." *La Vie socialiste*, 3 Feb. 1934.

———. "Après la constitution du cabinet Doumergue: Sang-froid et raison." *La Vie socialiste*, 17 Feb. 1934.

———. "Avant le Conseil central: Problèmes politiques et questions pratiques." *La Vie socialiste*, 24 Feb. 1934.

———. "Syndicalisme et corporation." *La Vie socialiste*, 17 Mar. 1934.

———. "Pour notre Congrès: Positions nettes et devoir clair." *La Vie socialiste*, 24 Mar. 1934.

———. "La Fin d'une controverse." *La Vie socialiste*, 7 Apr. 1934.

———. "Vers une nouvelle économie: Actualité de la corporation." *La Vie socialiste*, 7 Apr. 1934.

———. "Rapport moral." *La Vie socialiste*, 5 May 1934.

———. "Devoirs de vacances." *La Vie socialiste*, 14 July 1934.

———. "Autour d'une Constituante: Précisons notre tactique." *La Vie socialiste*, 13 Oct. 1934.

———. "Fronts et rassemblements." *La Vie socialiste*, 3 Nov. 1934.

———. "Pour l'élaboration d'un plan . . . d'un plan unique." *La Vie socialiste*, 24 Nov. 1934.

———. "Le Planisme et la tradition française." *L'Homme nouveau*, no. 12 (Jan. 1935).

———. "Après deux ans." *Le Front*, 2 Nov. 1935.

———. "Organisation sociale et philosophie." *Bulletin de la Sociéte française de philosophie* 37–38, no. 2 (Mar. 1938).

———. "Mourir pour Dantzig?" *L'Oeuvre*, 4 May 1939.

———. "Le Parti unique de la réconstruction." *L'Oeuvre*, 8 July 1940.

———. "Révolution nationale." *L'Oeuvre*, 10 July, 13 Oct. 1940.

———. "Solidaires dans l'épreuve." *L'Oeuvre*, 20 Oct. 1940.

———. "Le Tournant de la liberté." *L'Oeuvre*, 31 Oct. 1940.

———. "La Révolution nationale est dans l'opposition." *L'Oeuvre*, 14 Dec. 1940.

———. "De l'Action française au parti unique." *L'Oeuvre*, 15 Dec. 1940.

———. "Le Parti et l'État." *L'Oeuvre*, 21 Dec. 1940.

———. "Le Parti fera la révolution." *L'Oeuvre*, 22 Dec. 1940.

———. "Structure et fonction du parti." *L'Oeuvre*, 23 Dec. 1940.

——. "Révolution dans tous les cas." *L'Oeuvre*, 26 Dec. 1940.

——. "Rassemblement national-populaire: La Politique générale." Speech at the First Congress of the Rassemblement National Populaire, Paris, 14, 15 June 1941.

——. "Vers le parti unique." *Le National populaire*, no. 1 (6 June 1942).

——. Speech at the Palais de Chaillot, 26 Sept. 1943. *Le National populaire*, no. 65 (9 Oct. 1943).

——. "Ordre et justice sociale." *Le National populaire*, no. 89 (1 Apr. 1944).

De Man, H. "Pour un socialisme renouvelé: L'Anticapitalisme des classes moyennes." *La Vie socialiste*, 4 Nov. 1933.

——. "Le Plan national d'abord." *La Vie socialiste*, 6 Jan. 1934.

——. "Le Plan du Travail du Parti Ouvrier Belge." *Chantiers coopératifs*, 20 Mar. 1934.

——. "Planisme et réformisme." *La Vie socialiste*, 22 Dec. 1934.

——. "Le Socialisme devant la crise." *La Vie socialiste*, 22 Dec. 1934.

——. "Les Thèses essentielles du planisme." *La Vie socialiste*, 22 Dec. 1934.

Drieu La Rochelle, P. "Verra-t-on un parti national et socialiste?" *La Lutte des jeunes*, 4 Mar. 1934.

——. "Contre la droite et la gauche." *La Lutte des jeunes*, 11 Mar. 1934.

——. "Congrégations." *La Lutte des jeunes*, 22 Apr. 1934.

——. "Si j'étais La Rocque." *La Lutte des jeunes*, 20 May 1934.

——. "Sous Doumergue." *La Lutte des jeunes*, 27 May 1934.

——. "La République des indécis." *La Lutte des jeunes*, 10 June 1934.

——. "Mesure et démesure de l'esprit français." *Combat*, July 1937.

Dubief, H. "Front rouge ou faisceaux." *La Lutte des jeunes*, 27 May 1934.

Duveau, G. "Le Dialogue franco-allemand." *Esprit*, no. 43 (Apr. 1936).

Duverger, M. "La Situation des fonctionnaires depuis la révolution de 1940." *Revue du droit public et de la science politique* 57 (1940–41).

Fabrègues, J. de. "Une Mystique matérialiste: La Démocratie hitlérienne." *Combat*, Jan. 1937.

——. "Libérer le prolétariat." *Combat*, July 1937.

——. "Devant l'esclavage de la civilisation." *Combat*, May 1939.

——. "La Préoccupation de l'essential devant les menaces du monde." *Combat*, July 1939.

Fournière, E. "L'Idéalisme social." *La Revue socialiste* 23 (Mar. 1896).

Galland, P. "Proudhon et l'ordre." *Cahiers du Cercle Proudhon*, Jan.–Feb. 1912.

Gaucher, F. "Sur un programme qualifié de contre-révolutionnaire." *La Vie socialiste*, 3 Feb. 1934.

Gravier, F. "Deux démocraties: Une Seule Révolution." *Combat*, Dec. 1937.

Guionnet, J. "Où sont les socialistes?" *Le National populaire*, no. 31 (30 Jan. 1943).

——. "A propos d'un anniversaire." *Le National populaire*, no. 54 (10 July 1943).

Hitler, A. Interview by B. de Jouvenel. *Paris-Midi*, 28 Feb. 1936.

Izard, G. "Notre doctrine: L'Idée frontiste libérera tous les peuples." *La Flèche*, 11 May 1935.

———. "Classes moyennes, votre union est indispensable à la rénovation française." *La Flèche*, 27 Mar. 1937.

Jouvenel, B. de. "Qu'est-ce que l'anticapitalisme?" *La Tribune des fonctionnaires*, 16 Dec. 1933.

———. "Les États généraux du travail et la défense républicaine." *La Lutte des jeunes*, 15 Apr. 1934.

———. "Mes cinq points." *La Lutte des jeunes*, 27 May 1934.

———. "Deux opinions sur *Front commun*." *La Lutte des jeunes*, 3 June 1934.

———. "Bilan." *La Lutte des jeunes*, 14 July 1934.

———. "A propos de mon interview du chancelier-führer." *La Flèche*, 7 Mar. 1936.

———. "Nuremberg." *Gringoire*, 9 Sept. 1938.

———. "Il y a 15 ans, Hitler échouait." *Gringoire*, 10 Nov. 1938.

Lagardelle, H. "Au-delà de la démocratie: De l'homme abstrait à l'homme réel." *Plans*, no. 1 (Jan. 1931).

———. "Capitalisme." *Plans*, no. 9 (Nov. 1931).

———. "Supercapitalisme." *Plans*, no. 10 (Dec. 1931).

———. "La Fin d'une culture." *Plans*, no. 5 (May 1935).

Laurent, J. "Le Cri du jour." *Terre libre*, 15–30 Mar. 1910.

Le Corbusier. "Descartes est-il américain?" *Plans*, no. 7 (July 1931).

———. "Une Nouvelle Ville remplace une ancienne ville." *Plans*, no. 8 (Oct. 1931).

Leenhardt, R. "Le Vin nouveau et les vieilles outres." *Esprit*, no. 54 (Mar. 1937).

Lefort, H. "Comment faire la révolution." *La Lutte des jeunes*, 20 May 1934.

———. "Si j'étais Henri De Man." *La Lutte des jeunes*, 20 May 1934.

Lemmonier, G. "La Condition prolétarienne." *Le National populaire*, no. 90 (8 Apr. 1944).

Luxemburg, R. "Démocratie industrielle et démocratie politique." *Le Mouvement socialiste*, 15 June 1899.

Maire, G. "La Philosophie de Georges Sorel." *Cahiers du Cercle Proudhon*, Mar.–Apr. 1912.

Marc, A. "Jeunesse allemande." *Esprit*, no. 5 (1 Feb. 1933).

Marinetti, F. T. "La Nouvelle Sensibilité. *Plans*, no. 7 (July 1931).

Massis, H. "Quand Mussolini n'est plus devant la foule." *1933*, 1 Nov. 1933.

Mathon, E. "La corporation, base de la représentation des intérêts: Discours prononcé a la réunion du Comité des États généraux." *Cahiers des États généraux*, no. 6 (Oct. 1923).

Maulnier, T. "Une Jeunesse disponible." *1933*, 20 Dec. 1933.

———. "Le 'Fascisme' et son avenir en France." *La Revue universelle* 64, no. 19 (1 Jan. 1936).

———. "Le Socialisme antidémocratique de Georges Sorel." *La Revue universelle* 64, no. 21 (1 Feb. 1936).

———. "Les Deux Violences." *Combat*, Feb. 1936.

———. "Un Régime ennemi des arts." *Combat*, Apr. 1936.

———. "Le Seul Combat possible." *Combat*, June 1936.

———. "La Fin d'un ordre." *Combat*, July 1936.

———. "A bas la culture bourgeoise!" *Combat*, Oct. 1936.

———. "Libérons-nous du capitalisme." *Combat*, Nov. 1936.

———. "Sortirons-nous de l'abjection française?" *Combat*, Nov. 1936.

———. "Charles Maurras et le socialisme." *La Revue universelle* 68, no. 19 (1 Jan. 1937).

———. "Désobéissance aux lois." *Combat*, Jan. 1937.

———. "Il faut refaire un nationalisme en dépit de la nation." *Combat*, Apr. 1937.

———. "Les Nouvelles Conditions imposées à l'action politique en France." *Combat*, July 1937.

———. "Les Trois Grandes Démocraties." *Combat*, Oct. 1937.

———. "Pour un complot contre la sûreté de l'État digne de ce nom." *Combat*, Dec. 1937.

———. "L'État des forces en face de la société libérale." *Combat*, Jan. 1938.

———. "Pour un examen de conscience du nationalisme." *Combat*, Feb. 1938.

———. "La Mode est à l'Union sacrée." *Combat*, Apr. 1938.

———. "A propos d'*Au-delà du nationalisme*: Réponse à Drieu La Rochelle." *Combat*, May 1938.

———. "Notes sur l'antisémitisme." *Combat*, June 1938.

———. "Après les accords de Munich: Les Nouvelles Conditions imposées à l'action politique en France." *Combat*, Nov. 1938.

———. "Notes sur le fascisme." *Combat*, Dec. 1938.

Mauriac, C. "Les Tremplins de l'antisémitisme: Réponse à Bernard Lecache." *La Flèche*, 21 Oct. 1938.

Maurras, Ch. "Introduction aux *Aphorismes de politique sociale*." *L'Action française*, 15 Oct. 1900.

———. "Sur le nom de socialiste." *L'Action française*, 15 Nov. 1900.

———. "Politique mortelle et société renaissante." *Gazette de France*, 21 Dec. 1906.

———. "Liberté d'esprit." *L'Action française* (daily), 4 Aug. 1908.

———. "Besançon." *Cahiers du Cercle Proudhon*, Jan.–Feb. 1912.

Maxence, J.-P. "Pour l'avenir de l'intelligence." *La Solidarité française*, Oct. 1935.

Maze, J. "Non, M. Daladier, la défense nationale n'est pas la défense des trusts." *La Flèche*, 26 Aug. 1938.

———. "Vers la seconde Révolution française: Frontisme, espoir d'un peuple." *La Flèche*, 24 Feb. 1939.

Michels, R. "Les Dangers du parti socialiste allemand." *Le Mouvement socialiste*, no. 144 (Dec. 1904).

———. "Le Congrès des socialistes de Prusse." *Le Mouvement socialiste*, No. 149 (Feb. 1905).

———. "Le Congrès syndical de Cologne." *Le Mouvement socialiste*, no. 158 (July 1905).

———. "Le Socialisme allemand après Mannheim." *Le Mouvement socialiste*, no. 182 (Jan. 1907).

———. "Controverse socialiste." *Le Mouvement socialiste*, no. 184 (Mar. 1907).

Monconduit, A. "Qu'est-ce que le fascisme?" *Combat*, June, Nov. 1937, Jan. 1938.

Montagnon, B. "Bon courage." *Néo*, 14 Dec. 1934.

——. "Horizons révolutionnaires." *L'Oeuvre*, 4 Oct. 1940.

Mounier, E. "Réponse à *L'Ordre nouveau*." *Esprit*, no. 19 (1 Apr. 1934).

——. "*Esprit* au Congrès franco-italien sur la corporation." *Esprit*, no. 33 (June 1935).

——. "Adresse des vivants à quelques survivants." *Esprit*, no. 43 (Apr. 1936).

——. "Les Deux Grandeurs." *Esprit*, no. 44 (May 1936).

——. "Rassemblement populaire." *Esprit*, no. 45 (June 1936).

——. "Tentation." *Jeune Europe*, no. 3 (1936).

——. "Note sur la tactique et l'attitude politique d'*Esprit*." *Journal intérieur*, no. 19 (1 Oct. 1937).

——. "A l'intelligence française." *Marianne*, 21 Aug. 1940.

——. "Letter from France: A Personalist Leader, Editor of *Esprit*, Sends This Message to America from France." *The Commonweal*, 25 Oct. 1940.

——. "D'une France à l'autre." *Esprit*, no. 94 (Nov. 1940).

——. "Les Nouvelles Conditions de la vie publique en France." *Esprit*, no. 94 (Nov. 1940).

——. "Sur l'intelligence en temps de crise." *Esprit*, no. 97 (Feb. 1941).

——. "Fin de l'homme bourgeois." *Esprit*, no. 102 (July 1941).

Mounier, E., and G. de Santillana. "Dialogue sur l'État fasciste." *Esprit*, nos. 35–36 (Sept. 1935).

Mussolini, B. "L'Aurore d'une civilisation nouvelle." *1934*, 12 Dec. 1934.

Norgeu, P. "L'Esprit bourgeois." *La Lutte des jeunes*, 22 Apr. 1934.

Ollivier, D. "Éducation fasciste: Culte de la révolution." *La Lutte des jeunes*, 10 June 1934.

Perroux, F. "Intelligence de la nation." *Esprit*, no. 75 (Dec. 1938).

Prélot, M. "Le Socialisme français: Le Néo-socialisme." *Politique*, Feb. 1939.

Prévaux, B. de. "Demoiselles en uniforme." *La Lutte des jeunes*, 18 Mar. 1934.

Rebeix, L. "Socialismes et socialistes." *Le National populaire*, no. 99 (10 June 1944).

Renaudel, P. "Mon sentiment vrai, profond. . . ." *La Vie socialiste*, 26 May 1934.

Rivain, J. "Les Socialistes antidémocrates." *L'Action française*, 15 Mar. 1907.

——. "L'Avenir du syndicalisme." *L'Action française*, 15 Sept. 1908.

Roditi, G. "Du néo-marxisme au néo-socialisme?" *L'Homme nouveau*, no. 14 (1 Mar. 1935).

——. "La Solution corporative." *L'Homme nouveau*, no. 18 (July 1935).

——. "Mort ou naissance du néo-socialisme." *L'Homme nouveau*, 1 Sept. 1935.

Rouanet, G. "La Crise du parti socialiste." *La Revue socialiste*, no. 176 (Aug. 1899).

Roumanès, J. "La Tradition nationaliste." *La Lutte des jeunes*, 15 Apr. 1934.

——. "Révolution marxiste ou révolution spirituelle?" *La Lutte des jeunes*, 20 May 1934.

Saillenfest, J. "Fascisme et syndicalisme." *Combat*, Oct. 1936.

Sorel, G. Review of *Psychologie des foules*, by G. Le Bon. *Le Devenir social*, 1st year, no. 8 (Nov. 1895).

———. "L'Éthique du socialisme." *Revue de métaphysique et de morale* 7 (Mar. 1899).

———. "Y a-t-il de l'utopie dans le marxisme?" *Revue de métaphysique et de morale* 7 (May 1899).

———. Study of *L'Évolution créatrice*, by H. Bergson. *Le Mouvement socialiste*, nos. 191, 193 (Oct., Dec. 1907); nos. 194, 196, 197 (Jan., Mar., Apr. 1908).

———. "Aux temps dreyfusiens." *L'Indépendance*, 10 Oct. 1912.

Thomas, P. "D'où vient, où va le syndicalisme ouvrier?" *L'Oeuvre*, 4 Dec. 1940.

Thoyot, L. "Le Salaire d'association dans la corporation." *L'Accord social*, 10 Nov. 1907.

Valary, H. "Socialisme français." *L'Union ouvrière*, 5–12 Apr. 1902.

Valois, G. "L'Esprit proudhonien." *Cahiers du Cercle Proudhon*, Jan.–Feb. 1912.

———. "Notre première année." *Cahiers du Cercle Proudhon*, May–Aug. 1912.

———. "Sorel et l'architecture sociale." *Cahiers du Cercle Proudhon*, May–Aug. 1912.

———. "Sommes-nous des démolisseurs ou des architectes?" *Cahiers des États généraux* 1, no. 3 (June 1923).

———. "Patriotes et révolutionnaires." In *Histoire et philosophie sociales* (Paris: Nouvelle Librairie Nationale, 1924), 559–73.

———. "Les Rélations de l'État et des diverses classes sociales." *Cahiers des États généraux* 3, no. 18 (1st semester, 1925).

———. "Nationalisme et socialisme." *Le Nouveau Siècle*, 25–27 Jan. 1926.

———. "L'Autorité et la liberté ou la souveraineté et la représentation." *Le Nouveau Siècle*, 1 Feb. 1926.

———. "Erreurs et vérités sur le fascisme." *Le Nouveau Siècle*, 24 Apr. 1926.

———. "Origines françaises du fascisme." *Le Nouveau Siècle*, 27 Apr. 1926.

———. "Aux travailleurs français." *Le Nouveau Siècle*, 1 May 1926.

———. "Le Fascisme, conclusion du mouvement de 1789." *Le Nouveau Siècle*, 14 July 1926.

———. "La Victoire en chantant." *Le Nouveau Siècle*, 2 Aug. 1926.

———. "La Politique ouvrière du Faisceau." *Le Nouveau Siècle*, 26 Sept. 1926.

———. "Nous honorons la mémoire de Maurice Barrès." *Le Nouveau Siècle*, 26 Nov. 1926.

———. "Sur la voie glorieuse et rude de la pauvreté et de la réussite." *Le Nouveau Siècle*, 5 June 1927.

———. "A la recherche du parti nouveau." *Le Nouveau Siècle*, 19 June 1927.

———. "Les Socialistes découvrent le socialisme." *Le Nouveau Siècle*, 15 Jan. 1928.

———. "Chantiers 1928." *Cahiers bleus*, no. 1 (15 Aug. 1928).

———. "Commentaires." *Cahiers bleus*, no. 4 (1 Nov. 1928).

Vandervelde, E. "Après le Congrès du POB: Henri De Man et Marcel Déat: Analogies nombreuses et saisissantes." *La Vie socialiste*, 19 Jan. 1934.

———. "Planisme, néo-socialisme ou néo-réformisme?" *Le Peuple*, 6 Jan. 1935.

———. "Le Marxisme et le planisme." *Le Peuple*, 3 Feb. 1935.

———. "Retour à Marx et analyses marxistes." *Le Peuple*, 17 Feb. 1935.

Vaugeois, H. "Notes politiques: Nos trois proscrits." *L'Action française*, 15 Jan. 1900.

———. "Notes politiques." *L'Action française*, 15 May 1902.

Vincent, A. "Le Bilan de la démocratie." *Cahiers du Cercle Proudhon*, Mar.– Apr. 1912.

Vincent, R. "Le Miroir du siècle: Nécessité d'un surréalisme." *Combat*, Apr. 1937.

Works Published After 1944

Books

Agulhon, M. *La France de 1940 à nos jours*. Paris: Nathan, 1972.

Andreu, P. *Notre maître M. Sorel*. Paris: Grasset, 1953.

———. *Le Rouge et le blanc*. Paris: La Table Ronde, 1977.

Andreu, P., and F. Grover. *Drieu La Rochelle*. Paris: Hachette, 1979.

Aron, R. *Les Étapes de la pensée sociologique*. Paris: Gallimard, 1967.

———. *Mémoires*. Paris: Julliard, 1983.

Assouline, P. *Gaston Gallimard: Un Demi-siècle d'édition française*. Paris: Balland, 1984.

Avineri, S. *The Social and Political Thought of Karl Marx*. Cambridge: Cambridge University Press, 1966.

Birnbaum, P. *Le Peuple et les gros: Histoire d'un mythe*. Paris: Grasset, 1979.

Blum, L. *L'Oeuvre de Léon Blum*. Introduction by J. Texcier. Ed. by J. Léon-Blum, J. Cain, L. Fancon, and J. Texcier. 6 vols. Paris: Albin Michel, 1954.

Boisdeffre, P. de. *Maurice Barrès*. Paris: Éditions Universitaires, 1962.

Bredin, J.-D. *L'Affaire*. Paris: Julliard, 1983.

Byrnes, R. F. *Anti-Semitism in Modern France*. Vol. 1, *The Prologue to the Dreyfus Affair*. New Brunswick: Rutgers University Press, 1950.

Capitan, C. *Charles Maurras et l'idéologie d'Action française*. Paris: Éditions du Seuil, 1972.

Carter, A. E. *The Idea of Decadence in French Literature, 1830–1900*. Toronto: University of Toronto Press, 1958.

Charzat, M. *Georges Sorel et la révolution au XXᵉ siècle*. Paris: Hachette, 1977.

Dansette, A. *Le Boulangisme*. 15th ed. Paris: Fayard, 1946.

Deniel, A. *Bucard et le francisme: Les Seuls fascistes français*. Paris: Jean Picollec, 1979.

Dioudonnat, P.-M. *Je suis partout: Les Maurrassiens devant le tentation fasciste*. Paris: La Table Ronde, 1973.

Dodge, P. *Beyond Marxism: The Faith and Works of Hendrik De Man*. The Hague: Martinus Nijhoff, 1966.

———. *A Documentary Study of Hendrik De Man, Socialist Critic of Marxism*. Princeton: Princeton University Press, 1979.

Domenach, J.-M. *Barrès par lui-même*. Paris: Éditions du Seuil, 1954.

————. *Emmanuel Mounier par lui-même.* Paris: Editions du Seuil, 1972.

Doty, C. S. *From Cultural Revolution to Counterrevolution: The Politics of Maurice Barrès.* Athens: Ohio University Press, 1976.

Dupeux, L., ed. *Kulturpessimismus, Révolution conservatrice, et modernité.* In *La Revue d'Allemagne et des pays de langue allemande* (special number) 14, no. 1 (Jan.–Mar. 1982).

Duverger, M. *L'Autre Côté des choses.* Paris: Albin Michel, 1977.

Fabre-Luce, A. *Pour en finir avec l'antisémitisme.* Paris: Julliard, 1979.

Felice, R. de. *Mussolini il rivoluzionario, 1883–1920.* Turin: Einaudi, 1965.

————. *Interpretations of Fascism.* Cambridge: Harvard University Press, 1977.

Friedländer, S. *L'Antisémitisme nazi: Histoire d'une psychose collective.* Paris: Éditions du Seuil, 1972.

————. *Histoire et psychanalyse: Essai sur les possibilités et les limites de la psychohistoire.* Paris: Éditions du Seuil, 1975.

Furiozzi, G. B. *Sorel e l'Italia.* Messina and Florence: G. D'Anna, 1975.

————. *Il sindacalismo rivoluzionario italiano.* Milan: Mursia, 1977.

Gregor, A. J. *The Ideology of Fascism: The Rationale of Totalitarianism.* New York: Free Press, 1969.

————. *Interpretations of Fascism.* Morristown, N.J.: General Learning Press, 1974.

————. *Italian Fascism and Developmental Dictatorship.* Princeton: Princeton University Press, 1979.

————. *Roberto Michels e l'ideologia del fascismo.* Rome: Giovanni Volpe, 1979.

————. *Young Mussolini and the Intellectual Origins of Fascism.* Berkeley and Los Angeles: University of California Press, 1979.

Guchet, Y. *Georges Valois, l'Action française, le Faisceau, la République syndicale.* Paris: Albatros, 1975.

Hamilton, A. *The Appeal of Fascism: A Study of Intellectuals and Fascism, 1919–1945.* New York: Macmillan, 1973.

Harris, H. S. *The Social Philosophy of Giovanni Gentile.* Urbana: University of Illinois Press, 1966.

Heller, G. *Un Allemand à Paris, 1940–1944.* Paris: Éditions du Seuil, 1981.

Hellman, J. *Emmanuel Mounier and the New Catholic Left.* Toronto: University of Toronto Press, 1981.

Heurgon-Desjardins, A., ed. *Paul Desjardins et les décades de Pontigny: Études, témoignages, et documents inédits.* Paris: PUF, 1964.

Horowitz, I. L. *Radicalism and the Revolt against Reason.* London: Routledge and Kegan Paul, 1961.

Hughes, H. S. *Consciousness and Society: The Reorientation of European Social Thought, 1890–1930.* New York: Knopf, 1961.

————. *The Obstructed Path: French Social Thought in the Years of Desperation.* New York: Harper and Row, 1968.

Humphrey, R. *Georges Sorel, Prophet without Honor.* Cambridge: Harvard University Press, 1951.

Jouvenel, B. de. *Un Voyageur dans le siècle.* Paris: Laffont, 1979.

Julliard, J. *Clemenceau briseur de grèves*. Paris: Julliard, 1965.

———. *Fernand Pelloutier et les origines du syndicalisme d'action directe*. Paris: Éditions du Seuil, 1971.

Klemperer, K. von. *Germany's New Conservatism*. Princeton: Princeton University Press, 1957.

Laqueur, W., ed. *Fascism: A Reader's Guide: Analyses, Interpretations, Bibliography*. Berkeley and Los Angeles: University of California Press, 1976.

Lasierra, R., and J. Plumyène. *Les Fascismes français*. Paris: Éditions du Seuil, 1963.

Lefranc, G. *Histoire des doctrines sociales dans l'Europe contemporaine*. Paris: Aubier, 1960.

Lévy, B.-H. *L'Idéologie française*. Paris: Grasset, 1981.

Lichtheim, G. *Lukács*. London: Fontana, 1970.

Loiseaux, G. *La Littérature de la défaite et de la collaboration d'après "Phönix oder Asche?" (Phénix ou cendres?) de Bernhard Payr*. Paris: Publications de la Sorbonne, 1984.

Lottman, H. R. *La Rive Gauche*. Paris: Éditions du Seuil, 1981.

Loubet del Bayle, J.-L. *Les Non-conformistes des années 30: Une tentative de renouvellement de la pensée politique française*. Paris: Éditions du Seuil, 1969.

Lukács, G. *History and Class Consciousness: Studies in Marxist Dialectics*. Trans. R. Livingstone. London: Merlin Press, 1971.

McInnes, N. *The Western Marxists*. London: Alcove Press, 1972.

Marrus, M. R. *Les Juifs de France à l'époque de l'affaire Dreyfus*. Paris: Calmann-Lévy, 1972.

Marrus, M. R., and R. O. Paxton. *Vichy et les juifs*. Paris: Calmann-Lévy, 1981.

Massis, H. *Barrès et nous*. Paris: Plon, 1952.

Masur, G. *Prophets of Yesterday: Studies in European Culture, 1890–1914*. New York: Harper and Row, 1966.

Maulnier, T., and G. Prouteau. *L'Honneur d'être juif*. Paris: Laffont, 1971.

Mehlman, J. *Legacies of Anti-Semitism in France*. Minneapolis: University of Minnesota Press, 1983.

Meisel, J. H. *The Myth of the Ruling Class*. Ann Arbor: University of Michigan Press, 1962.

Mohler, A. *Die Konservative Revolution in Deutschland, 1918–1932*. Stuttgart: Vorwerk, 1950.

Mosse, G. L. *Masses and Man: Nationalist and Fascist Perceptions of Reality*. New York: Howard Fertig, 1980.

———, ed. *International Fascism: New Thoughts and New Approaches*. London and Beverly Hills: Sage Publications, 1979.

Mounier, E. *Oeuvres*. Intro. P. Mounier. 4 vols. Paris: Éditions du Seuil, 1963.

Néré, J. "La Crise industrielle de 1882 et le mouvement boulangiste." "Les Élections Boulanger dans le département du Nord." Unpublished works presented to Faculty of Letters, University of Paris, 1959.

Nolte, E. *Three Faces of Fascism: Action Française, Italian Fascism, National Socialism*. Translated from the German by Leila Vennewitz. New York: Holt,

Rinehart, and Winston, 1966. Originally published as *Der Faschismus in seiner Epoche: Die Action française, der italienische Faschismus, der Nationalsozialismus* (Munich: R. Piper and Co. Verlag, 1963).

———. *Theorien über den Faschismus.* Cologne: Kiepenheuer und Witsch, 1967.

Nye, N. A. *The Origins of Crowd Psychology: Gustave Le Bon and the Crisis of Mass Democracy in the Third Republic.* London and Beverly Hills: Sage Publications, 1975.

Ory, P. *Les Collaborateurs, 1940–1945.* Paris: Éditions du Seuil, 1976. (Paper edition, "Points-Histoire" series, 1980.)

Paxton, R. O. *Vichy France: Old Guard and New Order.* New York: Alfred A. Knopf, 1972.

Payne, S. G. *Fascism: Comparison and Definition.* Madison: University of Wisconsin Press, 1980.

Pierce, R. *Contemporary French Political Thought.* London: Oxford University Press, 1966.

Poulantzas, N. *Fascisme et dictature.* Paris: Seuil-Maspéro, 1976.

Rauch, W. R., Jr. *Politics and Belief in Contemporary France: Emmanuel Mounier and Christian Democracy, 1932–1950.* The Hague: Martinus Nijhoff, 1972.

Rémond, R. *La Droite en France: De la première Restauration à la Ve République.* Paris: Aubier, 1963. New edition issued under the title *Les Droites en France.* Paris: Aubier, 1982.

Riosa, A. *Il sindacalismo rivoluzionario in Italia.* Bari: De Donato, 1976.

Roth, J. J. *The Cult of Violence: Sorel and the Sorelians.* Berkeley and Los Angeles: University of California Press, 1980.

Schüddekopf, O. E. *Linke Leute von Rechts.* Stuttgart: W. Kohlhamer, 1960.

Schwarz, H. P. *Der konservative Anarchist, Politik und Zeitkritik Ernst Jüngers.* Freiburg: Rombach, 1962.

Schweierskott, H. J. *Arthur Moeller van den Bruck und der revolutionäre Nationalismus in der Weimarer Republik.* Göttingen: Musterschmidt Verlag, 1962.

Seager, F. H. *The Boulanger Affair: Political Crossroad of France, 1886–1889.* Ithaca: Cornell University Press, 1969.

Seliger, M. *Ideology and Politics.* London: Allen and Unwin, 1976.

———. *The Marxist Conception of Ideology: A Critical Essay.* Cambridge: Cambridge University Press, 1977.

Senarclens, P. de. *Le Mouvement "Esprit," 1932–1941: Essai critique.* Lausanne: L'Age d'Homme, 1974.

Sérant, P. *Le Romantisme fasciste.* Paris: Fasquelle, 1959.

Sontheimer, K. *Anti-demokratisches Denken in der Weimarer Republik.* Munich: Nymphenburger Verlagshandlung, 1962.

Soucy, R. *Fascism in France: The Case of Maurice Barrès.* Berkeley and Los Angeles: University of California Press, 1972.

———. *Fascist Intellectual: Drieu La Rochelle.* Berkeley and Los Angeles: University of California Press, 1979.

Stern, F. *The Politics of Cultural Despair: A Study in the Rise of Germanic Ideology.* Berkeley and Los Angeles: University of California Press, 1961.

Sternhell, Z. *Maurice Barrès et le nationalisme français.* Paris: Presses de la Fondation Nationale des Sciences Politiques, 1972. (Paper edition Brussels: Éditions Complexe, 1985.)

———. *La Droite révolutionnaire, 1885–1914: Les Origines françaises du fascisme.* Paris: Éditions du Seuil, 1978. (Paper edition 1984.)

Thibau, J. *"Le Monde": Histoire d'un journal: Un Journal dans l'histoire.* Paris: Jean-Claude Simoën, 1978.

Tucker, W. R. *The Fascist Ego: A Political Biography of Robert Brasillach.* Berkeley and Los Angeles: University of California Press, 1975.

Tweton, D. J. *The Marquis de Morès, Dakota Capitalist, French Nationalist.* Fargo, N.D.: Institute for Regional Studies, 1972.

Vajda, M. *Fascisme et mouvement de masse.* Trans. G. Valland. Paris: Le Sycomore, 1979.

Valiani, L. *Il partito socialista italiano nel periodo della neutralità.* Milan: Feltrinelli, 1977.

Vernon, R. *Commitment and Change: Georges Sorel and the Idea of Revolution: Essay and Translations.* Toronto: University of Toronto Press, 1978.

Wagar, W. W., ed. *European Intellectual History since Darwin and Marx.* New York: Harper and Row, 1966.

———, ed. *Science, Faith, and Man: European Thought since 1914.* New York: Harper and Row, 1968.

Weber, E. *L'Action française.* Paris: Stock, 1962.

———. *Varieties of Fascism.* New York: Van Nostrand, 1964.

———. *The Nationalist Revival in France, 1905–1914.* 1959; reprint, Berkeley and Los Angeles: University of California Press, 1968.

Weiss, J. *The Origins of Modern Consciousness.* Detroit: Wayne State University Press, 1965.

Willard, C. *Le Mouvement socialiste en France, 1893–1905: Les Guesdistes.* Paris: Éditions Sociales, 1965.

Winock, M. *Histoire politique de la revue "Esprit."* Paris: Éditions du Seuil, 1975.

———. *Édouard Drumont et Cie: Antisémitisme et fascisme en France.* Paris: Éditions du Seuil, 1982.

Wohl, R. *The Generation of 1914.* Cambridge: Harvard University Press, 1979.

Wright, G. *France in Modern Times: From the Enlightenment to the Present.* 3d ed. London and New York: Norton, 1981.

Zeldin, T. *France, 1848–1945.* Vol. 1, *Ambition, Love, and Politics*; vol. 2, *Intellect, Taste, and Anxiety.* Oxford: Oxford University Press, 1973, 1977.

ARTICLES

Allardyce, G. "What Fascism Is Not: Thoughts on the Deflation of a Concept." *The American Historical Review* 84, no. 2 (Apr. 1979), 367–88.

Andreu, P. "Les Idées politiques de la jeunesse inellectuelle de 1927 à la guerre."

Revue des travaux de l'Académie des sciences morales et politiques, 4th ser. (2d semester, 1957), 17–35.

Beetham, D. "From Socialism to Fascism: The Relation between Theory and Practice in the Work of Robert Michels." *Political Studies* 25, no. 1 (Mar. 1977), 3–24; no. 2 (June 1977), 161–81.

Bennett, R. I. "The Elite Theory as Fascist Ideology: A Reply to Beetham's Critique of Robert Michels." *Political Studies* 26, no. 4 (Dec. 1978), 474–88.

Bergounioux, A. "Le Néo-socialisme: Marcel Déat: Réformisme traditionnel ou esprit des années trente." *Revue historique* 260, no. 2 (Oct.–Dec. 1978), 389–412.

Byrnes, R. F. "Morès, the First National Socialist." *The Review of Politics* 12 (July 1950), 341–62.

Cointet, J.-P. "Marcel Déat et le parti unique." *Revue d'histoire de la Deuxième Guerre mondiale*, no. 91 (July 1973), 1–22.

Desolre, G. "Henri De Man et le marxisme: Critique critique de la critique." *Revue européenne des sciences sociales et Cahiers Vilfredo Pareto* 12, no. 31 (1974), 36–62.

Finer, S. F. "Pareto and Pluto-democracy: The Retreat to Galápagos." *American Political Science Review* 62, no. 2 (June 1968), 440–50.

Girardet, R. "Notes sur l'esprit d'un fascisme français, 1934–1940." *Revue française de science politique* 5, no. 3 (July–Sept. 1955), 529–46.

Grawitz, M. "Henri De Man et la psychologie sociale." *Revue européenne des sciences sociales et Cahiers Vilfredo Pareto* 12, no. 31 (1974), 75–106.

Gregor, A. J. "Fascism and Modernization: Some Addenda." *World Politics* 26 (Apr. 1974), 370–84.

———. "Fascism and the Countermodernization of Consciousness." *Comparative Political Studies* 10 (July 1977), 239–57.

Greill, A. L. "The Modernization of Consciousness and the Appeal of Fascism." *Comparative Political Studies* 10 (July 1977), 213–38.

Grossmann, S. "L'Évolution de Marcel Déat." *Revue d'histoire de la Deuxième Guerre mondiale*, no. 97 (Jan. 1975), 3–29.

Grynberg, A., and C. Singer. "Le Pouvoir de l'image: Les Pérégrinations du *Juif süss*." *Les Nouveaux Cahiers*, no. 75 (winter 1983–84), 41–43.

Guchet, Y. "Georges Valois ou l'illusion fasciste." *Revue française de science politique* 15, no. 6 (Dec. 1965), 1111–44.

Harmel, C. "A propos d'Henri De Man et de Léon Blum." *Le Contrat social* 9, no. 4 (July–Aug. 1965), 261–63.

Hoffmann, S. "Aspects du régime de Vichy." *Revue française de science politique* 6, no. 2 (Jan.–Mar. 1956), 44–69.

———. "Collaborationism in France in World War II." *Journal of Modern History* 40, no. 3 (Sept. 1968), 375–95.

Hutton, P. H. "Popular Boulangism and the Advent of Mass Politics in France, 1886–1890." *Journal of Contemporary History* 11, no. 1 (1976), 85–106.

Joes, A. J. "On the Modernity of Fascism: Notes from Two Worlds." *Comparative Political Studies* 10 (July 1977), 259–78.

Kennedy, E. "Bergson's Philosophy and French Political Doctrines: Sorel, Maurras, Péguy, and de Gaulle." *Government and Opposition* 15, no. 1 (Winter 1980), 75–91.

Kramer, S. Ph. "Neo-socialism: The Belgian Case." *Res Publica* 18, no. 1 (1976), 59–80.

Lefranc, G. "Le Courant planiste de 1933 à 1936." *Le Mouvement social*, Jan.–Mar. 1966, 69–89.

———. "La Diffusion des idées planistes en France." *Revue européenne des sciences sociales et Cahiers Vilfredo Pareto* 12, no. 31 (1974), 151–64.

Levey, J. "Georges Valois and the Faisceau: The Making and Breaking of a Fascist." *French Historical Studies* 8, no. 2 (Fall 1973), 279–304.

Linz, J. J. "Some Notes toward a Comparative Study of Fascism in Sociological Historical Perspective." In *Fascism: A Reader's Guide: Analyses, Interpretations, Bibliography*, ed. W. Laqueur (Berkeley and Los Angeles: University of California Press, 1976), 3–121.

Loiseaux, G. "Collaboration littéraire au service de l'Europe nouvelle." *Lendemains 29: Zeitschrift für Frankreichforschung und Französischstudium*, 1983, 9–33.

McInnes, N. "Les Débuts du marxisme théorique en France et en Italie, 1880–1897." *Cahiers de l'Institut de science économique appliquée*, no. 102 (June 1960), 5–51.

Mosse, G. L. "The French Right and the Working Classes: Les Jaunes." *Journal of Contemporary History* 7, nos. 3–4 (July–Oct. 1972), 185–208.

Müller, K. J. "French Fascism and Modernization." *Journal of Contemporary History* 11, no. 4 (1976), 75–107.

Olson, M., Jr. "Rapid Growth as a Destabilizing Force." *Journal of Economic History* 23, no. 4 (Dec. 1963), 529–52.

Ponty, J. "La Presse quotidienne et l'affaire Dreyfus en 1898–1899: Essai de typologie." *Revue d'histoire moderne et contemporaine* 21 (Apr.–June 1974).

Prost, A. "Le Rapport de Déat en faveur d'un parti national unique (juillet 1940): Essai d'analyse lexicale." *Revue française de science politique* 23, no. 5 (Oct. 1973), 933–65.

Rémond, R. "Y a-t-il un fascisme français?" *Terre humaine*, nos. 7–8 (July–Aug. 1952), 37–47.

Rens, I., and M. Brélaz. "Introduction." *Revue européenne des sciences sociales et Cahiers Vilfredo Pareto* 12, no. 31 (1974), 7–10.

Roth, J. J. "Revolution and Morale in Modern French Thought: Sorel and the Sorelians." *French Historical Studies* 3, no. 2 (Fall 1963), 205–23.

Rutkoff, P. M. "The Ligue des Patriotes: The Nature of the Radical Right and the Dreyfus Affair." *French Historical Studies* 8, no. 4 (Fall 1974), 585–603.

Santarelli, E. "Le Socialisme national en Italie: Précédents et origines." *Le Mouvement social*, no. 50 (Jan.–Mar. 1965), 41–70.

Schwarzchild, S. S. "The Marquis de Morès: The Story of a Failure (1858–1896)." *Jewish Social Studies* 22, no. 1 (Jan. 1960), 3–26.

Seton-Watson, H. "Fascism, Right and Left." In *International Fascism, 1920–1945* (New York: Harper Torchbooks, 1966), 183–97.

Sternhell, Z. "Anatomie d'un mouvement fasciste: Le Faisceau de Georges Valois." *Revue française de science politique* 26, no. 1 (Feb. 1976), 5–40.

———. "Fascist Ideology." In *Fascism: A Reader's Guide: Analyses, Interpretations, Bibliography*, ed. W. Laqueur (Berkeley and Los Angeles: University of California Press, 1976), 315–76.

———. "Strands of French Fascism." In *Who Were the Fascists? Social Roots of European Fascism*, ed. B. Hagtvet, S. U. Larsen, and J. P. Mykelbust (Oslo: Universitetsforlaget, 1980), 479–500.

———. "Sur le fascisme et sa variante française." *Le Débat*, no. 32 (Nov. 1984), 28–51.

———. "Emmanuel Mounier et la contestation de la démocratie libérale dans la France des années trente." *Revue française de science politique* 34, no. 6 (Dec. 1984), 1141–80.

Touchard, J. "L'Esprit des années 1930: Une Tentative de renouvellement de la pensée politique française." In *Tendances politiques dans la vie française depuis 1789*, ed. G. Michaud (Paris: Hachette, 1960), 89–120.

Trevor-Roper, H. R. "The Phenomenon of Fascism." In *European Fascism*, ed. S. J. Woolf (London: Weidenfeld and Nicolson, 1970), 18–38.

———. "Was Nazism Unique?" In *War der Nationalsozialismus ohne Beispiel?* (Opladen: Westdeutscher Verlag, 1983).

Turner, H. A. "Fascism and Modernization." *World Politics* 24 (July 1972), 547–64.

Valiani, L. "Il partito socialista italiano dal 1900 al 1918." *Rivista storica italiana* 75, no. 2 (June 1963), 269–326.

Van Peski, A. M. "La Critique du marxisme chez Henri De Man et chez quelques néo-marxistes." *Revue européenne des sciences sociales et Cahiers Vilfredo Pareto* 12, no. 31 (1974), 11–33.

Weber, E. "Nationalism, Socialism, and National-Socialism in France." *French Historical Studies* 2, no. 3 (Spring 1962), 273–307.

———. "About Marc Bloch." *The American Scholar* 51 (Winter 1981–82), 73–82.

Wilson, S. "The Ligue Antisémitique Française." *The Wiener Library Bulletin* 25, nos. 3–4 (1972), 33–38.

———. "The Anti-Semitic Riots of 1898 in France." *The Historical Journal* 16, no. 4 (1973), 789–806.

———. "Le Monument Henry: La Structure de l'antisémitisme en France, 1898–1899." *Annales*, Mar.–Apr. 1977, 265–91.

Winock, M. "Édouard Drumont et l'antisémitisme en France avant l'affaire Dreyfus." *Esprit* 38, no. 5 (May 1971), 1085–1106.

———. "Une Parabole fasciste: *Gilles* de Drieu La Rochelle." *Le Mouvement social*, no. 80 (July 1972), 29–47.

———. "Le Fascisme en France." *L'Histoire*, no. 28 (Nov. 1980), 40–49.

———. "La Gauche et les juifs." *L'Histoire*, no. 34 (May 1981), 13–25.

Index